About the Author

E. J. KAHN, JR., a staff writer for *The New Yorker* since 1937, is one of America's most brilliant reporters and writers. His work for *The New Yorker* and other major magazines has ranged from Profiles of important people to coverage of the Olympics, from humor to combat reporting. In addition he has written eleven books, dealing with such diverse subjects as the Coca-Cola Company, Frank Sinatra, and the story of the Japanese holdouts in the Pacific Islands after World War II ended.

Mr. Kahn was born in New York City and has traveled extensively in Europe, Australia, Japan, Korea, the U.S.S.R. and the Trust Territory of the Pacific Islands. He was graduated from Harvard cum laude, with a B.A. degree, and in 1962 his alma mater made him an honorary member of Phi Beta Kappa.

Mr. Kahn is married and has three teen-age sons. He lives in Westchester County, New York, and spends his summers at Cape Cod. There, in addition to writing books and magazine pieces, Mr. Kahn plays fierce—and usually victorious—tennis and contributes a weekly guest column to *Park Here*, a mimeographed newspaper published by his sons.

Other books by E. J. Kahn, Jr.

E. J. KAHN, JR.

THE
WORLD
OF
SWOPE

SIMON AND SCHUSTER
NEW YORK

FOR JINNY

A TOAST

Now here's to Herbert Bayard Swope.
God save the King. God help the Pope.
And God protect the President
From this demure, retiring gent.
He taught George Rex to put his crown on,
Queen Mary how to put her gown on,
And David Windsor, Prince of Wales,
To fall from horses and for frails.
Explained just how to outmaneuver
Depressions to our Mr. Hoover;
And for the Pontiff, as a pal,
He's written his encyclical.
His lessons finished to Lenin, he
Gave castor oil to Mussolini;
And after multiple attempts he
Coached Tunney how to K.O. Dempsey;
Instructed Lindbergh how to fly,
And taught Münchhausen how to lie,
Trained Washington to tell the truth,
Perfected batting in Babe Ruth.
He fertilized the many ova
Unjustly claimed by Casanova;
And, last and loftiest feat, inspired
The peerless nerve of Herbert Bayard.

—RALPH PULITZER
July 1931

PUBLISHER'S FOREWORD

In 1924—the year the publishing firm of Simon and Schuster was established—our most important book, and our first biography, was *Joseph Pulitzer, His Life and Letters,* by Don C. Seitz.

This is one of several reasons for our special pride in publishing *The World of Swope,* a biography of Joseph Pulitzer's most celebrated reporter, Herbert Bayard Swope, a legendary and fabulous figure in the annals of modern journalism, characterized by Lord Northcliffe as "the greatest reporter of our age."

Herbert Bayard Swope labored unceasingly to make journalism a learned profession and to keep it a free one.

He walked with the captains and the kings . . . but kept the uncommon touch.

His journalistic achievements contradicted Joseph Pulitzer's own dictum that every reporter is a hope, every editor a disappointment.

His fame as a reporter was matched by his later renown as the city editor and, finally, as the executive editor of the *World,* at the peak of that newspaper's history.

He regarded nonconformity and audacity as standard operating procedures, even to the point of seeming arrogance.

He enunciated no rules for success, but offered a sure formula for failure: *Just try to please everyone.*

He gloried in "accuracy, terseness, accuracy," as defined at 63 Park Row, and was ready to climb the highest mountain and cross the widest sea to verify a single fact.

He electrified any group he joined, and attracted so many VIP's from the seats of the mighty that literature was often inspired and history frequently made, quite literally, in a Swope-filled room.

A host of friends and associates felt a cubit or more higher for knowing him.

One of the most eloquent tributes to Herbert Bayard Swope was written for *The Saturday Evening Post* in 1938 by Stanley Walker, who qualified as an expert on the history of modern journalism, and whose appraisal is particularly meaningful because he spoke as one famous city editor assessing the achievements of another. (Walker was city editor of the New York *Herald Tribune*.) Here is a short excerpt from Walker's sketch:

More than once, important men—that is to say, men who were important to themselves, their wives or their associates—have been under the pleasant delusion that they were running something, say a political convention or a conference, only to discover, to their confusion and chagrin, that the real boss was, or seemed to be, Herbert Bayard Swope. He is as easy to ignore as a cyclone. His gift of gab is a torrential and terrifying thing. He is probably the most charming extrovert in the Western world. His brain is crammed with a million oddments of information, and only a dolt would make a bet with him on an issue concerning facts. He is fifty-six years old now; most of those years have been passed in a furious and highly successful endeavor to impress upon the consciousness of a stupid and lethargic world the fact that there exists, living and breathing and flashing fire, a man named Herbert Bayard Swope. Travelers returning from Europe have been known to report that the first question asked of them by high-placed foreign personages would not be "How are conditions in the United States?" but "How is Herbert Bayard Swope?"

In the days when he was a dynamic practicing journalist in New York, many other newspapermen were distinguished by their gall and brass, but the man who stood out among his fellows, like a snorting Caesar in a company of Caspar Milquetoasts, was Herbert Bayard Swope. The passage of years has done little to lessen his drive. He has worked and schemed until he is worth probably $3,000,000. He has talked himself into what amounts to a chronic case of laryngitis. He is always hoarse. . . .

At the [Versailles] Peace Conference [in 1918], easily the most impressive person was Herbert Bayard Swope. In top hat and cutaway, he received military salutes and crashed the gate to places where reporters were supposed to be barred. It was all highly effective. He was the first to get the outline of the terms of the treaty of peace. He was the first to get a copy of the Covenant of the League of Nations. He met all the big men of that momentous time, and he met them as an equal. He played golf with Lord Northcliffe. He captivated Queen Marie of Rumania. He put his hand to limericks to amuse President Wilson. This, then, was history, and Herbert Bayard Swope was in the middle of it, helping make it.

Had he been consulted on the choice of a biographer, Herbert Bayard Swope would not only have preferred, but would have vehemently insisted upon, a portrait that would show him honestly delineated as he breathed and lived—warts and all.

This book by E. J. Kahn, Jr., is that kind of biography.

—M. LINCOLN SCHUSTER

PREFACE

SOME MEN become memorable by doing something special—winning a
war, or committing a murder, or rescuing a maiden in jeopardy. Some
become memorable by *being* something special—Secretary of Defense,
say, or president of a large corporation, or both. Others achieve renown in a harder way—by being *somebody* special. As executive editor
of the New York *World* in its prime, and before that a celebrated
reporter, Herbert Bayard Swope was unarguably a something, and he
did quite a lot. But even before he attained journalistic eminence, and
also for the thirty years he lived after he retired from the *World*, he
was a Somebody—an often captivating, often infuriating, almost always
fascinating Somebody.

Swope's adult life spanned the first half of the twentieth century.
During those five bustling decades, the world he lived in rejected
isolationism and embraced psychoanalysis. Swope marched in step. He
had broad horizons and deep anxieties. But that was about as far as he
went in conforming to any pattern. He was an independent man, who
could not bear to be fettered by the conventions and routines that
govern most men's existences. From time to time, after he left active
newspaper work, he filled part-time posts: New York State Racing
Commissioner, consultant to the Secretary of War, member of the
American Atomic Energy Delegation to the United Nations, and
others. He held no steady job, though; he did not like to have his
freedom thus restricted.

In whatever enterprise Swope might be momentarily engaged, he
was a singular, and potent, catalytic agent. Human catalysts range
from diplomats to fixers, and sometimes they are both. Swope liked
to be an intermediary, and he didn't care how little in common his
vast and varied assortment of friends had as long as they had him in
common. He had a compulsive urge to get mixed up in other people's
affairs. As his wife once put it, "He had to be needed." Swope felt
equally at home in the fields of journalism, business, politics, the

11

theater, sports, and high society. Many of the leaders in these fields could frequently be found at *his* home, where, to cite one of hundreds of such examples, two political lions of the 1920s, Alfred E. Smith and Senator William E. Borah, met for the first time.

Swope introduced Charles Chaplin to Fiorello H. LaGuardia, Alice Roosevelt Longworth to Marion Davies, and Frank Crowninshield, the patrician editor of *Vanity Fair*, in whose columns the "Impossible Interview" flourished, to the anarchist Emma Goldman. During the First World War, Anne Morgan, the sister of J. Pierpont Morgan, Jr., wanted to raise some money for French war relief. Swope introduced her to the promoter Tex Rickard, who arranged a benefit prize fight for her cause. Swope did not confine himself to bringing the principals together. Miss Morgan said later he got so wrapped up in the venture that "I began to believe Swope was going to fight Swope."

Swope, being of an independent and unpredictable turn of mind, did not always say what he meant, nor did he always intend that the rules of behavior he was quick to lay down for others should apply also to him. One cannot be certain, for instance, that he would have thought that a book about him should conform to his views on biography—which were themselves ambivalent. When the author of this book wrote a *New Yorker* Profile, in the summer of 1951, about Swope's good friend John Hay Whitney, Swope was moved to send Whitney a discourse on biography that went, in part, "I want to know if a man is big in spirit, if he has purpose; clarity of mind; generosity; consideration. These are a few of the qualities that are important." Moving from the general to the particular, he went on, "In any event, Kahn did not belittle you; the story was frank and free from malevolence. You deserve that." But in a memorandum to himself, Swope concurrently observed, "The August Profiles of Kahn false in that it found nothing wrong with JHW."

When Swope was in a position to control biographical writing about himself, he was partial to words like "fabulous" and to phrases, describing his accomplishments as a newspaperman, like "the sagas of the Paul Bunyans of the craft." However, he thought the life stories of other men were too often overblown "exterior portraits." He once told a writer, "I want to know about the intrinsic qualities of the subject: Is he generous and not mean; is he decisive or vague; is he big or petty; is he loyal or does he abandon friends; has he principles or is he merely an expedientist [a word he liked; he made it up]? Why is Jesus remembered—because He had a curling blond beard or because of His spiritual makeup? That's the thing that counts."

I hope that Swope's intrinsic qualities can be ascertained from the pages that follow. This is an authorized biography, but of an unconventional sort. Swope might have liked that. In most authorized biographies, the close relatives of the subject have a say about what goes in, and also what stays out. In this instance, Swope's immediate family, while it gave me access to most of his personal papers and was generous in sharing its memories of him, had no editorial voice in the contents of the book. There may be parts of it the family will not like at all. And if Swope were alive, he might be kicking, too.

Swope's friends and relatives were so numerous that it would have been a never-ending task to try to get in touch with all of them. I am regretful if I overlooked anybody important. The length and variety of the list of those who were good enough to give me interviews, or recollective letters, or both, or to help in other ways, bespeaks the sweep of Herbert Swope's orbit. I am beholden, then, in alphabetical order to: the Earl of Amherst, George Backer, Dr. Alvan L. Barach, John G. Baragwanath, James W. Barrett, Bruce Barton, Bernard M. Baruch, Charles M. Bayer, S. N. Behrman, Irving Berlin, Edward L. Bernays, Lester Bernstein, Theodore M. Bernstein, Constance E. Bessie, Toney Betts, Victor Bienstock, Dr. Louis Faugeres Bishop, William Block, Preston Boyden, Ned Brown, John L. Burns, Abe Burrows, James M. Cain, Mr. and Mrs. Arthur Caplan, Marshall Cassidy, Turner Catledge, Samuel Chotzinoff, Richard M. Clurman, Margaret L. Coit, Marc Connelly, Katherine Cowdin, Russel Crouse, Jonathan Daniels, Paul Davis, Howard Dietz, Paul Draper, Martin Dunn, Ferdinand Eberstadt, Deltus M. Edwards, Harold Epstein, Morris L. Ernst, Douglas Fairbanks, Jr., James A. Farley, John Farrar, Edna Ferber, George Field, Jule Fink, Raoul H. Fleischmann, Rev. George B. Ford, Martin Gabel, Lewis S. Gannett, Arthur Gelb, Robert Gerdy, Nancy Gilbert, Bernard F. Gimbel, Arthur J. Goldsmith, Dan Golenpaul, Stanley J. Grogan, James Grossman, Lt. Gen. Leslie R. Groves, John Gunther, Harry Hansen, W. Averell Harriman, Alan Hathaway, Ben Hecht, James Henle, Joseph P. Hennessey, John Hersey, Max Hirsch, Laura Z. Hobson, Anna Rosenberg Hoffman, Dr. C. C. Hollis, Paul Hollister, J. Edgar Hoover, George A. Hough, Jr., Mrs. Malcolm Hubbard, Mrs. Henry Ittleson, Mock Joya, Herman Kahn, Leo Katcher, Horace K. Kelland, James L. Kilgallen, Donald Kirk, Arthur Kober, Norman Krasna, Maxwell A. Kriendler, Arthur Krock, Edward Lasker, William L. Laurence, Victor H. Lawn, Therese Lewis, Newman Levy, Ernest K. Lindley, Walter Lippmann, Paul E. Lockwood, David Loth, Samuel Lubell, Kendall Powell Lutkins, Leonard Lyons, Gen. Douglas MacArthur, St. Clair McKelway, John W. Martyn, Harpo Marx, E. V. Matthewman, Bill Mauldin, Charles Merz, Denning Miller, Alice Leone Moats, Raymond Moley, Mr. and Mrs. Sherman Morse, Robert Moses, Charles J. V. Murphy, Charles Nagel, John O'Hara, William S. Paley, Alicia Patterson, Mary Pickford, Margaret Leech Pulitzer, Dr. Daniel J. Reed, Mrs. Arthur Somers Roche, Mr. and Mrs. Richard Rodgers, Israel Rogosin, Billy

13

Rose, James N. Rosenberg, Samuel A. Rosenman, George F. T. Ryall, Aline B. Saarinen, Harry Salpeter, David Sarnoff, Joel Sayre, Arthur Schlesinger, Jr., M. Lincoln Schuster, A. Charles Schwartz, Gilbert Seldes, John F. Shevlin, Benjamin Sonnenberg, Francis Cardinal Spellman, Samuel and Bella Spewack, Frank Sullivan, Mr. and Mrs. David Swope, Mr. and Mrs. Gerard Swope, Jr., Henrietta Swope, Mr. and Mrs. John Swope, Mrs. Harold E. Talbott, Allene Talmey, Deems Taylor, Mrs. James Thurber, John Toohey, Nina Dumas Van Benschoten, Alfred G. Vanderbilt, Frank A. Vanderlip, Jr., Stanley Walker, Arthur Walworth, James P. Warburg, John N. Wheeler, John Hay Whitney, and Herbert A. Wolff.

I am appreciative, also, of the assistance given me by Constance Chafee, Ellen Stern, and Frances Ryder. And the depth of my gratitude to Merrill Pollack is fathomless.

A bibliographical note appears at the end of the book.

E. J. K.

Scarborough, New York
March 8, 1965

14

1

On JUNE 28, 1924, a fifteen-to-one long shot named Swope won the Great American Stakes at the Aqueduct horse-racing track on Long Island. After the race, Sam Hildreth, head trainer for Harry F. Sinclair's stable, turned to Herbert Bayard Swope and asked how much he wanted for the horse.

"Jesus Christ, Sam, you don't think I'd name a horse I owned after *myself*, do you?" asked the two-legged Swope.

"Of course," said Hildreth. "Why not?"

The horse belonged to Bud Fisher, the creator of "Mutt and Jeff." In New York, the comic strip ran in the *World*, of which Swope was the executive editor. Fisher and Swope had occasionally gone to the races together. One afternoon, while they were at the Empire City track with John N. Wheeler, the head of the North American Newspaper Alliance, Fisher mentioned that he was going to the August race meeting at Saratoga Springs. Swope gave him a letter to George H. Bull of the Saratoga Association for the Improvement of the Breed of Horses. Swope hoped that suitable courtesies would be extended to Fisher and that he'd be granted a complimentary admission badge—similar to the badges horse-owners proudly wore. Between the writing of the letter and its presentation, however, Fisher and Swope had a falling out. It was a routine Swope wrangle: it had to do with whether Fisher was right or wrong in not having his car deliver Swope somewhere, with the result that Swope had to take a taxi. Swope wired Bull, "IF BUD FISHER PRESENTS A LETTER TO YOU FROM ME, PAY NO ATTENTION TO IT. HE IS WELL ABLE TO TAKE CARE OF HIS OWN RACE TRACK PRIVILEGES."

Arriving at Saratoga, Fisher proffered the Swope letter, and

15

Bull parried with the Swope telegram. Fisher next wired Swope, "YOU OUGHT TO CHALLENGE HARRY K. THAW FOR THE EGOMANIA CHAMPIONSHIP OF THE WORLD, BUT OUT OF SPORTSMANSHIP GIVE HIM A HANDICAP." There were further bristling exchanges. Subsequently, Fisher, determined to get into the tracks on a bona-fide owner's badge, bought a couple of horses. He wanted to call one of them "Herbert Bayard Swope." However, the Jockey Club, which had charge of such matters, had a sixteen-letter limit on names and made him settle for a mere "Swope." The horse did quite well, and when Fisher decided to sell it he got more than double what he had paid for it.

Some years later, Stanley Walker, who once called Swope "the most charming extrovert in the Western world," gave up the city editorship of the New York *Herald Tribune* and moved to Texas. He began raising turkeys and was so impressed with one of his flock, an "imperious, upstanding, thirty-pound gobbler," that he christened it "Mr. Swope." Walker predicted that any gobbler with that name would spectacularly improve the breed of turkeys, and Mr. Swope did not let his owner down. "He must have sired between two hundred and three hundred fine turkeys," Walker said. "I kept him until he was almost two years old, at which time he weighed around fifty pounds. Gave an outdoor turkey feast for twenty University of Texas students and had enough left over for many purposes, including hash and turkey Tetrazzini. He was a noble bird, and right up to the last he gobbled, putputted, acted the big executive, and in every way was an honor to the great and good man for whom I named him."

Swope's friends could not help regarding him with fond irony. He was a serious man but given to such antic behavior that it was often hard to take him seriously. In the 1920s, a decade that itself in retrospect came to seem somewhat unbelievable, he was probably the best-known newspaperman in New York. But for all his esteem, even in that credulous era he attained the stature of a myth. James Thurber joined a table at a speak-easy one night. When a tall, stentorian, red-haired man to whom he hadn't been introduced got up and left, Thurber asked who he was. Herbert Bayard Swope, he was told. Thurber feigned surprise; he said he'd always thought Swope was a legend. Swope was pleased when he later heard the remark and more than once reminded the humorist of it when they got to know each other. Swope was not even displeased on learning that David Loth, a member of his staff at the *World*, said to a newly hired reporter asking for the low-down on the editor, "Oh, the man doesn't exist. Somebody made him up. He's my favorite character in fiction." The next time Loth asked Swope for a raise, the editor looked at him with mock severity and said, "What do you mean, I'm a character in fiction? Why do you have to say things like that to my brother-in-law?" The reporter had been Robert Bruce Powell, a younger brother of Swope's wife, who was working on the paper during a summer vacation from Yale.

A number of fictional characters *were* thought to resemble Swope. Heywood Broun went to work for him on the *World* in 1921. Soon afterward, Broun decided to write a novel and told Swope about it. "He took over the plot and the construction immediately," Broun said later. "I'd said that I was having some little difficulty in finding just the right name for my hero, and the next day he summoned me to his office and said, 'Why don't you call him Rufus Twice?' That sounded like a silly name to me, but I tried it. There was no doing anything with it. You kept running into 'Twice's' and things like that. So in the end I called the hero Peter Neale—but I kept Twice in the book. I introduced a character who was a managing editor—and he did get called Rufus Twice. But even that was only a fair approximation of the man's energy—the next time I write a book and have him for a character, he'll be called Rufus Hundredfold." The book was published in 1922 and called *The Boy Grew Older*. Its Rufus Twice was an editor who sent his staff telegrams like "Convey my respects to President Wilson and tell him I am solidly behind him" and of whom Broun had one character say, "I don't want to give you the wrong steer about Twice. Maybe you got the impression from what I said that he's just a big bluff. That's only about ten per cent right. He is a big bluff but in addition to that he's got the stuff."

It was one of Swope's saving graces that he could good-naturedly endure the kidding his friends were forever subjecting him to. He was unruffled when Ruth Gordon, who once came to visit the Swopes and found the atmosphere so agreeable she stayed for several years, brought out her play *Over Twenty-One* in 1944. One of its principal characters was a publisher called Robert Drexel Gow, the syllables of whose name were strikingly evocative of Swope's. Gow, the playwright said in her stage directions,

17

was a "tall, well-fed, handsome man, nearing sixty. His hair is grey. Grey, that is, to everyone but him. To him, it still looks red. He is a man of power and personality. Type-casting for a fictitious President of the United States? The world has been nice to him, and he acknowledges this by constantly giving it a graceful smile. . . ." Swope gave Miss Gordon's Mr. Gow a graceful smile himself.

No second-edition Swope, however, was any more outlandish or unbelievable than the original, who was himself something of a dramatic invention. Swope was occasionally credited with having invented Bernard Baruch. (Felix Frankfurter thought an apt epitaph for Swope would have been "Creator of Statesmen.") But while it is true that Swope had a finger in nearly every statesmanlike pie that Baruch baked from the First World War on, Baruch had attained the chairmanship of the War Industries Board in 1918, at a time when he and Swope were no more than casual acquaintances. Swope's grandest creation was himself. Other men have become inseparably linked to characters they portrayed throughout their careers, but most of them were professional actors, like Joseph Jefferson, alias Rip Van Winkle, or Edward Harrigan, alias Old Lavender. The role of Herbert Bayard Swope was more exacting than any of theirs, for to play it to the hilt required unlimited monetary resources, a circle of friends unrivaled in scope, access to the sources of real power in politics, industry, banking, and all the arts; and infallibility. No one but Swope would have had the temerity even to tackle the part, let alone create it, but he did, and he came close to playing it to perfection.

Was it because of the man, or character, who bore it that Swope's name itself came to enjoy such great éclat, or was the name *per se* something to reckon with? Would Hamlet have gone as far as he did if Shakespeare had called him Claudiussen? To be sure, Swope did not christen himself, but he made the most of the happy circumstance that instead of the mere "Gerard" his parents conferred upon their older son, who became president of the General Electric Company, he had something bigger and richer to work with. The middle name, it turned out, couldn't have been more aptly chosen. According to the legends of Charlemagne, Bayard was Rinaldo's bright bay horse, which "came rushing through the forest, regardless of rocks, bushes, or trees, rending everything that opposed his way, and neighing defiance." Swope never called himself "Herbert Swope" and rarely used

"Herbert B. Swope." Making a phone call in his newspaper days, he would always say, "This is Swope of the *World*—Herbert Bayard Swope." After 1928, when he was no longer on the paper, he had to drop the "of the *World*" identification tag, but his prologue was otherwise unchanged. There was a trochaic splendor to his full name that could be almost hypnotic; in 1939, the then Mrs. Vincent Astor opened a letter to him "Dear Herbertbayardswope." (On the other hand, Westbrook Pegler, on one of his sprightlier days, described his fellow journalist as "All gall, divided into three parts—Herbert, Bayard, and Swope.") When, in 1929, Swope decided he should have his own cable address, he was faced with a problem: The Central Bureau for Registered Addresses, which handles such matters, had a ten-letter limit on names. He finally applied for a stark "Swope," but the unaccommodating agency, which also had a seven-letter *minimum*, made him accept the lusterless nine-letter compromise "Herbswope."

Naturally, Swope did not expect his friends to use his entire name in ordinary parlance. While he could get fairly frosty toward anyone who called him Bert, he was tolerant of Bertie and even of Herbie-Derbie. He was proud that President Woodrow Wilson, who found it difficult to unbend enough to call many men by their first name, had at least got as far as calling him Bayard. To Baruch he was Herb and, on occasion, Swops or Swopsy. To Joseph P. Kennedy he was Jake, and he was Herbartus to Alfred E. Smith and Felix Frankfurter, who, after he became a Supreme Court Justice, would now and then solicit Swope's opinion of a Court opinion. Franklin Pierce Adams, while writing his column, the "Conning Tower," for Swope's *World*, called him Simon Legree (Swope called F.P.A. Uncle Tom), James F. Byrnes called him General, General George C. Marshall called him Doctor, and Senator Tom Connally called him Colonel.

Making puns on Swope's surname was for a time a minor but absorbing indoor New York sport. Swope himself liked to play—being partial to such phrases as "at one fell Swope." The oft-quoted "a Swope-filled room" is generally attributed to the publisher M. Lincoln Schuster, who is known to have uttered it in 1947 after watching Swope in omnipotent action at a directors' meeting of the Overseas News Agency. (Heywood Broun had said much the same thing, years earlier, without punning: "Whenever two or more executives are gathered together you have a group. Indeed, in my early days in journalism I always felt that when Herbert Bayard Swope was gathered together this was group enough for me.") "Abandon Swope, all ye who enter here" goes back to 1924, when some irreverent wag tacked it up outside Swope's office door at the *World.* The origin of "Where there's life there's Swope" is uncertain; several claimants exist, but their claims lack authority.

On July 14, 1938, when Howard Hughes landed at Floyd Bennett Field, Long Island, after a ninety-one-hour flight around the world with four companions, he was acclaimed as New York traditionally acclaims its heroes. The parade up lower Broadway, the ticker tape, the City Hall reception—all these conventional civic tributes were showered on the lion of the hour. But Hughes, in later years perhaps the most invisible and inaccessible of celebrated Americans, was even then an elusive lion. Less than forty-eight hours after his triumphal return, he disappeared from public view, although a posse of reporters was pursuing him. The New York *Times* reported, regretfully, on Sunday, July 17, that he had "managed to drop completely out of sight yesterday."

Early in the afternoon of July 16 a single-engine seaplane dropped into sight a few hundred yards off Prospect Point, a rocky strip of land jutting out into Long Island Sound at the seaward tip of Sands Point, one of the more affluent communities of the Island's elegant North Shore. Hughes, in his customary formal visiting clothes—open shirt, unpressed white pants, and dirty white sneakers—was at the controls. He landed smoothly and taxied toward a big gray house set on a bluff that dominated Prospect Point. It was Swope's house, and no one could have been less surprised than the head of this establishment that the aviator, after giving the worshiping rest of the world the slip, should have come calling on him. It always seemed meet and proper to Swope that anybody who was anybody would, sooner or later, turn up under his capacious and hospitable roof, and he greeted Hughes warmly, though with no more effusiveness than a feudal lord would normally extend to a visiting knight from another demesne.

To the hundreds of eminent pilgrims who did turn up, usually overland, the Swope house was a merry and memorable Mecca. John Hay Whitney, a long-time friend of Swope's and a man not unused himself to gracious living, once described the Swope ménage as "marvelous" and thought it was one of the gayest households he had ever visited. By the standards of its neighborhood, Swope's house was nothing out of the ordinary, but it had an unmistakable atmosphere of grandeur. In the spring of 1931, Alexander Woollcott, who for the previous ten years or so had attended many a dazzling Swope soiree, went to China to visit a college friend of his, Henry Ke-an Yuan. His father, Yuan Shih-kai, had been the first President of the Republic of China, and the Yuans were enormously wealthy. Writing to a friend about his jaunt, Woollcott said the Yuans had eight palaces and a regiment of servants. "As you see," Woollcott added, "they live just like the Swopes."

One singular factor in the life of Swope and his family was their scorn of conventional hours. Many owners of large homes like theirs employed night watchmen. The Swopes never had one, because more often than not they were still up at daybreak. It was a Christmas Day rule of the household, as in many others, that the two Swope children could open none of their presents, aside from the contents of their stockings, until their parents had arisen and could look on. It was sometimes two in the afternoon before the children got their chance. One time a governess of theirs, returning from a day off, was fired after being caught climbing in a window at two in the morning. In that household she should have known she couldn't get away with it. The Swopes rarely dined before ten. They had servants on call around the clock, among them a day chauffeur and a night chauffeur. (Once, complaining to the New York Telephone Company about what he considered the inadequacy of *its* service, Swope said, "I maintain a special night staff of servants, whose duty it is to answer the telephone. No one in my house goes to bed until at least three o'clock in the morning.") If the Swopes felt like showing their Saturday-night dinner guests—who might number forty or so—a movie, they would engage an entire Long Island theater and shepherd their crew over there at midnight, after the establishment's run-of-the-mill patrons had seen the end of the last feature.

A guest in the Swope home could request any kind of food or drink at any hour. Once, at three or four in the morning, a young woman asked for some chocolate cake and champagne, while others in the party were ordering hamburgers, chili con carne, omelets, and sundry dishes more or less appropriate to that time. A few minutes later, without any special fuss, she was served a bottle of champagne and a whole chocolate cake. Another woman who, close to dawn, asked if there was any chewing gum around was able a moment afterward to take her pick from six brands proffered on a silver salver. "Many will remember happily the night hours of clarity and high talk when the noises of the day were stilled and dull folks had long since gone to bed," Robert Moses said. "Here was no pretentious salon, but the atmosphere of the eighteenth-century coffeehouse and of an earlier romantic period when Gascons skilled with the rapier could compose a ballad to the ladies as they fenced against overwhelming odds." Swope, urbane, patriarchal, with a rapierlike tongue, presided over it all, and what made life in his household so elegant was not so much the special service or the crazy hours or even the celebrated guests but his own unparalleled and indomitable *panache*.

After Swope died, at the age of seventy-six, on June 20, 1958, a memorial service was held for him at the Sands Point place. Swope had many friends who were younger than he was, and among those present were the actress Arlene Francis and her actor husband, Martin Gabel. As they were leaving, Gabel said to his wife, "We'll never know a house like that again." Swope is unlikely to be duplicated, either. John Hay Whitney, after he became publisher of the New York *Herald Tribune*, was once told by John Fischetti, his staff cartoonist, that the trouble with most Americans nowadays is that they're all so much alike they're non-cartoonable. Whitney considered it significant that Swope was incontestably cartoonable. "The American tends to conform so much I've always admired enormously anybody who had stuff," Whitney said. "And Herbert had stuff. He had a tremendous quality. He was a bloody tiger."

Swope also had the physical stuff that appeals to cartoonists. He was an arresting figure, straight and slim, carrying a trim one hundred and ninety pounds on a six-foot-one-inch frame that looked even taller because it was crowned in his prime years by a thatch of bright-red hair—a beacon that perched like a magnificent dot atop an emphatic ramrod *i*. He admired big, noticeable men like himself. One time, asked to comment on a man being considered for an important journalistic job, Swope telegraphed his praise of the candidate's tenacity, intelligence, honesty, and judgment, but added, "AGAINST THESE QUALITIES I FIND QUESTIONS ARISING THROUGH FACT THAT IN SIZE HE IS SMALL AND UNIMPRESSIVE." In 1935, Peggy Bacon, who liked to amplify her

22

cartoons with captions, sketched a head of Swope for *Stage* magazine and annotated it: "Tall, architectural head like a department store, tomato bisque in color, topped by close, well-groomed frills of blond hair. Narrow forehead with square, jutting bones. Steep, pear-shaped nose, pinched in at the bridge, flanked by an inch of eyebrow, a circle of glass, and a wedge of eye. Scornful nostrils snorting with importance. Long upper lip of an early settler, suspending a mouth like a tailored buttonhole and a truculent chin with a slight dribble of flesh beneath. Big swinging stride: style, Lord of Creation. Voice like a dinner gong. Stuck-up, stiffened, starched, easily rumpled. Self-centered as the last dodo. Breathes fire, brimstone, and Big Business. The spirit of old Gotham."

John O'Hara summed up Swope more succinctly. "He had style," O'Hara said.

Swope's wife, Margaret, was something special, too. The Swopes were an unusually close-knit couple. Douglas Fairbanks, Jr., wrote Margaret Swope after her husband's death, "You were so much a part of him that we thought of the Swopes as one." Margaret Swope, often known as Maggie, was nearly a foot shorter than her arresting husband, but she was a formidable person in her own right, with a sharp mind and a sharper tongue. Edna Ferber thought the phrase for her was "acid in cream." Once the guests at the Swopes' included two men named Stephen. Margaret had a much higher opinion of one than the other, and as she came upon them standing together she smiled sweetly and said crisply, "Ah, the two Steves—common and preferred." For a woman in whom the social graces were most daintily lodged, she had an astonishingly rough-and-tumble vocabulary. Her husband had lived much of his life in newspaper city rooms, but sometimes his wife's uninhibited talk made him wince. "God damn it, you don't *have* to use words like that," he would say. Moss Hart, who once fondly described Margaret as the Bethlehem Steel Company, was moved on another occasion to observe that if her husband ever became President and she, like Eleanor Roosevelt, chose to write a daily column, it would presumably be called "My Damn Day." Leonard Lyons ran this item in *his* column; such are the vagaries of syndicated journalism that one cautious newspaper changed Hart's tag line to "My Horrid Day."

Margaret Swope, uncommonly devoted to and protective of her husband, was unremittingly concerned about his stature and his safety. Her fears for Swope's well-being would now and then

23

provoke her into extraordinary action. One night in 1938 she drove him to Pennsylvania Station to take a sleeper train to Washington. Riding back to her city apartment, she saw an odd glow in the sky, more or less above the Pennsylvania Railroad's right-of-way through New Jersey. When she got home she phoned a friend and was told that rumor had it a meteor had struck the earth. The meteor had, in fact, disintegrated fifty miles up, but Margaret was determined to ascertain that her husband was all right. She called the railroad's stationmaster in North Philadelphia, and though he told her he'd had no report of any train's being hit by any celestial object, she demanded that he furnish her with definite assurance of her husband's well-being. Swopes are hard to argue with. At the next stop, 30th Street, accordingly, a railroad emissary boarded the train, went to Swope's berth and shook him into wakefulness. Swope, thinking he had arrived in Washington, sat up and began to dress. He was half clothed before he realized what was going on. "They frightened him to death," Margaret said later, "but it appeased my mind."

Margaret was also uncommonly fastidious. She kept her homes spotless, and she would not sleep in a Pullman car or at a friend's place, if she could help it, without having her berth or bed made up with her own dependable linen. On her own premises she spent so much time emptying ashtrays and plumping pillows that some of her regular guests in due course found themselves performing these chores and could hardly arise from a Swope sofa without patting it back into shape.

Swope roomed for a while, as a young man, with John Barrymore, then a newspaper cartoonist, who later had a chance to act both on and off the stage. Swope, confined throughout to amateur theatricals, did his best to make his performances noteworthy. "All that I do is to avoid being commonplace," he once wrote a friend. Wherever he was was his stage; whoever he was with was his supporting player. There was a theatricality about Swope's costumes. Tailors loved him. In 1934 one of them, James W. Bell, asked Carr Van Anda, the managing editor of the New York *Times*, "Do you know Mr. Herbert Bayard Swope?"

"Yes, indeed," said Van Anda, no doubt smiling to himself that anyone would *put* such a question to a consequential New York journalist of that time.

"He came in here with Al Smith one day not long ago," Bell

went on. "What a figure of a man! The tailor's dream! If I made his clothes I would surpass even myself!"

Swope took pleasure in his clothes, and he had a flock of tailors, at home and abroad. He could never fathom Broun's determined sloppiness and once almost dragged him to a high-class clothing establishment he patronized, where the rumpled columnist grudgingly ordered a suit. Broun usually wore his newest suit until it fell apart, and then bought another. A year or so after Swope tried to prettify him, the two men were sharing a hotel room in Florida. Swope woke late one morning to see Broun, at a window, holding his trousers up to the sun. Light was streaming through them. "Looks as though they'll last another day," Broun said cheerfully. Swope—whose wife thought he had three hundred suits but who, according to his valet, rarely had more than seventy-five in circulation at any one time—was horrified.

One of the tailors Swope went to was Raymond G. Twyeffort, who had much to do with emancipating American mankind from its enslavement in drabness and with making men's clothes colorful, if not downright garish. A turning point in his crusade came in the giddy year of 1928, when midnight blue first was accepted as a substitute for black in evening wear. It was Swope, as a Twyeffort missionary, who carried off the dashing coup. (Swope was also credited with being the first man brave enough to wear zippered bathing trunks.) After that, it was by relatively easy stages that Twyeffort goaded Swope into a claret evening jacket. Arthur Brisbane said in his column that nobody could understand why Swope needed it. "In his house there can't be any mistake about the host," Brisbane wrote.

Swope's friends were both amused and awed by his wardrobe. Robert Moses, for all the multiple state and city jobs that kept him so frenetically occupied, would still find time every now and then to sneak into Swope's dressing room on Long Island and count his sets of underwear. Moses, the chairman of the Long Island Park Commission, once reached fifty sets before Swope, a vice-chairman, charged in and broke up the numbers game. Swope occasionally took such inventory himself. On Sundays his weekend house guests—perhaps Broun, or Edna Ferber, or Frank Sullivan, or any of a hundred other luminaries—would go up to the host's bedroom and find him in bed counting his neckties, and like as not screaming at his wife or his valet or another servant that one of his pet Charvets was missing. One afternoon when Swope, who had an awesome reputation for tardiness, was late for a croquet match on his lawn, the other players deputized one of their group to see what was holding him up. "You know what the son of a bitch was doing?" soon came the report. "He was upstairs counting his shirts."

Swope had special brass tie hangers built into his closets, designed so that each of his items of neckwear would be individually visible when he got around to selecting one. He was partial to monogrammed socks, which he bought in near-wholesale lots and which, since he himself was always ready to do favors for others, it seemed reasonable to him should be delivered by highly placed errand boys. He once instructed Bernard Baruch to bring him a dozen pairs of white wool socks from Paris. (When some socks Swope bought closer to home displeased him, he airily returned them, a year later, to the then president of Macy's, Richard Weil. "Throw 'em away or use 'em yourself—that's the sort of fellow I am," Swope told Weil.) Swope told John D. Hertz, when the financier was in Paris, to fetch him back two dozen evening ties from A. Sulka—one dozen each of black and of white. The list of credits in the program of the 1953 play *Men of Distinction*, of which Martin Gabel was a co-producer, read, "Mr. Robert Preston's black tie on loan from the Herbert Bayard Swope, Sr., collection." Gabel had hoped that this odd note might result in some publicity that would in turn boost ticket sales, but before the full impact of the news of this unusual borrowed plumage could spread among the theatergoing public, the show routinely succumbed to adverse notices.

David Sarnoff, one of Swope's oldest friends, once said, "Herbert Swope had enough initiative and enough brass so that if you wanted to meet God, he'd arrange it somehow." Swope, who enjoyed operating as a social catalyst, introduced Sarnoff to Winston Churchill, to whom he also introduced the junior Fairbanks, who in turn met his second wife under Swope's hospitable roof. George Backer met both his wives through Swope. Backer, a real-estate man and publisher who became one of W. Averell Harriman's chief advisers when Harriman went into politics, was introduced to Harriman by Swope. Swope brought Harriman together with Harry Hopkins at the start of the 1930s and did the same a few years later for Hopkins and Robert E. Sherwood. (Sherwood, while working on his book *Roosevelt and Hopkins*, wrote Swope,

"Going through [Hopkins'] papers, I find many letters which begin with the words, 'Having had the pleasure of meeting you at Swope's . . .'") In 1954 Harriman became governor of New York, after earlier careers as a Cabinet member, Ambassador to England and Russia, and a Presidential adviser. Still, he had never before held elective office, and Swope, evidently feeling that he needed some good local connections, not only gave him a dinner at the "21" Club, attended by a number of highly placed politicians and the publishers of half a dozen New York daily newspapers, but also volunteered to serve as a bridge across which the Democratic Harriman could march to meet that long-entrenched Republican power in New York, Robert Moses. Since both men were intimates of Swope's, this was easy enough to arrange, and from time to time during Harriman's administration when he had a message to transmit to Moses he would send it to Swope and ask him to recouch it in language calculated not to ruffle its recipient.

When the Princeton undergraduate son of a friend of his needed an actress to interview for a *Daily Princetonian* feature, Swope swiftly provided Beatrice Lillie. When Swope's own son, Herbert, Jr., was a freshman at Princeton in the spring of 1934, he asked his father to furnish some speakers for a meeting of a campus debating society. It was to be on a Sunday. Swope called Moses, invited him to participate, and said he would pick him up at 4:00 P.M. on the appointed day. Moses tried to beg off. Like any Moses, he believed in the institution of the Sabbath, and Sunday was his only day of rest. But Swope, as he so often did, prevailed. When the day came, Moses was surprised to have Heywood Broun turn up at his apartment at four. Broun said he had been told to be there then. A few minutes later, Raymond Moley arrived. The next person to show up was James J. Lyons, the Borough President of the Bronx. At five or so Swope swept in and urged everyone into his car; he said they were late. On the way to New Jersey, Swope, a Democrat all his life, told Lyons that he should talk about practical politics. To Broun he said, "You're a radical. You talk left wing." To Moley he said, "You talk New Deal." To Moses he said, "You're a conservative and a stick-in-the-mud. You take the Republican line." Here was catalysis at its purest. Swope had so many shades of political opinion represented for the debate that there was no need for him to talk at all.

As a middleman, Swope was forever finding himself in odd

27

situations. When, during the Second World War, the National Association for the Advancement of Colored People suspected that a patriotic organization, in a let's-all-make-socks-for-our-boys crusade, might be withholding knitting yarn from Negro women, it was to Swope that Walter White, the head of the N.A.A.C.P., turned for confirmation. Swope replied, "I was unable to get satisfactory evidence on the refusal . . . to give Negro women knitting yarn. I am told it is true. If so it should be exposed." Then, having disposed of that matter, Swope continued, "Are living conditions in Harlem any better? Are prices still outrageous? It makes my blood boil to see the conditions imposed upon the colored population in this great state." Swope was easily vexed by the imperfections of society, and also he had a mind that jumped.

To the general public, which does not always understand the intricacies of high-level intrigue, it might have seemed that Adlai Stevenson was pretty well fixed with the Navy in the spring of 1944, when he was Special Assistant to its Secretary; but when Stevenson heard, that May, a rumor that his name was being considered for an Assistant Secretaryship of the Navy, a job he coveted, it was to Swope he wrote asking that a favorable word be dropped in the ear of James Byrnes, then President Roosevelt's director of war mobilization. (Stevenson was not appointed, in spite of Swope's having spoken on his behalf not only to Byrnes but, as he confided to the aspirant, to "the big boss" himself.) On another occasion, when a number of Navy admirals were vying for selection as Chief of the Bureau of Navigation, one of the candidates, on sea duty in the Pacific, appealed to Swope confidentially to present his case to the President. Swope tried so hard to be of aid that he caused the admiral some embarrassment —by sending him messages about his efforts on an open radio circuit, as a result of which they were overheard by competing admirals who had been applying through routine service channels.

It was rare that Swope had to confess that there was any person of consequence with whom he was unacquainted. Once, though, asked to help a New York City police captain get elevated to Deputy Inspector, Swope had to reply that he would do what he could but "as it happens, I do not know [the Commissioner of Police], so I shall have to work through the Mayor." But he had made his point all right: Anybody working through Swope knew he had not far to go to reach his ultimate objective. In Swope the American tradition of getting things done by knowing the right people came to finest flower. Just the sight of him could inspire some people to jump to conclusions. Once Morris Ernst was asked to meet with a lawyer whom he knew to be close to the scoundrelly Arnold Rothstein, who had himself been close to Swope in earlier days. Ernst made a habit, when associating with men of conceivably shady reputation, always to be seen with them in the most public of places, and accordingly he took the Rothstein attorney to a big midtown New York restaurant. Presently Swope swept in, stopped at Ernst's table to say hello, and moved on across the room to join Bernard Baruch. "What a cockeyed world," Rothstein's man said. "Look how easy it could be for me to get straight to the President. Me to A. R. to Swope to Baruch to the White House."

2

I N THE ordinary course of events there is a great gulf between
businessmen and the non-mercantile world. Industrialists are
apt to be enormously impressed by admirals and generals, for instance, and admirals and generals no less impressed—Dwight D.
Eisenhower was a good example—by outstanding men from the
marts of commerce. At Swope's house a Ridgway or a Halsey or,
for that matter, an Eisenhower, could often be found shoulder to
shoulder with a Sarnoff or a Skouras, and if the one group
couldn't always understand everything the other said, Swope
stood ready to interpret—and to do so with such knowledgeability
and unflagging vitality that frequently both groups would just
lapse into silence and listen to him. After Swope had taken over
the weekend itinerary of one lieutenant general visiting New
York from his headquarters in Washington, the officer's thank-
you note said, "The thrill of a first night performance and the
meeting of New York and Hollywood celebrities would alone
have made the social side of my visit noteworthy. But I was particularly delighted to have the opportunity to meet your charming
wife and to become better acquainted with you personally. I
found my discussions, not only with you but with your friends,
highly stimulating and, I hope, profitable, not only from a personal standpoint, but for the betterment of our national defense
organization."

For much of Swope's life a good part of his income was derived
from large corporations, which paid him annual retainers as a
policy consultant and which could readily afford thirty thousand
dollars or so apiece a year to associate with a man who seemed to
know everybody and everything. Swope's connections could be

useful to his clients. If, say, the Radio Corporation of America had a bone to pick about a *Fortune* article on its operations, Swope had only to make a couple of phone calls to arrange for David Sarnoff to have lunch with Henry Luce. (Sarnoff could undoubtedly have picked up a phone and made the same arrangement himself, but when big business has hired a man like Swope it hates to waste him.) Conversely, when Arthur Krock's television set went on the blink in Washington, Swope was able to take this maintenance problem up with Sarnoff directly.

Some people have astonishingly fast physical reflexes. Much of Swope's value to his clients lay in his fast mental reactions. What was more important, his mind was finely attuned to how people in general would react to something—so much so that Krock once reminded him admiringly of "your capacity as the global public." Mrs. Eleanor Roosevelt described Swope in an obituary tribute as "one of those who understood how to communicate with the people of the country," and she added that he "helped many others to do so." He often helped a client to do so by anticipating how the public would react to some contemplated word or deed. Baruch, whom he assisted more than anyone else, told Swope in 1948, "You are editor emeritus of Public Opinion."

"I have confidence in my own opinion because, as you know, that is my chiefest occupation—evaluating an event in terms of public reaction," Swope once wrote Felix Frankfurter. Sometimes, after Swope had made his assessment of an event, he took the position that there was hardly any point in discussing it any more. When Judge Irving Kaufman sentenced Julius and Ethel Rosenberg to death in 1953 for espionage, the whole world was stirred. The Communists were, naturally, making the best propaganda use of the case that they could; the foes of capital punishment were getting their licks in; and a good many persons with varying motives were arguing loudly that the Rosenbergs' punishment was excessively severe. Swope reflected on the question and then telegraphed Judge Kaufman: "YOU HAVE RENDERED A RIGHTEOUS JUDGMENT SO GIVE THE MATTER NO FURTHER THOUGHT FOR SOUND PUBLIC OPINION IS WHOLLY WITH YOU."

So infectious was Swope's self-assurance, whether large or small issues were involved, that people now and then tended to believe he was right even when their own common sense argued strongly against him. He could be magnificently wrong, but it was hard

31

for others to tell, in his case, the difference between exuberance and divination. In 1948 Groucho Marx and Norman Krasna wrote a comedy, *Time for Elizabeth,* and as the curtain fell on its Broadway opening the collaborators feared the worst. But they brightened when Swope strode backstage, teeth gleaming, hand outstretched, and in an unequivocal voice yelled, "You're in!" They were so buoyed by his verdict that, despite twinges of misgiving when they read what the professional critics had to say the next morning, they remained confident of success for the entire run of the play, which closed, as almost everybody but Swope had foretold it would, after three performances.

Swope did not limit his sphere of operations to evaluating American reactions. He was constantly making notes to himself—in part to refresh his memory, in part to have evidence of how his restless mind was working. Al Smith was a close friend of his, and Swope was responsive to Smith's famous interjection, "Let's look at the record." Swope always liked to have a record of his own to look at. Thus in 1956, after the Soviet Union had begun the spirited downgrading of Stalin, Swope suggested in a memorandum for his own eyes that he had a pipeline to the Russian public mind, too. He thought the Kremlin had wrongly judged the rest of the world's attitude toward *its* attitude toward Stalin, and he added, "A good man would have been able to point this out." Swope saw quite a bit of the Soviet emissaries to this country while he was working with Baruch in 1946 on the American plan for the international control of atomic energy, and in 1949 he wrote to Secretary of State Dean Acheson, "My period of contact with [Andrei] Gromyko taught me that their formula was simple: Anything we wanted, they were opposed to. It seemed to me that they hoped to create Confusion [Swope had an old-fashioned fondness for capitalizing abstract nouns], which is to be followed by Collapse, then Chaos, then Communism [he liked Alliteration, too]. That formula is a conjecture on my part, but this is factual: They rely upon information regarding Public Opinion in America that is wholly invalid." The Russians, conceivably to their loss, never sought to retain Swope to set them straight.

"The public mind is like a baby's stomach," Swope was fond of saying. "You must feed it one thing at a time, and damn little of that." Swope's own ingestive capacity was huge, and it pleased him that he could digest what was in the public mind even when

32

the contents of that delicate and colicky apparatus were at variance with thoughts in his own mind. On March 7, 1935, halfway through Franklin Roosevelt's first term, Swope wrote to James A. Farley:

Things ain't too good. I am not referring now to business conditions. I am referring to a sense of fear that is beginning at the top, growing downward and spreading as it goes, which, lacking realization, takes the form of misgiving about the President. I say this as one of his warmest supporters, but I cannot doubt the evidence of my own senses, much as I should like to. I do not agree with this misgiving; I think it is baseless—nevertheless, it exists. It has not yet spread among the lower strata. There far more hope exists than doubt, but the fulmination is beginning to work and we must look out.

At least one historian of the Roosevelt era was later to confirm Swope's diagnosis. In *Roosevelt: The Lion and the Fox*, James MacGregor Burns wrote, "When Herbert Bayard Swope wrote Farley early in 1935 of a sense of fear that was beginning at the top, growing downward, and spreading as it grew in the form of misgiving about the President, he was reporting on an essentially irrational hatred of Roosevelt that had begun long before the second Hundred Days had given the business community some kind of rational basis for that hatred."

President Roosevelt frequently used Swope as a sounding board for his ideas, having been impressed by, among other things, Swope's perspicaciously pouncing on the words "New Deal"—first used in a not widely noticed paragraph in a 1932 Roosevelt speech drafted by Raymond Moley and polished by Samuel Rosenman—and telling the President that the two little words were just what the public then wanted.

Whenever Swope felt clearly enough tuned in on public opinion, he was quick to amplify and relay his findings. On February 29, 1940, he warned the Marquess of Lothian, the British Ambassador to the United States, "I discern in the American mind the belief that purpose is disintegrating among the belligerents—that the war is more a state of mind than a state of being." Swope's achievement at detecting a state of mind within a state of mind was perhaps no more remarkable, in a different degree, than Lord Lothian's reply, which characterized Winston Churchill as a man whose consistent foolishness kept him from becoming Prime Minister.

It is a relatively short step from analyst to oracle, and Swope found it hard to resist playing the prophet. Mulling over probable postwar conditions in September 1944, at a time when comparatively few men had yet begun to voice concern about subsequent Soviet-American relations, Swope wrote to Sir Keith Murdoch, the publisher of the Melbourne *Herald*, "I think the Russians will take an important part in the situation. In fact, I think the future of the world depends upon our relations, and those of the British Empire, with Russia. I see clouds in the sky."

Swope's favorite predictions were political, and he liked to handicap potential candidates for high offices, much as if he were running a future book on the Kentucky Derby. While his prognostications, like those of many a horse-race handicapper, were far from faultless, Swope delivered his political judgments, like all his others, with such certainty that other men eagerly awaited them and even courted them. In June 1948, for instance, Senator Owen Brewster of Maine was a delegate to the Republican National Convention at Philadelphia. A month earlier Swope had told Brewster that Dewey was the favorite for the Republican nomination. On the eve of the convention the Senator wrote Swope and asked for a more up-to-date prediction, to be sent straight to Philadelphia, presumably to help guide him in his deliberations. Swope obliged, though he might have done better not to, for this time he switched to Senator Arthur H. Vandenberg.

Swope foresaw in 1948, however, that Adlai Stevenson would be the Democrat to reckon with in 1952, and as early as 1947 he was making bets (he got nice odds) that Dwight Eisenhower would be the Republican candidate five years after that. In the case of John F. Kennedy, Swope did even better. He was fourteen years ahead of the bandwagon. On November 6, 1946, the day after Kennedy won his first election to Congress as a Representative from Massachusetts, Swope, who had known him since Kennedy was a boy, dictated a letter of congratulation. Then he added a footnote: "My crystal ball reveals you as the center of a fascinating drama—one that carries you far and high. I hope I'm a true prophet."

Toward the end of Swope's life, Mayor Robert F. Wagner of New York appointed him head of a do-gooding civic body called the Commission on Intergroup Relations. But when James Farley, who once said he regarded Swope as an institution, wrote to congratulate him on the new post, Swope replied, "The prospect is not very pleasing; I like to hunt alone." Swope gave the impression of being a fierce and fearsome fighter. "The man for whom Herbert had drawn his sword could have depended on him in all circumstances," Baruch once said, though no one knew better than he that there were circumstances in which Swope could be unreliable. And Gerhard M. Dahl, a big man in municipal transit in the rapid-paced 1920s, was moved to exclaim, "His intrepid spirit is such that he could lead a defeated army away from a losing battlefield with the air of supreme victory." Swope was often in combat, but except while he presided over the *World*, in many of the struggles in which he was clashingly engaged he was more of a ranking staff officer than a front-line soldier.

Still and all, Swope was a remarkable man, and what made him—to use one of Baruch's phrases for him—*sui generis* was his early recognition of his singular potentialities and his dogged determination to exploit them to the fullest. While the phenomenal surface gaiety and glitter of his life shrouded much inner doubt and worry, he made a solid impact on his fellow men by the sheer force of his personality. And people who were unacquainted with him, or to whom at the very least he was unknown, missed out on one of the most colorful sights, and sounds, of their time. It was as if they had failed, through obtuseness or indolence or ignorance, to attend a first-rate and memorable show.

Swope was highly intelligent, but not an intellectual in the conventional sense of the term. Realities were his forte, and he indulged in abstractions mainly when communicating with himself. Late in 1928, at the time of his departure from the *World*, he wrote to himself:

I am coming into equilibrium with life by easy swings instead of being forced into extremes by a fear of false duty. False because it is imposed from without instead of being a flow from within; false because it ignores real values and seeks merely consonance with the herd—always to be busy; never to be idle; always to be conforming; never to be self-determining; always to be a part of the mass; never to dare to be individual; never to think, act and be one's self but always to follow a set plan and pattern. Men work to avert death or the thoughts of death. Sometimes a substitute for this can be found. Work alone is not salvation. It is often harrowing and, like religion, merely an anesthetic. It is better to live freely than only to work hard.

For Swope to be apart from others, though, was not enough; he had to be above them, too. "He always wanted to be top boy," said his wife. Whenever Swope joined any gathering, or any gathering was drawn toward him, there was no question in his mind—nor, as a rule, in that of anyone else present—but that he would dominate the assemblage. Some people enter a room like a breath of fresh air. Swope habitually came in like a gale, and his friends often thought of him as analogous to violent natural phenomena. A British lady who knew him only slightly once described him to an acquaintance as dynamic, and the acquaintance, who knew him well, said, "No, cyclonic." The composer and critic Deems Taylor likened him to a tornado. Dudley Nichols, in the late twenties a star reporter on the *World* and after that the writer of *The Informer* and other movies, compared him to a comet; *Time*, to a typhoon; and Sir Wilmott Lewis, of the London *Times*, to a natural force second only to Niagara. Mrs. Harold E. Talbott, describing Swope for her grandchildren, who she feared without firsthand testimony might grow up to believe he could not be true, mentioned an *unnatural* force. "Long before Sputnik was invented, Herbert Swope was," she said.

Swope sailed through life like an ocean liner, leaving a wake behind him that rocked everything within his horizon, and frequently small-craft warnings were flown in anticipation of his approach. Even when Swope was sick, Franklin P. Adams once said, he had "more vigor than most of the men I know who are whole." Nobody could ignore him. After marching alongside Swope in a New York unemployment-relief parade in 1933, Arthur Brisbane wrote him, "All I can say is that you looked grand in the procession, something I should say like Achilles, when he got over his sulks, because they took his girl away from him, and came striding out of his tent."

Those who knew Swope slightly were usually scared of him. Those who knew him well were frequently annoyed with him. "There was never any middle course with Swope," said a man who worked for him for many years. "That personality of his would either repel you or charm the life out of you." Sometimes it did both. "I loved Swope, but he was an arrogant bastard," Raoul H. Fleischmann, the publisher of *The New Yorker*, once said. "He knew that I thought he was a bastard and I think he thought he was one, too. I've never known a man who was so likable and had so many faults. I was devoted to him, even though

36

every so often he would spit in my eye, just to put me in my place." *

Swope's ability to dominate a group was never better exemplified than on the evening of November 8, 1935, when he was one of eight hundred men attending the thirtieth annual show of the Society of Illustrators at the Heckscher Theater on upper Fifth Avenue in New York. It was a stag affair that attracted many of the senior bons vivants of the city—magistrates, bankers, publishers, sportsmen, artists, and others—and the cast included several dozen girls, a few of them decoratively underdressed. The production, though hardly suitable for a church, was considerably less naughty than most burlesque shows, but nonetheless the police chose to raid it. Two plainclothesmen climbed up onto the stage, said the show was indecent and must be stopped, and invited the audience to leave quietly. The spectators roared with laughter. They regarded the incursion as one of the high comic points of an evening that, while satisfying as far as the girls went, had not in its skits achieved a level of wit comparable to, say, that of *Anything Goes!* at the 46th Street Theater downtown. The cops were perplexed. The more they tried to prove their authenticity, the more the audience howled with glee. It was not until Swope, rising to the emergency, took center stage himself and assured his fellow spectators that the place really had been raided and that five scantily clad girls were at that moment being dragged out a backstage exit that anyone present would take the incident seriously.

Fiorello LaGuardia, then the Mayor of New York and of course in command of the police who had conducted the raid, was a sciatica patient at Mount Sinai Hospital that night, four blocks south of the Heckscher Theater. After wishing him a speedy recovery, Swope filled him in on the episode. ". . . It was fun," he said, continuing with a barbed ". . . It proved a gentle relaxation for the [Police] Department after the hardships involved in hunting for the perpetrators of the seventeen recent murders." After

---

* A promotional brochure put out by *The New Yorker* in December 1925, less than a year after its struggling birth, promised that its editorial columns would furnish the answer to, among other throbbing questions of that day, "Is there a Herbert Swope?" The magazine made a go of it without ever getting around to fulfilling the pledge, although in 1948 it published a short, ostensibly humorous piece by the author of this book, purporting to answer the question "What is Herbert Bayard Swope?"

thus reprimanding the Mayor, he served up a placatory tidbit of gossip: ". . . between us, Bernie Baruch was coming up but, arriving late, he saw the police cars and turned and fled."

On his personal stage, Swope was a player who both strutted and fretted. Some thought him a pompous man, and he was unquestionably a solemn one. He talked a lot, but it was seldom small talk. The weather as a conversational topic concerned him only if he had a croquet match scheduled or planned to bet on a horse with a known distaste for mud. He lived in a society where mirth rated high, but he almost never laughed aloud. He often *looked* as though he were laughing, but the ordinary sounds of risibility failed to emerge from his contorted features. His laugh, or non-laugh, was akin to the bark of a barkless basenji.

Swope was paradoxical in other respects. He was capable of extraordinary kindness, and he could also be extraordinarily rude. Quite often he did unsolicited favors for people he scarcely knew. Once, hearing that the young son of a casual acquaintance was collecting match packets, Swope sent the boy five rarities, including one that he proudly identified as having been swiped from Dwight D. Eisenhower. Shortly afterward, following a session with Baruch, Swope sent the boy another collector's item—a packet marked "B.M.B." On the other hand, when Swope decided he had to dress down a government official who had been unable to give a job to one of Swope's distant relatives, he wrote, in part, "I suppose, once you are in politics, one goes the way of all politicians. Ingratitude is a chief characteristic of that evolution. I remember, when you were fired from ———, in the late '30s, I extorted a job for you from ——— in ———. . . . When ——— needed a job . . . and badly, and turned to you for help, the answer is no. I am disappointed at this revelation of your makeup."

There was always doubt that Swope, so quick to generalize about another man's makeup, ever clearly understood his own. Dudley Nichols, after he had moved to the West Coast, wrote Swope once that he had spent the previous night with Oliver H. P. Garrett, another *World* alumnus. Garrett was working on a movie script about a newspaper managing editor who was to be a combination of three well-known New York journalists. "But mostly you," Nichols added, "or the outside of you. Not many know the inside. Do you?" It was a good question, but there is no record of Swope's having answered it, and one wonders whether he honestly could have with an unqualified affirmative.

The outside Swope was stately, suave, and unshakably self-sufficient. Inside Swope there was constant turmoil. For one thing, he was recurrently the victim of real or fancied slights; the skin that so many of his acquaintances thought was impenetrably thick was in fact painfully thin. Swope once got so upset when the Arthur Hays Sulzbergers turned down a couple of last-minute dinner invitations from the Swopes that Mrs. Sulzberger felt constrained to write him, "Both times I was sorely tempted to break our engagements so that we could dine with you but, unfortunately, I have never been able to get over my very excellent upbringing, and I could not be rude to friends whose invitations we had already accepted." Swope was appeased, and the day he received Mrs. Sulzberger's letter, learning that she was going abroad, he sent a telegram to her ship: "IT LOOKS TO ME AS IF YOU WERE FLEEING TO EUROPE TO ESCAPE FURTHER INVITATIONS BUT WE WILL GET YOU YET . . ." Swope must have concluded that he had struck just the right note for bon-voyage greetings to ladies of stature in New York morning-newspaper publishing circles. The following month, at any rate, when Mrs. Ogden Reid of the *Herald Tribune* boarded a ship, he sent her the parting salute: "I SUSPECT YOU ARE RUNNING TO EUROPE JUST TO ESCAPE THAT LUNCHEON BUT I WILL GET YOU YET . . ."

When Swope hit upon an idea or phrase that pleased him, he was apt to use it over and over. Early in the Roosevelt era, when James A. Farley was Postmaster General, he inserted the word "irregardless" into a speech he made in Boston. A local purist, a Harvard man, took him to task. He told Farley that for the first Catholic in a Presidential Cabinet to visit the seat of American culture and make such an error was abysmal. Farley, after genially inviting his critic to serve thereafter as grammatical watchdog of his public utterances, told Swope about the incident. Swope began using the taboo word himself, though with a caveat. For twenty-five years he would drop into his letters an " 'Irregardless,' as Jim Farley says. . . ." Farley, for his part, never used the word again in his life after that first Boston gaffe.

There was nobody at whom Swope did not stand ready, if he thought himself injured, to get angry. When Baruch chided him about his tendency to blow up, Swope wrote back, ". . . Anger is merely a corrective application of a code of ethics. I do become irritated momentarily when I, rightly or wrongly, suspect inconsideration, but with you the flash dies down quickly, for your affection always pulls me back." To Felix Frankfurter, after one impulsive tantrum, Swope confided, "Sometimes when I do things in a temper I am a little uncertain as to the wisdom of my course."

Wisely or unwisely, Swope indulged himself to the extent of getting sore at the Chief of Staff of the United States Army during the First World War for not returning a telephone call quickly enough to suit him, and at the Commander of the United States Army Air Forces during the Second World War for not responding with alacrity to a routine Swope letter. Presidents of the United States were not exempt from his wrath. On January 7, 1924, Swope wrote Baruch, to whom he often confided his frustrations, that he was "frightfully hurt" because Woodrow Wilson had ignored him. Three months earlier, at a third party's bidding, Swope had written the former President asking for an autographed photograph. "It was the sort of request anybody would [grant] for a bootblack," Swope told Baruch, "let alone for one who has battered his head against a stone wall, as I did for many years, for him." Swope went on to say that he thought Wilson had "deliberately ignored the entire matter," adding, "Sometimes I am afraid W.W. has streaks of meanness and littleness in him. If these suspicions are true, then Wilson will never take a great place in history, for the star of Greatness is not dependent upon success or failure, but upon the spirit of Bigness in which either is accomplished." The timing of this lament was unfortunate. Wilson was gravely ill when Swope uttered it, and less than a month later Baruch would be in Washington attending his funeral. Swope had the same kind of bad luck less than three weeks before President Roosevelt died. At that time Swope was collecting money for a fund to memorialize Al Smith, and, thanking Governor Thomas E. Dewey of New York for a fifty-dollar contribution, he could not resist adding, "Confidentially, the President sent ten dollars. Pretty shocking, isn't it? I was astounded and distressed."

It is not unusual, of course, for a newspaperman to have friends and acquaintances in high places. Often the best newspapermen have the most. Swope was justly proud of being on amicable terms with Presidents, in and out of office, and was quick to react to any intimation of estrangement. Presidents, for their part, welcomed and valued his friendship. In 1937 Herbert Hoover and Swope attended a public dinner at the Waldorf-Astoria. Swope wrote Hoover immediately afterward, "I thought you either had failed to recognize me, or, for another reason, failed to respond to the warmth of my greeting." Hoover at once invited Swope to a private lunch.

Dwight Eisenhower was still only president of Columbia University when, in the fall of 1948, he received the Swope letter: "What has happened to disturb our relations? When friendship is present, explanations usually can clear misunderstandings. I know of none, but it is evident that something has occurred. Or doesn't it matter?" General Eisenhower replied that Swope's curt note had made him fairly bounce out of his chair. He could think of no reason for Swope's outburst other than that Swope's name might inadvertently have been omitted from the guest list at his installation as president of the university, and he begged Swope not ever again to harbor such distressing thoughts about him as he had expressed in his letter. If Swope ever did harbor them, Eisenhower went on, wouldn't he please just come right up to the campus in person and not let anyone keep him from telling them to the General face to face?

Swope had begun his letter of inquiry with a somewhat cool "Dear General." Eisenhower had signed his reply "Ike"; now, starting off with a warm "My dear General Ike," Swope replied: "I am touched by your letter and reassured by it. Now it makes no difference what reasons animated my previous letter; you have effectively silenced all doubt"—a doubt that, he could not resist adding, had been raised when, after his non-attendance at the ceremonies, "Busy tongues tried to make it a breach between us, and represented you, without any reason being given, as sore at me. . . ."

Reassurance was what Swope always craved. Two years later Eisenhower, on the dais at a formal dinner, spotted Swope among the guests seated below and prudently hastened down to tender him a special greeting. Swope in turn hastened to apprise Baruch of the nice gesture. Baruch, who understood Swope well, wrote him, half sternly, half kindly, "I wish you would stop depreciating yourself with yourself."

It is the young who most frequently need to be petted and consoled and made to feel wanted, and there was something engagingly childlike about Swope during his entire three score and sixteen years. Perhaps it was significant that *Alice in Wonderland* was perennially one of his favorite books, along with the Bible, the *World Almanac* and any book at all that contained a reference to himself. "All of us still are children," he wrote Westbrook

Pegler in 1933, when Swope was nearly fifty-two, "seeking praise at any cost; relishing it most when it is deserved; taking it, nevertheless, when it is not deserved, and resenting criticism as being unfriendly, if not criminal."

Swope had a small boy's relish for the new experience and the unexpected treat. Given an office at the Pentagon during the Second World War, where he functioned as a part-time civilian adviser on public relations, Swope wandered once into a nearby room and there saw a new kind of duffel bag that the Army was planning to issue to some of its men in the field. If there was anything that Swope, a sedentary man, did not need, it was a duffel bag, and to move a wardrobe he deemed minimal would, in any event, have required something as capacious as an L.S.T.; but notwithstanding he asked to have one of these latest clothing carriers, and the Army gladly gave him one. He was delighted in one sense because it made him tangibly privy to a military secret and in another because it enabled him, like any kid stealing a march on his peers, to play with a new toy before it became generally available. Swope was on good terms, at one time or another, with both celebrated sets of American Marx brothers—the acting clan and the toy-making clan. The latter, when Swope was seventy, sent him a batch of *their* newest toys for distribution among his grandchildren; for good measure they sent him a second set, with the jocular explanation that these were for himself.

Like a child, Swope's enthusiasm for games was insatiable, and this was to lead, in the late Twenties, to the name of a famous game. Two recent college graduates, Lucien Esty and Justin Spafford, decided then to compile a book of quizzes on general intelligence, and they understandably elected to try out their project on Swope, having heard of his reputation for omniscience. Swope answered their questions—in some 95 per cent of the instances correctly—for five stimulating hours. By that time his inquisitors were exhausted, but the ordeal had a happy titular outcome when, as they were groping for excuses to call the marathon session to an end, Swope, flushed with victory from just having rattled off the line of poetry that follows "And what is so rare as a day in June?",* cried out, as excited as a boy in the finals of a spelling bee, "Ask me another!" When a book bearing that title was soon published, its dedication read, "To Herbert Bayard Swope, who

---

* "Then, if ever, come perfect days."

might have dictated the answers to these questions and spared the authors the trouble of looking them up."

Every man's home is supposed to be his castle, but over every such palace there does not preside an authentic king. Few could deny that Swope had the regal touch. The sports writer Dan Parker, reflecting once upon the Stuart kings of yore, described them as "those primordial Herbert Bayard Swopes." Brendan Bracken, who like many another illustrious European made Swope's home a port of call during transatlantic journeys, referred to the Sands Point establishment as "Schloss Swope," and some of Swope's friends thought it a pity that, inasmuch as his family was of German origin, he did not spring from sufficiently high-born Teutonic stock to call himself Herbert von Swope. And, of course, he looked the part. John Baragwanath, the mining engineer, once said of Swope to his wife, the artist Neysa McMein, "He has the face of some old emperor." When Edna Ferber and George S. Kaufman wrote *The Royal Family*, produced in 1927, quite a few people thought it was based on the Swope household, which the collaborators had often visited. It was not. The playwrights had toyed with the idea of trying to capture the atmosphere of that ménage on stage but had abandoned the project. "It never crystallized because the Swope household was too fantastic for fiction," Miss Ferber said. "It left nothing to the imagination."

Swope, who once astonished the Long Island social set by cutting in on the Prince of Wales during a dance at Clarence Mackay's, demanded the deference customarily accorded to royalty. "When Herbert came into a room, you couldn't help yourself; you felt like standing," said the Reverend George B. Ford, the Catholic scholar. In Swope's home, as a rule, there was no choice in the matter. When he walked into a room, he expected all present, including his wife and children, to rise to their feet. Instead of being resentful, most people were amused by this, as they were by his other blustering antics. (He himself was disappointed when a niece reached twelve and her mother insisted that the girl was too old to continue to curtsy to him.) Once after he entered a room in which his daughter Jane, by then herself the mother of grown children, was slumped in a chair, she avoided a reprimand only by saying quickly, "I'm terribly sorry, Daddy, but I have an awful headache." Another time, after a croquet match, Swope strode onto the sun porch of his Sands Point place.

43

Oscar Levant, a chronic house guest, was sitting there, and as his host approached he called out, "Hello, Mr. Swope." But he stayed put, and at this lese majesty Swope, who had lost at croquet and was feeling uncommonly put upon, stopped, glared, and replied, "God damn it, when I come into the room you stand on your feet!" About the only person for whom Swope regularly waived this calisthenic house rule was Mrs. Henry Ittleson, Sr., whom Swope had known as a boy in St. Louis and who was several years older than he.

Swope talked like royalty. "He never conversed in an ordinary sense," Marc Connelly said. "He gave you dicta from the throne." Now and then Swope would affect the courtly, English style of letter-writing—bracketing the typed body of a communication with a handwritten beginning and closing. He was partial to red crayon, which he used in bold, imperious strokes. This, along with his white stationery and bright blue typewriter ribbon, gave his correspondence a forthright patriotic appearance. For many years he exchanged letters with Franklin D. Roosevelt. (During the Second World War the proprietor of a Washington restaurant who wanted to get a message to Swope and didn't know his address sent it to him at the White House, which swiftly forwarded it.) On March 31, 1941, using the English style, Swope wrote the President about a speech he had made. Replying, four days later, Roosevelt started off with a handwritten "Dear Bayard," closed with a handwritten "Royally yours, Franklin D. Roosevelt," and beneath that, where a secretary had typed "Hon. Herbert Bayard Swope," crossed out the "Hon." and substituted a handwritten "H.R.H." "Your new form of salutation and subscription is truly regal," the President said in the text of his letter. "You must have inherited it from the Chevalier Bayard who was, as I remember it, the left-handed offspring of the Calif Haroun al Raschid. Whenever I get a letter from present Emperors, Kings, Grand Dukes, etc., that is just what they do. The salutation and subscription are also written longhand. . . ."

Swope and Roosevelt shared an addiction to a kind of sophomoric humor. At the end of 1940, a few months before the President delighted Swope by putting him in the same category with his unimpeachably blue-blooded correspondents, Swope had sent a telegram to the White House comparing another speech of his to one of Pericles'. Roosevelt wired back, "WHO IS PERICLES NEVER MET HIM F.D.R." To this Swope responded, "WHO WAS PERICLES?

44

WHY HE IS MY SLIGHTLY NON-ARYAN UNCLE HAPPY NEW YEAR. BAYARD." Three days later it was Roosevelt's turn again: "WHOM DO YOU MEAN—CONFUCIUS? I ALWAYS KNEW YOU WERE RELATED TO THE GRAND LAMA F.D.R." Within hours Swope had come up with, and duly dispatched, "LAMA TELL YOU THIS: I WOULD HAVE TO LOOK FOR A LONG TIME TO FIND A PHILOSOPHER AS WISE OR A WARRIOR AS BRAVE AS ONE I COULD MENTION." The next day, while the President was conceivably still seeking a rejoinder, Swope dictated, but did not send, yet one more wire: "LAMA ASK YOU ANOTHER. CAN YOU USE A SENTENCE WITH THE WORD MERETRICIOUS IN IT? GIVE UP? MERETRICIOUS AND HAPPY NEW YEAR. I'LL BET THAT WILL HOLD YOU. BAYARD."

In May 1935, after a drive through the New Jersey countryside, Swope wrote Marguerite, or Missy, LeHand, one of the President's secretaries, that he'd been astonished at the number of tent caterpillars he saw. "It occurs to me that the boss could use relief workers for the purpose of curing these blights," he suggested helpfully. President Roosevelt did not at once act on that tip, but he found some of Swope's counsel sound. Robert E. Sherwood observed in his Hopkins book that on June 23, 1941, just after the Nazis invaded the Soviet Union and the President was wondering what he should say to the American people about this turn of events, it was Swope who provided the most intelligent guidance in a memorandum to Hopkins for Roosevelt:

We are opposed to the Communists' formula and we are opposed to the Nazi formula.

In the twenty-seven years since Russia became Communistic, our national interests and our way of life never have been seriously threatened by the Soviets. But in the two years of Hitler's mad drive for world enslavement, our very existence, as a free people, has been gravely endangered.

Attempts to divide us have been made by would-be Quislings, acting within our borders. They have tried to create racial and religious differences; they have promised peace and quiet through Nazi appeasement.

Now we see what a grim tragedy a Nazi peace treaty is. Now we see again the fate that has overtaken fifteen nations which, relying upon Nazi promises, were destroyed, one by one.

We are not for Communism, but we are against all that Hitler stands for. He and his Godless Nazis are the pressing threats to a world of peace and justice and security. In his defeat lies our safety.

45

At this time, as ever, we must keep in mind that our greatest strength is in unity; our greatest danger in discord.

As a king, Swope did not construe his realm of sovereignty to be confined to his own home. Outside it, his behavior was equally regal. Speed limits and traffic lights were not for him; he believed in *droit du roi*. This attitude, to be sure, occasionally got him involved in automobile accidents at busy intersections, but his vehicular progress through the plebeian world was made somewhat less perilous than it might otherwise have been by his being able to bedeck his car with New York State Racing Commission and Long Island Park Commission medallions and by his having as a license plate, on the principal car in his personal fleet, the plain letter "S." He got it originally through Governor Al Smith, who might have saved it for his own use when he left the State House at Albany and had to give up the Governor's "1," but was fond of Swope and on retiring from that office made do with "4" and "5." When Swope died, his badge of honor was offered by the state authorities to Francis Cardinal Spellman, who had been getting by with the plate "H," a legacy from his predecessor as Archbishop of New York, Patrick Cardinal Hayes. But Cardinal Spellman—who was to attest to the catholicity of Swope's friendships by becoming, with Harpo Marx, one of the last two contributors to a Swope memorial at the Columbia University School of Journalism—graciously decided to stick with his "H," so that Swope's widow might continue to enjoy the automotive distinction that was part of her inheritance.

When Swope traveled farther afield, he sowed the path ahead with regal edicts. In 1944, when he and his wife were planning a transcontinental train trip, he instructed a busy corporation lawyer in Chicago, Preston Boyden, to meet him at the LaSalle Street Station there, where passengers switched from the Twentieth Century to the Far West run. Swope's orders were specific. He told Boyden to have two taxis waiting, one for the Swopes and one for their luggage, and to have prepared and to bring along a picnic lunch for three—"cold chicken, about ten sandwiches, six or seven hard-boiled eggs, salt and pepper, apples, etc." Four years earlier, on another trip, Swope knew he'd have an hour or so to kill between trains at Washington. He wired an even more eminent attorney, Felix Frankfurter, to hustle over to Union Station and join him during the layover. Frankfurter, who was extremely fond of Swope and quite accustomed to his ways, wired back, with restraint, that he would be most pleased to see him and that Swope could hop into a taxi at the station and be at his chambers in the Supreme Court building within two minutes.

When he traveled abroad it was much the same. In 1929 Swope turned up in London, accompanied by his wife, his two children, his mother-in-law, and a colored servant, Mae Fielding, who for many years was the major-domo of his household. The entourage moved into the royal suite at Claridge's. (The rooms had been re-decorated, not long before, in honor of an Asian potentate; the bedroom walls were studded with glittering imitation jewels.) One night the Swopes had some guests up for dinner. Dissatisfied with the brands of champagne the sommelier stood ready to pro-vide, Swope drew upon his own splendid resources. It was during the time of Prohibition at home, but he had nonetheless brought with him, as a hedge against the possible inadequacy of European potables, a trunk full of choice whiskies and wines.

People who knew Swope were sometimes disappointed when his actions lacked the touch of grandeur. In the late 1920s Ralph Pulitzer, the proprietor of the *World*, was returning from a trip to Europe. Swope, in the tradition of the day, arranged to ride out into New York harbor and welcome Pulitzer on a cutter that took Immigration, Health, and Customs officials to Quarantine. Swope, late as usual, missed the cutter. Undaunted, he took a ferry to Staten Island, chartered a speedboat, and came abreast of Pulitzer's ship concurrently with the cutter. Aboard this craft was the *World*'s ship-news reporter, John Parker. As Swope arrived, wreathed in spume, Parker leaned over the rail and called out, "I knew you'd make it, boss, but I really thought you'd come down the bay on a battleship."

Pulitzer was a man of considerable distinction himself—son of the legendary founder of the *World* and, before it, of the St. Louis *Post-Dispatch;* husband first of a Vanderbilt scion and then of the historian Margaret Leech; and publisher of New York's journalistic jewel. Even so, he was in Swope's shadow, both figuratively and literally. Pulitzer used to tell with amusement of a time the two of them went together to a heavyweight prize fight. It mattered not at all to Swope that, technically, he was only the second-ranking *World* man in the party. Instead, as they were trying to shoulder through the crowds to get to their seats, Swope shouted, "Make way! I am Herbert Bayard Swope, the executive editor of the *World!*" A way was quickly made, and Swope sailed

47

through it, with Pulitzer meekly in his wake. Pulitzer also wrote from time to time. Among his published works were some light-hearted editorials in the *World* and a satirical novel on high society. Among his unpublished works was a satirical poem, entitled "Ballade of Envy," that indicated he, too, regarded Swope as a man on whose head a crown would comfortably sit:

> *When he enters my room with a crash and a bang,*
> *Sits down at my desk with a bang and a crash,*
> *Springs onto his feet as no man ever sprang,*
> *Hurls open my window 'most out of its sash,*
> *Bespatters my papers with cigarette ash,*
> *Flips into my basket his match still aglow,*
> *Pours forth braggadocio brilliantly brash—*
> *I wish that he'd stub his toe!*

> *When he wagers ten thousand without a pang*
> *And coppers the market without a smash,*
> *Once explained to Caruso how singers sang*
> *And now teaches Jane Cowl how to act with more "pash,"*
> *When he suddenly makes a society splash*
> *And he hypnotizes both high and low*
> *And cuts such a naïvely dauntless dash—*
> *I wish that he'd stub his toe!*

> *When this man (as he'd put it) of "sturm and drang,"*
> *Whom nothing can feaze and none abash,*
> *Gives the date of the birth of Li Hung Chang*
> *Or the derivation of Sabre-Tache*
> *Or the numbers of millions of U.S. cash*
> *Or the speed of the Mississippi's flow*
> *And is always right, it's enough to fash—*
> *I wish that he'd stub his toe!*

> ### L'Envoi
> *Prince, you who are crowned with the flare and flash*
> *That nothing but genius may bestow*
> *Can afford to smile at this futile trash:—*
> *I wish that he'd stub his toe!*

Pulitzer—like a great many other men Swope knew—had access to practically unlimited sums of money. To Swope, Life and Happiness, as he once counseled a young friend embarking on marriage, depended on "Respect, Love, Health, Money and Position." Swope fought a never-ending struggle to obtain enough money to pay for the stylish kind of life he led. Swope was a glorious, reckless, pleasure-seeking spender. "We are all of us hedonists at the bottom, aren't we?" he asked the playwright Harry Kurnitz rhetorically in 1952. Whether Swope happened to have a couple of hundred thousand dollars or not in any given year did not especially concern him; he spent that amount annually, whatever his earnings happened to be, just to run his opulent households. At the peak of his hospitality, his food bills alone ran to a thousand dollars a week. Gracious living was for him not the means to any end; it was an end in itself. The actual physical nearness of money, moreover, made him feel comfortable. He habitually carried large sums of it, and sometimes in the course of a conversation he would abstractedly haul out a wad of bills and count them. Once, at Sands Point, he boyishly tried to impress—and indeed did impress—a group of his guests, most of them far wealthier than he, by flashing a ten-thousand-dollar bill. Nobody present had ever seen one, and it was passed around from hand to hand, until eventually someone teased Swope by hiding it in a glove belonging to Cissy Patterson, the publisher of the Washington *Times Herald*.

People who are *really* very rich—like such cronies of Swope's as Jock Whitney, Averell Harriman, Harry F. Guggenheim, Alfred G. Vanderbilt, and, of course, Bernard Baruch—devote very little time to worrying about money. They have hirelings to handle their financial affairs for them, and they themselves rarely carry much cash. Harriman is notorious for having to borrow a dime whenever he wants to make a pay-phone call. Swope at his peak was never worth much more than twelve million dollars—after the 1929 crash his net worth for a while was a minus figure—and he worried about money all the time. There can have been few other men who, like him, instructed their banks to send them statements of their account every week. Swope liked to be kept informed. In March 1929, while he was frolicking at Palm Beach during the height of the stock-market boom, his secretary felt constrained to advise him that his housekeeper back in New York had received a shipment of two hundred and five bottles of beer he'd ordered, two of which were broken. Swope's attitude toward money was perhaps best set forth in an obituary he wrote for the *World* in 1918 upon the death of Diamond Jim Brady. "Never a first night theatrical performance was complete without him; never a great sporting event did not attract his presence; never a big political gathering but what he was there; never a restaurant could call itself well known until it had been honored by Brady's patronage," Swope wrote. Every word of this could have been true about himself, and there was another passage in the obit, a long and eulogistic one, that sounded, apart from the statistics, even more autobiographical: "Mr. Brady died worth perhaps five million dollars. Fully twice that sum could have been left by him had he lived only to make money, but he was frankly a devotee of pleasure, not merely for himself but for all those with whom he came into contact."

3

I N ONE of Swope's introspective memoranda to himself, he said, on August 29, 1952, when he was past seventy and seriously concerned about where the next hundred thousand dollars was coming from, "My whole capital is my knowledge of things and my acquaintance with people." He had long had both these assets in abundance, and he liked to display them both at every opportunity. That Swope should have referred to a knowledge of *things* was significant. Facts were his province. He had a reportorial knack of acquiring and marshaling vast masses of information, much of it superficial but much of it, by the same token, beguiling. His knowledge of politics was solid; he knew boxing and horse-racing and a good deal more society gossip than most gossip columnists. His mind skittered and swooped. He would alight on a fact like a gull on a stranded clam and gobble it up with birdlike alacrity. If any university, in its quest to spread knowledge among the young, had established a Professorship of Odd Facts, he would have been an ideal choice for the chair. But he did not aspire to scholarship. In an era of restlessness and change and indecision, he had the curiosity and volatility that many men aspired to but few brought to such clarion consummation.

Whether or not a man whose brain is a storehouse of unrelated information is the mental superior of, say, one with a deep and penetrating understanding of a single subject is debatable; but the all-around man is often more fun to be with. In 1927, after looking over *Ask Me Another!*, F.P.A., in his capacity as a contemporary Samuel Pepys, made the diarial entry, "Now I do not believe that a person who could answer every question correctly in the book would for that reason be a better or more useful or interesting

51

person than he who could not answer half. But I have observed that it is usually the vague, dull, sloppy-minded persons who say, 'These tests are no absolute index of knowledge or wisdom,' as though anyone said that they were. But I know this: That a hundred persons who can answer three out of four questions on general information are more successful, more interesting, and happier, too, than a hundred persons who can answer one or two. For the race is oftenest to the swift."

Swope, in this respect, set a pace it was hard for others to match. He was not quite as omniscient as he hoped others would think he was, and there were peculiar gaps in his knowledge. Of painting and music he knew little, for instance, and although he was a newspaperman for thirty years, one of the few questions he muffed on one quiz he took was the identification of "qwertyuiop" —the familiar left-to-right anagram, of course, of the second line of keys on any standard typewriter. But what he did know usually impressed his associates. Charles M. Lincoln, who was managing editor of the *World*, in 1917, while Swope was one of its star reporters, said of him then, "He could probably define every bit of the insignia of all branches of the Army and Navy service with as little difficulty as naming the left halfback on the Princeton eleven of 1899, or telling you what the Senate did to that thing the House put through, in which you are interested, but cannot for the moment recall." It delighted Swope to be able to disseminate information. Knowledge was a form of wealth he was eager to share. Addressing a luncheon of advertising men, he would urge them to follow his example: Why didn't his listeners who advertised linen handkerchiefs do so, he would ask, by telling the public that the quality of the finest linen was achieved by patiently beating the cloth on rocks on the shore of the Ypres? On the Belgian side of the river, of course, he would add knowingly. And to liven up ads for llama wool, he would go on, why didn't the sponsors of that product let the public in on the absorbing, if arcane, knowledge that llamas, when angry, spit on the objects of their ire?

Swope looked on every new acquaintance as a potential contributor to his magpie trove of facts, and he could pick brains with the skill of a neurological surgeon. Once, while Ruth Gordon was staying with the Swopes, she brought to see them a Wall Street man who was eager to elicit from Swope some inside information he hoped he had on a pending international transaction.

Before the visitor had a chance to bring up the subject, Swope learned he was a wiping-material importer. For all the breadth of his acquaintances, Swope had never before met a wiping-material importer, and he proceeded to extract from his guest all sorts of intelligence: how these materials, which were mostly washed and sterilized rags purchased from Japanese textile manufacturers, were shipped over in five-hundred-pound bales and sold to automobile makers in carload lots; how the wily Japanese would now and then pack the rags wet, so that by the time an ostensibly quarter-ton bundle reached this country it would weigh, dry, a mere knavish four hundred and seventy-eight pounds; and how . . . But then, Swope realized, he was already impossibly late for his next engagement. He rose, escorted his caller to the door, slapped him on the back, thanked him for the edifying dissertation on wiping materials, and ushered him out. As the benumbed Wall Street man was about to drive off, he heard a shout. He looked back, and there was Swope, in one last ringing testimonial to his own insatiable curiosity, crying out, "Send me a bale!"

"If you don't know something, the next best thing is to know where to find it," Swope once said. "The other day Baruch asked me the derivation of the custom of Easter bunnies and Easter eggs," he wrote to one information bureau in 1938. "The question of the egg was not difficult to answer. The egg is a symbol of resurrection and dates from Pagan days. But where does one find the answer of the Easter bunny?" A lot of people in search of abstruse information thought Swope himself the most likely offhand source. Did the sons of the writer Herman J. Mankiewicz, out in California, want to know for a school paper they were preparing what the average annual salary was of American state legislators? Mankiewicz hurriedly wrote Swope for the answer. Could the *New Republic* find out if, following the First World War, the Japanese had refused to evacuate Siberia until the United States embargoed steel shipments to Japan? Bruce Bliven, its editor, had been told that Swope was the one man who would know the answer if anybody did.

Swope's main textual fount of information was the daily press. "Few realize how great is the dependence upon Journalism for general knowledge," he once wrote. "It is the farflung news coverage of the world that gives many their only mental life. Through it the people learn of the big and the little things that make life better or worse, for it is equally as important a function for the press to record evil as to chronicle virtue." To Swope, journalism was "a priestly mission," and he read newspapers as faithfully as any minister ever read the Bible. (Swope was also a dedicated Bible reader.) When Bruce Barton wrote an article for the January 3, 1925, *Collier's*, entitled "What Difference Does It Make?," in which he boasted of having gained an extra precious half hour every day by giving up newspapers, Swope followed with a rebuttal entitled "It Makes a Lot of Difference." He quoted one of his favorite Jeffersonianisms—"Were it left to me to decide whether we should have a government without newspapers or newspapers without a government, I would not hesitate for a moment to prefer the latter"—and he helpfully informed Barton that there would be an eclipse of the sun three weeks later, at eleven minutes before nine in the morning.* "Newspaper readers will have this information," Swope said. Barton could not recall, years later, whether Swope's admonition had had any direct effect on him, but the advertising man did concede that he was reading four newspapers a day.

"The newspaper might be called the common denominator to which current information is reduced for public information," Swope had told an interviewer in 1924, and he added, "Information is the thing that counts, whether on a race track, on Wall Street, in literature, art, or science. If every child could be trained early in life to get the facts and trained how to use the facts, there would be saved a vast amount of waste effort and energy now dissipated. People are dependent on newspapers. . . ." Swope's dependence was made manifest by the newspaper strike that afflicted New York City in the fall of 1953. It was a bad enough time for most people, but for Swope the absence of the daily papers hurt almost as much as a physical injury. That strike was nothing compared to the 1962–1963 one, which lasted one hundred and fourteen days, but at the end of its eleven-day duration Swope was as starved as if *he* had been on a hunger strike. The day the New York *Times* resumed publication, it ran one feature story under the headline "CITY GLAD TO HAVE NEWSPAPERS BACK." The first resident of the city to be quoted on his feelings was, appropriately, the Mayor. The second was Swope, who said, "I do not like to have my education interrupted."

As a student of renown in that field, Swope felt qualified to

---

* The eclipse was at eleven minutes after nine.

give advice to relative fledglings. When Clare Boothe Luce went to Washington as a newly elected member of Congress in 1943, Swope wrote to her, in no-wasting-of-words fashion:

DEAR CLARE:
 This may be a good method for you to follow:
 Every day look at the first page of the New York *Times;* the *Herald Tribune;* the Washington *Post* and the Washington *Times Herald.*
 Read the editorials in the New York *Daily News;* read Arthur Krock and Anne O'Hare McCormick in the New York *Times.*
 Look over Drew Pearson in the *Post.*
 Look at the news index of the *Herald Tribune* and its editorial page.
 Read *Time* each week.

It took a Swope to adjure a Luce to read *Time.**

Swope spent three or four hours a day reading newspapers, often with a pair of shears at hand so that he could cut out items he found appealing and put them in his morgue. He was undoubtedly one of the few individuals who maintained a private morgue. He operated it just like a newspaper-office morgue, folding his clippings neatly into long envelopes and cross-referencing liberally. Every so often the *Times,* which has a good morgue of its own, would avail itself of some yellowing rarity from another paper that Swope had in his files. After the *World* ceased publication, in 1931, the *Times* became for Swope the holiest of scriptures, and he approached it on two levels—first, as a disciple, and second, as a chaperon. He hovered over the *Times* like a mother proud of her daughter but fearful she might err; and when Swope caught the paper in what was or seemed to him a mistake he was quick to chide the offender. Once he complained to Theodore M. Bernstein, the assistant managing editor, of the inadequacy of a one-inch item buried deep in the financial section. Bernstein, the *Times*'s own guardian of rightness and the author of *Watch Your Language,* in replying to Swope, addressed him as "Dear Preceptor" and explained that Swope had been quite correct; the little story had been longer, and clearer, in the first edition but had been cut to save space. He implied that the entire *Times* was

---

* Swope was one of that magazine's earliest cover subjects, having achieved that distinction on January 28, 1924.

55

contrite that Swope had been put to the inconvenience of being confused.

At Christmastime Swope even plowed through the *Times*'s daily rosters of contributors to its Neediest Cases Fund, and not, as many people do, merely to ascertain what, if anything, their friends are publicly donating. During the Depression Swope wrote to Adolph S. Ochs, the publisher:

> Day by day I found myself drawn to the reports of the donations. At first I wondered if last year's mark would be topped. Then, from merely wondering, I found myself concerned by a possible failure. Why? Because, to me, the Fund had become a symbol. Would it be ignored and forgotten because of the recent financial smash? Or would it show that, even though money was not as easy as last year, humanity was just as kind? That has been shown. In fact, it shows that humanity is even kinder, because, with less money to give, more money has been given. Then, too, in common with many others, I kept my eye on the daily receipts because they took on the nature of a weather vane—a straw showing the way the financial winds were blowing.
>
> Now that last year's total has been exceeded, I feel certain that all who watched the struggle toward the top feel that things cannot be as bad as the alarmists have pictured; the times are not so desperate but that people can still lose themselves in thoughts of others. Breaking last year's record takes on spiritual, charitable and economic aspects, and for such a monument, so long and painstakingly created, the entire community owes a heavy debt to the *Times*.

So far from miserly was Swope with the information he gleaned from newspapers, other reading, and random chats with wiping-material men that almost every one of his friends could recall some incident in which he had been stunned, if not demolished, by Swope with a fusillade of facts. Frank Sullivan reminisced once how, arriving at the *World* for a job interview in 1922, he had prepared "a gracious address" to deliver to Swope. "My speech was not delivered as planned," Sullivan said. "It was not delivered at all. H.B.S., however, gave me a trenchant address on the ethics of journalism in general, the place of the *World* in particular, my own good fortune in being tapped for that paper, the influence of Stanton in Lincoln's cabinet, the best method for making raised biscuits, the Tacna-Arica dispute, and the Schick test for scarlet fever."

Swope spoke with such authority on practically any subject that few people dared dispute him. In the 1920s a group was playing an intellectual game on Long Island and Swope, asked to cite and identify a composer whose name began with "K," said unhesitatingly, "Kananovich." Samuel Chotzinoff, the music critic of the *World,* was present and, alone of those in the room, was certain Swope had invented the man, but Chotzinoff kept silent while his boss was asked to expatiate on Kananovich. Swope went into a brilliant twenty-minute discourse, which included a complete biography and a bibliography of the composer's major and minor works. When Swope finally ran out of steam Chotzinoff said, "Herbert, quit your kidding. There's never been such a person."

"O.K.," said Swope mildly.

Another time, when Swope insisted it had been Heine who wrote *"Der Erlkoenig"* and Chotzinoff, who knew better, said no, it was Goethe, the mere fact that Swope had endorsed Heine prompted Alexander Woollcott, Ralph Pulitzer, Averell Harriman, and one or two others on the scene to bet on the question against Chotzinoff, who collected several hundred dollars because of the others' misplaced faith in Swope's positiveness. No one had more faith in Swope than Swope. Playing a geography game one time in which the participants were required to name places starting with "E," Harrison Williams, the utilities man, said "Elyria." Swope said there was no such place, unless Williams happened to be thinking of Illyria, the ancient Greek community. Williams persisted. Swope offered to bet him ten thousand dollars on the question. Williams urged Swope not to bet. Swope insisted. Williams said he didn't want to take Swope's money on a sure thing. Swope said he'd never heard such nonsensical talk and demanded that Williams accept the bet or stop playing. Williams shrugged, and he was soon ten thousand dollars richer, as he had known all along he would be, inasmuch as he had been born a few miles from Elyria, Ohio.

The affectionate—and, sometimes, not so affectionate—insult was much in vogue in Swope's circle, and while he often confined himself to a snarling "Flathead!" when someone failed to have on the tip of his tongue an answer Swope thought should be there, he sometimes went further. The first time Martin Gabel ever dined at the Swopes' his host turned to him without warning and said, "By the way, Gabel, when did they stop using bagpipes in the Turkish Army?" Gabel said he hadn't any idea. "You don't *know?*" roared Swope. "If you're that ignorant, what the hell are you doing here—are you rich or something?"

"No, it's not that," Gabel blurted out. "You've asked me ten or eleven times, and I finally came." At that, according to the actor's recollection of the incident, Swope's wife jabbed Gabel sharply with her elbow, and he left the table in mortification.

Some of Swope's friends thought him an intellectual bully and whispered to each other that he was not really all that smarter than they were; that he probably boned up for his scintillating performances, like a lawyer before a trial. (One of his favorite books was *The Art of Cross-Examination,* by Francis Wellman.) When he would intone, "Of course, you all know what Benjamin Franklin said about . . ." and would then go on to quote Franklin at length, Swope's auditors suspected he had forehandedly memorized the passage. It was even nastily rumored that Swope tried to lure people into betting him on facts he had just previously looked up. (He certainly hadn't entrapped Harrison Williams.) Such mean allegations were largely inspired by envy, but Swope was aware of them and took them in reasonably good grace. He was not even offended when Arthur H. Samuels, one of *The New Yorker*'s many early managing editors, took to marching imitatively up and down the corridors of Swope's own home shouting, "I'll bet you ten thousand dollars I was never wrong on a fact in my life!" (Samuels held another distinction: he was one of the few men of Swope's acquaintance who could walk into a room while Swope was talking, say "Shut up," and get away with it.)

Swope, fortunately, had the redeeming quality of recognizing and being amused by his own foibles. In 1962 James M. Cain, once an editorial writer for the *World,* recalled an incident that had occurred at the paper some forty years earlier:

> Ordinarily, Swope's skin seemed made of rhinoceros-hide, covered with brass studs, like medieval armor. But he could get thrown off balance by some little thing, in the most astonishing way. Once, when a delegation of teachers, some Middle Western bunch, descended on the *World*, we were all told off to help with their entertainment, and I drew a group of a dozen or so, headed by a twittery little creature who looked like Zazu Pitts and was dressed in a knock-out creation by the Oshkosh Balenciaga. A few feet away, Swope was addressing his group at the top of his voice, em-

phasizing everything in a most positive way, and getting a thrilled reaction. My little chairman wanted to know who he was, and I told her, but obviously she had never heard of the Great Reporter. So I told her: "He knows everything, he's a human encyclopedia —well, if you don't believe it, try him. Ask him when did Steve Brodie jump off the Brooklyn Bridge. Go on, I dare you." So sure enough she did. She plucked him by the arm, asked: "Mr. Swope, when was it that Mr. Brodie jumped off the Brooklyn Bridge?" Without a moment's hesitation, he barked: "July 23, 1886!" and went on with his address. I said to the lady: "See, what did I tell you?" and she was agreeably bedazzled. But a second or two later I was spun around by the shoulder, and there was Swope staring at me. "What the hell's the idea?" he growled. "Why did you put that dame up to it, to ask me a thing like that?"

"Nothing," I said. "All in the spirit of good, clean, boyish fun. Giving you a chance to show off your vast erudition."

"You think I like to show off?"

"Yes. Yes, yeah, and yop."

He turned away, as upset as a young girl might be, on discovering her slip was showing. But as he walked off he stopped, seeming to know I'd be looking after him, and gave me that quick, startling smile that was one of his odd characteristics, but a slightly sheepish one too. And I realized two things, one that I'd already known, the other new to me: He was the least resentful man in the world, being able to take a joke, even one on himself, with a cheerfulness almost pathetic. And if caught by surprise, he could be as red in the face as anyone.

Like an eccentric owner of more tangible wealth impulsively flinging coins to the street from a window, Swope sometimes passed out dividends from his capital of knowledge in unpredictable ways. If he thought of a fact he wished to transmit, he would cheerfully break in on anyone else who might be talking. Swope knew his friends were aware of this impetuous proclivity, and he was not above kidding about it himself. During one conversation about abstract paintings, he had an urge to reveal some information he'd recently acquired about ordnance. When even his facile mind could devise no logical transition, he cleared his throat, jokingly yelled "Boom! boom! Speaking of cannon . . ." and was off and running. Being serious and sticking slightly closer to the subject under discussion, he broke into a conversation on politics another time to ask if anybody in the room knew the derivation of "elder statesman." After a respectful pause he explained that the phrase originated, as any flathead ought to know, in the palaces of the Emperors of Japan, who kept a retinue of knowledgeable graybeards around to prevent them from making avoidable mistakes.

Swope sometimes seemed to view himself as just that kind of elder statesman, doing his utmost to keep everybody in the world on the path of rightness. In a 1954 note to Supreme Court Justice Robert H. Jackson, Swope described himself as "a kind of St. George charging the Dragon of Confusion." The world was full of such Dragons, often disguised as Flatheads, and they were constantly conspiring to upset Swope. They attacked him early and never let up. (They misspelled his wife's middle name on the engraved announcement of his own wedding. On a letterhead printed for his family's use after he moved to Sands Point, they had it "Sand's Point.") John O'Hara Cosgrave, a Sunday *World* editor during the First World War and afterward, often tried to reshape Swope into a mold akin to that of ordinary men, and wrote him, in January 1918, "Being perpetually right is about as dangerous an indulgence as I know. It is the most rancorous and antagonistic of all the virtues." Swope was unafraid of danger and cared not that his virtue clanked. Had not St. George, in all likelihood, confronted his dragon with sharp-tongued threats and celebrated its demise with full-throated exultation? And if it was difficult always to practice accuracy, did that make the preaching of it any the less desirable—nay, mandatory?

Throughout his life Swope echoed the gospel of Joseph Pulitzer, who in founding the *World* also gave it the motto "Accuracy, Terseness, Accuracy." ("Accuracy is to a newspaper what virtue is to a lady," Pulitzer once said.) It was hard to know Swope even slightly without becoming aware of his allegiance to the bread of Pulitzer's sandwichy pledge, although when it came to terseness he sometimes backslid. Senator John L. McClellan, in an exchange of letters with Swope in 1949, referred to his predecessor from Arkansas as "Joseph T. Robinson." At once Swope wrote McClellan, "Merely as a matter of interest: I notice you refer to our dear friend, the late Senator Robinson, as 'Joseph.' In the many times I was with him he always referred to himself as Joe. How did he sign his documents? This is a matter of historical accuracy, on which I want to be right." The "Joe" was indeed right, as McClellan apologetically reported after consulting the Senate library.

Swope was not fazed when other sources of information disagreed with him. He besought a number of men, including President Franklin Roosevelt and various members of the staff of the *Times*, to fall in behind him as he battled to have the final "i" omitted from such proper nouns as "Argentinian" and "Floridian." Swope was disappointed when the President chose to go along instead with Dr. Samuel Johnson, Shakespeare, and Chaucer; and he was even more put out when the *Times* reminded him that not only did Webster's Dictionary prefer "Floridian" to the Swope-backed "Floridan" but that people who lived in Florida preferred it, too. "Very well—let's correct a mistake in usage," Swope replied blandly to the *Times*. "There is no excuse for 'Floridian.' Custom cannot justify it. We'll have to pound on Florida. . . ." It was almost as if he visualized himself as a hurricane gathering its forces to strike from the Caribbean—a word against the spelling of which there is no evidence that he ever took a formal stand.

Swope's granitic espousal of accuracy was commendable. There are far too few people around who either care about or adhere to such niceties. To Swope, the misstatement of a fact or the misuse of a word was something a gentleman simply did not do, and he construed it as the duty of a gentleman—*his* duty—to raise the appallingly low standards of the masses. But, alas, man is an imperfect animal. In June 1938, for instance, unable to find a copy of Professor Zechariah Chafee's *Freedom of Speech* at a bookstore, Swope wrote to Felix Frankfurter, then, like Chafee, at the Harvard Law School, for assistance. Frankfurter borrowed Chafee's own copy and sent it along. In December, Swope wrote the author, "Dear Prof. Chafee: Not long ago, I was called upon to address the National Encampment of the Veterans of Foreign Wars on 'Free Speech.' In preparing myself I bought a copy of your book *Freedom of Speech*. I found it to bear your signature, also containing many clippings of the reviews, especially from the English papers. It occurred to me the book may have come from your own library, having been loaned out by somebody, who lost it, or sold it. Do you want it back? If so, I shall be glad to send it to you."

On October 21, 1947, after reading a newspaper account of a speech by the President of a Catholic university on the overemphasis of campus athletics, Swope addressed a letter to the Right Reverend John J. Cavanaugh at South Bend, Indiana:

DEAR MR. PRESIDENT:

Ask the boys on the campus or the alumni who is the President of Notre Dame, and you will get one correct answer in twenty. Ask them who is the coach of the football team, and all the answers will be right.

This seems to me to be a clear support of the highly interesting and provocative position you took on Sunday. After all, are these institutions for higher education in football, or are they, at least, theoretically devoted to scholasticism?

I think you did a bold thing; a wise thing, and an effective thing. You had far more guts than the average schoolman, and I applaud you for that.

Alas, poor Swope! A few weeks later he got an answer—not from Indiana, however, but from the president of Fordham University, the Reverend Robert I. Gannon:

DEAR MR. SWOPE:

I appreciated very much the note that you sent on the occasion of my indictment by the sports writers and was delighted to know that our opinions coincided.

An unexpectedly humorous touch was added to your communication when your secretary sent it by mistake to the Rev. John J. Cavanaugh, President of the University of Notre Dame, who ranks today as the great high priest of big time football. He sent it to me with this laconic note attached—"This man appears to be one of your admirers." The addressing of the letter was a *felix culpa*, as it must have given them something to think about in South Bend.

A lesser man might have regarded such a *culpa* as mortifyingly *infelix*, but Swope took it quite in stride and told Father Gannon that he, too, found the mixup amusing.

"*My whole capital is my knowledge of things and my acquaintance with people.*" That Swope knew just about everybody of front-page consequence among his contemporaries—or at worst could by one well-placed phone call obtain access to any unfamiliar source—was indeed a valuable asset. Did someone want information about a convict in the death house at Sing Sing? The chances were that Swope knew the warden, the prisoner, and the executioner as well. Had Lord and Lady Mountbatten been robbed of some jewels while staying with the Joshua Cosdens? The hosts and their guests were all chummy with Swope, and if the thief had been caught, he might well have proved to be an acquaintance, too. Did the Chairman of the Federal Communications Commission wish to have a private huddle with David Sarnoff of NBC and William S. Paley of CBS? Swope took them all to lunch.

The story is told that in the mid-Thirties Herman J. Mankiewicz, on the verge of leasing a New York apartment through a snobbish real-estate agent, was asked to furnish six character references, preferably from very important people. "Well, there's Herbert Swope . . ." Mankiewicz began.

"But he's on everybody's list," the agent said.

As far back as 1917, when Swope was thirty-five, the managing editor of the *World* acclaimed his acquaintances as "all-embracing." Not long after that, Swope's wife decided they had to stop sending out Christmas cards; they knew too many people. Swope was often kidded about his mania for collecting friends. It was a joke around the *World* office, when Swope was executive editor, that before a reporter set out to interview anybody whose name had ever been heard of, Swope would send him off with an amiable "Give him my regards." Once a year, in Swope's reportorial days, the *World* staff had a banquet, and a feature of this get-together was the publication of a humorous house organ called *The Overset*, which spoofed the eccentricities of all hands. Swope was its favorite target. In 1914 it ran a fabricated letter, to which it signed Swope's name and in which it had him alluding to, among other cronies, Andrew Carnegie, the Mayor of New York City, the Governor of New York State, the President of the United States, the King of England, and the Czar of Russia. For all their joshing of Swope, however, his colleagues at the *World* could not help being impressed when a governor *did* telephone him from Albany to ask his advice on this or that affair of state, or when, as happened one day in 1917, a man stepped up to an editorial-floor receptionist and wondered if by any chance Mr. Swope would have a minute or two to spare for John D. Rockefeller, Jr.

To be a good friend to Swope was not easy, and many of his friendships drowned in a spate of incompatibility. Swope expected people to work at being his friend. After his relationship with Robert Sherwood had become somewhat cool, Swope replied to a note from the playwright, "What disaffected me, at least a little, was that I told you once that we had drifted apart but, it seemed to me, you did nothing about it." It would not have occurred to Swope to do anything about it himself. In a way, it was a rare tribute to his magnetism that he could retain people's affections in spite of behavior that could often lead straight to alienation.

One psychoanalytically oriented doctor who knew him well, and not infrequently scrapped with him, believed that Swope was the kind of insecure person who must continually challenge the affections of others, to prove to himself that he can retain their love no matter how insufferably he may act toward them. "In believing that the highest friendship involved the attempt to establish an ever-increasing sincerity," the doctor said reflectively after Swope's death, "he challenged it as no man of his time had ever done, in my memory. We exchanged blows that would not have been possible in any other relationship in his relentless attempt to secure an honest understanding of our differences in belief. In that way, a relatedness developed in which friendship reached a unique eloquence, on his part more than mine, for he had an indomitable will to uncover what was shadowy. There were men to whom this challenge of straightforward speaking was not to their liking. He probably suffered more from the disruption of friendship because he saw its profound possibilities more than others. He was as capable of admiration as he was of criticism. Although he knew that sincerity was a two-edged sword, he took the risk of hurting with the sharp blade by using it to the hilt, in the hope that the glory of an enhanced intimacy would be the result—once his provocation of honesty and personal assault was deeply understood as a search for truth. He was the only man with whom I lost my temper in more than three decades, but the consequence of our battle was that of unlimited continent of discussion. Having weathered that storm, there was never any question that we could not reach an area of understanding, even in the absence of agreement. . . . His own suffering was at times a fee, but he paid the fee, to steer his course with an honesty unique and special."

For Swope to be happy he not only had to know important people but, despite the provocation he might give them to avoid him entirely, to know them well. Some of his friends played a game: Conversing with Swope, they would get him onto British government or world politics and would secretly bet among themselves, beforehand, on how many times Swope would mention his good friend "Winston." Reviewing a book of memoirs by James W. Gerard, Swope referred to the author, an old friend who was eighty-three years old when the book came out, as "Jimmy" in the first sentence, adding that "Everyone who knows him calls him that." On the other hand, after Swope once sent a note that began "Dear Ernest Hemingway," the author, calling Swope "kid," replied, "How come you started full-naming me? I don't have to address you as Dear Herbert Bayard Swope, do I? If I do though I will." Swope got off a "Dear Pappy" answer as fast as he could.

Swope felt quite strongly about the rights and wrongs of first-naming. He was a faithful listener to radio and, in due course, television programs. He was especially partial to shows in which real people took part, and it went against his grain to hear someone who had obviously never before met someone else address that person, within universal earshot, in terms of intimacy. Swope once went out of his way to compliment Adlai Stevenson for bucking the awful trend and calling Edward R. Murrow "Mr. Murrow," and Swope would often beseech Murrow and others of consequence he knew in the field to bring a halt to the custom he deplored. But although Swope was himself in turn a director of the Columbia Broadcasting System and a consultant to the National Broadcasting Company, his appeals got nowhere, unless one can count the ultimate designation, on a CBS network program, of a talking horse as "Mister Ed."

Swope corresponded with so many illustrious folk that a part-time secretary of his, upon quitting his office, was moved to send him a note that went, "I want you to know how very reluctant I am to leave your employ, not only because I like the work, and like the people I work with, but also because I take such a deep pride in being even remotely associated with you. Handling your files is like having my finger on the pulse of the world."

Even when ill it comforted Swope to bask in the warm aura of the notable. From the Harkness Pavilion of Presbyterian Hospital, in October 1945, he reported to both Robert P. Patterson, then the Secretary of War, and Ferdinand Eberstadt, the investment banker, that he was having an interesting time, because Albert D. Lasker was in one nearby room and Surrogate James A. Foley of New York in another. Best of all, Mrs. Charles Evans Hughes was right next door, and the Chief Justice, when he visited his wife daily, also stopped by to have "jawing matches" with Swope—

who, in a triumphant footnote of name-dropping, was able even to let his acquaintances know that on his own release from the hospital his room was slated to be taken over by Edward R. Stettinius, Jr., who a few months earlier had been Secretary of State.

Even Swope's dogs were out of the ordinary. He had not much use for pets. He treated them much as he treated children—a pat on the head to connote affection, and then, like as not, dismissal from his presence. (He had the notion that all fauna were constantly hungry. Whenever his glance rested on a creature long enough for him to meditate on its needs, he would say to whoever might be present, "Feed it." One day he was sitting outdoors with a niece when a flock of gulls passed overhead. "Feed them," Swope said.) At one time or another the Swopes had a couple of pure-bred German shepherds, given them by Mrs. John Hay Whitney; two Pekinese, one obtained from Mrs. Irving Berlin and the other from Mrs. Howard Dietz; and an imported English pug for which they were beholden to Bernard Baruch. The pug was escorted across the Atlantic by Winston Churchill's son Randolph. The only dog the Swopes had of dubious origins at least could claim a pair of first-rate sponsors. It was a mongrel that Dorothy Parker and Neysa McMein came across one day while a drunk was kicking it. They retrieved it from a gutter and transported it to the fairyland that was Swope's.

It was indicative of the impact Swope had on his associates that once when an acquaintance asked his secretary what his religious views, if any, were, she replied, "He knew every Pope." (Swope used to say that the only two officeholders whom, out of deference, he would not address by their first names, no matter how well he might know them, were the Pope and the President of the United States.) In the early 1930s, when Felix Frankfurter did something that Swope found especially praiseworthy, Swope wrote him, "I nominate you for Pope." From then on, for the remaining twenty-five years of his life, Swope would periodically bestow this accolade. He nominated Frankfurter for Pope at least twice. Other double winners of the honor were Whitney and Baruch. President Eisenhower was nominated and also Adlai Stevenson. President Roosevelt doesn't appear to have made it, but Mrs. Roosevelt did, along with Clare Boothe Luce. Robert Moses, Westbrook Pegler, Averell Harriman, J. Edgar Hoover, Lewis S. Rosenstiel, the head of Schenley Industries, and Ernie Byfield, who presided over the Pump Room in Chicago, all attained this special Swopian state of grace. Once Swope nominated himself. Occasionally he varied the form of his tribute; he told Eberstadt one time that Rosenstiel wanted Eberstadt for Pope. In 1934 Swope nominated Joseph P. Kennedy and twenty years later his son John.

Swope learned relatively early in life that the world in which he lived and operated was, if not hieratic, hierarchic, and that the easiest way to get something done fast, provided you had the right connections, was to head for the principal source of power. When he wanted to buy an automobile he did not consult his friendly neighborhood dealer; he had Alfred P. Sloan, Jr., the president of General Motors, bring a Cadillac around to his house and demonstrate it. When Swope's son had trouble renting an apartment in a housing project financed by the Metropolitan Life Insurance Company, the father expedited the matter through the Metropolitan's Chairman of the Board. When a nephew, doing boot training in the Marines, complained in a letter home that he wasn't getting enough sleep, Swope transmitted the gripe to the Armed Services Committee of the House of Representatives and, in case the House shilly-shallied, alerted the Senate to boot.

To answer many of the questions that arose from Swope's unquenchable thirst for odd information, he did not often bother with such commonplace sources of research as libraries. How had the phrase "Queen of Battles" first come to be associated with the Infantry? Swope put it to the Secretary of the Army. Had American and Russian troops clashed in 1919? To accommodate Swope, the Vice-Chief of Staff of the Army had the Army's Historical Division prepare a suitable memorandum. And Swope habitually went straight to the top for action as well as information. A kinky telephone cord was enough to provoke him into correspondence with Walter S. Gifford, president of American Telephone and Telegraph; a misdelivered telegram enough to get him after Newcomb Carlton, president of Western Union. But Swope tried to help as well as nag. When an office assistant of his mentioned one day that a doctor had given him a prescription that did wonders for, or perhaps rather against, dandruff, Swope borrowed the prescription and graciously passed it along to the president of the Zonite Products Corporation.

Often, Swope went to the seats of the mighty for information he needed to settle a bet. In an attempt to adjudicate one with

Mrs. Hank Greenberg, the baseball player's wife, as to whether the average ball game was longer in the American or in the National League, Swope got in touch with the High Commissioner of baseball. To find out how many Chinese had migrated into Manchuria during one twenty-year period, he commandeered the services of the Japanese Ambassador in Washington. After one dinner-table conversation got around to whether or not there had ever been an authentic surviving basket case among American casualties in both world wars, the sort of subject on which Swope found it hard to dwell for long without making a wager, it was the Surgeon General of the United States Army whom Swope called in as an expert consultant. The Surgeon General dutifully reported that a search of the records of the First World War had revealed no basket cases and not even a triple amputation. The Second World War had produced nine triple amputees and two basket cases. Swope was thereupon able to inform his dinner companion, a lady internationally known for her beauty and delicacy, that she owed him a dollar.

Swope bet small and he bet big, but he bet, on anything and everything. He once won five hundred dollars from Ralph Pulitzer by coming closer to Kant's definition of the categorical imperative. He would bet on past political facts (had Woodrow Wilson carried Minnesota in 1916, and by how much? *), or on pending political contests. He sometimes bet for other people as well as for himself. When some Internal Revenue agents came around to see him one day to inquire into a rumor that he had won some three hundred thousand dollars in a winter-book bet on the previous Kentucky Derby, he deterred them by explaining that he was merely acting for a syndicate, one of whose members was President Roosevelt. On Roosevelt's 1936 victory over Alf Landon, Swope, although he had to give odds, netted nearly eighteen thousand dollars, a bit of which he shared with two co-bettors who were also Presidential assistants, Miss LeHand and Stephen T. Early. Roosevelt was himself called in to decide one wager in 1940. Swope had bet someone that the President, while making radio broadcasts, usually kept his face within eighteen inches to two feet of the microphone. Swope's inquiry arrived less than three weeks before election day, but the President

---

* Swope lost this one, to Albert D. Lasker. Making a note of the defeat for his voluminous files, Swope said, "Jove nodded."

took time out from campaigning to let him know that eighteen inches was about right.

Swope lost his share of bets, but there was true grandeur about some of his winning feats. In 1927 a play opened in New York called *Spread Eagle*. Swope subsequently showed up at a dinner party attended by Franklin P. Adams, and they got into an argument about the last line. F.P.A. thought it was "Stand up, you son of a bitch!" Swope said no, the imprecation preceded the imperative. He bet Adams one hundred thousand dollars to one dollar that he was correct. A few days later Adams read a Stark Young review of the play in the *New Republic* and was heartened to see the curtain line printed as "Stand up, you ———!" In his column, Adams wrote, "So I calculated upon what I should do with the one hundred thousand and one dollars H. Swope should give me on the wager, but my heart sank when I thought that perhaps Mr. Young might be as wrong as I was." Adams' foreboding was justified; the line was "You son of a bitch. Stand up."

4

OFTEN, before making a bet on some more or less readily ascertainable fact, Swope would insist that both parties agree in advance to abide by the *World Almanac*'s view of whatever was in dispute. The *Almanac* was his favorite reference work, and it was in a sense a mirror of his own far-ranging mind—a compendium of a hard core of information on a great many scattered subjects. Swope was so fond of the *Almanac*—"a book that was part of myself," he once called it—that on at least four occasions he tried to buy it and become its publisher. He also considered himself its perennial first-string critic. He read it carefully, and he often favored its editors with suggestions for improving it. When the 1951 edition, for instance, devoted nearly a third of a page to a table of figures headed "Four-suit and Five-suit Poker Hand Chances," Swope, by then a veteran of some fifty years of high-pressure poker-playing, took issue with the five-suit entry. "I never heard of that game being played," he wrote sternly to the editor, Harry Hansen, whom Swope had brought to the *World* twenty-five years before as a book critic. "It should be out. Further, I suggest instead of expressing chances of making different hands in terms of percentage, you give them in odds. For example, you give the chances of two pairs as being 4.8 per cent. Just what does that mean?" Hansen hastily mended his ways, and with the appearance of the 1952 edition, five-suit poker aficionados, and people who cared about odds expressed in percentages, had to look elsewhere for enlightenment.

When the eleventh edition of the *Encylopædia Britannica* was

70

published, in 1910, Joseph Pulitzer bought one hundred sets and distributed them to his staff, hoping to instill in them a proper reverence for accuracy, terseness, accuracy. Swope was a young reporter then, and it is uncertain whether he was thus honored, but he was impressed with Pulitzer's gesture and, a few years afterward, initiated a Christmastime variation of it that he carried on for the rest of his life. As each new edition of the *Almanac* came out, in January, Swope would have around one hundred and fifty copies specially bound, usually in morocco leather, and stamped with the names of a carefully selected and constantly reappraised list of recipients. Heads of corporations that engaged him as a policy consultant would make the roster, perhaps replacing a Cabinet officer who had left Washington for private life. When the business stopped retaining Swope, its president or chairman of the board would be dropped, perhaps to be supplanted by an Army general newly appointed Chief of Staff. Sometimes vacancies occurred as individuals incurred Swope's displeasure. Westbrook Pegler and General Hugh S. Johnson were both omitted for writing syndicated columns that irritated Swope.

There was usually a waiting list. Mayor Edward J. Kelly of Chicago, who knew that his co-worker in the Democratic vineyards, Mayor Frank Hague of Jersey City, had made the grade, once begged Swope to be admitted to the fraternity. Swope assented. When Frank J. Lausche was elected governor of Ohio in 1946, his secretary wrote Swope that she recalled from working for Harry Hopkins and Jesse Jones in Washington that they'd passed muster, and what were her new boss's chances now? Swope managed to squeeze the governor in. Richard Nixon didn't get tapped, though, until he was *re*-elected Vice President.

During the Second World War, two granddaughters of Professor Gilbert Murray, the British classicist, were among the many English children sent to this country. They stayed in Washington with Felix Frankfurter, and at the Justice's entreaty Swope put one of them on the list. At twelve, she was the youngest person ever to get there. That was a miserable year for Swope. His distribution system broke down. Young Miss Murray got the copy with Sam Rayburn's name on it, and Eugene Meyer, the publisher of the Washington *Post*, got Frankfurter's. Meyer's went to Supreme Court Justice Frank Murphy, and Frankfurter

71

got the one intended for Missy LeHand. Another eminent Washington lady, Cissy Patterson, publisher of the vigorously anti-Roosevelt *Times-Herald*, was also on the list, and Swope's dismay was acute when he learned that Missy had Cissy's.

Swope would herald the *Almanac*'s arrival with a late-December letter which usually went something like:

> If, as a friend, I were able to hold for you the interest, stability and value possessed by the book I am sending you, I should feel myself successful indeed. But even if I fall short of that standard, the little gift is sent with best wishes for many Happy New Years.
> This is a harbinger of the book's later arrival. It is a specially bound *World Almanac*, which should reach you upon publication about January fifteenth. It will help you keep your facts straight; it will settle arguments and win bets for you, and it will recall a great newspaper to which I gave many happy years of my life. Please let me know of its arrival.

Swope loved getting letters from big shots, and since nearly everybody on his list was of authentically large stature, he reaped each winter a bountiful harvest. He was gratified to have Al Smith describe the *Almanac* one time as "the most valuable book I have on my desk outside of the Bible" and to learn from Smith another time that his *Almanac* had provided him with religious information not in the Bible: he had used the reference book, he told his benefactor, to settle an argument about the makeup of the College of Cardinals. In 1938, when Harold Ickes, the Secretary of the Interior, had the temerity to have his secretary, instead of himself, acknowledge Swope's announcement that an *Almanac* was on the way, Swope got so angry he canceled the delivery order.

Swope was so insistent that recipients of the *Almanac* send him proper acknowledgment that some of them went to considerable pains to avoid any imputation of ingratitude. In 1953, his first year in the White House, President Eisenhower decided to take no chances and wrote two letters of thanks. (One of his White House assistants, playing it even safer, sent a third.) Alice Roosevelt Longworth perennially teased Swope by not responding at all, not even when he sent her a self-addressed, stamped post card on which she had merely to make a cross to indicate that his gift had arrived. Swope could not help admiring such unmitigated cheekiness, and she remained in good standing.

In 1933, when Swope was about to go to England, Felix Frank-furter gave him a letter of introduction to Harold Laski. "Swope, you know, was the guiding genius of the *World* in its greatest day," Frankfurter wrote, "and it would surprise even you, who know so much about us, if I told you the many and important words and deeds for which he has been responsible in recent American life, performing, as he mostly does—lusty nature though he is, anonymously. You will fight for your chance to talk when he is around—but the strange thing is that I have never heard him talk other than interestingly." Swope's verbal facility was ap-parent, it once developed, even to people who had never been within earshot of him. Frank Sullivan, as a *World* reporter, exhibited an example of Swope's handwriting to a Polish psychic, who deduced, "Here's a highly educated man, a very quick-minded man. IIe is a diplomat. He works too much. He can make others talk. I mean if you go to his office he can do much or little talking but he can talk so that you will say what he wants to find out. He understands a lot along every line. He has a mature brain. He knows what he wants and gets it almost always. He has great powers of criticism. He expresses himself very crisply. He doesn't like to have other people talk too much. He hasn't got any patience with people who do not come to the point. . . ."

There were those who, perhaps because of their own relative ignorance or inarticulateness, suggested snidely that Swope talked as much as he did to avoid thinking. There were perhaps just as many more, however, who regarded him, as he no doubt regarded himself—not without justification—as a devil's advocate, who, boldly and colorfully ornamenting any conversational topic that anybody could conceivably raise, piqued and clarified the think-ing of others. "The giants of our time recognized his stature and enjoyed the play of his mind and the sunshine of his smile," Robert Moses said. "What many of them sought was more than advice, more than encouragement, stimulation and amusement; it was access to his imagination."

Swope loved to argue. "Agreement is always the death of conversation," he would say, and it was nearly impossible for a conversation to languish, let alone perish, when he was in top form. He talked well, as so few people consistently do. His sen-tences, though rotund, were usually immaculately polished. He

73

also talked loudly.* Ethel Barrymore, en route to a country home into which the Swopes had just moved, was told by a mutual friend that she might have trouble finding the place. Nonsense, she said; she would just go to the edge of town and listen.

Sullivan once credited Swope with having invented the spoken word. Swope loved words. He was uncommonly fond of big, fancy ones and in plain conversation would use tongue-twisters that lesser men would hesitate to use in prose without first consulting a lexicon. Words like "rodomontade" and "strabismus" rolled smoothly off his tongue, and it was not, as some of his critics thought, pure rodomontade that made him use them. It was a relish for the special, the elegant, the flamboyant. At a party after the opening of S. N. Behrman's *End of Summer*, his fellow playwright John L. Balderston chided him for using the obscure —and, to most dictionaries, nonexistent—word "horizonal." Balderston said that characters like Behrman's simply didn't use words like that in ordinary conversation. Swope was present and leaped to Behrman's defense; there was *no* word, he argued, too precious or unfamiliar for the kind of civilized dialogue he espoused. Swope's own ability to turn a fancy phrase created a wide demand for him to serve as toastmaster at public functions. Robert Patterson once wrote him, "Your performances as master of ceremonies are so pre-eminent that you ought to charge a heavy fee for each occasion. I have never seen the like of it." Swope at once nominated Patterson for Pope.

Delayed in Washington one time on a business trip, Swope composed an explanatory telegram to his wife back in New York and asked an assistant to take it over to Western Union and have it sent. It was the sort of message that most men could readily have compressed into ten words. Swope's text, however, was not only so long but so flowery that the Western Union girl handling

---

* A poem of now unknown authorship that attained wide circulation in the city room of the *World* went:

> The French artillery's damnedest,
> Black Tom's awful roar,
> The shrieks of shells
> In the thousand hells
> In the European war—
> Are but the soft, sweet purling
> Of a brook on a gentle slope,
> To the mad whangdoodlearums
> Of ole Herbert Bayard Swope.

74

it, after spending a few moments counting the words in it with the point of a pencil, set down the pencil and read the telegram for, as she confessed, sheer pleasure.

In view of Swope's remarkable vocabulary, few people were brash enough to argue with him about the meaning or use of words. Clare Boothe Luce tried it once. Arriving at the Swopes' Manhattan apartment for dinner, she had scarcely yielded up her wrap when she asked Swope, challengingly, what some obscure and lengthy word meant. Swope snorted; this was child's play. She persisted, demanding a definition, and when Swope gave it to her she announced, triumphantly, that he was wrong. The word had two meanings, they discovered when they looked it up. Mrs. Luce had been thinking of one, and Swope had given her the other.

"There is nothing pedantic in employing a word," Swope once wrote a friend, "when that word has a specific and direct meaning; a writer is showing off only when he employs a heavy polysyllabic word, for which another and commoner usage can be substituted." In a letter to the *Times* in 1934, Swope used a word so far from being in common usage—it was "euhemeristic," and it was derived from Euhemerus, a fourth-century B.C. philosopher who took mythology as gospel truth—that before printing his communication a *Times* copy editor changed the adjective to "euphemistic." This slip-up in due course brought the *Times* more letters, among them a chiding one from Swope and a forgiving one from Leo L. Redding, who had been Swope's boss on the New York *Herald* some thirty years earlier. Redding recalled for the *Times* how he had told Swope at the turn of the century, "Bide your time, watch your step, and you will go far in this town." Redding implied that Swope had gone too far; back on the *Herald*, the old editor said, Swope could write in plain Anglo-Saxon terms and was also liable to a two-dollar fine that was levied on reporters who used an excessively ornate word. But from Swope's satisfied point of view, the climax of the "euhemeristic" controversy came when President Roosevelt, who had been reading about this whangdoodlearum of Swope's, wrote him:

Sir:
   The Typographical Union has lodged complaint under their code against you for submitting copy to the New York *Times* containing the word "euhemeristic." A hearing will be held by me at your

75

convenience. It is respectfully suggested that a jail sentence can be avoided by you if hereafter you will provide a dictionary of your own copy to all typesetters.

Very truly yours,
F.D.R.

P.S. By the way—what does the darn word mean anyway?

Swope had a naturally hoarse voice, and he used it so much, often abusing it, that he suffered recurrently from laryngitis, an ailment as crippling to him as a broken leg to a sprinter. Periodically he would seek professional help for this disability. After one visit to an elocutionist, Swope dictated, for his own guidance:

1. Practice sighing out sentences and whispering them.
2. Head nodding—chin forward.
3. Sigh faintly on high note.
4. Sigh in middle pitch—neck relaxed.
5. Talk in middle pitch.
6. Don't talk in open air or in vehicles.

Another time, his wife came upon him standing in front of a mirror and saying "Hello" in various ways. When she asked him, in her characteristic fashion, what the hell he thought he was doing, he said, "I'm placing my voice."

"Just yell, and it'll come out where it ought to be," she replied cheerfully.

In full command of his lungs, Swope was spectacular. The British sculptor and author Clare Sheridan, who worked for him on the *World* for a spell, once recalled sitting alongside him at a 1921 dinner party given by Maxine Elliott. "I asked him, when I was able to get a word in edgeways," she wrote, "how he managed to revitalize, he seemed to me to expend so much energy. He said he got it back from me, from everyone, that what he gives out he gets back; it is a sort of circle. He was so vibrant that I found my heart thumping with excitement, as though I had drunk champagne, which I hadn't! He talks a lot, but talks well; is never dull."

Mrs. Sheridan, whom Ina Claire portrayed on stage in Behrman's *Biography*, did portrait busts of Winston Churchill, her double cousin, and of Lenin, Trotsky, and Marconi. She also did a bronze head of Swope that is now on display in the room memorializing him at Columbia—a project instigated and largely underwritten by Bernard Baruch. It testified to Mrs. Sheridan's verve and charm that she got on well with Swope even though, while dining with him and some others at the Ritz-Carlton three nights after the Elliott party, she demonstrated ignorance of a sort that, in the case of a less attractive sinner, would have been regarded by Swope as beyond redemption. Baruch was in the party, and Mrs. Sheridan had apparently never heard of him, thought his name was Brooke, and asked him if he was by any chance related to the poet Rupert. Swope not only forgave her but hired her almost immediately afterward.

Helen Hayes, reflecting once on Swope's monopolistic conversational behavior, said, "Never have I heard a man talk so much and say—so much." Swope's own wife, who naturally listened to him more than anybody else, took pleasure as a rule from his prowess, but there were limits even to her redoubtable tolerance. One night the Swopes were dining with, for them, an exceptionally small group—Averell Harriman, Herbert Swope, Jr., and a contemporary of the son, Robert Gerdy, a *New Yorker* editor. The senior Swope went galloping off on some recital or other, and, when he finally halted to cool his throat, his wife remarked, "As I've often told Gerdy, I'm anti-semantic."

In full conversational flight Swope could have an almost hypnotic effect on his auditors. "He was never halfhearted about anything," said the writer Abe Burrows, himself a talker of high repute. "He never wobbled. If he told you a fact or a piece of political information, he said it as though it were about to be carved in granite. I can't think of anyone who would question or doubt anything Swope had to say while he was saying it, or for at least an hour after he had said it. After a while you might disagree with what he had said or find some other flaw in his logic. But while he was talking to you his impact was overwhelming." Albert Lasker sent an advertising aide to have lunch with Swope one day in 1931 and sound him out on a business proposition. The man reported afterward, "We will have to make up our minds about associations with him quite away from him and after allowing several days to intervene after a visit with him before considering the matter. Otherwise my judgment, at least, is very apt to be swayed."

John F. Kennedy's sister Kathleen, later the Marchioness of Hartington, worked for the Washington *Times-Herald* in 1942. That December Miss Kennedy described Swope in verbal action.

"First there's a long clearing of the throat, everyone is called to attention," she wrote. "Then comes the readjusting of the glasses, the pause for enough breath to carry him through any amount of opposition, and 'Swope speaks.'" Swope would from time to time punctuate a conversation he was dominating, graciously, by gesturing toward a silent spectator and saying "As Joe here has so sagely observed . . ." and would then attribute to Joe some sage observation that might or might not have ever crossed Joe's mind. Joe could be counted on to listen, if only to learn what sagacity he had spawned. With as many dinner guests as there usually were at the Swopes', it was sometimes hard for the paterfamilias to keep everybody's attention riveted on him, but he did his best. If a lady far down the table seemed inattentive, he would pause in full discourse and shout, "Betty, you are a very intelligent woman. I want you to reflect on this next . . ." and he'd be off again.

One night Swope addressed some parenthetical remark to the columnist Martha Blair, later Mrs. Arthur Krock. He was astounded when Miss Blair not only replied but, daringly, kept right on talking for fifteen minutes. Swope, atypically, made no attempt to interrupt. When she had finally finished and all present waited for his riposte, he merely shook his head in amazement, grinned broadly and said, "I must be in love with the woman." Usually, however, it took more than feminine charm to check him. Early in 1933 Harpo Marx, Cornelius Vanderbilt Whitney, and John Baragwanath gave a stag dinner—or a dinner, at any rate, at which all the women were young, pretty, unmarried to any of the male guests, and known for the evening as Miss Benson. The Miss Benson seated at Swope's side was a blonde eyeful, but he was mainly concerned at that moment with the throbbing struggles of the New Deal. He was speaking eloquently on the history of domestic American politics and some of the ancillary international repercussions that stemmed from them when the pangs of hunger made him stop long enough to put a forkful of food into his mouth. The girl next to him, who had with some difficulty tried to follow his monologue—it went all the way back to McKinley—gazed at him through her long curly lashes, batted her baby-blue eyes, and murmured, "Hey, hey, big boy!" Baragwanath, for years afterward, would utter the phrase whenever he thought Swope was becoming excessively talky; Swope always roared with indignation at the affronting memory.

Compulsive talkers are apt to be hotly competitive. Soon after the 1928 Presidential campaign, Swope was toastmaster at a banquet attended by Mayor James J. Walker of New York. Both were notorious for their tardiness as well as their gabbiness. (Swope, to maintain his reputation for lateness, or perhaps to put a friendship to the hard test of patience, once deliberately kept another mayor of New York, the usually impatient LaGuardia, waiting thirty minutes for an appointment when Swope was only one block away from their rendezvous at the designated hour and had nothing else to do.) At the banquet Walker, who had earned Swope's envy by letting it be known *he'd* been forty minutes late for an appointment with President Coolidge, heard Swope say that he'd not long before spent twenty-eight minutes at the White House with Coolidge. Walker broke in to announce that he not long before spent *thirty* minutes with the President. Swope quickly amended his elapsed time to thirty-one minutes. "Yes, Herbie," the Mayor said, "but you are including the three minutes you permitted Mr. Coolidge to get in a word."

Pitting Swope against Coolidge in a talking contest would, of course, have been an arrant case of mismatching. (At a party at Mrs. William Randolph Hearst's one night after he left the White House, Coolidge approached Swope's wife. "You're Mrs. Swope, aren't you?" he asked. She said, "Yes." He said, "You're not as talkative as your husband, are you?" She said, "No.") Swope's friends were always on the lookout for some other renowned talker to match him against. Westbrook Pegler, in the days before he soured on Swope and on much of the rest of the world, used to refer to him as "my man" and to dwell lovingly on Swope's victories against such celebrated talkers as Albert Lasker, the advertising man, and Isaac Marcosson, the journalist. At a New York dinner for a visiting London editor, in the 1920s, international affairs had so relatively low a priority that to keep the party going somebody got the idea, which quickly won favor, of putting Swope and Marcosson in a private room and seeing who could outtalk whom. Swope was the underdog, largely because he had a boil on his neck and it hurt him just to turn his head, but in spite of the handicap, less than half an hour after they had been sequestered Marcosson came out, asked for his hat and coat, and went home in tongue-tied humiliation. Swope did less well at the sportswriter Grantland Rice's home in a similar test of strength against Fielding H. Yost, the University of Michigan football

79

coach known as "Hurry Up." Yost maneuvered the conversation onto football and kept it there for what spectators later said, possibly exaggerating, was three uninterrupted hours, while Swope fumed on the sidelines. Finally, to illustrate some play he was explaining, Yost grabbed a nearby hat—it was, inevitably, Swope's—and drop-kicked it the length of the room. Some say it sailed out a window; others that it landed in a bowl of whipped cream. In any event, Swope retrieved his hat and left, at what was for him the ridiculously early hour of 11:00 P.M.

In 1928 Heywood Broun drew up an All-America talking team. Yost was not on it; Broun may have had him in mind for coach. Broun's selections were Clarence Darrow, George Jean Nathan, Irvin S. Cobb, Max Eastman, Al Smith, Alice Longworth, Alexander Woollcott, Dorothy Parker, Will Rogers, Floyd Dell, and Swope. "Indeed, there is one danger in including Herbert Bayard Swope," said Broun. "If he is on my team I rather fear that all his fellow players won't get a chance to do much talking." Broun, who from time to time would mention with pride his having once interrupted Swope and silenced him for somewhere between fifteen and thirty seconds, reminisced over the radio one night about a dinner he'd attended with H. G. Wells, six Japanese newspapermen, and Swope. Broun said:

These Oriental journalists were anxious to learn what the great English novelist thought about a number of topics, but they let him get all the way to his demitasse in peace. Then the spokesman for the Japanese began the interrogation. I forget what the question was. I think it had something to do with birth control—but it doesn't matter. Mr. Wells started to answer—and it was going to be at length, I guess—that is if one may judge by the writing of H. G. Wells. But this time he made a fatal mistake—he paused to clear his throat—erhem, like that—and no man can afford to take a chance like that while Swope's around. He's as quick as a Notre Dame halfback to see an opening. H. G. Wells never got started this time. He cleared his throat to no purpose, for the booming voice of my beloved boss cut through the respectful silence of the Japanese journalists, and he spoke up loud and clear, saying, "I think Mr. Wells means to say about as follows." And for the next half hour he held us all—including H. G. Wells—spellbound.

Years later, when Broun heard that Wells—who once inscribed a book, "To Herbert Swope, who taught me how to be a performing seal"—had had a talk in Russia with Joseph Stalin, the columnist wrote, "I venture to say that not since Mr. Wells worked for HBS under the gold dome of the old *World* has he met any man who brushed aside his views as unceremoniously as did Secretary Stalin."

In July 1939, while Swope was laid up briefly with a streptococcus throat infection, the New York *Post* said, "Though unable to see visitors or talk over the telephone, Swope's condition is not serious. . . ." To anyone who knew Swope at all, it was hard to believe that he would not consider a separation from the telephone serious, if not critical. In his Manhattan apartment and his Long Island place, he had a couple of dozen telephones, among them direct lines to his Wall Street brokers. For years, whenever he visited Washington, he was partial to the Hotel Carlton, mainly because it was the only hotel there with telephones in its bathrooms. Before the Second World War, when he went to Saratoga for the August racing, he often stayed at Jock Whitney's. Whitney had amenities enough to satisfy most guests, but to take care of Swope, and at the same time make telephonic communication with the outside world available to the rest of the household, Whitney had a separate, unlisted phone installed in the guest room that Swope usually occupied. It was for Swope's exclusive use. Such was Swope's impact on his fellow man that, twenty years after he stopped staying at Whitney's and four years after he died, the phone was still there, although silent. Dozens of other guests have slept in that bedroom since, but in the Whitney ménage the chamber is still referred to as "Swope's room."

Arthur Krock once said that Swope invented the telephone as an accessory of men's evening dress. At any hour of the day or night, in any social circumstances, Swope would drop everything else to talk on the phone. When he was a working newspaperman it was understandable that he should have got accustomed to making calls at all hours. He never broke the habit. In a footnote to a 1947 letter to Baruch, he wrote, "By the way, whenever you're awake before 3:30 A.M., why don't you call me up? I never get to sleep before then, and it's a quiet time for a talk."

For many years Swope was so close to Baruch that hardly a day passed without their talking to each other. Yet Swope resisted visiting Baruch's splendid South Carolina plantation, Hobcaw Barony, because its owner wouldn't permit a phone on the premises. It was necessary to make a half-hour trip, partly by boat, to get to a phone. Baruch, like President Roosevelt, was a big man fond of small jokes. Calling Baruch, Swope would sometimes identify himself by one alias or another that they both thought hilarious—"Mussolini," say, or "Mother Levy." While Winston Churchill was visiting Baruch one time, in a New York apartment that did have phones, a servant announced that President Hoover was on the line. "It's Swope," Baruch told Churchill, and, picking up the phone, said, "How are you, you big cheese?" There was a pause, after which President Hoover said, "Did you say 'chief' or 'cheese'?" Baruch, convinced more than ever that Swope was up to one of his japeries, shunned the graceful way out the President had offered him and plunged on. "I know whom I'm speaking to," he said. "I said *cheese*."

Baruch probably spoke on the telephone to Presidents more than Swope did, but Swope did his best to keep up with his friend. It was necessary that the telephonic bells that tolled for him should have the ring of authority. Once, suffering from a rash, Swope thought it might be psychogenic, and he consulted a psychiatrist. The psychiatrist sent him to a dermatologist. An hour or so later the dermatologist called the psychiatrist and said, in effect, "This patient needs you even more than me. I don't know who he thinks he is, but while he was in my office I couldn't keep him from using the phone and he claimed to be talking to Bernie Baruch, the Governor, and, for God's sake, the President." The psychiatrist, who knew Swope well, told his colleague not to be alarmed; that that was Swope at his most unimpeachably normal.

5

I T SOMETIMES seemed to members of Swope's circle that his majestic actions and attitudes could not possibly have sprung from the environment which he created and in which he flourished, but that, rather, they must have been inherited. "Mr. Swope was born taking charge of things," Damon Runyon once said. More or less the same conclusion was reached by another columnist, George Sokolsky, who said, "Herbert Bayard Swope possessed qualities of aristocratic bearing and noble living which are genetic, not cultivated, and which opened to him doors which were closed to others."

Whatever it was in Swope's ancestors' genes, his parents' only two sons were a remarkable pair. They both ended up taking charge of things, and there were few doors through which either or both could not readily pass. As president of the General Electric Company during its evolution into one of the most powerful corporate entities on earth, Gerard Swope was not merely an industrialist of consequence, but his enlightened views on the responsibility of big-business management to its employees, and on its responsibility toward the public at large, had a good deal to do with reshaping the corporate image of America. And in 1922, when Gerard was chosen president of G.E., his brother, nine years his junior, was already running the liveliest paper in the largest city in the world. It was quite an achievement for two scions of a family whose members were anything but aristocratic and noble but were, instead, solid, middle-class, German-Jewish, and no more nor less distinctive than thousands of Central European emigrants who flocked to the United States halfway through the nineteenth century.

Isaac Swope, their father, came to America, at the age of twenty-six, in 1857. He was a native of Lengsfeld, a village near Eisenach, in Thuringia, and his name was Isaac Schwab. His son Herbert, for all his preciseness about historical facts, tended to be vague about his origins. "My grandfather's name was Schwob or Schwoppe," he once wrote a friend. "Probably the name grew from Swabia, or Swobenland. His name became Swope, having been anglicized. . . ." Actually, the grandfather, Hirsch Schwab, who died in 1878, never changed his name at all. There was nothing unusual, however, about such anglicizing. As far back as 1720 an unrelated German Schwab had migrated to this country and then become a Swope. (Another unrelated namesake, Charles M. Schwab, did all right here without altering his patronym.)

Hirsch Schwab had three boys and five girls; of the eight children, five were to make America their home. The oldest son, Joel, was the first to cross the Atlantic, in 1842. He stayed a while in Cincinnati, and then settled in St. Louis, where he went into the wholesale shoe business. In 1867 his youngest brother, Meier, joined him. By that time all three brothers had changed their name to Swope. Joel and Meier branched out into the retail business. The Swope Shoe Company was the oldest retail foot-wear store in the city, where their horse-drawn delivery wagon —shaped like a boot—became a familiar sight. The driver rode over the toe, and the upper was used to carry merchandise.

Isaac Swope was a gentle, pale-faced, and unassertive man, five feet eight inches tall, with blue-gray eyes and dark-brown hair. As a young man he was not overly ambitious. He wanted to get sufficiently established in the new country to go back to Europe and find himself a bride. Following Joel's path, he, too, went first to Cincinnati and then on to St. Louis. He started a watch busi-ness, manufacturing cases and filling them with movements im-ported from Switzerland. Things went well enough during the Civil War years. In 1865 he returned to Germany and was soon engaged to Ida Cohn, then living in Muehlhausen, fifty miles northeast of Eisenach. Ida was only seventeen—half his age. She was bright and bustling, with ivory skin, wavy chestnut hair, and strikingly dark and shining eyes. Sometimes, when she was tired, she would snap them shut and in a moment open them again. They seemed brighter than ever, and she seemed refreshed. (Herbert, when he grew up, also gave the impression of being able to turn his vitality on and off, like a G.E. bulb.) Ida was short and plump and was impressed with height—as Herbert was later to be, too. In 1859, at the age of eleven, she had written her father, Gerson Cohn, a birthday poem that began:

> Papa, whom I honor as a child,
> If only I were taller, so that
> I could reward your tenderness
> With deeds! . . .

Herbert's maternal grandfather, Gerson Cohn, who died the year his daughter composed those sentiments, was a man of considerable academic attainment. He was a theologian, a doctor of philosophy, and a history and language teacher by vocation, but at the age of thirty-one he had had, in his word, a "call" to become a rabbi in Dessau, his home town. "I followed this call, though the position is, in financial respects, in no way outstanding," he later said. "I did so with the intention of helping the people of this community by doing good and needed things." His rejection of material rewards left his wife and four children, upon his death, in difficult circumstances, and the widow and her oldest daughter had to go to work. They moved to Muehlhausen and were running a dressmaking and millinery shop there when Isaac came to court Ida.

The Schwabs, like the Cohns, were faithful to Orthodox Jewish customs. A few weeks after Isaac and Ida became engaged, he wrote her a letter from his parents' home; but because it was a Saturday, he had to write it secretly. Had his mother caught him, she would have considered his action a violation of the Sabbath. Now that he had found a fiancée, he kissed her goodbye and went back to the United States. Notwithstanding the time and effort it took to cross the Atlantic in those days, he wasn't prepared to get married until he had a home ready for his wife and had his business on an even sounder footing. "First work, then play," he enjoined her as they parted, taking a view of marriage that, considering his normal serious mien, was somewhat lighthearted. They were engaged for seven months before he returned to Europe. In the interim he tried by mail to condition her for life in an alien land:

> . . . My dear child, I tell you frankly that some go to America without knowing what to expect; I think it is my duty to tell you also, my dear child, that I will care for you with loving hands, but

over and above that one should be prepared for all eventualities. There are times in life which demand that a person control himself, be his own servant and understand himself in every respect; there are times in life in which a person needs to remain composed in the face of demanding situations into which he might be thrown. And I think it is better to prepare one's self for it than to look forward only to agreeable and nice and abundant times; don't you think I am right, dear Ida? Hasn't experience already taught you that people who think they have everything later on need help from others? That has happened and will happen again. . . .

All this he wrote in German. But toward the end he added an affectionate English postscript, and at his suggestion Ida, in her letters to him, would also scribble a few lines in the language she knew she would soon have to cope with all the time.

In the spring of 1866 Isaac felt secure enough to go claim his bride. On board the steamer *Germania*, approaching the coast of England, he wrote her that he wanted to buy her a present in Paris. "But as I have absolutely no idea what to get you," he went on, "I have finally decided to present you with a gift in the form of a man, a man who will stand at your side forever, a man who has a business in America and who intends to have it there always. His name is Isaac Swope." He did present her with an additional gift, though—a watch.

Back in St. Louis as newlyweds, Isaac and Ida took up residence in a brick house on Olive Street, so close to the manufacturing center of that fast-growing city that it was often wreathed in soot and smoke. St. Louis, with a population of three hundred thousand, was then the fourth largest city in the United States, and to Ida there was a welcome Teutonic *gemütlichkeit* about the place. ("St. Louis is a sort of nice fat lady," Herbert Swope wrote after he'd moved to New York.) Of the eight daily papers in St. Louis, three were published in German. It was assumed by people in other cities that everyone in St. Louis spoke German. Nonetheless, Isaac was determined to be American always, and English was always the dominant language in the household. Herbert's German was never fluent, but he assimilated enough of it to be able to translate a speech, years later, for Albert Einstein, soon after the physicist came to the United States.

Isaac and Ida, moreover, soon forswore their Orthodox religious upbringing. When they began raising a family, they sent their children from time to time to a reform-synagogue Sunday school, but they had the relaxed attitude toward religion shared by many German Jews who had adopted a new way of life, and many of whose children became Episcopalians, Unitarians, Christian Scientists, and unlabeled unbelievers. The Isaac Swopes' first child, a girl named Golda, was born in 1867, when Ida was still not yet twenty. Gerard came five years later, and Julia, known to her family and friends as Dolly, three years after him. Herbert, the baby, was born on January 5, 1882. Two years before that, his parents had completed their naturalization proceedings and had become American citizens.

The Swope household fitted into another German-Jewish pattern of that time: it was matriarchal. Isaac would go off to work early, come home for lunch, go back to work, and come home again late—often without scarcely saying a word, let alone giving any orders. He was so taciturn that some of his friends called him Silent Swope. He let Ida run their home, and he was pleased and amused, and probably relieved, at her energetic stewardship. His detachment from mundane affairs was not the result of any particular intellectual bent. He was simply a placid, unimaginative man. Ida, who had spent the last six years before her marriage in a household run by women, didn't mind assuming responsibilities. By the time she bore Herbert she was no longer an inexperienced foreign girl in a strange country. Meanwhile, Ida's young brother Max had followed her across the ocean, and he joined Isaac in the watch-case business. Years later Gerard would reminisce about Max: "He was a talented man, played the piano well by ear, and had an acceptable singing voice, and was popular with everybody and cheerful and wanted to have and have others have a good time." Gerard thought that Herbert, though nonmusical, took after their Uncle Max.

In 1885, when Herbert was three, his sister Golda went to Germany to visit relatives. She met and married a banker, Albert Cohn, had three sons, and never returned to the United States. The whole family traveled to Germany, in 1887, for her wedding. Some fifty years later Herbert recalled that, as a five-year-old boy, he had enlivened the ceremony, which was held on a Saturday, by deciding that the guests were a bunch of silly, prattling geese and by asking loudly, "*Queckeln den die ganze auch on Sonntag?*" Swope's parents were not surprised. At that early age he had exhibited an aptitude for iconoclasm. His mother hated tardiness as much as dirtiness; his disdain for punctuality even then rivaled that of most boys for soap. "Earliest recollection is that I wanted to die before my mother," he noted reflectively after her death. "Probably selfish, but I did not want to have the grief." Ida died in 1925, and her two sons planned to escort her ashes to St. Louis from New York by train. Gerard, a man who liked to do everything on time, had to escort the urn alone. Herbert was late for the train going to his mother's funeral, but got there after some scrambling.

Herbert was a loner as a child. Gerard, more than nine years his senior, was too old to be a playmate, and, besides, their interests were antithetical. Gerard installed a workshop in the Olive Street basement, where he built an electric cloth-cutter to oblige a friend whose father was a haberdasher; Herbert, in his turn, converted the basement into a theater, where he staged shows and charged the neighborhood children two cents' admission. Gerard had no use for gambling. As a college undergraduate he got inveigled into a poker game and came out ahead. "The winnings burned in my pocket," he later said, "and I wasn't happy until I had spent it all on hot chocolate and sandwiches for all of us." While Gerard was thus putting out the fire, Herbert, then aged eight, was at the St. Louis Fair Grounds discovering the enchanting world of horse-racing.

Like his brother before him, Herbert went to the Stoddard School, which ran through the eighth grade. Unlike Gerard—who took after his father in subscribing wholeheartedly to the virtues of walking, which not only promoted health but saved carfare—Herbert kept an eye constantly cocked for gaudier means of locomotion. His favorite vehicle was his uncles' shoe-shaped delivery wagon. Whenever he spotted it he would hail the driver, who, recognizing him as the proprietors' nephew, would let him hop aboard. Herbert would ride in overshod splendor throughout the city, and if this occasionally meant his missing a day of school entirely, he was not abashed. When his mother told him one time how bad it made her feel to have to be inventing excuses constantly to his principal for his truancy, Herbert explained that the trouble with school was that his teacher kept telling her class the same old things over and over again, and that since he was perfectly capable of comprehending what she was saying the first time, her idiotic repetitiveness bored him unbearingly. He said he preferred being out of doors, where he could more often be exposed to new sensations and experiences and could probably learn more. His mother pointed out to him sharply that he never seemed to object to going through the unchanging routine of eating a hearty home-cooked dinner every day. "Oh, that's different," he said. "I bet with myself: Will it be lemon, cherry, or apple pie, or maybe pudding, for dessert? Lots of times I win."

The depression of 1893 hit Isaac Swope hard. Even before that his business had been slipping. His brother-in-law Max, although delightful when singing harmony, left something to be desired as a commercial partner, and the Swope Watchcase Company had been slumping before the trend became nationwide. Herbert's educational prospects looked bleak. His father had put both daughters in private schools, and Gerard, aspiring to a career as an electrical engineer, was at the Massachusetts Institute of Technology. But now there was no money left for such educational indulgences. Isaac Swope was downcast. At his most euphoric, moreover, he had never had the forcefulness necessary to control his younger son. Gerard, himself still under twenty-one, decided to take Herbert in hand. He was to have more influence in shaping Herbert's character than any other individual. Herbert's lifelong rebellion against many of society's conventions was simply an extension of his boyhood rebellion against his brother's severe strictures.

Even before Gerard, with his mother's acquiescence, stepped into the child-raising picture, Herbert had made it clear that he was going to be a handful. At twelve he was graduated from Stoddard, but he had hardly entered Central High School, the following fall, when he was expelled for all-around unruly behavior. From M.I.T., Gerard wrote him:

> To say I was pained and grieved at the intelligence my letter from mother and father brought me today is putting it but mildly indeed. It has been a constant source of thought and sorrow all day and this evening I thought I would write to you and tell you what I think about it and try to appeal to your better nature and character.

After dwelling at some length on the pain Herbert was ostensibly causing his parents, Gerard went on:

> Then think—and this I think is the most important of all—try to think of the effect on yourself of all this. Is it not necessarily degrading? And have you lost all sense of shame and decency? Can't you see that you are hurting yourself far more than you hurt anyone else—even your parents and teachers?

89

Herbert got himself readmitted and ultimately finished school, but it was touch and go.

Gerard was short and dark and serious. Herbert was light-haired and frolicsome, and at fourteen he was taller than his twenty-three-year-old brother. Herbert was far from handsome—gangling, freckled, spindly, and bespectacled—but as a teen-aged boy he was a chromatic sight. One neighbor with a patriotic turn of phrase recalled him later as "the red and white and blue boy of long ago. Skin lustrous white, hair redder than titian, large wonderful eyes bluer than the lakes of Venice." But Herbert was not as tranquil as the lakes, let alone a whirlpool. At home for lunch, on school days, he was almost always expelled from the table. He would get to talking, and then to arguing, and then to shouting, and soon, while Silent Swope looked mutely on, Ida would order the boy out of the room.

In 1895 Gerard was graduated from M.I.T. and—degrees in electrical engineering then having little vocational value—got a seven-dollar-a-week job as a factory hand in the Chicago shops of the Western Electric Company. He was working a fifty-six-hour week, but he found time, as he did later while progressing rapidly up the electrical ladder, to keep a vigilant eye on his brother, to whom he was fond of transmitting such counsel as "Let us look the facts squarely in the face and I am sure you will agree with me in what I say." Gerard noted that Herbert seemed to be making satisfactory headway in football and track (the high jump and shot put were his events), but the older brother became increasingly dismayed at what he was hearing of the younger's study habits. Writing on January 25, 1896, Gerard said:

There is only one reason why you aren't able to study now, and that is because you never *knew* how. Formerly you were accustomed as I understand to simply glance over your lesson hastily and by the aid of your somewhat retentive memory to retain a super-ficial smattering of the lesson—which in the grammar school days you found sufficient to impress the teacher that you *knew*—and *really knew*—your lesson. And now when you come to studies which require a little more application—like Latin, Greek, etc.— you are unable to meet this demand—in other words the fruits of your early training—or lack of it—now begin to make themselves manifest. This is what I think of the disease—now for the remedy. The remedy is by no means easy—though it is *possible* with some exertion and a little trouble on your part. You must first unlearn the evil results of your former pernicious habit and then by steady uphill work lay the foundations of a better method, and really learn how to study. Without this powerful adjunct—the knowing how to study—it is perfectly useless for one to even dream of studying a profession or even going to college.

He went on like that for four more pages, and he instructed Herbert to furnish him each week, in writing, a report on his behavior.

Herbert still hoped somehow to go on to college and maybe law school after that. His family's friends in St. Louis, however, were beginning to think of him as a hopeless ne'er-do-well, and some of them were even predicting he'd end up in jail. In the summer of 1897 his stock took a momentary turn upward. He got a four-dollar-a-week job as a delivery boy, and he won an essay-writing contest sponsored by a department store. For a treatise on why the store was the fastest-growing such establishment in St. Louis, Herbert received fifty dollars, a handsome prize at the time. Gerard's pleasure at Herbert's windfall was tempered by the news that the money had gone for a fancy new bicycle, and from Chicago he wrote:

You won fifty dollars as a prize, and are making a certain amount each week out of which instead of saving a little you indeed spend more than you make and are constantly borrowing from mother. My point is this—if you so earnestly desire to study you would be less ready to satisfy every selfish wish of your own and try to save and help yourself a bit, instead of first satisfying your desires for pleasure and then depending on someone else to supply the money for the education which you have so much at heart. Why didn't you think of college when you spent fifty dollars for your wheel? And why if the thought is ever patent to your mind do you spend every cent you earn and more beside? . . . You are now getting four dollars a week of which as I understand you are to pay one-fifty for board; your carfare costs you one-twenty a week making your expenses two-seventy a week and leaving a balance of one-thirty each week for incidentals. (Clothes, shoes, etc.) Now if you are in earnest and wish to study and help yourself—save as much as you can and I will help you in this way—for every dollar you save I will give you another, thereby doubling your savings and helping you to get along faster. You may deposit your savings with mother if you wish and whenever you have five dollars saved I will deposit five dollars to your credit here in the bank. Or if you wish, every dollar you save you may send me direct and I will deposit two to your credit and allow you interest on your money besides. Whenever you need money for anything extra (such as clothes, etc.) and draw from the fund if it is a necessary and legitimate expense, all well and good. If *not* I will draw an equal amount from what I have deposited to your credit. Is this plain? You must, however, pay your board regularly and not overdraw and if you deposit with mother she must send me a statement each time of the amount and also whenever you draw from your savings she must send me a statement of how much you drew and *exactly* for what purpose and her approval of it. Is this fair?

Herbert was overjoyed at the notion of having Gerard match his savings, and in less than three months he was able to report impishly that he'd made five dollars gambling and would Gerard, in consonance with his previously stated offer, please send him an additional five? Gerard exploded. "To this as you know I object most strongly and am most decidedly opposed to encourage such 'saving' by doubling that amount," he replied.*

In 1898 Dolly Swope, like her sister before her, went to Europe and married a German, Herbert Lewin, a broker. This time the whole family could not afford to attend the wedding. Herbert Swope was in his last year of high school and was applying himself somewhat more sedulously to his studies, especially to Greek. Twenty years afterward he was to write his old Greek teacher at Central High:

> I have found that, at least, an elementary knowledge of Greek is not only valuable but interesting. It becomes of special worth to those seeking proficiency in English. Its virtue as a mental discipline requires no new commendation. I believe that the war is bringing a change in the public viewpoint and that in the new order peace will create, there will be a swing-away from the ultra-practical to the things of cultural interest. In that class the study and enjoyment of Greek surely belong.

He added that he could still rattle off the Greek alphabet. Indeed, from high school on, when he wanted to write himself a note that

---

* Although Herbert rarely followed Gerard's advice, he thought it was sound in principle. In 1918, when Herbert himself stood *in loco parentis* to a young brother-in-law, he heard that the boy had contributed five dollars out of his savings to a war charity and swiftly called him to task: ". . . Five dollars is a pretty husky gift for a boy your age to make, so when you make it you should be satisfied that the cause to which you are giving is worth so large a proportionate part of your capital. . . ."

most other eyes, should they come upon it, could not decipher, he would transliterate English words into Greek.

There was nothing arcane, in St. Louis just before the turn of the century, about Herbert's reputation as a rake. "I want to eat all the food in town, drink all the liquor in town, and sleep with all the women in town," he was reported to have said. His sister Dolly's best friend was Blanche Frank, who married the financier Henry Ittleson and who was to become one of America's spriest and most charming octogenarians, as well as the country's pioneer psychiatric social worker. "At seventeen, Herbert was such a great ladies' man," Mrs. Ittleson recalled when she herself was eighty-six, "that he was thrown out of every St. Louis house with a girl the right age and a father capable of propelling him." One girl at Herbert's school got pregnant, and he was the nearly unanimous community choice for culprit. Not only was he innocent but he knew who the guilty boy was—a friend of his whom, however, he declined to identify. Instead, Herbert stoically endured a reprimand from a St. Louis lawyer who was a close family friend and had helped Gerard through M.I.T. For the rest of his life Herbert never forgave the lawyer. Gerard, on the other hand, named a son after the man.

Perhaps in part because of this hurtful interlude of notoriety, Herbert decided he might like to become a newspaperman. When he dutifully confided this ambition to his brother, Gerard replied:

Well, the gist and sum and substance of the matter is I don't think well of it at all. . . . My objections to the reporter idea are—you are too young—your character is not so strong that it can be depended upon to meet with safety the temptations such a life would open—you are growing and need more rest than such an occupation would allow—you are nervous and excitable and therefore must refrain from such a life and try and lead a quiet and regular one—your mind is not mature enough to carry the burdens of such a position. These are a few of my objections. I could give you a great many more but these I think will be sufficient. No, I do not approve and you must give up this idea at all events for the next year or so or as long as you remain at home.

Gerard thought Herbert might be better off in some healthy line of work like military service; Herbert had drilled a bit after school with a Missouri National Guard company. Better yet, if Herbert insisted on writing, why not go to a logging camp out west and write about *that?*

93

The experience of a lumber camp will be fine, healthful and invigorating, novel and interesting too. I think it absolutely essential that you go away from St. Louis as soon as it can be arranged. I must decline however to lend you five dollars as I haven't it in the first place and in the second I don't see why you need money when you are not paying board and not working.

That was in the fall of 1898, when Herbert was not yet seventeen, and Gerard wanted him out of St. Louis because he was becoming apprehensively convinced that Herbert was succumbing to bad habits. He hadn't quite fulfilled his ambition about the food, the drink, and the women, but he was staying out late, was gambling, and, worst of all, had bought a topcoat with some of his winnings. "I told you explicitly *not* to buy a topcoat," Gerard wrote. Gerard had to such a degree usurped the role of Herbert's mentor that at one point when the boy *was* working Gerard wrote at length to their father, asking for all kinds of information about Herbert and concluding, commandingly, "Did Herbert turn over his wages to mother last week? Answer this letter in detail as soon as you have found out about the above questions."

Isaac Swope must have been puzzled by the odd relationship that was developing between his sons and by his own abnegation of authority. But his health had been getting increasingly poor, and early in 1899, when Gerard was twenty-six and Herbert barely seventeen, their father died. Not long afterward, Ida went back to Germany and stayed there for most of the rest of her life with her daughters. There was no doubt now that Gerard was the head of the family—a two-man family. One of the first things he did after his father's death was to make a careful inventory of Isaac's estate. Its net value was slightly over seven thousand dollars. Herbert, who had not yet entirely abandoned thoughts of higher education, hoped his share might help him go to Harvard, but instead he took a trip to Germany, visiting his sisters, and while there attending a few lectures at the University of Berlin. That was as high as his formal education ever got, although in subsequent years he was to receive honorary degrees from Colgate and Hobart. Colgate set a fraternal precedent by thus honoring both Herbert and Gerard at the same ceremony. Hobart made Herbert an honorary member of Phi Beta Kappa.

Gerard did manage to wean his brother briefly from the temptations of St. Louis. He got him a job as a workman in the Western Electric shop in Chicago. Manual labor, however, was

94

not Herbert's forte. He took the post to please his brother, but after discovering what intense displeasure it gave *him,* he quit it abruptly and returned to St. Louis, where he had heard there was an opening more suited to his tastes—a cashier's job at the Fair Grounds race track. At that point, Henry Ittleson intervened.

Ittleson, who was to found the Commercial Investment Trust in New York, had been born in Berlin in 1870, the son of a Russian bookbinder, and had come to America at nine. He was a studious, sedentary man who thought he might become a rabbi but instead, when his family settled in Kansas, turned to law. While riding horseback through a Kansas blizzard to study under a country attorney, he took sick and lost the hearing in one ear. His parents concluded that the law was too debilitating for him and Kansas too cold, so they moved to Colorado and opened a general store, which he helped run. In 1889, at nineteen, Ittleson moved to St. Louis to manage the local branch of the May Department Stores. He soon met and married Blanche Frank. As a department-store executive, he learned his way around local newspaper circles. Now, feeling that Herbert could do better than spend all his time at the race track, and aware of the boy's earlier yearnings to be a reporter, Ittleson sent him over to see the city editor of the *Post-Dispatch,* Florence D. White, who was also to play a big part in Swope's life.

White had begun on the *Post-Dispatch* as a political reporter. He ultimately became its managing editor and in all spent more than fifty years working for the Pulitzer newspapers. While Swope was executive editor of the *World,* White, by then transferred to New York, was its general manager. His wife later was named godmother to Swope's son. Their early association in St. Louis was not, however, of long duration. Swope, taken on the city staff at eight dollars a week, found his new journalistic stature exhilarating, and he soon made himself noticed. (He was remembered for years afterward as the first reporter in St. Louis to wear spats.*) He liked to say in later life, perhaps stretching things a bit, that his hours at the *Post-Dispatch* were from 7 A.M. to 11:30 P.M. He would also recall, with an old-boy chuckle, that he was suspended three times—twice for fighting in the city room and once for playing college football, under an assumed name, for

---

* Twenty years later he won further acclaim as the only reporter at the Paris Peace Conference who wore spats.

St. Louis University against Christian Brothers College, which his boss, White, had attended. Swope recalled later that the university was to have paid him ten dollars for playing in the game, in which, he added, two men on the opposing squad were killed. At the end of the fracas he got only two dollars. If he had known in advance he was to be cheated, perhaps the carnage would have been more devastating. Swope owned up to these shenanigans when he returned to St. Louis, in 1945, for a party in honor of the sixtieth birthday of Joseph Pulitzer, Jr. Swope was met by Pulitzer's car, on arriving in the city, and he won a cigarette off Pulitzer's chauffeur, who rashly bet him that Roosevelt had carried Missouri by at least three hundred thousand votes in the 1944 election. The driver should have been warned that his passenger was a man who was likely to know that the margin was only 46,182.

As a cub reporter on the *Post-Dispatch*, Swope was assigned one day to go out with an artist—photographers were rare then—to cover a routine feature story. Swope flagged down a horse cab, jumped in with his companion, settled back, stuck his thumbs inside his vest, drew a deep contented breath, and said, "Ah, this is the life!" On his return to the office and his presentation of an expense account, he was quickly informed that if he wanted to be a successful leg man he had better get used to walking. Soon afterward his employers got the impression that he was seeking out far too many stories at the race track, and they fired him, but he had incontestably become a newspaperman.

Gerard Swope, in Chicago, had taken to spending much of his time at Jane Addams' slum settlement, Hull House. There he met Mary Hill, the social-worker daughter of a banker, and in 1901 they were married. Miss Addams officiated at the ceremony. A few months earlier Western Electric had transferred him to St. Louis as its local manager. The Gerard Swopes moved into the family home on Olive Street, and Herbert, once again at loose ends but now determined on a journalistic career, switched cities with his brother, went to Chicago and got a job on a daily called the *Inter-Ocean*. Ben Hecht, a Chicagoan who made journalists glamorous in *The Front Page*, described Swope as a newspaperman in the real Chicago tradition. That he may have been, but he did little in Chicago to merit the accolade. He wasn't there very long. A talent scout from the New York *Herald* came through Chicago while touring the hinterlands to recruit promising young men for that paper. Swope liked to say much later that he had taken the man out and got him drunk. Whatever his condition, the *Herald* herald sensed in the nineteen-year-old boy a still largely untapped flair for reporting and offered him a job. From then on New York City was Swope's city.

Herbert Swope's extravagance was legendary; so was Gerard's thriftiness. When Gerard, after he became president of General Electric, left his office at the end of a work day and went to his suburban home, his employees were confident they wouldn't hear from him until morning; he disapproved of frivolous long-distance telephoning. The celebrity-studded world in which Herbert moved with kingly ease was all but unknown to his brother. Major Edward Bowes was for years a neighbor of Gerard's, and once, at the height of his amateur-hour fame, he invited Gerard and Mary Swope to a party in New York. Gerard, not quite catching the name of one vaguely familiar-looking man he was introduced to, asked his wife what business the fellow was in; the fellow was Clark Gable.

Gerard could not comprehend Herbert's late hours and social habits. Once while the younger brother was abroad, Gerard and his wife spent an evening with Herbert's wife. Gerard wrote Herbert afterward, "Margaret, Mary and I went off to the theater one night and did not get back until the wee hours of the morning, following in your footsteps, and about a week ago Margaret and I went off alone to do the same thing. But I confess that I am either too logical or too old [Gerard was then forty-seven] to enjoy these midnight follies—it seems to me they give mighty little in the way of entertainment, and it is altogether on too artificial a basis and therefore far from giving simple enjoyment."

There was a peculiar ambivalence to the brothers' attitudes toward each other. As an adult, Herbert's affection for Gerard was tempered by awe and a trace of fear. When he would say to his secretary, "I've got to go see Gerard," he sounded like a schoolboy on his way to discuss an unsatisfactory report card with an irate father. Withal, Herbert had a deep respect and admiration for his brother. At the age of seventy, Herbert would tell Gerard, ". . . You were always an example to me in all the qualities I most admire; that I failed always to take advantage of them was my fault—not yours." Asked once to list the ten greatest men with whom he had been on personal terms, Herbert named Baruch, Clemenceau, Woodrow Wilson, Justices Holmes and Brandeis, Presidents Theodore and Franklin Roosevelt, Winston Churchill, Al Smith—and Gerard Swope.

Gerard, for his part, was puzzled and a trifle saddened that all his conscientious upbringing of his brother seemed to have been in vain, but he had a continuing fondness for him—half fraternal, half paternal. He too realized that none of the basic virtues he had tried so hard to instill in Herbert seemed to be firmly lodged. And yet while Gerard enjoyed the financial security and the world-wide repute that Herbert craved, he envied Herbert's capacity for being *liked* by so many different kinds of persons. Gerard was a prince of industry, but what Herbert did and said often got the attention that a big man in business could not readily command. Heywood Broun happened to be at White Sulphur Springs, in 1938, concurrently with a convention of leaders of the electrical industry. He reflected airily that these eminent men were so far from striking in appearance that they were indistinguishable from run-of-the-mill tourists. "Here, for instance, is Gerard Swope, brother of Herbert Bayard Swope, chairman of the Racing Commission of the State of New York," Broun wrote. "I believe Mr. Gerard Swope has something to do with the General Electric Co. His interests, therefore, may be as large in the eyes of the public as that of his younger brother. But Gerard Swope presents no such eye-filling picture as does Herbert Bayard Swope, the Commissioner. Indeed, if you were to see the two Swope brothers approaching a public rostrum bearing news you would bate your breath for the message of Herbert rather than Gerard. And that would hold true even if the Commissioner begged to announce that Jockey John Doe had been set down ten days for rough riding, while Gerard Swope announced that G.E., in its laboratories, had succeeded in devising a way to transmit electric power without wires. It is my belief that the average two bystanders would proceed to fall into a fierce debate as to the merits of the punishment of John Doe. One would feel that the suspension was an imposition and the greatest crime against American liberty since the days of Nathan Hale."

David Sarnoff, who was well acquainted with both Swopes, said, "If you didn't know Gerard and Herbert were brothers, you'd never have believed they had anything in common. There

98

were no two men in the world more different. Gerard was austere and hard to approach; you could never have a back-slapping relationship with him, no matter how well you knew him, but you could with Herbert. With Gerard, you had to talk sense; with Herbert, you could talk nonsense. With him, your relationship was warm and close; with Gerard friendly and formal." The younger Swope liked to display photographs of celebrities he knew, most of them effusively or intimately inscribed. Among his collection was a portrait of his brother. It was inscribed, "Sincerely, Gerard Swope."

Herbert Swope heard it said so often that Gerard was a comparatively stodgy fellow that occasionally, with fraternal fervor, he would issue a trumpeting denial. One time a literary agent who hoped he could get Heywood Broun and Alexander Woollcott on a radio show General Electric was sponsoring asked Herbert to put in a good word for the pair with Gerard. "Gerard Swope doesn't have to have anybody tell him about Broun and Woollcott," Swope replied with asperity. "He knows them as well as you do. For you to think he is out of touch with the situation is a reflection upon yourself. Judging from your letter, one would be justified in thinking you believed Gerard was some remote, spineless, austere, purse-proud, blue-veined Money Bag. He isn't. . . ." It would have pleased Herbert had he been present at a lively dinner party one summer night when Gerard, over eighty, fell into coquettish conversation with a woman some fifty years younger, and, on taking his leave of the festivities, borrowed her lipstick and wrote his phone number on her trim bare back.

One thing the brothers did have in common was a concern for their relatives. They devoted much time and money to their sisters in Germany. Dolly had a particular run of trouble. Her husband drowned in the North Sea while she was pregnant with her only child, a boy. The son was killed in a motorcycle accident soon after graduating from college. Through her brothers Dolly got a job as a receptionist at the American Embassy in Berlin, where she stayed until 1939, by which time the Nazis had made her life intolerable. She finally returned to the United States that year and died two years later.

Ida Swope's birthday was December 24, and Gerard and Herbert always made a point to dine together on Christmas Eve, along with their families. (Gerard's daughter, Henrietta, became a noted astronomer. When, as a student at Harvard, she discovered some new stars in the Milky Way, Gerard was quietly proud; Herbert burst into a dinner party and cried exultingly, "At last the name of Swope is forever enshrined in the heavens!") The December 24 reunions were held at Gerard's home. As a rule he liked to have his dinner served precisely on the dot of seven. As a concession to Herbert, the annual dinner in their mother's honor was scheduled for eight. Even so, Herbert would sometimes show up as much as three hours late. Mary Swope, caught in the middle between her meticulous husband and her dilatory brother-in-law, finally evolved a compromise: she decreed that the Christmas Eve meal would be served exactly two hours after the time it was set for, whether Herbert had arrived or not.

Gerard's first home in the New York area was at New Brunswick, New Jersey, his wife's birthplace. When he became president of General Electric, in 1922, he bought a house more befitting his new position. It was a Tudor mansion, known as The Croft, four miles north of Ossining, New York. It had been built in 1914 by Arthur Stannard Vernay, an antique dealer, big-game hunter, and orchidologist who decided to put up an authentic reproduction of a feudal British country house. Vernay imported nearly all the materials from England, including forty-three thousand roof tiles, some of them three hundred years old. There were oak beams weighing half a ton each, and one fireplace dated back to 1357. Englishmen were of short stature in the fourteenth century, and some of the doors at The Croft were only five feet eleven inches high. For Gerard this represented no hardship, but for Herbert it was a serious hazard. His movements were always abrupt, and he kept cracking his head against things. John Hersey told in *The New Yorker* about Swope's skulling himself on Baruch's car door at Saratoga one time and crying, "Abominable car! You'll have to get a bigger car, B.M., if you want my patronage." ("If a man's head gets too big, no car will contain him," Baruch replied. "I mean that generally. No reflection on yourself, Herbert.") Lying in a lower berth on a train passing through Texas one morning, Swope sat up and smacked the underside of the upper berth with such vigor that he had to be removed to a hospital for first aid. Almost every time he visited The Croft he would, while moving from room to room, often talking to someone behind him, bump his head against a door frame. It was almost as if his brother had finally figured out a way of trying to reform him by corporal—in a sense, capital—punishment.

Although the Swope brothers did not mix much socially—both considered their most productive hours nine to five, but Gerard was an A.M. man and Herbert a P.M. man—the paths of their careers often crossed. During the First World War both held consequential posts with the War Industries Board, Gerard as an official of the military supply service, and Herbert as an assistant to Chairman Baruch. When David Loth was doing research for a biography of Gerard, he interviewed one former W.I.B. staff member who told him about a meeting at which Gerard and Herbert had both talked so volubly and uninterruptedly that finally the president of U. S. Steel, James A. Farrell, said to one of them in exasperation, "Young man, have you ever heard the adage, 'Don't Swope until you're Swopen to?'" Loth checked the story with Herbert, who thought it was true and that it was he whom the steel man had singled out for jocular attention. Then Loth checked with Gerard, who said that the incident had happened all right but that Herbert's recollection was wrong in one respect. Gerard said the steel man had been talking to *him*.

Both Swopes were friendly with, and helpful to, Franklin Roosevelt, who in his instinctive way of sizing up situations seemed to have been aware of the jealous love they had for each other. Sometimes, in conversation with Herbert, the President would refer to Gerard as "your little brother." When, in late October 1935, Herbert sent Roosevelt a telegram signed "Swope the Lesser," the President replied, "I do not know why you call yourself 'Swope the Lesser.' As a matter of fact, you and Gerard between you should rate not as twins but as quintuplets! And, strictly between ourselves, you amount to a whole lot more than the Dionnes." Since the two Swopes by then had lived a total of one hundred and fifteen years and the five Dionnes altogether a total of less than eight, the compliment to the boys seemed hardly fair to the girls.

Inferior though Herbert may sometimes have felt to Gerard in some fields, when it came to journalism he knew who was top boy. In the spring of 1917 Gerard went to Asia on business for Western Electric, whose international operations he was then supervising. "He was provided with letters to various officials, especially dignitaries of the Japanese government," Herbert wrote a cousin of theirs. "It may amuse you to know that in each of them the obloquy was put upon him of being characterized as my brother. At last I have escaped the indignity of being known merely as his brother." In Japan, Gerard had an interview with Prince Shigenobu Okuma, who had been Prime Minister the year before. When Gerard told his brother this, Herbert urged him to write up the encounter for the *World*, adding, "In spite of your fear that you might be unequal to the task, I have no doubt you will be able to give an adequate and clear narrative of your experience, if you make up your mind to tackle the job." Gerard, conceivably astonished at receiving such nose-to-the-grindstone advice from that source, dropped the whole idea.

To the very end of a long and vigorous life, Gerard Swope kept hoping his kid brother would ultimately toe the line. In 1957, a few months before Gerard died, at eighty-four, Herbert, then seventy-five, had an appointment at Gerard's office. A secretary new to General Electric was asked afterward by a junior executive what she had thought of Mr. Swope's famous brother, Mr. Herbert. "He was forty minutes late, and when he came in I was frightened," she said.

"Oh, he yelled at you," the executive said. "Herbert yells at everybody. It doesn't mean a thing."

"I wasn't afraid for *me*," she said. "When I opened the door to Mr. Swope's office and said, 'Mr. Swope, your brother is here,' I never heard his voice so cold. He said '*Send . . . him . . . in.*' And then after I closed the door—and it's a thick one, you know—the shouting, though muffled, was something awful to hear. I gathered Mr. Swope was bawling out Mr. Herbert for not being on time."

Even from beyond the grave, Gerard kept trying to reform Herbert. The careful older brother was among several benefactors who would now and then lend the carefree younger one money. Shortly before Gerard's death Herbert borrowed $41,000 from a bank. To secure the loan, Gerard put up some G.E. stock. To secure this collateral, Herbert assigned some of his life insurance to Gerard. Then Gerard died. Herbert didn't repay the bank loan, and the bank got the stock, and when Gerard died his executors felt they couldn't forgive the life-insurance assignment. Herbert said that Gerard had told him conversationally he planned to do so, but the older brother's will, to Herbert's disappointment but by then perhaps not to his surprise, contained no forgiveness clause. The bank ended up with the life-insurance money and Gerard's estate with the G.E. stock. Herbert ended up thus indirectly having to repay the $41,000. It was Gerard's last lesson in thrift.

6

THE NEW YORK to which Swope migrated at the turn of the century was a multiple-newspaper city, with more than a dozen dailies in Manhattan alone and still more in the newly assimilated borough of Brooklyn. Swarms of reporters covered the city, usually assigned to a specific district—downtown, midtown, Harlem, and so on. There was an office in each district—often a second-story room above a horse barn or saloon—that was shared by all the reporters posted in that area. Each man had a direct telephone connection to his own city desk. There was one outside line, the cost of which was split among all the papers, and over this wire the district men talked to hospitals, fire houses, police stations, and other routine news sources. The reporters were not terribly well paid and, by and large, were not considered terribly respectable. They associated with low characters, wore their hats indoors, rarely went to church, and drank a lot. With no actuarial data available to disprove the assumption, it was widely believed that the life expectancy of a newspaper reporter was forty. Gerard Swope was not without reason for having qualms about his younger brother's chosen calling.

New York—blatant, rowdy, uncultured, but pulsating with life—fascinated Herbert, then barely twenty. His favorite district, on or off duty, was the Tenderloin, a gaudy midtown oasis of fun and sin, music and gambling, girls and bars, cops and robbers. Morning newspapers like the *Herald* seldom went to press before 3:00 or 4:00 A.M., and it was easy, especially for a young and energetic bachelor, to form the habit of hardly ever going to bed before sunrise. Swope loved the excitement of big-city night life, and he came to love New York itself with an engagingly intimate affection. He referred to the city on occasion as "she," as if it were a ship, and his attitude toward it, or her, was that of a salty seafarer who, though not actually in command of a lovely vessel, had unquestioned and irrevocable access to the bridge.

The Mayor of New York, whoever he might be, was always *his* Mayor. Swope felt toward the chief occupant of City Hall as residents of small New England towns feel toward their selectmen. When Swope encountered some civic lapse—a malfunctioning traffic light, say, or a residential area insufficiently staffed by foot patrolmen—he would take the matter up with the Mayor personally, and more often than not he would get quick action.*

For the entire half century he was part of New York, Swope could not bear not to be involved in every aspect of municipal life. To him, idolizing New York was like embracing a religion that demanded total immersion of its adherents. When, in the mid-1950s, Swope had behind him more than fifty years of devotion to the city, the columnist H. I. Phillips enumerated for the New York *Sun* a list of institutions that he said typified New York: Grover Whalen, General Sherman's horse, Sophie Tucker, *Variety*, the flea circus, and Swope. Another time, in the *Journal-American*, Louis Sobol devoted his column to his notion of a "Mr. New York." Swope at once wrote Sobol describing *his* version— a fellow whose image might have appeared to Swope out of a mirror:

> He loves parades, and he likes to look at what he calls the big shots, irregardless (one of his slips) of whether they are the big shots of sport, pictures, business, or crime. He has a healthy curiosity that makes him want to know how this type moves, breathes, and walks and talks. . . . He has one fault: the swiftness and savagery of life in the city has made him a worshipper of success, which he spells with a dollar sign. He has an envy for those who've won it. At the same time he has a quite understandable and wholly human relish for those of the mighty who are found with their pants down. He has a sort of suspicion of manners that makes him seem somewhat impolite when he is unexpectedly spoken to, but he is good-hearted and always tries to be helpful. If the other fellow is surly,

---

* Swope believed in direct action in all circumstances. Once, when his view of a baseball game at Yankee Stadium was impeded by an umpire who happened to plant himself solidly between Swope's seat and the pitcher's mound, Swope wrote to the High Commissioner of baseball suggesting that he instruct his officials to keep moving around, like ballet dancers.

so is he, but if the other fellow is nice, he is, too. These are just some of his characteristics.

The New York *Herald* still basked in the reflected glory of the days when the elder James Gordon Bennett had made it world-famous. One of the paper's prized relics was a desk that Henry M. Stanley had used before he set off in 1870 to find Dr. Livingstone, and Swope, like other newcomers to the premises, often gazed reverently at this wooden shrine. But the *Herald* for which Swope toiled, while proud of its record of far-flung exploits, was basically a small-town paper that emphasized popular small-town doings like mayhem. The paper, accordingly, had no managing editor. Its chief editorial executive was its city editor, Leo Redding. Redding, who happened also to be a native of St. Louis, shared further with Swope an addiction to poker, which may have worked to the advantage of the young reporter, for Swope quickly established himself as a strikingly individualistic employee. When Redding complained once about his coming to work four hours late, Swope blandly replied, "But, Leo, whenever I come in, I'm still worth any two other men you've got on your staff."

One other reporter who served his journalistic apprenticeship on the *Herald* was George Jean Nathan. After Nathan became a drama critic, he made much of his youthful appearance, and this always irked Swope, who knew that Nathan was his age, or, at any rate, a mere forty days younger. When Swope was executive editor of the *World*, he got to talking one day with James M. Cain about Nathan's determinedly boyish mien. "George is forty-five years old," Cain recalled Swope's saying. "And how I know that is that he was born the same year I was—1882. Okay, look at me. Do I look like a college boy?"

"No," Cain replied. "Beautiful, but not collegiate."

"I'm forty-five, I look forty-five, and, thank God, I act forty-five," said Swope, his voice rising. "He's forty-five, he looks forty-five, and, God damn it, won't act forty-five. What the hell is he trying to get away with?"

"I don't know," Cain said, "and I can't ask him, as he cuts me dead every time I see him."

Swope seized the opening. "And that's another thing!" he thundered, staring at Cain through the pince-nez that was one of his cherished props. "You know why he cuts you dead? He's nearsighted. He's not quite sure who you are! How collegiate is an

106

old buzzard that can't even see, and won't wear glasses for fear they won't be youthful!"

As a fledgling reporter, Swope met quite a few persons connected with the theater. One was John Barrymore, who had not yet become a full-time actor but hoped rather to be a painter. Barrymore's father had enrolled him at the Art Students' League and had paid a full term's tuition in advance. His son quit after one day. He soon broke even that speed record when, hired as a cartoonist for the *Morning Telegraph* and instructed to make a line copy of Gainsborough's portrait of the Duchess of Devonshire, he quit after twenty minutes. Then he got a job on the *Evening Journal*, where he hung on somewhat longer and illustrated Arthur Brisbane editorials on, of all things, the evils of drink.

Barrymore liked newspapermen. In the rollicking company of three Manhattan reporters, he once stole the sculptured sword from the Hand of Victory on the Dewey Memorial Arch at Madison Square. When not engaged in such vigorous pranks Barrymore was, by his own account, a "very indolent person," and in Swope, who as a young boy had been uncommonly hard to rouse in the morning, he found a sympathetic companion. They became roommates, sharing a furnished flat above a Times Square restaurant, a base of operations that was handily close to the city's fleshpots, not to mention the flesh.

Since the one worked for a morning and the other for an evening paper, their free time did not much overlap, but when they could they went out together, and sometimes Barrymore would tag along as Swope set forth on an assignment. One night Swope was ordered to interview a minister. Barrymore accompanied him to the reverend's home, and, spotting a saloon across the street, said he would wait over there—conceivably to get inspiration for illustrating Brisbane's next temperance screed. The interview over, Swope headed for the saloon and saw Barrymore at the entrance, surrounded. "Hey, Herb, I got us a fight lined up!" Barrymore yelled gaily. Swope looked at the raffish claque which was menacingly ringed around Barrymore and recognized them as members of the Hudson Dusters, a gang notorious for its casual attitude toward homicide. Fortunately, at that moment the clergyman crossed the street to impart to the *Herald* reporter one last pious anecdote he had just recalled, and in the hush that followed Swope and Barrymore made their escape.

On the *Herald*, Swope became an increasing trial to his city editor. Sent out one day to cover a section of the city where anybody with eyes and ears and a little patience was bound to observe some newsworthy occurrence, Swope telephoned the city desk and said he had arrived at the designated location, had looked in all four directions, had seen nothing of consequence, and was therefore taking the rest of the day off. He then hung up, before the sputtering man at the other end of the line could pull himself together and speak.

After a few such unsettling incidents, Swope and the *Herald* parted company, and he went off on a brief theatrical fling himself. In the winter of 1903 the producing firm of Klaw and Erlanger hired him as what he was later to describe as a "literary agent." He always hated to associate himself with the term "press agent." Swope's job was to beat the drums in advance of a touring company headed by the English actor Martin Harvey, who was starring in *The Only Way*, a fairly loose adaptation of *A Tale of Two Cities*. Traveling one week in advance of the troupe, Swope spent the winter traipsing from Albany to Philadelphia to Washington to Ottawa to Toronto to Montreal to Cleveland to Pittsburgh to Cincinnati to Columbus to Indianapolis. St. Louis was among his ports of call, too, and his appearance in that huckstering role cannot have buoyed Gerard Swope's hopes for his future. Herbert's principal task was to stir up local newspaper interest in the forthcoming production, and he found some editors he approached disappointingly unreceptive. He notified the producers of this journalistic obtuseness, and Marc Klaw tried to reassure him with a blast at the press:

> As for the Chicago newspaper men and the Chicago papers, we cannot control them and we are not going to try. Newspapers in this country, so far as theatricals are concerned, have fallen to the level of burlesque, and the public evidently does not believe them or in them, because the firm of Klaw and Erlanger, which is the object of their bitterest attacks, draws more money with their attractions than any other theatrical firm in the world. That is the best answer to them.

Despite Klaw's misgivings about newspapers, Swope renounced theatricals and returned to them, getting a reporter's job, back in New York, on the *Morning Telegraph*. His boyish enthusiasm for horse-racing had not slackened, and working for the *Tele-*

graph, though it was then a more general paper than it was to become, gave him a gratifying entree into the stable-and-paddock set. He was not particularly happy there, however, and was delighted, toward the end of 1904, when Leo Redding agreed to take him back on the *Herald*.

So far, Swope had made no great journalistic splash, and he was in a tough competitive field. Some city rooms had as many as forty or fifty reporters on the payroll, working as a rule for a seven-dollar-a-day minimum and up to eight-dollars-a-column space rates for stories that got into print. For exclusive stories they were apt to be paid at double these rates. Given a second chance on the *Herald*, Swope embraced a philosophy of independence that was pretty much to characterize everything he did afterward: If you can't join 'em, lick 'em. He began to make it increasingly clear that he was a man apart. Reporters, being not terribly well paid, were not terribly well dressed. An exception was Jackson Slaght of the *World*, the fashion plate of his journalistic day. Slaght covered Theodore Roosevelt, who was so taken with the reporter's outfits that he asked to be introduced to his tailor. As soon as the tailor landed Roosevelt as a customer, he gave Slaght his clothes for nothing.

Sartorially, Swope progressed rapidly from the journalist who in St. Louis had been noticeable for his spats. In New York he went in for gloves and canes. As he walked along Broadway, his stride was so springy that with his ever-present cane he reminded onlookers of a man on a pogo stick, and the hand that brandished the cane was encased in a yellow chamois glove so brilliant that his envious rivals were convinced he either had two dozen pairs or threw each pair away after a single wearing. At night, preparing to hobnob with the theater and opera crowd, he would don white tie and tails; for a reporter, it was unheard of. While other reporters huddled together grubbily in the district offices, Swope grandly toured the restaurants, table-hopping with a vivacity, and with a rewarding harvest of city gossip, that was perhaps not to be duplicated until Leonard Lyons materialized a generation or so later. Periodically, Swope, who as a city-desk reporter outranked the district men, would descend upon an office where a group of them had been gathering details about the latest rape or robbery, and would say, "What's new, boys, what's new?" Most of the other reporters, who had no special love for his free-wheeling methods, would ignore him, but there was usually at least one compliant fellow around who would fill him in on what was happening. Swope would pick up a phone and relay his findings to the *Herald* city desk. Then, with a genial wave, he would sail off again into the waiting night.

Swope was less visible in the city room itself, or in any of the district offices, than in establishments like Browne's Chophouse, a popular meeting place he sometimes used as a mail drop; or Jack's, where society blades made rendezvous with chorus girls; or Churchill's, a restaurant run by a retired police captain, where officers of the force could usually find a poker game in session, not infrequently with Swope participating and his city editor, too. Swope did not confine himself to poker. Six blocks north of Herald Square there was a spot called Scotti's. Many of the places on the fringes of Times Square had a back room where the whores hung out; in *its* rear chamber Scotti's had a billiard table, which was generally used for shooting craps. One night Swope breezed into the *Herald* office and asked Ned Brown, a reporter who so magnificently fooled the life-span experts that he was still active in the sports world when well past eighty, if he could borrow some money. There was action at Scotti's. Brown had a ten-dollar bill and a two-dollar bill in his wallet. Two-dollar bills were thought to be unlucky, but Swope, graciously ceding the larger bill to its owner, took the smaller one and headed for the pool table. Brown's recollection was that Swope did not return to the *Herald* for six weeks, having run the two dollars up to six thousand and departed at once for Atlantic City to spend it while it was fresh. Other contemporaries put Swope's winnings in that game as high as eighty thousand dollars, but it was the fashion of that day to exaggerate.

By the fall of 1905 Swope was suffering from exhaustion, not surprisingly, and he had picked up a touch of tuberculosis. He landed at Dr. Edward L. Trudeau's celebrated T.B. sanitarium at Saranac Lake, in the Adirondacks. Gerard Swope visited him there, and in mid-November, while relieved that Herbert had been pronounced physically fit again, Gerald was distressed at his brother's request for funds to help him make ends meet in New York. "I don't know how I can make it plainer . . . but I can't give you money to live there," Gerard wrote. "I will help you to go *West*." There was a government irrigation project in Arizona on which he thought he could help Herbert get a job. "I hope you will soon decide and hope too that you will go West," Gerard went on, "and if so you can count on my assistance and best wishes, but if you don't go West—go to New York and get to work."

Swope returned to New York just in time to be assigned by the *Herald* to the reportorial retinue of a titled tourist who was dazzling local society, which held all visiting royalty in deep and respectful affection. This was Prince Louis of Battenberg, a rear admiral commanding the British Navy's Second Cruiser Squadron, who cruised into port aboard the flagship *Drake* and was wined and dined at a merry clip. The local papers assigned eighteen reporters, among them Swope, to dog his footsteps and report his every regal move. On November 18, 1905, His Highness, whose brother Henry had married a sister of King Edward VII, dined with the August Belmonts, saw Maxine Elliott in Clyde Fitch's *Her Great Match*, and then changed from evening clothes to tweeds and went slumming in Chinatown. There was no question about one stop he would make on this instructive tour. It had been fashionable among the upper classes for a year or so to frequent a music hall at 12 Pell Street called Nigger Mike Salter's, whose proprietor was neither a Negro nor a Chinese but a Russian Jew. The fox trot was allegedly spawned at Nigger Mike's, but what made the place alluring to the society slummers was its reputation as a haven for opium peddlers and white-slave traders. Few such recognizable types had actually been *seen* there, but there was always the exciting possibility that one might turn up.

When the Prince and his party entered Nigger Mike's, the house pianist, known as Professor Nicholson, hospitably banged out "Strike Up the Band, Here Comes a Sailor." Then two of the singing waiters on the premises, teen-aged boys called Izzy and Bullhead, serenaded the royal patron. Izzy, whose surname was Baline and who while business was slack had composed a song called "Alexander's Ragtime Band," waited on the Prince's table. When Prince Louis tipped him a dime, Izzy announced he would frame the coin. The hovering reporters diligently made note of this avowal. Then, with Professor Nicholson playing "God Save the King" and all hands—singing waiters, salesmen, slummers, and Swope—lustily joining in, Prince Louis marched out and went nearby for some chop suey.

Not too long afterward, Prince Louis changed his name from Battenberg to Mountbatten, Izzy Baline changed his to Irving Berlin, and Swope became celebrated as the man who had first

111

called attention in print to the composer's existence. It was Alexander Woollcott, in a biography of Berlin published in 1925, who put the stamp of authenticity on the episode. Writing about the Chinatown lark, Woollcott concluded, "Thus it befell that the next day Irving Berlin made his first appearance in the public prints. The reporter who thus exploited him was a ruddy and impressive lad named Swope, who has since made himself heard even above the din of our noisiest city and who is today the editor of the New York *World*." While the *Herald* covered the Prince's outing at some length, it never quite got around to mentioning the singing waiter, although other papers did. But the Woollcott version became generally accepted, and one is loath to cavil with it; what could have been more apt than if Swope had been Berlin's first chronicler?

In any event, Swope and Berlin became fast friends. In 1940, when Berlin decided to give his earnings from "God Bless America" to charity, he called on Swope for advice. Berlin had written the song in 1918, planning to use it in the finale of *Yip Yip Yaphank*. But he thought then that the number was "a little too stickily patriotic" and tucked it away until the fall of 1938. That year, just after the Munich Conference, Kate Smith was looking for a suitably nationalistic song to sing on an Armistice Day radio program. Berlin dug up the old tune, made a few changes in the lyric, and gave it to her. It was so swift a success that Berlin's publishers had forty thousand requests for the sheet music before they could get their presses rolling.

Berlin had it in mind to give the proceeds to the American Red Cross, but when he consulted Swope, who by then had a son and a daughter, he was urged instead to give them to the Scouts. In the spring of 1940 Berlin established a God Bless America Fund, with three trustees—selected, at Swope's suggestion, as carefully as a New York political ticket. Berlin made Swope, who was Jewish, the chairman; his colleagues were Gene Tunney, a Catholic, and Theodore Roosevelt, Jr., a Protestant. Swope at once foresaw a difficulty. As far as the Boy Scouts were concerned, there was no real problem, but in his philanthropic handling of young girls should he deal with the Girl Scouts, the Campfire Girls, or both? He thereupon wrote to Harry Hopkins at the White House and asked him to ask President Roosevelt which of the two sororities he preferred. Hopkins was too shrewd even to present such a politically explosive question to the President.

112

Instead, he took it up with Mrs. Roosevelt, and he soon reported back to the God Bless America Fund trustee that the First Lady's informal opinion was that it would be nice if the two rival girls' groups combined. Eventually, Swope and his associates cut them both in, and the melon they shared with the Boy Scouts was juicy indeed; in twenty years "God Bless America" blessed them all with more than a quarter of a million dollars.

The song had its detractors. Swope was one of its most loyal and outspoken defenders. When a clergyman complained in a letter to the New York *Times* that the anthem was "mawkish" and "doggerel," Swope retorted in a letter of his own, "In simple style [Berlin] has brought tears of affection and the thrill of patriotism to millions of his fellow-Americans, who sing it, I dare say, with greater avidity than they struggle through 'The Star-Spangled Banner.' " And while he was on the subject of *that* he could not resist making a sly dig; its melody, he said, was merely borrowed from a "ribald" drinking song bearing the title "Anacreon in Heaven." As usual, Swope's independent declaration provoked controversy. In this instance, the next blow was struck, in still another letter to the *Times*, by Dudley Fitts, dean of the English faculty at Phillips Academy, Andover, Massachusetts, who said that in the first place the correct title of the drinking song was "To Anacreon in Heav'n," and added, "Either I am so far gone in sin that ribaldry no longer affects me, or Mr. Swope's sensibilities have been so demoralized by the tin-can banalities of 'God Bless America' that he is more easily shocked than most persons. If 'To Anacreon' is ribald, 'Drink to Me Only with Thine Eyes' is salacious, and the University of Maine's 'Stein Song' is downright bawdy." The Boy Scouts, Girl Scouts, and Campfire Girls, perhaps not wishing to rock a boat so laden with riches, refrained from comment.

Swope's sojourn at Dr. Trudeau's sanitarium improved his health, but it did not noticeably alter his habits. Once he was dispatched to Philadelphia by the *Herald* with the cartoonist Edwin Marcus, whose work later appeared for many years in the Sunday New York *Times*. They shared a hotel room. Swope shook the cartoonist into wakefulness at 4:00 A.M., said he was in a poker game and had temporarily run out of funds, borrowed Marcus' last five dollars, and loped off into the dawn. "It seemed one could always do pretty well at gambling," Swope wrote not long afterward. "If you won, you had lots of money, and if you lost, why, the problem was simple; all you had to do was to go out and borrow some money and start over again." In New York he continued to gamble whenever he could. Occasionally, when some assistant editor at the *Herald* would try to give him an assignment, he would mutter "Got to see Redding," and would head for Churchill's gaming tables—where there was, in fact, a not bad chance he might see his editor after all.

Swope learned other maneuvers. It was customary at the *Herald* for the day city editor to turn over his schedule of assignments for the next day's paper to the night city editor at 6:00 P.M. It would take them fifteen minutes or so to execute this transfer. Swope would turn up at 6:04 or 6:05, too late for the retiring editor to assign him anything. On seeing the two editors in conference, Swope would scoot to a cubbyhole where his mail and messages and assignment orders were deposited and would then leave a few minutes later, before the night editor took over and had time to tell him to do anything. But no one could say he had not reported in for work.

When Swope did work he could be brilliant. Ned Brown liked to describe him, reportorially, as a "stick-out fellow." (Billy Rose, in later years, was to accord Swope a variation of this Broadway accolade; to Rose, Swope was a "stand-up fellow.") Swope once listed his criteria for a good reporter: accuracy, judgment of news, sense of public duty, understanding of professional ethics, and ability to write. All these assets Swope possessed, and his associates on the *Herald* were constantly impressed by what he could do with them when he could be cornered. One evening when Redding was out of the office an assistant named Deltus M. Edwards, an alumnus of the Associated Press and the New York *American* who was then the *Herald*'s night city editor, glanced at an account sent in by a city-wide wire service about a family who made fireworks at home and had been the victims of a spectacular explosion while at the dinner table. Edwards thought Swope could rewrite the story capably. To make sure he caught his man, Edwards postponed the six-o'clock conference and stationed himself at Swope's cubbyhole. He had him trapped cold. In Edwards' words:

> Herb slid in, and was almost out of the door again.
> "Herb! Come here! Here's a good story. . . ."

"Oh, dammit, I can't. I gotta get up Broadway. Big news date!"
Everyone grinned; just the same old poker-game alibi.
"Come right here!" I called.
"Hell and damnation, I can't. Gotta get up and see Redding, right away."
"Let Redding wait! You come and write the story!"
"You'll get hell from Redding!" he growled.
"O.K., but come here. You can write this yarn in half the time you're fussing about it. Come on; get to work."
He shuffled over, protestingly. Stopped at his desk just long enough to remove his yellow gloves and place them very carefully on his desk with his cane.
"Gimme the damn thing!" He snatched the copy out of my hand, tearing the flimsy a bit. Grumbling, he went back to his desk. Kicked a chair around. Slammed his typewriter desk open. Sat down. Read the story for a minute or so. Calmed down. Read some more. Then, turning, he shouted: "Hey! This is a helluva good story."
"O.K. Whip it up. Give us one of your old masterful Herb Swope stories. You know—first-page stuff!"
"O.K.," Herb returned with an amiable grin. Herb, like most of us, appreciated a little flattery once in a while—for flattery in a newspaper office is about as rare as ice cream on Old Nick's dinner table. In less than fifteen minutes Herb finished his story: about 800 words.
He kicked back his chair with a racket. Slammed down his desk top. More racket. Came over:
"Here's your damned old yarn. See if you like it!"
And then Herb set up his life's record. He stood still, actually, for almost five minutes. Stood patiently. Didn't move. Didn't say a word—a really remarkable record! If you knew Herb Swope.
"It's a cracker-jack, Herb! Swell! A regular Herb Swope masterpiece."
He whirled away. Grabbed up his things and fussily putting on his yellow gloves, loped down Brain Alley and disappeared out into the dizzy Broadway whirl.
About half-past nine, Redding walked leisurely into his room, picked up the early proofs and looked them over. Holding a proof in his hand he came to his door and called me. When I entered, he was sitting, waving the proof.
"Here's a great story, this fireworks yarn. Schedule it front page. Who wrote it?"
"Herb Swope!"
"Herb Swope?" he almost shouted, incredulous. "A good story like that. I can't believe it. Not Herb Swope!"
"Yes, Herb Swope."

"No, no, no. Are you sure?"

"Of course I'm sure. Standard News stuff, I gave it to Herb to rewrite!"

Redding slapped the proof down on his desk. Pushing his chair back, he exploded:

"So Herb Swope wrote a story! Miracle! Now, will you tell me how in hell you can get that lazy so-and-so to work—to write anything? I can't—and I pay his salary!"

Gambling was not the only avocation that Swope found diverting. The city was full of attractive and available young women. Swope lived in hotel rooms then, for the most part—the Longacre, on West 47th Street, was one of his favorites—and there were quite a few rooms in Times Square hotels other than his own in which he was welcome. Embedded in his left leg for the rest of his life was a bullet that, many of his acquaintances had been told at least once, he had acquired as a souvenir of a fortuitous but triflingly delayed exit from the window of a bedroom in which his welcome was challenged. The attentiveness demanded of Swope by his extracurricular activities finally persuaded Redding, at the end of 1907, to drop him again from the *Herald*'s payroll. Swope didn't care. By then he had decided that the *Herald* was a "rotten" paper, and as years went by his retrospective opinion of it became more and more bilious. The paper was, he said long afterward, "the graveyard of ambition, and it killed all individualism . . . a soul-devastating, spirit-destroying, mind-mechanizing, stencilled, stereotyped, patterned institution." Fortunately, the wounds it inflicted on him were, while momentarily painful, no more permanently crippling than the romantic bullet in his leg.

Being out of work did not faze Swope. The restaurants he went to were generous with credit. Churchill's still welcomed him in 1908, although he had an unpaid account there running back eighteen months—two hundred and forty-three dollars for on-the-premises consumption and two hundred and ninety-five dollars for cash advanced. Banks were somewhat stickier. One to which Redding had introduced Swope, and which had loaned the reporter three hundred and twenty-five dollars, wearied of trying to catch up with its debtor and appealed to the editor to get the matter straightened out. But when one source of funds dried up there was always a new one to tap. Swope continued to be seen in the right places with the right people. In the fall of

1908, for instance, John Wheeler was covering baseball for the *Herald*. That was the year of the close National League pennant race between the New York Giants and the Chicago Cubs, when a playoff was required because in an earlier game Fred Merkle had failed to touch second base. Wheeler was assigned to get a statement from John McGraw, the Giants' manager, about this awful lapse, and tracked him down to Rector's. He found McGraw at a table with two companions—the gambler and racing-stable owner Davy Johnson and the unemployed newspaperman Swope.

Swope was getting to know other gamblers-about-town, too, principal among them Arnold Rothstein. Swope would often say later on, when asked about his acquaintance with Rothstein, that he believed it the duty of a conscientious and effective reporter to get to know all potential news sources, without making moral judgments about them, and in a column about Swope Westbrook Pegler echoed this viewpoint: ". . . whether a reporter likes or doesn't particularly admire an important and prominent person, he should meet him if he can find an occasion. I guess Herbie Swope has known as many in his time as any other reporter in the world. . . . Have it anyway you like but I say the best asset in a reporter's life is his acquaintanceship which widens and widens with experience and extends like, you know, the ripples on a pond."

Swope knew Rothstein, however, a good deal better than many reporters know many sources. Rothstein differed notably in some respects from Swope: He was soft-spoken, conservatively dressed, and anything but flamboyant. They were the same age, though, and came from similar backgrounds. Rothstein's father was an honorable dry-goods merchant who sternly deplored, but could do nothing to change, his son's compulsive need to gamble. Just as Swope's urge to bet led him to consort with such as Arnold Rothstein, so was Rothstein's urge to lead him from being a mere bookmaker into far deeper channels of iniquity and in due course to assassination. Rothstein played in one high-stake floating poker game called the Partridge Club, which met in various Manhattan hotels and restaurants and was often presided over by a lawyer, George Young Bauchle. Swope was admitted to this circle, where he soon found himself playing with wealthy gamblers like Harry F. Sinclair, the oil man, and Charles Stoneham, the owner of the New York Giants. "Bet a Million" Gates once tried to get in the game, but Rothstein would not let him in.

Rothstein considered him a pigeon who was to be plucked alone, and not when his rich feathers might have to be shared with others.

Swope professed to have mixed feelings about Rothstein. In 1929, a year after the gambler was fatally shot, Swope, who hadn't been seeing Rothstein for a while, wrote an acquaintance, "Make no mistake as to my attitude. I have no paean of praise to sing for him but, on the other hand, I can see that injustices have been done in having every crime on the calendar charged to his account." Swope did not add that *his* account with Rothstein could possibly have affected his attitude; he had been heavily in debt to Rothstein, and the gambler had been quite lenient about repayment. While some men tend to despise their kindly creditors, others may be more tolerant in judging them than they would be in judging recalcitrant debtors. One time, when Swope was city editor of the *World*, August Belmont, the chairman of the Jockey Club, barred Rothstein from the clubhouse at Belmont Park. The gambler had been warned about the size of his bets, which were giving the track a bad reputation, and when he persisted in the practice the Pinkerton Detective Agency, at Belmont's instruction, closed the clubhouse doors to him. Swope tried to intercede with Belmont. On September 12, 1917, he wrote the Jockey Club chairman that Rothstein had promised not to offend again, and added, "While he is a sporting man, he comes of a decent, respectable Jewish family, and I am inclined to think that once his word is given he will offer no further cause for complaint." Not long afterward, though, Swope was inclined to think that he himself might be complained about if he continued to see a great deal of Rothstein, and he informed the gambler that they'd have to curtail their association. "You're too much of a liability, Arnold," the editor told his friend.

One of Rothstein's ambitions was to win a million dollars on a single horse race. He came within a hundred and fifty thousand dollars of that goal in 1921 with a betting coup on a horse from his own Redstone Stable—the Redstone, of course, being an anglicization of his surname. The horse was a colt by Star Shoot out of Milky Way, and it was called Sidereal. It was named, as were half a dozen other Redstone horses, by Swope, but there were so few race track habitués familiar with the kind of words that appealed to him that in betting circles the horse was most commonly known as Side-reel. (Swope was very good at naming horses.

118

One of his most felicitous inventions was Sunset Gun, for a filly by Man O' War out of Eventide.) Sidereal, a horse that had never won a race before, was in a barn at Belmont Park the day Rothstein decided to plunge on him. The horse had been entered in the last race at Aqueduct, but its trainer, Max Hirsch, had planned to scratch him. When Rothstein decided the horse was ripe to win, Hirsch barely got him to Aqueduct in time to be saddled. The bookmakers were offering thirty to one on Sidereal, but Rothstein laid so much money on him that the odds dropped to four to one by post time. One legend had it that Swope, late as always, raced to the track to bet on the horse he had christened but didn't get there until it was no longer a bargain. The story is probably apocryphal. As Swope's son has pointed out, "Even he could not have been late for the last race."

In the fall of 1908, at a tea at Sherry's, Swope met a shy, slim, petite, dark-eyed, eighteen-year-old Far Rockaway girl named Margaret Honeyman Powell. Her maternal grandfather was an elder of the Scotch Presbyterian Church. Her father, James Scott Powell, a Long Island Railroad employee who had risen from conductor to stationmaster, had died five years earlier. He was a pleasant but taciturn man who left behind him two legends: first, that he had a secret wife and child in his past; and second, that he had Indian blood in his veins. (In 1926 the English artist Olive Snell, who did portrait sketches of a number of American women high in society, said after Margaret Powell Swope had sat for her, "She has a touch of the Indian about her, with a rather secretive look and a calm and poised lift to her head.") James Powell's undisputed wife, born Jane Black, was a placid woman who bore him three children, a girl and two boys. Margaret, the oldest, was named, against her father's wish, after her maternal grandmother, whom James Powell detested. Since the mere sound of the word "Margaret" upset him, he insisted that his daughter be called Pearl, derived from the Greek word for the jewel, *margaron*. She was universally known as Pearl (Herbert identified her in confidential notes to himself by the Greek letter *pi*) until around 1920, when a friend in the international Prince of Wales set told her Pearl simply would not do. She became Maggie except to some of her long-time friends and, on occasion, to her husband, who hated to abandon a nickname beginning with the letter "P" and called her Pug.

At eighteen, Pearl Powell was radiantly beautiful, with pale, nacrine skin, striking deep-set eyes, and a handsome figure. For several summers her widowed mother had rented their Far Rockaway house to a young New York attorney, James N. Rosenberg, who was practicing law in partnership with Joseph M. Proskauer. Both were to go far—Proskauer as lawyer, judge, and politician, Rosenberg as lawyer and painter. In 1904 their two-man office was absorbed into the firm of James, Schell and Elkus, then run by the surviving member of that triumvirate, Abram I. Elkus, who was later Ambassador to Turkey. In 1907 Rosenberg, knowing his summer landlady's daughter needed a job, brought Pearl into the firm as a file clerk. "She set the office on its ear," he recalled fifty-five years later. The law clerks took an interest in the files that was unprecedented, but Pearl never gave any of them a second thought once she had been set on her own ear, at Sherry's, by the sight of a tall, carrot-fringed, young boulevardier with a jauntily held walking stick and the most dazzling pair of canary-colored gloves she'd ever glimpsed.

The courtship that ensued was tempestuous. To Swope, sentimentality and punctiliousness were unrelated. He would invite Pearl to the theater, ask her to meet him at a restaurant first for dinner, and keep her waiting there alone from seven to eleven. One night, coming in late and leaning forward to greet her, *he* was greeted by having a pair of torn-up theater tickets flung in his face. But when Swope got into a scrap with a third party, as boulevardiers occasionally did in those free-swinging days, Margaret proved a valuable ally. As his one hand clenched to strike an adversary, his other would remove his pince-nez and toss it to one side. He knew that Margaret would nimbly catch it and hold it for him until he had finished with his foe.

Many women might have disapproved of Swope's penchant for gambling. Pearl, however, was all for it. "I liked Herbert as a gambling fellow," she would say. "I was always on his side and sort of rooting him on. It was exciting not to know whether we had ten cents or a million dollars." She accepted with equanimity the periodic need, when she was first married, to pawn her engagement ring to raise household cash. Pearl was something of a gambler herself, but on becoming Mrs. Swope she usually played in women's games where the stakes were lower than those her husband fancied. The most she ever recalled winning in a single poker pot, for instance, was nine thousand dollars. Some of the

Swopes' friends liked to tease them about their mutual affection for games of chance. When in 1937 Robert Moses was asked to join something called the National Advisory Board of the Society for the Suppression of Gambling, Inc., he at once told Swope, "I wrote this man that his purpose is entirely outside of the scope of my interests and activities, but that I was sure you would join and take an active part in putting the program across. I told him that you were really an Evangelist on this subject, but that you had been hiding your light under a bushel. You may therefore expect to hear from him almost any day." In a postscript Moses added, "I told him I thought Margaret would also join."

Margaret was not *always* at Herbert's side rooting him on. They sat together at the Dempsey–Tunney fight in Chicago in 1927, but he was betting on Tunney and she on Dempsey. When Tunney went down for the famous long count, Maggie began yelling, "Stay down! Stay down!" Swope removed his pince-nez, looked at his wife and said, "Really, my dear, I have an enormous bet on Tunney." He took his gambling seriously, and he took hers seriously, too. One winter they spent a Palm Beach holiday at the Henry Ittlesons'. Swope had to return to New York ahead of his wife, and on the eve of his departure he wrote out for her the kind of memorandum another sort of husband might have devoted to having the car greased or the gutters cleaned or the cat spayed. Swope's memo went:

> Get from your uncle Frank Keogh [an unrelated employee at Bradley's Casino] the exact amount you owe this year, inclusive of everything. Tell him you will pay him in full your present debt and you will send him part of the balance from last year. Make it evident that it is your own operation. As I recall it, your debts will include the $1,000 you signed for chemy [chemin de fer]. Is that right? Be sure of this, as I want to keep an accurate account. Am I right in assuming you made three ventures? The first time you won $500; the second time you lost a net of $800, and the third time you won $160. That makes a total you are up $140. As I recall it now, the second play (when you signed two markers of $500 each) you had $200 left, which you gave me, making you a gross loser of $1,000 and a net loser of $800. On the third play, which was Saturday night, I think, if my memory serves me right, you won $160. You gave me this, didn't you? Therefore, I make your total operations $880 loser and $660 winner. Is that right?

121

In August 1909 Swope took Miss Powell to Saratoga for the racing season. Arnold Rothstein was there, and he had with him a twenty-one-year-old actress named Carolyn Greenwald, who had gone on the stage several years earlier and for professional purposes had dropped the woodsy suffix from her name. As Carolyn Green she had been a show girl in *The Chorus Girl, Fascinating Flora*, and *Havana*. A poll of the audience at the Casino, when she was playing there in *The Social Whirl*, had voted her the prettiest young woman in the cast. Rothstein, who knew many of the show girls in town, had fallen in love with Carolyn, and she made quite an impression on most people who met her. "She was more of a lady than most ladies I know," Margaret Swope once said. On August 12, 1909, Carolyn was married to Rothstein, in Saratoga, by a justice of the peace. Herbert Swope and Margaret Powell were the witnesses. In its account of the ceremony the *Morning Telegraph* said that the other girls in the cast of *Havana*, to whom the bride was known as Carrie, were disappointed that she'd slipped off to get married without letting them in on the excitement. To the *Telegraph*, Carrie was the chief attraction at the wedding; the bridegroom, who got only a brief mention, was described as a broker. The attendants were not mentioned at all.

On May 16, 1917, Rothstein organized a poker game in a room at the Hotel St. Francis, on West 47th Street, down the block from the Longacre. A dozen or so other men, some of them prominent but none of them Swope, were present. Three masked and armed intruders, apparently tipped off by one of the players, walked in behind a bellboy at 2:00 A.M. and walked out with five thousand dollars in cash and a four-thousand-dollar diamond stickpin of Rothstein's. He usually carried close to one hundred thousand dollars in cash on him, but he saved his bank roll as the thieves entered by kicking it under a rug. The next day Swope talked to the New York City Police Commissioner, Arthur Woods. No complaint had been made to the police, because, according to the *World*, the incident was "apparently one of those cases in which the victims are supposed never to 'squeal' and seldom do, to the police, at any rate." But everyone would talk to Swope. Soon he was in touch with Rothstein, asking what he planned to do about the robbery, in a dialogue that Rothstein's biographer, Leo Katcher, subsequently reconstructed after consulting Swope.

"I'll take care of it," said Rothstein.

"The police know about it," said Swope.

"So what?" asked Rothstein.

"Arthur Woods says you're too yellow to report this," said Swope, goadingly.

Rothstein showed Swope the diamond stickpin he'd lost the night before. "People know better. I never take my troubles to the cops," he said. "Why do I need them? The fence got this back to me before breakfast."

"They're laughing at you, Arnold," said Swope. "The word is out that you're buffaloed."

"I'll show them who's buffaloed," said Rothstein. "No one can laugh at me."

Rothstein accompanied Swope to a police station, reported the robbery, and picked two faces out of a rogues' gallery of photographs. The two men he identified were arrested, and Swope next prodded Rothstein by saying Commissioner Woods had offered to bet him that Rothstein, however far he might already have gone in violating the code of the underworld, would never identify the gunmen in a courtroom. Rothstein did, and the two were convicted. All this shuttling back and forth between the Commissioner of Police and the Commissioner of Crime was enormously helpful to Swope, of course, as a gatherer of news—in this instance, moreover, as a maker of news as well—but even beyond that it was an exciting catalytic role for someone who, unlike most boys, was in the happy position of, as an adult, being able to go right on playing cops and robbers.

Although during much of 1908 and 1909 Swope held no steady job, he had not entirely dismissed from his mind the idea of gainful employment. At one point, in fact, he tried to embark on a career as a public-relations consultant. He formed a partnership with a man twenty years his senior, Willis Carle Pratt, who had been a reporter on the *World* and the *Herald* and, while covering New York State politics at Albany, had worked out in a boxing ring with Theodore Roosevelt. Anybody who could say he had punched a President in the nose was the kind of person who appealed to Swope. And Swope appealed to Pratt; in 1905 Pratt had helped pay the younger man's bills at Dr. Trudeau's sanitarium. To a long list of corporations and individuals, including the General Electric Company and five Vanderbilts, the two men sent a soliciting letter that is interesting in the light of Swope's bread-and-butter work after he left the *World:*

In the marked trend toward publicity in every department of political, professional and commercial activity that has characterized the last few years, there has developed a need for the services of trained newspaper men who shall act in the capacity of advisors to those whose prominence, individual or corporate, in the world of affairs frequently brings them in the public eye.

We propose acting in this capacity; first, with a view of protecting those we serve from misrepresentation when their acts are the subject of general comment; and second, gaining for them the legitimate benefit that accrues from intelligently directed publicity and dignified exploitation.

In addition to advising as to the proper course to pursue on occasions where publicity is desirable or inevitable, we will undertake to map out complete publicity campaigns with a view of gaining public attention and sympathy.

Long and varied experience which covers every field of newspaper work fittingly qualifies us for this new line of endeavor. For considerably more than ten years we have been connected with the most prominent New York papers, including the *Herald* and the *World.* We are familiar with the methods employed by reporters and we are cognizant of the importance of avoiding the danger that lies in the ambiguous statement.

We know the general point of view from which the city editor of any one of the great New York dailies will consider the material collected by his reporters and just how it will be treated in the news and editorial columns. In short, from our experience we know what is "news" and what the papers want.

Through this knowledge we will be able to put into proper shape the subject for which you wish to gain publicity. Much good matter that has every right to be printed goes into the wastebasket because the real "story" is lost through being improperly presented.

While in no sense do we seek to become press agents, yet we feel that there is a distinct field for our services as confidential advisors in all matters that have to do with newspapers. We believe that we can be of signal aid to all those whose efforts make it expedient to them to have the public ear.

Our past affiliations have brought us into close contact with practically all those in authority in the offices of most of the big dailies in New York and other cities, and we will be glad to supply references from persons in public and private life. These references will deal with our integrity and ability to perform such services for our clients as come within the scope of our specialty.

We will call on you at your request and submit our terms and a more detailed exposition of our aims and our facilities for achieving them.

Swope, it would thus appear, was ready to retire from journalism, in his twenties, even before he had any solid journalistic achievements behind him. But the letter he and Pratt drew up failed to bring them any clients, and the two men soon drifted apart. How far they drifted was indicated by a letter that Pratt, who lived to be one hundred and died in 1962, sent Swope in 1931, when Pratt was nearing seventy. Pratt had been trying, unsuccessfully, to call on Swope, and he wrote that he hoped they could get together for a few minutes and that Swope could help him get a job.

Pratt also reminded Swope of a conversation they'd once supposedly had at the Longacre Hotel, in which Swope had said: "Bill, you may have a better mind than I have, but, I have a better intelligence. Do you get what I mean? You come to the right conclusion, perhaps more often than I do, but my wheels go faster than yours." Swope replied, "I am at a loss to understand your letter of January 13th. I am not aware of any change in me, except that effected by age, for I have not grown younger. Who has? I always liked you and still do. Our paths have not crossed in the last fifteen years because of the difference in our work—not because of any disaffection between us. Therefore, it was wholly unnecessary for you to assume an attitude that I might have outgrown you. Incidentally, I do not recall the conversation you refer to as being held in the Longacre. I am quite sure I never admitted willingly that anybody had a better mind than I had." He may have meant this last line to be ironic.

7

IN THE second half of the twentieth century the ambition of most young reporters in, or heading toward, New York has been to work on the *Times*. In much of the first half the *World* enjoyed much the same exalted status. Its very building—on the site of the old French Hotel at the corner of Park Row and Frankfort Street, a block from City Hall—had a shrinelike air. Finished in 1890, the *World* building was fifteen stories high and was surmounted by a gilded dome, from inside which its proprietors could look out, and down upon, the Mayor's office and the relatively lusterless quarters of the *Times* and other squat competitors. Even the ground floor of the *World* building had a special charm. Located there was a combination drugstore and saloon called Perry's Hole-in-the-Wall, and to this oasis came reporters from all the papers in town, as if they hoped their hanging around long enough might somehow result in an invitation to proceed on upstairs to the Olympian heights they longed to scale.

The *World* had begun in 1860 as a religious daily. For the next twenty-three years it went through a number of hands and phases; its most consistent aspect was its avowed faithfulness to Democratic politics. One of the *World*'s owners was Jay Gould. In 1883, considering the paper, which then had a circulation of less than ten thousand, as the least promising of his many investments, he was glad to sell it, for three hundred and forty-six thousand dollars, to what he took for a Midwest sucker, Joseph Pulitzer. Born in Hungary, Pulitzer had migrated to St. Louis in 1865. Three years later he was a reporter on the German-language *Westliche Post*, and ten years after that, in 1878, he was the publisher of the English-language *Post-Dispatch*. In New York he quickly converted the *World* from a neglected and nearly bankrupt plaything of Jay Gould's to a fiery, crusading, liberal newspaper that stood against just about everything Gould stood for: "The *World* is never content with merely giving the news. It conceives itself as the attorney for the People. It abhors injustice and dares expose it. It can be depended on to defend the oppressed." Hammering away at the iniquities of the rich, the *World* became so distasteful to some leaders of high finance that as late as the Wall Street crash of 1929 J. Pierpont Morgan refused to open his mouth before any group of reporters that included a representative of Pulitzer's nagging daily.

By 1887 the *World*'s circulation had risen to more than two hundred and fifty thousand, and Pulitzer was expanding. In addition to his morning paper, which was always known simply as "the *World*," he had a *Sunday World* and an *Evening World*. For many years the city editor of the evening paper was Charles E. Chapin, who went to prison in 1918 for shooting his wife. He spent the rest of his life in jail, and one story had it that, asked if he was happy there, he replied, "Well, no, not happy. But this is better than the *World*." It was assumed in newspaper circles that he meant the evening paper; few journalists would have said that of the morning one.

Pulitzer, who died in 1911, spent little time in New York. In 1887, the same year he started the *Evening World*, his health collapsed, undermined by his relentless dedication, in St. Louis and then in New York, to his publishing interests. He had a severe nervous breakdown, and he started going blind. He never saw his glittering *World* building at all, and after 1887 he was never physically at the *World* office, except for one brief visit in 1908. Thereafter, the chief editorial voice at the *World*, for nearly a generation, was that of Frank I. Cobb, the son of a Midwestern farmer. Unlike Swope, Cobb *had* worked in a lumber camp. Born in 1869, he was writing editorials for the Detroit *Evening News* in his twenties, and at thirty he was chief editorial writer for the Detroit *Free Press*. He was found there in 1904 by Pulitzer—or, rather, by an agent whom the publisher had sent to Boston, Buffalo, Cleveland, Chicago, and, finally, Detroit, with the mission of holing up in a hotel room at each stop, reading editorials for a few days, and looking for signs of unusual talent. In Cobb he spotted it.

Although Pulitzer's doctors urged him to dissociate himself entirely from his papers, he could not. Much as James Gordon

127

Bennett, Jr., became an absent and peripatetic proprietor of the *Herald,* so did Pulitzer reign from a series of homes in this country and abroad, or from his majestic yacht *Liberty,* aboard which he shuttled across the Atlantic, accompanied by an entourage of physicians, valets, and secretaries with pencils poised to transmit his orders by wireless to his underlings in the golden dome. When, after a lengthy spell at sea, his yacht would pull into a port where a batch of *Worlds* awaited him, the air would soon crackle with criticism. One time, sensing that the paper was becoming a mite too staid, and reflecting that most of the men putting it out were known for their sobriety, Pulitzer commanded that an old-fashioned, reeling-drunk reporter be taken on to liven things up. His editors found one, suitably bleary-eyed, in a park, and they obediently put him on the staff.

Swope—whose own ingestive excesses while at work ran more to pig's knuckles than to whiskey—thought Pulitzer was one of the four greatest journalists of his time. The others were William Randolph Hearst, whom Swope ranked first; Adolph S. Ochs, who came north from Chattanooga to infuse in the *Times* the same revivifying spirit that Pulitzer brought to the *World;* and Lord Northcliffe, the publisher of the London *Daily Mail.* It was a mutual admiration society. Northcliffe once called Pulitzer "the ablest newspaper man of our time," and he called Swope "the most alert, if not the ablest, of the younger American newspaper men." Northcliffe edited the *World* for one day—the January 1, 1901, edition. He had not yet attained the peerage, and as Alfred Charles William Harmsworth he was invited by Pulitzer to put the paper to press the night before. The *World* editorial staff, in deference both to New Year's Eve and to their temporary boss, turned up at the office that night in evening clothes—with one holdout, the city editor, Pomeroy Burton. The guest editor liked men of independence, and soon afterward he hired Burton to work for him in England. Burton became both a British subject and a knight. Subsequently, after Lord Northcliffe got to know Swope, he made *him* a similar offer. "Maggie would have a lovely time," Northcliffe said. "I make all of my editors at least barons." But Swope, who because of his thoughtful habit of sending out letters of praise was fondly known among journalists who received them as "Sir Hubert," resisted the temptation to become universally known as Sir Herbert.

Pulitzer and Swope had several traits in common. Swope subscribed heartily to the *World*'s platform, which Pulitzer, on his sixtieth birthday, in 1907, cabled home from Rome and which after his death appeared every day on the paper's masthead and also on that of the *Post-Dispatch:* "An institution that should always fight for progress and reform, never tolerate injustice or corruption, always fight demigods of all parties, never belong to any party, always oppose privileged classes and public plunderers, never lack sympathy with the poor, always remain devoted to the public welfare, never be satisfied with merely printing news, always be drastically independent, never be afraid to attack wrong, whether by predatory plutocracy or predatory poverty." (It was in keeping with Pulitzer's ideals that the *World* set up a Bureau of Accuracy and Fair Play to investigate cases where people mentioned in the paper thought it had been unfair to them.) Like Swope, Pulitzer was a newspaperman who believed that it was the proper function of a journalist to be not only an observer of events but an all-out participant; in Missouri, Pulitzer had served concurrently as the *Westliche Post*'s state legislative correspondent and as a member of the legislature. Pulitzer, too, was enamored not only of accuracy but also of odd facts; he like to conduct what he called Question Bees, in which he bombarded his employees with requests for information he thought they should have at the ready. Pulitzer was, one of his biographers said, "the most incorrigible busybody of his day and age."

Physically, also, Pulitzer and Swope were not unalike. Pulitzer, to be sure, had a beard most of his adult life (the closest Swope came was a mustache, which he grew experimentally one summer in the Twenties but shaved off at his wife's insistence), but both were tall, slim, and had large, prominent noses. When Swope became executive editor of the *World* he hung a portrait of Pulitzer behind his desk. Perhaps because of the proximity of the two commanding heads, perhaps because Pulitzer had been a young man in St. Louis when Swope was born, word soon spread around the office that Swope was Pulitzer's illegitimate son. Swope was reported to be rather pleased by this and to have done nothing to scotch the rumor. Not only were the two men not related, however, but it seems doubtful that they ever even met. It was just as well. For all they had in common, in one respect they differed strikingly. Pulitzer couldn't stand noise.

129

Swope liked to describe the front page of a daily newspaper as "the mirror of the world in which a man lives." He began to live in the world of the *World* on Monday, November 15, 1909, when the paper's circulation had gone up to more than three hundred and fifty thousand. The *World* cost only one cent then, in Greater New York and Jersey City; elsewhere, and on trains, it was two cents. The day before, the leading story in the paper had been an account of a Yale-Princeton football game (Yale won, 17-0), and lesser page-one headlines went MANGLED BABY RESCUED FROM DOG WITH HOT IRON and CHASES MANIAC TO ALTAR OF CATHEDRAL. (In those days, newspapers freely used "maniac," a word that was to come into disrepute unless it could be pinned on someone who had murdered at least six people and could be confirmed to have escaped from an institution for the criminal insane with an inadequate budget for therapeutic rehabilitation.) On Swope's maiden day the front page of the *World* reflected at least two—but only two—events of any general consequence: The Federal government was bringing anti-trust proceedings against the American Sugar & Refining Company, and there had been a fatal mine explosion in Illinois. The rest of the big news was rather small: The minister of the Cathedral of St. John the Divine, inspired by the John Jacob Astor divorce suit, had preached a sermon against class privilege; Mrs. Augusta Stetson, the thorn in the side of the Christian Science Church, had had new charges leveled against her by that body; a man had jumped off the Brooklyn Bridge and died; another man, at the Morris Park Race Track, had narrowly missed being struck by an ascending airship; roses were blooming, unseasonably, in Bloomfield, New Jersey (also dandelions and honeysuckle); and it had been revealed that turkeys suffer from appendicitis.

Swope was hired for the *World* by its city editor, Sherman W. Morse, who had been a fellow reporter on the *Herald* and who for the rest of his life, a long one, regarded as his principal achievement having brought Swope into the Pulitzer fold. City editors lead a nerve-racking existence and traditionally have a life expectancy lower even than that of reporters. Morse retired from the *World* two years after taking on Swope and took himself to raising apples in upstate New York, a comparatively tranquil vocation. He lived to the age of ninety-three. He started Swope in at a guarantee of seven dollars a day for a six-day week —plus the usual space rates. (On Fridays, every reporter would clip his stories from the previous week's papers and send the cuttings to the Accounting Department, which would compute what he had coming to him.) Swope liked space rates, because he liked to write long stories. An editor for whom he'd worked five years earlier on the *Morning Telegraph*, Spencer Bull, once described him as a "master of turgidity." Years later Swope liked to tell about an early assignment he had on the *World*. He covered a warehouse fire, returned to the office, and began typing a story. After a while one of his superiors called over to him, "What page you on now, Sonny?" Page eleven, Swope replied. "Well, mark the next one 'Page three,' " the man said.

Less than a month after he joined the *World*, Swope came up with his first exclusive story, which he was permitted to recount at considerable and considerably remunerative length. On November 30, 1909, the lead story on the front page of the paper—bylines were rare then, and it was unsigned—began:

> Into the old-fashioned, simple life of Miss Louisa Ewen, member of an old New York family now extinct save for three maiden ladies—sisters—who still bear the name, a romance has come. Her fifty years has been spent in the well ordered regularity that belongs to another generation, and she has always devoted herself and her wealth so wholly to her charities that her friends can scarcely credit the report that she is to be married.

After that slow-paced, teasing start, Swope went on to say how Miss Ewen, who was worth two hundred and fifty thousand dollars, was being pursued by an unscrupulous fortune hunter half her age who called himself Baron Boto von Koenitz and who not long before had been advertising in the Pittsburgh papers that he was available for any heiress seeking to acquire a title by marriage. (The daughters of big steel men had the reputation then of being title-hungry.) Baron Boto, a whiskey salesman, had obtained an introduction to Miss Ewen through the proprietor of a travel club with whom Von Koenitz had a written contract; the travel man was to get 10 per cent of whatever the Baron got from his bride. In that first day's story, it later developed, Swope did not tell all he knew. With an eye on space rates, though, he covered a good deal of ground, throwing in such leisurely digressions as "The three Miss Ewens are of that class of gentle spinsterhood that writers of New England stories love to delineate. They have grown old in ignorance of the ways of the world, and re-

131

mained untouched by sophistication even in the midst of the materialism and hurly-burly of New York life."

The next day Swope had a good deal more to reveal. The so-called Baron, the *World* stated, had learned that the paper was going to divulge his shameful story, had spirited Miss Ewen to Atlantic City, and had married her. The bride and bridegroom were in seclusion. Now Swope played a card he had been holding back and demonstrated the effectiveness of his special way of gathering news. Some months before, it appeared, he had been at Browne's Chophouse, as had been Von Koenitz, who was drunk. Boto had babbled about his heiress-plucking scheme and had said something about a contract with a man who was going to find him a plump pigeon. Swope had feigned skepticism, and the Baron had showed him the contract. Then Swope got Boto *really* drunk. He passed out, and before he came to Swope had rushed the contract off to a photographer, had a copy made, and returned it to its still unconscious owner. On December 2 the *World* not only reproduced the document but showed that Boto's handwriting was markedly similar to that of an ex-convict who had been in a New Jersey jail ten years before on a blackmail charge.

For more than a week the *World* played up Swope's scoop—in part because *it* was being concurrently scooped by the *Times*, which had an exclusive about some skulduggery stemming from the polar explorations of Dr. Frederick A. Cook. The *World* tracked the hapless Miss Ewen to St. Augustine, Florida, where she and her husband were registered at a hotel as "Mr. and Mrs. Anderson." By then Louisa had given Boto fifty thousand dollars, and her grieving spinster sisters had retained Arthur Train to try to curb the flow of her philanthropy. Eventually she was per-suaded to get an annulment, after Boto ran away with somebody else. Train kept her memory fresh in one of his autobiographical Ephraim Tutt stories. Swope, the lawyer recalled, had been the first to tell him the facts of the case, "with an air of authority, if not of ownership."

By January 1910 Swope too was in the South, but on a different assignment. He had taken a train to Atlanta with some Federal marshals who were escorting a celebrated prisoner to the peni-tentiary there. This was Charles Wyman Morse, a prominent New York banker unrelated to, and much richer than, the *World*'s city editor. Morse had been in the shipping and ice business. Mayor Robert A. Van Wyck of New York had been ruined politically when it came out that in return for some half a million dollars' worth of stock he had made the municipal docks exclusively available to Morse for bringing ice into the city; the criminal lawyer Abe Hummel had gone to prison for perjury after getting Morse's wife an annulment from a previous marriage. Now, following the 1907 depression, Morse himself had been found guilty of manipulating bank stocks in such fashion that two banks closed and the president of one killed himself.

Swope's first story from Atlanta had a prologue—W. E. Henley's "Invictus." On the train to Georgia, Morse had remarked that while he was in the Tombs, in New York, awaiting sentence, a friend had sent him the poem, from which he had derived much comfort; but he had left it behind. Swope admired "Invictus" so much himself that he had memorized it, and he wrote out the words for the banker, so he would have some agreeable and inspirational reading matter in the bleak months to come. Having thus helped create a newsy sidelight to the case, Swope followed the text of the poem, in his first account of Morse's tribulations, with:

> Ten minutes after the big steel door of the United States Penitentiary here swung shut behind Charles W. Morse, but yesterday a man of millions, he had ceased to exist socially. He had become convict No. 2,814, and clad in an ill-fitting suit of rough blue clothes was marched into the big dining-hall and with negroes, Indians, Chinamen, and whites of every condition took his first meal under the roof that is to shut out his liberty for fifteen years.*

Morse stayed at Atlanta for only two years, being pardoned by President Taft early in 1912. Swope stayed there for nearly one week, interviewing the warden and, for the Sunday paper, writing a three-column wrap-up feature about Morse that, to vary things a bit, concluded with "Invictus." He told in great detail how No. 2,814 would live and work behind bars and what he would eat. The prisoners munched raw onions like apples, Swope said; the smell in the dining hall was strong, but the onions had medicinal properties. What was more, according to the warden, the prisoners stayed healthy because much of their food was cooked

---

* Later, as executive editor of the *World*, Swope initiated the now common newspaper practice of capitalizing the word "Negro."

in vegetable oil. Years afterward an Atlanta newspaperman confessed in a letter to Swope that back in 1910 he'd had a side job as press agent for the Georgia cottonseed-oil industry and that he'd persuaded the warden to stress the healthful aspects of vegetable oils to out-of-state reporters. And, the Atlanta man added, on the strength of Swope's favorable account of Morse's diet *he'd* been engaged as director of advertising for a big cooking-oil company. Now, thirty years later, he just wanted to thank Swope for having inadvertently launched him on a successful career.

Swope was barely back in New York when he was asked to look into another bizarre heiress, a young woman named Antoinette Elizabeth Gazzam, who had got herself mixed up with a Los Angeles spiritualist, astrologer, and palm reader named Marshall Clark, who also went by several other names, principal among them Professor Niblo. Miss Gazzam, who, at twenty-five, had a fortune of three million dollars and lived alone in a mountaintop marble mansion at Cornwall, up the Hudson River from New York, had got interested in psychic revelations and had, by her own account, already managed to communicate with her dead mother. But that was not enough. She went to California in search of a clairvoyant who could broaden her horizon even further, and she stumbled on Professor Niblo. After ascertaining what she was worth, he told her he would help her find her true affinity, in the shape of a man she could love. On Miss Gazzam's payment of a modest deposit, Professor Niblo tolerated additional visits from her. In the course of one, to demonstrate how little money meant to him, he tore a one-thousand-dollar bill in half and gave a piece of it to a cigar-counter attendant as security against a small outstanding account. In the course of another he was pleased to be able to inform her that the identity of her true affinity had been revealed to him—Professor Niblo himself! She was not immediately overwhelmed, since the Professor was past fifty, was physically unprepossessing, and, worst still, was married. But Miss Gazzam was willing to make the best of this. Then his wife, who was in business with him and was known professionally as Madame Mizpah, broke in on the two of them, roughed the girl up, and sued her for one hundred and fifty thousand dollars for alienation of affections. Madame Mizpah was prevailed upon to accept a settlement of twenty-five thousand dollars.

Miss Gazzam returned east, and, just after a blizzard, Swope was sent to her snow-covered aerie to get her story. Two other reporters showed up—Max Henrici of Bennett's *Herald* and Henry H. Stansbury of Hearst's *American*. Miss Gazzam not only let them in but invited them to stay for the weekend. Her lawyer, trying to stop her from talking, charged up the mountain by sleigh, but she insisted on telling all, and, at space rates, it was a gratifying weekend. "It must be borne in mind that she spoke with the deepest sincerity and with a freedom so great she seemed quite oblivious of the varying effects produced upon her hearer —incredulity, skepticism, and at times almost a fear that game was being made of him," Swope said in the *World* Monday. "But when she went on in the same even way her absolute faith in the marvels she talked of as mere incidents became pervasive. It is difficult to convey her intensity and abandon in written words; it may be conveyed only by those who feel the faith themselves." Having concluded that she was "a little wacky" but "a sincere and pure-minded girl," however, Swope did his best to convey her faith, in slightly more than four columns of type. Miss Gazzam was so pleased with the outcome of the weekend that a few days later she sent all three reporters silver loving cups, and to Swope she also addressed a note saying, "Nothing short of a divine miracle has been this day revealed to me—the truth that your soul through the medium of your pen has succeeded in translating me to what I deem the most exalted pinnacle of spiritual fame!"

By conventional standards, Swope's exaltation of Miss Gazzam did not constitute an exclusive story. By his standards, it did. Sometimes, while out of the office gathering information, he would telephone in and urge his editor to hold open three or four front-page columns for a scoop he was bringing in. When that happened once, and Swope's story turned out to be a rehash of what an afternoon paper had already published, he was not flustered. "The exclusivity is in the treatment," he said.

Swope was working hard now and was becoming more and more interested in politics. Two weeks before he joined the *World*, New York City had elected a Mayor, Judge William Jay Gaynor, and a District Attorney, Charles Seymour Whitman. Gaynor, the first Irishman ever to attain the mayoralty, had beaten two rivals, one of them William Randolph Hearst. The following August, when a disaffected ex-dock worker, James J. Gallagher, shot and nearly killed Gaynor, the *World* was anxious to prove that the assailant had been prompted by Hearst's vengeful editorial attacks on the man who had defeated him the previous November. Swope went to Hoboken, where Gallagher was locked up, and asked him—hoping he would reply *"Journal"* or *"American"*—what newspaper he read regularly. "The *Times*," the man said, while Henry Stansbury, who was there for the *American*, roared with laughter. The best the *World* could do was run a picture of a not terribly inflammatory *Journal* editorial that a policeman claimed he had found in Gallagher's pocket.

In dispensing patronage, Gaynor appointed Charles H. Hyde to the post of City Chamberlain, who was responsible for depositing municipal funds in banks and administering certain trust funds over which the city had jurisdiction. Hyde was a nephew of Gaynor's first wife and had practiced law with Gaynor. In December 1910 the Northern Bank collapsed (banks collapsed in those days with alarming frequency), and a month later the Carnegie Trust Company followed suit. A legislative committee charged that two Carnegie officials had bribed Hyde to tell the president of the Northern Bank that unless he loaned the Carnegie some money to help it out of its miseries, the City Chamberlain's office would withdraw its deposits from the Northern. There were allegations, too, of mishandling of trust funds. But when the committee tried to get hold of Hyde for an explanation, he was nowhere to be found. A subpoena was issued for him early in January 1911; for more than a month before that, his family and his office staff insisted, they had had no word from him and had no idea where he was. Everybody wanted to find Hyde, and the *World* ran a cartoon—it was captioned "Hyde and Seek"—showing a sleuth searching for him under a bed, on the moon, inside a crocodile, inside a shark, and in both heaven and hell.

Swope had his own notion of where to look. Hyde had a houseboat, berthed in Camden, New Jersey, and it was generally believed he had headed south aboard this craft. A man resembling him had been seen, a few days before Christmas, near the waterfront in Beaufort, North Carolina. Swope headed south again himself, picking up clues as he moved along, and on January 13 the *World* was able to splash across its front page:

THE WORLD FINDS HYDE;
DISCOVERED IN FLORIDA,
HE DODGES REPORTER
City Chamberlain 45 days Missing,
Is Seen Aboard His Houseboat,
Aground on River Mud Banks, but
Hurries Below, and Wife and Father-
in-Law Deny He is Aboard
RELATIVES MAINTAIN SECRECY,
THOUGH HE IS RECOGNIZED
Staff Correspondent of This Newspaper Who
Makes Discovery Sees Porthole Stealthily
Opened as He Asks Questions—Voyaged by
Canal, in Which Secrecy Could Be More
Easily Maintained

The day before, Swope had tracked Hyde to St. Augustine and
had watched him head south from that port, through the St.
Augustine–Daytona canal, on his boat, called the *Stop-a-While*.
Swope waited until the houseboat had got past the one point at
which it would have been easy for someone to get off—following
the inland waterway, the craft would then have to stay out in
the middle, in a channel—then hopped a train, got ahead of his
quarry, hired a launch at Daytona, and cruised upstream to meet
the *Stop-a-While*, bow to bow. As Swope's boat drew near he
saw Hyde on the quarter-deck of his, unpacking a barrel full of
what appeared to be bottles. Hyde saw him and ducked below.
Swope closed in on the houseboat, and a man on deck shouted
at him, "Don't come aboard! There ain't nobody here that you
want!" Swope dropped his anchor and yelled to Mrs. Hyde that
he wanted to see her husband. She insisted he wasn't aboard, and
Swope insisted he'd seen him aboard. Then the *World* recounted:

At this moment one of the portholes was stealthily opened, and the
correspondent, speaking toward it, said: "The *World* wants to
know why Mr. Hyde is running away. Why he did not testify before the Legislative Committee regarding the race track bribery
fund when it was common gossip that he had represented the
Brighton Beach Association in the steps taken to prevent adverse
legislation, and, above all, why he has not returned to New York
to straighten out the tangle the city's finances have been thrown
into by the failure of the Northern Bank and Carnegie Trust
Company."

It was quite a speech to make to a porthole, and there was a good deal more to come. But Hyde wouldn't show himself again, even when, the following day, the vigilant Swope generously helped pull the *Stop-a-While* off a mudbank into which it had drifted. The Chamberlain eventually returned to New York, without having to answer Swope's questions. Swope didn't mind too much by then, for the day after his first disclosure appeared a flotilla of boats had joined his, each chartered by a reporter from a rival paper. Hyde gave them all the slip when a heavy fog covered the area. At its densest the reporters were lured from the houseboat by a fake distress call downstream. By the time they returned to their watch, Hyde had escaped upstream in a rowboat. Swope did, however, get to talk to one of the oarsmen who had spirited the Chamberlain away. The fellow told him that a passenger in the rowboat, who had a gun in his lap, had said as they were fleeing, "I am not going to let any damned reporter intercept me; he'd better not if he knows what's good for him."

On March 25, 1911, while District Attorney Whitman was still trying to unravel the Hyde case, New York suffered one of its worst fires. The Triangle Shirtwaist Company's premises, at Washington Place and Greene Street, burned down, and one hundred and forty-five lives were lost. Whitman was talking to half a dozen reporters at his office when Swope burst in and said, "That will be enough, boys. The Triangle building's on fire, and I think the D.A. ought to be there." Swope marched them all to the scene, and after they had been there for a while marched them back to Whitman's office, where Swope said, "I think this is what the D.A. should say about the fire for the morning papers." Whitman meekly approved a statement that Swope then dictated.

Swope's colleagues at the *World* were more accustomed than rival reporters to his whirlwind tactics. Reporters had no telephones at their desks then; when they wanted to call anyone they used one of several telephone booths at one end of the city room. Swope would breeze into the *World* office, direct three copy boys to occupy three booths, and give each a number to call. Then he could move from one source to another without losing time—although meanwhile a District Attorney or Tammany Hall leader or bank president or bookmaker might be waiting impatiently on one of the lines that was being held open to suit Swope's convenience. Before not too much longer he had people with news for the *World* calling *him*, which he thought was as it should be.

After he became executive editor he once bawled out one of his reporters, Russell Porter, for missing out on a juicy scandal story that the other papers had. Porter observed that Swope had ordered him back from the spot where the main source of information on the story was located. "That doesn't make any difference," Swope said. "You should have impressed your personality on him so much that he would have called you up and given you the story." Porter walked out angrily, walked over to the New York *Times*, and stayed there for forty years.

While some reporters on other papers admired Swope's methods —Damon Runyon once said he "carried the power of the press like a flaming beacon when he was a reporter, and fairly intimidated his way to news"—others were less enthusiastic. Frank Ward O'Malley, the *Sun*'s reporter, once said cynically, "If Swope should say, 'I've bought a new pair of shoes,' I'd want to see those shoes," and to an anonymous critic is credited the saying, "Swope will go far if he isn't caught stealing the gold leaf off the *World* dome." But even Swope's detractors were compelled to admit grudgingly that, with the blazing-headed young reporter around, the *World* could now properly be said to be distinctive for two brilliant domes.

Meanwhile, Swope was still wooing Margaret Powell, though in what she, as she gradually overcame her girlish diffidence, began to conclude was an unacceptably backsliding fashion. In 1911, visiting, in his absence, an apartment he occupied on West 113th Street, in the then genteel vicinity of Columbia University, Margaret saw a photograph of an attractive woman unknown to her. She took it out of its frame and on the back of it found a photographer's name and a number. She phoned the photographer and, on the pretext that she wanted to order some extra copies, got the subject's identity out of him. The picture was that of a society matron who had gone to Reno to divorce her husband and who, on her return east, expected to marry Swope. When the woman got back to New York she at once called his apartment to say she was free. Margaret answered the phone and, when the woman asked who *she* was, replied sweetly, "Mrs. Swope." The woman left for Europe the next day.

On learning what had happened, Swope was so charmed by Margaret's cleverness that he at once proposed to her. They were married on January 10, 1912, in Baltimore, and they were to enjoy for forty-six years what Arthur Krock called "the most devoted relationship that I have ever seen revealed." While Margaret Swope could be just as caustic to her husband, in public, as she was to everybody else, in private he represented to her the embodiment of all the virtues, without flaw. "You are the most unceasingly satisfactory human in the world," she would write him, in cream unmixed with acid, or would say that she had "the blind feeling that you are God and nothing can shake it."

Margaret recalled, however, that she giggled throughout her wedding. It was conducted in a church, by a minister, but her uncontrollable levity may have stemmed from the circumstance that the only attendant was H. L. Mencken. Mencken appealed to Swope because he had, Swope said, "the most controversial mind I have ever known." Mencken, for his part, esteemed his friendship for Swope because it was, Mencken said, "born of mutual distrust and affection." What may have added a special touch of hilarity to the nuptials was the memory that not long before, when Swope had been in Baltimore, Mencken and he had escorted six chorus girls to a bawdy house, where the resident women, evidently regarding the incursion as a challenge to their security, had set upon the actresses tooth and nail, in a donnybrook so lively that most of the customers present, fearing for their lives, had fled in disarray.

The newlyweds lived first in the West 113th Street apartment. In the fall of 1912, with Margaret pregnant—their daughter Jane was born in December—they moved into a larger apartment one block north. The bride's family moved in with them. Swope's mother-in-law, known to all generations as Mimi, lived with him until she died thirty-five years later. She was a cheerful, vague woman of whom he was fond enough—he liked to have his feet rubbed, and she was expert at this—but like most mothers-in-law she had her eccentricities. Although her father had been a Presbyterian elder, she was converted to Christian Science, and along with faith-healing she had other therapeutic convictions. For common colds she advocated tying raw onions to the feet—when, it went without saying, they were not being rubbed. Her predilections could be a trial to Swope. One time when she had the flu, out on Long Island, Swope phoned a busy Manhattan doctor and begged him to rush out there and tend to his mother-in-law. The doctor did so, reluctantly, and as he was entering the house was jostled by a departing Christian Science practitioner, whom the patient had already summoned on her own.

Mimi brought her other children to live with the Swopes, too. There were two boys, Kenneth and Bruce, who in 1912 were thirteen and six. Kenneth in due course grew up, got married and had a family of his own, but Bruce—except for a brief unsuccessful venture into matrimony in 1926—was always a member of the Swope household. He was more like a son to Swope than a brother-in-law. Swope supported and educated him. (When Swope asked Mencken in 1916 for his opinion of a Maryland boarding school to which he was thinking of sending Bruce, Mencken replied that its founder was "a mortgage shark of the standard model, and when he died it turned out that he owned nearly the whole northeasterly portion of Maryland, not to mention a bank or two in Baltimore. He was a man who feared God and kept such of the ten commandments as met his views, but I am privately informed that he slept in his undershirt all his life.") Bruce, who went to Tome and Yale, had not long been under Herbert's aegis when he developed a stammer that was to plague him his entire life. Sometimes, when Swope wanted to communicate some stern paternal injunction to Bruce Powell—his admonitory letters to his young brother-in-law strongly echoed those of Gerard Swope to his younger brother—he would write a letter and mail it to him, even though they resided in the same building. Bruce, like his mother, lived with the Swopes until he died, at the age of forty-nine. The constant presence in her home of her own blood relatives was pleasant for Margaret, who loved companionship and the exercise of matriarchal power, but to Herbert it may sometimes have seemed a mixed blessing, and it once inspired Alexander Woollcott, with the cruel humor at which he was so adept, to remark, when someone mentioned that Swope was looking a bit off his feed, that it was probably just a recurrence of his chronic ailment—Powell trouble.

By 1912, having just turned thirty, Swope was one of the *World*'s top reporters. He was usually given good assignments, and he handled them, usually, with distinction, or with ingenuity, to the extent that when newspapermen gathered his means were as often discussed as his ends. Once, sent to the state prison at Dannemora to interview an inmate who was petitioning for release, Swope arrived a few hours ahead of any other reporter, and he was soon credited with either having chartered or, as some versions had it, commandeered an entire railroad train, when in fact he had merely got a head start on the reportorial pack and caught a scheduled train. Of course, this itself was quite a feat, for Swope. He had no use for published transportation schedules. As he grew older, wishing to catch some train like, say, the Commodore Vanderbilt or the Congressional Limited, he would have his wife or his secretary call a stationmaster and say he was on his way, please hold the train. And since the stationmaster was apt to be a good friend of Swope's, the train was likely to be held, although if a railroad president or two were also traveling on it the delay sometimes proved difficult to arrange.

When the *Titanic* hit an iceberg and sank, on April 15, 1912, with a loss of fifteen hundred lives, Swope took the first train to Halifax, Nova Scotia, where it was thought the survivors would probably be landed. A cable ship did turn up with the bodies of three hundred victims, and the local British authorities ordered a ring of policemen around the dock where the gruesome cargo was to be unloaded in order to keep prying American reporters back. Some of the Americans there were phoning the State Department in Washington, demanding that it intercede on their behalf. Swope sized up the situation, went to a naval officer commanding the port, and dictated to him a set of special credentials, addressed to the Chief of Police of Halifax, which read, "Pass Mr. Herbert Swope into dock yard at all hours until further notice."

Realizing that additional telegraphic facilities would be needed to handle the copy of all the correspondents who were converging on the scene, Swope next had himself appointed their spokesman, went back to see the commander, and began a long, impassioned speech about how freedom of the press required that news flow freely. Specifically, Swope wanted a telegraphic switchboard installed at once. The commander tried to reply, but Swope talked on through him. When at last he paused, the man said, "Mr. Swope, have you quite finished?" Swope hadn't quite. He summoned enough reserve breath to deliver one last ringing summary of his position, following which the commander was able to say what he'd been trying to say all along: that his staff, anticipating the journalists' needs, had already installed the switchboard.

Meanwhile, the liner *Carpathia* was steaming toward New York from the *Titanic*'s grave, carrying eleven hundred more bodies and seven hundred survivors, among these J. Bruce Ismay, the managing director of the White Star Line, who was reported to have grabbed lifeboat space for himself in a manner incompatible with the traditions of the sea. The *Carpathia* was due to dock late at night on April 18. Swope rushed back from Halifax. Because so many Americans—including John Jacob Astor, Isidor Straus, Benjamin Guggenheim and Judge John B. Thayer—had been on the *Titanic*, the United States Senate had set up a special investigating committee, with William Alden Smith of Michigan as its chairman, and instructed the committee to go to New York and ask questions. President Taft sent along his Secretary of Commerce and Labor, Charles Nagel, who was also concerned with the plight of the steerage passengers who were still alive—immigrants who might have no friends or relatives in America to look after them and had undoubtedly salvaged nothing from the tragedy but their own mortality. On the afternoon of April 18, Nagel and the Senators boarded the Congressional Limited in Washington. They planned to arrive in New York early in the evening and take a revenue cutter down the bay to meet the *Carpathia*. But the incoming ship was ahead of schedule, and the rumor had spread around New York that it was going to make a fast turn-around, to give the inquiring Americans as little time as possible to ask embarrassing questions. The first the Washington party knew of this was when their train was flagged down in New Jersey, at Swope's direction, so a message from him could get to Senator Smith: proceed with all haste from Pennsylvania Station to Pier 54, where the *Carpathia* was to be berthed.

Swope met the group at the station and accompanied it on a hair-raising carriage ride to the pier. So many New Yorkers had congregated there that, as the investigators got within a few blocks of their destination, the going became difficult, and finally a police sergeant told them they could proceed no farther. "I am Secretary of Commerce and Labor," Swope the next day quoted Nagel as saying, "and as such I am in command of the police on an occasion of this kind. I don't propose to be held up in this manner." Nagel may have said it, but the style was suspiciously Swope's. The police escorted Nagel and his retinue to the ship, where the Secretary found seventy-five miserable steerage passengers, who, because their papers weren't in order—most of them were, of course, no longer in existence—were about to be hustled by immigration authorities to Ellis Island. Nagel, taking command of that situation, too, arranged for these unfortunates to be disembarked with a minimum of red tape. There were a few spectators present who felt that if the Secretary of Commerce and Labor hadn't managed to turn the trick, Swope would have stepped in and done it on his own.

Swope's biggest story of that year, and in his lifelong view the biggest of his entire career, came in July. There were four principal characters (not counting Swope himself, who was a principal character in any story he tackled): District Attorney Whitman; Herman Rosenthal, a gambling-house proprietor; Charles A. Becker, a police lieutenant; and Jack Rose, a gambler and versatile criminal.* In keeping with his practice of cultivating all potentially useful sources of information, Swope knew the lot of them. Becker, forty-two years old, had been on the force since 1893, was a favorite of Police Commissioner Rhinelander Waldo, and in June 1911 had been given command of Special Squad No. 1, more commonly known as the Strong-arm Squad. Becker had been in and out of trouble but had always survived his misadventures, protected by a loosely organized coalition of policemen, politicians, and crooks that Lincoln Steffens had called "a system" and that Swope promoted to *the* system. As head of the Strong-arm Squad, which raided—or, for a suitable fee, was prepared not to raid—various premises providing illegal services, Becker had in ten months banked something like one hundred thousand dollars while earning a salary of twenty-two hundred. Jack Rose, an immigrant from Poland who was notable for his complete hairlessness and his long, tapering, white, gambler's fingers, was Becker's chief collector, abetted by a couple of raffish subalterns named Bridgie Weber and Harry Vallon. Rose had got to know Becker when the police lieutenant raided *him*, and they had both concluded that life would be simpler and more profitable if they thenceforth operated in cahoots. All this was suspected around town, but it was hard to get evidence against Becker or any other policeman. Whenever outraged citizens complained to Mayor

---

* He also had a cocktail named after him: One jigger of applejack, juice of half a lemon, half an ounce of grenadine. Shake with cracked ice and strain.

Gaynor, for instance, he would turn their complaints over to Commissioner Waldo, who would turn them over to Becker for investigation. Becker's investigations always exculpated Becker.

In November 1911, at an Elks Club Thanksgiving ball, Becker met Herman Rosenthal. Rosenthal was chiefly known then as the ex-president of the Hesper Club, an institution that, under the protective wing of the Tammany Hall politician Big Tim Sullivan, put on an annual ball of its own. There was no fixed price for the tickets, but people who wanted to stay in good with Big Tim were expected to buy them, each according to his means. Becker and Rosenthal became chummy. They spent that New Year's Eve together, along with their wives, and early in 1912 they met frequently at fraternal parties, Turkish baths, and other sociable spots. Rosenthal needed some cash to set up gambling facilities in his home, at 104 West 45th Street, and Becker advanced him fifteen hundred dollars—in exchange for a mortgage that the policeman had made out in a dummy's name. For a pledge of protection, Rosenthal promised Becker 20 per cent of his gambling-house profits. Rose, designated the lieutenant's liaison man, was cut in for 15 per cent himself.

The alliance was short-lived. Becker, himself oddly pressed for cash early in the spring, asked Rosenthal for five hundred dollars. Rosenthal begged off, and on April 15 the Strong-arm Squad raided his premises. Then Becker had two policemen detailed to Rosenthal's place, where they sat around the clock, inhibiting operations and also interfering with the gambler's home life. Irritated, Rosenthal decided to make public everything he knew about police corruption, which was plenty. (The time was ripe for such a disclosure. A group of citizens, convinced that there was little chance of their getting any action through conventional municipal channels, had engaged William J. Burns' private-detective agency to look for evidence.) Rosenthal asked Arnold Rothstein for advice, and Rothstein, a man of prudence, offered *him* five hundred dollars and suggested that he leave town until he had calmed down.

Becker did not want to take a chance on Rosenthal's remaining silent, anywhere, so he instructed Jack Rose to hire some gunmen, for one thousand dollars, and have Rosenthal killed. This was easy for Rose. He soon had lined up four mercenaries named Frank Muller, Louis Marks, Frank Ciroficci, and Harry Horowitz—or, to give them the nicknames by which they were to become far better known, Whitey Lewis, Lefty Louie, Dago Frank, and Gyp the Blood. Rosenthal had decided not to leave town after all, and on July 7, guns ready, the four men tracked him to a Seventh Avenue café. They refrained from shooting him, though, when they found his wife at a table with him.

Rosenthal's tongue grew looser daily. On July 11 he asked a magistrate's court to enjoin the police from camping out on his premises, and he told a few reporters that a conniving police lieutenant was responsible for this humiliating state of affairs. But Rosenthal's reputation for unreliability was so widespread that nobody took him seriously. Next he turned to Swope, whom he had known for some time and who, he realized, was inclined to take gambling men seriously. Swope urged Rosenthal to tell what he knew, in full, to the *World*, and the gambler did—first in an interview, then in an affidavit signed at the *World* office. On July 13 the *World* published part of his account. Becker was not mentioned by name. Although the story made page one, it got only a one-column headline. From that day on, however, for more than a month, the Rosenthal–Becker entanglement would preoccupy the *World* and most of the other papers in town, and Swope would be in the thick of things.

July 13 was a Saturday, and District Attorney Whitman was spending the weekend at Newport as a guest of the Oliver H. P. Belmonts. The question in Swope's, and the *World*'s, mind was: Would any officials act on Rosenthal's accusations against the police? Specifically, would Whitman announce that he'd put Rosenthal in front of a grand jury, which, if convinced by his tale, could hand down some indictments? Swope took off for Newport to persuade Whitman to move, and the next day the *World* was able to report that the District Attorney would indeed give Rosenthal a chance to talk under oath. "I have had Rosenthal's charges under investigation for some time," Whitman said. "I have no sympathy for Rosenthal the gambler; but I have real use for Rosenthal, who, abused by the police, proposes to aid decency and lawfulness by revealing conditions that are startling. The trail leads to high places. . . . This man will have a chance to tell his story to the grand jury."

The *World* was elated. "WHAT YOU SENT SAVED THE STORY," Swope was told in a telegram to Newport from his city editor, William A. Thayer. While Swope was in Rhode Island, Rosenthal continued to talk. That Saturday he confided to James W. Barrett of the *Morning Telegraph*—himself later a *World* city editor—that he'd gone to the *World* office and signed an affidavit incriminating Becker. It didn't take long for Becker to learn of this, and he went over to the *World*, accompanied by his lawyer, and asked to see the document. He pronounced it a pack of lies.

That same day the magistrate whom Rosenthal had asked to evict the sentries who were living with him refused to do so, and on July 14, along with Whitman's statement to Swope, the *World* published a photograph of one of the gambler's uniformed house guests. He was sitting in a chair, with his cap on, reading a book. The chief cop of them all, Commissioner Waldo, was spending the weekend in Toronto at a law-enforcement convention, where three days earlier he had made a speech denouncing graft. Now he came back to New York, hurriedly. His secretary, Winfield R. Sheehan, who had earlier been a *World* reporter and was later a Hollywood movie producer, had nothing to say to the press. Nor did Mayor Gaynor. The *World* said, jubilantly, "POLICE SCANDAL BRINGS WHITMAN AND WALDO HOME," and Swope, still writing from Newport, digressed from his prodding of the District Attorney to turn out a feature story on gambling at that resort. His thesis was that while gambling was permitted to flourish there for the rich, the opportunity to lose money was unfairly denied to the poor—a point of view that, Swope may have reflected while composing his copy, fitted in perfectly with the philosophy of the *World* as set forth years before by Joseph Pulitzer.

On July 15 Rosenthal went back to see Rothstein. Rosenthal had changed his mind; he thought now he would take that five hundred dollars and leave town. Rothstein said it was too late and that the offer no longer stood. Rosenthal then went to Whitman's office, and the District Attorney made an appointment for him with a grand jury for the following day. That night Rosenthal was at the Hotel Metropole, on 43rd Street just east of Broadway. A few minutes before 2:00 A.M. he was told a man wanted to see him at the front entrance. He stepped out onto the sidewalk and was shot down by Jack Rose's hired gunmen. Half a dozen policemen were in the area, one of them only fifty feet away, but none managed to stop Whitey Lewis, Lefty Louie, Dago Frank, and Gyp the Blood from escaping in a getaway car. The police did manage to obtain several license numbers for this vehicle—all different and all wrong. A bystander who jotted down the correct number and took it around to the neighborhood station, on West 47th Street, was clapped in a cell for his pains.

Where Swope was at the moment of Rosenthal's murder is uncertain, but he was back in New York from Newport and at that hour was probably not too far from Times Square. In any event, he heard about the killing almost at once after it had taken place. And at once he acted. He telephoned Whitman, who was asleep at his apartment in the Madison Square Hotel, on East 26th Street, and told him that inasmuch as the police were unlikely to try very hard to catch the murderers, he should take personal charge of the hunt. Within an hour Whitman appeared at the West 47th Street police station, where he succeeded in getting hold of the right automobile-license number before the police could lose it. Also he released the man who had furnished it. Rosenthal's body had been taken there, too. Becker arrived at the station not long after Whitman and, according to testimony later given by Jack Rose, said after inspecting the gambler's corpse, "It was a pleasant sight to me to look and see that squealing Jew there, and if it hadn't been for Whitman, I would have reached down and cut his tongue out and hung it up somewhere as a warning to future squealers."

Within a few hours after Rosenthal's death, the *World* was on the streets with a brief account of it, and the following morning —July 17—the paper ran Rosenthal's own story of his relationship with Becker, a narrative the *World* described as the gambler's "death warrant." That day's leading editorial began, "Herman Rosenthal was murdered in cold blood by the system." The police were dragging their feet. There were numerous demands for Becker's superiors to scrutinize his affairs—let alone look into whatever part he might have played in the killing—but Gaynor told Waldo not to rush into anything. "Do not bend a single bit to clamor," the Mayor was reported to have told his Commissioner, "and especially to clamor chiefly created by hired press agents of the gamblers with whom you are at war, and those corrupt newspapers which have been all along and are now at the service of such gamblers and against you." He did not mention which newspapers he meant.

Whitman would have to do his own investigating, it was clear. The Burns private detectives helped him, and so did Swope. It was Swope who, traveling to Staten Island, a part of New York normally as alien to him as a savings bank, dug up the facts about the mortgage that Becker, under a false name, had given Rosenthal. It was Swope who, after Jack Rose, concerned about his own safety, had given himself up as an accomplice, persuaded Rose's lawyer, Max Steuer, that Rose, Weber, and Vallon should confess. (Swope wangled a copy of Rose's confession, and the *World* ran it in full.) For turning state's evidence, the three men avoided prosecution. When the police, ostensibly searching for a newsboy who'd been one of the last persons to talk to Rosenthal at the Metropole, sent an expedition to Saratoga, it was Swope who found the boy, in a movie theater on Eighth Avenue in New York. Swope worked with such vigor on the case that some of the reporters covering it for other papers got sick. One of them, Woollcott, who represented the *Times,* had to go off for a rest. Swope observed years later in one of his notes to himself that Woollcott, once he recovered, "swore he would never be a reporter again." *

Whitman had enough evidence against Becker by July 29 to arrest him, and the following day the *World* devoted its entire front page to this development. Becker was twice tried for first-degree murder. He was found guilty that October, but after months of legal wrangling the conviction was set aside. (At space rates, Swope earned $320.88 in one five-day period during the trial and $324.41 in a subsequent six-day period. The virtuous, too, can profit from graft.) Meanwhile, the four assassins were tried in separate proceedings, were convicted and, in April 1914, with Swope looking on, were executed. Thirty-three years later, when Robert Sherwood was working on his Hopkins book, he wrote Swope, "In going through the records of Harry's early life— which I am merely sketching in to trace the development of his character—I was very interested to learn that his arrival in New York from Iowa was the summer of the Rosenthal murder. Later, he was profoundly shocked when, in the course of his social-uplift activities, he saw a meeting of a boys' club observe two minutes' silence, standing, in tribute to the memory of the four gunmen who had just 'died game' at Sing Sing. This was part of Harry's education in the facts of life."

---

* Woollcott, whether or not he ever took such an oath, did return to reporting, but not for long.

In May 1914 Becker was tried again. By this time Swope had been rewarded by the *World* for his work on the case not only with a bonus but also with a byline, and on the twenty-third of that month, under his name, the lead story in the paper began:

"Guilty of murder in the first degree."

For the second time Charles Becker heard that sentence when the jury, after having been out one hour and fifty-nine minutes, came in at six minutes to five last evening with the verdict that he is the man who procured the killing of Herman Rosenthal—the verdict that means death to him unless it is upset by the Court of Appeals, as was the one spoken nineteen months ago.

There was a hunted look in his eyes and his hands gripped the rail before him when the boyish looking foreman, Meredith Blagden, pronounced the finding, but otherwise the bold-faced, stalwart Becker showed no stress. He had schooled himself well. His cheeks went just a trifle grey; his voice once broke on a whimpering little cough. There was a touch of the wistful as he answered "married" when his "pedigree" was taken, but it took close watch to catch these suggestions of despair, for on first glance he appeared the coolest man in the room.

His head was unbowed, his shoulders thrown back defiantly, his glance was level and not once did he take it from the twelve men who had ended his fearful suspense of seventeen days—ended it in a way he had convinced himself could never be. Almost it seemed he was glad it was all over, though the conviction came as a surprise, so sure he was that the worst he could get would be a disagreement, while hoping and believing it would be acquittal.

The reverberations of Becker's exposure and downfall were felt in New York for quite some time. Mayor Gaynor took out his displeasure at all newspapers by asking Commissioner Waldo to investigate three addresses on West 58th Street, where he thought prostitutes might be operating. The properties belonged to Gaynor's arch-enemy, Hearst. (Some years later, by chance, Swope moved into one of the buildings.) Gaynor did not run for re-election in 1913, and the Tammany candidate who tried to replace him was roundly beaten by a reform-minded man, John Purroy Mitchel. Becker was electrocuted at Sing Sing, on July 30, 1915. Swope did not attend. It was said that Becker, dying no less gamely than his associates, had one final message before the switch was pulled; he asked that word be sent to Swope not to worry. Becker's last vain appeal for clemency was denied by the newly elected Governor of New York, Charles S. Whitman. Whitman achieved that office almost entirely because of his success in prosecuting Rosenthal's murderers, and Swope—the Daniel, some liked to say, to Whitman's Nebuchadnezzar—became famous as the reporter who'd made him Governor.

8

NOT LONG after Herman Rosenthal's murder, the *World* raised Swope's basic pay to a flattering one hundred and twenty-five dollars a week, and restaurant headwaiters, no less flatteringly, began to point him out to other patrons. He had attained—as some men do attain and others wish they could—a plateau of recognition sufficiently high to become an acceptable subject for public jokes. At one Broadway theater a special performance of a play was scheduled early one morning, for the benefit of morning-newspaper staffs and other night-workers who could not attend at regular hours. The curtain was supposed to go up at 2:00 A.M. In describing the event the New York *Sun* said:

> But at 2:10 A.M. the boxes assigned to Herbert Bayard Swope were still vacant, and consequently nobody dared start the show. At 2:12 A.M., however, sounds were heard far up Broadway. As the roar increased, some timid folk began nervously to study ex-reporter Bob Adamson's line on the programme: "For heaven's sake look around now and choose the nearest exit. In case of a mixup walk (not run) to that exit." And finally there was one mighty crash, a clanging of lobby doors, a knocking over of lobby tables covered with programmes, a clatter of box chairs being arranged and rearranged, a general rising and waving of the Chautauqua salute by the entire audience toward the last of the boxes to be occupied, a crash of the opening strains of "Hail to the Chief" by the orchestra, and then a final flutter as the audience, now that everyone was present, settled back to compose itself and try to keep its composite mind off that particular box and concentrate upon the show.

The performance ended at dawn. "And finally," said the *Sun*, in the same facetious manner, "there were three rousing cheers and everybody stood while Mr. Swope showed the audience how to reach Broadway."

But if kidding Swope was now a popular sport, he was also treated with real respect. The city's law-enforcement agencies, impressed by the vigor with which he had shaken up the Police Department, took him very seriously.* Whitman's successor as District Attorney, for example, asked Swope to become his chief administrative assistant. Swope declined. And when the young lawyer, and future writer of light verse, Newman Levy, got a job as an assistant D.A., he considered it no less helpful to his candidacy that his father, Abraham, was one of the city's top-flight criminal counsel than that Swope wrote a letter endorsing his application to Charles F. Murphy, the boss of Tammany Hall.

Swope was getting more and more involved with politics. While he liked crime stories ("Journalism is life reflected in ink," he would say, "and it must partake of the ugliness as well as the beauty of life"), he liked political stories even more. In 1912, when not busy on the Becker case, he was pleased to be assigned to cover part of Woodrow Wilson's Presidential campaign. The bang-bang Theodore Roosevelt was much more Swope's type of man than the austere and scholarly Wilson, but in the case of others Swope often preferred performance to personality as a yardstick to measure his admiration and allegiance. To Swope, Wilson loomed big. "I was in love with him," Swope said in after years. Wilson may have formed the habit of calling Swope "Bayard" because the name had a particular sentimental appeal to him; a number of men with the surname Bayard had been important on the Princeton campus.

That was the year in which Roosevelt, a Harvard man, ran against Wilson. (Swope claimed that Wilson, who generally spoke on a lofty level, described Roosevelt to him at the time as "the bandit of Oyster Bay.") The Harvard–Princeton football game was played at Cambridge on the Saturday before Election Day,

* After the Becker business, Swope found it hard to take the police seriously. He had a notice posted in the *World*'s city room that went, "Once more reporters are cautioned under all circumstances to get both sides of every story, especially when an unfavorable reflection is involved. Also, members of the staff are doubly cautioned not to take the oftentimes irresponsible utterances of the police as final or authoritative. What the police agents give in the way of information is to be subjected to the same investigation and verification as would be the case with any other information."

and Swope covered it. Inevitably, his story reflected a search for microcosmic political portents. "Harvard Red-socked Princeton today," he started off in Sunday's *World*, continuing, "Her sons, following the lead of another of their ilk, turned faunal naturalists and proved nature fakers of those who said that the Tigers can't be tamed. And T. Roosevelt, Esq. will have a mark to shoot at from now on, for he never even bagged one Tiger, let alone eleven, at the same time. . . . And tonight . . . there is a monster torchlight and red fire parade for Woodrow Wilson. The students made it their own. Having beaten his college, they turned around and by outward and visible signs showed that they hoped he would escape that fate."

A few weeks later, after Wilson Orange-and-Black-socked Roosevelt, the President-elect gave Swope some advice, which Swope ignored, and Swope gave him some advice, which Wilson accepted. Wilson's advice to Swope was, as Swope once confided to Lyndon B. Johnson when Johnson was a Senator, "When you have won your point, stop arguing." Swope, for his part, was able to be of service to Wilson when the President-elect told him he thought it would be politically desirable to appoint a New York Democrat—one not connected with New York City or with Tammany Hall—to a reasonably important Washington job. He asked Swope for a recommendation. Swope consulted with Frank Cobb, and the two of them agreed that a young Harvard graduate from Hyde Park, about to start a second term in the state legislature, seemed suitable; at their suggestion Wilson named Franklin D. Roosevelt his Assistant Secretary of the Navy.

As Wilson was elected President in 1912, New York voters chose for their next Governor Congressman William Sulzer, a Tammany wheelhorse who tried to ape the physical appearance and forensic manner of Henry Clay. The *World* backed Sulzer, although it changed its mind about him when he was shown to have falsified reports about his campaign contributions, as a result of which the state legislature—Al Smith was then presiding over the Assembly—threw him out of office. Shortly before Election Day, Sulzer called on Swope at the *World*. What happened then Swope once recounted in a letter to James M. Cox, the Ohio publisher whom the Democrats ran for President in 1920:

Stretching out his long legs, and letting go a wad of tobacco juice, he said: "Swope, I've been following your career for some

time. I told Mr. Pewlitzer (giving it the wrong pronunciation) *
what a likely fellow you are." I said: "Thank you very much, Bill,
what do you want?" Smiling a little selfconsciously, he then told me
he was going to close his campaign that night among his "friends,
the Jews, up on Second Avenue," in, I think, the Seventh Assembly
District, and he would like to have me see how highly he was
thought of by those who properly appreciated him.

So that night I went up, along with Ed Hill, of the *Sun* (who is
now on the air), and Frank O'Malley, the *Sun*'s star; also Dill of the
Herald, and others. We sat in front of the pulpit in a synagogue,
which was literally packed with Bill's neighbors.

Bill appeared upon the rostrum, and there was a wild shout of joy.
He raised his hand to still the tumult and, after shooting a large and
juicy mouthful (which just missed the ark of the Covenant), looking
exactly like Henry Clay, with the forelock, and posturing like him,
began in his sepulchral tone and accentuated slowness of speech in
this way: "My friends, and I call you my friends advisedly, his-
torians say that the Jews are an ungrateful people. William Sulzer
denies this. (You will recall he always talked about himself in the
third person—that enabled him to be more self-laudatory than if he
used "I"). Mark you, and mark you well, when William Sulzer was
chairman of the House Committee on Foreign Affairs, he drafted
and had passed a resolution of protest to the Czar of all the Russians
anent the Kishinev massacre. And from that day to this the Roosians
never dared have another massacre."

The crowd went wild. They cheered and yelled and wept. Again
he raised his hand, and again let go another large projectile in the
form of more tobacco juice—this time just missing the press bench—
and went on: "Because of that there are fifteen million Jews on their
knees every night thanking their God for William Sulzer!"

I leaned forward from my seat and said, in a stage whisper: "Bill,
the Jews don't kneel when they pray." In his anxiety to make his
point he swallowed part of his cud. With a voice hoarse and ecstatic,
strained to a yell, he said "My learned young friend Mr. Herbert
Bayard Swope, of the New York *World* (at which I tried to cut
in by saying "Thanks for the ad, Bill"—which he ignored), says the
Jews don't kneel when they pray. They may not kneel for others,
but they kneel for William Sulzer."

At that the crowd went completely delirious. They screamed:
"We do, Bill, we do."

And they did, for next year, when Bill was impeached and removed from the Governorship of New York, he was sent back to
Albany as an Assemblyman from the Sixth District; and the Demo-

---

* "Pull-"—rhyming with "full"—was correct.

crats never dared unseat him, although it was a violation of the constitution for him to have been given another elective office.

Swope had several stories about himself that he liked to tell, and did, over and over. He would recount them with the gusto a gourmet devotes to an especially memorable meal. The Rosenthal–Becker episode was Swope's meat-and-potatoes story. The-night-the-Jews-agreed-to-kneel-for-Billy-Sulzer story was a brandy-and-coffee yarn. Swope told this one so often that some of his friends could give a creditable imitation of his rendition. Baruch sometimes told it. So did Jim Farley. So did Al Smith. So did Arthur Krock. Henry Cabot Lodge had his own version of Krock's version of Swope on the subject of Sulzer. So closely were the two linked in the minds of some of Swope's friends that on November 7, 1941, the day after Sulzer died, Supreme Court Justice Frankfurter sent Swope a telegram. The entire message was "I HOPE THEY WILL KNEEL WHEN THEY PRAY FOR BILLY SULZER."

From the start of the twentieth century to the outbreak of the First World War, there was no subject better fitted to grip the imagination and interest of newspaper readers—combining as it did the novel, the bizarre, the dangerous, and often the fatal—than the development of aviation. The papers were quite aware of the good new thing they had to latch onto, and they encouraged the spread of the sport, or business, or self-destruction, or whatever it might prove to be, by offering prizes for each step forward in the conquest of what was then reasonably considered outer space. In the spring of 1910, for instance, Glenn H. Curtiss collected ten thousand dollars from the *World* by negotiating the one-hundred-and-thirty-seven-mile distance between Albany and Governors Island, off the tip of New York City, in one hundred and fifty-two minutes, with two stops. The *World* and the *Post-Dispatch* were so pleased by the attention focused on this feat that they jointly put up thirty thousand dollars for the first flight between New York and St. Louis.

By 1914, at which time the *World* even found a *retired* aviator to interview, a biplane was racing a mile against an automobile (Barney Oldfield, in the car, won by two seconds), and newspapers everywhere were trying to extend the horizons of aviation. That year, Lord Northcliffe's *Daily Mail* offered ten thousand pounds—the equivalent of fifty thousand dollars—for a flight in either direction between Canada or the United States and Ireland or England. There was a seventy-two-hour time limit, but no restriction on the number of stops en route. At Hammondsport, New York, in the Finger Lakes section of the Adirondacks, Glenn Curtiss was commissioned by L. Rodman Wanamaker to build a contender for this prize. Curtiss fabricated a twin-engine seaplane, weighing over three tons fully loaded. It was a biplane, with a seventy-two-foot upper wing. To pilot it Wanamaker imported a British Navy officer, Lieutenant John Cyril Porte, who, showing for that sort of career man an uncommon dislike for surface craft, had not long before switched from the submarine service to naval aviation.

In the spring of 1914, as Wanamaker's plane neared completion and Porte arrived at Hammondsport for a month or more of test flights, the area rapidly filled with reporters. Hammondsport had two rival drugstores, one harboring the local Western Union concession, the other Postal Telegraph. The facilities of both pharmacies were taxed. The *World* sent up Swope. Until he got there, early in June, Lieutenant Porte had been standoffish toward the press. Swope changed that. The morning after he arrived, the other reporters, waiting in a hotel lobby for the pilot to show up for breakfast and hoping to get a crumb of news from him, were astounded on his appearance to hear him tell the maître d'hôtel, "Mr. Swope says he will be down right away. He wants you to have his breakfast ready: Orange juice, two poached eggs with crisp toast, a rasher of bacon, and piping-hot coffee."

While he was at it Swope also tied up the American rights to Porte's first-person story of his adventure—ghostwritten by Swope. Swope had Porte reveal that he was training hard for the flight and that he had embraced temperance. "I shall not take a drink until after the flight, should I succeed," the pilot was said to have said. "It is within the realms of possibility that I might be induced to take a wee drappie then." (Reader response to this sort of thing may have been discouragingly apathetic. The *World* was moved one morning to put over a front-page story from Hammondsport the explanatory headline "ATLANTIC FLIGHT WORLD EVENT, NOT SPORTS NEWS.") On June 22 the plane was christened the *America*. On June 23 it took to the air for the first time, and in the *World* that day Swope, evidently sensing that the other reporters on the scene were getting miffed at his monopolizing of

157

Porte's time and thoughts, had the pilot saying, "And as to the American press correspondents, I want to express my opinion that they are a fine lot of chaps, always ready with suggestions when asked for and showing an understanding of the subjects they are asked to 'cover' (I am told that is the right word) that reflects creditably upon their educations and mentalities. I am free to say that many of the American newspaper men and their personalities and methods might be copied with profit in my own country." The *Daily Mail* might, in the circumstances, have taken umbrage at that, but Lord Northcliffe's paper refrained from comment.

For the next few weeks the *America* made frequent flights, often carrying passengers. They acted as ballast in lieu of sandbags, and, said the *World*, "not one of the eight correspondents whose fortune it was to be selected as ballast would have surrendered his post for the royal suite on the finest liner afloat." Whether Swope was in this lucky octet was not made plain. On June 28 Porte's plane was raked by a hailstorm and barely survived. That same day, across the Atlantic, the Archduke Francis Ferdinand and his wife were assassinated at Sarajevo. The ominous news from Europe did not at once much affect the American press. The only story from that area deemed important enough to make the front page of the *World* three days after the shooting at Sarajevo was an interview with a London vicar who had officiated at a heavyweight prize fight in which an Englishman, Bombardier Wells, had knocked out an Australian, Colin Bell.

The plan was to have Porte's plane, once it had passed its tests, dismantled, shipped by train to St. John's, Newfoundland, and reassembled there for the first leg of its flight—a twelve-hundred-mile hop to Horta, in the Azores. Early in July the *World* replaced Swope at Hammondsport with another staff man, Norman G. Thwaites, an Englishman who had been one of Joseph Pulitzer's secretaries for the last seven years of the publisher's life and had then joined the paper as a reporter. Swope was posted to the Azores, so he could welcome Porte there and ghostwrite a first-person account of that phase of his journey.

Swope took his wife along. They left New York on July 4 aboard the Austrian steamer *Franz Josef* and landed five days later at Horta, on the island of Fayal, where a local Portuguese newspaper, *O Telegrapho*, to which the arrival of an American correspondent was big news, greeted them, under the disconcerting headline "MR. HERBERT HAYARD," with the story:

158

Encontra-se n'esta cidade, desembarcando hontem do paquete austriaco *Franz Joseph*, Herbert Hayard Swope, reporter do importante diario americano *The World*.

O sr. Herbert vem acompanhado por sua esposa e tenciona demorar-se no Fayal tres semanas.

O principal motivo da sua viagem e colher impressoes da passagem por esta ilha do hydroplano *Curtiss*, esperado de 25 do corrente a 2 de agosto.

Os distinctos visitantes estao magnificamente impressionados pelas bellezas da nossa terra, tencionando visitar outras ilhas.

Aprentamos os nossos cumprimentos ao illustre representante do *World*.

One of Swope's purposes in visiting a number of outlying Azorian islands was to assure the inhabitants that if an angel materialized from the sky, it would be a friendly angel, and to entreat them not to shoot at it. Margaret had never been abroad before, and she had not much use for travel anywhere. Her stay in the Azores did not allay her xenophobia. The place was hot, and there was no ice, and when she craved oranges there were no oranges. She fell ill, and—having somehow got the impression that it was the local custom to dispose of corpses as if the place were a ship, and having the further impression that the waters surrounding the Azores teemed with man-eating jellyfish—begged her husband, "Don't let them bury me at sea." She was restored to health in part because of the kindly ministrations of the British consul, who sent her some barley water. Swope was distressed by her indisposition, and he was also irritated. He always found it hard to cope with human frailties, and sickness—his own or that of anyone close to him—he regarded as a great inconvenience. Anything he couldn't handle—disease, accident, misfortune—was to him hateful. Moreover, he was an exceptionally fastidious man, and the sanitary arrangements on Fayal were primitive. Every morning he would wait until all others had used the rudimentary facilities. Then, after instructing a chambermaid to scrub and disinfect them, he would stalk disdainfully toward them, sprinkling toilet water ahead of him to sweeten his path.

Hanging around the Azores to receive an angel was frustrating for Swope, furthermore, because he could not abide small-town life, in any small town anywhere. Here it was summer and the height of the racing season back in the United States, and not only was there no race track to visit of an afternoon but he couldn't even get a bet down. Forehandedly, though, he had made some arrangements before his departure, recruiting various sporting cronies to cut him in on their ventures. One such agent he had was the celebrated horse-breeder, John E. Madden, who had once given Mrs. Payne Whitney some betting advice that Swope thought a philosophical gem of its sort: "One thing you must learn is to lose as if you like it, and win as if you're used to it." Madden, twenty-six years older than Swope, was a man of many talents. Aside from breeding six Kentucky Derby winners, he was a sparring partner of John L. Sullivan's and he made a sizable fortune in Wall Street. Swope named a number of race horses for him, and once pleased Franklin P. Adams by persuading Madden to call a horse "Conning Tower," after his column. Now, in 1914, Madden, back at his Kentucky farm—where out of his love of racing he established a horse cemetery and an old horses' home—was trying to make Swope's enforced separation from betting circles less unbearable by wagering fifty dollars for him on what Madden called "all impromptu affairs."

After the *Second* World War, Swope confided to an acquaintance that it had been the *World*'s intention more than thirty years earlier that when Porte landed at the Azores, Swope would climb aboard the *America* and fly on to Portugal with him, thus becoming eligible to write a legitimate first-person account. Whether or not any such scheme existed before the First World War is hard to tell. Swope never said anything about it to his wife. If she'd had any idea he was going to fly off and leave her alone in the Azores, she would probably have thrown him to the jellyfish. Whatever Swope may have had in mind soon proved to be of no consequence anyhow, because Porte never got under way. There was delay after delay, and as it became increasingly likely that England was going to war, Porte—and Thwaites, too—took off to join the British Armed Forces, while Swope impatiently exchanged cablegrams with the *World* office in New York.*
On July 16 Charles Lincoln, Swope's managing editor, cabled him that Porte would fly to the Azores on August 1, and on July 24 the managing editor said, "SHE SOARED TONIGHT WITH SIXTY-ONE HUNDRED POUNDS BARRING ACCIDENTS WILL BE AT ST. JOHN'S AUGUST 1ST." But the next day he was saying, "DEFINITELY

---

* Thwaites, before being badly wounded in France, sent the *World* excerpts from a diary he kept while fighting at Ypres.

OFF UNTIL OCTOBER ANYWAY." Only three days after that the *World* editors concluded that with war imminent in Europe, and Swope halfway there already, he might as well move on east. On July 28 Lincoln cabled, "GO TO PARIS."

That same day was an eventful one in the Azores. The day before, the German cruiser *Strassburg* had appeared unexpectedly at Horta. On the twenty-eighth it began to take on coal as fast as it could, and the next day it steamed off at top speed for its homeland, hoping to get there before war was declared. At the time the *Strassburg's* exact whereabouts were unknown—the "will-o'-the-wisp of the ocean," some called the ship—but four British destroyers spotted it in the English Channel and escorted it all the way to the Kiel Canal, with guns and torpedoes aimed, ready to blow it out of the water the instant word came that the war was on. But the *Strassburg* made it to a home port just two hours before hostilities broke out. Later, Swope was able to resolve the mystery of where the cruiser had begun its last frantic dash to safety:

> On the morning of July 27, at about 4:00 o'clock, I was awakened in the Hotel Grand Horta, by the sound of constant booming, and I sat up with a start, for those sounds could come from nothing but a cannon. The sea was in view from my window, and riding into the harbor, saluting and being saluted, was a dingy, sea-worn cruiser, which I was later to learn was the *Strassburg*. As she was coming in her crew was making ready to take on coal, and no sooner had anchor been dropped than boats put off for shore.
>
> Now at Horta there are two coaling companies, one a Portuguese concern, Ben Suade & Co., and the Fayal Coaling Company, which is owned by "Pat" Keating, an Irishman, who forced the monopoly from the other concern. There is an agreement by which these vessels alternate in coaling all vessels that enter the harbor, and this was the Fayal Coal Company's turn. Rear Admiral Reuber Paschwitz, Commander of the cruiser and once Naval Attaché to the German Embassy at Washington, rushed the coaling squad. Every available craft was put into use, and when her regular capacity of seven hundred and fifty tons was reached the Commander ordered more and more coal. Then it was learned that the Portuguese concern was coaling also, and Keating ordered his men to halt. In vain Admiral Paschwitz urged that he must have reserve coal; that the emergency was great. The Irishman was adamant, and finally the Portuguese concern was left with the field for its own.
>
> When the *Strassburg* finally steamed she had coal even in her

forecastle. She must have carried about thirteen hundred tons more than her gross carrying ability.

With all funnels spouting smoke and her ensign fluttering bravely, the *Strassburg* steamed to sea and was lost in the night, and lost, too, to all sight, apparently.

Not many hours after the *Strassburg* left Horta, but under somewhat less pressure, the Swopes sailed out—"*a Europa em visita a differentes cidades*," according to *O Telegrapho*—aboard the small French passenger liner *Roma*. They planned to debark at Marseille, but when war began while they were at sea the ship headed for Lisbon, where they went ashore. The cities Swope most aspired to visit, despite his managing editor's terse instruction, were German ones, and after the couple had made their way to London, Swope received a letter from Ralph Pulitzer approving this plan. The *World*, like much of the United States, was not then openly antagonistic toward Germany. Not only did the paper feel that most of the news from Europe was weighted in favor of the Allies, but the *World* was even running a campaign to collect toys to send to German children at Christmas. Pulitzer, who did not yet know his reporter well—he addressed him as "My dear Mr. Swope"—instructed him, in a handwritten letter dated September 2:

> I am disgusted at the way in which all the sources of war news are monopolized by the anti-German nations, with the result that the New York (i.e., the American) papers are giving their readers grossly one sided, partisan news, this being the only news that they can get.
>
> I want you to go to Germany for 3 main purposes: 1—to get news from the German side. 2—to get in interviews or articles from prominent Germans the German point of view or interpretation of events. 3—to devise some method to get these views and news before our American readers, after passing the German censors, but without having to run the gauntlet of English and French censors. It seems to me that no man in Germany is too prominent to be willing and eager to help you in these efforts, which should offset the bad impressions so far made by false news. The Press of America, my papers included, would never have assumed the attitude of unfair hostility to Germany which they have assumed, if they had been able to get news out of Germany as well as out of England, France, Russia and Belgium.
>
> I hope you will succeed in getting these presentations of affairs

from prominent Germans whose names will carry weight with our readers, and will also get what unbiased, truthful news the censors will pass, and will find a method of getting them before the Readers of the N. Y. "World," the St. Louis Post-Dispatch, and the World Syndicate of American newspapers.

Faithfully yours,

RALPH PULITZER

Pulitzer hoped Swope would get an interview with the Kaiser, but Swope could not bring that off. Sending Margaret home from England, he went on to Germany alone and reached Berlin in mid-September. Almost at once he ran into the trouble that usually besets correspondents in wartime. "There is no certainty that the stuff goes out . . . when it is filed," Swope bewailed in a September 22 letter to Lincoln. "Great bodies move slowly, and the Germans are great bodies." At the start of the war, the only cable line linking Germany and the United States had been cut by the Allies, who were then able to maintain tight censorship over all westbound news dispatches, not to mention ordinary mail, which they intercepted when they could. Swope's best chance was to use a courier service to London, via The Hague, but once his stuff had reached London he was at the mercy of the British censors. To James M. Tuohy, head of the *World*'s London bureau, Swope was writing concurrently, "Whenever you and [John J.] Spurgeon [a *World* man there who was later executive editor of the Philadelphia *Public Ledger*] think London is a bad news source give a little prayerful consideration to this burg. My Gawd—it is fearful. We get most of our news from London." He also thought that maybe the *World* ought to reconsider its Christmas-toy project and send plain money instead, "as in many cases bread is more necessary than toys."

On September 22, 1914, in the North Sea, off the Hook of Holland, occurred what Swope then appraised as "the greatest exploit in Naval history." A German submarine, the *U-9*, with a complement of twenty-six, commanded by a thirty-two-year-old Kapitänleutnant named Otto von Weddigen, left its base on the Kiel Canal that morning and, before it returned in the evening, had in a single hour's spirited action torpedoed and sunk three twelve-thousand-ton British cruisers, first the *Aboukir* and then, when they steamed toward their stricken sister ship, the *Hogue* and the *Cressy*. The three cruisers carried among them more than two thousand men, and some fifteen hundred drowned. It was a disas-

163

ter of first magnitude, and it brought about a change in British admiralty policy; after that, every vessel in the Navy was supposed to protect itself, no matter what might happen to another ship.

The foreign correspondents in Berlin at first could add little to the London coverage of the episode, beyond the romantic footnote that von Weddigen had been wished Godspeed as he left that memorable morning by his bride of five weeks. Swope felt, as he was later to write to Joseph Pulitzer, Jr., that it was "easily the most picturesque incident that the war had produced up to that time and, furthermore, was the worst blow England's sea power had sustained in hundreds of years." Swope learned that Captain-Lieutenant von Weddigen was at the Wilhelmshaven naval base and decided to get a firsthand story from him. When he made overtures to naval headquarters in Berlin, however, he was told that Admiral Alfred von Tirpitz, the ranking officer, was unalterably opposed, not wanting the enemy to learn anything it might not know and also not wanting to glorify any individual German sailors—except for von Tirpitz himself. Swope went next to a telegraph office on the outskirts of Berlin—to avoid observation by any other correspondent—and wired von Weddigen at Wilhelmshaven. "IN THE NAME OF ALL WHO APPRECIATE HEROISM," began Swope, in German, "I, AS CORRESPONDENT OF THE NEW YORK WORLD, THE ST. LOUIS POST-DISPATCH, AND OTHER INFLUENTIAL AMERICAN NEWSPAPERS, CONGRATULATE YOU EARNESTLY ON YOUR BRILLIANT FEAT WITH THE U-9. THROUGH THIS COMMUNICATION I BEG TO ASK IF IT WOULD NOT BE POSSIBLE FOR YOU TO MAKE A STATEMENT OF YOUR REMARKABLE SUCCESS EITHER IN THE FORM OF AN INTERVIEW OR THROUGH A SELF-WRITTEN ARTICLE, WHICHEVER WAY IS MORE FEASIBLE TO YOUR PURPOSE." Swope offered to donate the equivalent of three hundred dollars to the officer's favorite charity, and added that "THE PUBLICATION OF A SUCCINCT AND AUTHORITATIVE ACCOUNT OF THE DESTRUCTION OF THREE GREAT CRUISERS WOULD HAVE A DEEP IMPRESSION ON THE SENTIMENT OF THE WORLD, ESPECIALLY IN AMERICA WHERE IT WOULD BE A REAL AID TO THE SPIRIT OF FRIENDSHIP TO GERMANY IN QUARTERS THAT ARE LUKEWARM NOW BECAUSE OF THE FEAR OF ENGLISH SEA POWER."

A day or so later von Weddigen telegraphed a polite but firm refusal. That night Swope had dinner at the American Embassy in Berlin. James W. Gerard, a lifelong friend of Swope's, was the

Ambassador, and among the other guests was a friend of von Tirpitz's. Von Weddigen was naturally much on everyone's tongue. When Swope mentioned the rebuff he'd had, von Tirpitz's friend offered to intercede. He telephoned the Admiral the next day and won him partly over.

Swope still failed to obtain a face-to-face meeting with von Weddigen—who died less than a year later—but with the German Navy's blessing he talked to him briefly on the telephone, and he also got the first-person narrative he was after. Upon putting this into publishable form and having it passed by the German censors, Swope sent it to The Hague on September 28, but it took nearly two exasperating weeks for the story, once it reached London, to clear through the British admiralty, of which Winston Churchill, then not yet personally acquainted with Swope, was First Lord. (Churchill had especially good reason to be unhappy about von Weddigen's exploit; not long before, the Englishman had confidently predicted that the German U-boats would be "dug out like rats.") Swope, anticipating difficulties with his dispatch, had wired the *World*'s liaison man in Holland to have Tuohy, in the paper's London office, "ASK CHURCHILL HIMSELF TO INSTRUCT CENSORS TO PASS IT AS IT CONTAINS NOTHING INJURIOUS TO ENGLAND AND STORY SHOULD NOT BE MANGLED," and to request this "ON GROUND OF TRADITIONAL ENGLISH FAIR PLAY." Swope's appeal to fair play may have prevailed. For the British, though somewhat sluggishly, cleared the dispatch—even the first sentence of Swope's introduction, which began, "Through the kindness of the German admiralty . . ." There were only a few deletions. Missing from the published story, for instance—though there is no more evidence now that it was excised by Winston Churchill in the admiralty than by Charles Lincoln on Park Row—was Von Weddigen's statement that "What our little ship has done our big ones can do, for the same spirit animates every man in Germany—a spirit that brooks no check and knows no defeat." What with one delay and another, it was October 11 before the *World*, under a five-column page-one headline, ran the still-exclusive dispatch. Lincoln cabled Swope, "HEARTIEST CONGRATULATIONS FOR WEDDIGEN STORY FINE ACHIEVEMENT NOTHING BETTER BY ANYONE ANYWHERE DURING WAR . . ." and a few days later, in a letter, the managing editor said, "That story alone was worth all the time and money you spent in Germany."

In five weeks there, obviously, Swope did not confine himself to one naval engagement. He spent some time—and, presumably, money—on the east Prussian front, where von Hindenburg was pushing the Russians back. From Berlin, Swope had mentioned tales of Russian atrocities; on his return from the front he spelled them out in detail. His tour was a guided one, and his atrocity stories were all related to him by others, but they were an impressively gory lot, and it must have been with relish that his German hosts read his prefatory remarks about them:

> . . . Torture, murder, incendiarism, robbery and attacks on women —these were five characteristics that marked the Cossacks wherever they appeared as the advance guards of the Russian armies in their so-called "march on Berlin." As I had heard charges of outrages against troops as made in France and England and had been able to find on the occasions little real basis for the accusations, I entered upon the investigation with a mind disposed to believe that the accounts were overdrawn and that the alleged misconduct had been justified perhaps by the rules of war. But I found the actual conditions to be so bad, the play of unchecked passions so terrible, that the account almost defies belief.
>
> And it should be said that, on the other hand, the Germans who later entered Russia in pursuit of the fleeing armies of the Czar were held under such an iron discipline that not one single instance was I able to gather of misconduct on their part. Every soldier was held personally responsible to his direct officer and they in turn held accountable to their superiors, so that there could be no misbehavior without an immediate reckoning.
>
> It may be that the charges against the Germans that were made in Belgium had a salutary effect; but whatever the reason it is simple justice to say that the soldiers in Russia never once departed from the iron rules governing the military in their relations with the civilians. I personally saw and spoke to many inhabitants of Russian villages—most of them Jews but with representatives of other religions as well—and they rejoiced in the coming of the Germans and were free in expressing the hope that they would stay. . . .

After thus analyzing—with perhaps a mite less dispassion than he, as an editor in the years to come, would have condoned—the differences between the two nations' warriors, Swope returned to London, where he besought an interview with one of his literary heroes, Rudyard Kipling. Swope was asked to join the writer and his wife one morning at Brown's Hotel, but Kipling added, "What frightens me is not that you are a newspaper man, or even

166

a *World* man, because I used to know and like Pulitzer a long time ago—but that you are a friend of Mr. [Irvin S.] Cobb. He came to my house as the friend of a friend of mine, and used the visit for newspaper purposes and also described a fellow-guest whom he met under my roof. But I shall be glad to see you if you will regard the visit, as you have written, *not* for publication." Swope may have been glad, too, for, unencumbered by any responsibility to report the proceedings, he was able to devote most of the get-together to an account of his pursuit of von Weddigen's memoir.

Swope returned to the United States early in December 1914. He had been in Germany, and he had been in England, and—like many other Americans who had visited neither warring country —his feelings about the conflict were strongly neutral, with, if anything, a slight predisposition for the Central Powers' cause. Months later, on October 20, 1915, he would write Charles M. Schwab, who sailed back across the ocean with him, "If you will recall our long conversations on the *Adriatic*, in which I related some of my experiences and impressions of the wonderful German army and the still more wonderful patriotism and devotion every man, woman, and child in that empire feels, you will recall I prophesied that Germany, while she might not be wholly victorious, certainly would never be defeated. I believe this more strongly today than ever before." And six weeks after that Swope would write his mother, in Germany, "With you, dearest mother, I hope for an early peace—a peace with honor to all concerned, especially to Germany, who has waged so wonderful a fight against such heavy odds. Thus far her every campaign seems to have been successful, and I think she is on the high road to even greater victories."

So, in his own campaign for journalistic glory, was he.

Swope had hardly returned from Europe when the *World* made him its city editor. Nearly four years earlier, when Sherman Morse, the city editor who had hired Swope, had retired to grow apples, he had suggested that Swope succeed him. The three most influential men concerned with the paper's coverage of news— Ralph Pulitzer, Florence White, and Charles Lincoln—had heard Morse out, and each had pronounced him daft for entertaining the wild notion. Now the same three men, six months separated from Swope's clanging voice and what Lincoln liked to call his "crashing methods," thought it a perfectly sound idea. For Swope, it seemed at first an exciting prospect. War or no war, the competition for local news was still what kept New York's papers scrappy and lively. Before accepting the new job, typically, Swope talked it over with himself on paper, and the conclusions he set forth went, in part:

> Realize it big opportunity so will take it but want conditions so that I can make good.
> Willing to have all necessary supervision over me but want single and undisputed authority over all city news.
> This includes sporting news. Sports is too big a part of City Department to permit me to omit that from my plans. Willing to be responsible to others but want all City Department responsible to me.
> Must be able to operate independently, since I must work out my own salvation and accomplish results. Therefore I must be permitted to use my own methods and select my own instruments. . . .
> My own personality must play a part. I think I understand the spirit of the paper and the objectives we seek; I must be allowed wide sway in doing this work.

Equally typically, as he did when taking many major steps in his life, on January 15, 1915, the day after his appointment as city editor became effective, Swope wrote his brother about the job: "There is endless detail to be mastered, and the transition from the 'line to the staff'—from an outside job to one of an executive nature—is so sudden that I feel my first task to be to train myself not to try to do everything in person. Cursed as I am with the Swope characteristic of love of system—or perhaps I may call it a desire for thoroughness—I have an ever-present impulse to handle most of the work myself."

As city editor Swope operated from a dais at one end of the long city room on the twelfth floor of the *World* tower. At a level slightly below him sat his principal assistant, John H. Gavin, who had begun at the paper as an office boy and worked his way up to within a few inches of Swope. Gavin, who left the *World* in 1926 and subsequently became Surrogate of Hudson County, New Jersey, liked to describe Swope as a "steam engine in boots." Just behind Swope's perch was a bronze plaque. It memorialized a city staff reporter who in the spring of 1913 had died in the line of duty. He was Gregory T. Humes, a thirty-five-year-old bachelor, and still another St. Louisan who had become a New York journalist. On his day off, he was aboard a Boston-to-New-York train that had an accident at Stamford. Fatally injured, with two fractured ankles and his hips crushed, Humes was carried off the wrecked train, and his last recorded words were "Call up the New York *World* right away and tell them there is a wreck here —a big story. Also tell them I'm sorry I won't be able to work on the story because I'm smashed up. Call up my mother, too." After Humes' death, Swope's old Chicago paper, the *Inter-Ocean,* said editorially, "Nothing finer nor more heroic can be imagined." The *World's* own editorial tribute to him, headed "Faithful Unto Death," declared that "many a towering shaft the whole earth around commemorates loyalty less notable and bravery less admirable."

One impulse that Swope quickly demonstrated as city editor was to leap four square into the midst of every news story, although it was not now he who chased the elusive fact or the elusive municipal official. James Barrett, whom Swope hired as a reporter in 1916, said, "He attacked the news with such zest that the staff was galvanized—also partly paralyzed and partly amused." Swope took a beguilingly possessive attitude toward the news. "Who is covering my subway accident?" he would shout. "Who is covering my murder?" Once he looked out of a window on a wintry day, frowned, and barked at an assistant, "Who is covering my snowstorm?"

Ideas for stories—some good, some bad—sprayed forth from him like precipitation from on high. Was there a plan afoot to start a charity drive to build a clubhouse in New York for newsboys? Swope got Diamond Jim Brady—an ex-newsboy who had climbed high enough in the world to lavish jeweled toys upon the children of such friends of his as Swope—to make the first contribution. "It will make a good story that will go all over the country," Swope told Brady exuberantly, "and I will see that it is properly handled." How should the paper cover a Billy Sunday revival meeting in New York? Swope, sizing up the evangelist as primarily an actor, invited George M. Cohan to comment for the *World* on Sunday's performance. Cohan shared Swope's estimate, but begged off. "It would not be fair for me to publicly criticize Billy Sunday," he wrote Swope, "because after everything has been said and done he is a showman offering an entertainment to the public, and it would be nothing short of unprofessional for any other showman to knock his game. The only difference between Barnum and Sunday is that Barnum charges admission and Sunday lets 'em in free and charges 'em to get out."

Swope had not long been city editor when, to his own disgust, he fell ill. In April 1915, feeling well enough at least to do some reporting, he got the *World* to send him to Havana to cover the heavyweight fight between Jack Johnson, the champion, and Jess Willard, the contender for the crown and America's white hope. Swope had a low opinion of most full-time sports writers; he thought them infantile. But whenever he could cover a sporting event himself, he was delighted. This was a particularly interesting event. The aging Negro champion, fat and flabby, was hated by many Americans, especially in the South, because he had had three white wives. (When Johnson had successfully defended his title against Jim Jeffries in Reno, in 1910, there were race riots all over the country, and a couple of dozen people died in them.) Willard, whom Swope described as "an unspoiled, well-behaved, clean-living, upstanding, quiet-mannered young countryman," beat Johnson in twenty-six rounds, and Swope told about it in some four thousand words, beginning, "The last ten seconds that Jack Johnson held the world's prize-fighting championship were the most dramatic of his career. He lay on his back with his mouth wide open, eyes staring straight into the sun, belly heaving convulsively, half hearing but not grasping the slow counts of Referee Welch that took away from him the great prize and gave it to the grinning, lean-faced, youthful Jess Willard, who stood over him, awaiting for the 'ten' that made him rich and famous."

One could write freely then about race relations, and Swope did:

John Brown was a friend of the negro. He came from Ossawatomie, Kansas, and operated about fifty-five years ago. Jess Willard comes from old John Brown's stamping ground, hailing from Pottowatomie, Kansas, but he certainly had no love for the colored brother in his heart, judging from the way he tore after Johnson this afternoon, and never in the history of the ring, which stretches back hundreds of years, was there such a wildly, hysterically, shriekingly, enthusiastic crowd as the fourteen thousand men and women who begged Willard to wipe out the stigma that they and hundreds of thousands of others, especially in the South, believe rested on the white race through a negro holding the championship.

And Swope devoted an entire paragraph to Johnson's current wife, whom he thought "pretty in spite of the paint on her cheeks and the rouge on her lips":

She wore a white lingerie frock, thin white coat and a white straw with a long white feather sticking straight up in the air. Her shoes and stockings were white and she wore many diamonds, but in no way was her attire extreme. She is of medium height, rather slender, with a thinnish face that breaks into a smile too readily, and shows too much teeth and gums. She seemed to fairly enjoy her importance as she entered and equally she seemed to bitterly resent her slide into obscurity as she left. Her transition was abrupt—from the wife of the world's champion, frowned upon and adulated, she had become merely the white consort of a fat and unusually homely, middle-aged and very dark negro. The women present had eyes for her and sneers for her as she left dethroned.

Not long after his Johnson–Willard story, which Charles Lincoln called "a classic of sports writing," Swope got sick again. This time his propensity for talking undid him. Playing tennis one day, he worked up a sweat, finished his match, got to chatting with somebody in the locker room, neglected to take a shower, came down with a chill, and ended up with rheumatic fever. He was laid up for several months. When he recovered and returned to the *World*, he was restless. His predictions about the course of the war were not coming true. The public, moreover, was slowly beginning to consider foreign battles more lastingly consequential than local murders, and as a reporter who had been a correspondent abroad so recently, he chafed at his detachment from the scene of big events. It was a relief to him when, in 1916, the *World* decided to send him back to Germany.

9

_____

I N THE summer of 1916 there was still little news coming out of Germany that bore the stamp of credibility. Most of the American correspondents on the Continent, fearing that if they attached themselves to the Central Powers they would never be able to send back anything of consequence, chose to stick with the Allied armies. (There was, however, no complete blackout of news from Germany. A number of American newspapers kept correspondents there, and there were occasional temporary reporters of more than passing interest; in the summer of 1915, for instance, Ralph Pulitzer had gone to Europe and had reported about a flight he took in a French plane over the German lines.) America was still ostensibly neutral. That was President Wilson's firm official position, and even the ordinarily bellicose Teddy Roosevelt had joined his Democratic rival to espouse an attitude of moderation. The sack of Belgium and the sinking of the *Lusitania* in May 1915 had stirred American passions, but a year after that the Germans pledged that they would not engage in indiscriminate submarine warfare. And if there were many Americans who, because of their country's historic ties to Great Britain, favored the Allies, there were millions too whose forebears, like Swope's, had come from Germany and who had their own understandable sympathies. But however Americans might feel about the rights and wrongs of what was going on across the ocean, it was generally conceded that they were getting precious little information out of Germany itself that they could consider neutral.

The *World*, like other papers, had its own man in Germany—Karl H. von Wiegand. Many of his dispatches, though, had given the impression, even to his own editors in New York, that he tended to be overly friendly to the nation to which he was assigned. It was to redress in part that lack of balance that the *World* sent Swope to Germany again, to look around and on his return to write a series of articles. Swope was in many ways the ideal choice. He had a disdain for the red tape in which a less aggressive man might have found himself hopelessly snarled. He knew Germany and had been there at the beginning of the war, so he was qualified to detect changes. And, Charles Lincoln pointed out to him, if the Germans tried to make things difficult for him as a correspondent, he could always affect the guise of a loving son and brother who had come to visit his family. For occasions when he could openly be what he was, the *World* invested him with the title of Special Staff Observer.

Again, Margaret repressed her fear of travel and went along, though by now they had two small children. Their son, Herbert, Jr., known from infancy as Ottie (the nickname derived from some obscure doggerel), had been born November 30, 1915. The Swopes left the children, with their Grandmother Powell, a maid-nurse, and a cook, in an apartment at 448 Riverside Drive into which they'd moved just before the boy's birth. Prior to sailing for Europe, Swope armed himself with an array of credentials. He had a letter from Frank L. Polk, the Counselor of the State Department and its Acting Secretary, asking in the country's name that he be accorded favorable treatment. He had a letter from John Purroy Mitchel, the Mayor of New York, describing him to whom it might concern as a personal friend and an eminent citizen of Mitchel's domain. He had a letter, too, from President Wilson. Swope had called at the White House on July 13, 1916, to discuss with the President his pending trip, and on the 18th he wrote Wilson:

My dear Mr. President:

I would be doing myself an injustice if I did not tell you how interesting I found our talk of last Thursday and how helpful I found your suggestions in the formulation of plans for my trip abroad. Surely you will understand it as a compliment when I say that you showed a fine newspaper judgment in the suggestions you made of the subjects most worthy of attention and of the subjects in which the deepest public interest would lie.

Because my previous experience abroad taught me the great value of thorough identification, I take the liberty again of making the request—about the granting of which you were in doubt on Thursday—that you send me a letter, not necessarily of introduction, but which would serve to have me recognized as being actually known to you as Herbert Swope, a newspaperman. I think it is unnecessary, my dear Mr. President, for me to assure you that the most remote possibility of the misuse of such a letter would be thoroughly guarded against.

In expressing the hope that you may be re-elected, I am actuated more by a desire to see the true interests of this country served than the wish to witness merely your personal success. With all my heart I believe that if ever a man deserved the devotion of his countrymen, you are that man. That is the message I am personally charging myself with in my trip abroad, and whether or not you can see your way clear toward giving me the letter for which I ask, the sincerity of this message will be none the less pronounced.

I am, my dear Mr. President, with regard,

Faithfully,

HERBERT BAYARD SWOPE
City Editor

The next day Wilson obligingly sent Swope two letters, one of them an explanation that he could not go beyond the other, which said:

MY DEAR MR. SWOPE:

Thank you sincerely for your letter of July eighteenth. I hope that your trip abroad will afford you just the experience and just the information you seek, and this letter is sent to express my best wishes for your safety and happy return.

Cordially and sincerely yours,

It was a restrained communication at best, but Swope told the President that it was just what he wanted, adding, "In event of my identity being doubted, it proves conclusively who I am, and proves it impressively with the testimony of the President of the United States."

Thus reassuringly identified, Swope descended again on Berlin. James Gerard was still Ambassador there, and it soon became apparent that Swope had far freer entrée to the Embassy than von Wiegand, or practically anyone else. Two years earlier von Wiegand, who by now, to distinguish him from Swope, had the title "Special Staff Correspondent," had been calling Swope "my dear old 'war chum' "; now, resenting Swope's chumminess with

Gerard, von Wiegand became bitterly angry and even returned to the United States to protest that Swope's presence in Germany was, for him, not only an embarrassment but an impugnment of his honor. What was more, von Wiegand complained after Swope himself had returned, while other correspondents were going to nerve-racking pains to get their material out of Germany, Swope had done it painlessly, and unsportingly, by the device of using the Ambassador as his messenger. Von Wiegand was not the only envious journalist to feel that Gerard was treating Swope with excessive consideration. When, the following year, a movie was made based on the Ambassador's reminiscences of his wartime post, the New York *Sun*, which took special glee in teasing Swope, said in a tongue-in-cheek review, "There was only one disappointing scene, one which left the spectators sharply in doubt. Mr. Gerard at a secret interview confides an important state paper to a messenger who memorizes its four pages on the spot. The messenger did not turn his visage to the audience, so that the audience went home not knowing whether the messenger was just an ordinary messenger or Herbert Bayard Swope."

Swope stayed in Germany, in and out of the Embassy, for nearly two months. Again he missed the Kaiser, but he did get to see the Chancellor, von Bethman-Hollweg, and the Minister for Foreign Affairs, Dr. Alfred Zimmerman. Swope went to parts of occupied Belgium and northern France, toured a combat area at the Somme, escaped an incoming artillery burst by several yards, and had a long colloquy with the young flying ace von Boelcke, whose knightly attitude toward battle much impressed Swope. One day he turned up at Cambrai, where the Germans had a camp for Allied prisoners, just after two young British pilots were brought in. The commandant at the camp, when the *World* man asked for permission to interview the captives, said he could do that and could also notify them they were soon to be court-martialed—and would probably be convicted and executed —for using incendiary ammunition. "I was unwilling to be the bearer of such unhappy news, and I did not tell them," Swope recalled later. Instead, as soon as he next saw Ambassador Gerard, he told *him*. Gerard, as a neutral envoy, was representing British interests in Germany, and he got the men's lives spared. Nearly thirteen years later one of the two, having just then learned how felicitous Swope's intercession had been, was to thank him "for what you did on our behalf, and to state that I shall never lose sight of the fact that it is an American citizen to whom I owe my life."

Swope found the Germans united, determined, and unafraid. "We Germans don't want to fight, but so long as we are forced to, you may be sure we will, and fight so that we shall never be beaten," von Boelcke, the flyer, told him three weeks before he was killed in a crash. The *World*'s Special Staff Observer concluded that the Germans could never conquer the rest of the world, that they themselves could never be conquered, that they were in surprisingly better economic and spiritual shape than most of the rest of the world was aware, that they would not accept any peace terms to which the Allies were likely to agree, and that they had a powerful dislike for all Americans.

In September the Swopes left Germany. Ambassador Gerard was sailing home to report to President Wilson, and Swope, alert to the advantages of getting the voluminous notes he'd been taking into neutral territory inside a diplomatic pouch, accompanied Gerard to Copenhagen and thence home on the Danish steamer *Frederik VIII*. There was one last-minute hitch: Margaret balked at crossing the ocean. Asked once why she disliked sea travel so much, even in peacetime, she replied, "Because if I get halfway out across the Atlantic and I change my mind and ask the Captain to turn back, he won't." Now, in Copenhagen, she changed her mind at the dock, and after going aboard she retreated down a gangplank, where she dug in, mulishly, and refused to be budged. Forty minutes after the ship's scheduled departure time, the Captain told Swope he really couldn't wait any longer. Swope dragged his wife back on board, stowed her in her cabin, locked the door, and stood guard outside until the harbor pilot had drawn away and the ship was too far off shore for Margaret to swim to land. "After three or four days, things were all right," she said subsequently. "I relaxed, and the people on board were fairly amusing."

To proclaim its neutrality, the *Frederik VIII* had its sides painted with large Danish flags. But German U-boat commanders did not always observe the niceties of war. Ambassador Gerard had particular reason to be edgy; one of the things he wanted to talk to President Wilson about was his conviction that the Germans, pledge or no pledge, were about to revert to the practice of torpedoing any ship they chose to, without advance warning.

Gerard confided this opinion to Swope, who wrote a long dispatch on the subject. He had trouble getting it to the *World* by wireless; it was held up for a full day, while the *Frederik VIII* headed warily toward New York, because radio channels were being kept clear for the calls of distress from a ship struck down by a U-boat not far away.

When the Ambassador landed, on October 10, he was greeted by a morning *World* with an eight-column streamer headline on its front page:

GERARD IS COMING SOLELY TO TELL OF U-BOAT MENACE;
GERMANY MAY DECIDE TO ABANDON ITS SUSSEX PLEDGE;
PRESIDENT WILL DEMAND A "COMPLETE FULFILLMENT"

Under Swope's byline there followed a story that showed he had put to good use some of the time on shipboard he might have devoted to shuffleboard or stargazing. He began:

The *World* can state positively that Ambassador Gerard, who is on board the Frederik Eight, arriving in New York on Tuesday, carries no message from Germany to President Wilson requesting his good offices to make peace.

Such reports are wholly false, and are probably the outgrowth of a stock-jobbing plot having its origin in Copenhagen and being imposed upon the United States. The Ambassador resents the efforts to use the President and himself, especially as his visit is fraught with such seriousness that a misconstruction may add to the gravity of an already delicate situation. Mr. Gerard is making his first visit to America in three years to report to President Wilson in person on a matter vastly more important to America than the subject of peace, important as that is. He comes to describe the heavy black cloud hanging over German-American relations in the form of the submarine menace, which is growing day by day, and which, even the most friendly German statesmen agree, will break open after election unless the unexpected occurs and peace intervenes.

Mr. Gerard will report that Germany is nurturing no false hopes or delusions on this point. She does not believe peace is a likelihood or will be a probability for a long time, so she is concerning herself with means of war, ignoring the plans for peace. Therefore it is proper to say the diplomat's visit has to do more with the war and the possibility of our becoming involved than it has to deal with peace through our agency. It is, of course, true that the Ambassador has received a communication from the Kaiser and the members of the German government on the subject of ending the war, but these are all indefinite and formulated in plans lacking any immediacy. On the other hand, I am able to state that the real purpose of the Ambassador's journey is to present to the administration in concrete form what every intelligent visitor to Germany recently has been impressed by—the sure and rapid weakening of German opposition to a "ruecksichtslose" U-Boat campaign, and the deliberate preparations being made to resume the practices objected to by America in the cases of the Lusitania, Arabic, and Sussex, to mention only three of the most prominent instances.

Swope let the Ambassador report to the President first. Then he went to Washington himself, gave Wilson his views of the German situation, and was pleased when the President told him, according to a letter that Swope sent to Joseph Pulitzer, Jr., that his U-boat scoop was a "really notable piece of journalism."

To spend two weeks at sea and come home to find oneself monopolizing the front page of one's paper that very day is a reporter's dream. Swope's triumphant return was suitably observed at the *World*. He found his city room draped with bunting, and it took little persuasion for him to climb upon a desk and regale the staff with some of his adventures, including that of the incoming artillery shell, which, as in all old soldiers' yarns, kept landing closer to him every time he thought about it. He was much in demand as a speaker at banquets. He told the annual dinner of the Columbia Club that "I do not think there is one individual in the [German] empire who would not willingly sacrifice his or her life and all they had in the world beside, if it was thought that by so doing they would assist the Fatherland in this hour of need"; and he told the annual dinner of the Sports Writers' Association of Greater New York that "the soldiers had come to look on the war as a sport, the greatest ever devised, and . . . how different officers had spoken proudly of the feats in hand-grenade throwing and in the time the soldiers made in sprinting from one trench to another." Otto H. Kahn asked him to lunch, John D. Rockefeller, Jr., asked him to address the twentieth annual dinner of the Young Men's Bible Class of the Fifth Avenue Baptist Church, and late one evening he restored Damon Runyon's flagging spirits about the war situation:

I am in the Prince George tap room the other night punching the bag with Herb Swope, the newspaper guy, who has been over in

178

Germany giving the war the close up, and after he explains what a roughhouse it is, we get to talking about the chances of this country horning in on the squabble, which we agree are great. Herb makes a terrible hit with me because he is the first guy I meet in a long time who will admit that this country has a chance in any kind of a jam. I am reading in the magazines and newspapers for over a year about how we are going to get a smearing if we stick our beezer into a fuss, and I am feeling pretty much discouraged about it.

I am brought up to believe that the U.S. can tie its hands behind it, and put its feet in a hole, and still lick anybody in the world, but after reading these magazines and newspapers I get to thinking my early teaching is away out of line, until I run into this Herb. Now I am Jake again. . . .

When not on the banquet circuit, Swope was turning out a series of articles on his observations. He was in a hurry; he wanted to get into print before his impressions were out of date. To speed things up, he assigned to himself a young *World* reporter, Lewis S. Gannett, whom Swope had hired for the city staff the previous spring, when Gannett was trying to make up his mind whether to become a journalist or a truck driver. Gannett knew German, and he could type fast. Swope decided they would work at night, beginning at eight. Then he advanced the hour to ten. But it was so hard for him to concentrate on any sustained effort when there was anybody around to talk to that finally he settled on 3:00 A.M. For the better part of six weeks, from that hour to seven in the morning, he rattled off dictation to Gannett, who wrote to Swope, when the stint was over, "For a young reporter it was a rare privilege to work so closely with one far advanced in the profession, and to have the opportunity for such intimate observation of the making of a journalistic landmark. And it was a pleasure as well as a privilege."

Some of Swope's detractors later suggested that Gannett had actually written the landmark himself, but in fact he had a creative hand in only two installments. "As I recall it," Gannett said subsequently, "he read them, said they were fine, but needed punchy first and last paragraphs—that was about all anyone read, anyway—and he provided them, and taught me a lesson in journalism." (After Gannett had forsaken reporting and become the *Herald Tribune*'s literary critic, he referred to Swope in one of his reviews as "the yellingest editor in newspaper history." Swope probably was, but he didn't like others to emulate him. One day at the *World*, a reporter using one of the city-room phone booths was talking in a loud voice, with the door ajar. When he emerged, Swope grabbed him and asked to whom he'd been speaking. To City Hall, the man said. "Why did you bother to phone? You could have just opened the window," said Swope.)

The first installment of Swope's series ran in the *World* on November 4, 1916, a Saturday. The following Tuesday there was a Presidential election. The *World* naturally gave the contest between Wilson, its choice, and Charles Evans Hughes the favored position on its front page—the upper right-hand portion; at the top of the left-hand side it ran a Swope piece that was headlined 9,000,000 HERE ARE READY TO DO HER BIDDING TO MAKE KULTUR RULE WORLD, GERMANY BELIEVES. To many of the ardent pro-Germans in the United States, who were rooting for Hughes as the candidate less likely to take overt action against the Fatherland, this was arrant anti-German propaganda. They were even angrier when, in the text beneath this headline, Swope quoted Ambassador Gerard as replying, to someone who'd said the United States would never fight Germany because there were five hundred thousand Germans in America ready to bear arms against it in such an eventuality, "There may be, but there are five hundred thousand lamp posts in America to string them up on if they ever try it." The German-language press in the United States began to look sourly upon Swope. A newspaper called the *German Herald* said he was "hopelessly wrong in everything he writes in respect to Germany," and one called *Germania* said that "He is merely a conscienceless slanderer against whom German readers of English newspapers should be on their guard." On the other hand, Louis Wiley, the editor of the New York *Times*, thought the series "the most striking journalistic achievement since the outbreak of the war."

On Election Day, Swope, still technically city editor but unwilling even at a time normally so burdensome for editors to stay long at his desk, roamed the town. Shortly after midnight he visited Republican headquarters, at the Hotel Astor, in time to see Charles Evans Hughes, Jr., fling open the door to his father's suite and announce to the reporters waiting outside, "Gentlemen of the press, I present to you the President-elect of the United States!" The Republican candidate was not, of course, alone in thinking he had won. When Swope then went back to his office he found that the *World* had conceded to Hughes. Swope, though, had not. He tried to convince Lincoln, who was getting the next morning's first edition to press, that the outcome was still doubtful, but he managed only to persuade the managing editor to hedge in the punctuation of the banner headline "HUGHES ELECTED IN CLOSE CONTEST?" (It was two more days before the *World* elected Wilson—with an exclamation point.) Swope had been in touch with some of his gambling friends and had heard that although the odds by that late hour were twenty-five to one in Hughes's favor, money was still being laid on Wilson. Why? He did some more checking and learned that one New York brokerage house with a "fast wire" to its San Francisco office had been getting information throughout the night that the returns from northern California were puzzling politicians who had earlier put that state's pivotal electoral votes in the Republican column.

At around three in the morning Swope went to the Hotel Belmont, where the Democrats had their New York headquarters. He marched through the rooms where the hacks and hangers-on were gathered and barged into a sanctum occupied by four of the party's biggest names: Vance McCormick, the Pennsylvania publisher, who was chairman of the Democratic National Committee; Thomas L. Chadbourne, the corporation lawyer; William G. McAdoo, Wilson's son-in-law and subsequently a Senator from California; and Bernard Baruch. "They were in their shirt-sleeves, and a more despondent crew you never saw," Swope later recalled in a letter to Arthur Krock. The four men had reason to be glum. McCormick was still perfunctorily insisting that Wilson would win, but he was also aware that the President had already prepared a message congratulating Hughes.

Swope lit into them. "You fellows are a lot of damn quitters," he shouted. He warned them that—the judicious expenditure of funds then being a not insignificant factor in both getting out the vote and counting up the ballots—they had better have some fiscal operatives move fast into the upper California counties that could evidently decide the race one way or another. ("And how right you were," Krock wrote him later, "in making the point that, if the National Democrats that night completely quit claiming, the local Democrats everywhere would begin trading off what votes they had to the Republicans.") McCormick at once began transmitting never-say-die instructions to the West Coast. It was not then or subsequently claimed by Swope or anyone else that

181

Wilson might not have carried California and retained his office if the *World* man, instead of going to the Belmont, had, say, gone home to bed, but it is possible that Charles Evans Hughes would have been just as happy if Swope had stayed in Europe for another month or so.

Swope's German series kept coming out. Late in November, H. L. Mencken asked for a complete set. He, too, was going to Germany. "I am eager to see your discussion of the facts of America's unfairness toward the Germans," said Mencken, whose jaundiced view of the Allied cause was no secret. "As you say, there is imbecility on both sides, but it seems to me plain that the campaign of lying was started on this side. Surely the Germans in the beginning of the war were eager enough for America's friendship." Mencken asked Swope for some letters of introduction to prominent German officials and urged him to be cautious in phrasing these; he was afraid "our English friends" might intercept them. Swope obliged, but he was finding it hard to please everybody; Mencken hadn't been long in Germany when he was sending back word to the United States that on the basis of *his* observations there Swope's reports on the state of that nation were "cock-tales."

(Not that Mencken, of course, always stuck to unvarnished fact. In 1941, when he was preparing to indite a tract about city editors, he wrote Swope, "You are naturally mentioned. I described how we met at a Y.M.C.A. in Scranton, Pa., and later toured the country together as singing evangelists." Swope knew better than to try to duel on Mencken's level with Mencken's weapons; in replying, he confined himself to a dissertation on the species old-time city editor: ". . . The men of those days were able, as they are now, to control and anticipate the handling of their back yard news better than they could the news that came from a distance. The Circulation Department always would be wanting a juicy murder, in a choice neighborhood where the reporters would not have to strain their imaginations in describing the actors as being Society people.")

There were nineteen long parts in Swope's German series, and they appeared, outside of New York, in the *Post-Dispatch* and six other newspapers. "The Coast papers did not take them," a *World* syndicate man told Swope, late in November. "I understand that out there they hardly know a war is on, so far as the newspapers are concerned." Meanwhile, the Century Company was rushing to bring out the material in book form. With a foreword by Ambassador Gerard, who called it "an important contribution to contemporaneous history," the book came out early in January 1917 bearing the title *Inside the German Empire*.*

The pro-German press had no more use for *Inside the German Empire* than for the articles on which it was based, but in more broad-minded circles the book won, on the whole, a commendable reception. The New York *Times* called it "invaluable," the *Herald* "the very last word in regard to Germany," the *Tribune* "indispensable," the *Morning Telegraph* "most readable," the *Literary Digest* "highly interesting," and the *Outlook* "remarkable and illuminating." O. O. McIntyre said that even though he hadn't read the book "I know that it will prove to be the most accurate and perhaps interesting array of facts about Germany yet published." There were some dissenters. The New York *Globe* thought testily that Swope was wrong in suggesting that Germans were not anxious to make peace and that they hated Americans, and the Los Angeles *Times*, commenting on Swope's assertions that Germans were getting enough to eat, said, "Somebody is a liar. It is either the publicists of the Allies or Herbert Bayard Swope." However little might generally be known on the West Coast about the war, the *Times* believed it knew enough to go along with the publicists. The New York *World*, reviewing "our author," said, "In all the literature of the war, to date, there is nothing just like it."

Inside the German Empire, which Swope dedicated to his mother, appeared only one month before President Wilson broke off relations with Germany.† As soon as the United States declared war, in April, the book's detached point of view was considerably at odds with the national attitude toward Germany—and, when it came to that, with Swope's attitude, for by June 1917 he was

---

* When John Gunther brought out his first "Inside" book, in 1936, he was unaware that Swope or anybody else had ever pre-empted a similar title.

† When he did, Swope had a notice posted in the *World* city room that went, "You are requested to avoid sensationalism in the writing of war stories. Only simple presentations of facts, without embellishments and without conclusions, are wanted. Particular care is to be observed in the investigation and writing of matter bearing upon Germans and German-Americans, so that there shall be no undue inflammation of race feeling. Remember—we are not at war with Germany, and, if we were, remember that decency begets decency, and as we act, so will the Germans."

sweepingly characterizing all the subjects inside the Empire as "those damned Germans."

Just two months after America went to war, Swope's published observations on Germany earned him the first Pulitzer Prize ever awarded for reporting. His citation credited him with "the best example of a reporter's work during the year, the test being strict accuracy, terseness, the accomplishment of some public good commanding public attention and respect." As a trail-blazing Pulitzer Prize winner, Swope took a personal, almost proprietary, interest in all such awards for the remainder of his life, and it was a rare playwright, novelist, cartoonist, editorial writer, photographer, or reporter who, on attaining the honor, did not also get a letter from Swope welcoming him into the fraternity. When Walter Lippmann won a Pulitzer Prize in May 1958, a month before Swope died, Swope wrote him, "I take the Pulitzer Prizes very seriously, so you will know how sincere my congratulations are to you on achieving this proud distinction."

With the cachet of a Pulitzer Prize, *Inside the German Empire* enjoyed a respectable sale in the United States, although the total was less than one-third of the thirty-one thousand figure Swope got into the habit of giving out. There were editions in England and Japan, too. (An Englishman who sat next to Swope at a banquet was asked by the man on his other side if he'd read the book. "No, I haven't, I'm sorry to say," he replied, "for, judging from Mr. Swope's conversation of the last half hour, it must be very comical indeed.") Swope reported to his publishers in June that the Japanese edition was "going enormously well," and he may have had visions of exotic Oriental royalties, but four months later he was informed by a Japanese friend who made inquiries on his behalf that of a total printing there of three hundred copies, only eighty had been sold.

The transmitter of this sobering news was a journalist named Mock Joya, who had been on the staff of the *World* when Swope joined it in 1909. Joya's first name at birth had been Moku. When he came to the United States in 1907 his new American friends called him Mok, and then Mock, and finally he adopted that first name himself. He went back to Japan in 1915 as an Asian correspondent for the *World*, and he later became managing editor, in Tokyo, of the Japan *Times and Mail*, an English-language daily. He was forced off the paper by his government during the Second World War but returned to it afterward—it had by then become the plain *Times*—and during the MacArthur occupation years he wrote a column that explained to American servicemen some of the customs, traditions, and legends of Japan. For many years Joya and Swope carried on an extensive correspondence, and it was characteristic of Swope that now and then, when Joya would tell him of political developments in Asia, Swope would pass along his letters to the Chief of Staff of the United States Army, suggesting that they might help his Intelligence people. During the postwar years, when Joya, like many Japanese, was leading a marginal existence, Swope sent him food and clothing and books and medicine. When Swope died, Joya, who had not seen him for thirty-five years, said, "I have lost my best friend."

One of the most persistent buyers of the American edition of *Inside the German Empire* was Swope himself. He bought more than two hundred copies. He gave the book to John D. Rockefeller, Jr., to Diamond Jim Brady, to Theodore Roosevelt, to Supreme Court Justice Louis Brandeis, to Herbert Hoover, and to Woodrow Wilson, to whom he sent an accompanying note that went, in part, "If [the book] possess merit, it lies in the effort to preserve an actual neutrality in approaching all the facts in issue, and that neutrality had its inspiration and support in the precept and example you set down." He gave the book to Franklin P. Adams and asked for a plug in F.P.A.'s column. "The Conning Tower" duly carried the item, "Read this day *Inside the German Empire* by H. Swope, the pamphleteer, and I found it a book full of interest, yet less interesting than the author himself." Quite some time later Swope was still giving away copies of his book. He gave Leonard Lyons one in 1949, and in 1951, when celebrities were asked for some personal item of theirs to auction off for the Heart Fund, Swope produced a copy in mint condition. In 1953 he gave one to the West German Consul General in New York.

To have hoarded copies for distribution thirty-seven years after publication was not unusual for Swope, who liked to save things. In his study at Sands Point he kept on display until he died some mementos of his wartime trips to Germany—a collection of helmets that he hung on hatracks along one wall. The last part of *Inside the German Empire* was a section called "A reporter's notebook." In consisted of "brief, random notes of scattered facts and fugitive impressions." One note read, "Nothing is permitted to be carried off the battlefields as souvenirs. The debris is carefully sorted over, and every article that German ingenuity can bring into usefulness again is sent back to the Quartermaster's Depot." The Germans had not reckoned on anyone as acquisitive as Swope. One of his favorite battlefield souvenirs—no Quartermaster surely would have begrudged it to him—was a five-card poker hand he picked up in an abandoned dugout also strewn with German and British helmets. It was a relic of warfare that to a man of Swope's predilections must have had an especially warm appeal, for the hand was a ten-high spade flush.

10

___

W HEN THE United States went to war, in April 1917, and
the government began to mobilize its manpower, Swope
was thirty-five and in reasonably good health. Quite apart from
questions of patriotism or conscience, his irrepressible desire to be
involved in consequential events made the idea of getting into
uniform attractive. Moreover, war was the biggest game, for the
highest stakes, yet devised by man, and when there was a big
game going on he wanted to be in it. At the same time there were
his wife, small children, and dependent in-laws to consider, and
there was the *World*, too. The paper's ranks were almost daily
being thinned by the departure of young and single men for
whom no plausible justification for deferment could be found.
Having sent more than fifty men into the armed forces during
the first two months of the war, the *World* hoped Swope would
stick around as long as he could.

Nevertheless, in March 1917, a month before Congress declared war, Swope tried to get a Reserve Army commission in
the Quartermaster Corps. He had references from, among others,
the Mayor of New York City, the Governor of New York, and
the President. Wilson wrote to his Secretary of War, Newton D.
Baker, "I do not know whether you know Herbert Swope personally or not, but he is a very active-minded person and I dare
say might be genuinely useful." (Another time, when Swope was
in Washington, Wilson told Baruch that Swope had the quickest
mind in the capital.) Swope hoped that on being commissioned
and called to active duty he'd be assigned to the Army War College, in Washington, in Intelligence. The commandant, Brigadier

General Joseph E. Kuhn, was an old friend; as a colonel, he had been Ambassador Gerard's military attaché in Berlin, and in 1916, when the Germans refused to let Kuhn join other neutral nations' military representatives in an inspection of the front, Swope had generously shared *his* observations with Kuhn. When there proved to be no room in the Quartermaster Corps for any more reserve officers, General Kuhn thought he might be able to get Swope commissioned in the Cavalry and told him to "get out your riding breeches and practice a bit." But before Swope could act on this advice (as far as horsemanship and its accouterments were concerned, he'd have had to start from scratch), that plan fell through, too.

While trying unsuccessfully to become an Army officer, Swope continued working for the *World*, which sent him to Washington in November 1917 on an undercover mission. The paper had been consistently loyal to President Wilson. All across the country, however, voices were saying ever more shrilly that the Administration was derelict in its prosecution of the war. A high official of the United States Chamber of Commerce, indeed, had flatly asserted that the war was already lost. Swope's assignment was to nose around Washington and ascertain just how things *were* going. His superiors had authorized him, if he saw fit, "to blow the Administration out of the water"; and because the *World* realized that an attack on Wilson coming from a traditionally friendly source would have wide impact, it had lined up several other newspapers to run Swope's findings, which his editors assumed would be explosive and splashy.

One of the men Swope most wanted to talk to in Washington was Baruch, who before the outbreak of war had been a member of the Advisory Commission of the Council of National Defense and was now handling war materials for the War Industries Board. Swope and Baruch had met, of course. There had been the early-morning session at the Hotel Belmont the year before, when Wilson squeaked past Hughes, and back in 1910, not long after Swope had joined the *World*, the paper had assigned him to try to get a statement from Baruch on some Wall Street development toward which the Pulitzer paper was taking its habitual churlish view. Swope tracked Baruch to the bar of the old Waldorf-Astoria, where the Empire State Building later rose, accosted him as he emerged, and put a question or two to him. Baruch declined to answer, and it may have been significant, in the light of the relationship that was subsequently to grow between them, that Swope did not try to bully him into a reply.

Swope must have felt that he had made little impression on Baruch at any of these brief early meetings. For at the end of 1917, as he set forth to probe Washington, he bore several letters of introduction to him. In soliciting one of them, from Dr. John H. Finley, then Commissioner of Education of New York State and later the editor of the New York *Times*, Swope explained, "While I know Baruch, my acquaintance with him is so slight that I believe your sponsorship would help greatly to put me on that basis of understanding and of an approach to intimacy that is essential if he is to help me and I to help him." Even before Swope knew Baruch, then, he sensed that a close association between them might be mutually assistive.

For nearly two months Swope reconnoitered Washington. He talked to Wilson's private secretary, Joseph P. Tumulty, to Cabinet members, to Senators and Congressmen, to members of the Diplomatic Corps, and, naturally, to Baruch. Baruch never got over his amazement at an interview he granted Swope on the production of French .75-millimeter artillery shells. Baruch was supposed to be the expert and to answer questions. Instead, he found himself listening to a lecture by Swope on the subject. On January 23, 1918, Swope sent a lengthy memorandum to Ralph Pulitzer, which Swope specified was not for publication. (The memorandum was marked "Confidential," but he gave a copy to the President's chief adviser, Colonel Edward M. House. Swope had met House in December 1916, obtaining an introduction from Henry Morgenthau, the American Ambassador to Turkey. "I regard an acquaintance with him," Swope told Morgenthau, "apart from the pleasure it affords, as essential to a complete newspaper equipment.") Pulitzer must have been surprised at Swope's report, for it was almost entirely the opposite of what he had been expected to produce. What he had to say was as revealing about his approach to such an assignment as it was about the state of the nation:

> The President asked me to come to see him yesterday. Tumulty called me up in the morning to find out if I could come. I was with him almost an hour. It was most enlightening. He told me that he had known from the first day what my purpose was in Washington and that he had told Tumulty to keep away from me so that I might be able to form unbiased conclusions. He added that he was quite

189

willing to have the administration's war conduct judged by a man in whose "honesty, ability and vision" (the quotes are his) he had such faith. That he had asked me to come only because he had heard directly that I had reached a verdict that things were, after all, pretty fair and that there was more room for praise than for censure. He said he valued this in coming from me more than he would from another and less independent source and (if he ever does that sort of thing) gave me a little more taffy. I was pleased, for he is not the kind that praises loosely. He must have been told my position by Tumulty, Baruch, McAdoo, Lane, and some of the others with whom I have been speaking recently in checking up certain of my conclusions. [The name of Baruch here was apparently an afterthought; it was written in ink after the original version had been typed.] I told him that the report he had received was correct and he answered that he would have been as willing, though not so glad, for me to have reached the opposite opinion, had I thought conditions justified it. He added that he hoped I would not hesitate to tell him where I found error.

Please bear in mind that he did not see me or use any influence upon me until after he had heard that I had reached a judgment. I liked that. It was no effort on his part to sway me, for my decision had already been formulated. Had I been censorious I should have availed myself of the opportunity to say all that I had found to criticize.

I tell you that I believe that no other man could have done the things he has done in this war; he lacks a certain faculty of making his results apparent—he is not a good Press Agent for himself because he talks best about abstract things, but the more closely I study the situation here, the more certain I am the Nation's program has achieved a record outmeasuring all the other belligerents, and most of that program has been due to him. We have done all that should be done; some things, perhaps, could have been done better but we have profited by the experience and THERE HAS NOT BEEN ONE SINGLE ERROR THAT HAS BEEN REPEATED. That is the index of efficiency and execution.

He talked frankly of his aims, his plans, and his purposes and not once did he seek to preach the counsel of perfection. He even particularized as to certain shortcomings which is MORE than any of the administration's critics have done. He answered freely all the questions I had to ask him and even directed me along the lines of the weaker parts of the program. He explained his opposition to a Planning Body by explaining that the Supreme War Council now sitting in Versailles where General Bliss had returned, is laying out the main theme of action, and the detail planning was being done by the several departments. We are, after all, a participant in a war that is, at this time, dominated by our "associates" and we must follow the lines they indicate. There is more of this that I will tell you later.

Since I have been in Washington I have seen everyone, almost, whose mind is worth having. I have talked intimately, and many times, in their offices or their homes to Baker, Daniels, Lane, Polk, Creel, Houston, Gregory, Simmons, Crowder, Biddle, Squier, Brandeis, Baruch, Hoover, Garfield, Hurley, Colby, McCormick and Chadbourne (of the War Trade Board), Tardieu, Jusserand, Da Gama (Brazil—a very intelligent man) and others who may be said to possess an understanding of what the administration is doing and how it is doing it.

For the opposition I have spoken to Harvey, Chamberlain, Lodge, Wadsworth, Harding, Davison, Child, Garrett, and a whole slough of "big business" men who are opposed to what Wilson stands for.

I made it a point to seek every bit of opinion that would help me to form a judgment to be taken IN CONJUNCTION WITH MY OWN OBSERVATIONS, BASED ON MY FIRST-HAND INVESTIGATIONS AND THE INFORMATION I GATHERED. I used practically the same methods I employed in Germany. I put myself in the position of a seeker for the truth who had no pre-commitments and had no advanced judgments. So my mental processes were free from any warp, except that, perhaps, which I got from friends in New York who unconsciously sought to influence me adversely to the administration. My conclusions, from a newspaper standpoint, are to be regretted, since obviously there is more "news" in censure than in praise. So even my professional instincts were aligned against the final decision I reached.

I am firm in my own mind that today the two big things to consider are, first, if public confidence is deserved by Wilson; and, second, if it be, to prevent it from being undermined by honest error in criticism or by insidious political chicanery, such as Penrose and some of his ilk are using.

I am certain that the conduct of the war has been GOOD; that it is not perfection but that it has come as near 100% efficiency as reasonably could be expected; that it has been marked by a spirit of nationalism and democracy which makes it noteworthy; that it has been astonishingly free from graft and corruption, in sharp contradiction to the Spanish War and to the preparations of France and Britain, both of which countries have many instances of graft.

That while the President may not have been as quick to accept outside suggestions as his critics have wished, that this has been due to the fact that he felt he alone was responsible for success or failure, so he chose to select his own methods of procedure. That in one form or another, most of these suggestions have been incorporated in the war program in different ways.

That Wilson has played a far larger part than anyone has suspected in the details of the program though in a quiet way. That these things are getting better each day—not worse—AND THAT WE HAVE OUTSTRIPPED THE PROGRAM T. R. HIMSELF OUTLINED AS A MAXIMUM AT THE BEGINNING OF LAST AUGUST. More of this later; I have it in black and white.

The opposition, including the honest element, has dwelt emphatically upon isolated instances that do not reach below the surface; that are not truly characteristic. The matter of guns is a case in point. There was a supply that was noteworthy *not* because of its poverty but because of *its* abundance. How many of the administration's critics know that the ordnance program calls for something like three billion dollars worth of steel of a sort that was never before produced in this country beyond nine hundred million dollars in value. There had to be vast industrial expansion to allow for the increased demand, and no man familiar at all with business can expect the development can be done overnight or overyear. There is labor to be thought of; construction work to be considered; special machinery to be built, and all the while the pressure upon our whole industrial fabric has been increasingly great as the program of the Air Board, the Navy, the Shipping Board, the Allies' Supplies and other agencies got under way.

And as regards clothing; the outfitting was done on a scale of supply for four million five hundred thousand to seven million individuals. This was because of the need of having an immediate reserve supply of such things as uniform breeches and coats, and changes of underwear. Also, because of the great variation in sizes. The whole wool industry in the country had never before even approached an output sufficient to supply a fraction of the need. And the whole manufacturing industry of the country had never before been able to produce anything like the figures required. Every unit of industry was employed in which the prices were within reason. (This qualification explains probably why certain of the better-class New York plants were not used.) By conversion of purpose, plants making non-essentials were employed to make the needed materials. This is true all through the list. Production was stimulated after a classification of needs and ability had been made. One illustration along this line will be enlightening: How many have ever heard of manganese ore? Yet it was realized that the needs of ourselves and our Allies would in another two years over-tax the mines where it is found. So prospectors were encouraged to find new ones and arrangements made to expand the ones now being worked. There has been such provision that there is today *no real lack of any essential that is not being supplied, sometimes slowly, but, nevertheless, being supplied.*

And what about the biggest thing of all—conscription? Look at our own history and the record of the many draft riots and fights against the Navy Press gangs. Look at the bitter battle they had in Britain and in Canada over conscription. Look at the defeat of the measure in Australia. We did it in such a way as to astound the students of politics. When Britain accepted conscription Germany was aghast but her leaders felt certain that America, as they told me, would not dare make the essay because of our loosely knit form of government and because of the lack of popularity of the war (for it is unpopular—largely because of its lack of nearness and the consequent inability of the people to visualize the causes that made our entrance inevitable).

Yet we did the thing in such a way as to make the transition—perhaps the most significant in our history—stand out as our proudest accomplishment. Do you believe—can anyone believe—that if this had not been done with superb skill; with supreme wisdom; with rare delicacy; with an all pervasive knowledge of the hearts and minds of our people, that it could have been done at all? What would Roosevelt have done? He would have, perhaps, forced it upon the nation with a Big Stick. I have no doubt that the Republican philosophy would have caused a Republican administration to have brought about the result by the use of rifles and bayonets. *But Wilson did it differently. He did not do it; he had the people do it.* The government did not conscribe the Army; the people themselves selected those who were to serve and, through their own agents, sent them to the government to be trained. In the history of the world has ever an army been more truly democratic or chosen with a greater freedom from the hated element of Force?

There is another phase of the situation that should not be permitted to be put into the background of the picture by the opponents of the administration. That deals with the spiritual side of the war. When in the story of America has it held such a place of leadership, even among our enemies as it does today? When have we possessed the spiritual insight into world problems as now animate our international relationships? When was America looked to as other than the home of the dollar and the dollar chaser? It is a part of this war that Wilson enunciated the doctrine, which will in after years bear his name, that this nation shall never seek territory by conquest or aggression. Measure that with the "I took Panama" of T. R.

While this war was forced upon us by those who still preach and believe in the philosophy of force; by those who live in the past and regard the archaic methods of by-gone years as being the only ones calculated to bring them that power they mistakenly regard as a virtue, and though we have been compelled to defend ourselves and our rights with arms, we still have kept burning the light of the day—which is world peace and world freedom. We fight for those things alone. We do not fight to punish, or to revenge ourselves; not to gain money or land; not to advance our commercial prospects. We fight for nothing that can be measured by a physical standard except the right to live in peace and to help all nations equally to gain that right.

How is it possible to make a survey of the American war program without considering the ethical side of the problem? And if one does, would a single change be made in our adventure? It has been said that Germany is winning the war. She will never WIN it, even though her armies march down the streets of Paris, London and Washington simultaneously, for America has called into life those forces that not all the cannons in the world can kill; those elements of Justice, of Right and of Liberty that no conqueror can long hold prisoner. Sooner or later they will rise and overwhelm the part of the German spirit which still worships the gospel of might. This war will go far toward ever stilling that creed, and the greater part of the victory—if it comes now or if it be deferred—will belong to us, and to us because of the vision of the President.

But we shall not lose the war, even in a physical sense, and nowhere is this realized more clearly than in Germany. In that country the fear is greater over our political offensive than over our military might. Slowly but surely the whole fabric of the empire is being permeated by the spirit of unrest; of doubt; of a feeling that it is better to be at peace and happy than to be at war and powerful. This sentiment is spreading, and we are its protagonists through Wilson. And if it does not grow fast enough and the question finally resolves itself into one of force, stripped of all other considerations, *we shall win*, then too, because Germany cannot finally conquer (the most pessimistic admit this as axiomatic) and if the outcome be delayed the delay makes our victory the more certain, for Time fights with us and as our man-power increases Germany's slowly wastes away. We are ready now, and adding to our readiness each day, to make the decision by arms. And that brings me back to my point of departure—our war conduct.

As I see it, we have done well in every single phase of the task that we have undertaken. Therefore if my conclusion be correct (returning to the two main themes laid out for discussion) it is our duty Not to add to the volume of misinformed and often vicious criticism but to change it; not to stifle it, but to make its injustice and baselessness apparent. Expressing this in positive terms, I think we should seek to prevent the undermining of public confidence by all the means in our power. We are winning the war and nothing should be done to interfere with that end. The surest way of blocking it would be to permit the disaffection of public opinion, the

194

support of which is deserved (even to a far greater extent than it now gets), by the administration for the way the war is being conducted.

This is a hasty outline of my thoughts on the subject. I have not tried to set down the detailed processes by which I reached these conclusions; I have tried only to put in words the reactions of a fairly well-trained and accurately observing mind. I have not been, and I am not now, a fanatic either in support of or in opposition to the administration. I could not be either without doing injustice to myself as well as to it. And I cannot find ground for condemnation without doing greater injustice and injury to the country which needs to be guarded today against all tendency to lose faith where faith is so richly deserved, and where it is essential to success.

If I have written in solemn strain it is because one cannot be near this thing without feeling solemnly. I am *not yet sure* that, if criticism is not justified or wise, praise is the best thing to give. That might have a tendency to react unfavorably. Also, it might tend to overconfidence on the part of the public and the officials.

The real nature of our participation soon will be revealed more surely than any laudatory articles could bring about, and besides a certain amount of criticism is a healthful stimulus which should not be checked. But there are certain aspects of the situation that can be reduced to terms of easy understanding and, if it were thought wise, at this time, they could be made the subject of an expository series. But that must be talked about further; the time may not be right; it might look like special pleading and that must be avoided for no such necessity exists and it would be a mistake to give, however innocently, that impression.

By the start of 1918, Swope was finding Washington a more exciting base of operations than New York. The nation's capital, to the delight of the journalists who were permanently stationed there or who, like Swope, drifted in and out more or less at their own pleasure, swarmed with the quaint and colorful characters who flare up and sputter out so often on the periphery of warfare—inventors, expeditors, red-tape cutters, red-tape manufacturers, lobbyists, evangelists, spies and counterspies, and the sole repositories of the secrets of secret weapons. Early in 1918 the nation's attention was briefly focused on the odd activities of the sculptor Gutzon Borglum, who was later to blast and chisel away much of the face of Mount Rushmore, in South Dakota, and to substitute Presidential faces. Woodrow Wilson (who never made the mountain) had a high opinion of Borglum; for one thing, the artist had fashioned some gargoyles that adorned a dormitory Wilson's class at Princeton had donated to the university.

Borglum, a pilot and aviation enthusiast who thought of himself as a latter-day Da Vinci, was disturbed by a rising clamor for a Congressional investigation of aircraft production, which was alleged—Swope's views notwithstanding—to be hospitable to graft and inefficiency. The sculptor wrote Wilson proposing that to head off Congress the President deputize him to make a one-man investigation. Wilson gave the project his blessing. The report that Borglum submitted to him in February, supposedly a confidential one, was a blistering indictment of, among others, the Army's Chief Signal Officer, who had charge of military aviation.

Swope persuaded Wilson to let him have a look at what Borglum had come up with, and on March 21 and 22 the *World* printed a good part of his findings, appending the disclaimer, "The *World* prints it with no attestation to its accuracy, but solely with the view of permitting the public to be informed of conditions regarded as sufficiently serious to justify investigation. By full publicity it is certain that the impression will be gained that there is nothing to conceal. If good, the public should know it; if bad, the right to that knowledge is equal." (This didn't seem to jibe with what Swope had told Pulitzer in his lengthy confidential memorandum, but in journalism principles often succumb to the charms of exclusivity.) The Borglum hubbub soon died down, but not before the New York *Tribune* had run a stinging editorial denouncing the *World* for having used the story and the President for having made this possible. And the magazine *Air Travel* had in a more flippant vein observed that "The sculptor suffered the rare privilege of having Mr. Swope carve his report."

At the time the *World* was exposing Borglum's assault upon the Signal Corps, Swope was being tendered a public-relations-officer's berth by the Army Ordnance Department, which may have felt that a Swope in hand was worth two on the loose. But after flirting with this further chance of being commissioned, Swope spurned it—acting, he informed Ordnance, on the advice of Colonel House, whose advice had a manifestly high rating, since it was what the President himself often sought and got. By mid-1918 Swope was pretty much reconciled to spending the entire war on the *World*. This pleased the newspaper. In one promotional advertisement about its coverage of current events it proclaimed, "The *World* is publishing the most important dispatches coming out of Washington. With unequaled sources of information Herbert Bayard Swope is regularly giving the *World's* readers the best presentation of the developments of the war in the National Capital. Mr. Swope is an international authority and the value of his work is not approached by that of any other writer in Washington."

Having—at least for the time being—made up his mind, Swope suggested to his managing editor that maybe the *World* should handle his Washington dispatches differently. He thought he should be displayed as a commentator rather than as a straight reporter, under a departmental heading like "Washington Day by Day" or "News and Views of Washington." "Such a method would prevent that constant straining-after-news effect in the headlines that so often works disastrously," Swope told Lincoln. He had a point, for it must have been a struggle for *World* desk men to come up with headlines for no-news Swope stories like one from Washington on March 7, 1918, the whole first paragraph of which went:

> There should be no misunderstanding regarding the situation existing today between the United States and Japan over the latter's proposition to send armed forces into Siberia. If the public is puzzled, it is due less to the complications of the problem than to the fact that the Administration, contrary to its usual method, has not made clear its position. Whatever doubt has arisen has been due to the absence of any public statement by the President; and with him silent there is no one in Washington to speak for him.*

Every year the *World* employees had a banquet, and for their amusement put out their waggish intramural paper the *Overset*. One of these appeared two weeks after Swope's excursion into Siberia, and it featured a spoof of this kind of Swope story:

'NO NEWS' BIG NEWS FROM GREAT SCRIBE
Bertie Untired Hope Holds Overset
Readers Breathless Until He Solves
Vast Problems of State.

---

* The headline put over that was
TOKIO IS EXPECTED
TO GIVE GUARANTEE
ON ITS INTENTIONS

FORTHRIGHT SENSATIONS ASSURED FOR TO–MORROW.

Uncensored Story Reveals How Government Rests Pending Writer's Advice.

The Overset herewith publishes an article of international signifi-cance from its Washington correspondent, and, as requested by him, not a word has been deleted by the news censor.

By Bertie Untired Hope.

WASHINGTON, March 23.—It can be stated on the very highest au-thority that there is no news in Washington to-night—for two highly important reasons.

(Note to editor: Do not cut a word out of my story to-night, as it bears deep significance; the wanton emasculation this morning was, I may say, exceedingly painful.)

Not to reiterate, but to emphasize the enormity of the international situation as it exists at present, the correspondent of *The Overset* is privileged to announce on the very highest authority, as stated pre-viously, that there is no news in Washington to-night.

(Note to editor: Full face part of foregoing sentence, beginning with "emphasize" and ending with "to-night.")

There should be no misunderstanding of the irrefragable conditions with which the Administration is confronted, nor any misapprehen-sion as to the two highly important reasons for the lack of news from the National Capital to-night.

The whole matter can be boiled down to this manifestly simple statement:

(Note to editor: Indent the following two paragraphs.)

First—The correspondent of *The Overset* has not had opportunity properly to adjudicate certain weighty problems of state that were propounded to him to-day by high Governmental officials.

Second—Pending such decisions the affairs of the Government natu-rally are held in abeyance. Therefore there is no news, and conse-quently nothing about which to write. . . .

A couple of days after that parody appeared, Swope was en-gaging, on a more serious level, in the kind of jockeying for position that often marked, and sometimes marred, his relations with his managing editor. Swope wired Lincoln from Washing-ton, "I'M SENDING ABOUT TWELVE HUNDRED [words] ON INNER MEANING OF GERMAN DRIVE SO FAR AS ITS EFFECT UPON AMERICA IS CONCERNED. IT'S WRITTEN BY REQUEST AND IMPORTANCE IS ATTACHED TO HAVING IT PUT OUT."

So unfailingly did Swope profess to be in touch with the White

House that his editors may occasionally have wondered whether the President of the United States had time for anyone but him. In this instance, at any rate, Lincoln wired back, "AT WHOSE RE-QUEST IS 'INNER MEANING OF GERMAN DRIVE' PUT OUT?"

Swope replied, "I AM SURPRISED AT YOUR QUESTION, BUT THE STORY WAS THE OUTCOME OF MY TALK WITH THE SECRETARY OF WAR AND THE STATE DEPARTMENT."

To this Lincoln retorted, "WHY BE SURPRISED AT SUCH A QUES-TION? I'M MUCH INTERESTED IN KNOWING WHERE STUFF COMES FROM. NATURALLY."

Naturally, Swope liked to have the last word. And the last words that are known to have been transmitted in this particular exchange were in a letter of his: "I'll tell you why I am surprised at your query: I regarded both the substance and the tone as unpleasant. I consider my news judgment as being sufficiently good to have it accepted without question. If you are pleased to override it, that's your affair, but I do not intend to be questioned as a cub reporter would be. I know as well as you or anyone else what ought and what ought not be printed, and I will not acqui-esce in any attitude of toleration or patronage on your part. The time for that sort of thing has passed."

But for all the skepticism, and even antagonism, that Swope aroused, he did occupy a good many of the President's wartime hours. Sometimes before filing a story Swope would ask Wilson to go over it, and the President would take out a word or two, like a college professor helping an especially gifted student with a term paper.*

Swope favored the White House with memoranda he had no particular thought of publishing—outlines for, say, a program governing postwar labor relations, or for establishing a single executive agency to oversee the operations of all others—and usually Wilson replied to him at once and at length, often closing with some phrase like "Don't you agree?" or "Don't you think

---

* In another dispatch about Siberia, Swope had written, ". . . America's non-assent to the suggestion of Japanese intervention in Siberia checked the original plan. . . . Nothing is to be done along that line until there is actual military necessity for the step, in which case America will give her consent." Wilson asked Swope to delete "in which case America will give her con-sent," explaining, ". . . I should like to leave that idea out, in view of the many impressions which are beginning to cluster around this extremely difficult and delicate subject."

there is something in that?" To Swope's proposal of the over-all agency ("If it did nothing more the Bureau would almost justify itself by relieving you of the outpourings of the thousands of well-meaning saviors of the Nation who daily take their pens in hand to instruct you on how to win the war, in which dread group I hope you will not include your very sincere . . ."), Wilson replied, the very day he got Swope's communication, ". . . I am afraid that you do not realize what irritation and, perhaps I might say, even resentment would be created if I were to institute a process of constant inquiry into the efficiency with which the innumerable jobs of the Government were being carried through. Inasmuch as I deal with sensibilities every day, I know how much, as a rule, they play in efficiency itself, and I do not think it would be wise to risk ruffling them all the time. Besides, it would mean a very big piece of machinery indeed and one which would attract a great deal of public attention to keep such inquiries up to date with regard to the whole range of our present work. Don't you think so?"

Late in the winter of 1918 Wilson decided to give the War Industries Board broader powers than it had previously had and to put Baruch in charge of the strengthened agency. Swope, learning well ahead of the official announcement that Baruch was to get the post, wrote him a note of congratulations, to which Baruch replied, prophetically, "I have often heard repeated your many pleasing and flattering remarks regarding me, and might I be so bold as to say that I think you are prejudiced, as I think you and I understood each other and became friends as soon as we met. I trust that the future will help to ripen our meeting into a lasting friendship." Three days later Baruch's appointment was made public, and in writing about it for the *World*, Swope said, "That he possesses the President's confidence to a marked degree has been known for some time; that he deserves it is now generally admitted even by those who opposed him."

Swope liked to write nice things about important acquaintances. A month later, when Charles M. Schwab was made Director General of the Emergency Fleet Corporation, Swope described him as a "genius," and the story was so glowing, all in all, that it evoked immediate warm thanks from Schwab, who was quoted by the *World* the following day (Swope's byline was modestly omitted) as saying, "First of all, I want to express my delight over the story in the *World* this morning telling of my appointment.

It was written in that spirit that I want injected into every ship that is built. There must be a spirit of encouragement and praise and not one of faultfinding."

While Swope thought that the Administration had enough to do, by and large, without having to be constantly fending off the thrusts of carping critics, when *he* felt disenchanted with the progress of the war, that was something else again. He was particularly upset by the suppressive attitude of Secretary of War Newton D. Baker toward disclosing military information. It is customary during wars, of course, for the military to favor exclusion of news and the press to favor inclusion. Swope believed that Baker, and the generals on various echelons of command beneath him, were excessive in their restraint. While the civilian population back home was being urged to make sacrifices because of what the boys were doing in the trenches, there was very little appearing in print about just what any individual boys—or even whole regiments—*were* doing. One day, learning privately that the five hundred thousandth American soldier was about to embark for Europe, Swope stormed into the Secretary's office and begged him to make an occasion of this statistical event. He wanted gongs struck and fireworks launched. "We have got to sell this war to the people," he told Baker. But it was hard to sell that idea to the Army. Years afterward, a senior officer, Major General Johnson Hagood, would write Swope, "I think that the military and naval censorship during the World War was one of the greatest among the many great mistakes we made. It caused no embarrassment whatsoever to the enemy but very great embarrassment to ourselves and resulted in irreparable damage to American prestige in one of the greatest undertakings of all time. . . . News must be built around human interest. The Marines realized this but the Army fed the public on dregs."

On April 24, 1918, when the United States had been at war for more than a year, Swope was urging Baker to bring fifty soldiers who had seen action back to the United States, to push the sales of Liberty bonds. This proposal, Baker wrote Swope two weeks later, had "led to a thorough discussion on the whole subject of publicity with General [Peyton] March [the Chief of Staff], and he and I are now in cable communication with General Pershing to get more advantage from the exploits from our American soldiers than we have heretofore taken. I thank you very much for the suggestion." He was to end up further in Swope's debt.

That June, when the Secretary addressed the graduating class at West Point, he based his speech on some notes furnished him by Swope. The Secretary of the Navy, Josephus Daniels, not wishing to have the Army get any edge on him, promptly asked Swope for some help on a commencement address *he* was concurrently giving to the graduates of Annapolis.

Active though Swope was on the Cabinet level, he did not confine himself to that stratum. In June, for instance, writing about an abortive scheme the President had to station three high-ranking officials in Europe—one representing Wilson, one the Army, and one the Navy—Swope dwelt at flattering length on the man who was slated to go abroad for Daniels, Assistant Secretary of the Navy Franklin Roosevelt. The next day Roosevelt wrote, "Dear Swope: When my office staff read the New York *World* this morning, they remarked unanimously, 'Swope can come again. We will be glad to see him.' Ditto."

By the spring of 1918, more and more of Swope's contemporaries had joined the armed forces, and his own comparatively comfortable course had him worried. Furthermore, because of some of the things he had written following his two trips to Germany, gossip had it that he was pro-German. He voiced his qualms in reflective notes to himself: "I feel myself a slacker—can't stand it. . . . Feel myself trifling when such big things are going on. . . . It will mean much in years to come. . . . My patriotism has been aspersed—must go to vindicate it. . . . Am unhappy—everyone going—I'm only slacker—affects my work. . . . I've learned what others think—want to really *do* something. . . . It's way I'm built. . . . Other concerns have given up their men—ten years of service entitles me to something. . . . R.P. [Ralph Pulitzer]—what does he want? . . . Will he agree to my going? . . . Little left for me to do. . . . Things will work themselves out. . . . I'm slacker and disaffected. . . . Hurts me, my work, and paper. . . . Will come back refreshed."

Swope even thought he might enlist. When he confided this intention to Florence White, the *World*'s business manager wrote him sternly:

. . . What your children will think of you, is what the children of every other man so placed by the law and natural responsibilities will think of them.

As to any reflection on your loyalty for any broad-minded ex-

pression or analysis of situations of a year ago—that is preposterous. . . .

You, a highly intelligent young man, represent the fountainhead,
the most independent guidepost in the United States—the *World*—
to erect which, over one hundred million dollars has been used in
thirty years. Is this not opportunity enough to satisfy any man's
conscience on doing his duty? Can you name a successor there, in
whom you would have as great confidence as you have in your own
ability and inspiration? I cannot. . . .

Before Swope could get around to do anything about enlisting,
both the Army and Navy came along with new offers of a commission. The Navy's idea—that he become a lieutenant commander and put his knowledge of Germany at the disposal of its
Intelligence branch—seemed the more attractive. Although he
changed his mind before he could be sworn in, he came close
enough to being in the Navy to feel justified in telling an admiral
subsequently, "I was a bit of a webfoot in the last war." In the
long run, actually, the Army outmaneuvered the Navy. Swope
never saw a day's active duty in either service, but for a while
between the two world wars he was in the Army Reserve, as an
Intelligence officer.

Swope was vastly impressed with what Baruch was doing in
Washington. On June 9, writing a speculative piece for the
World about a new notion that was circulating in Washington—
Swope attributed it to the Secretary of Agriculture, David Houston, but it may have been his own—he started off, "And now for
a Supreme Economic Dictator for the Allies and America!"
Swope's candidate was Baruch, whose "name is frequently mentioned as the one for the job should it be created." That particular
job never was created, but just as Swope was on the point of
becoming a webfoot, Baruch suggested that he come over to the
War Industries Board. Unable to make up his mind which way to
turn, Swope again besought the President's advice. "I value your
personal interest in me too highly to jeopardize it by too often
intruding my affairs upon your notice," he wrote Wilson, "but I
feel the need of the guidance which I never failed to obtain from
you, and that need is my justification for this note. . . . Will
you, out of your friendship for me, indicate along which path my
duty lies? Sometimes impulse obscures judgment. Your clarity of
vision will enable me to see more clearly." Wilson urged him to
forget the Navy and go with Baruch, and on August 19, with

relief at having the decision made for him by the Commander-in-Chief, Swope wrote Joseph Pulitzer, Jr., "I have the satisfaction of knowing that this is the thing the President regards as a duty." Three days later Swope's appointment to the W.I.B. was announced, and he scrawled himself a note about Baruch: "Going with him because of him and his work and future possibilities—putting my eggs in his basket." It was as accurate a long-range prediction as Swope was ever to make.

Bernard Baruch had a knack of attracting to him and retaining the loyalty of able and colorful men, for he himself was a fascinating figure, as stimulating to the imagination as he was arresting to the eye—with his huge, spare, erect frame, his sharp, patrician features, and, even back in the First World War days, when he was in his late forties, the thatch of snowy hair that crowned him with the splendor of a glacial alp. Baruch was always close to the sources of real national power, and occasionally—though as a rule he preferred the nonresponsible role of adviser to the responsible one of decision-maker—he himself exercised great power. Whatever he did he did with the poise and dash and skill that had earlier characterized his subjugation of the stock market. (It was Swope who, when Woodrow Wilson had some reservations about Baruch because Baruch made no bones about his being a speculator, had reassured the President by pointing out that this should be no drawback; Baruch had been a *successful* speculator.)

At the War Industries Board, Baruch corraled his customary stable of expert assistants. There was the florid, erratic, but brilliant general, Hugh S. Johnson, who functioned for some years as a sort of personal aide-de-camp to Baruch. There was the ever-faithful, staid, methodical investment banker, John M. Hancock, who, if service stripes had been issued for fealty to Baruch, would by the time he died, in 1956, have earned an armful. There was Alex Legge, the onetime cowboy with such an affinity for mechanization that he had become the head of International Harvester, and another big industrialist who had come a long way up the corporate ladder, J. Leonard Replogle, the steel man. There was Eugene Meyer, who was to become publisher of the Washington *Post*. There was Albert C. Ritchie, later the Governor of Maryland, who in 1932 might have taken the Democratic nomination for President away from Franklin Roosevelt but for the handicap of a divorce. And there were three men whom Baruch liked to call his "flying executives"—the investment banker Clarence Dillon, the utilities man Harrison Williams, and Swope. These were men who could size up situations rapidly and make judgments unhesitatingly. After one conference, for instance, a manufacturer who had never before met Swope said to a man on the W.I.B. staff, "What kind of a fellow is this—who can walk into a meeting on how to make bricks cheap or cut down on the size of nails, and grasp things so quickly?"

Swope was designated an associate member of the W.I.B. and assistant to the chairman, and he moved with full force into the Board's offices, in one of those ramshackle buildings—this one on the bank of the Potomac River—that proliferate in Washington during wars. Baruch had only one room; Swope began with two rooms and spread out into three. Baruch's job was by the very nature of it unpopular. Nobody, whether a consumer or manufacturer, likes to be told how much he can or can't have of what he thinks he needs, and it was Baruch's obligation to make more raw materials available for defense purposes by persuading nonessential users of them to get by with less. Swope's main function was to explain to the public what Baruch was doing—to help sweeten, as it were, the bitter pills that Baruch had to dispense. By Baruch's fiat, nobody else at the W.I.B. could issue any statement about the Board until it had cleared through Swope. After the war, while the two men were together once, somebody began extolling Baruch and the W.I.B. Swope said to Baruch, "Were we *that* good?" "Sssh, they'll hear you," said Baruch.

Typical of the chores that Swope did for Baruch was one handed to him shortly after he began working on the Board. Baruch had had a request from Mayor John F. Hylan of New York City. Hylan wanted some building materials made available so he could construct schools. A Democratic administration is loath to affront the mayor of the largest Democratic bailiwick in the country, especially when he appeals in the name of children. Baruch, however, felt that he couldn't authorize the new construction and delegated to Swope the job of formulating a polite but firm rejection, which could serve as a precedent if similar requests came in from other cities. "Out of New York's needs for school buildings," Swope's first draft for Baruch's signature began, "which you have set forth graphically in your letter to me dated September 6th, there flows a condition that is nation-wide and has its final reflex on the very edges of that no man's land which is being changed, in blood and glory, to the frontier of freedom." Before the letter went out, though, Swope had pruned his prose and had come up with a succinct "civilian order of the day: He serves best who saves most." On his own copy of the final draft Swope later scribbled, "The President called this a 'great' letter." *

Baruch was often called to the White House, and sometimes Swope went with him. One day the President told them about a book he'd been reading; its thesis was that all human beings were reincarnations of animals. The three men got to speculating about various acquaintances. Wilson said William G. McAdoo reminded him of a tiger and Colonel House of a fox. "Turning to Baruch," Swope later recounted, "he said he was at a loss to find his proto- type, especially when Baruch was in deep thought, or in disagree- ment with the one he was listening to, when he had the habit of scrunching down in his chair and piercing his companion through with a look. I said that at the War Industries Board we said that when Baruch assumed that attitude he was like a snake in the grass (in the pleasanter sense), ready to strike at the first sign of weakness. Then I added that this was not especially true; that I thought Baruch's real prototype was the elephant—the Asiatic ele- phant, which has five toes, as against his African brother, which has only three, it being agreed that Baruch would have all the toes that nature permitted. The Baruch elephant, representing the embodiment of all animal wisdom, would be walking along a nar- row path and come to a deep river, across which was thrown a flimsy bamboo bridge. First the elephant would try it with his trunk; then with his right foreleg; then with his left foreleg and, backing up to it, repeat the process with both hind legs. Having completed his inspection, the elephant, turning to his followers, would announce: 'This bridge is perfectly safe and will carry my weight—but I guess I'll let some other sucker cross first!'"

Baruch loved Swope's elephant story. Until 1938, by which time the chairman of the W.I.B. had outlived many of his under- lings there, Baruch periodically gave reunion parties for his war- time staff. Swope was always the master of ceremonies, and it was rare that an evening went by without, at Baruch's insistence,

---

* A few years later, when there were no restrictions, Swope irritated Hylan with a slambang crusade for more New York City schools; "'a seat for every child" was the *World*'s slogan.

Swope's giving his pachydermatous analysis of his old friend's cautious habits.

Swope had never held a job that required him to get anywhere reasonably early in the morning, and the War Industries Board operated on a normal daytime schedule. Swope did his best to adjust to this distasteful state of affairs. In a letter to Florence White, who had expressed amazement that he was observing conventional work hours, Swope said, "I am at my office every day between nine and nine-thirty and usually do not leave until the same time at night." And to White, Swope also took occasion to express a mounting dissatisfaction he was beginning to harbor for the way Ralph and Joseph Pulitzer, Jr., were running their father's papers. Swope thought they were becoming imperious—they looked upon themselves, he said, as "little branches of an autocratic trunk"—and he told White, "The day of that thing has gone by. Our whole war is directed against it. Their reformation had better come before it is too late, and sometimes I fear that the 'too late' hour has already struck." That was ten years before Swope left the *World*, and over twelve years before the *World* left the world, but already Swope had sensed the paper's doom.

On joining the War Industries Board, Swope had borrowed from the *World* his secretary there, Alexander Leo Schlosser, who was named after two Popes. Schlosser, who stayed on at the *World* until its demise and ended up as assistant city editor, had joined the paper in 1904 as a fifteen-year-old copy boy. He was a warm, kindhearted, but obsequious man whose attitude toward Swope was deferential almost to the point of slavishness. Like most men in such a position, Schlosser hit upon ways of compensating; two nephews lived with him, and he paid each of them twenty-five cents a week to run to the front door whenever he approached with a companion and cry out, "Three cheers for Uncle Allie!" Schlosser found the pace in Washington too grueling, and Swope let him go back to New York after a few weeks. He then commandeered as a personal assistant a young *World* reporter, George A. Hough, Jr. Hough, from an old New England publishing family, was to become a noted Cape Cod journalist as editor of the Falmouth *Enterprise*. He joined the *World* after graduating in 1917 from the Columbia School of Journalism.* He'd been

___

* That class, which included Howard Dietz, Morrie Ryskind, Merryle Rukeyser, M. Lincoln Schuster, and George Sokolsky, later added one more big name to its roster when it made Swope an honorary member.

drafted into the Army and, when Swope put in a bid for him, was stationed in a hospital at Camp Upton, on Long Island, where he spent much of his time on bedpan duty attending soldiers sick with influenza. He was glad to go to Washington instead and attend Swope.

Hough was still in a private's uniform when he reached the capital. "My God, get out of that," Swope said. Hough said he'd be overjoyed to, but pointed out that the government, aroused about draft-dodging, had agents all over the place pouncing on young men in civilian clothes and that he would therefore appreciate some credentials attesting to his right to be in mufti. Swope said not to worry, that he'd get some suitable papers right away. He gave the matter no further thought. "I was so confident in Swope's protection," Hough said later, "that *I* never thought about it again, either." Soon after the Armistice, in November, Swope took off for Europe, and as he was leaving Washington, in his usual rush, Hough asked what *he* should do. "Do whatever you like," Swope said cheerfully, and bade him a grateful and affectionate farewell. Hough had a terrible time getting out of the Army, because from the moment of his being assigned to Swope there seemed to be no official record any place of where he was or even who he was. Luckily, his wife had an uncle working at the War Department who managed after a couple of months of struggle to retrieve for him his mislaid identity.

Another young man at the W.I.B. was Billy Rose. Nobody had summoned him. At nineteen he was a champion shorthand reporter, a veteran of many contests in that special field, with a capacity for taking two hundred words of dictation a minute. Rose heard that the Board's stenographic staff averaged only around eighty or ninety—too slow for transcribing any conversations verbatim—and that it was stuck with sluggish typewriters also. He got in to see Baruch and offered to recruit for the W.I.B. a whole battery of top-speed shorthand people, if Baruch would only procure some new quick-action typewriters. Baruch admired his brashness and accepted his offer. Later, Baruch told President Wilson, a shorthand man himself, about his new office protégé, and Wilson asked Rose over to the White House, where they took turns dictating to each other.

Rose, an observant and articulate man, saw Baruch and Swope in joint action then, and years later he reflected, "I always had a hunch Bernie fell in love with him the way you'd fall in love with a beautiful show girl—one who'd also had an education." As for why Baruch liked *him*, Rose would say, "I think Bernie thought, 'This little guy's stuck on me and thinks I'm a hell of a fellow.'" Rose was stuck on Baruch, too, and although the two of them had only an employer-employee relationship in Washington, afterward they became good friends, like an ingénue and a character actress.

In 1935 Rose, by then an established songwriter, night-club operator, and theatrical producer, embarked on his most ambitious project. He put on *Jumbo*, a gargantuan musical comedy with one hundred animals in the cast, ranging in size from an elephant on down. John Hay Whitney and his sister, Mrs. Charles Shipman Payson, were the principal backers, and a third investor of proportions was Baruch. For reasons never made clear, he chose to remain anonymous; as far as the public or, for that matter, Rose and Whitney knew, Swope, who had never before been a Broadway angel, was the other *Jumbo* backer, a twenty-eight-thousand-dollar one—but it was all Baruch's money. Writing to Baruch's secretary at the time, Swope said, "If there is a loss it is to be B.M.B.'s. I am merely the agent in the matter. If there is to be a profit, it is to accrue with me. Does that agree with your understanding?" It did not agree with Baruch's; he was willing to shoulder the losses, he soon let Swope know, but he thought he ought to get the profits, too. The show had a five-month run, but it was so expensive to operate that the backers were out nearly their entire investment, in spite of Swope's having composed an advertising testimonial for Alfred E. Smith, who agreed to be quoted as saying, "I think *Jumbo* is grand. It's as new and as funny to my grandchildren as it is to me, and that's a great test for any entertainment."

Jumbo was so sprawling a production that Rose had to rent two riding academies for the preliminary rehearsals. The only theater in New York that could possibly accommodate the show was the Hippodrome, on Sixth Avenue between 43rd and 44th Streets. The producer, who had signed up Jimmy Durante and Paul Whiteman, among others, thought he also had the Hippodrome in hand. But just as he was about to bring in his menagerie for onstage rehearsals, he learned that the owners of the property, the English branch of the Astor family, were balking. A thin-lipped New York banker who handled the Astor real estate told Rose he'd rather rent the theater for a Max Reinhardt production of *The Eternal Road*, with an exclusively two-legged cast. Rose was chastened but undaunted. "I knew I had to bring in the biggest gun I could think of," he said. That weapon was Baruch, who was crossing the Atlantic on the *Normandie*. Rose sent him an anguished radiogram—one of the few instances of an S.O.S. going from shore to ship. Baruch responded swiftly, and forcefully, with a message to the president of a big bank that controlled the Astor bank. The next morning the big-bank president invited Rose to his office. The producer went there and found the thin-lipped banker present. "I just want to have a look at the fellow Baruch is so excited about," said the big banker. After looking at the diminutive Rose—a sight that may have made him blink—he turned to the subsidiary banker and said, "Give him the keys."

Rose's headaches didn't end once he was inside the Hippo-drome. There were staging problems of appalling complexity. It took Barnum & Bailey about forty-five minutes to set up a lion cage on the floor of Madison Square Garden. The pace of *Jumbo* called for a like installation in forty-five seconds. What with one such thing and another, there were twenty-one weeks of dress rehearsals before the show was ready for its première—an interval so protracted that Charles MacArthur, who with Ben Hecht wrote the book of the show, remarked that there was hardly any point in opening at all, since everyone had seen it. This was not entirely in jest. The Whitneys and the Swopes—Margaret loved circuses—were there night after night, accompanied by parties of friends lugging hampers of food and buckets of champagne. Whitney and Swope referred to the Hippodrome as "the Club." Swope may have been an angel wearing borrowed wings, but on the very day of the much-postponed opening he performed a providential service for Rose that the producer was never to forget. That morning a fireman inspected the theater and said that the show couldn't go on; he pronounced the Hippodrome a "house of violations." Rose told an assistant to get hold of Swope, and twenty minutes later Swope bore down upon the theater— "like a north wind," Rose recalled. "Herbert took that fireman aside and began talking to him, and I don't know what he said, but pretty soon he had the fireman charmed and bedazzled, and we opened that night and played for five months and never heard another such complaint." The fireman had learned something that to most of Swope's old acquaintances was elementary knowledge: that it was far simpler to put out a fire than to cope with Swope in full elocutionary flame.

11

WHEN Woodrow Wilson sailed for Paris on December 4, 1918, to take personal charge of the American mission to the Peace Conference that was designed not only to settle past scores between victors and vanquished but also, almost more important to the President, to achieve a permanent, effective, and universally pacifying League of Nations, all other American news became momentarily inconsequential. The *World* had its normal complement of seasoned correspondents in Europe—Tuohy of the London bureau; Lincoln Eyre, Arno Dosch-Fleurot, and Louis Seibold on the Continent—and they were ready to converge on Paris. So, in New York, were Ralph Pulitzer and Charles Lincoln. Frank Cobb had already taken a leave of absence from his editorial page to join Wilson's staff and help draft the agreements that the President hoped the nations assembled in France would approve.

As the star reporter, Swope naturally wanted to be in on a big-name spectacle. He was already distressed that the one time he *hadn't* been in Europe during the war, as combatant or correspondent, was while Americans were actually fighting there. Moreover, with an armistice in existence, there was no remaining *raison d'être* for a War Industries Board. Although he had, as he wrote Baruch that November, "fallen completely under your spell," he shook himself out of this trance and joined the *World*'s transatlantic task force. ("When two men understand each other as I know we do," Swope told Baruch on leaving the W.I.B., "expression in words becomes superfluous." He then went on, "My experience in the War Industries Board has been valuable in shaping my judgment and rounding out my mental processes. I have been helped much. I hope that I have been able to help a little. But by nothing have I been helped so much as by the influence you have exerted upon me. It has stood for all that is fine and kind and decent. I do not believe that an impure thought could find lodgment in your mind. I feel myself a better and a sounder man from my all too brief association with you. . . .")

This time Margaret did not go along. The European situation was far from stable, her mother's mother was ailing, she herself was not feeling too well, and there were the children. Besides, Swope didn't expect to be absent for more than six weeks, and nobody had yet devised a better way to cross an ocean than by steamer.

Swope sailed from Hoboken on December 1, 1918, three days ahead of the President, aboard the American transport *Orizaba*. It carried more editors, reporters, photographers, and typewriters, the papers observed with pride, than even Henry Ford's heavily populated "peace ship" had ferried over three years before. (Lincoln was on the *Orizaba*, and he learned at sea that Swope's earnings from the *World* that year—eighteen thousand dollars—exceeded what he, the managing editor, was getting. "I tell you what, Charlie," Swope told Lincoln consolingly, "when I see Ralph Pulitzer next I'll speak to him for you.") Swope, inevitably, almost didn't make the voyage. The *Orizaba* was scheduled to sail at noon, and all newspapermen had been told to be aboard not later than ten-thirty. At twelve, when the Captain was informed that Swope hadn't yet appeared, he agreed to wait half an hour. At twelve-thirty, just as the last lines were being cast loose, a baggage wagon thundered down the pier like a Roman chariot, propelled by two fleet longshoremen. Swope was on the cart, astride his luggage, and as he approached the gangplank he was shouting last-minute instructions to Alex Schlosser, trotting along at his side.

Conceivably nettled at Swope's having delayed the departure, the ship's officers later dressed him down severely for having ignored an abandon-ship drill. Swope insisted he had been maligned; he had, too, turned up, in his pajamas, but after attendance was taken. The trip was not, however, without its satisfactions. En route, the journalists decided to organize themselves into a United States Press Delegation to the Peace Conference, and when time came to vote for officers there was little question in anyone's mind that Swope was the natural choice for President.*

President Wilson reached Paris on December 14, and on that day Colonel House received a letter jointly signed by President Swope and by one of his colleagues, Lawrence Hills of the New York *Sun*, later editor of the Paris *Herald*. They were disturbed by the lack of arrangements for covering the Conference, and they hoped that House would have a press center established—the British correspondents already had one—and would make himself or Secretary of State Robert Lansing or, better yet, the President available to meet regularly with the American press contingent and keep it posted.

Swope was no mere detached observer anxious to get as much news as he could. He was also an enthusiastic advocate of Wilson's policies, and the President could hardly have wished for a more acclamatory account of his arrival than that cabled to the *World* by Swope:

> France took America deep into its heart yesterday. Paris was France and Wilson was America. It was a pageant of peace that greeted the American President, not one of war. . . . It is true that thousands of soldiers lined the five miles of streets through which the procession went, and thousands of guns marked the passages, but the soldiers smiled and the guns were empty, and flags flew gaily to winds that seemed to whisper of peace not of war.
>
> Mr. Wilson, who had done so much to bring peace to the world, brought joy to Paris. The city was *en fête* hours after the President had passed, and the streets were filled with dancing, cheering crowds, to whom the arrival of the American peace delegates came as the outward and visible signs of peace—peace that should endure and be lasting.
>
> The President's coming renewed the outburst of happiness that attended the armistice. The visit seemed to be the seal of confirmation on the truths which shall be finally translated into terms of peace that within the next thirty days will be written in this capital. . . . Men who know Paris say that never in the many comings of Emperors and Kings, of dignitaries great and little, has there ever been the like in the City's history to compare with this coming of Wilson.

---

* The arrival in Paris of this self-constituted body occasioned some amusement among the American correspondents already in that city, who considered themselves authentic press delegates, too, but had been disenfranchised.

And on December 20, Swope was saying in the *World* that the President "has projected his personality to the furthest end of the nation" and that he had the power to upset the government of France, should he choose to, and probably the government of England as well. Swope's effusiveness in this and other dispatches did not sit well with all his colleagues on the paper. For years he carried on a periodic and peppery dialogue with the editor of the *World*'s Sunday magazine, John O'Hara Cosgrave, an Australian by birth who before coming to the paper had edited *Everybody's* and *Collier's Weekly*. Cosgrave, eighteen years Swope's senior, was a courtly, old-world journalist—also a gourmet and for many years one of the prime movers behind the Dutch Treat Club. His wife, Jessica Finch, founded Miss Finch's Finishing School. Ralph Pulitzer always called him "Mr. Cosgrave"; Swope called him "Jack." Now, from across the Atlantic, Cosgrave, who didn't much care for President Wilson, was pursuing his chronic habit of giving Swope what he no doubt construed as older-brother advice—the very last sort of guidance, of course, that Swope fancied. On December 21 he wrote Swope:

> To say that a visiting President has more power in France and in England than Poincaré or Clemenceau or Lloyd George and Asquith is, I submit, going a bit far. And as to the truth of this assumption— on what position is any man, however clever, whose French is fragmentary and whose residence is not two weeks in length, to boldly assert it? . . . The performance makes the judicious grieve. You were not guilty of such facile and exuberant presumptions when you were dealing with Germany. The apparent rigidity and fixity of the Teutonic institutions impressed you. Doubtless you had fuller opportunities of acquainting yourself with the facts. Furthermore it was not necessary to identify yourself by expression until you had really mastered conditions. . . .

Cosgrave went on to argue that Swope, in Washington and now, he deduced, in Paris, was so eager to be on terms of intimacy with Wilson and his Cabinet that he could not be objective, and that whatever he might be gaining in personal prestige from his associations he was losing in journalistic accomplishment. (He stopped sermonizing long enough to confide, in younger-brother fashion, that he had no interest in his wife's adolescent wards and that in anticipation of Prohibition he had laid in one hundred and forty cases of wines—for his use, not the young ladies'.) What

Cosgrave, and other critics of Swope's, failed to reckon with was his mercurial changeability. Swope could not long remain any man's unquestioning disciple. Within less than a month after Wilson reached Paris, Swope would write:

A curious ostrich-like policy is being maintained by most leaders of public opinion on the question of a social uprising, evidence of which is seen on all sides, but which seemingly is to be checked by the mere denial of its existence. Nor is the President himself free from the criticism of ignoring the situation. He preaches a vast political reform, and is succeeding in substantiating his words by his practice, but he is silent upon the bigger social questions, which are, after all, the taproots of world politics.

In France, there were a good many ceremonial rituals to be got out of the way before the President could sit down with Georges Clemenceau, David Lloyd George, Vittorio Orlando of Italy, and the spokesmen for all the lesser participating countries. On Christmas Day, Wilson, accompanied by many of the four or five dozen American reporters in Paris, went to A.E.F. headquarters to join General Pershing in reviewing ten thousand United States troops —an event that inspired Swope to write:

There have been great days in President Wilson's life, but none will live longer in his memory or in the memory of those who participated in the occasion than the scene upon the plowed field between Humes and Langree in the department of the Vosges. It combined grandeur and humaneness, gravity and joy and charity as well, and the whole fabric was shot through with the strain of spirituality and sincerity, characteristic of President Wilson's best efforts.

That Christmas evening, with the press on his heels, the President crossed the English Channel. The following day, Boxing Day, there was a reception for him at Buckingham Palace. The American reporters had been held up at Calais, and by the time they got to Dover they were so late for the reception they were hustled onto a London train and from the Charing Cross Station were escorted directly to the Palace, without having a chance to wash up. Arriving, they were at once presented, in their disheveled state, to King George V and Queen Mary; Arthur Krock said it was a legend that the Queen, immediately after shaking hands with him, with Swope, and with all the grimy rest of the lot, threw her gloves away.

The schoolmarmy Cosgrave, in dwelling on Swope's supposed eccentricities, had written him, "I shall now approach a more delicate phase of your personality. Though you'd be prone at first to deny it, the truth is that you rather love a Lord. No one would dare call you a snob in my hearing, but you are prone to seek contact with the great. I'm quite sure you are unaware of any such tendency, but it is a fact." Swope was probably quite aware of it. The year before, from Washington, he had written Florence White, "It will please you to know that I met Earl Reading yesterday for the first time and today got a bid for a private lunch for tomorrow—but I can't go as I'm booked for Baltimore. And I didn't have anybody 'fix it up' for me as F.I.C. [Frank Cobb] did through [Sir William] Wiseman [the banker]. So there!" Lord Reading was England's High Commissioner and Special Ambassador to Washington during the war. In Paris, after the Armistice, Swope ran into him again, in the lobby of the Ritz. While they were chatting a young man in a loud checked suit and a derby approached. "Who's that dreadful person trying to horn in on us?" demanded Swope. "Oh—you mean my son, Lord Erleigh?" asked Reading. Swope recovered as quickly as he could. "Oh, no, that man going out the door," he said.

Cosgrave could not know that within a week of his joshing Swope about lords, Swope, at one of several lunches and dinners given the Presidential press party by British journalists, would annotate his menu by inscribing on it the names of all peers present, but no commoners; and that one of the relics he brought home from that European journey would be a chewed-up pencil stub that he preserved forever afterward in an envelope marked "Lord Bryce's pencil." *

Back in Paris, the Peace Conference formally got under way on January 19, and in the week preceding the inaugural session Swope, as a spokesman for the American press, had all but declared war on the peacemakers and had issued one ultimatum. The first of the celebrated fourteen points that Wilson brought to France had been an espousal of "open covenants, openly arrived

---

* Viscount Bryce of Dechmont, O.M., had published *The American Commonwealth* in 1888, had been British Ambassador to the United States, and in 1919 was an ardent advocate of the League of Nations and the main propagandist for Armenian independence.

at." When, however, the Supreme Council of the Associated Nations met to formulate procedures—it was a five-nation council, but though Italy and Japan were nominally supreme, Britain, France, and the United States were pretty much running the show —they ruled that no member of any nation's delegation could discuss anything substantive with the press beyond what might be divulged in official and, it was not hard to surmise, unrevealing communiqués. Indeed, the French had proposed, with American and British concurrence, that communiqués should mention only "established facts, suppressing all matters under consideration."

Swope and his colleagues grumbled about gag rule, and all other negotiating activities among nations were suspended while the world's leaders negotiated with the press. Swope, Krock, and a few others were appointed a special grievance committee, and they told the President that unless they had reasonable access to information they'd pack up and go home—naturally explaining to their readers why. (Concurrently, Swope, on his own, was putting pressure on Colonel House. "I think we are being trifled with," the *World* man told him, "and the thought is not pleasant.") Wilson was sympathetic to their cause. "I suggest the complete publicity of all that happens," he told the Supreme Council. But Lloyd George sided with the French against the President, and the best concession he could obtain was that a limited number of reporters would be admitted to plenary sessions of the Conference and that violations of the rule barring staff men from talking to reporters—not that enforcement would have been very easy in any event—would be viewed with tolerance. Swope and the others felt justifiably proud that by their intransigence they had assured that whatever open covenants might ultimately be arrived at would at least not be reached in tight-shut secrecy.

Swope, who hailed the journalists' entrenched stand as "one of the finest demonstrations ever seen of the thoroughly patriotic spirit of the American press, and a close reflection of the Nation's ideals and principles," was lucky when straws were drawn for the seats allotted to the American reporters at the opening session, held at the French Foreign Office on the Quai d'Orsay. In his account of that historic meeting he said, "Of great import, too, was the presence of representatives of the Press of the world, who had their positions in the room forming a part of the main chamber, witnessing the proceedings. They represented the public

218

directly [if Wilson, as directly chosen a representative as anybody in the room, had read that, he might have chuckled], and through their attendance, against which strong influence had been furtively directed, recognition was given to the part that public opinion has in the final formation of the relations which are to make the rule of the many supreme over the rule of the few." From his point of vantage, Swope enjoyed a good view of Clemenceau,* with his "singularly strong face, virile and set uncompromisingly," of the five Japanese delegates, "suave and quite baffling in their pose," and of their counterparts on the American mission. "They were headed," Swope wrote, "by a tall, distinguished figure, Bernard M. Baruch, who will handle all questions of the world's raw materials, so vital at this period of reconstruction." A few weeks later, Cosgrave wrote to Swope, "Use your relationship to Baruch. He has aspirations through which you may realize your own. That main chance must be seized, sooner or later." Even to others, Swope's eggs were beginning to loom large in Baruch's basket.

The Peace Conference dragged on for months. Swope had more than his share of good stories. He furnished the *World*, ahead of all other papers, with a transcript of the proceedings at the first meeting at which the League of Nations was officially proposed. He had an exclusive interview with the venerable Marshal Joffre

---

* When the French Tiger was shot and nearly killed on February 20, 1919, Swope sent an obituary cable to the *World*. The Premier survived and lived another ten years, and when he did die the *World*, if it still had Swope's obit on file, decided against using it. That was a shame, for it was vintage Swope. It began, in cableese, "Clemenceau is dead and heart France is broken stop Clemenceau is dead and his nation dash nation he lived and died for undash feels sense loss that leaves it groping blindly for consolation stop Clemenceau is dead and countrys fears comma those fears he mastered singlehanded comma live again stop part Frances future dies with favorite son comma the future she hoped to achieve through strong peace he making when stricken down by assassins bullet stop." Swope went on for several hundred more words, before concluding with "In all Frances history rich in number her great sons and daughters there can be found few greater figures than the one that will forever live in hearts of people Joan of Arc and as she saved her country so did he and like her he died martyr stop Richelieu has been called Frances greatest minister stop history may change verdict for Clemenceaus claims rest not only on what he did for France but even more on what he did for humanity his body lies still in death but his soul dash that soul which ten million enemies couldnt frighten or destroy undash marches on forever comma immortalized by all true men everywhere as quote le pere de victoire unquote end Swope."

219

("Because the matter is fraught with deep significance to the whole world and the time is propitious for a new and firm foundation for lasting peace, and because also errors of omission may create greater errors of commission later, France's great soldier gave to me permission to publish his views. . . . When we had finished the business of the visit, he took me upstairs, where he keeps his war souvenirs. I asked to see his Marshal's baton. Such is his lack of vanity that he could not recall where he had put it and had to search for it. . . ."). He had an interview with Queen Marie of Rumania ("I rather fancy some of us left the apartment rather regretting we were not Rumanians, remembering she had said she loved them and was loved by them. A man could think of a far worse fate. . . . She is not too young and not too old; a little above forty, I should say confidentially, though she does not look over thirty. Her height is about five feet eight inches, and she has a well-rounded figure, neither spare nor stout. About her head are thick curls of bronze-gold hair, all quite her own, surmounting a fair face, marked by a classical nose and blue eyes wide apart, under darker lashes, her mouth and chin are firm but womanly. At the audience she wore a dark-blue velvet frock, belted with an antique gold chain girdle. Her skirt reached her shoe tops, show-ing long, narrow feet and pretty ankles. Her dress was cut low and topped by a white roll collar, and around her neck hung a double rope of beautifully matched pearls the size of small hazel-nuts. . . .").

Off duty, Swope found Paris and its environs agreeable. The Longchamps race track was an attractive and convenient magnet, as winter ended and spring began, and there were plenty of com-panions who were horse-fanciers. Baruch, of course, was one. Another, while Wilson was in Paris, was the President's naval aide and personal physician, Rear Admiral Cary T. Grayson, who had his own racing stable. Baruch, Grayson, Swope, and Charles Merz, then of the *New Republic* and later the editor of the editorial page of the New York *Times*, went to Longchamps one day when formal dress was *de rigueur*. All had suitable top hats save Merz, who was sporting a cap. The gatekeepers were for keeping him out, but he got in after Swope exuded the same irresistible charm with which he would later beguile the fireman at the Hippodrome.

Swope's own attire had already won him much admiring com-ment. Among foreign correspondents, as among domestic ones, his sartorial pre-eminence was all but unquestioned. In Paris,

Arthur Krock, who had been impressed on first meeting Swope back in America because he'd never before seen a reporter in white tie and tails, blinked at "the bulgingest, whitest, stiff-shirt bosom east of Troy" and at Swope's "laundered, confident breast"; Admiral William F. Halsey, then a lieutenant, recalled that on catching his first glimpse of Swope, in France, "I looked at him with much awe." Swope had no valet in Paris to keep his plumage unruffled, but he came close to making a gentleman's gentleman out of a young reporter, F. Darius Benham, who'd just been mustered out of the French Foreign Legion.

Benham, eight years Swope's junior, had been hired by the *World* before the war, largely on the strength of scoring a reportorial beat when J. P. Morgan was shot on Long Island. During the Peace Conference, Swope got Benham a job as a *Post-Dispatch* correspondent, and Benham gratefully tagged along behind him, performing chores somewhat more menial than those customarily done for one newspaperman by another—like packing his bags when he took off on a jaunt. Benham told later of one occasion when seven reporters covering the Conference were invited to Switzerland. Swope, who had selected the group, was a half hour late for their train, then delayed them another thirty minutes while he had a private chat with an ex-Emperor of Austria, then lost eighteen thousand dollars in a Geneva casino, and then failed to show up at all for a dinner being given in his honor by the Swiss President. Or so Benham recalled it.

Years later, Benham founded the Circus Saints and Sinners, a New York lunch club given to fraternal pranks, and he also founded an organization of office workers called the Seraphic Secretaries of America. In establishing this sorority, he was acting on advice he'd had from Swope: If you want to make contact with important public men, establish a cozy relationship with their private secretaries. After launching his secretarial group, and getting friendly with dozens of important secretaries, Benham found himself hindered in communicating with *them* by the uncooperative attitude of office switchboard girls. At once, pursuing Swope's theory one step further, Benham formed an organization of switchboard operators, and he installed the chief White House switchboard operator as its principal officer. Benham by then, it almost goes without saying, was a press agent.

Among the many American correspondents in Paris was Damon Runyon. He came down with influenza, and when Swope stopped by one night to see how he was, and asked what kind of medical attention he was getting, Runyon said he was doing all right—a Y.M.C.A. doctor was treating him at his hotel. Swope said that would not do at all. He left and soon returned with Admiral Grayson in tow to minister to Runyon. By now Swope was acknowledged on all sides to be a very special sort of correspondent. When William C. Bullitt and Lincoln Steffens arrived in Paris late one evening, after a fact-finding mission on Wilson's behalf in Moscow, Colonel House wouldn't let them report to the President at that hour, so they reported to Swope. It was then that Steffens uttered his memorable summary of the Bolshevik regime: "I have seen the future, and by God, it works!" Swope's account was tamer. He said in the *World*, "William Bullitt, who went to Russia for the American mission, returned today. He was instructed to say nothing for publication, in conformity with the new efforts to hide the peace proceedings under a veil of secrecy. In spite of this restriction, it may be said that he and Lincoln Steffens found conditions in Moscow under far better control than had been pictured, and their reports will tend to show a degree of permanency and stability in Russian affairs which puts a new face on the Russian situation."

To correspondents and delegates from other nations, Swope was becoming a spectacle not to be missed. Harold Nicolson was in Paris on Lloyd George's staff, and not long after meeting Swope—"the star turn in the American journalistic world," Nicolson entered in his diary—they had a private get-together. "Lunch at the Meurice with Swope, an American correspondent," Nicolson wrote in a further entry. "He bursts with boost. He is very vulgar. He is a nice man. My liking for the Americans is becoming a vice. I like the scholarly sort, such as Coolidge, Seymour, Day, and Allen Dulles, because they are quiet and scholarly and because they like the truth. I also have a weakness for the noisy sort such as Swope, because he is so unlike myself. I feel like a mouse much impressed by a jaguar."

For all the exuberance that Swope radiated, he was upset by the news he was getting from America. His wife, who could not stand her long separation from him, kept pleading with him to come home, and when it became clear that he would or could fix no date for his return, she suffered a nervous breakdown. But he was determined to see the Conference through, and there were

moments of elation that more than compensated for the disloca-
tion of his family life. At the start of April, for example, he managed to get hold of the text of the near-final revisions of the League
of Nations Covenant, and the *World* had this document ahead of
any other paper. The Paris *Herald*, reprinting Swope's story,
called it "the great journalistic success of the Conference."

What must have pleased Swope almost more than successfully
breaching the veil of secrecy was a sense of taking part in the
dramatic creation of such a document. At lunch with the President one day, for instance, Swope got to discussing Article Ten
of the Covenant, which pledged the signatories to support any
incumbent government against insurrection. Swope remarked to
Wilson that some of the opponents of the League were complaining that strict adherence to the terms of this Article would inhibit
national uprisings against tyrants. Wilson's reaction to Swope's
comment delighted the *World* man. "Jumping up from his place,"
Swope would write later, "he came over to where I sat and,
poking me in the chest with his finger, he said, 'My boy, if I
thought that, by direction or remote implication, any clause or
phrase in the Covenant forbade to any peoples the sacred right of
revolution, I would tear up the Covenant with my own hands.' "

Even before the Peace Conference had begun there had been
considerable speculation about what reparations claims would be
incorporated into the final treaty. Lloyd George's selection as
Prime Minister in 1916 had been brought about in part by his
assurance to the British that he would make Germany pay vast
sums of atonement. After many discussions of this prickly and
politically explosive subject, England, France, Italy, and the United
States agreed upon a reparations section of the treaty—which they
hoped to keep secret as long as possible—and it diplomatically
avoided any mention of exact amounts of indemnity. Swope got
his hands on this document, too, and on April 10 he sent it to the
World via Tuohy in London. Giving himself an eight-hour head
start, Swope then shared the document with Hills of the *Sun*, who
cabled the text directly from Paris to New York. To Swope's
dismay, the *Sun* got his big scoop before the *World* did.

It was two days before Swope learned what had happened.
Then he found out from Tuohy that the British had refused to
transmit his copy from London to New York. They wanted to
hold it up until after April 15, when Lloyd George was scheduled
to speak in the House of Commons, whose members could be

expected to ask him some searching questions about reparations if they knew the vague terms to which he had assented. While Swope had no idea, at first, what the British were up to in London, he was aware that his still undelivered dispatch had annoyed the British in Paris. Lloyd George had asked Wilson, in fact, to try to persuade Swope personally to delay his story. Flattering though it was to have the leaders of the world's two greatest nations preoccupied with a single reportorial dispatch, Swope got furious. He might have gone along with the Prime Minister's request in ordinary circumstances, but now that he'd learned from Tuohy what was happening across the Channel, he wanted no part of any concession. He cabled Lincoln:

. . . IVE NO DESIRE TO IMPEDE PROGRESS PEACE CONFERENCE AND AM ALWAYS WILLING TO ACCEDE TO PRESIDENTS WISHES BUT I OBJECT TO SURREPTITIOUS METHODS EMPLOYED WITHOUT WILSONS KNOWLEDGE INSTEAD OF RELYING UPON GOOD FAITH AND WILLINGNESS OF PAPER TO FULFILL PRESIDENTS REQUEST STOP I GAVE STORY IN QUESTION WHICH WAS EXCLUSIVE TO SUN CORRESPONDENT WHO FILED IT EARLY FRIDAY MORNING STOP HAS SUN PRINTED IT OR WAS THAT ALSO HELD UP ILLEGALLY STOP NOTIFY ME IMMEDIATELY STOP ENFORCED SECRECY AND QUESTION-ABLE METHODS HAVE GIVEN MATTER UNPLEASANT ASPECT AND I THINK IT DUTY TO CLEAR UP SITUATION IN WHICH WE ARE BEING CLUBBED INTO SUBMISSION STOP LLOYDGEORGE REQUESTED PRESIDENT TO ASK FOR SUPPRESSION OF DISPATCH AS VOLUNTARY ACT BUT HIS ORGANIZATION MEANWHILE HAD ALREADY STRANGLED IT STOP TODAY SUNDAY I WAS FURTHER ASKED TO AUTHORIZE BRITISH CENSORS TO HOLDUP STORY AL-THOUGH IT HAS NEVER BEEN SENT SO THAT I MIGHT SEEMINGLY BE PLACED ON RECORD AS APPROVING THEIR IMPROPER ACTION STOP THIS IVE DECLINED TO DO END SWOPE.

The same day that Swope sent that message the *Sun* printed the story that he'd obtained exclusively for the *World*. Lincoln didn't know *what* was going on. The next day he cabled Swope, "YOUR REPARATIONS DISPATCH FILED APRIL TENTH REACHED ME MONDAY MIDNIGHT. . . . ALTHOUGH TRANSMITTED BY MARCONI URGENT RATE DISPATCH BEGINS QUOTE ENLIGHTENMENT AFFORDED BY PUBLICATION TERMS END QUOTE MANGLING EVIDENT OUTRAGEOUS TREATMENT TRY HARD TO GET TO BOTTOM OF IT." Simultaneously, Swope was cabling him, "REPARATION STORY RELEASED AFTER STORY EXPOSING TRUTH WAS FILED STOP SUGGEST YOU USE IT INDICATING BY LARGE TYPE WHERE BRITISH CENSOR DELETED DISPATCH PARALLELING IT WITH

LLOYD GEORGES PERSONAL ASSURANCE GIVEN AT END OF DECEMBER THAT ALL CENSORSHIP OF NEWS AND COMMENT HAD ENDED STOP. . . . WHOLE MATTER IS HEARTBREAKING BECAUSE NOT ONLY WAS I DENIED BIG EXCLUSIVE THROUGH OPERATION OF CENSORSHIP THAT LLOYD GEORGE STOOD FOR AND ASKED PRESIDENT TO HAVE ME AUTHORIZE BUT STORY WAS PRINTED IN SUN TO WHICH I GAVE STORY EIGHT HOURS LATER BUT WHICH FILED OVER FRENCH LINE STOP WHEN THEY LEARNT SUN HAD STORY THEY TRIED TO STOP THAT BUT FAILED STOP AM HEARTILY DISGUSTED AND HOPE THAT WITH STUFF I SENT YOU YOU CAN MAKE BIG EXPOSURE OF DELIBERATE DECEPTION REGARDING NO CENSORSHIP STOP BESIDE DELETED STORY RELEASED MONDAY NIGHT HAVE YOU EVER RECEIVED COMPLETE STORY STOP."

The *World* did eventually receive the complete story. It came limping in bit by bit, and the paper didn't get to run it until April 18. Meanwhile, Swope had told President Wilson, in front of several statesmen, that he thought the Prime Minister had behaved insufferably. Swope voiced his complaint in such blunt language that one of Lloyd George's deputies, Philip Kerr, later Lord Lothian, moved toward him with fists clenched. Admiral Grayson, a doctor in this instance practicing preventive medicine, stepped between them before any blows could be struck.

On April 18, the same day that Swope's reparations story finally made the *World*, the paper also ran a later dispatch of his in which he summarized his feelings about the whole aggravating conference:

More and more clearly does it appear as the days of the Peace Conference near their close that the final treaty to be signed will be merely an incident in the world disorders and not an end.

Unsatisfied ambitions and unrealized hopes are poor foundations upon which to build a permanent peace structure, and the structure itself is of the political type of architecture, remote from the new problems of a social nature confronting the world and to which the Conference has addressed itself but little, if at all.

The wrath that is being stored up will show itself for many years to come, and its manifestation can be met only by force. It is a realization of this condition that has made France insist upon and receive from Great Britain and America something more tangible in the way of assurance of protection than is afforded by the League of Nations. France is to gain this security, but what about the other nations which are even more in need of defense? With them, unless the League of Nations achieves success, it will be as always has been

the case—a survival of the fittest—and the edifice so carefully con-
structed by precept will fail in use.

There are today questions of pressing nature which the Conference cannot settle, and it requires no gift of prophecy to say that
they will continue to plague future generations for years to come.

Swope's apprehensions about the Conference—which were to
prove unhappily true in years to come—were not then shared by
the *World*'s editorial page. Frank Cobb had returned to the paper
by that time, and on April 19 the lead editorial in the *World*,
taking what seemed to be a dig at its principal Paris reporter, said,
"While it is possible that the correspondents in Paris could draft a
more satisfactory peace than Wilson, Clemenceau, Lloyd George
and Orlando are capable of doing, still the President and the Prime
Minister are officially charged with the work, and it might be just
as well to give them another chance." *

Nobody ever found out for certain how Swope got hold of
the reparations text that precipitated all the fuss. On that same
April 18 Frank Polk of the State Department was writing to
Secretary of State Lansing about Swope: "He frequently published stuff that came from one well on the inside. I think I can
guess who the man is, and I imagine you can, too." This seemed
to most people who heard about Polk's and Lansing's guessing
games to point to Colonel House (whom Swope, incidentally, described then to a friend as "swelled up like a poisoned pup"), but
Swope subsequently denied that House had been his source and
said, "In fact, frequently the correspondents supplied him with
more information than he supplied them." There were some who,
knowing Swope's closeness to Baruch, thought *he* was the source.
This Baruch denied. It was *his* understanding that Swope had
asked Colonel House to let him see the document and that House,
after protecting himself by saying that of course he couldn't do
anything of the sort, had told Swope that the text was right there,
lying on that table in front of them, and had then excused himself
from the room they were in. "Herbert always knew a way of
getting things done," Baruch said.

Swope never gave a better demonstration of how he could get
things done than on May 7, at the Petit Trianon outside Paris at

---

* Years later, Westbrook Pegler remarked, "Clemenceau was just another
French politician to Herbert and you would have thought Woodrow Wilson
was his assistant at the Paris Peace Conference."

Versailles, when the Allies presented Germany's representative, Count Ulrich von Brockdorff-Rantzau, with the peace treaty. As on other momentous occasions, the number of tickets allotted to the press was sparse. Eight American correspondents were to be admitted—one each from the Associated Press, United Press, and International News Service, and five others, chosen by lot. This time Swope didn't draw a lucky straw. But that was of no account. As the ceremony was about to start, an American Army sedan swept up to the palace, flying a general officer's flag. It was a car that Swope had borrowed for the day from an accommodating military friend, Brigadier General Harry H. Bandholtz, who as General Pershing's Provost Marshal was the chief of military police of the A.E.F. No soldiers or gendarmes directing traffic were likely to stop General Bandholtz's car, Swope knew well.

When the car reached the entrance to the Petit Trianon, the passenger it let out looked so magnificent and important that it never occurred to anyone to question his right to enter, either. Swope had costumed himself in a diplomat's formal morning clothes—cutaway, striped pants, and a glistening top hat that sat so cocksurely upon his head William Allen White said afterward Swope looked as if he'd been born with it on. Swope strode inside, escorted by a retinue of three less elegantly dressed correspondents carrying attaché cases, who were assumed by the doortenders to be lackeys of the commanding figure whom with bows and salutes they passed on through. Swope perched himself composedly on a front-row spectator's seat in a section reserved for the diplomatic corps, and he had a fine view of the entire proceedings.

After the meeting, the press gathered in a tent that had been pitched on the palace grounds, where the eight correspondents who had been legitimate eyewitnesses were to brief their colleagues on what had happened. Richard V. Oulahan of the New York *Times*, one of the five non-press-association men who'd been admitted, began to give his report, but he was interrupted by Swope, who felt that one aspect of Oulahan's account needed clarification, amplification, and ornamentation. Swope held forth for a few minutes, and then *he* was interrupted by Charles A. Selden of the London Bureau of the *Times*. How did Swope, Selden demanded, know what had taken place, since he hadn't been inside the palace? Oh, but he had, Swope said matter-of-factly, and he explained what he'd done.

227

When Selden returned to the American press headquarters that were now in existence in Paris, at the Hotel de Crillon, he took a telegraph blank of the Anglo-American Telegraph Company and typed on the back of it, "Members of the organization of American correspondents attached to the Peace Conference who resent the action of Mr. Swope in violating the rules for attendance at the Versailles meeting and who think that Mr. Swope should not continue to be a member of the organization's committee may indicate their feelings in the matter by signing this paper." Selden appended his own signature, posted the sheet on a bulletin board, and stood by to see how many other names his grumpy petition would attract. A few minutes later Swope walked in. He read the protest and, in bold red crayon, signed "H. B. Swope" directly beneath Selden's name. Selden knew when he was licked. He took down his protest and handed it over to Swope, who proudly added it to his collection of souvenirs.

Swope might have conquered the press in Paris, but the press was still far from satisfied—when was it ever?—with the treatment it was getting from the government. In June, while the world was still anxiously waiting to see whether the Germans would accept the terms the Allies were seeking to impose on them, Swope was once again fighting, at the highest level, for his occupational rights, and fighting on behalf of himself, Selden, and all the rest. President Wilson had been invited to make a state visit to Belgium, and the correspondents naturally wanted to go along, but their requests to accompany him were coolly received. On June 15 Swope wrote the President:

How can even so devoted a friend as I hope I have been and am to you and to what you stand for, view the exclusion of myself and other special correspondents from your Belgian trip as other than a studied insult? We are informed that there is trouble over having an extra car attached, yet it is difficult to believe that but little effort would not have succeeded in gaining accommodations for us had you so desired. It would be out of place to say anything as to the embarrassment the situation has caused to our work, for that is a problem each of us must face continually, but it is proper to express a keen sense of disappointment at being subjected to such indifferent personal treatment, especially when the Belgian government has indicated its wish to make particular arrangements for our convenience in "covering" your visit, which takes on an importance that makes it essential for the special writers over here to see it personally. I am sure one word from you will rectify the matter. It may not be too late to speak it. Will you do it? If not, I, for one, will know how little consideration you think those of us who are seeking to help you are entitled to. I feel deeply over this matter and therefore I write frankly, which I am sure you prefer to disingenuousness.

At the same time, Swope was urging Admiral Grayson to put in a word for the journalists. Under pressure from all sides, Wilson capitulated, and Swope was able triumphantly to record, on his copy of his disingenuousnessless letter to the President, "He spoke the word." Riding the train to Brussels, Swope might well have sat back and basked in the glory of his having brought about his being there, but he had a reporter's ever-open eye, and on the way he remained unfalteringly—indeed, astonishingly—observant. "Other columns will have told the route the party followed," he told the *World*, "but perhaps nothing has been said of the fact that there were to be seen only twenty cows on the whole trip and half as many chickens, the Germans having accounted for the great balance once teeming in the countrysides."

The Peace Treaty was signed on June 28. For this ceremony Swope routinely acquired a ticket of his own, but just to keep his hand in he wangled an extra one for Lincoln Steffens. Swope's account of the signing, delivered in the orotund style to which his readers were by now thoroughly accustomed, went:

They who had drawn the sword perished by it. There was to be found in the scene that shall never sink from the memory less of the spectacular—indeed, it was almost disappointing in that respect —than of the spiritual. It marked the triumph of the strength of right. . . . The road is clear. It is hers [Germany's] to follow or to abandon it for more devious routes. It is within Germany's power to remove the taint now resting on her by new ideals and by service. Will she take this course or will she bide her time to spring anew upon mankind, seeking revenge for her thwarted ambitions?

At the *World* in New York, some of Swope's associates thought he would come straight home after the treaty was signed and that he would write a long analysis of what had gone on, much as he had done following his 1916 visit to Germany. John O'Hara Cosgrave, in his usual fashion, thought that Swope would be derelict if he didn't do that. "The very excellent advice suggested in my note and emphasizing that given you by White, I understand has been discarded," Cosgrave wrote in a sarcastic letter to Swope shortly before the treaty signing:

> You proposed, after your serious labors in Paris, to take a vacation in Europe. You are not to return ahead of the President and tell the inside story of the proceedings at Paris. Wearied after your labors as a member of the Conference you must rest and you prefer to relax over there than to return here where you'd have perforce to write.

Furthermore, Cosgrave, who seemed to take special delight in teasing Swope, said that he didn't think much of what his colleague had been writing all along. There was too little of it, he believed (Ralph Pulitzer, who had to pay the cable tolls, believed at times there was too much), and Swope the man, in Cosgrave's judgment, had made a bigger stir abroad than Swope the newspaperman. Cosgrave continued his lecture:

> You are not employed as the President's or Colonel House's confidant, but to translate as much of what is told you as you may into the *World*. It's the stature of the paper that counts, not yours. The understanding is that you contribute that stature of yours and what it brings you to the *World*, and to do less is a betrayal.
>
> The trouble is that you are expressing yourself and that's oratory and not journalism. You reserve your gifts for a little group of admirers and deny them to the institution that pays your salary and expenses, and wagers its reputation on your capacity as its correspondent.
>
> Can't you realize how illogical, how unintelligent, how unfair this is to us—to yourself? Your rewards are here, not there. Gratification to personal egotism you may gather by word of mouth, but enhancement to your reputation you can only achieve by your pen. For heaven's sake, suspend your emotional personal excitement, let your analytic brain reassume its normal function, look at the situation from the *World*'s point of view, from mine, from White's, your sincere friends, and make good. Come back as soon as possible and repeat the success you gained out of your German series. Tell us ahead of the President what happened in Paris. Draw the curtains aside and show us the tragedy and the comedy. Characterize the dramatis personae with insight and understanding. Help the *World* to a big series and help yourself to a renewed prestige. . . .

Swope was unswayed. By the end of June he had been away for more than six months, but he nonetheless hung around Europe, mostly vacationing, until mid-August, and he might not have returned that soon but for a despairing cable from Margaret. His prolonged absence subsequently proved evidential. The previous January 19 three New York City policemen were shot while trying to break into a room where a crap game was being held. Arnold Rothstein was caught on a fire escape outside the room, carrying a gun, but he escaped prosecution. It was rumored he had paid thirty-two thousand dollars to have the case dropped. And Mayor Hylan, who had no love for Swope, suggested to his Police Commissioner that he look into another, ancillary rumor—that Swope had been the payoff man. Swope was subsequently absolved by a grand jury when he was able to point out that he had been abroad throughout the period under scrutiny.

Swope landed in New York, on a troopship appropriated from Germany, along with F. Darius Benham, whose horizons of service were widening. By now, while not busy attending Swope, Benham had other responsibilities, and he was fulfilling one of them by escorting a dog Baruch had acquired overseas. Swope found at the *World* an atmosphere of restlessness and discontent. Few of the top men there were on good terms with all of the others. Ralph Pulitzer was having his differences with Frank Cobb, the exacting Cosgrave had many faults to find with Lincoln ("If I knew a good story that I desired to suppress, I'd accomplish my object by telling it to Charlie," Cosgrave wrote Swope), and Florence White was a general manager of whose managerial jurisdiction most of his associates had quite varying interpretations.

Pulitzer wanted to distill some order from this chaotic executive ferment, and he decided that Swope was the man who could best carry this out. Neither Cobb nor Lincoln thought much of the idea. Lincoln could not help having reservations about a man whose work habits were so conspicuously different from his own; it was *his* custom to get to the office at ten in the morning and to stay until midnight, and his legendary lunch was a single apple, which he could eat without wasting time. Pulitzer resolved to go along with Swope notwithstanding, and to start off he invested him with the title of assistant to the publisher. (John Gavin replaced him as city editor.) Neither Swope nor anyone else was certain what his functions were. "No one knows New York better than yourself," Cosgrave wrote him. "No one has more contacts, relationships. You *know* news better than anyone else in the game, and you can cooperate. Also you have ideas. Why could you not sit in on a daily news council? Personally I would not tie you down to any desk job, because the transaction of routine is not your metier, and the expression of your ability is rather feeding power to a machine than serving beside it. You are gasoline, not an apparatus. If you imagine there is any element of detraction here, just remind yourself that one does not require inspiration of a clock. . . . They also serve who keep others waiting." *

Swope strode around the *World* office for several months, inspiring here, refueling there, until, in the fall of 1920, Pulitzer suggested that he assume a newer title, one that had never been used at the *World* before, that of executive editor. Swope seemed to have some doubts about accepting the position. "Confidentially, we are in the throes of some big changes at the shop," he wrote Krock, who was in Kentucky, "and, curiously enough, I have no inclination to accept the peacock feather they want to hand me. In fact, I have practically rejected the kingly crown, at least for the time being." But for a man of regal bent a kingly crown and a mantle of peacock feathers were hard to resist for long, and Swope soon consented to his enthronement. At that, Lincoln, who had been managing editor of the *World* since 1915, quit and went to work for the *Herald*. It wasn't long before most New Yorkers readily got the point of a cartoon drawn for the old *Life* by Roland Young. It showed Swope, his chest puffed out and his stomach sucked in like a drill sergeant's, in the lobby of the *World* building, and he was towering over the well-known window there with two stained-glass hemispheres of the globe.† Beneath the drawing was the caption "*Le Monde c'est moi.*"

---

* Years later, Cosgrave, harboring second thoughts about punctuality and routine, had Swope's Dutch Treat membership revoked because of his spotty attendance record at the club's weekly lunches.

† The window is now in the Swope memorial room at Columbia University.

12

THE ELDER Joseph Pulitzer once said, "Every reporter is a
hope, every editor a disappointment." It was a debatable
aphorism, but it appealed to Swope, though he did not mean it
to apply to him. He was one of the few men in newspaper annals
who achieved success on the same paper in the customarily antithetical roles of reporter and editor.

Swope spent eight lively and contentious years as executive
editor of the *World*—or, as he occasionally chose to call himself,
Chief Executive Editor. There was not a little titular confusion
at the paper. Swope's two immediate assistants, William P. Beazell
and J. Earle Clauson, transmitted communications on letterheads
inscribed "Office of the Managing Editor," and they were known
themselves as assistant managing editors, but there was no managing editor, let alone a Chief Managing Editor. Beazell was the
assistant day managing editor and Clauson the night man. Both
were solid, dependable, faithful workers—ideal counterbalances
for a volatile and unpredictable superior. Both, by coincidence,
were aviation buffs. Clauson, who also edited a volume called
The Dogs' Book of Verse, handled many aeronautical assignments
after joining the *World* in 1911; and Beazell, whose service on the
paper began the year before, was the first civilian observer to
attend the Army's experimental training schools for its Air
Service.

Technically, Swope did not run the *World*. Ralph Pulitzer
not only represented the ownership of the paper but, from 1924
on, after Frank Cobb died, called himself the editor. Cobb was
succeeded as editorial-page editor by Walter Lippmann, whom

Swope hired away from the *New Republic* in 1923 and who, like his predecessor, had an understandably determined protectiveness about his department. In the spirit of fraternal competitiveness that prevailed at the paper, Swope was expected to keep his hands off the editorial page, as one brother is expected to lay off another brother's prized possessions.

To the other strong and sometimes clashing personalities on hand—the captious Cosgrave and the cautious White—was soon added Arthur Krock, whom Swope began trying in 1921 to lure to the *World* from the Louisville *Courier-Journal* and who finally came north in 1923. For a while Krock was a part-time editorial writer under Cobb. Then, after Lippmann took over, Krock was hired full-time, as an assistant to Pulitzer, in which somewhat vague capacity he at once found himself caught among the various forces pulling and tugging at the helm of the paper. Lippmann didn't particularly want Krock writing editorials, and Swope, who didn't want anybody intervening between Pulitzer and himself, tried to shunt the newcomer out of the way by suggesting that he go to Washington and write a signed column from there, which was, of course, what Krock eventually ended up doing, for the *Times*.

But whoever was entrusted with whatever responsibilities, at the *World*, between 1920 and 1928, Swope was conceded to occupy a unique, Olympian niche. "Swope never thought, I am sure, that he belonged to the *World*," said one of the paper's reporters, Donald Henderson Clarke, in a memoir. "He felt that the *World*, including Ralph Pulitzer, belonged to him. His ambitions were too vast to be limited by personalities or properties. He was a Conqueror: an Alexander, Caesar, Genghis Khan, Napoleon." Swope often inspired historical allusions. Dudley Nichols, who as a *World* reporter developed a lifelong admiration for his energetic boss, once said that even in relative repose Swope seemed like a Hercules between tasks.

Swope's *World* was, like the man who got it out, an exciting, argumentative, boisterous, cocksure, and entertaining journal. "What I try to do in my paper," Swope once told Heywood Broun, "is to give the public part of what it wants and part of what it ought to have whether it wants it or not." And on another occasion Swope justified the *World*'s pick-and-choose approach to news by saying:

The paper of record has an enormous claim upon all of us, but I submit that there is necessarily no merit per se in a report that is merely comprehensive, that is merely enveloping without the needed lift of intelligence in selecting the important from the unimportant. There is less merit in that process than there is in the effort to make the presentation of news rest upon selectivity. Throwing away is as important as printing everything.

This was to a degree a rationalization, for even if Swope had wished to he could not have competed with a paper of record—or, specifically, with *the* paper of record, the *Times*. The *World* was making money in the early 1920s, and had been for some time, but Joseph Pulitzer's three sons, the chief beneficiaries of its profits, tended to drain these off instead of plowing them back either in the form of better equipment or a larger staff. Swope simply didn't have the facilities or the manpower, either in New York or at outlying bureaus, to make his paper comprehensive. He could and did, however, make it colorful—make it, in the phrase of Denning Miller, Alice Duer Miller's son, "a bright and glistening candle in the singularly materialistic and conscienceless times."

Swope's credo was "Pick out the best story of the day and hammer the hell out of it," and the economics of the *World* gave him little choice, as far as news was concerned, to do otherwise. But as a paper the *World* was a great deal more than a mere dispenser of news. Not long after *The New Yorker* began publishing, in 1925, it said in a promotional ad that it hoped to be a weekly comparable to the *World*. Among the daily's qualities that the new magazine aspired to emulate were intelligence, reasonable good taste, honesty, courage, good news sense, freedom from oppressive sensationalism, respect for the rights of privacy, "and, above all, interest, interest, interest." To its contemporaries, Swope's *World*, however incomplete it had to be, was interesting.

Swope's office as executive editor was in the northwest corner of the twelfth floor of the *World* tower, just beyond the big city room. Dudley Nichols, who characterized his editor as a man "who always loved nothing better than pushing the strong around and giving a hand to the weak," described the office as a lion's den. Down one corridor were the *Evening World*'s offices. One floor below Swope was the Sunday Department, one floor above him the *World*'s restaurant. On the fourteenth floor were Pulitzer, Lippmann, and Krock, and at the very summit of the building were the other editorial writers—at one time or another, James M. Cain, Allan Nevins, and Maxwell Anderson—and Rollin Kirby, whose incisive cartoons illuminated the editorial page. When the *World* building was new, the public gladly paid admission to ascend to its top. After one visitor had had Ralph Pulitzer pointed out to him as "Mr. Pulitzer," he inquired, "What Pulitzer was that?" Kirby was walking by. "The hand we do not bite," said the cartoonist.

Alluring though the tower might be to outsiders, to its inhabitants its charms were something less than overwhelming. The place was drafty, for one thing, and when a reporter died of influenza in 1922 Swope complained to Pulitzer that he had probably succumbed to the twelfth floor's malign atmosphere. Swope was equally critical of the restaurant, which was widely thought to embody all the worst traits of institutional dining. The food and service, Swope would say, were abominable, and he would send a copy boy out for an order of pig's knuckles or some other robust snack rather than patronize the establishment.

He was not alone in his disdain. Frank Cobb wouldn't set foot in the restaurant, no matter how pressed for eating time he might be, and it was a favorite intramural joke around the *World* that the only good thing ever to come out of the place was *What Price Glory?* The play evolved in part from the mealtime huddles of Maxwell Anderson and Laurence Stallings, who began at the *World* as a Broadway reporter but, because the artificial leg he'd acquired after being wounded at Belleau Wood bothered him, was shifted to the more sedentary job of book-reviewing.*

Swope's office was a hub—an *étoile* of sorts—of a ceaseless swirl of editorial traffic. Reporters, copy-readers, and others drifted in and out at will. Sometimes half a dozen of them would be lined up, hoping to have a word with him when and if he got off the telephone, but in no particular hurry. For just to listen to him on the phone, when he was in fettle, could be as beguiling as attending a concert. Once Swope put in a call to an unapproachable

---

* In the restaurant one day, Stallings turned to Deems Taylor and said, "I suppose you think every now and then it must be pretty horrible to lose a leg." Taylor said yes, he did. "Well, I think that all the time," Stallings said.

foreign diplomat from whom the *World* was anxious to have a statement. After several minutes of captivating talk, Swope hung up and beckoned to a waiting reporter. The envoy, Swope said, had agreed to see a *World* man. The reporter went to the designated rendezvous, and when he identified himself the diplomat frowned and said, "Oh, I thought Mr. Swope was coming." The reporter said there must have been some misunderstanding. "Oh, well, it doesn't matter," the foreigner said. "I have no statement for you and I'd have had none for him, but I was so fascinated listening to him on the phone that I wanted to see what he looked like."

Just outside Swope's office, a spacious one, sat a secretary he acquired in 1920, a spinster named Helen A. Millar. She remained in his employ for more than thirty years and defended him with unflagging fidelity against real or fancied incursions. (S. N. Behrman, after trying vainly to get past her once to reach her boss, was moved to refer to Swope's "papal inaccessibility.") Miss Millar, who sometimes referred to Swope as "our impetus," was typical of those office assistants who seem to have no life outside their employer's; and Swope had enormous confidence in her loyalty and discretion. He ran accounts with bookmakers in her name, and when, though supposedly a reform-minded Democrat, he wanted to give Tammany Hall a thousand dollars, he gave that in her name, too. She feared no one except Margaret Swope, and she rarely entered the Swope home; but in her own lair, Swope's office, she reigned with a firm hand.

Miss Millar could be blisteringly short with people whom she found tedious. One time in 1936, when Joseph P. Kennedy was receiving calls at Swope's office, a man wrote him that he had been rudely rebuffed on the phone and added, "I am curious to know the identity of anyone in this day and age so evidently discourteous." Several years after that, Mrs. Arthur Hays Sulzberger, after trying to reach Swope on the phone, wrote him, "I am not able to get past your dragon-like secretary. She seems to be under the impression that she is guarding the treasure of the Rhine. I agree that you must be wearing the Tarnhelm, for you seem to be invisible."

At the *World* it was impossible for Miss Millar to keep Swope in operatic isolation, but when he was away from his desk she would protect it valiantly. She waged a running battle with John H. Tennant, the managing editor of the *Evening World*, who would wander into Swope's office, ostensibly to use a water cooler, when the morning-paper editor was off somewhere. Should Tennant's glance happen to stray toward the top of Swope's desk, Miss Millar, concerned lest the evening paper ascertain what schemes the morning paper was hatching, would carry on like a brood hen until he'd slaked his thirst and gone back to his own province.

Neither she nor Swope had much use for the *Evening World*. As executive editor, Swope's salary was fifty-four thousand dollars a year, and he also had a 2 per cent share of the profits of the morning and Sunday papers, but he got no part of the proceeds of the evening. Swope believed a newspaper should have character, which he defined for Ralph Pulitzer in 1922 as "an appeal to intelligence and thought." He felt that the evening paper, which was avowedly more raffish than the morning, lacked this essential. Analyzing Tennant's journal, at Pulitzer's request, the following year, Swope said, "It is sawdusty. It is the sort of a paper that Warren G. Harding would have made and that President Harding would have been much pleased with." Harding, for his part, once suggested that Swope would make a good President of the United States.

What Swope liked best of all—and naturally tried to hide from prying rivals' eyes—were journalistic crusades, on which the *World* embarked with unabated relish, whether they were against slum landlords or for the League of Nations, against ethyl gasoline or for daylight saving, against reckless driving or for better subway service. "When we locked horns, we really locked," said Ernest K. Lindley, who worked on some of Swope's more spirited crusades.

Underdogs were often involved. In 1920, for instance, the United States was agitated about foreign agitators. It was a year of Red scares, and at one point Ellis Island harbored two hundred and twenty New Yorkers of alien birth who had been branded as Bolsheviks or Anarchists or Communists and were slated for deportation. The previous November, five admitted Socialists from New York City were elected to the State Legislature. When they arrived at Albany in January at the start of the annual legislative session, their colleagues in the Assembly refused to seat them. Instead, they were lined up, excoriated, and hustled out of the Assembly chamber by the sergeant-at-arms, pending a formal disposition of their status by a legislative judiciary committee.*

The public at large was not unduly aroused about this turn of events, and most newspapers accepted it calmly. The *World* was outraged. Frank Cobb thundered on his editorial page, "The most revolutionary blow ever dealt to representative government in the United States was struck by the New York Assembly when five Socialist members were suspended." Meanwhile, Cobb's associates on the paper had set up a "Representative Government Fund," which had as its goal the raising of twenty-five thousand dollars to help the Socialists retain their seats, but which said it would accept contributions only from people who would stipulate they were not Socialists themselves. The Press Publishing Company— the corporate entity that controlled all the Pulitzer papers—got the fund rolling with a gift of two hundred and fifty dollars. The first listing in the *World* of contributors indicated that Swope had been busy soliciting himself; Baruch and Thomas Chadbourne were each down for one hundred dollars, as was Ralph Pulitzer. The next day Swope came through with twenty-five dollars and an accompanying statement:

> It is not Socialists the members of the Assembly are putting on trial, strive as they may to project that illusion; it is Americanism that is being put on the rack, though, blinded by prejudice, they do not perceive that fact. So in enclosing my check for twenty-five dollars I am helping to defend myself; I am observing the law of self-preservation. If the public opinion that the *World* is helping to create does not block the "Albany idea," which may be fairly defined as "believe my way or be damned," it can readily be the turn of five others after the new Torquemadas have finished with their inquisition of the present group.

There was a strong undercurrent of liberalism in nearly every crusade that the *World* launched, and this was in a decade when Republican conservatives were entrenched in the White House,

---

* The adjudication took so long that the legislature accomplished very little else that session. In April, all five Socialists were expelled from the Assembly, and a special election to replace them was announced for September. All five ran again and were re-elected. This time, the Assembly, with ebbing enthusiasm for its harassment of them, threw out only three of the group. The two who were allowed to occupy their seats sat in them long enough to claim victory, and then resigned.

when apathy and isolationism were the distinguishing marks of American foreign policy, and when most residents of the United States were principally concerned with making money on the stock market and trying to get around the tiresome enforcement provisions of the Volstead Act. It was an environment not terribly hospitable to the propagation of unpopular viewpoints. But the *World* stuck in the main to the trail that Joseph Pulitzer had blazed four decades earlier. At Swope's suggestion, for example, the paper published a series of articles, in 1922, by Emma Goldman, who had been deported to the Soviet Union two years before. Her observations, to be sure, were conservative in one sense—she was writing about her disillusionment with life in Russia—but her mere appearance in the paper brought down upon it the scorn that liberalism so often attracts from two sides: Many of her followers were incensed that she was featured in a capitalistic medium, and many of the *World*'s followers felt exactly the same way.

From defending Socialists, a smallish group, the *World* moved on to attacking a larger and far more influential body, the Ku Klux Klan. In the 1920s the Klan, resurgent since the end of the war, was no comic-opera hooligan outfit but a consequential social and political force. Even before the paper began an enlightening series on the operations and membership of the organization, in the fall of 1921, the Klan may have perceived in Swope a threat to its shrouded serenity. Sixteen months earlier, while the *World* was preoccupied with Albany, a small and crudely wrapped package addressed to Swope was delivered to the newspaper, with a note affixed saying that the building would "be blowed up by we all, Ku Klux, tomorrow, at noon." The contents—some rubber tubing and wires and a broken cigar—were harmless enough, and nothing happened the following day. Whether the *World* was really in danger or the parcel was some prankster's hoax was never determined. In any event, if Swope was expected to be the target of any violence, its perpetrators couldn't have known him well, because the chances of finding him at work at midday were as remote as finding him in a torchlight procession with a pillowcase over his head.

On Sunday, October 10, 1920, the *World*'s weekend feature section carried a front-page story from Atlanta that began, "The old Ku Klux Klan of Reconstruction days has been revived. Hooded night-riders in long, flowing white gowns parade the thoroughfares and bypaths of the South in the dark hours when innocent people are abed." Some of the information for this account came from Swope's friend Walter White, of the National Association for the Advancement of Colored People. White, who once called Swope "an irascible, valuable, impatient, courageous editor," had, in the guise of an Anglo-Saxon Southerner living in the North, been corresponding with William Joseph Simmons, the ex-Methodist circuit rider who reconstituted the Klan and was its Imperial Wizard and who was later convicted of white slavery. In his letters to White, Simmons blabbed all sorts of incriminating confidences that he would not, had he known his communicant's identity, have told to one of the country's most militant Negro leaders.

Other newspapers fought the Klan, but as James A. Farley, then a New York State legislator, said at the time, the *World* battled "most consistently of all papers the growth of this organization that has for its principle the arraigning of classes and creeds against one another." The paper's biggest barrage was fired for twenty-one straight days, beginning September 6, 1921. A retired Army captain from Chattanooga, Henry P. Fry, had joined the Klan early that year, because he was a Mason and felt the Klan was a sociable fraternal order. He quickly advanced to the rank of Kleagle and almost as quickly became disenchanted. He got hold of a membership list by the device of professing to his brethren to be an ambitious snake-oil salesman—the kind of businessman the Klan held in high and sympathetic esteem. In June, Fry came to Swope and Beazell with his files, which contained, among other things, the texts of secret oaths and of membership application questionnaires. Swope bought the material and assigned Rowland Thomas, one of the *World*'s most facile reporters and rewrite men, to get it in shape for publication.

At the time the *World* ran its exposé of the Klan, there were many other interesting news developments—Babe Ruth was on his way to a fifty-nine-home-run year; President Harding was being welcomed at West Point by the Superintendent, General Douglas MacArthur; and Franklin D. Roosevelt was in the hospital with what the *World*, in an inside-page story, called a "slight attack" of infantile paralysis—but for the entire twenty-one days Thomas's pieces occupied the *World*'s leading page-one spot, with a good deal of impassioned spillover into the rest of the paper. There were numerous illustrations, one of them a photograph of the authentic Klan handshake. The stories were available for syndication, and a few papers in the South, along with many in the North, picked them up, but to Swope's disgust the St. Louis *Post-Dispatch* was cool to them. In New York, where the *World* had many Catholic, Jewish, and Negro readers, the paper's circulation went up by sixty thousand the day after Thomas's first installment appeared. The result was about the same in Philadelphia, where the *Public Ledger* had picked up the series. In Detroit, where the Klan pieces weren't running, single copies of the *World* were selling for fifty cents. Even so, Pulitzer and Cobb and Florence White all thought that Swope was overplaying the story. Swope disagreed. He argued that it would take legislation, on a local or perhaps even Federal level, to put the Klan out of business, and that no effective laws could be expected to be enacted without every possible bit of pressure being exerted on lawmakers.

Not long after that the *World* framed a bill for the New York legislature, outlawing organizations that operated anonymously, and the bill was passed. It was introduced by the dapper Jimmy Walker, of whom Swope would say, after his mischievous regime as Mayor of New York, that "lacking though he may have been in other things, [he] had a sense of public service." Swope's own sense of public service was recognized, too. A few months after the Klan series Swope went to Pittsburgh to speak in favor of the League of Nations at the Carnegie Institute of Technology. Just before he started off, with the remark that every reporter was a hope, every editor a disappointment, six robed and hooded undergraduates marched to the rostrum and ceremonially presented him with a twenty-foot papier-maché fountain pen—symbolic of their gratitude for his having performed valiant service in the perpetual struggle for might between the pen and the sword.

For its Ku Klux Klan stories the *World* won a Pulitzer Prize. Tennant of the *Evening World* was one of the few Pulitzer employees who did not share in the general jubilation. He had hoped that his paper would get the award for a series on slum housing, written by Bella Spewack, a young reporter who had served her apprenticeship on the Socialist *Call*. When it was announced that the morning paper had won, she took the defeat in stride, but Tennant, once again thwarted by Swope, broke down and wept.

The *World* soon won another Pulitzer Prize for another Southern exposé. This involved a North Dakota farm boy named

Martin Tabert, who had migrated to Florida to seek work and had been beaten to death in a lumber camp with a horsewhip. Running out of money on reaching Florida, Tabert had ridden a train without buying a ticket and on being arrested was given a choice of a twenty-five-dollar fine or ninety days in a county jail. He telegraphed home for the money, but when his family sent it it was returned by the county sheriff, with the message "Party gone." The party, like other county prisoners, had been leased out by the sheriff to work in the lumber camp. After Tabert was killed, his family was notified he had died of malaria and pneumonia. The family, unconvinced, asked the State Attorney General of North Dakota to investigate, but he could get nowhere with his counterpart in Florida. So he turned to the *World*.

Swope, who once said, "In general, boil over whenever wrong is done the little fellow," had his staff start digging into the story. The paper found a man in Brooklyn who'd been in the lumber camp and had kept a telltale diary, and the reporter Samuel Duff McCoy went to Florida. He stayed on the story for two months, revealing in one dispatch that a Florida state senator owned a turpentine camp that also used, and abused, convict labor. McCoy told all in the kind of purplish prose that colored many a crusading feature:

> The facts which the *World* here reveals about Florida are not those which have to do with the Florida known to the half million tourists who visit the State each winter.
>
> It is not the Florida of glorious sun and blue skies and of white surf beating lazily on the beaches of Miami or Palm Beach. It is not the Florida which the traveller, looking from the windows of trains gliding northward from Key West, looks at and regrets to leave, a land where the dogwood already is spreading its beauty of white blooms through the forests and jonquils are glowing golden in every dooryard.
>
> It is not the Florida of fruit and flowers, sunshine and contentment which the whole world thinks of when it hears the name. The last of the winter visitors lounging on the verandas of hotels on the southern coast hears the throbbing dance music of perfect orchestras; he has not heard and may never hear a quite different sound— the scream of a human being under the lash of a convict captain.

As with many of its crusades, the *World* got results with its disclosures about conditions in Florida. The Pulitzer Prize was one reward. Another was the indictment of the lumber-camp horsewhip man on a first-degree murder charge. Still another was the passage by the Florida legislature, though by a narrow margin, of a statute forbidding the use of the lash.

The South at that time was, of course, a fertile field of inquiry for a liberal Northern newspaper seeking evidence of inhumanity. There were plenty of lynchings, and the *World* ran plenty of lynching stories. Walter White, who was so light-skinned he looked whiter than many white men, would occasionally risk his life by obtaining firsthand information on lynching bees, and would pass along the hair-raising details to Swope. The *World*, in due course, acquired the reputation of being pro-Negro. It was more than the contents of its news columns and editorial page that earned it this cachet. Laurence Stallings, for instance, in reviewing one of Walter White's books, referred to the author as "Mr." and for that gall was all but ostracized in his birthplace, Macon, Georgia.

Swope had already decreed that the word "Negro" would be capitalized in the paper. He issued this order partly at the instigation of a colored journalist, Lester A. Walton, another native of St. Louis, whom Franklin Roosevelt was to appoint Minister to Liberia in 1935. (Walton held the post for eleven years, and Swope, often eager and usually able to do favors for his friends, arranged for up-to-date American newsreels to be shipped to Africa so the Minister could show them to Liberians, who had had to make do for years with stale, outmoded newsreels. Sometimes they were a whole Channel swimmer behind.) Walton, like Swope, got his start on the *Post-Dispatch*. Moving to New York, he became managing editor of a Harlem weekly, the New York *Age*. In 1917, feeling that the Wilson Administration and the white newspapers of the North were soft-pedaling lynchings, and regarding Swope even then as somebody who could redress the balance, Walton wrote him, "You had better pay more attention to this Negro question. Take this tip."

As soon as Swope was in a position to do something, he commissioned Walton to write a series about Southern Negroes who had migrated above the Mason and Dixon Line. Then, in 1922, Swope went one step further and invited Walton to write a column each week for the Sunday *World* on news of the Negro community in New York. The circulation of the Sunday paper, and of the daily, too, shot up in Harlem, to the not unalloyed joy of the *World*'s business executives. They complained that other papers were underhandedly telling advertisers that the *World* was excessively partial to Negroes and was read *only* in Harlem. Pulitzer refused to be swayed by his advertising department's requests that he countermand Swope's recognition of a colored society, the significance of which was subsequently appraised by another Harlem paper, the *Dunbar News*, which said in 1931 that Swope's hiring of Walton "may be taken to mark the beginning of a new day in American journalism," and went on:

It had been seldom that space was given to news about the Negro, except for purposes of laughter or disparagement. The black man was front-page material when accused of rape or burglary or arson but not when he wrote a poem or sang the folk songs of his people or built a business. The life and labor of the great wholesome masses of the people had no news value at all but the holdup man had much. The *World* gave no little space to items about men and women of color which were of some real meaning in terms of social progress. It gave detailed accounts of Negro advancement in industry, business, education, literature and art. . . . The generous and enlightened policy of the *World* stimulated editors of other daily papers in and out of New York to select and publish significant news in which the Negro people figure, although previously many of these editors had been apathetic if not hostile to this new sort of thing.

By no means all of the features and stunts in which the *World* reveled were solemn. The paper, for example, had a peculiar fascination with the occult. The big play given to Swope's youthful adventures with Antoinette Gazzam, the unlucky girl who fell afoul of the spiritualistic Dr. Niblo, was characteristic. The paper devoted much space to, among other sprightly personalities of the era, Mrs. Augusta E. Stetson, a stubborn and outspoken Christian Scientist who was long at odds with the governing faction of her church. On July 31, 1927, when Mrs. Stetson, a lady who was close-mouthed about a few things, was estimated to be eighty-five years old, the *World* ran an exclusive front-page story quoting her as saying that she would achieve physical immortality and, what was more, that Mrs. Mary Baker Eddy would return in full and animated vigor to the earth. Mrs. Stetson died of a heart attack in Rochester, New York, a year later.

The *World* was also much taken with Harry Houdini. At the

height of his fame, in the mid-1920s, he presided over a Sunday feature section called "Red Magic." Walter Lippmann was chiefly responsible for Houdini's association with the paper. While studying philosophy at Harvard Lippmann had been influenced by a psychologist whose avocation was exposing the wiles of mediums. Houdini, when not extricating himself from awful physical predicaments, was also fond of deflating the claims of mind-readers, table-rappers, and folks who professed to enjoy a chatty relationship with the dead. Hearing that Lippmann shared his interest, Houdini called on him at the *World* and invited him to a sleight-of-body demonstration in the swimming pool of the Shelton Hotel, where the magician bafflingly emerged alive after spending fifty minutes under water in a sealed coffin.

In 1925, while Houdini was playing a vaudeville engagement at the Hippodrome, there was much excitement about a news development from England. Professor Gilbert Murray, who like Sir Arthur Conan Doyle and other reputable Britishers attached considerable importance to spiritualism, announced that in the course of a thought-transference experiment with Earl Balfour he had read the peer's mind from thirty-six feet away. Pulitzer thought there might be something to all this and wanted to pursue it. Lippmann wanted to debunk it. He arranged with Houdini to set up a much more dimensionally impressive performance at the magician's home, a brownstone on West 113th Street. The audience consisted of Lippmann, Pulitzer, Arthur Train, the psychiatrist Edward J. Kempf, Houdini's wife and brother, Swope, Margaret Swope, and, at Swope's invitation, Baruch.

Houdini went up to the third floor, where he was locked in a room. The others assembled in a ground-floor parlor and wrote out some thoughts, which were then whispered around three times. Houdini's relatives were not allowed to say anything, even in a whisper. Lippmann's thought, appropriate for him, was "I'm thinking of Lord Curzon in the Foreign Office last January." Baruch's was "Don't give up the ship." Dr. Kempf came up with "Buffalo Bill's monument in Wyoming by Mrs. Harry Payne Whitney." Houdini was called downstairs. He flubbed Lippmann's entry, but for Baruch's he came up with "A sense of heaving water and a ship," and for the psychiatrist's "I get the picture of a man killing cattle—no, buffalo! I see him bringing meat to men building a railroad. He has long hair."

Then Houdini was escorted back upstairs, stripped naked and

encased in a cabinet. The cabinet was hoisted onto a couple of chairs, and Lippmann and Pulitzer stood watch over it, while two stories below the rest of the assemblage concentrated hard on a portrait painted by Mrs. John Barrymore. Again Houdini came up with only a partial answer, but an impressive one: He got the name Barrymore. He never would explain how he accomplished any of this, but he assured his audience there had been nothing supernatural involved. It was just one of the many tricks in his bewildering bag.

As it pleased Swope to have the halls of his home aswarm with celebrities, so was he fond of parading them in the columns of his paper, as contributors. He captured H. G. Wells to cover a 1922 international conference on disarmament in Washington which the *World* was sponsoring. It was widely believed in that giddy bygone era that conferences could achieve disarmament. The following year, Swope obtained the exclusive New York newspaper rights to a new poem by Rudyard Kipling. Elated at his success with leading English literary lights, Swope also tried to cajole George Bernard Shaw into coming to the United States to cover a heavyweight championship fight. Shaw begged off, even though he loved money and though Swope, according to his later recollection, offered him fifteen thousand dollars for the stint. Clinging to his conviction that dramatists were somehow especially fitted for covering fisticuffs, Swope later asked Eugene O'Neill to write up a fight for the *World*, but O'Neill also declined. He explained that he doubted he had the ability.

Swope was always looking for new journalistic angles. As assistant to Pulitzer after returning from the Paris Peace Conference, he had been asked to revamp the *World*'s syndicated feature service, which had long been in the doldrums and was earning a paltry five thousand dollars a year. Swope converted this limping enterprise into a profitable offshoot of the Press Publishing Company. (By 1928 the syndicate was netting eighty thousand dollars a year.) His widespread connections made it relatively easy for him to find new ways to cover old stories. For a special approach to a world economic conference held at Genoa in 1922 he signed up Frank A. Vanderlip, the head of the National City Bank, and guaranteed him one thousand dollars an article—maybe five or so pieces altogether, Swope suggested. Vanderlip, showing the fiscal acumen that made him a pillar of banking, proceeded to write more than a dozen, which were relayed to New York by Samuel

Spewack, who was in charge of the straight-news coverage for the *World* at Genoa.

Spewack was born in Russia and was fluent in both his native tongue and German. In 1921 he was on Swope's city staff, earning sixty dollars a week but eager to be a foreign correspondent. He kept asking Swope to send him abroad, and some six months after his first request Beazell called him in one afternoon. The assistant managing editor had good news. Spewack could go to Vienna, but, since it was a big opportunity for him and since living costs in Austria were allegedly moderate, he would have to accept a cut to forty dollars a week. Spewack consented, not altogether happily. At midnight Swope came to work. At once he summoned Spewack and countermanded Beazell's instructions. The reporter would be going not to Vienna but to Moscow, and instead of a reduction in salary he'd be getting a raise, and there'd be an expense account to boot. Spewack was never able to figure out whether this reversal was prearranged between Swope and Beazell, who were quite close as a rule. But he left Swope's office in a state of euphoria, convinced that Swope was the greatest and most generous man alive.

On his way to Moscow, Spewack went to Genoa. It was his responsibility, to save communications costs, to translate Vanderlip's prose into cablese. Feeling that the financier's copy was on the whole rather dull, he took the liberty, while he was at it, of slashing whole paragraphs. Vanderlip knew nothing of this until the mails came in, by ship, and when he saw his truncated texts he at once cabled Swope and demanded that Spewack be fired. To Swope, a good reporter was the equal of a Union League Club's worth of bankers, and his only reply to Vanderlip was to tell him that the articles he was writing were the talk of the nation and to keep up the good work.

That same year, Swope turned up in Europe again himself. In the spring of 1922, Kaiser Wilhelm let it be known that his memoirs had been written and would be available to the highest bidder. His agents were reportedly asking a flat one million dollars for publication rights and were asking ten thousand dollars just for authorization to look at the book and see if anyone wanted to make an offer for it. The *World* was interested, as were numerous book and magazine publishers and other newspapers. Pulitzer decided Swope should go to Germany to negotiate in person. In May, Swope scrawled a cablegram to one of the Kaiser's representatives in Leipzig. He gave it to Miss Millar and told her to have David Loth, who Swope knew had a good command of German, translate it. Swope's message went, "Will leave as soon as I can get transportation. Please have manuscript ready for examination." Loth, the young man from St. Louis whom Swope had hired largely as a favor to his brother Gerard, knew nothing about the context of the message. In innocent ignorance he thought Swope was trying to rig a deal to get his expenses paid. In translating, accordingly, Loth used the phrase, "*sobald ich fahrgeld bekomme*," which could best be translated back into idiomatic English as "as soon as I can scrape together the fare." Miss Millar sent off the message.

A few hours later Swope found out what had happened, called Loth into his presence and after a few preliminary "Flathead!'s" got so worked up that the reporter thought he was going to be flung out of a twelfth-story window. When Swope could talk again he said, "God damn it, I can pay my own way." Loth suddenly realized what all the commotion was about and burst out laughing. The effect of *that* was to convince Loth that he would not only be hurled from a window but, worse still, would be fired. "I guess I never was," Loth said later, "because occasionally Gerard would say to Herbert, 'How's David Loth doing?' If Herbert had had to say he'd fired me, Gerard would have asked, 'Why?' and Herbert would have had to answer, 'He laughed at me.'"

Once Swope got his transportation problems straightened out he sailed for Europe, taking Margaret along. He was racing against time. The Kaiser's agents had set a date by which sealed bids for the precious memoirs had to be submitted. Swope, however, did not seem to be in any great hurry. Arriving in Paris, instead of taking the first train to Germany, he and Margaret moved into a suite at the Ritz and spent a restful day there. Alexander Woollcott called on them at noontime. "Margaret was in bed," he wrote to Edna Ferber, "garbed in pink and altogether too beautiful. Herb was receiving correspondents, being shaved by an imported *coiffeur* and describing London hotel prices. There were silk stockings and fragments of toast and huge bunches of roses in pleasant profusion, but nothing much to do, so Margaret and I shot craps while Herbert talked."

By the time the Swopes got up steam again, a group consisting of the New York *Times*, the McClure Syndicate, and Harper & Brothers had all but obtained the rights to the Kaiser's memoirs and were ready to sign a contract. But there was still time to outbid this combination, and the word in Europe was that Swope was en route with what the *Times* called a "cargo of cash." He was late, as usual, and missed his chance, for which the *World* was profoundly grateful, inasmuch as the Kaiser's reminiscences proved to be overpoweringly dull. Cosgrave remarked that Swope's failure to execute his mission was a striking example of his extreme good luck.

Stopping off in Berlin for a few days, the Swopes found Spewack there, about to go to Moscow. (Not long after Spewack reached Russia, he sent back a series of articles that Swope decided to entitle "Behind Red Curtains." This may have been the first use of "curtain" in connection with the Soviet Union.) At the Genoa conference, Spewack had met George Tchitcherin, the Russian Commissar for Foreign Affairs. Tchitcherin, too, was in Berlin, heading home. When Swope, by now being shaved by a *barbier* at the Hotel Adlon, learned that the Russian was also registered, he asked Spewack to arrange an interview. Spewack did, for eleven o'clock the following morning. At ten-thirty, Spewack went to Swope's room to escort him to the session. On rapping at the door, he got no response. Worried, he persuaded a waiter to let him in with a pass key. The Swopes were fast asleep, and Spewack woke them. "What's your hurry?" Swope said. Spewack pointed out that Russia was an important country, despite America's not having recognized its government, and that the Commissar might take it as a national as well as personal affront if Swope kept him waiting. Swope grudgingly arose, bathed and dressed, all the while talking—a rehearsal of what he planned to say to Tchitcherin.

Meanwhile, Spewack got the Russian on a house phone and explained that his editor had been lamentably detained by a transatlantic call of the gravest urgency, but would be along soon. Some fifteen or twenty minutes late, Swope arrived at Tchitcherin's room. After they were introduced, Swope sat down, cleared his throat and said, "Now, one thing you people don't understand is that we, too, are a revolutionary country. Let me tell you about the revolution of 1776." With that, he was off, and for one and one-half uninterrupted hours Swope gave the Commissar a lecture on American history, spiced with quotations from, among others, Thomas Jefferson and Thomas Paine. Tchitcherin listened in dazed fascination. Swope concluded by saying that if the Russians would behave themselves, diplomatic recognition by the United States would probably be merely a matter of time. Tchitcherin just blinked. Then, having had no breakfast and feeling hungry, Swope rose and bade the Commissar a gracious farewell. Three days afterward, Tchitcherin ran into Spewack. "That Mr. Swope of yours . . ." the Russian began. "Yes?" said Spewack, wondering if an international incident was brewing. "He's very informed on American history," said the Russian mildly.

In a 1928 memorandum to himself that he headed "My Laws of Work," Swope reflected, "Some men must be measured by time-clocks. Others cannot be. Their brilliance or efficiency is affected by it. My satisfaction found in multiplying this in others. To stimulate and direct others to creative effort is the highest form of executive capacity. Irregularity is not a drawback if efficiency goes with it. . . . Greatest satisfaction is to multiply your self-efficiency by stimulating others." Stimulating Swope undeniably was, and he was also gruffly protective toward his employees. One secretary at the *World* remembered for years how touched and flattered she was when she went to the theater with her mother and Swope, spotting her in the lobby during an intermission, stopped and chatted with her, although up to then she'd had no idea he even knew who she was. "It was like talking to God," the giddy girl recalled.

The *World*'s copy boys, who knew the withering force of Swope's voice better than most mortals, also knew that he was their champion. One day Swope asked one of them to run out and get him a copy of the Philadelphia *Evening Ledger*. Unable to find one at any nearby newsstand, and not daring to come back emptyhanded, the boy took a train to Philadelphia and bought one there. When he submitted a voucher for his travel expenses, Florence White refused to honor it—refused, that was, until Swope heard what had happened and bellowed his insistence that the messenger be repaid for his perseverance.

To Swope, his reporters were a special breed and the most precious of all his employees. He gave them wide latitude, respecting initiative and enterprise and glossing over such minor frailties as tardiness, flightiness, and drunkenness. One time the

251

World got a tip that a colored magistrate had handed over to the law a young Negro wanted for shooting a policeman. Spewack was assigned to write a story about this upstanding, law-abiding elder citizen. Looking into the matter, Spewack found out that the boy, who was out on parole, had been regularly beaten up by the policemen he had to report to, and, unsettled by their cruelty, had fired at one of them. Then he had fled and gone to the magistrate for help. The magistrate, who ran a speak-easy on the side and was anxious to stay in the good graces of the cops, had promised to do what he could for the boy and had promptly done nothing except to turn him in. Spewack wrote a sympathetic story about the boy, and Swope, though the assignment hadn't worked out quite as originally anticipated, gave him a bonus. "The function of a good reporter is not just to cover a story but to uncover a story," Swope once said.

Reporters and rewrite men on the *World* were encouraged to use their imagination and to add colorful, anecdotal flourishes to their stories. (Several of them became successful fiction writers, and one, Henry Sydnor Harrison, was an established novelist before he became a newspaperman.) Swope was not of a particularly humorous turn of mind himself, but he encouraged his writers to be funny. Even the financial columns of the *World* were infected with the virus of gaiety that he condoned. To Pulitzer's dismay, the chief financial writer, S. S. Fontaine, sometimes covered Wall Street as if he were in the sports department. Once he attributed to an anonymous investor an order to his broker that went, "Buy me one hundred Coca-Cola. We may get a little kick out of it."

One of Swope's reporters was Joseph Van Raalte, a dour-faced man who cared so little for time clocks he sometimes didn't show up for a week at a stretch. He had a way, though, of adding light, comical touches to a story. He was in the city room one day when a young woman came in to air a lament. She was a blackmailer who'd been acquitted in court because, in an era when ladies' legs were rarely glimpsed, she had hiked her skirts up high while on the witness stand and had mesmerized the jury. Now, she complained to the *World*, she was being retried, and the wily district attorney had tried to thwart her by fencing in the witness stand. Van Raalte was so touched by her plight that in a number of novels he subsequently wrote, the best known of which was *The Vice Squad*, he usually included a spirited defense of blackmailing, which he upheld as the logical punishment for nasty, rich old men who preyed on innocent girls.

When St. Clair McKelway was a Swope reporter and was on rewrite duty, a brief, unadorned item came in over the wire of the City News Association. It was about a grieving mother and father who, without telling each other, had separately visited their son, a prisoner in the Tombs. The then city editor was Joseph J. Canavan, who was subsequently Governor Herbert Lehman's secretary and chairman of the New York State Parole Board. An emotional Irishman, Canavan loved sentimental stories, at the most lachrymogenic of which he would quite literally burst into tears. Canavan turned over the bare-boned City News item to McKelway, who without bothering to ascertain any additional facts spun out a touching yarn about the worried and uncommunicative parents. He invented a breakfast scene between them. He had oatmeal going into their mouths and dialogue coming out.

McKelway was pleased when Canavan, on reading his copy, wept copiously, and he was even more pleased when Swope, who well knew how much a word of praise from on high meant to a young reporter, sent him a "Good job, Mac" note. Then, however, the mother of the lad in the Tombs wrote to the *World* that the story was incorrect: There had been no oatmeal on her breakfast table, she said, and how dare the paper suggest any such outlandish thing! Her complaint was turned over to the paper's Bureau of Accuracy and Fair Play. Swope soon summoned McKelway and asked where he had got his information. "I just made it up," McKelway said. "We do it all the time." Swope growled a bit, paternally, and then sent him off without further reprimand.

Frank Sullivan, another reporter who was given a good deal of leeway, and indulged in a good deal of levity, in his treatment of news, described the years he spent on the *World* as "the happiest of my life." In 1922 Sullivan was working, contentedly enough, for the *Sun* but like many reporters in New York wanted more than anything else to be on the *World*. When Swope asked him to drop over and talk about switching, Sullivan said he'd be right there. "The first meeting with Swope," he said, "was happy and typical. He was far from a difficult man to meet. But some friend on the *Sun*, who had something in his crop against Swope and who thought I was making a mistake in leaving, said to me, 'Well, you'll go over there and Swope will put on a show to impress you—probably by telling his secretary to get Governor Smith on the phone. It will all be an act.' So help me God, I wasn't in Swope's office for more than a minute or two when his famous secretary, Miss Millar, interrupted and said, 'Mr. Swope, Governor Smith is on the wire and would like to talk to you.' Well, my friend at the *Sun* had been half right. Swope did talk with Al, but it was Al who called Swope, not vice versa."

Swope had two ways of getting from the twelfth-floor elevator landing to his office. He could go through the city room, or down a corridor separated from it by a thin partition. If he chose the latter path, he couldn't be seen, but he could be heard—his stride, Sullivan would say, sounded like a man on horseback—and the familiar ring of his gallop would galvanize all hands into furious activity. Sullivan came to work one day in a new pair of shoes, without rubber heels. After making sure Swope wasn't around, he clip-clopped down the corridor in a spirited and persuasive imitation of the genuine article, accompanied by a salvo of suddenly activated typewriter keys. Not to have reacted instantly to even a spurious Swope would have been regarded with suspicion at the *World*. A cub reporter who'd been there a month was standing near the city desk one day when Swope cantered into the room and yelled at the city editor until the windows rattled. When he left, the cub asked the city editor who *that* was. "You've been on this paper for a month and you mean to say you don't know who that was?" demanded the incredulous editor. The reporter said no, he didn't. "You're fired," said the editor.

Sullivan would probably have been fired himself, not long after he joined the *World*, had it not been for Swope. One night Sullivan was on rewrite duty when a tipster phoned Swope that Mrs. Charles Cary Rumsey had died. She was the daughter of Edward H. Harriman, and Swope rushed out and told Sullivan to handle the big story. Swope assumed that Sullivan would verify the facts of her death, and Sullivan assumed that somebody else would, or already had, and that he was supposed only to write up an account of her life. He did this, and his story, which never mentioned how or when she was supposed to have died, appeared on the first page of the first edition.

Only then, after the other papers in town, wondering how they had got scooped, began making inquiries, did the *World* learn that it was another Mrs. Rumsey who had died. The mistake would have been bad enough in any circumstances for any paper. It was particularly unfortunate for the *World* because the senior Harriman had had a long-standing feud with the senior Pulitzer. Harriman's widow thought this false account of her daughter's death was just another typically mean trick of the hateful Pulitzer press. The Harrimans were so globally prominent that the *World* not only printed an abject retraction two days running but, Swope would recall, tried to set the matter as straight as possible by notifying newspapers in Paris, London, Berlin, Rome, and St. Petersburg. Sullivan expected the worst, and when he was called to Swope's office and found there, with grave expressions, all the top men of the *World*, he in one stammering sentence conveyed his regrets and tendered his resignation. But Swope refused to accept it.

Many gifted reporters worked for Swope—so many that he found it hard to believe that anyone who was any good had not. As an elder statesman of journalism, long after he left the *World*, he would refer to Russel Crouse, for instance, as "one of my boys," but though Crouse had worked for a number of New York papers before he became a playwright, and though his first wife was Alison Smith, who moved from the *Evening World* to the morning paper's drama department, Crouse was never Swope's boy. Swope may have regarded this lapse as an oversight for which he was prepared to confer retroactive absolution.

The roster of those who did unarguably serve under Swope was glittering, and many a man who later went on to marked success remembered vividly how Swope gave him his start. Henry Luce would say of Briton Hadden, who with Luce founded *Time*, that Swope "had a very special place in his life." On graduating from Yale in 1920, Hadden went to the *World*, breezed into Swope's office while the vigilant Miss Millar was momentarily away from her sentry post, and, when the editor tried to get rid of him, said, "Mr. Swope, you're interfering with my destiny." Swope couldn't resist asking what Hadden thought his destiny *was*. Hadden said it was to work on the *World* for a year, getting experience, and then to start his own publication. They talked for a few more minutes, and Swope was so impressed with the young man's earnestness that he took him on.

Whoever the *World* men were, wherever they came from, and wherever they might go, they all unquestioningly—and, in most cases, affectionately—recognized Swope as the top man at the paper, and many of them would call him "Boss" for the rest of their productive and prosperous lives. Among the other reporters who graced the *World*'s pages were two men of political éclat— Charles S. Hand, who became Mayor Jimmy Walker's right-hand man; and Charles Michelson, who handled press relations for the Democratic National Committee. Michelson covered the Scopes trial for the *World* in 1925. While in Dayton, Tennessee, he got a telegram from Swope, who in the *World*'s irreverent fashion instructed him to ask Williams Jennings Bryan if he believed the earth was flat. Michelson obediently put the question to Bryan, who went into a towering rage. "I'll have you know, sir," he replied, "that I am a classical scholar and will not stand for any of this impertinence."

Still another member of the versatile reportorial staff was J. Otis Swift, the nature man, who was to found the Yosian Brotherhood, an outdoorsy fraternity that hiked for years up and down the Palisades, sniffing flowers, harking to bird calls, and breathing fresh air in gulps that Swift faithfully recorded. He was a run-of-the-mill reporter until Swope read a murder story he wrote. The body had been found under a yellow pine tree, which Swift had knowledgeably described as a *pinus echinata*. Swope was always impressed with that sort of thing, and at once he took Swift off crime and put him on nature. Swope would subsequently consult the erudite Yosian, who called his department "News Outside the Door," when some special outdoors situation arose. It was to Swift that he turned for advice, not that anything ever came of it one way or the other, when Florence White, concluding one day that the executive editor's crusades were too heated and that maybe the *World* should embark on one less inflammatory than, say, exposing a cartel in aluminum, urged that the paper start a drive to collect funds so New York City could put up scattered dovecotes for refugee pigeons.

One of the *World*'s most brilliant writers under Swope was William Bolitho, the author of *Twelve Against the Gods*. He was born in South Africa and his real name was William A. Ryall. After being wounded in the First World War he went into journalism. For a while he was the Paris correspondent of the Manchester *Guardian*. In 1923 he began sending pieces to the *World*. One of his earliest was an account of a race that the great French horse Epinard ran at Newmarket, in England. The

World's home-office racing man was George F. T. Ryall, who was born in England but was unrelated to the South African. When the paper came out carrying two horse-racing stories from different continents with Ryall bylines, Swope judged that life was complicated enough for his readers without their being subjected to that. He cabled William Ryall and suggested that he change his name. Bolitho was that Ryall's mother's maiden name, and he submissively gave up his true identity. (Later, George Ryall, too, forsook his patronym, signing his *New Yorker* racetrack column "Audax Minor.") Bolitho, like Swope a redhead, spent most of his short life in Europe—he died, in France, after a country doctor prescribed a laxative for a ruptured appendix—but he came to New York and to the *World* office for several months in 1928. An anti-Fascist book of his published two years earlier, *Italy Under Mussolini*, was dedicated to Swope, whom Bolitho, with more feeling than style, called "the type of those newspaper men who are not allowed in Italy under Mussolini."

Another book respectfully dedicated to Swope was the published version of the play *Five Star Final*. Its author, Louis Weitzenkorn, who went to the *Evening Graphic* when the *World* stopped publishing, was feature editor of the Sunday *World*. His dedication went, "To Herbert Bayard Swope. The greatest newspaper man I ever knew. The ethics of journalism I learned from him made the author of *Five Star Final* a failure as a tabloid editor." (Swope's ethical code would have driven a tabloid right out of business. He refused to let the *World* publish anything about divorce cases until they reached the courts. It was also part of his ethics that when a divorce case involving well-known people got that far, the *World* would write about it even if one of the principals happened to be Ralph Pulitzer.)

Weitzenkorn was a short, vain, Napoleonic man. He adopted a lordly air toward most people, but toward Swope his attitude was one of unadulterated hero worship. The playwright had a merry social life—he was married five times—and he would permit no one to rouse him before noon, unless Swope wanted to talk to him, at which special summons he would leap from his bed, or from somebody's bed. Weitzenkorn had his own modest eleventh-floor domain at the *World*, which was populated by, among others, a society editor, Mrs. Josephine Ober, of such exquisite manners that she seemed to spend half her time saying polite how-do-you-dos to people straying in and out of the office she shared with half a dozen other writers. She was celebrated at the *World* for the ladylike "Good morning" with which she once greeted a cat that jumped onto her rolltop desk.

Another Weitzenkorn factotum, later also a dramatist himself, was Norman Krasna, whom the Sunday editor once solemnly enjoined, after the *World* folded, "Always remember, when you feel the newspaper racket is the blackest, that there's a chance that Herbert Bayard Swope may buy a paper." Krasna, the son of a Bronx sewing-machine operator, got a copy boy's job at the *World* as a teen-ager, while taking pre-law night courses at Columbia. He became so enchanted with journalism, real and make-believe, that he gave up the law after attending a matinee of *The Front Page.*

It was typical of the free-wheeling way in which the *World* functioned that Krasna had barely been employed there when Weitzenkorn appointed him judge of a high-school letter-writing contest the paper was sponsoring. All went well until the *World*'s promotion department arranged for the judge—who, the promotion men were unaware, was no older than some of the students whose work he'd assayed—to make speeches around the municipal high-school circuit. Swope rescued Krasna by insisting that it would be unthinkable for a man operating in a judicial capacity to court notoriety.

Next, Krasna, who knew nothing about the theater or its off-shoots, found himself reviewing the variety bill at the Palace. He was so naïve when he began that he thought movies were shown there, too. But after a few weeks he was affecting a floppy black hat strikingly evocative of the sartorial trademark of George Jean Nathan. One night a theatrical press agent introduced Krasna to a man whose daughter was in a small Palace act. While shaking hands the father pressed a twenty-dollar bill into the *World* critic's palm. Krasna, aflame with youthful idealism, spurned it and strode off huffily. When he returned to the office he recounted the whole sordid adventure to the then night city editor, Benjamin Franklin, an older and more cynical man. Franklin asked him what he'd done with the bribe. "I didn't take the filthy money! I'm from the *World!*" cried Krasna, his normally high-pitched voice going up an octave or so. "Search him!" commanded Franklin. A half dozen lounging reporters leaped to their feet, gabbed Krasna, turned him upside down, and shook him vigorously.

Krasna was so upset by both the physical and the spiritual violence inflicted on him that for some time he vengefully castigated *all* the acts at the Palace. The result was that a man from the *World*'s advertising department, located four stories beneath the city room, came up to Franklin and reported that the Palace was threatening to withdraw its ads from the paper and that maybe the cheeky kid who was responsible for this should be taken off that assignment, or at the very least toned down. If there was one thing Swope's subordinates well knew, it was that he, like any self-respecting editor, was ever watchful for and resentful of business-office interference in his bailiwick. Between the editorial and advertising departments of a publication, Swope insisted, there should be an "unbridgeable gulf." Franklin, who had started all the fuss by teasing Krasna, grabbed the advertising man by the lapels, shoved him toward an elevator and said, "I never want to see you step one foot above the eighth floor again." The fate of the girl whose father tried to grease the *World*'s palm is unrecorded.

13

―――――――――――――

THE MOST celebrated and, it was widely thought, most gifted among Swope's stable of writers were those who pranced and capered on the page opposite the editorial page, many of the readers of which, following Swope's time-saving example, came to call it the Op. Ed. page. When he assumed the executive editorship the page had no particular sobriquet and no particular distinction. It was a catchall repository for obituaries, society news, advertisements, reviews of books and plays, and the disclosure that certain out-of-town buyers were in town. Referring to the genesis of the Op. Ed. page, Swope once wrote Gene Fowler :

> For a long time while I was on the outside, and later when I was first the City Editor, I would notice, from time to time, that the opinion stories which had crept in, in spite of our hard and fast principle of having little or no opinion in our news columns, had been dominantly interesting. It occurred to me that nothing is more interesting than opinion when opinion is interesting, so I devised a method of cleaning off the page opposite the editorial, which became the most important in America . . . and thereon I decided to print opinions, ignoring facts.

Swope soon began to round up writers—among them Heywood Broun, Alexander Woollcott, Franklin P. Adams, Deems Taylor, Laurence Stallings, Samuel Chotzinoff, Harry Hansen, and St. John Ervine—who converted the page into quite possibly the most refreshing journalistic oasis of its era. History will probably not judge them all towering literary figures. Woollcott, for instance, had enormous prestige and influence in his day, enhanced by the flow of his syrupy voice, over the radio, into thousands of homes where he evangelistically preached the gospel of reading. But what he himself wrote was evanescent, and his reputation as a guide to others' works may eventually have to stand, or fall, on his impassioned espousal of the novelist James Hilton.

Still, Woollcott and his Op. Ed. confrères were a lively and intelligent group, even though the page they graced may in retrospect seem a mite better than it actually was. At times it was flat and at other times excessively cute, but for a daily commodity it was consistently good. And it was fresh in both senses of that word. Its contributors were encouraged by Swope, who never wrote a line for it himself, to say whatever they liked, restricted only by the laws of libel and the dictates of taste. To keep their stuff from sounding stale, moreover, he refused to build up a bank of ready-to-print columns; everybody wrote his copy for the following day's paper. Swope never entirely succeeded in cleaning advertising off the Op. Ed. page, but he tried. Occasionally, too, the page harbored news stories—such as a travel item that appeared, at the end of the 1924 Democratic National Convention, under the headline "B. M. BARUCH SAILS, LAUDING 2 LOSERS"—but the page was largely devoted to short and perceptive commentary, much of it funny and most of it free-flowing.

Some critics of the *World*, both off and on the staff, thought that Swope's preoccupation with the Op. Ed. page was so intense that the rest of the paper suffered by neglect. Certainly that page, his favorite of any, was a heavy drain on his editorial budget. The funds at his disposal were limited, yet when in 1923 he hired Woollcott to replace Broun as his drama critic—Broun moving over to write "It Seems to Me"—he offered the newcomer fifteen thousand dollars a year, with the fringe benefit of a three-month vacation. And while the Op. Ed. page attracted a devoted and enthusiastic following among New York's intellectuals, their delight in it seemed to point up ever more strongly the disparity between the *World*'s two main groups of readers—the urbane and cultured on the one hand, who for straight news, though, often preferred the *Times;* and on the other hand a larger body who seemed to prefer the rest of the *World* to its Op. Ed. page and who comprised what Ralph Pulitzer called "the lower fringe of population."

An early prize catch for the Op. Ed. page was Adams. F.P.A., who joined up at the start of 1922, was in no sense a discovery of Swope's. His "Conning Tower" had been running in the *Tribune* since 1914. Three months older than Swope, Adams, for all the casual air of his column, was a man of savagely puristic literary standards; if a poem that was supposed to rhyme or scan had the slightest flaw, he spurned it. (He, too, once honored his editor with a dedication: "To Herbert Bayard Swope, without whose help and friendly counsel every line of this book was written.") Adams brought over to the *World* the men and women who—though he never paid a penny for anything he ran—considered it a high honor to be published in "The Conning Tower," people like Dorothy Parker, Marc Connelly, E. B. White, George S. Kaufman, Ring Lardner, Edna Ferber, Samuel Hoffenstein, Gellett Burgess, Newman Levy (who signed himself "Flaccus"), Nate Salisbury ("Baron Ireland"), and Howard Dietz ("Freckles").

The contributors to "The Conning Tower" even had a club of their own, called the Contribunion. It held an annual dinner, and Adams would bestow a gold watch upon the writer who'd pleased him most in the preceding year. Initially, the Contribunion met at Scheffel's Hall, above a saloon at Third Avenue and 17th Street. Many writers had a double purpose in making submissions to F.P.A. They wanted to get into print and into the dinner. In time the eligibility list got so big that the affair was shifted to the Waldorf-Astoria. At the last dinner, in the mid-1930s, by which time Adams had moved over to the *Herald Tribune*, Swope was the master of ceremonies. F.P.A. never went himself. He claimed he didn't want to get to know his contributors too well, so his judgment of their work wouldn't be swayed by personal factors. (Swope's viewpoint, of course, was just the opposite; he wanted to get to know *everybody* well.) Adams was perhaps wise to take that position. He could be so ornery and irascible that if some of his contributors had become too intimately acquainted with him they might have stopped sending him their squibs.

At an early meeting of the Contribunion, Adams deputized Robert Benchley, a recent Harvard graduate, to present the watch on his behalf. Fidgeting, adjusting his tortoise-shell glasses, and clearing his throat, Benchley hauled forth a bulky sheaf of manuscript and declared that, inasmuch as a timepiece was involved in the proceedings, he thought his audience might be interested in some statistics he'd brought along about the watch business. The audience groaned. Benchley droned on, owlishly, the audience shuddering, and it was not until he said something about his figures being of course "ad valorem" and not "per capita" that the audience began to catch on and to titter. Soon the whole room was roaring, enraptured by the first performance of what was to become Benchley's "Treasurer's Report."

Benchley worked briefly for the *World* himself, writing mostly about books. When, in 1920, Swope asked him to become the paper's drama critic, he replied, "About the theater stuff: I don't think that I could do regular newspaper theater reviews, because I don't know enough about the theater or about what the public likes." The next year Benchley went to work for *Life*, and Swope wrote Krock, "Benchley flared, burnt steadily, flickered, wabbled, and practically went out, so I turned him over to David Lawrence, who had begun to seduce him."

Residence on the Op. Ed. page was sometimes transient. Stallings left after the success of *What Price Glory?* and was replaced as book critic by Harry Hansen, who had been on the Chicago *Daily News*. Hansen felt awe-struck at the prospect of being featured on the Page. "From Chicago, F.P.A. and Broun and Woollcott and all the rest of them looked very tall," he said. He soon felt he had enough stature himself to complain, when Swope stopped by his office one day to see if he was comfortable, about a partition that cramped his cubicle. "Get an ax and sledgehammer and break it down," Swope said benevolently and sailed on off. The partition was ultimately removed, in routine fashion.

The *World*'s music critic, when Swope assumed command, was James Gibbons Huneker. He couldn't stand noise and was beset by the clacking of typewriters all around his office. Swope let Huneker use his own relatively quiet office—when, it went without saying, he was not present himself making its walls ring. Huneker died in 1921, and Swope got Deems Taylor to replace him. Taylor was a composer and not a critic, but Swope liked him. Furthermore, it was prestigious for the *World* to have a man who could be reviewing the Philharmonic on one column of the Op. Ed. page, while a column or two away there could be excerpts from the flattering things that other papers' critics were saying about his own music.

One night Taylor's double life got him in jeopardy. He had composed some incidental music for a Jane Cowl production of *Pelleas and Melisande* and was eager to attend the première. But he also had a Mischa Levitzki piano recital to cover. Taylor had heard Levitzki play most of the scheduled program before, so he took a chance. He went to Miss Cowl's opening and prepared in advance a Levitzki notice that mentioned a "lucent and imaginative reading" of a Chopin sonata. At the last minute the pianist decided not to play the Chopin at all. After Taylor's imaginative, if not exactly lucent, review was published, the *World* received a number of questioning letters from music-lovers who'd been at the recital, but Swope was sufficiently amused by Taylor's embarrassment to let him off with a scolding.

Taylor fared better when the Philharmonic played a symphonic poem he'd written years before, "The Siren Song." Swope let him review it himself. Calling it "the novelty of the evening," Taylor embarked on a lengthy, parodic analysis:

> . . . We thought it a promising work with a certain freshness of feeling and a disarming simplicity of utterance that partly atoned for its lack of well-defined individuality. . . . The thematic material is, on the whole, good and offers possibilities for development, of which the composer has not always availed himself. . . . We should like to hear more works by the same composer.

After four years on the *World*, Taylor quit to concentrate on composing more works for others to hear. In his stead, Swope took on Samuel Chotzinoff, a pianist who'd accompanied Jascha Heifetz and Efrem Zimbalist.* Chotzinoff was a little more experienced than Taylor had been when he started in, but not much; the newcomer had written a few articles for *Vanity Fair*. The genesis of one of these had been accidental. He'd run into George Gershwin, and Gershwin had invited him to the first public performance of the *Rhapsody in Blue*. Learning that Taylor was leaving the *World*, Chotzinoff asked Arthur Samuels, then an

---

* Chotzinoff's assistant, for forty-eight hours, was Paul Draper, then eighteen and just out of school. His mother Muriel knew Swope, who took him on and let him review two unimportant concerts. Each time Draper wrote a gush of words, and each time his copy was cut to little more than a bare announcement of the numbers performed. He complained to Swope, who asked, "Are you interested in literature or journalism?" Draper mumbled something about a critic's right to unfettered expression, and was at once given a week's pay and his dismissal. He next went to *Musical America*, a journal so relatively harsher than the *World* that it assigned him to sell subscriptions. He was glad after all that to abandon music criticism and take up dancing.

advertising man, how to get to Swope. Swope was abed with the flu, and Samuels had an article that Chotzinoff wrote about Gershwin's piece mounted, as if it were a presentation to a client, on a huge sheet of cardboard, carried to Swope's bedside, and draped across him. Swope agreed to hire Chotzinoff if only somebody would move the weight off his chest.

Swope, whom Chotzinoff once described in music-critic's jargon as a man who "was so brilliant vocally and had such virtuoso knowledge and was so voluble that he overwhelmed people," tried to make things as easy as he could for his new Op. Ed. man. When Chotzinoff, on his first assignment, reached a theater where an opera company was holding forth, he was pleasantly surprised to find Alison Smith in the lobby. Swope had sent her over to keep him company and stem his nervousness. Notwithstanding, Chotzinoff was in such a panic he didn't hear a note of the music, and when he got back to the *World* office he was sure he couldn't write a word.

Swope, whose solicitousness for a new and hesitant employee was often boundless, had made arrangements there, too. Joseph Canavan, the city-desk man who often cried, came over and told him not to worry, that there was no rush, that the presses would be held until whenever his copy was finished. After a couple of hours, Chotzinoff still hadn't written a word. Canavan, on one of his periodic tours of inspection, found him collapsed over his typewriter, in tears. That set the Irishman to bawling himself. At around three o'clock Chotzinoff dried himself off and turned out a review of sorts. He thought it was awful and that he would lose his job as soon as Swope saw it, and in despair he went home and threw himself on his bed with all his clothes on. At six o'clock, while he was still lying there, rigid with apprehension and mortification, his phone rang. It was Swope. "Jesus Christ, that's a God damn good first piece," Swope said. Chotzinoff took off his clothes and went to sleep.

Swope's musical ignorance was often a source of amusement to his staff. Popular culture was the only kind he understood well. Once he urged Chotzinoff to go downtown to Little Italy and review whatever he could hear from street corners—largely organ-grinders' recitals. Another time Swope told him that the kind of musical writing he liked was exemplified by a piece Alison Smith had done after listening to *Siegfried*. She compared the dragon's eyes to the headlights of a subway train. Except for the annual opening of the Metropolitan Opera Company, which was as much a social as a musical event, Swope rarely went to an opera or concert. Occasionally, however, Chotzinoff would take Margaret Swope to the Philharmonic, for which, in the Twenties, tickets were avidly sought. (He was offered as much as a hundred dollars for one of his.) Chotzinoff escorted her to ·a Leopold Stokowski concert at Carnegie Hall one night. By then Chotzinoff was an old hand at music criticism and had figured out a way of sleeping unnoticed at Carnegie Hall, where the atmosphere could be quite stuffy. He would put an elbow on one arm of his chair and cover his eyes with one hand, simulating deep thought. Happily, he didn't snore. The night he took Margaret was especially humid, and Stokowski was conducting a long, dreary Russian symphony. Chotzinoff quickly fell asleep, but his elbow skidded off its perch and rammed his boss's wife in the ribs. He awoke, appalled. Margaret graciously put him at ease. "Don't worry," she said before he could apologize. "I was asleep, too."

Swope could be equally reassuring. He called Chotzinoff in one day, pointed to a stack of letters on his desk and thundered, "You see these? They're all about your reviews. One hundred and fifty of them, and all against you." Chotzinoff could only say, "You want me to leave?" "Hell, no," said Swope. "If one hundred and fifty people say they don't like you, it means they read you."

For much of Chotzinoff's tenure as the *World*'s music critic, Woollcott was its drama critic. One night in 1926 the Spanish performer Raquel Meller opened in New York. She was celebrated, but hard to classify. She sang and danced and liked to be billed as a *diseuse*. Swope had a hard time deciding who should cover her première. He finally concluded she was primarily a dramatic artist and sent Woollcott. (Since part of her performance consisted of pelting her audience with violets, he might have sent J. Otis Swift, the nature editor.) Swope was at the opening himself, in his customary man-about-town role, and though he published Woollcott's estimate that Miss Meller was a "rare artist" comparable to Charles Chaplin, Ruth Draper, and Eleonora Duse, he disagreed with it. Then Swope instructed Chotzinoff to write about the *diseuse*, too. Chotzinoff appraised her material as second-rate and the lady herself as anemic and monotonous.

For the most part, Swope gave Woollcott a free hand, even when he was dissatisfied with a show and went after it with unmitigated waspishness. Sometimes Woollcott's acerb judgments distressed Pulitzer. The publisher thought it inexcusable when Woollcott called *A Masque of Venice*, starring Arnold Daly, "a pretentious bit of sedulous lunacy" and added that "a large and exceedingly bronchial audience assembled to watch Arnold Daly go down for the third and last time." Swope conceded that perhaps Woollcott had gone a mite far, but only once or twice did he feel constrained to curb his splenetic reviewer. Before Eugene O'Neill's *Strange Interlude* opened, in 1928, Woollcott wrote a piece for *Vanity Fair* expressing misgivings about the play. Swope thought a man who had already taken a public stand about a dramatic offering was disqualified from reviewing it objectively. *Strange Interlude* was probably the most important new play of that season, but Swope nonetheless ordered Woollcott to step aside and let Dudley Nichols substitute for him. Then, to demonstrate there was nothing personal in it all, Swope gave Woollcott his own first-night ticket. The muzzled critic escorted Swope's wife to the performance.

Swope's insistence that the contributors to the Op. Ed. page be allowed to function without interference—except, on occasion, from himself—put him in the position of having frequently to defend them from assaults by his less indulgent colleagues. The business department, with an eye more to Pulitzer's "lower fringe of population" than to the cerebral folk who liked Woollcott, Broun, and Adams, would keep pointing out whenever Swope would listen that much newspaper advertising space was sold on the basis of the quantitative, not the qualitative, nature of a paper's circulation. Florence White thought that Swope let his Op. Ed. writers run wild and that he tolerated irreverent and even off-color nuances in their work that were entirely inappropriate for a daily newspaper, and, what was worse, were irritating to advertisers.

Moreover, White wondered worriedly, why did Adams, in his relentless struggle to elevate the standards of grammatical usage, always have to be picking on mistakes he spotted in advertisements? "Why not order F.P.A. to ignore advertising copy in his criticisms?" White said in a memorandum to Swope. "He has the whole book world to shoot at. Why not, at the same time, order him to stop advertising stores in his column. . . . No other newspaper in this country would stand for this deviltry of an employee. Why do we?" The answer, as White well knew, was that the *World* stood for it because Swope stood for it. The only time he ever changed a line of Adams' column was when an item that had been factually correct when F.P.A. turned his copy in had become inaccurate by press time. Adams, thanking Swope in print one time for extending him such freedom, said that "as never in all my life have I been let go my own way, his leaving me alone being almost ostentatious."

No one in the other executive departments of the paper could ever be sure what would crop up next on the Op. Ed. page. Swope considered the commentators whom he nurtured there exempt from the general rule of the paper that the news and editorial departments should not, if it could possibly be avoided, be in overt conflict. Sometimes it seemed as if his Op. Ed. boys went out of their way to proclaim their iconoclasm. One day in 1926 Walter Lippmann wrote an editorial attacking a couple of novels. He thought their main characters were thinly disguised and scandalously drawn facsimiles of real and prominent individuals, including an ex-President. "Both these books should be withdrawn at once," Lippmann wrote. "No other course is open to the publishers." The very next day, on the Op. Ed. page, Harry Hansen was publicly arguing with him. *He* thought one of the books was tedious and the other second-rate and tasteless, but, looking the page opposite the page opposite straight in the eye, he added that he did "not agree with the *World* that it should be withdrawn."

The Op. Ed. men, to the further annoyance of some of their associates, had an irrepressible tendency to engage in log-rolling. Broun would write about having played cards with F.P.A., and F.P.A. would write about Woollcott's neckties or Stallings' imprecise use of the English language. Lippmann thought that when they all began taking in one another's wash like that it was a "ridiculous performance," and Krock complained that "our critical gentlemen are revolving around the others all the time." He cited as a particularly whirly instance a long telegram that Adams ran—a message from Stallings replying to an Adams rebuke for a misapplied word in *his* department. Most of the Op. Ed. writers were close friends outside of the office, and since Broun's "It Seems to Me" and F.P.A.'s weekly, Pepys-like diary were highly personal, their intramural references perhaps inevitable. One day in 1926, separated by a thin single column of type, Adams was writing about Broun and Broun about Adams. Broun's wife then was Ruth Hale, a Lucy Stoner of first magnitude, who would never permit herself to be addressed as "Mrs. Broun" if she could help it. Some of her husband's readers who were unaware of this may have missed the point one day when he, in a general discussion of marriage and divorce, quoted Ruth Hale without identifying her as anyone of particular intimacy and added, "We think that Miss Hale means to say that monogamy, far from being an impossibly high ideal, isn't good enough to stand as man's final solution of the problem of human relationships." *

Swope had brought Broun, like Adams, over from the *Tribune* and had told him right off that his writing should be provocative and controversial. Broun was an uncommonly hard worker. At one point in 1922 he was covering the theater, writing three other signed columns a week, doing a drama piece and a book piece for the Sunday paper, writing a weekly sports department for *Judge*, contributing an article each month to *Collier's*, *Vanity Fair*, and the *Atlantic Monthly*, and working on a novel. In what time remained, he led an active social life and brooded about the world. He had an ambivalent attitude toward Swope. The shaggy columnist was genuinely fond of his polished editor, but Broun was also suspicious of all men who held positions of authority anywhere, and at the *World* Swope represented authority. Broun achieved what was for him a satisfactory compromise: Although he was often and contentedly in Swope's company, on the most cordial of terms, he never called him anything but "Mr. Swope."

Swope often appeared in F.P.A.'s diary—"Mistress Margaret Swope" was similarly featured, as a glittering hostess—and Broun would write about him too, almost always kiddingly. One night in the spring of 1927 the Swopes and Broun were invited to a dinner party Bernard F. Gimbel was giving at his Westchester home for Gene Tunney, then the heavyweight champion. The Swopes offered Broun a lift. On the way, at 8:15 P.M., there was a collision, and both Swopes were injured. (In the course of liti-

---

* A joke of the era went, "A Lucy Stone gathers no boss." Swope rarely originated bons mots, but it was sometimes attributed to him. He had a feeling George S. Kaufman was supposed to have said it first, and, this being the kind of thing Swope could not resist pursuing to the point of absurdity, he wrote Kaufman and asked him to set the record straight. Kaufman, whose wit was prolific and really didn't care what off-hand jokes he might be remembered for, replied, "If you will meet me at my lawyer's I shall be happy to deed over to you all rights in and to and against that joke about Lucy Stone. I doubt if the transaction will really stand up in law because (a) I don't know if I really said it, and (b) I don't think it's much of a remark anyhow."

gation that ensued, a lawyer representing the driver of the other car tried to elicit from Swope the admission that, since he was going to dinner at that hour, he must have been late and his chauffeur must have been speeding. Swope, who had already infuriated the presiding judge by appearing at 3:15 P.M. for a court session that had been set for 10:00 A.M., professed astonishment. He said he imagined dinner was to have been served at around 8:30 or 9:00. "*What?*" exclaimed the lawyer cross-examining him. "Somewhere between 8:30 and 9:00," continued Swope. "Country dinners are usually indeterminate." "Country dinners are *what?*" asked the lawyer. "Is usually a non-fixed feast," the transcript quoted Swope as replying. "Your idea of the country people is they dine about 8:00 or 9:00?" "City people in the country, yes," Swope said. The lawyer abandoned that line of questioning as hopeless.)

Broun, who was unhurt in the accident, devoted a column to it. He led off, "For ages I have been curious to know what would happen if the nose of a great editor was shattered. I find that it bleeds." Then he quoted a headline that had appeared over a Yonkers *Statesman* story about the crash:

WORLD EDITOR
AND WIFE HURT
IN AUTO CRASH

———

Swopes are Injured
On Central Ave.—
Broun Shaken.

Broun added that his fans in the *World*'s city room thought the headline might better have gone:

HEYWOOD BROUN
ESCAPES DEATH
IN AUTO CRASH

———

Columnist Has Narrow
Call on Central Ave.
—Swopes Hurt Too.

Broun, who of all the Op. Ed. galaxy was the greatest trial to his editor, had the misfortune, three months after the smashup, to

270

collide jarringly with the *World*'s management at a time when Swope was not present to give him all-out support; the horses were running at Saratoga. The Sacco-Vanzetti case was the cause of the difficulty. The two men had been sentenced to death and their case was being reviewed, at the direction of Governor Alvin T. Fuller of Massachusetts, by a three-man committee headed by the president of Harvard, A. Lawrence Lowell. Broun was a Harvard man himself, but the bonds that tied him to his alma mater had ever been gossamer. When the Lowell committee upheld the death penalty for Sacco and Vanzetti, the editorial page of the *World*, which had been for clemency all along, said temperately that while the law of the land had to be obeyed, it still seemed possible that an injustice had been done. On the opposite page Broun had a good deal more than that to say:

. . . What more can the immigrants from Italy expect? It is not every person who has a President of Harvard University throw the switch for him. If this is lynching, at least the fish-peddler and his friend, the factory hand, may take unction to their souls that they will die at the hands of men in dinner jackets or academic gowns, according to the conventionalities required by the hour of execution.

The following day, there was a *World* editorial begging Governor Fuller to be merciful and to commute the men's sentences to life imprisonment, and opposite it there was a Broun column that said, "Shall the institution of learning at Cambridge, which we once called Harvard, be known as Hangman's House?"

Pulitzer had gone to Harvard also, and he had had about enough of that sort of thing. Then the *Times* came out with a lead editorial which tried to put the Sacco-Vanzetti case into the general context of the national concern about radicals of explosive militancy. Providing its own capitals, the *Times* said, in part, ". . . if we are to measure out condemnation for cowardly bomb throwers, we should not overlook men like Mr. HEYWOOD BROUN, who asks in the *World* whether 'the institution of learning in Cambridge which once we called Harvard will be known as Hangman's House.' Such an educated sneer at the President of Harvard for having undertaken a great civic duty shows better than an explosion the wild and irresponsible spirit which is abroad. . . ."

Pulitzer had barely swallowed that bitter pill dispensed by an honored rival when Broun turned in a third column attacking Lowell. That did it. The *World* continued to run editorials pleading for the condemned men, but its readers who wondered what Broun would say next found instead at the top of the Op. Ed. page a boxed statement headed "Regarding Mr. Broun:"

> The *World* has always believed in allowing the fullest possible expression of individual opinion to those of its special writers who write under their own names. Straining the interpretation of this privilege, the *World* allowed Mr. Heywood Broun to write two articles on the Sacco-Vanzetti case, in which he expressed his personal opinion with the utmost extravagance.
>
> The *World* then instructed him, now that he had made his own position clear, to select other subjects for his next articles. Mr. Broun, however, continued to write on the Sacco-Vanzetti case. The *World*, thereupon, exercising its right of decision as to what it will publish in its columns, has omitted all articles submitted by Mr. Broun.
>
> RALPH PULITZER
Editor, the *World*

Broun was out of the paper—on what he called a "permanent strike" and what Pulitzer called in columns other than his own a "witch's sabbatical." He stayed out for four months, writing for a string of publications. Then, after all sorts of sub-rosa negotiations and face-saving gestures, he came back. "We always have been properly impressed with the value of Mr. Broun to the *World*," Swope announced upon his homecoming. "Mr. Broun has learned the value of the *World* to him. We are glad that he is returning." Broun, for his part, stated that he realized he would now be liable to some editing; and with that confession, the shining integrity of the Op. Ed. page seemed somehow to have been irreparably, if not fatally, tarnished.

Had Swope been on hand when Broun was disciplined, sparks would undoubtedly have flown at a meeting of the *World*'s top executives, who when formally assembled were known collectively as the Council. This policy-making group had been established by Pulitzer in the spring of 1920. The Council was, at the start, supposed to meet every afternoon (later, three sessions a week were deemed sufficient), and frankness was to be the overriding factor in its deliberations. Pulitzer, White, and Swope were usually in attendance, along with the head of the editorial page. Krock sat in after he arrived. Cosgrave was there, too, and he usually kept the minutes, which recorded innumerable discussions of past mistakes, prospective crusades, dilatory reporters, double entendres, and other matters that seemed to require high-level attention.

The Council met in Pulitzer's office on the fourteenth floor. Arguments were frequent, some of them ending in what Cosgrave felt obliged to record were "violent recriminations." Swope was usually a heated participant. Once, in a rage, he bolted out of the room, cursing loudly and colorfully. Pulitzer's secretary was seated outside the door. As Swope emerged, his face crimson and the air blue, she looked up and caught his eye. She had been around a newspaper office long enough not to be shocked by anything she heard, and her glance was free of reproof. Swope, however, she recalled, "looked quite startled, clapped a hand to his mouth, and just seemed to shrink. And then he turned and fairly tiptoed back into the meeting. I was very much amused at the small-boy behavior, and rather touched by the big man's embarrassed reaction."

Sometimes the Council would argue about the scantiness of the paper's news coverage. It incensed Swope that the editorials kept referring to stories that had appeared not in the *World* but in the *Times*, and that the editorial writers, to keep their own files of source material comprehensive, clipped the *Times* instead of the *World*. The editorial writers would retort that they had no alternative; the news in their own paper was too skimpy to serve their purpose. Allene Talmey, a *World* reporter before she went on to an editorship of *Vogue*, once said in a magazine piece that Pulitzer would come out of such meetings "looking like a pair of pants, pressed between the immovable mattress of Lippmann, and the springs of Swope." *

Often there were arguments about propriety. In the 1920s, such self-appointed anti-vice crusaders as John S. Sumner were riding high, and the men who made the *World* spent much time wondering to what extent a newspaper should be a guardian or an arbiter of public morals. Pulitzer, for instance, thought it unwise that the drama department, reporting on a revival of *'Tis Pity She's a*

---

* As Swope's male reporters were his boys, Miss Talmey was one of his girls. Some years after she served a journalistic apprenticeship on the *World*, Swope reminded her, with somewhat heavy-handed humor, how he had "picked her out of the gutter" and given her a job. He had hired her six days after she left the Wellesley campus.

Whore, had seen fit to print its entire title. Swope said it was the paper's duty to publish news and that one could hardly inform the public of the presentation of a theatrical classic without identifying it. White said the show should be given the same treatment as a sodomy case: Ignore it.

While he was at it, he reverted to the by then familiar theme of the independence of the Op. Ed. writers. He said, according to Cosgrave's faithful minutes, that "Ideas of liberalism in vogue on the *World* at present were playing hell with the interest of the paper. Our readers do not share prevailing liberalism." If that was what the *World* wanted to espouse, White continued, why didn't it subsidize a new paper with another name and let Adams, Broun, Stallings, and the others run riot in its pages? "Let us save the *World* while there is still time!" he declaimed. Swope, rising to the defense, insisted that there were fewer pornographic details in the news columns of the *World* than in any other contemporary newspaper. White said that even if this were true, no one in New York would believe it. And so the debates went on and on.

One of the principles that Swope clung to his entire life, losing his grip only briefly every now and then, was a dedicated and outspoken antipathy to censorship, which he termed "a thug and a throttler." He himself had a curious puritanical streak—he thought lingerie advertisements showing women in brassières and corsets were obscene—but as an editor he was a persistent advocate of free expression, which endeared him, if not to his peers on the Council, to the Op. Ed. men who raised the Council's hackles.

Many of the plays produced in the Twenties, though tame indeed compared to some of the aberrational dramas that came along thirty or forty years afterward, were considered daring at the time. Many, to be sure, seemed to have been put on with no discernible motive except to titillate a clearly receptive public. In an era when the tabloid newspaper was establishing a foothold—the *Daily News* began in 1921 and the *Mirror* three years later—they were the tabloids of the stage. To what extent a responsible newspaper should condone, applaud, or decry such productions—or, perhaps, ignore them—was frequently discussed at Council meetings. A trashy play about a pitiable whore, called *A Good Bad Woman*, opened in February 1925. It was about to close, that same week, when the *World* ran an editorial about its "gutter orgies"—for good measure throwing in a slap at a wobbly sister show called *Ladies of the Evening*. The next day the news department chimed

274

in with a story headlined "PUBLIC SUPPORTS WORLD'S PROTEST AGAINST FILTH ON NEW YORK STAGE." Business picked up instantly at the box offices of both theaters, and the plays enjoyed quite lucrative runs.

One of the thorns that continually pricked the Council was Swope himself. He was almost always late to its meetings. Pulitzer began one session by presenting an agenda, with "Punctuality" as the first order of business. (In the capacious morgue that Swope kept up his whole life, there was but a single item filed under "Punctuality." It was a column of Broun's, about a goody-goody boy who'd never been absent and who'd never been late in thirteen years of attending school. Broun wondered if this seeming paragon would make out all right in life. He doubted it.)

Swope's sometime inaccessibility was another problem. The stereotype of a successful editor is a man so selflessly devoted to his newspaper that he has little, if any, time for the avocational interests that ordinary men pursue. (James Barrett furnished an example of this in his dedication for a book about the paper, *The World, the Flesh, and Messrs. Pulitzer:* "To my wife, who was jealous of my affection for THE WORLD . . .") Swope was as fond as any *World* man of the paper, but it was not his only institutional darling. Horse racing was one love, and the quest of money was another. Swope moved through the then unbridled world of high finance with ease and assurance, getting stock tips here, giving them there, and all the while making astonishing sums of money in an ascending stock market. Newspaper editors are not supposed to be rich. Swope was not only comfortably fixed; he was an authentic millionaire. While most of his colleagues sweated out their weekly pay checks, he could and did calmly discuss with his brokers, day in and day out, transactions involving hundreds of thousands of dollars.

It was no wonder that his associates on the paper, who could not afford to engage in *that* kind of speculation, began speculating whether, in return for the inside market information he appeared to be getting, he was not perhaps compromising his position as an editor who should play no favorites and grant no privileges. He made no secret that he hobnobbed with the likes of Baruch and Chadbourne, Otto Kahn and August Belmont, and those two pyrotechnical oil prospectors, Joshua S. Cosden and Harry F. Sinclair.

But these men did not fare especially well in the columns of the

World. Sinclair's involvement with the worst elements of the Harding Administration, which eventually got him jailed, was painful to Swope, who hated to see any of his friends humiliated, but the *World* covered his lapse from grace as it would have anybody's else. And when Cosden's teen-age son got arrested for rowdyism and the father called Swope to ask if the story could be left out of the *World*, Swope not only declined but gave the relatively unimportant incident a bigger play than did most other papers in town. As for Baruch, while there was no question in anyone's mind that any public statement he cared to make would find a refuge in the *World*'s columns, Swope extended himself not much beyond sending a memorandum to an assistant in the spring of 1926 that went, "Please tell the Sports Department in referring to Mr. Baruch never to call him 'Barney.' His name is Bernard M. Baruch, and he is to be referred to in that way, or as B. M. Baruch."

Swope's employees at the paper had long been aware of his rapport with Baruch, but they refused to be awed by it. After returning to the *World* from the Paris Peace Conference, Swope told Baruch he ought to write a Sunday feature about the postwar views of Woodrow Wilson, who was ailing and unable to speak for himself. Baruch scarcely ever wrote for *himself*. This time, to help him turn out a publishable manuscript, Swope chose a callow reporter who'd recently graduated from Yale, John Farrar. Later the head of his own book-publishing firm, Farrar had been a counter-intelligence agent in the A.E.F., but he was so naïve about economics and politics he had never heard of Baruch. Swope, who naturally could imagine no such possibility, called Farrar in and told him merely to go to Baruch's Long Island place—it was at Syosset—and put himself at his host's disposal.

Farrar withdrew to the city room and asked a couple of reporters if they knew who this fellow was the boss was carrying on about and where he lived. Deadpan, the reporters thumbed through a Long Island phone book and directed Farrar to an address in Kew Gardens. He went there, rang the doorbell and asked a woman who answered if her husband was home. She said he'd be back from work in an hour and told the reporter to wait outside. A couple of hours later Farrar timidly rang the bell again. This time the woman asked what he wanted, and he soon learned that her husband was a man named Baroo who worked for a railroad. Farrar retreated in confusion to a drugstore phone booth. He called Swope, told what had happened, and asked for clarification. Swope's roars of "Flathead!" nearly carried to Montauk Point.

Swope's chief difficulties at the paper were not with the reportorial staff or with the editorial page but with the business department. The Pulitzers and the various deputy administrators were so frugal that even the paper and ink used to put out the *World* were notoriously inferior to those of other dailys. By the end of 1927 the *World* was spending less than half of what the *Times* was, moreover, to obtain what it printed, let alone what its editorial matter was printed on or with. (The average weekday size of the *Times* was fifty-nine pages, of the *Herald Tribune* forty-six, and of the *World* thirty-two.) Swope asked once to be allowed to buy five minutes' worth of radio time each evening, to herald some of the attractions that would be on the Op. Ed. page the following day. His wish was not granted, partly because of what the *World's* circulation manager complained to Pulitzer was "systematic starvation of promotion enterprises." (The kind of promotion enterprise the paper did then go in for was a contest to discover New York City's champion girl jacks player.) The *World's* profits were dwindling. The morning paper had earned half a million dollars in 1922, and while this figure had been severely reduced by 1925, the paper was still in the black. But none of the gravy was being poured back into the operation.

At the start of that year, the Council made a decision—with Swope and Krock vociferously dissenting—that proved costly and possibly suicidal. The *World's* newsstand price was raised from two cents to three. The January 3 paper carried an unsigned, page-one box justifying the change. Expenses had increased, the statement said, and the *World* didn't want to make its advertisers foot the extra charges by raising their rates. "The *World* believes that it is unsound for any independent, aggressive, uncontrolled newspaper to have to rely to so great an extent on support other than that which comes from its own readers," the statement continued. Adams and Broun both took jesting note of the new price, the latter promising *his* readers that thenceforth they would get a fancier, three-cent column from him.

But the readers were fickle, as Swope and Krock had feared they'd be. The *World's* average daily circulation, just before the price increase, had been over four hundred thousand. A year later it had dropped off by sixty thousand, and two years later by an

277

additional twenty thousand—a 20 per cent decline over-all. The Council, now unanimously, reversed itself, and on January 2, 1927, there was another front-page statement, this one signed by Pulitzer: "There is a type of newspaper which can be content with a commercial success and a stationary circulation. But to the *World* a stationary circulation is a stagnant circulation and the half a million dollars a year which the extra cent brings in [there was nothing stagnant about the *World*'s arithmetic; it churned like a millstream] cannot begin to pay for even the risk of stagnation. . . ."

Swope was vindicated, but he was far from happy about the flip-flop performance. The downward revision in price brought back to the paper's fold only about half the vanished circulation, and advertisers were quick to perceive this infidelity. Swope did his best to make a banner occasion, when the new change went into effect, of what the Council proclaimed as "Two-Cent Day." He whipped up a complementary crusade, but it was a pale shadow of some of his earlier ones, and it was one he could hardly have had his heart in. It was a campaign against the sale in New York of allegedly pornographic magazines—precisely the sort of prurient antics against which Swope's literate commentators had persistently and eloquently wailed.

The reporter assigned to the pornography beat was a sardonic Jesuit, Hugh O'Connor, who'd been trained as a civil engineer and had come to the *World* as an assistant music critic—the versatile type who appealed to Swope. O'Connor, presumably with Swope's blessing, or at any rate without his express disapproval, proceeded to turn out a tongue-in-cheek exposé of the horrible situation. The headline above his first revelation was straightforward enough—"OBSCENE MAGAZINES OVERRUN NEW YORK; OFFICIALS POWERLESS"—but the story that followed was impish. The publications under assault—some twenty of them, with a total and hardly terrifying circulation of a hundred and fifty thousand—were popularly known as "art" magazines. The reporter selected as his first civic-minded individuals to comment on them two men who weren't even in New York. They were professors at the Yale School of Fine Arts, and the gist of what they had to say, in solemn tones, was that such art magazines as those the *World* abhorred were unnecessary for Yale art students. O'Connor threw in a quotation he ascribed to an unnamed publisher of one of the suspect journals. "Smash New York, and

278

you've killed the fake art magazine," he said. The inference was that he regarded New Haven as a hick town.

The next day the *World*'s front page trumpeted, "CITY ACTS TO BAN FAKE NUDE 'ART' AS PROTESTS RISE." The *World* had had a "flood" of calls, it said. "So spontaneous and numerous were the communications that it appeared to be a prime instance of the intelligent guidance of public opinion rather than its creation." (That sounded like a crack at some of the paper's earlier, and more substantial, crusades.) The mayor, Jimmy Walker, got into the spirit of things and divulged to the *World* his earnest determination to clean up the newsstands. (Lippmann's editorial page seconded the motion, dutifully if not thunderously.) The following day was a Sunday, and the *World* appropriately ran front-page pictures of a priest, a minister, and a rabbi, all of whom pronounced themselves aghast at the besieged magazines. This pictorial spread had the desired effect, for the Monday paper was able to say, "WORLD'S WARFARE ON PORNOGRAPHY HAILED IN PULPITS." A couple of preachers got carried away in their contemplation of sinfulness and digressed from the main theme to attack rum. This may have displeased the *World*, which was steadfast against prohibition, but on the whole the clergy responded admirably to the paper's clarion call. (Broun got into the act, too. He said some of his readers were wondering why he hadn't spoken out on the art-magazine question. He said he hadn't because he was puzzled—not knowing quite what tack to take inasmuch as he himself was a painter with a leaning toward nudes.) Some reverends were still belaboring the fake nude art pornographic magazines the following week, by which time the *World* had squeezed all it thought it could out of that sordid issue and was focusing its attention on a revolution in Mexico.

Meanwhile, Swope had been getting apprehensive about still another cloud that was casting a shadow over his working horizon. It was becoming clear at the *World* that the youngest and richest of the elder Pulitzer's three sons was somebody to reckon with. Joseph Pulitzer's last will and testament decreed that the profits from his publishing enterprises should be split into peculiar fractions. His namesake, running the *Post-Dispatch* out in St. Louis, was to get one-tenth. Another tithe was set aside for half a dozen senior employees, like Swope. One-fifth was to go to Ralph. The remaining three-fifths belonged to Herbert, who was fourteen when his father died in 1911.

Herbert Pulitzer, an amiable, soft-spoken man known as Tony, had spent much of his boyhood in the south of France. He'd returned to the United States to attend St. Mark's and Harvard, where he was chiefly noted for a Rolls-Royce. Back in Europe, in 1921, he'd had a fling as a foreign correspondent. He accompanied an American relief mission to Russia, and he sent the *World* a dispatch saying that capitalism was on the upsurge in the internal economy of that nation and that the beds in the Moscow hotels were full of bugs. His account came in to Swope, who handed it over to David Loth to prepare for publication. Since the story had been written by a Pulitzer, and a three-fifths-of-the-profits Pulitzer at that, Loth assumed he was supposed merely to correct the grammar and spelling. When he handed Swope the edited but not much altered piece, Swope said, "Jesus Christ, can't you make a better story out of it than *that?*" "Yes, but this is what the man wrote," Loth said, "and it's Herbert Pulitzer." "Oh, Christ, pay no attention to *him!*" Swope yelled.

Before much longer, however, the youngest Pulitzer would be commanding a great deal of Swope's attention. Late in 1926 Herbert Pulitzer visited the United States again. He did some work on the *Evening World*, and he began to drop in at Council meetings to air his views. After a while there was no doubt around the office who was meant when members of the staff would speak to one another, with mock respect, of the Young Master.

The first issue of the *World* to come out under Swope's aegis was dated November 3, 1920, and carried news of Warren G. Harding's victory over James M. Cox. The last was dated January 1, 1929, and carried news of Franklin Roosevelt's inauguration as Governor of New York. These were fitting brackets for his stewardship of the paper, since politics was his special field of interest. He had neither the ambition nor the sustained drive nor the common touch that would have enabled him to run successfully for office, although he was often urged to do so, but he was fascinated with politics and with politicians. It was they who exercised power, and Swope was drawn to leaders and wielders and movers and shakers and manipulators as a moth is to flame. "I always knew you were far more a politician than a newspaper man," H. L. Mencken once told him. Mencken was half joking, but there were serious overtones in what he said.

Swope loved the raw excitement of political conventions, and he attended a good many of them, as reporter, editor, or, a couple of times, delegate. Whatever part he played in the proceedings, he made it his business to be as close as possible to the men who were involved in the big decisions. Charles G. Ross, the St. Louis journalist who became President Truman's press secretary, recalled Swope as a man he was always running into at nominating conventions, "in roles that I did not always fully understand but that seemed portentous."

Being a Democrat, Swope was never as intimate with the leaders of the Republican party as with those of his own, but he knew the top men on both sides. Of all the occupants of and aspirants to the White House whom he knew, the one he admired most was Alfred E. Smith, who Swope thought was "touched by genius that makes him the embodiment of the ideals of dreams." Few men were as close to Smith as Swope was. On the surface they had little in common. But Swope was always fond of underdogs, and Smith's crude and lowly origins and his raucous manner attracted the editor, who also saw in him, early and perceptively, the makings of a national leader of enormous promise. "His life represented the romance of America," Swope would write Smith's daughter after Smith died in 1944.

Smith, for his part, recognized in Swope a man who had no particular personal ax to grind, was widely acquainted and vastly informed, and was ever ready to provide a quick, unwavering answer to any question of public policy on which his opinion might be sought. Smith, moreover, was amused by Swope's boyish exuberance and by the glittering social orbit in which he spun. Smith was a man of relatively simple tastes and never tried to become a part of Swope's group, although he would have been welcome. Swope, though, became a part of Smith's. He was admitted to that inner circle of rough-hewn politicians who convened at William F. Kenny's Tiger Room, a male New York retreat on West 23rd Street to which Franklin Roosevelt never quite gained access.

Swope got to know Al Smith, then a lower East Side alderman, before the First World War. The *World* man even then foresaw that the Protestant stranglehold on national political offices was weakening. In the summer of 1917, for instance, Swope wrote to Mayor John Purroy Mitchel of New York, "Personally, I think you have opportunity for other and higher things than the

Mayoralty if you want to go after them. You are the first Irish-Catholic in America of whom this can be said and it becomes almost a duty to our political system for you to demonstrate that national or religious prejudice is no longer a vital factor."

Mitchel, who died in a plane crash soon afterward, didn't even get re-elected Mayor that fall, losing to John Hylan, a Tammany hack with whom Swope and the *World* waged a spirited feud for years. Smith, running for Sheriff of New York County, was on the winning ticket. "Al is a true humanist," Swope once wrote Robert Moses. "He saw good in all men and helped to bring that quality out in them." After the 1917 election, Swope saw much good in Smith, if only he could shake himself clear of the opprobrium of Tammany Hall. Swope hoped to be able to help bring out that quality in him.

After Smith had risen to the governorship of the largest state of the nation, Swope began to entertain real hopes that he could go all the way to the White House. Smith's Catholicism was, of course, the main drawback to that goal, and the extent to which Smith, as a public official, was influenced by his religious adherence was a chronic concern of Swope's. He urged the Governor once to take his children out of parochial school. As the head of a sovereign state, Swope said, Smith had a responsibility to uphold the public-school system, and he could best do that by precept. Smith acknowledged that Swope was right, in principle, but said it was too late for him to do anything about it; if he'd switched the children when he first went to Albany, that would have been one thing, but to do it afterward would smack of expediency. In 1926 there was a Eucharistic Congress in Chicago. The Papal Legate dispatched by the Vatican, John Cardinal Bonzano, stopped off in New York on his way west. Governor Smith, welcoming him, knelt and kissed his ring. The *World* made no mention of this obeisance, although the *Times* did, but Swope upbraided Smith privately. "What did you do that for?" he demanded. "You weren't acting as a Catholic. You were acting as Governor of a state, in your own bailiwick. You shouldn't have knelt to him or anyone else. *You* were the authority."

Swope never held any official position under Smith, but he was as trusted a counselor as were Belle Moskowitz, Robert Moses, or any of the full-time hands. "I sat on the coach's bench and gave advice on public evaluation—advice which occasionally was followed," Swope once said.

In the summer of 1924 Calvin Coolidge, having succeeded to the Presidency on Harding's death, was practically a shoo-in for the Republican nomination, but the Democratic candidacy was wide open. The principal contenders were Smith and William G. McAdoo. Not since 1868 had there been a national convention in New York City. With prohibition and the Ku Klux Klan the two major issues, and New York a city the majority of whose inhabitants were, like their governor, hostile to both restrictive institutions, Swope reasoned that the Smith forces could operate at fullest strength in his home environment. Furthermore, it would enhance the *World*'s reputation if the paper could receive credit for bringing the big convention to New York.

On April 11, 1923, more than a year before convention time, Swope asked the *World* Council to approve the idea. The Council, Cosgrave recorded telegraphically, "agreed success improbable but endorsed campaign." (Swope not only thought success probable, but was so optimistic he visualized starting a supplementary campaign to bring the Republican convention to New York in 1928.) For weeks the *World* advocated the scheme in its columns, while off the record Swope sought to win over Boss Murphy of Tammany Hall and other Democrats who would have a say in the matter—among them Chadbourne, the party's convention entertainment chairman; Joseph P. Day, the auctioneer; Morgan J. O'Brien, the former presiding judge of the Appellate Division of the State Supreme Court; and Tex Rickard, who ran Madison Square Garden, where the convention would presumably be held.

In January 1924 the Democratic National Committee met in Washington, D. C., to pick a convention site. Chicago, St. Louis, and San Francisco were New York's principal rivals. The New York contingent—O'Brien carrying a check for one hundred and fifty thousand dollars—set off for Washington, in a private railroad car, on what some called "Swope's wild-goose chase." Swope was not dismayed. "I'd rather put this over than anything else I ever did!" he announced as he was departing. "They think I can't do it!"

In Washington, Swope assembled a staff of *World* men—Charles Michelson, Charles Hand, and John J. Leary, a labor reporter, who had not long before won his paper still another Pulitzer Prize, for an exposé of working conditions in West Virginia coal mines. Among them they telephoned every one of the more than one hundred voting delegates. It was not easy going. Mrs. J. Borden

Harriman, for example, who finally did vote against New York, tried to dissuade Swope from even forcing the issue to a ballot. The Tammany Hall boys, she predicted, had no comprehension of what people from other parts of the country were like and would make one gaffe after another.

Swope persisted. He got two breaks. One was that when San Francisco came up with a cash offer of two hundred thousand dollars, O'Brien and Rickard magically produced enough extra money to bring New York's bid up to two hundred and five. Even more important was the blessing of McAdoo. The Senator from California had good cause to be alarmed about how his candidacy might be received in New York, though Baruch was his foremost supporter, but he was finally convinced that even if the big-city newspapers didn't endorse him, they would at least treat him fairly, and he failed to lodge any strong objection. On the third ballot New York squeaked through with a bare majority of the votes. Asked for a comment, Swope, ecstatic that he had captured what Percy Hammond of the *Tribune* would call "his pet convention," predicted wildly that *all* future political conventions would be held in New York City.

The 1924 Democratic convention began on June 25. It was, through circumstances beyond Swope's control, a fiasco. It was so memorable a nightmare that twenty years later, when Swope suggested mildly to Franklin Roosevelt that the Democrats think of returning to New York, the President reminded him of what he called the "Madison Square bullfight" and added that if he had anything to say in the matter, there would *never* be another such Democratic gathering in the city. Roosevelt had good reason to remember the occasion vividly. Struggling on his braces, he had taken his first clumsy steps toward a political resurrection after his crippling attack by climbing to the podium and nominating Smith with his "Happy Warrior" speech.

Like a good many other Democratic leaders, Roosevelt had been in doubt about the ascription of Wordsworth's felicitous phrase to Smith. Roosevelt thought, in fact, that the entire speech, which Joseph M. Proskauer had written, was too poetic, and he had written his own substitute address. Proskauer didn't like *that*. With Roosevelt and his amanuensis at a stalemate, both Proskauer and Smith suggested that Swope be called in as a mediator. At the Roosevelt town house on East Sixty-fifth Street, Swope was handed the two speeches, without being told which was whose.

He pronounced the "Happy Warrior" text a knockout, and Roosevelt yielded, though not without trying, as the conference went far into the night, to salvage some of his own words. "I recall vividly how I . . . had thrown away lavishly F.D.R.'s material," Swope wrote Proskauer later. "He wanted to save part of it and he crawled around the floor in his harness, picking it up."

Madison Square Garden was not air-conditioned, and it was midsummer in New York. A convention of conventional length would have been grim. This one dragged on for fourteen days and one hundred and three ballots, until the phrase "Alabama casts twenty-four votes for Underwood" became a national joke. The heat was so oppressive that Cordell Hull, the chairman, fainted several times while presiding. Everything that could have gone wrong did. When the delegates from Georgia demonstrated, the band that Tammany Hall had hired, in a blaring exhibit of the gaucherie Mrs. Harriman had foreseen, played "Marching through Georgia." * The intended compliment almost precipitated a riot. When Roosevelt nominated Smith, the hullaballoo raised for over an hour by a band of partisans who'd packed the auditorium not only didn't help the Happy Warrior's cause much but gave most of the delegates headaches, literally as well as figuratively.

McAdoo, what was more, quickly became disillusioned about his municipal reception. Friend of Baruch's he might be, but in the *World*'s view the Ku Klux Klan was also friendly to him. Three weeks before convention time, when it was too late to switch the site, the *World* was attacking McAdoo editorially with

---

* Irving Berlin was a Democrat then, and the *World*, which devoted page after page to the convention proceedings, ran the lyrics of a special campaign song he'd dashed off. It was called "We'll All Go Voting for Al," and it concluded:

> The White House will be ready,
> The room where dear old Teddy
> Made history is waiting for our pal.
> The servants are preparing
> To give the place an airing;
> They're dusting off the furniture for Al.

One earlier line went "Every fellow and every gal from Maine to Texas, They'll mark their X's in the Democratic circle for Al." F.P.A., who thought Eugene Debs, the Socialist candidate, deserved equal time, promptly came up with a lyric in "The Conning Tower"—"Every king and every queen From Fort Lee to Desbrosses, They'll mark their crosses In the Socialistic circle for Gene."

such blunt statements as "His devotion to liberty is open to question." (To the *World* anybody who wasn't strongly on record against the Klan was found wanting. An editorial calling on Coolidge to speak out on the subject said, "For Calvin Coolidge, this is a test of his Americanism and his manhood.") The Republican *Herald Tribune* ran a cartoon showing McAdoo in a Roman toga, near a marble column. "They say Caesar was too ambitious," went the caption. Behind the column, knives poised to stab the unwitting Senator, stood a bunch of assassins—all of them prominent in Democratic circles. Al Smith was in the lurking gang; but the first man in line, his blade nearest the victim, was Swope.

After the first hundred or so ballots it was obvious that McAdoo and Smith were hopelessly deadlocked and that neither could win. A conference was held at the Ritz-Carlton. The two contenders were there and three or four middlemen, Swope among them. The embittered rivals agreed to withdraw, and soon John W. Davis was nominated by the delegates, most of them too limp by then to care. They were also in many instances flat broke, not having figured on staying so long in so costly a city.

By the time the whirl was over, the *World* had dropped the notion of suggesting that the Republicans stop by in 1928. While it was true that the Broadway Merchants Association thanked Swope profusely, as well it might have, for bringing all the visitors and their money to the city, and while the *World* itself ran the face-saving headline "NEW YORK GAINED IN GOODWILL BY THE WORLD'S WORK," the whole episode was generally regarded as a political flop. Will Rogers, who was fond of Swope, said in a commiserating column that his bringing the 1924 convention to New York was a "crowning defeat," and added, "The Kaiser was exiled for life for less than that."

Swope resolutely continued his efforts on Al Smith's behalf, and he was probably as responsible as any other individual for his getting the nomination in 1928—at a convention held in Houston, Texas. On Smith's attaining the goal he had so long sought, Swope wired him, exultingly:

YOU HAVE BEEN NOMINATED TO BE PRESIDENT OF THE UNITED STATES. YOU, THE FISH-MARKET CLERK, THE STREET NEWSBOY. NO MAN HAS GIVEN YOU THIS GREAT HONOR THAT HAS COME TO YOU. YOU HAVE WON

IT BY WORK BASED ON INTELLIGENCE, JUSTICE, HONESTY AND PERSIST-
ENCE, ALL WELDED TOGETHER BY A FLAMING LOVE FOR AND UNDER-
STANDING OF THE COMMON PEOPLE, A PASSION YOU SHARE WITH
ABRAHAM LINCOLN. YOU HAVE DONE MUCH FOR YOURSELF, BUT MORE
FOR YOUR FAMILY. WITH THEM, YOUR FRIENDS FIND HAPPINESS IN YOUR
VICTORY; AND THE THOUSANDS WHO DO NOT KNOW YOU HAVE EVEN A
GREATER RIGHT TO REJOICE, FOR YOU HAVE MADE THEIR DREAMS COME
TRUE. IN YOU THEY SEE THEMSELVES LIFTED TO THE HIGH PLACES. IN YOU
THEIR FAITH IN LIFE AND MAN IS RENEWED AND STRENGTHENED. BECAUSE
OF THESE THINGS YOU CANNOT FAIL IN THE FINAL BATTLE YOU NOW
FACE. YOU WILL WIN THAT, AS YOU HAVE WON THE OTHERS, AND IN
THAT BELIEF I GO INTO THE FIGHT WITH YOU, BRINGING ALL I HAVE
IN STRENGTH, COURAGE AND DETERMINATION. WITH AFFECTIONATE
REGARD . . .

Swope hurled himself into the Smith campaign that summer and
fall with such energy that he even skipped Saratoga, and friends
who had never ceased to marvel at the perfection of his speech
were astonished to hear him saying "raddio" and "ain't." Back in
1920 Swope had been so eager for Hoover to become President
he felt that if the Republicans didn't nominate him the Democrats
should. But now Hoover was the enemy. Determined to beat him
by any means, Swope even had the London bureau of the *World*
try to confirm a few old rumors about him—one being that he
had spent so much time out of the United States he had somehow
forfeited his right to be President. The day after Hoover won, it
was with relief that the *World*'s chief London man, John L.
Balderston, reported to Swope, "This office will now cease to be
a detective agency and try to get back to journalism."

By Election Day Swope had already resolved to get out of
journalism himself. His decision had nothing to do with Smith's
prospects. Should Smith win, Swope had no special wish for a
personal reward; earlier, he had written Krock, "Incidentally, if
he is elected President of the United States, I want to tell you
what I am going to do: Pray God that I be let alone to try to run
the news end of the New York *World* bravely, intelligently, and
successfully." On election night Swope got so excited that for
the first time in nearly thirty years of his association with the
World he was seen to take a drink of hard liquor in the office. All
through the evening he was on the phone, checking returns from
across the country and growing increasingly glum. When Democratic hopes were all but gone, Smith's daughter Emily called

Swope and asked if it was true, as she'd heard on the radio, that her father was losing Virginia, North Carolina, and Florida. Swope said it was, and he had even worse news for her: Smith was losing New York. (The previous June, while attending the Republican convention at Kansas City, held just before the Houston conclave, Swope had been willing to bet twenty-five thousand dollars, at even money, that Hoover couldn't carry New York against *any* Democrat; but, as Swope informed Baruch ruefully, he could find no Republican takers.) It was a chastened Swope who, when he was finally persuaded there was no hope that the tide against Smith could turn, picked up a phone, called the Democratic nominee, and told him—thus, as far as the editor was concerned, making the hurtful verdict official—that he had lost.

A fortnight after Election Day, the Democratic National Committee began selling off the furnishings it had used in its New York campaign headquarters, at the bargain rates that customarily prevail in such forlorn circumstances. Swope, who knew he'd be opening up an office of his own at the start of 1929, made a gesture that nicely combined sentimentality and economy. For a mere five hundred dollars he acquired a batch of only slightly used walnut furniture, not to mention a hundred or more yards of Presidential-caliber carpeting. His prize item, Smith's very own campaign desk, was in due course adorned with an inscribed plate that said, "To my friend Herbert Bayard Swope. This desk and chair were used by me in national headquarters during my campaign as Democratic candidate for the Presidency of the United States. Alfred E. Smith. 1928." * Thus it became Swope's lot to occupy, for as long as he lived, the discarded throne of one for whom he had served valiantly as a would-be kingmaker.

---

* After Swope died, his widow gave Smith's desk to one of the Happy Warrior's grandchildren.

Above left, Margaret Swope at Horta, the Azores, in 1914, wearing a local *capote*.

Above right, as a young *World* reporter, in pre-First World War days. H.B.S. relaxes aboard the U.S.S. *Missouri*, with a naval escort.

Below, Germany 1916: H.B.S. and a fellow correspondent, James O'Donnell Bennett, with Captain Fritz von Papen, who before that was German military attaché in Washington, after that, attaché to Hitler.

Above left, crossing the Atlantic in October, 1916, with James W. Gerard, United States Ambassador to Germany.

Above right, H.B.S. in the working-press section at the Dempsey-Carpentier fight, Jersey City, July 2, 1921.

Every Sunday THE WORLD has 127,131 more city circulation than the *Times,* and 252,111 more city circulation than the *Herald Tribune;* an intensity of concentration unique in its field.

The World EXTRA

VOL. LXIX. NO. 24,396—DAILY.   Copyright Press Publishing Company (New York World) 1928.   NEW YORK, SUNDAY, DECEMBER 23, 1928.   FIVE CENTS IN MANHATTAN, BRONX AND BROOKLYN   TEN CENTS ELSEWHERE

SWOPE QUITS

Swope Quits, Swope Quits, Swope Quits, Swope Quits

By John L. Balderston

Swope Quits, Swope Quits,

Swope Quits, Swope Quits, Swope Quits

Swope Quits, Swope Quits, Swope Quits

Swope Quits, Swope Quits, Swope Quits

TIME

The Weekly News-Magazine

HERBERT BAYARD SWOPE
"Dynamic?" "No—cyclonic!"
(See Page 24)

VOL. III   NO. 4

JAN. 28, 1924

H.B.S. in a catalytic pose while Franklin D. Roosevelt and Al Smith go through the motions of friendship during the 1932 political campaign. (Smith to Roosevelt: "You old potato.")

At an Elsa Maxwell costume party in January, 1937. Left to right, Mr. and Mrs. Douglas Fairbanks, Mrs. Ogden Mills, and H.B.S. (*International News*)

Championship form: While Howard Dietz looks admiringly on, H.B.S. lines up a shot during a croquet tournament in 1938.

At Hialeah Park in Florida, 1939, with James A. Farley and John Sloan of the N.Y. Racing Commission. *(Photo by C. C. Cook)*

Bernard Baruch, John Hancock, and Trygve Lie solicit a word of advice from H.B.S. during a U. N. Atomic Energy Committee session in 1946. In the background: Dr. J. Robert Oppenheimer.

The very epitome of an elegant racing commissioner inspects one of his tracks (Lt. Gov. Charles Poletti, right rear, background). *(Photo by Gordon Morris)*

General Eisenhower, then Chief of Staff of the Army, decorates H.B.S. with the Medal of Merit in September, 1947.

Robert Moses, chairman of the Long Island State Park Commission, and H.B.S., his vice-chairman, confer in August, 1957, with Governor W. Averell Harriman of New York.

The stained-glass window once in the lobby of the *World* building on Park Row now ornaments the room memorializing H.B.S. at the Columbia University School of Journalism.

14

I N 1921, soon after becoming executive editor of the *World*
and moving into the thousand-dollar-a-week earned-income
bracket, Swope also moved into a then fashionable neighborhood,
renting an apartment at 135 West 58th Street, which he was to
occupy for ten years. He started off with a spacious fifth-floor
apartment, but soon found this too confining. He acquired the
apartment above his, spliced the two, and ended up with twenty-
eight rooms, eight baths, and twelve telephones. The upstairs
living room had such jewellike sparkle, with silver walls and
crystal sconces, that Elinor Wylie wrote a *New Yorker* story
about its glitter. Swope treated it as a throne room. Once he was
addressing a group of some forty friends at one end of the salon
when he became aware that at the other end a half dozen additional guests, their voices barely audible, were holding a conversation of their own. Swope stopped and yelled across the void that
separated them, "Am I to be interrupted in my own house?"

Swope's guests, an endless stream, were often on the scene
before he was, since he rarely got home from the paper before
midnight. He would usually arrive bursting with some tidbit of
late news that it pleased him to be able to divulge a few hours
before it would reach the newsstands and become public knowledge. In some respects the 58th Street ménage was less like a
private home than a public establishment. Samuel Chotzinoff lived
across the street. After attending a concert and writing his review,
if he didn't feel like going home, he would stop by the Swopes',
whether or not they happened to be on hand. He knew that food
and drink were always hospitably available. "It was like going to
Child's," he said.

Some of the more memorable parties of the party-loving Twenties took place in the neighborhood. A typical one was given at the apartment Chotzinoff shared with S. N. Behrman, later his brother-in-law. Chotzinoff's party, a bring-your-own-bottle affair to which the Swopes ferried a fleet of guests across the street, carrying whole cases of potables, cost the host only ten dollars, which he spent on salami. The entertainment, to hear which much of the general public would gladly have paid a ten-dollar admission fee, began with a piano recital by George Gershwin. Then F.P.A. and Pauline Lord acted out a skit. Then Irving Berlin played the piano. Then Gregory Kelly and Harpo Marx did a comedy magic act, with Marx costumed as a female Oriental.

The high spot was an endurance contest, featuring five of the greatest living violinists—Joseph Fuchs, Jascha Heifetz, Paul Kochanski, Albert Spalding, and Efrem Zimbalist. They all simultaneously played Paganini's showy, accelerated *Moto Perpetuo*. As soon as each got to the end, he was supposed to begin again. The one who lasted the longest would win. Marc Connelly started off the gifted quintet by firing a blank pistol, and as they all sawed dexterously away, the other guests egged them on by throwing money on the floor, as a prize for the survivor. One by one the virtuosos sagged and fell out of line. Heifetz got so tired he had to brace his bow-holding arm on the top of the piano. Then he collapsed. Fuchs prevailed, fiddling on for twenty-one minutes. It was days before any of them was ready again for Carnegie Hall.

There were many other friends living near the Swopes, among them Broun, Edna Ferber, Noel Coward, and the Wall Street man A. Charles Schwartz. He and his older brother Morton, a horse-fancier who came to New York from Kentucky and made a million dollars before he was twenty, were two of Swope's steadiest playmates. (At the Turf and Field Club enclosure at Belmont Park, Charles Schwartz had Box 42, Morton had 43, Swope had 44, and Baruch had 45.) For several years Swope shared a rented house with the Schwartz brothers during the August race meet at Saratoga. Charles Schwartz was a skilled gentleman boxer, and now and then, at a charity benefit, he would put on an exhibition bout with a professional. In 1923, when Jack Dempsey was training to defend his heavyweight title against Luis Firpo, the champion turned up at Saratoga and Schwartz went four rounds with him. Swope was Schwartz's second.

Two summers later, at Saratoga, Swope narrowly missed having to demonstrate how he would make out against the man who could stand up to Dempsey. Swope had beaten Schwartz at croquet one afternoon. Later, while the loser was taking a bath, he reflected that the victor's most telling blow had been struck with a ball that had somehow moved out from beyond a tree without a mallet's touching it. From his tub Schwartz accused Swope of nudging the ball with his foot. Indignant, Swope spat at Schwartz, who, enraged that his bath had been sullied, leaped from the tub and, not pausing to grab a towel, set out after Swope, both fists clenched.

One of those childish tiffs on which mature energies are often expended was now in full flower. Swope, with his head start and his long legs, made it safely to his bedroom and bolted the door. Schwartz, stark naked, raced outside, to the mild surprise of a few onlookers who'd been attracted to the scene by the murderous threats he was screaming, and tried a flanking attack through Swope's window. But Swope had got there first, too, and had locked and shuttered it. Then Schwartz charged back inside, changed his tactics, knocked gently on Swope's door, identified himself as a valet, and asked dulcetly if he could please come in to lay out Mr. Swope's things for dinner. Swope was too familiar with Little Red Riding Hood's misfortunes to fall for that. Then dinner guests began to arrive, and Schwartz reluctantly abandoned the chase and went off to put some clothes on. It was a measure of the times that for long afterward members of the thoroughbred-horse-racing set would regale one another with the story of the time Herbie Swope spat, like an irate llama, in Charlie Schwartz's bath water.

At the same time that the Swopes moved to 58th Street, they rented a country place, a rambling Victorian mansion at Great Neck, on the north shore of Long Island overlooking Manhasset Bay. The house, belonging to Lottie Blair Parker, the author of *Way Down East*, was a big, square structure, three stories high, with frosted-glass doors, a wrap-around porch, and a mansard roof surmounted by a gazebo. Ring Lardner said it looked as if it had been built by a man with a scroll saw and plenty of time. Lardner lived a hundred yards off, across a field. "It is almost impossible to work at times and still more difficult to sleep," he once said. "Mr. Swope of the *World* lives across the way, and he conducts an almost continuous house party. A number of other neighbors

[Clifton Webb was one of them] do the same; there are guests in large numbers roaming these woods all the time. Apparently they become confused occasionally and forget at whose house they are really stopping, for they wander in at all hours demanding refreshment and entertainment at the place that happens to be nearest at the moment." Lardner said the only way he could ever get any writing done was to go to New York and take a hotel room. One of his most felicitous, and most satirical, lines was his inclusion, among the *dramatis personae* of a burlesque operetta, of "Herbert Bayard Swope, a nonentity."

The Swopes' country establishment, like their one in town, resembled a public place of entertainment. Shakespeare-spouting poets and, when it came to that, Shakespeare-spouting pugilists might be seen there, milling and churning among Senators, polo players, professional gamblers, Supreme Court Justices, and horsey debutantes; the house was like a decompression chamber between social extremes. The carefree hours that F. Scott Fitzgerald spent under the Swope roof were evoked in his setting for *The Great Gatsby*. The conversation was animated and unpredictable. Dorothy Parker was there for dinner one night along with Governor Albert Ritchie of Maryland. He was the most prominent political guest present, and many of his table companions were directing questions to him about the state of the union. One man who wasn't had had too much to drink, and in the middle of it all he suddenly burped, loudly. There was a brief, embarrassed silence, into which Mrs. Parker deftly moved. "I'll get the Governor to pardon you," she said sweetly.

Age or social standing meant little at the Swopes'. Herbert and Margaret were good friends of their children's friends, and the Swopes' children were friendly, on their own, with their parents' crowd. Dullness was the only unforgivable sin. "It was an absolutely seething bordello of interesting people," Margaret Swope would say. She herself had emerged with beating wings from her early cocoon of diffidence. Of all the people around, she was fast becoming one of the most fascinating in her own right. "Herbert used to say he made two big mistakes—first, teaching me how to think, and second, teaching me how to talk," she would say, with excessive modesty. "The thought of ever opening my trap was unheard of until I began to see how easy it was. I decided to talk up. It surprised Herbert, and I think annoyed him a little."

Margaret had become a woman not only of striking beauty and

292

charm but of good sense and perceptivity. What was more, she had a notable wit—far sharper, and more scathing, than her husband's. It was a time when gossiping and backbiting were at the height of their popularity. Once at a party at Heywood Broun's, where much of the Swope crowd also congregated, the conversation had gone on for a while, with many knives being turned in many backs, when Newman Levy interrupted to ask, "Hasn't any one of you a decent thing to say about *any*body?" It was an interesting and novel thought, and all present paused to meditate upon it. The ultimate consensus was that the only person known to any of them about whom nothing mean could be said was George S. Kaufman.

Kaufman's first wife, Beatrice, a perennial guest at the Swopes', searching around one time for a suitable present for her hostess, gave her the cable address "Sourpuss." The recipient was overjoyed. Margaret's crosspatch pose won the unalloyed admiration of all her peers. They would repeat with envy her reproof to a male guest who had brought to her house a woman with a notoriously scarlet past: "Everyone who comes here must have a visible means of support." And thirty years after the event they would smilingly recall Margaret's riposte when a pompous man, speaking of a young and extremely celebrated lady they both knew well, observed, "She's a charming woman, but somewhat free with her body." "Yes," said Margaret, "but that's the only way she can dispose of it."

With Swope himself she was ordinarily much gentler. He was attractive to women, though he usually felt more comfortable with men, and his predilection for gambling now and then led him into a mild flirtation. It was the sort of lapse that the Swopes' friends figured would, if detected, unleash a spate of invective beyond anything they had yet heard emanate from Margaret, but she sometimes disappointed them. Once, for instance, Swope came into a room where she was playing cards and announced importantly that he'd just been talking to Senator So-and-so on the phone. Margaret looked up at him, said in a calm voice, "In that case, wipe the lipstick off your face," and went on with her game.

As is the tradition at some of the statelier English country houses, the Swopes gave their guests considerable latitude, even dispensing with such customary American amenities as introducing them to one another. Conventional introductions were generally superfluous; everybody was supposed to know who everybody else was. One evening, while the Swopes were dressing for dinner, an out-of-town Swope, a cousin, happened to be in the drawing room as some of the guests began to arrive. He scarcely knew who *anybody* was, but he did his best—quite unnecessarily—to introduce the later arrivals to the early ones. As the room filled up he had a hard time keeping track of who was who, and he pulled what in the Swope set was considered a terrible boner by going over to Ginger Rogers and saying he was sorry but he couldn't remember her name. Swope's own daughter got so accustomed to having movers and shakers under foot while she was growing up that as a young bride in Washington, when she was invited by Mrs. Eleanor Roosevelt to a private dinner at the White House, she said she was already packed to go to New York that night and didn't want to bother to change her plans.

There are celebrities, though, who happen not to be acquainted with all other celebrities, and since it was possible to spend a weekend at the Swopes' without ever being told by the host and hostess who the other guests were, the consequences could be awkward. Robert Moses recalled arriving at the Swopes' and finding Margaret at a card table with three other women. Margaret looked up and said, pleasantly enough, "Get yourself a drink," but her companions didn't even raise their heads. The mealtime routine was elastic, and one guest might be having breakfast in one room while another was having afternoon tea somewhere else. Some guests might be playing games, others listening to a pianist. There was usually someone around to play —Gershwin or Irving Berlin or Deems Taylor.

Still another pianist, Oscar Levant, was for some twenty years practically a member of the Swope household. Levant was notable for his churlishness, and the Swope establishment was one of the few he was welcome in for long. When he behaved too outrageously, Margaret would banish him. "The iron gate's up again," Levant would tell acquaintances, and he would absent himself from the Swopes' until Herbert persuaded Margaret to reinstate him.

Levant was at the Swopes' one evening when an ornament of the Empire, H. G. Wells, was invited. Swope selected most of his family's guests, and on this occasion had decided S. N. Behrman would be a good person to have over to meet Wells. Behrman had idolized the Englishman since he was in college and was in awe of him. Levant wasn't in awe of anybody ever and carried on in his usual gruff fashion. Several years afterward, Behrman ran into Wells again in London and reminded him that they had met at Swope's. Wells at once said, "And how is that strange young man?"

The casual atmosphere of the Great Neck house had its appealing side. One well-traveled guest of the Swopes observed, in a bread-and-butter note, "I have found broad personal freedom in schedule in the Canadian west, and extreme grace in detail in London, but the Swopes' is the only place I have ever found them both present under the same roof." And nearly everyone who was under that roof had a good time. Raoul Fleischmann once said he liked it so much at the Swopes' he hoped he'd die there.

Many of the Op. Ed. writers, and other staff men on the *World*, turned up at their boss's homes. Late Saturday night, Swope would often shepherd a carload of them out to the country, where, like as not, they would be joined by a flock of theatrical folk, to whom the Swopes' late hours were a blessing—maybe Laurette Taylor, or Leslie Howard, or Helen Hayes, or a couple of Barrymores. Two theatrical press agents, John Peter Toohey and David H. Wallace, were frequently around also. Wallace—who, reflecting once upon a graduating class of a school of journalism, remarked, "Who knows but what in that list of clear-eyed young men and women there is not one who is destined to become Marbles Editor of the New York *World*"—achieved a reputation as a wit by uttering one word at the Swopes'. He was known to be something of a snob, and when a pretty girl was introduced to him there she said, teasingly, "I think I ought to tell you, Mr. Wallace, that my father is a grocer." Wallace said, "Wholesale?"

It was while staying at the Swope house that Leslie Howard got perhaps his most famous stage role, that of Peter Standish in John Balderston's *Berkeley Square*. Balderston had come from the *World*'s London bureau with the script of his play and asked Swope to read it. Soon afterward, at Great Neck, Swope presented Howard to Balderston's wife. "This is your Peter Standish," he said, dispensing with needless irrelevancies.

Margaret Swope never appeared to spend much time running her household, but it ran smoothly, around the clock. Should sixty people turn up for Sunday-night supper, the climax of the Swope weekend, she was not rattled. She had emergency standby arrangements with the local tradesmen. If she didn't have enough food, they would go to their shuttered stores, open them up, and deliver the necessary provisions. Her meals were simple but superbly cooked and served. (During prohibition, the Swopes would not give their guests any liquor that hadn't been analyzed and vouched for by a competent pharmacist.) To keep her household staff on its toes, she would assign members of it specific rooms to clean; thus no one servant could use another's negligence as an excuse for sloppiness.

Not that this was likely to happen anyway; the staff was beautifully trained and doggedly faithful. In 1963 Margaret still had in her employ three servants who'd been with her for a total of one hundred and twenty-two years—Lydia Stephens, her personal maid; Roy Robinson, her chauffeur and formerly Swope's valet; and Mae Fielding, who was more or less the Swope major-domo and adjusted to their hours, never arising before noon and remaining on duty until her employers had retired at dawn or thereabouts. Every detail of the Swopes' home life was meticulously planned and scrupulously executed, including the service of the paterfamilias's breakfast. He ate, in his dressing room, from a relay of trays, brought seriatim so his eggs and his coffee wouldn't cool while he was consuming his fruit.

One thing that nearly all of Swope's guests did, at the town apartment or the country house, was to play games. Usually a half dozen different spirited contests—backgammon or mah-jongg, parchesi or cribbage, poker or gin rummy—would be going on simultaneously. One group might be playing "Murder," which probably originated at the Swopes'; in this game the participants are supposed to solve a fictitious crime on the basis of prearranged clues. Swope generally monopolized the role of District Attorney, or, as F.P.A. put it, Inquisitor. Or the feature attraction might be a version of charades called "The Game," which was polished at Great Neck if it didn't start there; the idea of that one was to guess slogans or other phrases from watching somebody act them out, in whole or syllabically. Swope was an incomparable guesser. Other games, like "Twenty Questions" or "Who Am I?" or "Shedding Light," were equally popular, and a generation later would evolve into a plethora of radio and television quiz shows. The Swope crowd played these with such undimming enthusiasm that in the formal dining room at 58th Street guests would sometimes find pencils and pads of paper at their place settings.

Swope was so fond of guessing games—he had little use for

competitions in which he could not excel, and the broad and general range of his knowledge, plus his superior memory, gave him a natural edge in these—that he rarely passed up a chance to get a contest started. If on coming home from work he found no one around but his wife, he might greet her by saying, "I ran into a friend of yours today—guess who," and might then grant her twenty questions to come up with the answer. When Dr. Edmund E. Day was chosen president of Cornell University, Swope, in a letter congratulating him, said he was sure Day would be a good man for the job because he could remember how well the educator had comported himself in a game of "Twenty Questions" some years before. It was during one such test of wits at Great Neck, with Swope an ardent participant, that F.P.A. got off a remark for which he was long cherished. Trying to concentrate on a game of cribbage, Adams kept being distracted by Swope, who was in the next room interrogating a writhing victim about obscure German poets. When Adams heard Swope demand, "Who was Kleist?" he called out, "The Chinese Messiah."

William L. Laurence, who as the New York *Times'* star science writer won the Pulitzer Prize in 1946 for his account of the birth of the atomic bomb, got a reporter's job at the *World* a generation earlier by distinguishing himself in a game at Swope's house. Laurence, while attending law school at Boston University, made ends meet by tutoring inept students at Harvard. In 1925 he came to New York with a law degree but very little else and took a room at the Mills Hotel, the hangout of the city's derelicts. In the papers one day Laurence read that a favorite Cambridge tutee of his, John Gaston, of the Long Island set, was about to be married. Laurence phoned his congratulations, and Gaston said there was a prenuptial party on, that Laurence must come, and that he'd send a car for him. Soon a Rolls-Royce drew up outside the Mills, to the astonishment of all inside, and Laurence was escorted to an elegant Long Island country house where he was introduced to Harold S. Vanderbilt and a platoon of Whitneys. After a while everybody decided to move on to the Swopes'. There they found George Kaufman and Edna Ferber and F.P.A., and then Laurence's heart skipped a beat and his head swam, for he spotted Ethel Barrymore, with whom he was desperately in love, though theretofore unacquainted.

Somebody started a question-and-answer game. Laurence was trying to talk to Miss Barrymore, but strangers kept coming up and interrupting with sophomoric inquiries about phases of the moon or American Indian burial rites or little-known Teutonic versifiers. It all seemed fairly infantile to him, but to be polite he threw out the answers and then resumed his starry-eyed, parch-lipped pursuit of the actress. Suddenly he was conscious of a din. People were exclaiming, with admiration, that a champion had been dethroned. The results of the game had been tallied, and Laurence had come in first, with Swope second.

The next thing Laurence knew, a red-haired, red-faced giant was looming over him (Laurence stood five feet five inches). "Who the hell are you?" Swope was demanding. "And why?" Laurence said he was a law-school graduate looking for a job. Swope told him to be at his office at three o'clock the following afternoon. When Laurence learned the identity of the tall, bluster-ing, crimson fellow who'd carried on so, he decided to go around to the *World* and accept a reportorial job if he was offered one, as an expedient until he could get placed with a law firm. Any-thing was better than the Mills Hotel. The next day, accordingly, he went to the newspaper office at three. When Swope turned up, at five-thirty, he seemed to have forgotten all about the appoint-ment, but, on having his memory refreshed, he put him on the city staff. Laurence hardly ever saw Swope again at the *World*, but after the 1946 Pulitzer Prize Swope began referring to him as "one of my boys."

Arthur Krock was fond of fact games, too; he and Swope were forever trying to trip each other up with tricky questions. The lively exchanges they had with, among others, F.P.A., Woollcott, and Stallings paved the way, it was sometimes thought, for "In-formation Please." In 1938, when that program was a fledgling show still chirping for a sponsor, its official originator and pro-ducer, Dan Golenpaul, asked Swope to appear on it. Not to have asked him would have been like asking someone other than the President of the United States to throw out the first baseball of the major-league season. But Swope kept begging off. For one thing, Margaret was afraid that instead of the aplomb he habitu-ally exhibited while throwing and fielding questions at home, in an alien setting he might prove to be all thumbs. A single error could crack, if not shatter, the smooth image of his infallibility. And he himself, for another thing, suspected that everybody connected with the show would be trying extra hard to stump him—prob-ably, he once said, with a series of questions on bird calls or some such nonsense. "Does your sucker join the Board without preparation?" he asked Golenpaul in one note of declination. "How are the questions distributed? How does one know he won't be framed? For example: I know I can answer many more questions than F.P.A., and many, many more than George Kaufman, but there might be some questions especially cooked up which even I could not answer."

Golenpaul finally persuaded Swope to go on "Information Please," but only once, and then in special circumstances. Mrs. Ogden Reid wanted the program put on at the Waldorf-Astoria in October 1940 as a promotional tie-in with the *Herald Tribune*'s annual forum for students from around the world. Golenpaul said she could have "Information Please" if she would get Swope, and she did. He appeared with Adams, John Kieran, and Deems Taylor —as well as, of course, the master of ceremonies, Clifton Fadiman.* Mrs. Reid herself introduced Swope, by saying just the sort of thing his wife had been worried about: "So far as I know, Herbert Bayard Swope has never, up to the present, been asked a question that he could not answer." (A cynic pointed out afterward that while it was certainly true he had never refused to answer any question, he did not always give the correct reply.)

Considering the pressure on him, Swope did quite well. He knew that Alfred Loewenstein was a Belgian capitalist who had killed himself by jumping from an airplane over the English Channel. He knew that Enoch H. Crowder had been Judge Advocate General of the Army in 1917. He astounded Fadiman, who wanted an identification for Dave Barry and had in mind the Barry who refereed the Dempsey–Tunney long-count fight in 1927, by coming up with another, perfectly acceptable, Dave Barry—one who'd been Sergeant-at-Arms of the United States Senate. "I can see you're going to cause me a lot of trouble this evening," Fadiman said. Swope slipped only once, and then, ironically, on a question that had probably been inserted for his benefit: He said it was the New York *Sun*, rather than the *Times*, that liked to use a period after its name. When Fadiman wanted to know what sport called for the wearing of one leather-soled

---

* In the New York *Times*, Kieran would now and then devote one of his columns to the deeds or, more often, the words of the man he regularly called the "Chevalier Bayard" and of whom he once fondly said, "He can recite a weather report and make it look and sound like John Barrymore playing the lead in *Reunion in Vienna*."

and one rubber-soled shoe, Swope answered correctly—it was correct then, at any rate—"bowling." "On which foot is the leather sole and on which the rubber sole in your case?" Fadiman went on. Swope replied, "The left foot, I think, for the leather sole." Fadiman said, "Are you a right-footed or left-footed bowler?" Swope said, "I am whatever makes that answer right." And on that note of triumph he retired permanently from public exhibition of his peculiar talent.

That the games at the Swopes went on throughout the night did not necessarily mean that they were long games, because of the hour at which they began. Dinner was customarily served so late that it might be long after midnight before the after-dinner coffee was out of the way and the postprandial amusement could begin. (Once, at 9:30 P.M., Swope phoned George Kaufman and said, "George, what are you doing for dinner tonight?" "I'm digesting it," Kaufman said.) But while the Swopes' adoption of the kinds of hours that were more normal on the Côte Basque than the North Shore was understood and accepted by most of their guests (except one or two novices who'd had early lunches), when they themselves went out, clinging to their own routine, it made for difficulties. They were the despair of cooks the length and breadth of Long Island. One bold hostess, when they arrived two hours late for a dinner party, greeted them with an icy "How do you do and you'll never come to my house again."

The Swopes were inveterate theatergoers, and they went almost exclusively to opening nights. Margaret didn't like second or subsequent nights, because, as she put it, the people in the audience were so bloody dreary and had to catch all those trains to the suburbs. That theater curtains regularly went up, especially at premières, some time before the Swopes' regular dinner hour was a circumstance they found irritating but tried to cope with. They never quite succeeded. Most playwrights and producers of any experience knew them and knew their habits and would try to lie to them—again usually without success—about curtain times. Marc Connelly swore up and down to them that *The Green Pastures* would begin half an hour before it actually did. George Kaufman wrote them before his *Fancy Meeting You Again* opened, "Eight o'clock, and the whole plot is in the first thirty-six seconds. After that the play goes steadily down hill. Will count on your being in your seats." Leland Hayward wrote Swope at *Call Me Madam* time, "Why don't you quit that campaign you

300

have been running for years now, and just get to openings on time, because you have the worst reputation of anyone in America for being late on opening nights. Everyone loves you all the rest of the year except the night they have an opening, and then you become a real villain."

If villain he was, Swope was a picturesque, swashbuckling villain—the kind one hates to see bested by time-clock-punching heroes. (Asked once by the management of a building in which he was renting an office if he'd like a time clock installed, Swope replied that he could foresee no conceivable instance in which he'd have use for one.) Actually, he made an extra-special effort to get to the theater on time, and his favorite moment of entrance was just as or after the lights began to dim, when he and his petite consort could sweep royally down an aisle toward the seats in front he always favored. If he timed it right, he and the rising curtain met head on. At some musicals, Swope almost made it seem as if the overture were his overture. No matter how many celebrities there might be at any opening night—Marlene Dietrich, Tallulah Bankhead, or whoever—his entrance was one that attracted attention. The house would be divided into three groups: those—as a rule the majority—who were old acquaintances and would nod or wave as he marched by; those who would poke a companion in the ribs and whisper, "That's Herbert Bayard Swope"; and finally those—presumably out-of-town relatives of some obscure member of the cast—who would say, with hushed admiration, "Who is *that?*"

Swope became so much a part of the opening-night décor that playwrights would now and then pay him tribute from *on* stage. In Sidney Kingsley's *Detective Story* there was a scene in which a criminal lawyer brandished a photograph of a client; the playwright used Swope's picture. In *State of the Union*, Russel Crouse and Howard Lindsay had a scene in which their leading character, a Presidential candidate, was looking over some congratulatory telegrams with his wife, an unsophisticated type. This aspect of her character was to be illustrated, at the opening, when she looked up from one telegram and exclaimed, "Who is Herbert Bayard Swope?" The authors felt sure this would get a big laugh at the New York première, and it did. Then they planned to change the line. But before they got around to it, Crouse said afterward, "We noticed that *all* the audiences were laughing at it, and this continued to be true at all performances, even those of

301

the road companies in such places as Amarillo, Texas, and Sioux City, Iowa, where you would think no one had ever heard of Swope. We never were able to explain this and quit trying."

In the Twenties it was unthinkable for someone like Swope not to be seen at, and to have a good perch from which to see, the championship prize fights it was then fashionable to attend. Most prominent sporting men naturally wanted to sit in the ringside section, which unscrupulous promoters sometimes managed to extend far, far back from the ropes. Swope insisted on being *at* ringside—that was, in the first row directly behind the working press. If he was taking a large number of guests, he would accept some seats as remote as, say, the fourth row, but he demanded at least a couple of front-row tickets. Promoters usually humored him, and sometimes they even wooed his attendance. "It won't seem like an important contest without your presence," one matchmaker wrote on hearing that Swope was passing up his bout. But now and then there would be setbacks. Learning once that he had been assigned tenth-row seats, Swope, to whom that sort of location was the equivalent of the bleachers, confided to Damon Runyon, "To sit there would be shocking to normalcy."

To get Swope more or less on time to New York fights, which were usually held either in Madison Square Garden or at a baseball stadium, a compliant Police Department often furnished him a motorcycle escort. (It was understandable that a metropolitan police force would be eager to accommodate a consequential metropolitan editor.) After treating his guests to dinner at the Colony restaurant before one fight, Swope took them to the arena in a fleet of limousines. Riding in his car were Ailsa Mellon Bruce, Andrew Mellon's daughter; Margaret Emerson, Alfred G. Vanderbilt's mother; and Baruch. They represented around a half billion dollars' worth of companionship. A young woman of comparatively modest means was in Swope's party on one such ride, and as their car, behind wailing sirens, careened uptown toward the Yankee Stadium, weaving in and out among the elevated pillars, she exclaimed delightedly that she felt like Caesar's wife en route to the Coliseum in the imperial chariot. Walter Lippmann accompanied Swope on a similar sortie and had a different reaction. He was certain they were going to kill somebody and thought it might be embarrassing for the *World* if they did. Still, he had to admire the way Swope arranged things. "There was no perquisite or privilege you could have, get, or wangle that Swope didn't have," Lippmann said.

Two of the biggest fights in the Twenties were between Dempsey and Tunney. Their first set-to, in 1926, was to have been held in New York City, but the New York State Athletic Commission, of which James A. Farley was chairman, interposed so many obstacles that the fight was moved to Philadelphia. Swope, who was barely acquainted with Farley, hoped unavailingly that he'd change his mind, made a dinner date with him at Billy the Oysterman's, turned up late, and at once, according to Farley's memoirs, "proceeded to give me his candid and very uncomplimentary opinion of the way in which the Athletic Commission was conducting itself. 'Farley,' said Herbert, 'if I didn't have a high regard for you, I wouldn't be here tonight. You have just issued the most asinine statement ever issued by a member of the Commission.' It was a very strong beginning. . . ." It was also the beginning of what was to become a very strong friendship.

Swope went to the first Dempsey-Tunney fight in the private railroad car of Harry F. Sinclair. The following year, when the two fighters met again in Chicago, Swope rented a railroad car of his own. It was a comfortable way to travel, and Swope once engaged such a vehicle to transport his family and servants to Palm Beach for the winter season. The Chicago trip cost him slightly over three thousand dollars for rail fares, not counting tips. His *World* associates who worried about his high-living habits and outside sources of income might have found it disquieting to read an explanation he gave the Income Tax Bureau about a Pullman car he rented the following year: "My business is that of a speculator and investor, which requires me to maintain extensive contacts."

Tex Rickard, at whose funeral Swope was a pallbearer, promoted the Chicago fight, and he came through handsomely with sixteen one-hundred-dollar tickets, all in the very first row. On the way to Illinois, Swope's guests—among them Joshua Cosden, J. Leonard Replogle, Harold Talbott, Charles Schwartz, Clarence Dillon, and Harry Payne Whitney—understandably got to making some bets on the fight. There was a good deal of pro-Dempsey money aboard, and the Tunney crowd, which included Swope, had raised only thirty thousand dollars to back its man by the time the train was nearing its destination. "Let's make it fifty thousand," said Swope, and he added his check for twenty thousand dollars to what proved to be the winner's pool.

After the fights, the itinerant sportsmen often played cards. On the way home from the Philadelphia bout, there was a friendly poker game. Nobody got hurt badly; the biggest single pot— there were two pat hands, and Talbott's straight flush beat Cosden's full house—amounted to thirty-two thousand dollars.

When Swope was playing serious poker, it was with men like Whitney—or later his nephew Jock—or Cosden or Sinclair or Samuel Goldwyn, all of whom were vastly richer than he was and could unblinkingly win or lose a hundred thousand dollars in an evening—and this at a time when the dollar was hard. In 1922, for instance, there were two games a couple of weeks apart. In the first, Goldwyn won $155,000, and in the second he lost $169,000. There was a sense of balance to thinks. Some of Swope's acquaintances thought *he* made a lot of money playing poker or betting on horses, but, like most gamblers, he had his good moments and his bad. He kept careful records of how he made out. His summation for one notably heady year in the Twenties—covering poker, chemin de fer, horse races, prize fights, elections, and random wagers—showed a net profit, before he gallantly subtracted his wife's relatively modest losses of $11,975 over the same period, of $186,758. But most of the time, however defiant Swope might be of ordinary rules, he was no less subject than anyone else to the law of averages.

Perhaps the most celebrated running poker game of the Twenties, though far from the steepest, was one that attracted the men, and a few women, who comprised the Algonquin Round Table. This game, when it began in 1922, was christened by one of its participants, John Peter Toohey, the "Young Men's Upper West Side Thanatopsis Literary and Inside Straight Club." The Thanatopsis endured, with a shifting population, for more than a decade, until, according to Franklin Adams, it "foundered on a reef of seven-card high-low stud." Along with Adams, the players included Robert Benchley, Heywood Broun, Marc Connelly, Raoul Fleischmann, George Kaufman, Jerome Kern, Neysa McMein, Harpo Marx, Harold Ross, Donald Ogden Stewart, and Alexander Woollcott. There would be occasional out-of-town players, too, like E. Haldeman-Julius, the little-blue-books publisher. Swope sat in from time to time, more because he liked the company than the competition. The stakes were too tame for him. It was rare that any individual won or lost as much as five thousand dollars in an evening.

For quite a while the Thanatopsis convened in a second-floor suite at the Algonquin. It pleased Frank Case, the proprietor of the hotel, to have so illustrious and amiable a bunch of sportsmen on his premises, and he would see that they were well plied with food and drink when they assembled. Swope, however, found the culinary standards of the hotel unsatisfactory. One night when he was going to play he arranged, without telling anybody in advance, to have a lavish supper catered by the Colony, which sent over a squad of waiters, accompanied by gleaming steam tables and snowy napery. The poker players were dazed, and so was Frank Case. When the Thanatopsis men returned to their accustomed suite the following week they were greeted by a sign Case had put up. "Basket parties welcome," it said.

There were frequent poker games at Swope's apartment and country house. One of them ended in what Woollcott called Swope's "immortal dismissal" of a man who galled him. A Rumanian prince attached to his country's embassy in Washington came to dinner one night and agreed to take a hand after explaining that he didn't really know very much about poker, and after asking ingenuously whether he was right in believing that two pair were better than three of a kind. After a while, with a good deal of hesitant fumbling, he bet heavily on one hand of draw. Swope, who had three aces, stayed with him, chuckling to himself, and when only the two of them were left in the pot, a large one, the prince quietly laid down a full house. Swope felt he had been taken in, and he called out to his valet, "Roy, the prince's hat and cuffs!"

There were occasions, however, when other players probably wished they had been as abruptly barred from further involvement in Swope's poker games. Now and then some of the Thanatopsis set would play with him, for higher stakes than they were used to or could afford. The consequences were upsetting. Heywood Broun, staying in one game long after he should have pulled out, lost a house. Harold Ross, when he was just starting up *The New Yorker* and probably wasn't worth over ten thousand dollars, lost nearly thirty thousand in a single night at Swope's.

To Swope, there was nothing wrong about gambling for far more than one could possibly afford to lose. He was frequently out of his own depth. He didn't much care for sunshine—his fair skin tended not to tan but to turn a fiery and painful red—but in the wintertime, when the prosperous men he gambled with migrated south, he went merrily along. (In 1926 he even started up a Florida edition of the *World*. It was a two-page supplement to the Miami *Daily News*, and it furnished New Yorkers sojourning down there with the contents of the Op. Ed. page and other selected gems from each day's paper.) Many yarns have been spun about the Florida poker games of that era. An oft-repeated one, which may be apocryphal, concerned a wealthy man—his identity varied with the telling—who approached Swope, Baruch, and Florenz Ziegfeld one time and asked if he could join a game of theirs. On being admitted, he pulled out twenty thousand dollars, whereupon Swope, or so the story went, turned to Ziegfeld and said, "Give him one blue chip." Baruch could not recall, years later, that any such incident had ever occurred.

The biggest single poker game Swope is definitely known to have played in was held at Palm Beach in February 1923. It was a four-man fray. Ziegfeld, whose *Follies* were booming, was in it, along with Cosden, then at the apogee of his financial orbit and worth some seventy-five million dollars, and Replogle, who, while not quite in Cosden's class, was several times over a millionaire. Swope was a salaried newspaper editor unconverted to thrift. There were plenty of big houses in Palm Beach that could accommodate a card table. Cosden, at one time, had perhaps the fanciest place in the whole resort—a two-million-dollar edifice designed by Addison Mizner, with a ballroom that projected out over the ocean, and a staff of thirty servants. (He also had a three-hundred-acre estate on Long Island, with its own eighteen-hole golf course, and a thirty-room triplex apartment in Manhattan.) But when such men decided to have an intimate game of poker, they liked to get away from all the women and children and servants and secretaries who might interrupt them, and they often elected to hole up in a private railroad car parked on a siding.

On this occasion the four men adjourned to Cosden's car, a comfortable one, and they remained there for two days.* At the

---

* At the end of 1939 a moderately high-stake poker game got under way at Palm Springs, California. After it had been running three days and two nights and was still going strong—was going, in fact, well into 1940—David O. Selznick, who sometimes played gin rummy with Swope in sessions where $10,000 changed hands, wrote him about the poker game, which he described as "sort of a Swope memorial, I guess." Swope's curiosity was

end of the marathon session, there was some confusion about precisely how they had come out. Replogle and Swope finally arrived at a reckoning. They determined that Cosden had lost $443,100 and that Ziegfeld—at whose death most of his loss, which he owed Swope, was still unpaid—was out $294,300. Replogle won $267,100. Swope was the big winner. He had decided in advance that he would quit if his losses reached $150,000, but he didn't have to worry about that. He ended up ahead by $470,300.

---

whetted. "Who was in it? How long did they play?" he wrote Selznick. "To hell with who won; my interest is aroused by their endurance."

15

Several weeks before Al Smith's defeat in the 1928 Presidential election, Swope, then forty-six, was walking along Fifth Avenue with his wife one afternoon. Suddenly he stopped. "I don't want to be a hired boy any longer," he said abruptly. Swope, who often told his children that the most important thing in life was to make decisions, headed for the nearest pay telephone, called Ralph Pulitzer, and said he wanted to talk to him. Pulitzer had just returned to New York from a European honeymoon with his second wife, Margaret Leech, and their westbound voyage was to be a fateful one for the *World*, for Roy W. Howard, the head of the Scripps-Howard newspaper chain, was a fellow passenger.

In Pulitzer's absence, his brother Herbert had been running the paper. Ralph Pulitzer was a newspaperman, perhaps not as aggressive as some of his contemporaries, but at any rate a dedicated, full-time journalist. Herbert was a dilettante. Ralph got on well with his employees. Herbert was aloof. Once, indeed, he brushed past William L. Laurence, who had tutored him at Harvard, without a nod of recognition. Swope was upset at the way things were going with the paper, and with himself. He had suffered deep spells of depression and had had a few ineffective sessions with a psychoanalyst. "Have poured my life into the paper," he reflected in a moody memorandum he wrote that fall. "Uncertain as to future. Find no assurance of opportunity of improvement. Therefore I am inclined to think it would interfere with happiness. Not of greatest value to paper or paper to me. I am inclined to think inefficiency in business office has interfered with my usefulness because it dampens my ardor. Worked too long under handicap of being outdistanced by rivals. Can't make ideas take place of organization. The smart won't always substitute for the solid. . . . Don't want to settle down to another contract of routine which will make for a drab existence and rob it of all adventure. I have to fight my way through everything I want done. Getting too hard. The paper is slipping fast and I don't want responsibility charged against me."

Ralph Pulitzer, for his part, had become somewhat concerned about Swope's irregularity. The executive editor had been out of the office almost as much as he'd been in it. And when he was around he might keep the affairs of the paper pending while he attended to his own increasingly complex personal investments. Upon Swope's turning up at the *World* and saying he thought the time had come for a change, Pulitzer was agreeable. He could understand, he said, how Swope felt, now that he was a "very wealthy man," but even if he gave up the executive editorship wouldn't he stay on in some less trying capacity—perhaps to reorganize the very business office about which he had so long complained? A number of titles were discussed: Advisory Editor, Consulting Editor, Associate Editor. But after nearly a month of meditation, Swope decided to make a clean break and to leave the *World* at the end of the year. On October 16 he dictated the statement:

> I am leaving the *World* after many years of pleasant association because there are some things I want to do which I can do only as a free agent and, too, I am a little tired of being a hired man. It is bad to be a hired man too long. One falls into a groove—a groove that deepens and darkens when the future offers little change. All of us want to grow. All of us want to play. And it is hard to play as a hired man. There is always the feeling that it is resented by the boss. The *World* has my respect and affection, though I believe it would be more in keeping with the spirit of the day were it possible for those who make the paper to become part owners of the property. That system is increasingly used in every enterprise. The *World*'s position is limited because of the will of its founder. At the moment I have nothing to say regarding my plans, but I hope to have an announcement not without interest to make presently.

The public disclosure that Swope was bowing out caused quite a stir—both within the field of journalism and outside it. Newspaper editors commanded wide general interest then. *The Front Page* and *Gentlemen of the Press* were running on Broadway, and there was no question in anyone's mind that, however diverting and exciting the fictional editors portrayed in them might be, Swope was far and away the most brilliant and dashing *real* editor in circulation. "Park Row without Swope will seem to many like the *World* without the golden dome," lamented *Editor & Publisher*. Ralph Pulitzer's own reaction was expressed in a letter he sent Swope on October 23:

MY DEAR HERBERT,

Now that the very bare announcement of your retirement from the executive editorship of The World has been made, I want to try to overcome my damnable inarticulateness enough to give you at least a faint idea of the deep and abiding appreciation I feel for your outstanding contribution toward making The World what it is today. Your brilliant intellect, your amazing energy and your fine courage have been dedicated to the development of the paper. A multitude share my deep admiration for these qualities. But few know as I do the less obvious virtue of patience which you have so admirably displayed under vexations and difficulties.

If I owed you no other debt of gratitude than for the consistent thoughtfulness with which you have assumed the burdens of so many problems which you might well have unshouldered on me, that debt would be great. But I fully appreciate that you have done infinitely more than that. You have raised the standards of good taste in a paper which retained its fighting spirit, sacrificing neither to the other. You have made a paper which appealed at once to the intellects of the few and to the interests of the many.

You have been of ungrudging service to the paper in so many other ways that I cannot attempt to specify them.

For all these things I want to thank you from the bottom of my heart. In abiding admiration and friendship, I am

Yours

RALPH PULITZER

And Walter Lippmann said:

Your decision is, I think, a wise one. It has become increasingly evident to me in the last six or eight months that you had outgrown the possibilities at the office. As I see it you began as the greatest reporter New York has known in this generation. But you were more than a reporter. You were also an editor of the most original sort. To have done justice to that side of yourself, you would have had to have complete control of the whole paper and a free hand. That was impossible given the traditions of the *World*. You would,

310

had you been in complete control, have made something wholly new in journalism. You could only make your kind of newspaper, and the attempt to fit your peculiar and original genius to an old institution could not in the end result in justice to you or to it. I have never seen so clear a case, as it finally developed, of an irreconcilable conflict between a powerful temperament and a settled tradition. The *World* did you no injustice, though your own vitality was too much for it. All that has happened is that in the last five years you have come into full possession of all your powers, and for their proper and happy use you need to be your own boss. Had this not happened, the best that was in you would have been thwarted.

You may be certain that you have done an immense service to the *World* and made an enormous contribution to American journalism. What you have done, above all, I think, is to take a paper which was running on the inspiration of the past, and improve it with an inspiration suited to the modern age. You did for the *World* in the post-war period what Joseph Pulitzer did for it twenty-five years ago, and your place in the history of the paper, and therefore, in the history of American journalism is secure.

That ought to mean a good deal to you and to Margaret, especially since you have done that as a very young man. For to my mind you are today at the threshold of your mature career. Your very best years are all ahead of you, and no one ever had a finer prospect. Your only problem will be to choose wisely and imaginatively among the thousand opportunities which will present themselves. Fortunately, you will be able to choose it with absolute freedom.

It was inconceivable to newspapermen everywhere that Swope would not shortly reappear in their fold. Adolph Ochs wrote him, "I hope we are not to lose you in New York daily journalism, for you would be sadly missed. Your energy, enterprise and enthusiasm, combined with your uncanny news sense, have ever been inspiriting contributions in making New York newspapers alert and interesting; and your wholehearted and courageous cooperation in matters of mutual interest to the profession has been useful and constructive." From England, Lord Beaverbrook wrote, "I hope that you are not giving up journalism or indeed, developing any side lines, but that you are sticking to the main theme." Swope had no idea what he was going to do. But while perplexed, he was not unhappy. For within a fortnight of the announcement of his imminent departure, he achieved a paradoxical triumph. The *World* that reported the crushing, to him, news of Herbert

Hoover's landslide victory over Smith reached a circulation of five hundred and ninety-two thousand—the highest in the entire sixty-eight-year history of the paper.

The staff of the *World* memorialized Swope's leave-taking with a specially printed front page of the paper, consisting mainly of one hundred and thirty-six repetitions, in various sizes of type, of "Swope quits." He was tendered two farewell dinners. Ralph Pulitzer gave him one, at the Players Club, attended by the top executives; Swope was presented with a gold watch. Then several hundred of the paper's employees gathered at the Hardware Club to pay him further tribute. William P. Beazell was the master of ceremonies, and a number of speakers, including Lippmann, who called Swope "a lucky, fascinating devil," paid him tribute. Still another speaker was Alexander Woollcott, of whose contribution to the festivities James M. Cain would later reminisce:

> Instead of remaining near his place at the head table, perhaps stepping toward the guest of honor for the obligatory pat, he walked around the horseshoe, re-entered its open end, and stood facing his guest with anything but an admiring look on his face. It crossed my mind he looked like the Frog Footman in Alice in Wonderland. In fact, in the several seconds he took before speaking at all, various things crossed my mind, like the transformation in him, from the reasonably lean sergeant I had talked to, at the *Stars & Stripes* office in Paris a bare ten years before, to this fat, puffy personage, with eyes so dismayingly venomous, who briefly smirked his acknowledgement of the applause. It crossed my mind what terrible things money, success, and adulation, plus gnawing secret bitterness, can do to human appearance. But then, very quietly, he began to talk, leading off with some tale I don't recall, at the guest of honor's expense, and not in his praise at all. His response was a burst of applause. Then he reminisced about all sorts of things, especially police court days, and paying loving attention to Gyp the Blood, Lefty Louie, Whitey Lewis, Dago Frank, Jack Rose, Lieutenant Becker, Governor Whitman, and other dignitaries of 1912, with particulars about Swope's behavior in connection with them. He told the Versailles story, of the silk hat and cutaway coat that Swope had dressed himself in, to gain admission to the treaty signing —making it perfectly clear that this celebrated imposture was less to get the story than to appear a big shot at a big important time. . . .

But what fascinated me was Swope and how he took it. He sat there, to all outward appearance overcome with delight. If there was any resentment whatever at this waspish, malevolent recital, no hint of it showed on his face. And when at last it was his turn to speak, he did so with the utmost good humor, and to terrific applause. Indeed, amiability under spoofing was one of his most surprising, and of course most likeable traits.

At the big dinner, Swope received a handsome, red-leather-bound scrapbook containing letters from his colleagues on the *World* and other friends. Alison Smith said, in toto, "Dear Mr. Swope. 'Psalms: verse 3—chapter 138.' " * Dudley Nichols, playing a variation on the Biblical theme, pictured Swope entering the Kingdom of Heaven—along the way overtaking three Popes, seven Kings, three Presidents, four Dictators, and seventy millionaires, and upon his arrival instructing St. Peter to send down Gabriel and God. J. Otis Swift conveyed the warmest sentiments of twenty-five thousand Yosians. William Bolitho said:

DEAR CHIEF:
You reached over to England to give me help, and then you brought me to America; it was the last of a great number of interferences with my fate, which made you the most important influence in the best part of my life. I know you have been the same thing to innumerable others, but none of them is more grateful than I, or more sorry or bereaved tonight. I feel a deep sense of personal loss and a fear of what your actions may mean to me.
So the glittering progress of your past to this point has carried along all the way the careers of many other men, who all feel as if a great ship had disembarked them; we all feel sorry and lost, but not one doubts that for you this is the beginning of a still nobler and even more exciting voyage. I wave my handkerchief. I hope I may join you again.

Bolitho's hope was widely shared. For years afterward Swope would hear from his boys, begging him to become an editor once more so they could become his editorial assistants. And for years after he left the *World*, Swope would use wistful phrases like "when I get my paper . . ." In May 1930 he received a summons for jury duty. He replied, "I beg to state that I am a newspaper man and therefore exempted. I have been until recently Executive Editor of the *World*." The Commissioner of Jurors replied that

---

* "All the kings of the earth shall praise thee, O Lord, for they have heard the words of thy mouth."

only active newspapermen working for dailies were exempt, and he invited Swope to stop by and talk over his status. Swope had his secretary answer that one. Miss Millar explained that her boss had been a writer, reporter, and editor for twenty-five years. "He is still actively engaged in those three vocations," she added, "although momentarily on a holiday." It was a holiday that would last for the remaining twenty-eight years of his life.

Even before he left the *World*, Swope had been looking for another paper. He thought he might try to take over the *Morning Telegraph*, for a million and a half dollars, with the backing of John D. Hertz, the Chicago taxicab and drive-it-yourself man, and of, among others, Baruch, the Schwartz brothers, Irving Berlin, and Thomas Chadbourne. Nothing came of it, although some prankster, hearing of Swope's interest in the paper, sent its managing editor a telegram that went, "KINDLY REPORT TO MY OFFICE WORLD BUILDING SATURDAY AT TEN HERBERT BAYARD SWOPE." After Swope left Park Row he had a man investigate newspaper properties for him all over the country. Swope compiled a fat dossier of circulation figures and advertising revenues for dailies in, among other places he thought he might invade, Kansas City, Chicago, Cleveland, Miami, Boston, St. Louis, Atlanta, Tampa, and Memphis.

He hoped that if and when he made an offer for any of these papers, Baruch would provide the funds. "You have never been identified with newspaper work," Swope wrote Baruch one time. "While your record of public service is fine, I think an explanation would be asked for were you to enter journalism cold turkey. Some would say that you entered solely for the purpose of aggrandizement; others would say you entered for the purpose of revenge; a few would say you entered for the purpose of public service; but all would think it rather surprising if you yourself plunged into it in too forthright a manner. Your entrance with me would be different, first, because we are known as intimate friends of many years standing; second, because my whole life has been given to journalism, politics and other forms of public service; third, because it is known that I am seeking a new journalistic opportunity. What could be more natural than that you go along as my associate and principal backer?" Baruch, always willing to lend Swope a hand, expressed mild interest. But he never got enthusiastic about the idea, partly because he thought it was becoming difficult for Swope to sustain his interest for long on any single undertaking, and partly because of the advice given him by other friends, one of whom, the journalist Garet Garrett, told him, "What would you want a newspaper for? You can get on the front page any time you like without one."

Uppermost in Swope's mind was the hope that if the Pulitzer family should ever relinquish the *World*, he could return to it— not as a hired boy but as Commander-in-Chief. He discussed this eventuality with Ralph and Herbert Pulitzer, and he got the impression that, should they ever put the newspaper up for sale, he would be given the first chance to buy it. No formal option, however, was ever granted, an oversight that Swope would subsequently have cause to regret.

Swope felt no need to be concerned about earned income at the start of 1929. The stock market was soaring, and he was in synchronized orbit with it. When Chadbourne expressed misgivings about the speculation rampant early that year, Swope told him, reassuringly, "Don't kid yourself. We are going to take a pleasant ride, so climb up in the driver's seat." Swope's friendships with Wall Street insiders were paying off handsomely, and he was the envy of his peers. Arthur Brisbane was one of the most prosperous and best-connected journalists who ever wrote a line of copy, but when he was looking for a big corporate client for a New York office building in which he had invested, he turned to Swope, who was, Brisbane said, "the friend of the great and the rich and the powerful."

Day in and out, Swope was swapping stock tips with Baruch. When Baruch went abroad, as he customarily did once a year, Swope would pursue him with cable and wireless messages—some of them partly in code, to keep telegraphic operators from climbing up into the driver's seat with them—that sounded almost like professional market letters. It was easy to make money then if you had the right acquaintances. The Securities and Exchange Commission did not exist, and in the spring of 1929, when some of Swope's friends—John J. Raskob, Charles M. Schwab, Nicholas F. Brady, William F. Kenny, Walter P. Chrysler, and a handful of Fisher brothers among them—made nearly five million dollars in a pool operation on RCA stock that took only a week to consummate, they cut him in for $58,342.15 of their profits. It was a nice deal, because Swope, conceivably being entitled to some sort of finder's fee in the transaction, had put up not one cent of capital. Later that year, when RCA stock began to tumble, Swope made an additional hundred thousand dollars in a single transaction by selling short. In Chicago, he had a joint brokerage account, involving more than two million dollars, with John Hertz and Hertz's close associate, Albert D. Lasker. In New York, Swope had accounts, singly or jointly with Baruch and other men, at a half dozen brokerage houses. To facilitate communications with one such establishment, he had the telephone company install a private line connecting its order room with his home. "In those days, I thought I had all the money in the world," he said.

Some of Swope's acquaintances—even some far better off than he would ever be—began to surmise apprehensively that he thought *everybody* had all the money in the world. It was his merry practice, for instance, to make horse-race bets for friends without telling them in advance. Hertz got nervous about this in the spring of 1929 and begged Swope not to bet more than a thousand dollars of *his* money, in his absence, on any single race. Once, when Hertz *was* present and he asked Swope to lay as much money as he could with the bookmakers on an entry the Chicago man fancied, Swope came back and reported apologetically that the best he'd been able to get down was one hundred and fifty thousand dollars. Hertz gulped. Swope then said he'd be glad to take half the bet himself. The entry won. In the fall of 1929 Swope wanted to use Joshua Cosden's box at the Aqueduct track. Cosden, who was in Texas, wired his consent and added, ". . . BET ONE FOR ME ON THE FIRST WINNER YOU HAVE." Swope wired back, "DOES YOUR WIRE MEAN TO BET ONE HUNDRED OR ONE THOUSAND MUST KNOW IMMEDIATELY." Cosden hastily replied, "ONE THOUSAND NOT ONE MILLION."

Swope was no hoarder or miser. He was so openhanded with money that even some of the bookmakers he knew, when momentarily pressed for cash, would turn to him as a likely source of funds. At the beginning of 1929 he belonged to eighteen costly social clubs, most of which he hardly had time to set foot in. (A year later, after the Wall Street crash, he would write his brother, "I belong to so damn many clubs it is ridiculous.") In the fall of 1928 he had given up his rented Great Neck country home and, for $310,000, bought a thirteen-acre place at Sands Point, on the north shore of Long Island, a more fashionable community than Great Neck. Most of Long Island, in those days, was a rural area; no Levitt had yet built himself a town. On the North Shore,

Swope was surrounded by neighborly Bakers, Chryslers, Davisons, Fields, Guggenheims, Harrimans, Hitchcocks, Igleharts, Leedses, Mackays, Morgans, Phippses, Pratts, Sanfords, Schiffs, Sloanes, Stevensons, Tiffanys, Vanderbilts, Webbs, Whitneys, Woolworths, and others who did not have to mow their own lawns. In time, Frank Costello also moved out there.

The Swope estate was called Keewaydin, the name some bygone Long Island Indian tribe had given to the northwest wind. The main house, which Swope had the impression was designed by Stanford White, was a three-story structure of twenty-seven rooms and eleven and a half baths—"almost fifty rooms," Swope would say when feeling especially seignorial. The library alone measured fifty-two by twenty-four feet, and it had two fireplaces. To operate the establishment stylishly took a staff of twelve or fifteen. There were several outbuildings, among them a seven-room cottage and a seven-car garage, which was usually filled close to capacity with Swope's own vehicles.

Swope spent several hundred thousand dollars improving the place. Whatever he wanted he wanted the best of. He had almost a quarter of a mile of beach front, and on concluding that a retaining wall would be in order against the probable onslaughts of tide and tempest, he prevailed on Eugene Grace to send over some of the Bethlehem Steel Company's sturdiest sheet steel. To enhance his lawn, he had Albert Lasker put him in touch with a man Swope proudly described as the "world's greatest grass expert."

The Swopes put in an all-weather tennis court and a salt-water swimming pool, which they placed between the seaward side of their house and Long Island Sound. Swope didn't use the pool much himself. Like many a native Midwesterner, he did not take to water. He never learned to swim properly, being unable to coordinate the movements of his arms and legs. (He could never learn to drive a car properly, either, because his mind was often one move ahead of what his hands and feet were supposed to be doing.) But he would now and then take a dip, and at Sands Point, long before Hollywood embraced the vogue, he had a telephone installed that he could talk into from his pool.

Despite Swope's personal aversion to overexposure of the human form, some of his relatives and friends got into the habit, while he was indoors, of swimming naked, in a comparatively modest fashion: they would shuck their robes at the deep end of the

317

pool and quickly dive in. Eventually, although Swope was neither a party to nor partisan of the buff goings-on, he acquired the reputation of being an advocate of nude bathing, and a few of his guests went to quaint lengths to conform to what they wrongly took to be his accustomed ways. One of the nation's leading corporation executives shucked *his* robe while strolling toward the pool and then walked in stately bareness down the steps of the shallow end, to the amazement of all present. Another time, an aristocratic young woman emerged like an unclad Venus from Swope's waters and was leisurely about covering herself up. Meanwhile, a fellow guest observed that some men cruising on the Sound were taking in the pretty spectacle through binoculars, with admiring whoops and whistles that carried to shore. When this was called to the lady's attention, she remarked, "Oh, it's all right. I'm sure I don't know them."

To equip their new house, the Swopes spared no expense. They ordered close to one hundred thousand dollars' worth of goods and services from Elsie de Wolfe, or Lady Mendl, the reigning queen of interior decoration. They imported antique furniture from England, sheathed their dining room in hand-painted wallpaper, and for a while threatened to corner the antique sterling-silver market. (To divert their daughter, entering her teens and embarking on the horse-show circuit, they bought her a fifty-five-hundred-dollar mount.) Margaret ordered bed sheets from Paris at forty-four dollars the pair, and Herbert ordered a thousand dollars' worth of assorted haberdashery from the Paris branch of A. Sulka.

Royal families have the reputation of settling their accounts with tradesmen at a sluggish pace—perhaps once annually. The Swopes hardly glanced at their bills until they were a year overdue. Margaret had a particularly cavalier attitude toward people who concerned themselves with small sums of money. Money bored her. One morning a newspaper reporter called her home to solicit her reaction to having won a consolation prize in the Irish Sweepstakes. Her personal maid, Lydia Stephens, had standing orders not to wake her until she rang and refused to summon her to the phone. The reporter kept trying to reach her. After several calls he told Lydia he was sure her mistress wouldn't mind being disturbed to learn of her good fortune. Lydia asked how much she had won. "Five hundred dollars!" exclaimed the reporter. "I can't wake Mrs. Swope for no five hundred dollars," Lydia replied, and she hung up.

As befitted a Long Island country gentleman in the dizzy pre-depression days, Swope also acquired a racing stable. His colors were royal blue, with scarlet braid, and a scarlet cap. He began to accumulate horses at the Saratoga sales in the summer of 1929. On one day when the average price per horse sold was $5,500, he paid some $30,000 for a pair of them. It was not an immediately taxing outlay, however, for that same day he reputedly made more than $100,000 betting on other horses. He had even better days. At Saratoga two years earlier he had won $165,000 in an afternoon's play. The bookies he clipped were not overly per-turbed. "He'll probably lose it all back before the week's over," one of them said. When the New York *Post*, some years later, described Swope as "one of the biggest bettors in America," he responded, "That seems to me to be a hyperbolic statement, for while I have no knowledge of what others do, I know that when I bet my bets are moderate."

The *Evening Graphic* described Swope's first two race horses —a two-year-old filly named Curtsey and a three-year-old gelding named Lativich—as "smashing-looking," and the paper quoted their new owner as saying, in royal-blue-and-scarlet prose, "I shall have more horses—good ones. Platers will eat none of my oats." Curtsey made her debut in his colors at that Saratoga meeting. An unexpected bit of bad luck kept her from winning, at twenty to one. Swope had paid $17,500 to buy up the riding contract of George Rose, a fairish jockey, but in this maiden effort Rose's new scarlet cap flew off and brushed his horse. The mishap distracted Curtsey long enough to lose her the race by a nose. Lativich was Swope's favorite horse, and his most successful. It won six of its first ten races. But its purses added up to only $8,000, and Swope did not bet heavily on it; the most he ever won on a Lativich race was $12,000.

In all, Swope bought nine horses. The costliest, a colt called Parsifal for which he paid $23,000, caught cold and never ran in a race. Swope kept his stable going for a year and spent nearly $120,000 on horses and horse maintenance. He got back $15,270 in purses and a few thousand more when he sold his string. (Lativich, by then a bit winded, brought a mere $1,000.) And his net loss in betting on his own horses came to another $41,600. All he got out of that phase of the sport of kings was the royal blues.

Most of the men with whom Swope associated were successful and readily identifiable. His older brother Gerard was the General Electric man, Baruch was the Elder Statesman, nearly everyone in his circle had a clearly marked and legible tag. Some of Swope's big-business associates couldn't conceive of a man who *didn't* have one. After he left the *World*, Swope went to one banquet given by the International Business Machines Corporation. There was a printed guest list, and Swope's hosts, apparently feeling that everyone present should have a title, listed him as president of the Keewaydin Corporation—which was nothing more than a small, wholly Swope-owned family holding company.

Stanley Walker once said that Swope's "chief post-*World* project was merely to be Herbert Bayard Swope." Walker had a clearer understanding than many of Swope's acquaintances of just what he was up to. Swope was in a curiously anomalous position. He detested the kind of work that demanded routine, and yet he felt that an adult, healthy, vigorous, intelligent man *should* work. Back in 1919 he had written in a speech for Baruch to deliver, "Work is the cure-all for envy, malice, avarice, and general dissatisfaction. It is the talisman for contentment, comfort, self-respect, and above all peace." Now, ten years afterward, Swope seemingly had all the contentment and comfort a man could seek, but the self-respect and peace were proving elusive. He told Thomas Chadbourne in January 1929 that he felt "a foolish sense of guilt" without steady employment, and he told himself, in one of those introspective memoranda of his, "Need job for purpose of keeping my mind from spinning too fast. It is less a question of salary than a question of interest."

Not that there was any lack of activity. The stock market alone, during 1929, was a major preoccupation. Spending part of that winter in cozy idleness at Palm Beach, Swope instructed Miss Millar to telephone Baruch and Morton Schwartz at noon every weekday and to rush along to Florida whatever relevant market information she gleaned. Swope even toyed with the notion of buying control of a brokerage house and, if his prospective partner assented, to name the company "Baruch, Swope & Co." Baruch was not taken with the idea. Swope thought for a while, too, that he might join forces with Al Smith, who was himself, after his defeat at the polls, at loose ends. "I am glad to see," Swope wrote Smith in the summer of 1929, "we are both adhering to our double-barreled resolution: (a) that we shall 'rest' a long time before going to work and (seriously) (b) that neither of us shall go into any publication enterprise without consulting the other and preferably going with the other." Smith, though, went into banking on his own; when his bank moved into a new building, he told Swope (jokingly) he'd reserve the barbershop concession for him.

Swope's adventures were of unremitting interest to his friends, and there was considerable curiosity among them as to where this high-flying bird of such splendid plumage and shrill call would finally alight. In the first couple of years of his retirement from the *World*, some of them thought he should run for Congress. To the surprise of many of them, his first public appearance as an ex-editor was somewhat anticlimactic: He turned up in a testimonial for Lucky Strike cigarettes. "I find Lucky Strikes an immeasurable aid in helping me keep trim and fit," he was quoted as saying. "Whenever I am tempted to eat between meals, I light up a Lucky." (Swope got fifteen hundred dollars for the ad, but he went along with the testimonial mainly to help out his old friend Fred Benham, who was then in the testimonial business, and he also gave Benham the money. The ad, incidentally, had portentous overtones about the fate of the *World;* the American Tobacco Company ran it five columns wide in the *Times* and *Herald Tribune*, but in Swope's own paper it spanned only four columns.)

The Swopes moved their city residence to an East Side apartment not long after his retirement. In February 1929, a month after his resignation from the *World* took effect, he became the principal backer of a short-lived and ill-fated organization called the National Radio Press Association, which was run by the former radio editor of the paper. Radio was a relatively new and unexplored medium; the object of the Association was to furnish news to broadcasting stations much as the wire services furnished it to papers. Swope had no titular position in the N.R.P.A., but its secretary-treasurer was Helen A. Millar, and the money that she disbursed in her fiscal capacity—close to fifty thousand dollars of it before the venture fizzled out—was her employer's.

A month after the faltering N.R.P.A. was launched, Swope was off on another tangent. He had invested heavily in an English concern, the General Electric Company, Ltd., which was licensed to use some of the patents of Gerard Swope's General Electric

Company but was otherwise independent of its American name-sake. Around half the stock of the British G.E. was owned by Americans—among them Baruch and his brother Herman, Raskob, and Chadbourne, who in January of that year, at Herbert Swope's recommendation, had bought forty-five thousand shares, worth about half a million dollars. In March, British G.E. announced that it was planning an issue of new stock, which was to be known as British Ordinary Shares and would be available, at a price below the market price, to British shareholders only. The American shareholders considered this scheme rankly discriminatory. They asked the State Department to intervene, but it felt it had no jurisdiction. The Americans thereupon decided to act on their own and to send emissaries to England to argue against the proposed stock issue with the head of the British company, a German-born, hyperemotional, and outspoken industrialist named Sir Hugo Hirst, who had built up General Electric, Ltd., almost single-handed.

Chadbourne and Swope were picked as the negotiators. They were a striking pair. Chadbourne, silvery-haired and six feet, six inches tall, was one of the few friends Swope had who dwarfed him physically. He was far richer, too. He had a château in France and a hundred-and-seventy-five-foot yacht that carried a crew of thirty. He was a native of Michigan who, without any formal law-school education, had come to New York and founded one of the city's biggest corporation-law firms. It was originally called Chadbourne, Stanchfield & Levy. Chadbourne was an unusual corporation lawyer for his time, because he was genuinely sympathetic to the aspirations of labor. Like Swope, he was a Democrat, and like him, too, a gambler. They often went together to Colonel Edward R. Bradley's celebrated casino at Palm Beach. Bradley had a rule that no drinks would be served at the gaming tables. One night Chadbourne was having a run of hard luck at chemin de fer. He was two hundred thousand dollars in the hole and felt he could use a drink. When his wish was conveyed to Bradley, the proprietor said he wouldn't think of breaking his own house rule, but he'd be glad to give Chadbourne back his two hundred thousand dollars and let him step into an adjoining chamber and buy himself a drink.

Chadbourne and Swope set off for Europe in a blaze of publicity, issuing statements right and left, to the delight of the British press, which dubbed them the "United States Giants."

Gerard Swope had begged his brother to do nothing until he'd reached London and had a chance to confer with Owen D. Young, the chairman of the board of *his* G.E., but the younger brother did not, as usual, take the older brother's advice. On landing in England, Herbert kept right on spouting indignation and submitting to dockside interviews, to such a degree that John Balderston, still manning the *World* bureau in London, felt impelled to try to rein him in. He sent Swope a note suggesting methods for dealing with the British press—"a course," Balderston said, "directly opposite to that adopted on your landing." Balderston explained:

> The language is the same here as at home, the psychology different. . . . Half the strength of your position, apart from questions of equity, lies in the prejudice of the natives against Hirst's *un-English* manners and behavior, i.e., weeping at Board meetings and making threats or implied threats in public. . . . It is unheard of in this country for serious financial people to talk to *pressmen.* Talk to journalists if you like, but you haven't met any yet. These articles and interviews therefore make serious financial people and editors here regard you both as a pair of hell-raisers out for a fight, whereas your tactics should be to create the impression that you are serious investors, people of weight, which implies the same sort of attitude as adopted by people like your brother [and] Owen Young. . . . (Of course, this doesn't apply to talks with the *American* correspondents, but there you are on familiar ground and need no advice.)

The London pressmen were impressed with Swope as a talker. The *Daily Sketch* credited him with a world's record, contending that he had once delivered a four-hour nonstop monologue to Mary Pickford. This was close to the era of bunion derbies, dance marathons, and flagpole-sitting contests, and a man who could do anything for a protracted stretch without collapsing was regarded by his fellow humans with awe and, in some cases, admiration. But while Swope undoubtedly could have lectured Miss Pickford, or anyone else, for even longer than that, the actress had no recollection of ever having her ear bent to that extent. In any event, once the United States Giants got to conversing with Sir Hugo, they talked *him* into submission, and Swope was able to send Baruch a triumphant cable: "WE WIN COMPLETE ABANDONMENT NEW ISSUE . . . BIG VICTORY REGARDS."

The spring that was so financially sunny for Swope that year led to a fall that was sere. In September 1929 he was worth nearly fourteen million dollars—on paper. A month later, the stock market collapsed. Baruch, anticipating the crash, had got out unhurt himself and had tried to persuade Swope to sell while the selling was good, but Swope had refused to climb down from what he still thought was the driver's seat. Even on October 29, Black Friday, Swope was not unhopeful. "REAL BELIEF WORST IS OVER," he wired John Hertz in Chicago, after a meeting at Baruch's house with, among other big investors, Gerard Swope, Owen Young, Charles E. Mitchell, Thomas P. Lamont, Eugene Meyer, Charles M. Schwab, Albert E. Wiggin, and Clarence S. Woolley. Two days later, Swope's net paper worth was *minus* two million three hundred and forty-five thousand dollars. To Harpo Marx, another gravely wounded plunger, he wired, "THANK GOD WE'RE STILL ALIVE." It was at this bleak nadir of Swope's financial career that his mother-in-law, a lady insulated against the stresses of the time, turned to her daughter and remarked, "You know, Pearl, I do believe there's something on Herbert's mind." Seven years afterward, Swope still hadn't got himself even.

Swope did not, however, appreciably alter his *mode d'être*. True, he sold his racing stable, but in the main because he was displeased with the performance of his horses. He made ends meet, more or less, by borrowing—from, among others, his brother, Baruch, Hertz, and Lasker. But so far was Swope, seemingly, from viewing the disaster that had engulfed him as anything more than a momentary annoyance that on the New Year's Eve that linked the ghastly end of 1929 to what was to be a thoroughly dispiriting 1930 he invited seventy-odd guests to a bang-up party at Sands Point. And eight days after that, upon dropping $10,240 in a friendly poker game at Joshua Cosden's, Swope graciously thanked his host for what, despite all the fiscal lumps he had been absorbing, he was able to describe as "a pleasant evening."

16

Just prior to quitting the *World*, Swope became a trustee of a heavyweight-championship trophy—a bronze statue of a prize fighter by Mahonri Young that was put on display in the lobby of Madison Square Garden—commissioned by Gene Tunney, the then recently retired champion, and William Muldoon, the czar of boxing. The assignment was reasonably prestigious and relatively effortless. Swope and his fellow trustees—James A. Farley, Bernard F. Gimbel, Judge Jeremiah T. Mahoney, and John McEntee Bowman, who ran the Biltmore Hotel—were required simply to approve the inscribing of champions' names on the pedestal of the statue, a responsibility they could discharge by meeting for lunch at the Biltmore once every few years. The thorniest problem they ever had to come to grips with—they finally decided in the affirmative—was whether or not to put Max Schmeling's name on the roster after he'd taken the heavyweight title from Jack Sharkey on a foul.

Swope was a sports enthusiast, but he was not basically an athlete. Many of his Long Island playmates were all-around men who had the wealth and upbringing and physical prowess and determination to excel in a variety of competitive sports. There was Charles Schwartz, who might conceivably have had his name on the Muldoon–Tunney trophy himself, if he'd turned professional. (Baruch was a good amateur boxer, too.) There was Joseph W. Brooks, an insurance broker whose father ran Western Union and who was an all-American football player, a first-rate racquets player, and an expert fly-caster. Brooks once flabbergasted a bunch of Broadway hustlers by stopping in at a poolroom and offhandedly making a six-point run, a prodigious accomplishment,

325

at three-cushion billiards. There were the polo players of championship caliber—among them Tommy Hitchcock, Jock Whitney, Averell Harriman, and Harold Talbott—all good friends of Swope's and all proficient at almost any sport to which they chose to devote their time and energy and finely tuned reflexes.

Polo was a big game in the Twenties—so big that Swope once predicted it would one day eclipse football in popularity as an American spectator sport. On the eve of the International Cup matches between Great Britain and the United States in 1924, he assigned a member of the *World*'s sports staff, Peter Vischer, to bone up on polo. No other paper, not even the *Times*, which had a dog editor, had ever had a polo editor. Vischer applied himself so sedulously to his new specialty that he was soon editing the magazine *Polo*, of which, with a nice touch of reciprocity, he made Swope chairman of the board.

Swope, however, cut quite a figure at his own favorite mallet game. That was croquet. The croquet he played was a far cry from the juvenile garden variety, or back-lawn variety. In Swope's view, his kind of croquet combined, as he once put it, the thrills of tennis, the problems of golf, and the finesse of bridge. He added that the game attracted him because it was both vicious and benign. "The game gives release to all the evil in you," he once half jokingly wrote a man who asked him how he'd come to grow so fond of it. "It makes you want to cheat and kill. Conquer these impulses—or yield to them as I do—and the mere sport becomes a spiritual exaltation or debacle, as you choose. What I'm trying to say is that it's a good game."

The strategic aspects of croquet, as it came to be polished and refined under his aegis, also fascinated him. "It is the only game I know, barring chess," he said, "in which you can see three moves ahead, assuming you have that clarity of mental vision." Swope played with fierce concentration. He was preparing some clairvoyant move or other one day when he was notified that Al Smith was phoning from Albany to seek his advice on a pressing gubernatorial matter. "Tell him to hold the line," Swope said. "It's my shot." He spent twenty minutes making the shot and then proceeded indoors to see what was on the waiting Governor's mind.

Alexander Woollcott was another nonathlete who, if national rankings had ever been issued for croquet, would have been a strong contender. Woollcott once wrote that croquet "is no game for the soft of sinew and the gentle of spirit. The higher and dirtier

326

croquet can use the guile of a cobra and the inhumanity of a boa constrictor. Then, the general physique of a stevedore comes in handy, too." Woollcott maintained that the breakthrough in American croquet occurred in Englewood, New Jersey, one day in the spring of 1920. A group including Neysa McMein were playing the childish version there, on a smoothly groomed and narrowly constricted lawn. "Let's play without any bounds at all," Miss McMein suggested, and a revolution was under way. The word quickly reached Great Neck and touched responsive ears.

The Swope crowd would have no truck with the standard croquet sets that can be found in toy stores. Swope and his friends got some of their equipment from Abercrombie & Fitch, and they imported some directly from the old English firm of John Jaques & Son, Ltd., purveyors to croquet players since 1795. They used cast-iron wickets, so narrow that there was only three-eighths of an inch of clearance for a ball, and they placed these hoops at odd angles. They were partial to hand-made mallets, of ash or snakewood reinforced with metal bands. Howard Dietz had mittens to protect his mallet heads. Swope and Harpo Marx kept their favorite mallets in unheated rooms, fearful that high temperatures might throw them out of kilter. Averell Harriman, after giving up polo mallets for croquet mallets, had an extra-heavy croquet bludgeon that he carried around the world with him on his diplomatic missions—to London, Paris, Moscow, or wherever he went in the service of his nation.* Spending a weekend at a château in Fontainebleau while Ambassador to France, Harriman said the surface of the croquet course his hostess had considerately laid out for him was of inferior texture. He urged her to spade it up and as a bread-and-butter gift sent her a sack of grass seed.

The croquet course that Swope set up on the grounds of his Great Neck place was considered topnotch, under the rule that Miss McMein had been inspired to enunciate, because one could rap an opponent's ball into a downhill roadside gutter, along

---

* Harriman, like most of Swope's good friends, often kidded him about his tardiness. During the war, while Harriman was Ambassador to the Soviet Union, his mail was slow in reaching him, and in June 1944 he cabled Swope from Moscow: "YOUR THOUGHTFUL CHRISTMAS NEW YEAR'S GREETING JUST RECEIVED ISN'T THIS A RECORD EVEN FOR SWOPE OR DO YOU MEAN NEXT YEAR. . . ."

which the ball could roll for several hundred yards before it came to a halt, almost out of sight of the playing field to which its miserable owner was obliged to return it when his time came. After Swope moved on to Sands Point, the succeeding proprietor of the Great Neck house, a cotton broker and race-horse owner named Lee Rosenberg, would escort his guests around the area and point with pride to the scene of some of Swope's greatest croquet struggles, as if he were conducting a tour of a hallowed battlefield.*

Some of the Great Neck contests lasted well into the night. The summer days were long, but not long enough to satiate Swope's appetite for croquet, so he decided to play after dark. Harold Talbott, who'd been trained as an engineer, ultimately rigged up a lighting system, but even before permanent illumination was installed, Swope would encircle his field with automobiles and shine their headlights on it. One memorable game *began* at 2:30 A.M. Dorothy Parker and Marc Connelly were sitting on the Ring Lardners' veranda another evening, shortly after Swope introduced night games, when to their surprise they observed that all the cars parked at their neighbor's were moving around, as though his guests were leaving. Since it was only about 10:00 P.M. and the group at the Lardners' were certain dinner hadn't even yet been served across the way, they were puzzled. They realized what was going on when all of the car headlights converged on one spot, followed by the familiar crack of a mallet head meeting a ball. There was a moment of silence on the veranda. Mrs. Parker broke the spell. "Jesus Christ," she said. "The heirs of the age."

---

* Rosenberg owned Kerry Patch, an outsider that won the Belmont Futurity in 1932, at forty-five-to-one odds. The night before, there was an auction pool at Mrs. William Randolph Hearst's, for the benefit of the New York Infirmary for Women and Children. Swope presided. Kerry Patch was the last horse he auctioned off, and, to try to get as large a bid as he could for the hapless animal and thus enrich the hospital, he spoke of the horse in glowing terms. It really had a very good chance, he said, in a long-shot kind of way. The next day, just before the big race, Swope placed an enormous bet on the favorite, Ladysman. His wife went off quietly and placed a bet on her own. The race began, and as Kerry Patch came down the home stretch Swope realized that Margaret was rooting him home. "Why are you yelling for *that* horse?" Swope yelled. "I bet on him," his wife said. "Whatever made you do such an idiotic thing?" he said. "I only listened to what you said about him last night," Margaret replied as her horse charged down first under the wire.

328

Swope's Sands Point course was, in the view of some croquet fanciers, even sportier than his Great Neck one. If a player could propel an opponent's ball onto the driveway there, it could roll down toward the garage and, should the doors of that structure happily be ajar, roll on inside, where it might providentially lodge behind a spare tire or in a pool of grease. (Actually this was Swope's second Sands Point layout. The first proved to be too close to the Sound, and even though he built a restraining barrier, a ball would occasionally go out to sea.) The Swope course was universally conceded to be challenging, but there were other playing fields in the vicinity with stimulating characteristics. Harriman, whose Long Island place was a mile or so from Swope's, built a course on a hillside, and the conceivably exaggerated legend was that one wicket was so sticky a ball wouldn't negotiate it unless it was shot precisely across a certain blade of grass. Raoul Fleischmann's course, at Port Washington, adjoined a tennis court, and if an opponent's ball could be lashed in that direction, all kinds of diverting complications could ensue, including brief scuffles between croquet players and tennis players.

Margaret Emerson's course was generally conceded to be the most exciting. While not the largest—Swope and his set once converted an unused polo field into a croquet patch it was some two hundred feet long, and it boasted a venerable tree with gnarled, exposed roots. Swope was considered to be unrivaled at stroking an enemy ball into the roots, whence to extricate it might take three or four flailing mallet swings. Once Swope hit Fleischmann's ball so severely that it somehow skidded up the trunk of the tree and nestled in the crotch of a branch, too high for Fleischmann to reach it without a ladder. Swope insisted that Fleischmann try to play it out of there notwithstanding.

"Herbert was always inventing new rules," Mrs. Richard Rodgers said. " 'You couldn't shoot out of a shadow,' or 'You *had* to shoot out of a shadow'—it depended on whatever suited his position." Once after Mrs. Rodgers, a fine player, had beaten Swope in a match, he contended banteringly that she never would have managed it if she hadn't been wearing shorts, whereas, the rules clearly stipulated, women had to play croquet in slacks. It was the first anyone had ever heard of *that* rule. Ever afterward, Swope addressed the composer's wife as "Legs." Mrs. Emerson had another croquet course, at a camp in the Adirondacks, which boasted jutting crags of rock; and at his Neshobe Island retreat

Woollcott reigned over an arena so cluttered with hazards that some of the survivors of games played there said admiringly that the course must have been designed for mountain goats.

Swope's travels were less far-flung, and less eventful, than Harriman's, but whatever Swope's destination was, he too liked to find croquet awaiting him. Heading for Palm Beach to stay with the Henry Ittlesons one winter, he designated the writer Arthur Somers Roche, a full-time resident of the resort, to stake out a course for him on the Ittlesons' grounds. Heading for Saratoga to stay with the Jock Whitneys, Swope heralded his arrival by shipping a carton of mallets, wickets and other essential paraphernalia.* Descending upon Saratoga another time, to visit Charles Schwartz, Swope cast a practiced eye over the lawn abutting the house that Schwartz had rented and found it inadequate. "Therefore his beaming host was greeted on the threshold," Woollcott later reported, "with the announcement that, whereas it was charming of him to have extended the invitation at all, the too hasty acceptance would have to be withdrawn unless Mr. Schwartz could arrange next day to take a place with larger grounds. Mr. Schwartz moved the following morning."

Once Swope journeyed across the Sound to Connecticut—an adventure that to many Long Islanders was comparable to scaling the Himalayas—to play croquet on the Richard Rodgers course at Southport. It was late in the fall, and a few spots of crab grass that marred the tidy Rodgers lawn had turned brown. The Rodgerses feared that if Swope saw their blemished sward he'd invoke some thitherto unsuspected rule that would disqualify them even from picking up a mallet. So they hastily sprayed the withered blotches with green paint. Then their only problem was to keep Swope off the course until the paint had dried.

Swope now and then played croquet in Central Park, and once he and some friends contemplated renting the roof of a Man-

---

* Sometimes Swope would go there in Whitney's private plane. His pilot was his valet, Edgar, an aviator of considerably more daring than skill. He promised Whitney that he would stop flying if he ever got scared, but to his employer's dismay he never did. To Margaret Swope's subsequent horror, her husband and Whitney and Edgar nosed over on landing one time. Swope was flung out and shattered his pince-nez. "We tried it again, an evidence of true friendship or undaunted stubbornness," Whitney said. Margaret was furious, but nothing went wrong. "I was stuck with the situation," Whitney explained, "not wanting to hurt Edgar's feelings."

hattan garage and establishing a course suitable for midwinter play, but Sands Point was the focal area. The customary weekend schedule there called for a minimum of two four-hour croquet sessions every Saturday and every Sunday. Women were tolerated, if, like Mrs. Rodgers, Mrs. Emerson, Miss McMein, Mrs. Nelson Doubleday, and Alice Duer Miller, for instance, they had proven themselves able to stand up in competition with males. Margaret Swope never played croquet; about the kindest thing she ever had to say about the pastime was that she loathed it. Several of Swope's masculine kin, however, were highly proficient, notable among them his son, his brothers-in-law and a nephew, Peter Powell. (When Bruce Powell died, in 1955, Swope sent his obituary to the papers and mentioned in it that Powell was a croquet player.) The regular participants included Harriman, Fleischmann, Dietz, Schwartz, Harold Guinzburg, Ogden Phipps, George Abbott, John Baragwanath, William Rhinelander Stewart, and Joseph Brooks's brother Gerald, a Wall Street man. Woollcott once said that Gerald Brooks was the only literate stockbroker he'd ever met. Brooks was one of Swope's best friends, and to sustain that relationship imposed a strain on the broker. He specialized in arbitrage, and he had to be up and working in the morning when the London stock exchange opened—at 5:00 A.M. New York time, which was Swope's retiring hour.

Harpo Marx would join the group when he was on the East Coast. One afternoon Harriman and two other men were waiting for Swope to appear for a match. In due course he arrived, splendidly accoutered and followed by a retinue—his valet Roy Robinson carrying his coat and his major-domo Mae Fielding carrying his mallet. As Swope drew near he noticed a man unfamiliar to him and, walking up with hand outstretched, said, "What's your name? My name is Swope." "I'm Mr. Marx's chauffeur," the stranger replied. Swope's game was noticeably off that day, and every now and then, after muffing a shot, he would mutter, "*Gentlemen* have their servants in livery."

Gerald Brooks was strong and husky, and Swope liked him as a croquet partner because when he smote an opponent's ball there was no telling how far it might go. (Strength, as Woollcott had pointed out, was important. Moss Hart once achieved renown by swinging his mallet with such force that, although he missed the ball he was aiming at, he easily broke his own foot.) One afternoon Brooks and Swope took on Averell Harriman and

331

Raoul Fleischmann. That day Swope got a black ball, Brooks a blue one, Harriman red, and Fleischmann yellow. Before they went into action Swope gave his partner some instructions. Everybody knew, Swope said, that Brooks was allowed on the premises purely because of his brawn. Accordingly, he, Swope, would do all the thinking for their side, and Brooks's contribution was to be exclusively physical. Brooks meekly acquiesced, and play began. At the third wicket all four balls were clustered together, and it was Brooks's shot. Swope looked over the situation and commanded, "Listen, you moron with that great muscular system, your blue ball has struck that black ball, and now you will drive the black ball clear across that apple orchard." Brooks was perfectly aware that it was Swope's own ball that was being consigned to that fate, but, mindful of his orders, he shrugged, swung with all his might, and swatted the black ball into appleland with the force of a cider press. The ball had hardly begun its flight when Swope realized his error. "Brooks, you're worse than useless!" he screamed in dismay.

Brooks died in 1936, and his croquet-playing friends instituted a Gerald Brooks Challenge Cup Tournament in his memory. Margaret Emerson, who was widely regarded as the fairy godmother of the sport, provided a suitable trophy—a sterling-silver Tiffany reproduction of an eighteenth-century Dublin cup on display at the Metropolitan Museum of Art. (Mrs. Emerson once also offered a purse of ten thousand dollars for an East-West match between Swope's crowd and a California croquet coterie led by Samuel Goldwyn—who had two courses, with sand traps and built-in sprinklers—and Darryl F. Zanuck, but the contest never came off, although the two factions engaged in a good deal of cloying correspondence about it, involving such phrases as "with mallets toward none" and "no rest for the wickets.") There were many brisk duels for the Brooks trophy, which Swope's son, who was suckled on croquet and could hold his own in adult competition at the age of ten, finally retired in 1950. The junior Swope and Harriman were locked in one tussle during the fall of 1938 when a hurricane swept in; they went on playing until they were all but blown off their feet. Swope *fils* was the superior shotmaker, but Harriman was a master of psychological warfare. He played with such tortoiselike deliberation that he infuriated his opponents, and once they had lost their temper they were likely to lose a match, too. Herbert Swope, Jr., brought about Harriman's downfall by usurping his enemy's tactics and dragging his own feet. When Harriman began to complain that the young man was being insufferably poky, Swope knew his battle was as good as won.

The most bitterly competitive croquet players of all, probably, were Swope *père* and Woollcott. They would get so worked up and noisily argumentative that they were jointly called the Katzenjammer Kids, although, considering their respective builds, Mutt and Jeff might have been apter. The tall, lean Swope usually turned up for a match in impeccably tailored white flannels; the short, puffy Woollcott would try to disconcert him by wearing floppy green silk pajamas. (Swope never bet more than a thousand dollars on a croquet game, possibly having taken to heart the 1869 observation of a man who published a book on croquet rules and said, "It is too refined, too intellectual, ever to become a gambler's game.")

It was inconceivable, quite apart from their professional relationship, that Swope and Woollcott should not have become friends. Both loved to move in an eddy of other celebrities, especially those whose books or plays or paintings or songs were in the public eye and ear. Both loved to talk and be listened to, and to engage in lively intellectual byplay; and croquet was another firm, cementing bond. It was equally inconceivable that they could have stayed friends forever. Both were quick, in their personal relations, to shift from affection to scorn. What was perhaps most important, both needed to occupy stage center and during their glittering performances could not long countenance the presence of a co-star or even a featured supporting player. Woollcott liked to arrange things. It was perfectly agreeable to the diffident Harriman that Woollcott should practically dictate the guest list and arrangements at the annual Thanksgiving house parties for which Harriman was nominal host at Arden House, his castle on the west shore of the Hudson. (To play croquet there at that time of year, the guests sometimes first had to shovel snow.) But on Swope's home grounds he wouldn't stand for anybody arranging anything except himself.

Swope and Woollcott had had periodic flareups. Swope thought Woollcott overbearingly rude, and Woollcott, who prided himself on always being on time, was horrified at Swope's incurable tardiness. Once at Sands Point the pudgy critic sought to teach Swope a lesson. Woollcott dallied in the Swope swimming pool until he was sternly informed he was late for lunch, a feat difficult to achieve at the Swopes'. Making a show of abjectness, Woollcott rushed into the house, pulled a pair of trousers over his still damp bathing trunks, and settled himself solidly on an upholstered chair in the dining room. When he arose an hour later he had, as he had calculated he would have, geraniums and nasturtiums imprinted on the seat of his pants. The Swopes were not amused by the artistic innovation.

It irked Woollcott, moreover, that while almost every game of chance known to man flourished at the Swopes', nobody there ever seemed eager to play *his* favorite card game, which was hearts. But throughout the 1920s and into the '30s the two men saw a good deal of each other, and on Swope's departure from the *World* Woollcott wrote him, "If you ever take over the Great Neck *News,* I can tell you one thing about its dramatic critic. His guts will be hated by your whilom underling Alexander Woollcott." And a year after that, Woollcott concluded a letter to Swope by saying "that your heart is God's little garden and that the indurated habit of loving you has lasted so long I shall probably never get over it."

He did, though. At the Swope house in Great Neck, the guests had mostly comprised the artists and writers whom Woollcott found congenial. On Swope's moving to Sands Point and retiring from the paper, he began to associate more and more with business people—Sarnoffs and Hertzes and Laskers and Chadbournes and other formidable corporate entities. It was understandable enough that after Swope left the *World* and got involved in international stock issues the nature of his companionship should change. But Woollcott didn't like it and said so. "Herbert thinks he's going social when he's only going financial" was one of Woollcott's softer jabs.

The Swope-Woollcott relationship gradually worsened. Several sharp blows were struck—both verbal and epistolary. One skirmish got under way toward the end of 1931, when John Hertz decided to move from Chicago to New York. Swope still owed him more than half a million dollars, and he was hard put even to keep up with the interest payments, but on Hertz's driving himself eastward the straitened debtor did his best to make his prosperous creditor feel at home. Swope tendered Hertz a Lucullan feast at the Lotos Club—a terrapin-and-guinea-hen affair for some fifty prominent New Yorkers and Mayor Frank Hague of Jersey City.

Moreover, Hertz's arrival on the Manhattan scene presented Swope with an opportunity, he was happy to reflect, to do a big favor, at one intermedial swoop, for two friends. The transplanted Chicagoan was looking for suitable lodgings, and at the same time Joshua Cosden, who had gone broke, was saddled with his thirty-room triplex apartment, in a cooperative-apartment building at 450 East Fifty-second Street, called the Beekman Campanile. How tidily both men's problems could be solved, Swope reasoned, if Hertz leased the Cosden establishment!

Swope knew a good many of the other residents of the Campanile, among whom were the Ralph Pulitzers, the Harold Talbotts, Alice Duer Miller, and Woollcott. Swope also knew that no apartment in the building could be sold or rented to anyone unacceptable to a Campanile insider. When Cosden proposed Hertz as a tenant, Woollcott blackballed him. Swope thought Woollcott was being anti-Semitic; actually Woollcott had other personal reasons, two of the milder ones being that he regarded Hertz as a bounder and a social climber. In any event, Swope was furious at Woollcott and swiftly made his fury known. Woollcott felt impelled to write him that "I keep hearing rumors to the effect that you are denouncing me for discreditable behavior in the matter of the proposal to install the Hertzes in the Cosden apartment. I am resting comfortably in the assumption that you do not express or even harbor unamiable thoughts about me without finding out from me just what mischief I have been up to and why. I don't know what tale you have heard, but to save time I might volunteer the information that I have done nothing I am ashamed of, nor that I would not do again on the basis of the same information."

Swope retorted, in a letter he did not mail but had Miss Millar read to Woollcott, that he considered the Hertzes desirable tenants in any building. "I do not demand that you accept my judgment on them or on anyone else," he went on. "I do not say that the fact you met them several times in my home entitled them and me to any special courtesy. But I do say that while you have every right to view people as you wish, there is a price you must pay when you translate unkind thoughts into venomous action, and that price is my friendship." Woollcott tried to make the price not quite so steep. "If you are going to glower at me at parties and write me terse notes which put me in the preposterous position of volunteering excuses for my way of conducting my

335

affairs," he wrote Swope, "I cannot imagine what my next move should be—if any. But if you really have a friendly interest in my reputation for decency in human relations, and can remember to challenge me the next time I run into you, I promise to testify truthfully on any points that may still be troubling you. I cannot purely on a matter of principle break a twenty-year habit of preferring that you should think well of me."

But the challenge was never issued, the testimony never given. Instead, Swope and Woollcott sniped away bitterly at each other. Swope would soon be writing to Dudley Nichols that Woollcott's prose was "entertaining—just as an éclair is pleasant to eat. But, after you have read Woollcott, you have in your mental stomach only a confused gas; never the enrichment that is given by bone and sinew, and Woollcott is typical of many. He has had a profound influence on writers—all to the bad." And Woollcott, no less partial himself to the stomachic phrase, would be describing the Swope ménage at Sands Point as "pleasant, distracting, and singularly unnourishing."

There was more friction to come between the two men. Swope had never been a conventional father. He had no aptitude for small talk or horseplay, and the advice he gave his growing boy sounded as if he'd copied it out of an archaic parents' manual. When Herbert, Jr., was fifteen, his father, after looking over a school report card, wrote him, "Incidentally, I notice you were tardy once; why was this?" and continued, "Remember, you are going through a course of training now before you enter the ring. If you train well you will fight well. If you slough off training you won't know how to fight and won't be willing to fight, and the fellow who can't fight and keep his head up is the fellow who goes down and out in the early rounds of the battle of life."

Swope was one of those far from uncommon fathers who espouse don't-do-as-I-do-do-as-I-say child-raising. His son first went to a horse race at the age of five and sat in Harry F. Sinclair's box. Just before the last race the oil man said, "Sonny, what do you like?" "I don't know, Mr. Sinclair; what do *you* like?" the boy replied politely. "Friday the Thirteenth is an immortal cinch!" Sinclair exclaimed, and young Swope was persuaded to bet five dollars on the sure thing—with Sinclair himself gallantly volunteering to stand *in loco* bookmaker. A horse named Forest Flower won. "Too bad, boy!" said Sinclair. At that moment the senior Swope came along to retrieve his son. On hearing what had happened, he gave Sinclair the five dollars he'd won and all the way home lectured his son on the evils of gambling.

In the late 1920s the Swope son went to a country-day school on Long Island and lived the year round at the Great Neck house, with his maternal grandmother, while his parents, during the winter months, spent most of their time at the 58th Street apartment. The Swopes thought it would be good for their boy to have some male supervisory companionship, and a promising candidate turned up one weekend quite by accident. He was Joseph P. Hennessey, a bookstore proprietor who was an old friend of Margaret Swope's brother Kenneth. Kenneth Powell was also friendly with cats, to which his brother-in-law was allergic. Cats made Swope's nose run. Powell would keep sneaking cats into the Great Neck establishment. They always seemed to like to perch on a ledge outside Swope's bedroom window. He would wake up, snuffling and sneezing, and rush off to Saratoga or some other spa to cure himself of what he thought was a terrible head cold.

Powell brought Hennessey to Great Neck for a weekend, and he stayed on and on. It was not unusual for the Swopes to tender prolonged hospitality. When the Swopes were fond of someone they all but resented his being anywhere else. George Backer was for a time a steady weekend guest and even kept some clothes at the Swopes'; when he informed them once that he wouldn't be able to make it the following Saturday, Margaret Swope told him if he missed any more weekends she'd throw his things away. The writer Alice Leone Moats was another perennial house guest. She once described her début, on a Saturday, in that role:

> I took the train to Port Washington that arrived around noon so that I could be at the house in time for lunch. I was very worried because [a dowager in the neighborhood] kidnapped me at the station and insisted upon taking me back to her house for a drink and I was sure I would arrive late at the Swopes'. It was 1:30 when I finally reached the house. There wasn't a soul in sight. A servant took me up to my room and then I began to wander about, looking for my hostess. She appeared at three o'clock. Swope didn't show till tea-time. Accustomed to the kind of hosts one usually finds on Long Island, who greet one with the information that there's a fine train back to New York on Sunday afternoon, I expected to receive some hint as to when I should go home. Nothing, of course, was said and when, on Monday morning, I announced that I was leaving, Maggie made a frightful scene, and I didn't depart until Wednesday, promising to return on Friday.

But Joseph Hennessey's stay was exceptional, even for the Swopes. Invited originally for a weekend, he remained for five years. His status was never made explicitly clear. He became not merely a companion to the Swope son but also a superintendent of the house and grounds. He had the further duty of evaluating incoming morning telephone calls for the master of the house; he was supposed to awaken Swope if there seemed to be any especially turbulent action in the stock market. After a while Swope concluded—or so it was Margaret Swope's impression— that it was undignified for Hennessey to be hanging around in limbo and put him on a salary; but Hennessey did not share that impression. In any event, he was on the premises—after the Swopes moved to Sands Point they quartered him in an apartment over the garage—and the whole family had got comfortably used to him when, in the spring of 1933, he announced unexpectedly that he was moving on. It was bad enough that he was leaving at a time when the tennis court had to be got in shape. It was worse, as soon became known, that he was leaving to stay with and work for, of all people, Alexander Woollcott. Swope was as wrathful as any pre-Civil War McCoy would have been whose runaway slave had been found on a Hatfield plantation.

The final cleavage between Swope and Woollcott came a few months after Hennessey's defection. In the 1933 mayoralty campaign in New York City, Woollcott was an all-out advocate of the Fusion candidate, Fiorello LaGuardia. Swope was working equally hard for, and was treasurer of the campaign committee of, Joseph V. McKee, a Democrat running on a Recovery Party ticket. At McKee headquarters one day Swope proudly displayed to Beatrice Kaufman a handful of checks that had come in, and she happened to mention his boyishly enthusiastic flourishing of the money to Woollcott, who was about to make a pro-LaGuardia speech at Town Hall. In his remarks Woollcott said:

It is too bad, really, that the *World* is not being published now, for I am sure it would be for Mr. LaGuardia. At least everybody on the *World* at that time is for Mr. LaGuardia now—except Mr. Herbert Bayard Swope. Walter Lippmann, the chief editorial writer of the *World*, who is now the chief editorial writer of the world, is for LaGuardia. Heywood Broun is for LaGuardia. F.P.A. is for LaGuardia. In fact, about the only exception is Mr. Herbert Bayard Swope. Well, as you may know, Mr. Swope was executive editor of the *World* in the period before its finish. . . . It is with peculiar interest that I watch his connection with this campaign.

I have brought with me some files, showing that · distinguished company of citizens who went to the late James J. Walker four years ago, and urged him, please, please, to run again! "Who could say no?" was the reply of that dandy little gentleman. Mr. Herbert Bayard Swope was one of those distinguished citizens. And now he is passing the hat, as campaign treasurer, for Mr. McKee—passing it so furiously that only the other night he was flashing certified checks up to ten thousand dollars—checks he had collected for Mr. McKee—and where they came from, one does not know, but it will probably come out sooner or later.

Swope was doubly angered—both at the implication that there was something underhanded about his political fund-raising and that he'd been responsible for the downfall of the *World*. It was not surprising, therefore, that when, three years later, Woollcott, a man as fond of money as Swope himself, was paid by the Seagram Distillers to send his many acquaintances Christmas-time letters saying that he couldn't think of a nicer holiday gift than a bottle or more of Seagram's, Swope wrote the company, testily:

GENTLEMEN:
I had placed an order for your Pedigreed Bonded Whiskey, for personal use and for Christmas gifts, when Mr. Woollcott's "letter" reached me. As he never drinks whiskey and, therefore, is unable to judge its value—an inability that is not confined to whiskey—it follows that his letter must be regarded as deliberately misleading— a failing of which he is frequently guilty.

In these circumstances I have cancelled my order for your product, and I shall advise my friends to follow the same course.*

Throughout most of the 1930s there was hardly any communication between Swope and Woollcott. But at the start of 1939 (by which time Swope had had a falling-out of his own with John Hertz) Woollcott decided that Nazism posed a graver threat to peace on earth than their own personal squabble. On January 17, hearing that Swope was involved in a plan—which

---

* Swope may have been carried away by spleen. It is hard to see why he should have placed an order for Seagram products to begin with, inasmuch as the previous spring he'd become a consultant to its big rival, Schenley.

didn't work out—to set up a German exhibit at the New York World's Fair that would emphasize the non-Nazi aspects of German history and culture, Woollcott sent Swope a brief note: "I am writing this on the chance of your sharing my own conviction that the time has come to bury all hatchets—in Hitler's neck. More particularly, I was wishing I could lend a hand to the pre-Nazi exhibit at the World's Fair and wondering if a broadcast about it before—or, better still, after—the Fair opens would be an acceptable and useful contribution. My best to Ottie." Swope at once replied:

DEAR ALEC:

I was touched by your letter. The call of the years is hard to resist, so I, too, want the unpleasantness to end. Friends are few and far between and their rarity becomes greater as one grows older.

I think it would be best to talk out some of the details. That is what you suggested when the Great Schism first arose, but we never came around to it. Thereafter, perhaps unintentionally, you struck me a heavy blow. Did you know it? I shall tell you about it when I see you, and tell you how its effect is continuing. . . .

The heavy blow to which he referred was Woollcott's casual remark more than five years earlier about Swope and the end of the *World*. It was not for nearly another couple of years after this comparatively pacific exchange of letters, however, that the two men did get together. Then, in November 1940, Woollcott called at Swope's office one afternoon, and they had a chat. They parted on reasonably amicable terms, and Swope's wrath ebbed further when, the following month, he persuaded Walter Winchell, who commanded a larger audience than Woollcott, to say in his column, "Herbert Bayard Swope wishes people would remember that he quit the Morning World in 1928—long before it died." * But in the three years that remained of Woollcott's life he and Swope were never again to attain their bygone mutually agreeable state of snippy camaraderie.

---

* Winchell's own memory was no great shakes. After Swope's death, the columnist ran an item that had Swope editing the *World* six months before its death, in 1931.

17

NOTHING UPSET Swope more than to have Woollcott or anyone else assert, or even hint, that he was in any way accountable for the passing of the *World*. He sometimes bristled when people said the paper "died." At its sale, in the winter of 1931, the paper fetched five million dollars, and who would pay that, he demanded, for a corpse? But he was quibbling about words. For what had endeared the *World* to so many readers was its peculiarly animated quality—in Swope's own word, its "sparkle"—and people who admired its liveliness while it was around could scarcely be blamed, once it had disappeared, for considering it to have perished. A Morris Markey piece in *The New Yorker* about the cessation of the paper—"the greatest institution of them all," Markey called it—ran under the terse and, few save Swope would argue, unassailable title of "Obit."

As to just who killed off the *World*, three decades' worth of post-mortems did not produce a universally accepted verdict. Certainly, between 1928 and 1931, the paper lost much of the bounce and drive and dash and daring that had won and kept its readers. *The New Yorker* told of one New Yorker who, unable to give up the habit of scanning the *World* at breakfast, would unfold the paper each morning, reflectively read Joseph Pulitzer's ardent pledge that graced its masthead, and would then refold the paper and set it sadly aside. One thing the *World* clearly lacked during its fading years was a dominating personality—someone like the senior Pulitzer in his prime, or like Swope in his. There were those whose sharp hindsight perceived that at least part of the blame rested on Swope, because of his inattentiveness to detail during the last months of his regime. How far can a general who hopes to win a battle be, they would ask, from his troops? Others, among them Swope, thought Lippmann's cautiousness had proved debilitating. The *Daily News,* which stood to profit from the disaster no matter who was wrong, ran a neutral editorial blaming both Swope and Lippmann.

Herbert Hoover had his own theory. He believed that when the paper had to retract a charge of scandal it made against his Administration in 1930, "the exposure so discredited the *World* that it died soon after." The depression was probably as causal as anything else. Advertisers had severely curtailed their budgets, and they spent their limited funds on space in what they considered the more rewarding columns of the steadier *Times* and the flashier *News.* The death of the *World,* it would seem in retrospect, was brought about not by any single one of these factors but by a combination of all of them, along with, and perhaps chiefly because of, the penny-pinching philosophy of the second-generation Pulitzers.

Even before Swope left the *World* he had high hopes of some day returning to it, and after departing he kept a close—very nearly proprietary—eye on its fortunes and misfortunes. When he was out of New York he had Miss Millar get in touch almost daily with Beazell, who stayed with the paper, to pick up the latest interoffice gossip for him. The idea was firm in Swope's mind that if the Pulitzers changed *their* minds about selling the morning paper, he had an option to buy it. He did not know that ever since Ralph Pulitzer had returned from Europe with Roy Howard, the Scripps-Howard chain had the inside track and was running fast. Nor did Swope have any inkling that the owners were contemplating the sale not alone of the morning paper but of the evening and Sunday papers as well. This likelihood could hardly have occurred to anyone who, like Swope, was familiar with the provisions of Joseph Pulitzer's will. He had decreed, in language that to a layman, if not a lawyer, seemed explicit and binding:

> I particularly enjoin upon my sons and my descendants the duty of preserving, perfecting and perpetuating "the World" newspaper (to the maintenance and upbuilding of which I have sacrificed my health and strength) in the same spirit in which I have striven to create and conduct it as a public institution, from motives higher than mere gain, it having been my desire that it should be at all times conducted in a spirit of independence and with a view to

inculcating high standards and public spirit among the people and their official representatives, and it is my earnest wish that said newspaper shall hereafter be conducted upon the same principles.

Swope never had enough liquid capital, even at the peak of the market, seriously to consider buying the *World* properties, or whatever portion of them might be available, with his own money. He needed a patron, and for a while thought he had found one in the formidable person of William Randolph Hearst, whom Swope once described as "the most remarkable genius the profession of journalism has produced." (He also once said, though, that working for a Hearst paper was like being in a graveyard; that "men who go there die.") During Swope's reportorial days he had got to know Hearst, and as far back as 1917 the publisher and his wife Millicent had given the Swopes a brace of lovebirds, which, Swope said in thanking the donors, "will keep us in mind of you. I suggested to Margaret that we name them Willie and Millie. . . ." It was an ironic choice of names, for the lovebirds arrived just about the time that Hearst was meeting and falling in love with Marion Davies. It was typical of the catholicity of Swope's friendships that he was able to stay on good terms all his life both with Mrs. Hearst, who in 1931 bought Mrs. Oliver H. P. Belmont's estate adjoining his place at Sands Point, and with Miss Davies. Swope was one of the few of the publisher's friends who, when Hearst died in August 1951, had the honesty and decency to send a message of condolence not merely to the widow he rarely saw but to the mistress he adored.*

In 1928, while still at the *World*, Swope was thinking about aligning himself with Hearst, in whose employ, he was confident, *his* own energies would not be fatally sapped. Perhaps, he meditated, he might take over the New York *American*, which was having its own troubles, and might alter it, as he had earlier altered the *World*, by giving it "intellectual character" and fulfilling its need of "what people ought to read—not *want* to read." Another, nonintellectual idea Swope had stemmed from Mrs. Hearst's pet

---

* Swope must have been pleased and flattered by a selective question that *Time* used in one of its news quizzes two months afterward: "In his eighty-ninth year death came to capricious, inspired, ruthless and sentimental lord of the Press: 1, Col. Robert R. McCormick; 2, Roy Wilson Howard; 3, Herbert Bayard Swope; 4, Frank Ernest Gannett; 5, William Randolph Hearst."

charity—providing free milk for needy babies. Swope thought that if he ever ran a Hearst paper he would arrange to have deliveries made by milk wagons, with a copy of the paper wrapped around each quart. (It would have made a wonderful early-morning weapon for street fights.)

The following year Swope began to visualize Hearst as a likely prospect to take over the *World* and to reinstall him there in a co-proprietary role. Hearst came east from California at the end of 1929. Swope, who by then had decided that if he made a bid for his old paper he'd like to do so in conjunction with John Wheeler of the North American Newspaper Alliance syndicate and with Bruce Barton, had several meetings with the autocratic publisher and also with Ralph Pulitzer and Florence White. From the latter two, Swope deduced that the morning *World* might indeed be sold. But Hearst wanted the Sunday paper as well. The negotiations bogged down, moreover, because Pulitzer wouldn't set an asking price for the morning paper and Hearst wouldn't make a bid. Swope was in the difficult position of an agent trying to transact business between a seller who didn't seem sure he wanted to sell and a buyer who was equally uncertain he wanted to buy.

At the start of 1930 it became evident that Ralph Pulitzer was about to turn over the reins of all the *World*s to his brother Herbert, then thirty-four. The Young Master did assume command, on February 10, and hardly had he done so when some one hundred employees, many of them with long years of service, were summarily dismissed as an economy move. (By an unfortunate coincidence they were let out on the same day that Lippmann's editorial page chided Harvard for unceremoniously firing thirteen scrubwomen.) One of the sacked veterans, who had joined the staff fifteen years before Herbert Pulitzer was born, had the not terribly important job, except possibly to him, of reading other newspapers and comparing their contents to the *World*'s. On getting his notice, he turned in his daily report as usual, subscribed "1880–1930" beneath his signature, put on his hat, and left without a word. The mass involuntary exodus from the paper was interpreted to mean that the new management was going to retrench rather than try to resurrect the paper by pouring additional life-saving capital into it.

At the instigation of David Sarnoff, Swope joined the Board of Directors of Radio-Keith-Orpheum in 1929, and he thought it would be nice to go to Hollywood and see motion pictures made *in situ.* The trip seemed doubly worthwhile when Hearst, anticipating Herbert Pulitzer's takeover, phoned Swope in January from his San Simeon enclave and suggested that they continue their conversations about the *World* in California. What Hearst now apparently had in mind was acquiring the morning *World* and ultimately combining it with his own faltering *American,* with Swope the front man and Hearst's own involvement, for the time being at least, to be kept secret. (Swope loved intrigue and, in a spate of transcontinental messages he exchanged with Miss Millar, would refer to Ralph Pulitzer as "Dome," to the *World* as "Senior," and to Hearst as "Sansimeon." Anybody who wanted to break his code would probably have had little difficulty doing so.) The two men first had a lunch conference in Marion Davies' dressing room on the Metro-Goldwyn-Mayer lot, and Swope came armed with some fresh information that Miss Millar, after getting in touch with the obliging Beazell, had furnished on the sorry state of the *World:* "W.P.B. ADVISES DRASTIC CUTS ON SENIOR SINCE VISIT MAN FROM WEST [another code term for Hearst] ABOUT TWO WEEKS AGO SAVING ABOUT ONE HUNDRED AND TWENTY-FIVE THOUSAND IN EXPENSES IN ADDITION SIXTY-EIGHT THOUSAND MADE DURING FALL GRAVURE BE CUT TO FOUR PAGES MAGAZINE BACK TO NEWSPRINT PHOTOGRAPH DEPARTMENT CUT TWO-THIRDS REDUCTION DAILY COLUMNS TO TWELVE AND ONE-HALF EMS ALSO REDUCTIONS IN COMPOSING ROOM AND BUSINESS OFFICE. . . ."

In the next couple of days Swope and Hearst met again, once at Miss Davies' home in Santa Monica, once at Charles Chaplin's home in Beverly Hills, and the faithful Miss Millar by now had flashed: ". . . ADVISED TODAY OWNERS SENIOR IN PANIC. . . . OLD TIMERS OUT. . . . BOLITHO CONTRACT UNRENEWED PHOTOGRAPH DEPARTMENT WIPED OUT. . . . TWENTY PEOPLE IN ADVERTISING DEPARTMENT OUT ARE CUTTING RIGHT AND LEFT. . . . NOW IS PSYCHOLOGICAL MOMENT TO MAKE OFFER BY ANY INTERESTED PARTY. . . ."

The messages kept flowing in. But along with those from his secretary, Swope also got a telegram from his wife that may have given him pause: ". . . DON'T PLEASE SELL YOURSELF AND FREEDOM OF ACTION INTO SLAVERY AGAIN. . . ."

From Hollywood, Swope moved north to spend a few days with Sansimeon at San Simeon. Now, for the first time, Hearst got around to discussing terms. He thought somewhere between five and eight million dollars would be a fair price for the Pulitzers' morning and Sunday papers, and he summoned Arthur Brisbane, one of his main financial deputies as well as his star writer, to work out details with Swope. Brisbane was less prodigal in his estimates; he thought Hearst should make an opening offer of not more than four and a half million.

Swope headed home, jubilant. An affiliation with Hearst seemed closer than ever. Instead of the prudent Pulitzers, he would be working for—better still, if he could arrange things satisfactorily, working with—a powerful lord of the press whose spending habits were legendary. When Swope's eastbound train stopped at Albuquerque he wired Miss Millar to let Herbert Pulitzer know he would be prepared to make a definite offer on his return. Arriving in New York, however, Swope found the youngest Pulitzer still professing not to be sure the family wanted to sell at all. Swope nonetheless put forth his four-and-a-half-million-dollar proposition, keeping Hearst's name out of it, and he repeated the bid to Ralph Pulitzer, who said he'd think it over and that in any event, or so Swope got the impression, there would be no sale of the papers without Swope's foreknowledge.

Judging that there was no particular urgency, Swope thereupon betook himself to Florida, to partake of the agreeable hospitality of, first, John Hertz at Miami Beach and then Thomas Chadbourne at Palm Beach. While at Chadbourne's, Swope got a message from Miss Millar that shook him: "BEAZELL ADVISES SCRIPPS PEOPLE VERY BUSY. ANXIOUS BUY EVENING BUT YOUNG MASTER SAYS ALL OR NOTHING." It was the first inkling Swope had had that the Pulitzers had come around to the conclusion that they were under no filial obligation to perpetuate any kind of *World* in New York.

The *World*'s financial position was rapidly deteriorating—despite Herbert Pulitzer's stringencies, the morning paper lost $1,677,000 in 1930—and Swope and Howard were not the only journalists keeping a watchful eye on its downhill skid. Ogden Reid of the *Herald Tribune* coveted whatever the Pulitzers might yield up. So did Generoso Pope of the Italian-American *Il Progresso Americano*. So did Paul Block of Pittsburgh and J. David Stern of Philadelphia. Adolph Ochs met with Herbert Pulitzer and urged him to let his employees take over the morning and Sunday papers; the *Times*, Ochs said, would back the employees and share control with them. Pulitzer mentioned a figure of ten million dollars for the morning and the Sunday. He quoted the same figure to Swope afterward, adding that for that amount, however, a purchaser could expect no staff, no equipment, and no building—nothing but the daily-and-Sunday morning circulation and the use of the name *"World"* for a limited period, perhaps three or four months. Swope rejected that insubstantial package out of hand.

He still thought he'd have first crack at any more reasonable proposition the Pulitzers might make, but they instead embarked on final negotiations with Roy Howard. In December 1930, with Joseph Pulitzer, Jr., coming in from St. Louis to present a united fraternal front, the Pulitzers agreed to let Scripps-Howard have everything they had in New York for five million dollars. Nobody else was notified. The assets to be sold, though, were, under the terms of the senior Joseph Pulitzer's will, held in trust, and the rights of more than a dozen minor Pulitzer grandchildren were involved. Accordingly, any transaction would have to be approved by the Surrogate of New York County, James A. Foley. And his sanction would require an elastic interpretation of the clause in the Pulitzer will enjoining the old man's heirs to preserve the institution of the *World*. The Pulitzer sons' lawyers embarked on this last Pulitzer crusade—a muffled one—to change the face of New York.

The last two weeks of February 1931 were feverish for Swope and for the *World*. On February 13 Herbert Pulitzer, aware of Swope's long-standing partiality to the *World Almanac*, had Florence White tell him that the reference book was for sale, should he be interested. Swope was, but before he could get around to doing anything about it he heard more startling news. For several years, at Christmas time, the *Evening World* had been raising money to buy coal for the indigent. In 1930 Herbert Pulitzer made the morning paper a co-sponsor of this charitable project. The coal was bought and distributed before New Year's Day, but contributions kept dribbling in belatedly. On February 16 James Barrett, the *World*'s city editor, dropped into John Tennant's *Evening World* office to discuss what should be done with these surplus funds. Barrett thought maybe they should be held over, to give the following year's coal fund a head start. "There won't be any next year," Tennant said. "Scripps-Howard have bought the whole works." Only a handful of Pulitzer executives, he went on, had yet been let in on a dire secret: That on

347

January 31 a contract of sale had been signed and there remained merely some legalities for the *fait* to become *accompli*.

Barrett spread the bad tidings, and while nothing about the impending sale appeared in print for another fortnight, word got around fast and far. (Adolph Ochs heard the news in Honolulu, and, hoping to save the *World* from extinction, at once headed back to New York. But, transportation being what it was then, he might as well have stayed put and gone surf-riding.) Soon after leaving Tennant's office, Barrett telephoned Miss Millar. She told Swope, who turned pale. He swiftly got in touch with John Wheeler, who was about to sail to Europe. The *World* had become Wheeler's syndicate's biggest single customer (it may have been a portent of doom that this paper, once so proudly independent, should have turned into any canned feature service's principal client), and Wheeler called off his trip. Eager to talk to Swope at length in person, Wheeler tracked him down several hours later to a crap game at the home of a *World* sports writer, Walter Trumbull. The syndicate man was feeling low, and he felt even worse when, after he'd accepted an invitation to join the fray, Swope made seventeen straight passes. It was about the only bit of luck Swope was to have in those turbulent two weeks.

Later that night Swope, who was still uncertain how far Hearst would go to keep the *World* alive, decided with Wheeler that they'd make a last-minute stab at buying in on their own. They moved along to an after-theater party, and Swope began telephoning some of his wealthier friends. Gilbert Seldes was there, and looked and listened with awe as Swope "swept into action— the most dynamic, frenzied, violent man I'd ever seen." Within twenty-four hours Swope had promises of financial help from his brother, Baruch, Harriman, Hertz, Owen Young, Morton Schwartz, and Harrison Williams. Meanwhile, Wheeler went to see Herbert Pulitzer, hoping to persuade him to hold up whatever was in the works until Swope and he were ready to make a formal bid. Pulitzer said they were too late for anything like that. Swope, mindful of the other iron he still had in the fire, sent a stream of informative and questioning messages to San Simeon. And in a message he composed for his own files, he said, in bitter contemplation of the Pulitzers' failure to honor the priority of purchase he thought they'd pledged to him, "I regard myself as badly used."

At the *World*, the executives denied all the rumors that were buzzing beneath the golden dome. But Barrett knew that whatever arrangement had been made between the Pulitzers and Scripps-Howard would have to be ratified by the Surrogate, and his city staff found out from Foley, though the city editor was not allowed to print the news, that a matter involving the Joseph Pulitzer estate was slated to come up for a hearing on February 24. That day Ralph Renaud, Swope's successor at the *World*, called in Barrett and J. Earle Clauson. "Gentlemen, tonight we will get out the last issue of the *World*," he told them. "There will be no *Evening World* tomorrow. You may so inform the staff. All three papers are being merged with the *Telegram*, and the first edition of the *World-Telegram* will be published tomorrow. . . . I knew nothing about this until a few moments ago. The Pulitzer trustees [that was, Ralph, Herbert, and Joseph, Jr.] have been lying to me right straight along, from hell to breakfast. . . . They say now they had to do it."

Proceedings in the Surrogate's Court got under way a few hours afterward. These had hardly begun when there was a dramatic interruption. The lawyer Max Steuer rushed into the courtroom. He was representing Paul Block, the publisher, he said, who was on a train heading toward New York and was prepared to exceed any Scripps-Howard offer for the papers by half a million dollars. Couldn't everything be postponed until Block arrived? Foley granted a one-day reprieve, and on February 25 both the *World* and the *Evening World* were published. They now carried news stories about their own impending fate.

The pace of protest quickened. Block arrived and wangled a few more hours' delay from the Surrogate. At the *World*, Barrett took a telephone call from a prominent New York lawyer, Gustavus A. Rogers, who besought a favor. Rogers' daughter was going to Europe, and would the *World* be kind enough to mention her departure in its ship-news column? When Barrett replied wryly that he'd be glad to oblige if there was a ship-news column or a paper to print one in, it developed Rogers hadn't yet heard about the sale. On being enlightened, he urged the city editor to marshal the *World*'s employees for a last-ditch stand. They could buy the paper themselves and run it as a cooperative, Rogers suggested, and he'd be glad to plead their case before the Surrogate that same afternoon. Barrett checked with Swope, who endorsed the plan—the third plan, by now, for rescuing the *World* in which he was a participant.

By telephone, telegraph, and cable the *World*'s employees were alerted, and they rallied to the cause, sending in pledges of their own and soliciting further assistance from colleagues on other newspapers. The Surrogate withheld his decision for still one more day, and in that less than twenty-four-hour period of grace the Barrett forces, adopting the name Joseph Pulitzer Employees' Association, had conducted an emotional rally in the ballroom of the Hotel Astor and had raised half a million dollars. Albin Johnson, the *World* man in Geneva, cabled, "TEN THOUSAND. GOOD LUCK. REGARDS." The Paris bureau chief, Arno Dosch-Fleurot, had talked to Jo Davidson and reported that the sculptor could be counted on for "any reasonable sum." Balderston and the rest of the London staff could and would help. Samuel Duff McCoy canvassed some neighbors in Connecticut and sent word that the Westport Society, a group of artists and writers, would be good for a thousand dollars. Another thousand was pledged by H. V. Kaltenborn of the *Brooklyn Eagle*. The Nashville *Tennessean* staff pledged two hundred dollars and the Houston *Chronicle* two thousand and fifty. In Albany, the *World* man, Ernest Lindley, and his counterpart on the *Evening World*, William O. Trapp, had $5,150 in pledges from twenty-three state-house correspondents and two state employees, one of them Joseph Canavan, the former *World* city editor. Canavan was working for Lieutenant Governor Herbert Lehman, and Lindley, helped by a call to Lehman from Swope, got the Lieutenant Governor to promise one hundred thousand dollars. The publisher of *Az Ember*, a self-styled "poor" Hungarian weekly in New York City, asked to be put down for one hundred dollars.

There was considerable confusion. A Pulitzer lawyer charged before the Surrogate that Swope was the troublemaker who'd incited the employees to fight, instead of their sitting back serenely while the *World*—along with the jobs of most of them—quietly disappeared. The general public was beginning to get aroused. There was no Newspaper Guild then, but Samuel Gompers, the president of the American Federation of Labor, wired Swope, who Gompers evidently figured was in cahoots with Block, "STEUER MIGHT LIKE FOLLOWING STOP JOSEPH PULITZER REGARDED WORLD AS AN INSTITUTION AND IN WILL SOUGHT ITS PERPETUATION STOP CONTRACT WITH HOWARD IS NEGATION THESE WISHES WHICH COURT IS BOUND TO CONSIDER. . . ."

Swope didn't know by now just who his allies were. He had no idea whether Block, for instance, was representing himself or was representing Hearst. Hoping, reasonably enough, to find out if he should try to block Block or help him, Swope sought clarification from Hearst. A four-hour meeting on February 25 with Brisbane, who presumably knew what was in Hearst's mind, was not especially fruitful; it apparently took Brisbane that long merely to convey the word that Swope should do nothing until he'd spoken to Hearst. It was midnight before Swope could get through to San Simeon, and Swope found Hearst puzzled himself. He said he *believed* Block was his deputy but hadn't been able to get hold of him to find out for sure. But, Hearst went on, if Block *was* his man, and if he succeeded in upsetting the sale to Scripps-Howard, Block would take the *Evening World* and Hearst the morning and the Sunday—and however the properties were divided Swope would have a share.

The next morning Block, by then evidently as baffled as anyone else, withdrew his bid entirely. (It was a measure of his bewilderment that, according to Barrett, he thought he was bidding for Hearst not against Scripps-Howard but against Swope.) Then Howard called Swope. The employees' unexpected intervention had him worried, and he wondered if Swope wouldn't try to persuade them to abandon their efforts. Swope declined. Instead, he called Barrett, urged him to seek a further ten-day stay, and said he had some twenty million dollars lined up. But by then it didn't matter much who was offering what amounts. The Pulitzer brothers felt that the only relevant issue was whether the Surrogate would approve their action. That day, he did, finding it meet and proper for the trustees of Joseph Pulitzer's estate, regardless of his expressed wishes, to dispose of its principal assets, in order to protect the heirs by preventing the assets from shrinking any more than they already had. It was all over but the crying.

On February 27 Henry F. Pringle, a one-time *World* reporter who was then in California, wrote Swope, "It is perfectly incomprehensible that the *World* has really gone out of existence and I can hardly believe it yet. . . . But I did want you to know how I feel and I think that all of us, desolated by the thought of that long room on the twelfth floor of 63 Park Row deserted, are wondering what 'H.B.S.' is doing at the moment." What Swope was doing was to continue negotiating with Hearst. The squire of San Simeon had missed out on the *World*, but he was still receptive to the notion that Swope minister to his ailing *American*. That day Swope sent Hearst a long wire, which went, in part:

I BELIEVE ONLY WAY IN WHICH THERE IS REAL CHANCE OF ACCOMPLISH-ING REAL RESULT ON AMERICAN WHICH SO MANY HAVE TRIED TO LIFT AND FAILED IS TO BE GIVEN COMPLETE CHARGE OF PAPER SUBJECT OF COURSE TO CERTAIN LIMITATIONS. TITLE TO BE GIVEN ME AND MANNER IN WHICH IT IS DISPLAYED IS OF LESSER IMPORTANCE THAN FULL POSSESSION OF AUTHORITY WHICH MIGHT RARELY BE USED BUT NEVER-THELESS WOULD BE AVAILABLE WHEN NEEDED. I WOULD BE PERFECTLY WILLING TO RELY UPON YOUR PERSONAL ASSURANCES BUT I FEEL IT WOULD BE BETTER TO HAVE UNDERSTANDING IN WRITING WHICH I WOULD NOT WISH TO HAVE RUN FOR TOO LONG A TIME WITH SALARY SET AT A MINIMUM OF TEN THOUSAND DOLLARS A MONTH AND INCREASES IN EVENT OF CIRCULATION GROWTH. . . . A BIG HOLE HAS BEEN CREATED IN NEW YORK NEWSPAPER FIELD THAT IS NOT APT TO BE QUICKLY FILLED. . . . JOB WOULD NOT BE AN EASY ONE TO DO OR ONE IN WHICH RESULTS ARE EITHER QUICK OR CERTAIN BUT I THINK WITH FREEDOM OF ACTION AND WISE THOUGH POSSIBLY HEAVY EXPENDITURES IT MIGHT BE DONE AND THERE MIGHT BE SOME FUN IN DOING IT WITH YOU. . . . WHAT PAPER NEEDS ABOVE ALL ELSE IS NEWS REPORTED WITHOUT PREJUDICE AND WITH ACCURACY UNDERSTANDING AND AUTHORITY. ONE OF THE BIG-GEST PRESENT DAY TROUBLES IS THERE ARE TOO MANY AROUND SHOP WHO THINK THEMSELVES LITTLE HEARSTS AND TREAT NEWS AS MATTER OF POLICY. THAT IS TAINT THAT HAS STUNTED AMERICAN. ARE YOU COMING EAST SOON? ANYWAY WE WILL REMAIN FRIENDS WHETHER YOU GO TO WORK FOR ME [he chose to end on a comical note] OR NOT. REGARDS.

Hearst's reply was more laconic and less enthusiastic:

I NATURALLY AGREE WITH YOUR GENERAL PROPOSITION THAT NEWS SHOULD BE UNCOLORED BUT YOUR STATEMENT IS NOT SPECIFIC ENOUGH TO GIVE ME ANY DEFINITE IDEA OF WHAT YOU DESIRE. I DO NOT THINK ANY AGREEMENT IN WRITING IS NECESSARY. I NEVER INTERFERE WITH ANY PAPER WHICH IS DOING WELL AND I ALWAYS RESERVE THE RIGHT TO INTERFERE WITH ANY PAPER THAT IS NOT.

The two men had further probing exchanges, but whatever chance they had of working together ultimately vanished on account of Marion Davies. Swope, trying to find out just how free a hand he'd have under Hearst, asked how the publisher would react if a movie starring Miss Davies came out and a Swope-run Hearst paper decided to pan the picture and the actress. Hearst replied that no such eventuality was thinkable in any paper he owned. Swope concluded that if Hearst felt that strongly about his girl he would not fit in well as one of Hearst's boys. After the *American* folded in 1937 and was merged with the *Evening Journal*, Hearst apparently had second thoughts, for he wrote Swope then that "If you had been on the paper it would never have happened."

The whole of page ten of the last issue of the *World*, on February 27, 1931, was given over to a promotional ad for the emergent *World-Telegram* that crowed, in as great a tribute as was ever paid a hyphen, "4 Great Newspapers in ONE." The principal story on page one, logically, was an end-of-the-*World* account. The second main news item, which on an ordinary day would probably have ranked first, told of the strangling of a New York woman who'd been about to testify on alleged police corruption. How it must have pleased Swope, in this valedictory issue of his paper, to read in the lead paragraph that the discovery of the body "threw police authorities into the greatest tumult the city has seen since the killing of Herman Rosenthal in 1912!" F.P.A.'s last column in the *World* concluded, "And so to all concerned the Conning Tower, trying to stave off the final word like a child asking for another drink of water before the light is turned off, says 'Good-by.' "

Swope sent a farewell of his own to Ralph Pulitzer: "It's over, and my heart bleeds for you. In the death of the *World* [at that moment the word "death" did not strike him as inappropriate], all of us who loved it died a little, and none more than you. . . ." Pulitzer replied, a week later, "When I do see you let us not talk about something that I am going to do my best to forget. The wound is going to heal slowly enough without my turning the dagger in it."

The passing of what E. B. White fondly called "a sort of town gazette" was saddening enough to the *World*'s big-city readers, but to its nearly three thousand employees, not to mention its thousands of former staff members, it was a numbing emotional as well as financial calamity. St. Clair McKelway heard the news at the American Club in Tokyo and burst into tears. In New York, Franklin Adams and Heywood Broun, as if visiting a bereaved close relative of a decedent, turned up at Swope's apartment the night the last *World* went to press. The Depression was in full swing, and F.P.A., brooding over the prospect of the ranks of the unemployed being swelled by so many of his friends and associates, and quite possibly by himself, too, pointed to a bowl of fruit on a side table and said, "Mr. Swope, where have you been buying your apples?"

Swope couldn't bring himself to go down to the *World* offices, but he called Barrett and said he was sending a couple of emissaries. At three in the morning Broun and his wife turned up at the Pulitzer building, bearing some of Swope's best Scotch for the grieving staff assembled there. The last edition had rolled off the presses, and a composing-room quartet was wandering around, singing "Auld Lang Syne," while in other areas other singers improvised such numbers as "Old Joe Pulitzer is A-rolling in His Grave."

The staff moved on to an impromptu wake at a saloon on William Street, and two weeks later a more formal ceremony was conducted, with flourishes, in California, by men who'd worked for the *World* before migrating westward. The invitations were headed "*Sic Transit Gloria Mundi.*" The restaurant on Wilshire Boulevard in Hollywood at which the lugubrious affair was held was decorated with eight-foot funeral candles, a model of the *World* dome, and a flag at half-mast. Barrett had mailed out copies of the last *World* and the last *Evening World;* these reposed in a glass-topped coffin.

Among the mourners present were Dudley Nichols, Louis Weitzenkorn, Norman Krasna, Robert Benchley, Arthur Kober, Samuel Hoffenstein, Donald Henderson Clarke, Herman Mankiewicz, Arthur Brisbane, Will Rogers, and Winfield Sheehan. Swope sent a telegram "SALUTING THE SPIRIT OF THE WORLD—A SPIRIT THAT NOTHING CAN KILL, A SPIRIT THAT QUICKENS US ALL AND WHICH WILL BE KEPT AFLAME BY YEARLY CONVOCATIONS SUCH AS THIS." Nichols made a speech in which he said that "The only possibility of perpetuating the *World* would have been for some strong personality, such as Mr. Swope, to have gained absolute control of publication and policy." Nichols devoted much of his speech, Hollywood being Hollywood, to a eulogy of Sheehan, who though a mere City Hall reporter on the *Evening World* had become an executive producer out west and was thus a man to reckon with in that crowd of writers. Krasna was furious at what he considered inopportune kowtowing. "Mr. Nichols, you have broken my heart," he said. Weitzenkorn sobbed throughout the evening.

The *World* was gone, gobbled up by the *Telegram*, which was later also to swallow the *Sun*. (The Scripps-Howard evening paper in New York had a penchant for hearty eating, though what it ingested never seemed to make it appreciably stronger.) The *World*'s readers were downhearted. One of them took an ad in the *Herald Tribune* to say, "Frank Sullivan, where are you? Have looked in every paper. Can't live without you in this family." Sullivan replied, "I don't know but I am making every effort to find out. I was walking along minding my own business when something hit me from behind practically ruining my best pair of serge pants. It is all very strange. . . ."

Swope never got over the disappearance of the paper to which he had tried unavailingly to return. In May he was still dazed. "I yearn for activity," he wrote Nichols then. "I seek release for my creative and kinetic energies, but where am I to find them? . . . I find my soul to be awaiting a trumpet call to action. What it will be, when it will come, and where it will take me I cannot say. I only hope I shall have courage enough to follow the light when it appears."

One can merely surmise what Swope's reaction was fifteen years after that harrowing winter and spring when, at the age of sixty-four, he received a Selective Service questionnaire addressed to him as "Executive Editor of the *World*."

18

I N THE spring of 1932, when the Depression was at its most
oppressive and many Americans were casting about for
something, anything, to keep them occupied and eating, Arthur
Brisbane undertook to explain to his readers what Swope was up
to. "He deals in everything," the Hearst columnist said. By now,
Swope had reservations about working full-time no matter what
the economic climate might be. While the scope of his activities
was not quite as all-embracing as Brisbane thought, Swope became involved, for periods of varying duration, in a plethora of
part-time occupations—so many of them that one acquaintance
was moved to describe his life during that period as one of "frenzied inaction."

President Roosevelt was soon to propound his Four Freedoms.
Swope was zealously protective of what he had already advanced
as a personal fifth freedom—freedom to play. It was in the
Thirties that "café society," an agglomeration of bona-fide society,
wealth, creativeness, and plain notoriety, came into being and
flourished. In 1937 *Fortune* ran an article on this species, listing
one hundred and seventy New Yorkers who were "in," and
superimposing on this elite corps an even inner cadre of seventeen
men and women whom the magazine dubbed "The Regency
Council." The Council consisted of Mrs. Vincent Astor, Mrs.
Margaret Emerson, Elsa Maxwell, Charles A. Munn, Condé Nast,
Prince Serge Obolensky, Mrs. Charles Shipman Payson, Mr. and
Mrs. William Rhinelander Stewart, Mrs. Harold A. Talbott, Mr.
and Mrs. Cornelius Vanderbilt Whitney, Mr. and Mrs. John Hay
Whitney, Mrs. Harrison Williams, and—it was no surprise to any-
one who cared about such rankings—Mr. and Mrs. Herbert Bayard

Swope. In places like the Colony restaurant and the Stork Club, where the regents of café society beamed daily on their huddled courtiers, the Swopes were very much in evidence, and any head-waiter in any fashionable establishment who was loutish enough not to dip his velvet rope at their approach was imperiling his livelihood.

Much in demand as a toastmaster, Swope presided in regental splendor over countless starched-shirt banquets. "As an amateur in the field I have watched with envy and admiration your pro-fessional performances," Arthur Krock wrote him after one affair, "and I note that, where I am inclined to very brief sen-tences, an abundance of irony, and a modicum of sentiment, you work in the broad Roman manner—rounded sentences glittering with literary elegances."

Swope was particularly in evidence at gatherings of sportsmen, and he sometimes refused to attend their frolics unless he *could* be toastmaster. After illness had kept him away from one testi-monial dinner, to the broadcaster Clem McCarthy, the sports writer Tom O'Reilly observed in the *Telegraph*, "Now the reason I missed Mister Swope takes a bit of explaining. . . . Senor Swope has a way with him that turns innocent little parties such as this one upside down. It starts out as a party for McCarthy and Bertie is such a charming man that it turns out being a party for Swope." One of Swope's triumphs was to compete success-fully—at an elaborate testimonial in the Biltmore Hotel in 1931 to Joseph E. Widener, then the head of the Jockey Club—with an assemblage that included Franklin Roosevelt, Al Smith, Bernard Baruch, twelve thoroughbred horses with jockeys astride, four huntsmen accompanied by eighteen hounds, and an army caisson dragged through the chamber by four more steeds.

Swope was much sought after, too, by the organizers of civic committees who felt his name would add luster to their rosters. He put in appearances at such ceremonial New York events as the openings of the Empire State Building, the George Washington and Triborough Bridges, the Hayden Planetarium, and the West Side Highway. He graced the reviewing stand for the St. Patrick's Day Parade and cut a dashing figure at municipal receptions for distinguished visitors like the King of Siam, the Lord Mayor of Liverpool, and motley trans-Channel swimmers and transocean flyers. He was a Grover Whalen without portfolio. He became a director of the Municipal Art Society and of the New York

Humane Society (in which capacity he had the power to arrest maltreators of animals, in and out of hotel ballrooms). At the behest of Mrs. Roosevelt he joined an honorary committee putting on a benefit in 1934 to raise funds to set up rest rooms for unemployed girls in the city. Swope simply didn't have time to keep up with his committees. That same year, at Governor Herbert Lehman's request, he became a member of the New York State Planning Board, but he never attended a single one of its meetings, and at the group's final session the chairman told the other members that he wasn't sure Swope ought to be allowed to sign their report, since he wasn't familiar with any of its contents.

It was difficult, of course, for Swope to fulfill some of the obligations he assumed, because the world was full of imbeciles who persisted in holding meetings in the morning. Moreover, by the time a business or social session he'd said he would attend actually came around, he might be bored with the prospect of showing up. His old friends got accustomed to his sometimes dismaying habit of simply not appearing where he was expected to be. When Swope suggested amiably to Henry Pringle, the one-time *World* reporter, that they meet for a reunion lunch in 1936, Pringle replied that he'd be happy to, but only if Swope posted a bond guaranteeing his presence. Another *World* alumnus, Charles Michelson, was completing arrangements for the Gridiron Club annual dinner in Washington that same year and wired Swope, "HOPE YOU WON'T CANCEL AT LAST MINUTE AS USUAL." Baruch, when Swope notified him that a dentist's appointment would lamentably preclude his going through with a long-planned visit to the patriarch's South Carolina plantation, wrote, "Dear Old Friend, I knew you wouldn't come."

To some of Swope's acquaintances it seemed not illogical that, in the absence of a steady job, he would devote himself to writing. Book publishers and magazine editors were constantly after him. In the autumn of 1929, for instance, Ray Long of *Cosmopolitan*, soliciting a contribution on the then still robust stock market, had told him, "You seem to be an outstanding example of how a man can make a lot of dough in the market. I have an idea that your story is dramatic as the very devil." Swope did not bite at that lure, nor did he accede to a request from his old friend Mencken, soon after the *World* closed its doors, to give

358

his version of that sorry episode, even though the Baltimorean said, "Most of the stuff about the *World* that is getting into type at the moment is sentimental blah. What ought to be done is an intelligent account of the process whereby the paper came to grief. You know more about the inner workings of the office than anybody."

Even President Roosevelt could not sway Swope. In 1939 Swope thought that the visit to America of the King and Queen of England had been ill-timed and might hurt American relations with Great Britain. When he told the President how he felt Roosevelt swiftly suggested, tongue-in-cheek, that Swope cover the royal visit and write a documentary history about it. "I would guarantee that your manuscript would not be published for fifty years but that I could take a peek at it first," Roosevelt wrote him.

What beseeching editors and other eggers-on did not realize was that aside from a random book review Swope avoided writing for publication, immediate or future, in part because it was too much work and in part because he was not, as he may have been painfully aware, a consistently skillful writer. The bromide and the cliché came most trippingly to his pen. But he liked to foster the belief in others that he was always on the point of engaging in some literary pursuit, and toward the end of his life he himself came to have a swollen concept of his own output. He would refer to "some books I wrote." The only one, in point of fact, was his 1917-vintage *Inside the German Empire*. The other titles he sometimes included in biographical resumés were *Journalism—An Instrument of Civilization* and *Germany, France, and England*. But while there were such impressively named volumes of his authorship displayed in his own library, handsomely bound in green leather, the first consisted merely of the text of an address he delivered in 1924 at Hobart College, when he got his honorary degree, and the second of some random jottings from his European notebooks that the *World* had run one Sunday morning in 1922.

Instead of writing literature, or even journalism, Swope wrote personal letters. He churned them out as if he were a letter-press for thirty epistolarily fecund years. His letters had a cachet of their own regardless of their content. The flaming red signature, bold and confident, was a splendid sight to behold, and it bespoke the same sort of good wishes transmitted by a Christmas card from an old and absent but warmly thought-of friend. Swope loaded the mails with cheery notes not only to friends but to casual acquaintances and utter strangers. He was uncommonly considerate and conscientious about thanking people who'd done him favors or services. After a stay in a hospital he would write a note of gratitude to the nurse who'd briefly ministered to him in the X-ray room. Most patients don't even know the name of their X-ray nurse, let alone bother to send her a kind word once they're cured. When a New York City policeman found him a parking space during a World Series game at Yankee Stadium, Swope sent his thanks the following day in separate letters to the patrolman, his lieutenant, his captain, an inspector, the chief inspector, and the Commissioner.

Should Swope's friends be hospitalized themselves they could count on quickly hearing from him, usually in the form of a terse note containing some such hortatory admonition as "You're too good a man to be on the shelf. Up and at 'em!" Swope's up-and-at-'em messages seemed to have a tonic, therapeutic effect of their own. Gene Tunney wrote from a hospital bed that hearing from Swope had made him feel like shadow-boxing and skipping rope. Ring Lardner, after a protracted hospitalization during which Swope deluged him with communications, wired Swope, "CAN YOU SUGGEST ANY WAY TO END THIS CORRESPONDENCE AMICABLY STOP MY PERSONAL PHYSICIAN SAYS EXCITEMENT OF HEARING FROM YOU DAILY IS BAD FOR ME. . . ."

Often Swope signed such letters, and others, with a phrase, or a variation of it, that came to be his trademark—"Across the years." He thus concluded one letter to Laurette Taylor in 1945, after having been entirely out of touch with her for nearly two decades. "And after *all* these years!" she scribbled pensively on Swope's letter.

Swope's intimates could hardly keep pace with the letters they got from him. When Baruch was out of town Swope might send him three or four letters a day and might throw in for good measure carbon copies of a number of other current letters, "just to show you how my mind is running." Swope liked to have lots of people know how his mind was running. Periodically, for instance, he would compose a longish letter analyzing American political trends and portents for someone like Lord Beaverbrook in England; when the letter—more an essay, really, than a private communication—turned out especially satisfactorily, Swope would have it mimeographed and would share it with several dozen acquaintances.

Messages of congratulation or condolence were Swope's specialties. In 1936 the race horse Pompoon, owned by Jerome H. Louchheim of Philadelphia, was favored to win the New England Futurity at Narragansett Park but came in second. Swope's considerate reaction to this upset elicited from Louchheim a letter that went, "I wish I were able to tell you in words how much I appreciate your telegram of yesterday. Had Pompoon won, I imagine I would have received any number of telegrams of congratulations, the same as I did when he won in the Belmont Futurity, but you were the only one who was thoughtful enough to acknowledge that I had a great horse even in defeat." There can have been few individuals, moreover, who, like Swope, took the trouble to tell a high Federal official who'd just been sentenced to prison, "I believe in you. Good luck."

In Swope's capacity as the public mind he felt impelled to speak out regularly to the public's leaders, to let them know they were not functioning in a vacuum. When the Berlin blockade was lifted in 1949 he was swift to congratulate the Secretary of the Air Force. (Eight years earlier, after Pearl Harbor, he was no less prompt in sending his regrets to the Secretary of the Navy.) "When you have a generally favorable reaction about a situation," Swope once enjoined David Sarnoff, "it is a good thing to let the subject know. It encourages him and, incidentally, makes him think that you have got good judgment!" After a testimonial banquet for Baruch, Swope drafted a dozen thank-you notes for the guest of honor to send out and advised him further, "Anybody who made any particular reference to you, slap them down with thanks." On his own, Swope adopted a scatter-shot technique. When some big event occurred his outgoing mail burgeoned. Immediately after D-Day, for example, he fired off a barrage of congratulatory messages—to, among others, President Roosevelt, General Marshall, and General Eisenhower. On V-E and V-J Days, while other Americans were merely celebrating, Swope was also congratulating.

On paper, in contradistinction to conversation, Swope was partial to brevity. In the fall of 1949, when Omar Bradley was appointed Chairman of the Joint Chiefs of Staff, Swope naturally congratulated him. He said, in toto, "My Dear General: The country will be safe in your hands. Good luck." On Harold Talbott's becoming Eisenhower's Secretary of the Air Force, Swope confined himself to a combination of two of his favorite phrases. "I am wholly in your corner," he wrote. "Across the years." Talbott replied that he was having the letter framed, as a masterpiece of conciseness.

Eisenhower himself, while still a military man, wrote Swope, admiringly, "A number of times in this war I have been struck with the fact that you, in mighty few words, can give me a tremendous lift." Swope could not resist passing along a copy of that particular accolade to, among others, the movie man Joseph M. Schenck, whose reaction was, Swope felt, snide. "I was not so naïve as to send that to you for the purpose of showing that I maintained correspondence with him—or that he is my friend," Swope adjured Schenck sternly. "A man can screw around and get letters from almost anybody, although, as you say, it is pleasant to be on a basis of friendship." But to another film producer, David O. Selznick, Swope confessed, after sending along one of his political analyses, "I am a little uncertain as to just why I give out copies. It may be . . . that I am merely seeking your kind applause."

Swope's urge to communicate was so strong that when no telephone or stenographer was handy he communicated with himself. He kept his pockets full of stubby pencils and long strips of paper and was forever scrawling notes—many of these reminders of notes he planned in due course to transmit to others. When he ran out of relatively clean scratch paper he would turn to the backs of envelopes or any other handy medium. The lawyer Isidor Kresel, after once examining some of Swope's correspondence files, remonstrated with him, "I would suggest that in the future you do not mark up original letters with all sorts of pencil notations. A time may come when you may want to use these letters in court and they would not look so well with all your scribbling on them."

Swope especially liked to send notes of commendation to journalists of whose work he approved. Thanking him for such a letter in 1948, Phelps H. Adams, then chief Washington correspondent of the New York *Sun*, wrote Swope:

It reminds me of an occasion many years ago which you have probably forgotten. It was early in the New Deal, shortly after Roosevelt had taken office, that I picked up a copy of the *Sun* and found on the editorial page a letter from you commending a piece I had written. So far as I know, that was the first time anyone had ever bothered to write a letter to the *Sun* commenting favorably on a story of mine. Certainly, it was the first communication of the kind the *Sun* had ever printed. I remember that an editorial writer had headed it "Praise from Sir Hubert," and "Sir Hubert" you have been to me ever since.

Robert P. Post, in the London bureau of the New York *Times* in the 1930s, said:

Your letter about my story was one of the nicest I ever received. I only hope that some distinguished newspaper man did as much for you when you were young and struggling because I should hate to think that as a young reporter you never had such pleasure as you gave me. . . .

To Otto D. Tolischus, Berlin correspondent of the *Times*, Swope had written, characteristically, in 1935:

MY DEAR TOLISCHUS:
   For some time I have been wanting to do what I do now:
   Tell you that your work has been extraordinarily sound under trying conditions, and that your dispatches from Germany are comprehensive, understanding and written with real authority. You are doing a fine job.
   With high professional regard.
   Faithfully . . .

And Tolischus' reply was typical, too:

MY DEAR MR. SWOPE:
   When I was still in the Columbia School of Journalism, your name was pinned for us to the journalistic skies for emulation. It made me therefore proud and happy to receive your kind letter approving of my work, and I want to thank you for it most cordially. It is heartening in any case to discover that the stuff we shoot out of here more or less in the dark finds both readers and response, but it is doubly gratifying to win professional approval from an authority as eminent as yourself. Thanks again!

During the Second World War, when Ernie Pyle was one of the most celebrated newspapermen on earth, he wrote Swope,

"Your letter to me was just about the nicest anybody ever got, I think. I do appreciate deeply your thoughtfulness in writing me. . . . You'll forgive me for showing it around to a few select people with considerable pride." Hundreds of newspapermen felt the same pride when Swope demonstrated the same thoughtfulness, and Gene Fowler once wrote him, summing up the feelings of his fellow journalists, "You have been so God-damned fine to your fellow newspaper men that it may well be your greatest monument."

Franklin Delano Roosevelt's nomination and election in 1932 had special significance for Swope, in more than one respect. The dawn of the Roosevelt era, for one thing, put Al Smith's sun in permanent eclipse. But if that turn of events tended to dim Swope's own chance of exercising national political influence, at the same time his prospects were brightened by his party's conquest of the Washington heights for the first time since the Wilson Administration. Swope had kept open his lines to the White House during its occupancy by Harding, Coolidge, and Hoover. The messages he sent and received through these Republican channels of communication had, however, been something less than crackling. Toward the end of the Hoover regime, to be sure, Swope was advising Secretary of the Treasury Ogden Mills on setting up a federal economic planning board, and he was telling the President himself how to cope with the veterans marching on Washington in search of a bonus; but Swope nonetheless felt irritatingly detached from the center ring of the governmental circus. With the Democrats back in power, all would be different.

Swope had long been proud that he had helped call Roosevelt to Woodrow Wilson's attention and that the *World* had given F.D.R. some helpful momentum on his way up the elective ladder by vigorouly endorsing a campaign that Roosevelt, as a newly elected State Senator, conducted in 1910 against the appointment to the United States Senate of a Tammany wheelhorse called Blue-eyed Billy Sheehan. Early in 1932, though, when there was considerable doubt about who would be the Democratic Presidential standard-bearer the following November, Roosevelt was merely Swope's fourth choice. "I do not think he shapes up well in a fight," Swope wrote Mark Sullivan. "Personally incorruptible, he is not direct and straightforward in his intellectual processes. Of course, it may be that F.D.R. may get the nomination by default. If he does, it will be an empty honor, for, mark you and mark you well (as Bill Sulzer used to say), no man, given the Democratic nomination, can win the election without the complete and hearty endorsement of Al Smith. Al Smith's failure to go along would be a sign and a portent to the vast army of Irish Catholics that he, Smith, had been jettisoned solely because he belongs to a proscribed faith. And that would be the truth. . . ."

Smith was still Swope's first choice. As the party's most recent Presidential candidate, Smith was its titular leader, and one of his out-and-out partisans, John J. Raskob, had been installed as chairman of the Democratic National Committee. In the spring of 1932 Swope organized a preconvention fund-raising campaign for Smith. Swope didn't really think Smith had much of a chance, but he wanted at all odds to keep the nomination from going to Roosevelt, whom he called "the Boy Scout."

At the same time, Swope was looking with some favor on Albert C. Ritchie (". . . one of the real leaders of the Democrats . . . a true disciple of Thomas Jefferson. . . .") and on Owen D. Young, who had become Chairman of the Board of General Electric ten years before, at the same time that Gerard Swope became its president. On May 5, 1932, the younger brother informed the older, elatedly, that he'd just learned that Democratic headquarters was preparing a biography of Young. "This is a step never taken unless the need has appeared!" Herbert wrote Gerard. And to Thomas Chadbourne Swope wrote, "My job at present is to keep him [Smith] fighting with one man [Roosevelt] and, at the same time, keep the others fighting, too. This is important in the veto block but his importance is of lesser consequence when it comes to the nomination. Frankly, if I did not think O.D.Y. was to be nominated I should be less concerned than I am. It will please you to know that Young is growing in importance every day. It is extraordinary that this should be so, for he has never indicated by word or deed his willingness—that is being taken for granted. Not a thing is being done for him, although, of course, anything done against R. is helpful to him and to the others in opposition."

The 1932 Democratic Convention was held in July at Chicago, and Swope was a delegate from New York. The state's contingent was split between Roosevelt, the incumbent Governor, and Smith, his predecessor; when the New York delegation was polled during the first ballot, the Smith adherents (among whom Swope was so vociferously notable that he became known around Chicago as "Herbert Diehard Smith") prevailed, getting sixty-five and a half votes to Roosevelt's twenty-eight and a half. (New York never did go for Roosevelt; it probably would have on the fourth ballot, when he finally won the nomination, but he had enough votes before his state was reached in the alphabetical procession.) When it became apparent that Smith couldn't stop Roosevelt, Swope switched his behind-the-scenes support to Young, even though Young had earlier insisted he would not be considered as a candidate. Swope kept his brother posted through a series of telegraphic communiqués from Chicago. "NEVER IN MY EXPERIENCE WAS A CONVENTION SO RIPE FOR THE PICKING AS THIS WOULD BE WERE MY HERO FREELY AVAILABLE STOP," Herbert wired Gerard at 4:43 one morning, after a night of furious politicking on Young's behalf. "R. [Roosevelt] HAS MOST OF THE DELEGATES BUT NO FRIENDS THE OTHERS HAVE MOST OF THE FRIENDS BUT NO DELEGATES STOP AS I WIRED YOU WILL TAKE A MIRACLE TO BEAT HIM IF THAT MIRACLE OCCURS TWILL BE THROUGH A VOTE BLOC AND THEN THE NOMINATION OF MY CHOICE NONE OTHER CAN TURN THE TRICK HIS NAME ELECTRIFIES [probably an unintentional pun] THOSE WHO HEAR IT SO THERE MUST BE A CHANCE FOR DRAFTING LOVE."

There was no such chance, but Swope blew through Chicago like a storm off Lake Michigan. "No gathering of politicians or anyone else was so private or sacred that Herbert couldn't and didn't barge in," Jim Farley once observed. It was a way of behaving that another acquaintance, the lawyer Louis Nizer, once described as Swope's "interferiority complex." Just before Roosevelt was nominated, on the fourth ballot, there was a flurry of excitement when a rumor swept the convention that Smith, in his own diehard fashion, was going to try to stop the eventual winner by throwing what strength he still had to Newton D. Baker. William Randolph Hearst didn't like Baker. Hearst didn't much like Roosevelt either, but when the San Simeon man heard the Baker story, he decided to call off a stop-Roosevelt drive of his own, which centered around California and Texas and their favorite-son candidates, William G. McAdoo and John N. Garner, over both of whom the publisher had much influence. Hearst telephoned Baruch in Chicago to find out what was going on.

Swope was with Baruch, along with Raskob and other party leaders, and it was Swope who volunteered to go to Smith's hotel room and find out what he really had in mind. When Smith wouldn't say, Swope reported this back to the others. Hearst decided to adopt a lesser-of-the-two-evils policy and dropped his opposition to Roosevelt. The contest was over.

When Smith heard the bitter news that Roosevelt had carried the day, Swope once again was at his side. Five days later Swope wrote the far from happy warrior:

> You have lost nothing by a political defeat based, not upon principle, but upon superiority of numbers and expediency. On the contrary, you have gained much. In the minds of most men, because of your courage; because of your vision; because of your inspiration, you would have been the nominee of the party and the president of the nation, had it not been for one thing—your religion. That reason, however deplorable, cannot be removed in these days of continued bigotry. All that can be done is to work and wait, and to give yourself generously, as always, to the public good. You can follow no other course, even if you wanted to.

Smith replied the day he got Swope's letter:

> You hit the nail on the head. I hope you are pleased with the statement I put out. There is nothing to do but wait. All of these things right themselves.

And two weeks later, in one of those letters brimming with political gossip of which he was so fond, Swope would write consolingly to Young:

> Some personalities emerged from the cataclysm with enhanced reputations; the reputations of others dwindled, and some were so unable to make up their minds where they wanted the light to fall, that they resembled nothing so much as a poached egg looking for a piece of toast to sit down on.
>
> Hearst turned the trick. That is the long and short of it. It was his first demonstration of power in a national convention, possibly excepting 1908. He did it because of his fear of Baker, and because of his complete ownership of Garner, whose surrender was abject and somewhat contemptible. McAdoo, of course, was the third string to the harp. His quitting came after he had given assurance he would stick; but, somehow, I do not find it as easy to blame

367

him as I do others, for, after all, he had a stake in interest—the Senatorship from California—and Hearst, whose last political strength is in that state, has five papers there! . . .

Having done his best for the man—or men—he preferred, Swope now undertook to mend his political fences and do his best for the man the majority of the delegates wanted. By September he was dashing off memoranda to Roosevelt and to some of his campaign associates—principal among these Raymond Moley and Joseph P. Kennedy—conveying his views on issues like the five-day work week and tax revision. Swope was communicating directly with Roosevelt, too. Late in September the Democratic nominee was campaigning in the Southwest. He had been scheduled to go on to the Far West, but there was talk of his changing his plans and heading southeast instead. On September 27 Swope sent him a telegram to Colorado Springs:

BORN OF MY INTEREST IN YOUR SUCCESS AND MY ANTIPATHY TO CHANGES THAT MILITATE AGAINST IT LET ME ADD MY PROTEST AGAINST THE REVISION OF YOUR SPEAKING PLAN STOP FIRST IT IS OBVIOUSLY UNWISE TO SHIFT DECKS WHEN ALL THE CARDS ARE COMING YOUR WAY STOP THE WESTERN TRIP HAS BEEN GIGANTIC SUCCESS SO WHY TRIFLE WITH YOUR LUCK STOP SECOND WHISPERERS ARE ALREADY SAYING THAT THE TRIP MUST REALLY BE A BUST OR ELSE YOU WOULDN'T ABANDON IT STOP THIRD AND OF GREATER IMPORTANCE OTHER SCANDAL MONGERS ARE ZEALOUSLY CIRCULATING REPORT THAT CHANGE IS DUE ENTIRELY TO YOUR HEALTH STOP THAT'S UNTRUE BUT WHY GIVE TENABILITY TO RUMOR STOP FOURTH THERE'S NOTHING TO BE GAINED IN SOUTH WHILE THERE'S MUCH TO BE GAINED IN YOUR ORIGINAL TERRITORY ESPECIALLY SINCE MR. HOOVER IS JUST ABOUT TO VISIT THAT REGION STOP DON'T LET'S APPEAR TO BE RUNNING AWAY STOP SEVERAL OF YOUR WARMEST SUPPORTERS AGREED WITH THIS GENERAL VIEW AND URGED ME TO WIRE YOU IN HOPE THAT SUCH BELIEF AS YOU MAY HAVE IN MY ABILITY TO JUDGE PUBLIC PSYCHOLOGY MAY CAUSE YOU TO RECONSIDER WARM REGARD.

Roosevelt did reconsider and went through with his original schedule.

One of Roosevelt's biggest campaign problems was Smith. The 1928 candidate still commanded vast respect, especially among the Catholics and wets in the big Eastern cities. The electoral votes in Massachusetts in particular were thought by the Democratic strategists to be in doubt unless Smith came out for Roosevelt, and ever since the convention Smith had maintained a sulky silence. The Republicans were doing their best to exploit his differences with Roosevelt. Felix Frankfurter, from his professorial chair at the Harvard Law School, was among those most deeply concerned about the possible consequences of the rift. "For the affection we all bear to Al," he wrote Swope in mid-September, "even more than for the help he can bring, can't you persuade Al to leave his tent? . . . Here is a job that you ought to tackle—to make Al see that the situation, disagreeable as it is for him, calls for the bigness in him that is so much admired. . . . So you do your damnedest."

Swope did. He arranged a lunch with Smith, Frankfurter, and Baruch, and Smith agreed to speak out for Roosevelt in Boston. Swope was just getting his family settled in a new, sixteen-room, six-bath apartment at 895 Park Avenue, but he took time out to, as he put it, "accompany Al Smith to Boston to do God's work." On the train to New England, Swope helped Smith draft his pro-Roosevelt remarks, on a copy of which Swope later scribbled, "Written largely by me." Whatever reservations Roosevelt may have had about Swope's loyalty to him were exorcised by his helpfulness. On election eve, when the Democratic candidate took a motor tour around parts of New York City, he invited Swope to ride in his car on the Bronx-to-Queens leg of the journey. As the cavalcade, with sirens screaming, approached a ferry that was to transport Roosevelt over the East River, a child cried out, "A wedding! A wedding!" "That's right!" Swope shouted back. "He's the groom and he's going to marry Miss Prosperity!"

After Roosevelt's victory, with the electoral votes of Massachusetts contributing nicely to his total, Smith soon got himself enmeshed in the increasingly conservative web of the newly formed American Liberty League. Aware of Swope's intermediary effectiveness, Smith asked him to join up, too, and to bring along with him, if possible, Owen Young, Gerard Swope, and Baruch, all of whom could have contributed bountifully to the League's special pursuit of Liberty. But Smith was probably just making a routine gesture; he must have known that Swope would, as he did, decline to stray that far from the liberal path along which—for so much of the time in Smith's own footsteps—he had regularly walked.

On March 2, 1933, two days before Roosevelt's first inauguration, Swope sent the new President a "Dear Frank" letter wishing him good luck. "This is an emanation straight from my heart," he went on. "It is the last time I shall give myself the privilege of calling you Frank. I do so to please myself (as Al [Smith] says, there is always a kick in calling the Big Boss by his first name), and because this is so purely a personal tribute." Roosevelt replied eight days later, "That was one of the nicest letters I ever received and it will be tucked away with my treasures. I feel that we are off to a grand start and I hope I can accomplish some vital and important things while the general feeling is so friendly. I shall count on you for advice. Do let us know when you are in Washington." From then on Swope usually began his letters to the President "Dear Boss," although in speaking of him he generally called him "Great White Father" or, for short, simply "Father." *

The President would periodically repeat his invitation to Swope to stop around and see him. When Roosevelt's insatiable curiosity revealed to him one day that his secretary Missy LeHand had just typed out a letter of her own to Swope, the President hijacked her letter and wrote on the bottom of it, in longhand, "Dear Herbert: Come down soon and see us! F.D.R." Every so often Swope would yield to such entreaties, and when he did visit the White House his friends could be certain of hearing about it. In January 1936, for instance, Swope made a White House stopover one evening while on his way to Florida. He sat up a good part of the night discussing national affairs with the President. ". . . *He* kept *me* up to four o'clock in the morning talking and drinking," Swope told Walter Lippmann afterward.

Swope added, "F.D.R.'s charm continues unabated. His ability to make his visitor believe that he alone is essential to the presidential happiness continues. His new found ability and decisiveness have come to him without corresponding development in character, which must broaden and become more disciplined for the proper control of the qualities he possesses. He is an expedientist but, of course, that is the characteristic of every politician. He is sadistic, which probably is a corollary of his physical condition. That attribute makes him the more willing to have around him those who are apt to make mistakes. As between second-rate men,

---

* Alexander Woollcott called him "Big White Father." Swope was jealous that Roosevelt found a spot in his heart, and at his hearth, for Woollcott, too. "Are they renting any rooms at the White House?" Swope once wrote Grace Tully. "I am told that Woollcott makes it a regular stopping place, but he complains somewhat of the table."

whom he dominates, and the first-rate man who shines independently of him, he is for the lesser type every time."

To General Hugh Johnson, who had inquired what he was doing with himself, Swope wrote, "My recent history includes an overnight stay at the Weisse Haus, where the Great White Father kept me up until 4:15 A.M., both of us doing full duty to a couple of bottles of brandy. Your name came up. . . ." Roy Howard's name, Swope confided in another account of the evening (the consumption was put in this instance at "almost two bottles of brandy"), had come up "more than once." Swope's pleasure at being able to tell Howard about the exalted company he was keeping may have been somewhat dampened when he got the publisher's reply. Howard wrote while traveling from Rome to Paris and revealed that he, too, had been breathing rarefied air. He'd just had personal interviews with Hitler and Stalin, he was able to inform Swope, and, he added, thumpingly getting in last licks, he had had a similar talk scheduled with Mussolini but hadn't bothered to go through with it because the Italian had tried to shift the appointment to an hour inconvenient to Howard.

Throughout the Roosevelt years Swope's relations with the President were cordial, if not quite as close as Swope wished. For a while he entertained the hope that Roosevelt would ask him to fill the kind of intimate, confidential, advisory role that Harry Hopkins had. (When at the start of the second Roosevelt Administration it was disclosed that six new White House administrative assistants were to be appointed and that a criterion of eligibility would be "a passion for anonymity," a small Washington joke had it that the only sure bet for one of the jobs was Swope.) The President never made such an offer, but he was fond of Swope, finding him amusing, stimulating, and responsive, and from time to time he would call on him to perform small private missions—to report, for example, on the background and character of men whom Roosevelt was thinking of appointing to diplomatic posts.

Swope himself volunteered many a suggestion. Even before Roosevelt was sworn in for the first time Swope had urged upon him the adoption of a scheme to bring a little gladness into the lives of the millions of Americans then unemployed, and at the same time to strengthen their resistance to left-wing propaganda. Swope spelled out what he had in mind—and there were echoes of this in the subsequent activities of the W.P.A.—in a letter written on January 21, 1933, to Senator William E. Borah, the Idaho Republican:

> I think that we are stressing the wrong things in our present upheaval. We are saving bodies and losing souls. We are feeding the bellies and clothing the backs of our unemployed but what are we doing to feed their minds; to occupy their leisure; to preserve their morale and to prevent them from becoming the victims of every insidious form of dangerous propaganda?
>
> In a long talk I had with F.D.R. Wednesday I brought this matter to his attention. He thought it was of supreme importance and marveled at the fact that nobody had thought of it before. He wanted me to reduce it to a formula and then give him a memorandum suitable for a message. I am eager to get your reaction. Personally I think it of primary value and I should be glad if I had thought of a way of making a helpful contribution to curing our lot.
>
> What I should like to see done is an organization to arrange a vast series of regular meetings to be addressed directly and through the radio by really important speakers. I want to provide gathering places, both indoor and outdoor. Indoors I want to provide reading material. Outdoors, I want to provide facilities for recreation; games, public baths, gymnasia, etc. I think we should study what was done in Germany in '21 and '22 in the way of socialized effort that prevented that country from going Bolshevist, in the face of every temptation both of emotion and reason to do so.
>
> This, then, my dear Senator, is the Swope plan. I shall be complimented if it enlists your attention. Of course I am saying nothing about it for publication until we see if Franklin wants to take it up, which he says he does. Otherwise, I shall put the baby in your arms.

In the summer of 1936 Swope was again a delegate to the Democratic National Convention. Roosevelt's renomination was, of course, taken for granted, but there were minor crises, one being whether Herbert Lehman could be persuaded to run again that fall for Governor of New York and thus strengthen the Democratic ticket in that state. From the convention Swope cabled to Baruch, who was in Austria, that Roosevelt "HAD ME ON THE PHONE FREQUENTLY TO DO STUNTS STOP AT MOMENT IS PUSHING LEHMAN CONSENT PROBABLY GETTING IT LOVE." Early in the campaign that followed, Swope wrote to Roosevelt:

> I should think the major policy—the grand strategy—in this battle is to be firm without being ferocious; to be kindly rather than cold; to be hopeful instead of pessimistic; to be human rather than to be

economic; to be insistent upon every man having a chance, and, above all, to make yourself appear to be the President of *all* the people, to whom you are again submitting your candidacy—not merely to the Democrats, but to the Republicans and to anyone else who believes in what you have done, what you have tried to do and what you are going to do.

Roosevelt replied that he thought Swope's letter was grand and said, "I hope Saratoga was good to you, and wish I could have gone up there for a day of racing."

During the campaign that followed, there were many Democrats who felt that for old times' sake and party harmony, if for no other reason, Roosevelt should make a conciliatory gesture toward the estranged Smith, and the President did call in Swope one day (perhaps Roosevelt was thinking that another speech like the Boston one in 1932 might be desirable), asked him to try to mollify Smith and, as Swope noted, to "promise him something next year." Whether or not Swope actually passed along any such pledge is uncertain. In any event, Smith walked out of the Democratic party before the 1936 election.

Vast though the gulf might be that separated Roosevelt and Smith after the President's landslide victory over Alf Landon, Swope did his best to bridge it, or at any rate to maintain amicable contact with both sides. Less than twenty-four hours after that election, Swope sent a note of comfort to the onetime leader of all the Democrats, now commanding a one-man army. On November 5, 1936, Swope wrote to Smith:

> Now that the smoke of battle has cleared away let me tell you that the friendship that has existed between us for almost thirty years remains undisturbed. During that period of time we have had differences of opinion but they have always left us untouched. After all, each of us has preserved his independence and neither has followed blindly the other's political or religious principles. It has always been a matter of volition.
>
> As I told you several times, I thought the President and the Democratic party (although I know you did not believe that appellation the proper one) deserved renomination. I felt, too, that it would be dangerous to fight against the public confidence in F.D.R., which I saw becoming stronger every day. . . .
>
> It is a mad world, My Master.
>
> But there are things that will continue, and among them is friendship.

As Roosevelt embarked on his second term, Swope began to have increasing reservations about him. In May 1937 Swope jotted down three questions about the President that he felt had been theretofore unanswered:

1. Did he always have something, which we were incapable of discovering?
2. Did he have nothing but was something brought to him through the pressure of his illness?
3. Did he always lack something; does he lack it now, but are we dazzled by the glamour of his office?

Two months later, Swope's disillusionment was even greater, and to Raymond Moley he would say, with no interrogative qualifications, "It is a biting commentary upon our type of government when the welfare of the nation rests with one man; when the gradations from prosperity to adversity can be forced by a single individual. That is the case today and that is worse than military despotism. . . ."

But when Swope discussed dictatorship with Roosevelt himself it was on a chummy and jesting note. After the Soviet Union attacked Finland in the fall of 1939 Swope wrote the President:

As a symbol of our sympathy for Finland and as an evidence of our appreciation of Russia's wantonness, why would it not be good to have you write a brief note to Finland excusing her from the coming payment of interest and annuity on her debt? Probably she cannot pay, but to lift it from the question of necessity and make it a gesture of friendliness would be not merely right, but enormously popular. . . .

Roosevelt—who was shortly to help out Finland through a loan from the Export-Import Bank—replied:

You are a trusting soul in suggesting that I could waive the payment on the Finnish debt! I may be a benevolent dictator and all-powerful Santa Claus and though the spirit has moved me at times, I still operate under the laws which the all-wise Congress passes.

For example, when you get conscience stricken and send me a check for one hundred thousand dollars, which you have forgotten to include in previous income tax returns, I would love to say to you, Bayard old dear, I have such a sympathy for your present state of bankruptcy that I hereby remit the check to you. How I wish

I could help out you and Finland—brave souls both—but whether we like it or not Congress and God still live!

To this Swope answered:

Your letter of December 7th was a liberal education in the rights, perquisites, privileges, and appurtenances of a Dictator. The manner in which you worked out the course of action toward Finland is a far better one than the idea I had. After all, I am flattered to know we were thinking along the same lines, although yours was effective and mine was clumsy. . . .

By the spring of 1940, with most of Europe at war, Swope was convinced that Roosevelt had to run for a third term, but once again he found himself tight-rope walking. Jim Farley had split with Roosevelt over the third-term issue. Swope told Roosevelt that May, "There can be no question as to the world need of your remaining in office; it transcends politics; it rises above personality." But when at the nominating convention in July the New York delegation, with Swope again a member, again was polled, he cast his ballot for Farley. Walter Brown, Governor Lehman's secretary, tried to head him off, but Swope said stubbornly, "Mind your own damn business. I said I'm voting for Farley and I'm going to vote for Farley." He explained his motivation to Felix Frankfurter. "I would not have voted for Farley if my vote had been the one that would have made him President of the United States, or even the nominee. I did, however, cast a ballot for him as a symbol of appreciation of his honesty, his hard work, and his loyalty to party and to chief." *

For all the advice on public policy Swope was asked to give, or gave gratuitously, he never had to make high-level policy. In government, he never had to assume responsibility or to suffer accountability. But seldom did anyone look or act more authoritative. In the autumn of 1934 the movie *The President Vanishes*, written by Ben Hecht and Charles MacArthur, went into production. While seeking to cast the title role, it occurred to the

---

* Swope had become so attention-getting a fixture at Democratic national conventions that when he failed to put in an appearance at the 1944 conclave the columnist George Dixon observed that it seemed to be in violation of a fundamental American political tradition that Swope was not there to throw out the first Vice-Presidential candidate.

authors that they knew no one of more outward authentic Presidential stature than Swope, and they invited him to take a screen test at a studio on Long Island. Swope had reservations about the acting abilities of journalists. "Heywood Broun became an actor," he said. "He was terrible. Alexander Woollcott also became an actor. He said he was very good." But Swope agreed to try out for the part, to the delight of, among others, President Roosevelt, who asked to have a print of the test shown at the White House. Margaret Swope was not delighted; she told Hecht and MacArthur she'd scalp them both if her husband got the role. He didn't, but he turned up for the test, though so long after the hour set for it that the scenarists decided, while waiting, to play a trick on him.

Hecht and MacArthur had previously written a speech for him to deliver into the camera—a demagogic oration suitable for a Presidential candidate during a whistle-stop campaign. Swope was so enchanted with the notion of becoming a movie star— what would his old roommate John Barrymore think of *that!*— that he memorized his speech. Now, it occurred to Hecht and MacArthur to contrive a variation of the old vaudeville act of Professor Lamberti—the xylophonist who affected to think his audience was applauding him when it was actually reacting to a stripteaser performing behind his back. At the Long Island studio, when Swope finally arrived, he was placed at a rostrum, told to keep his eyes straight in front of him, and cautioned not to glance back if he heard any distracting sounds; there would probably be stagehands and prop men moving around behind him and he should just ignore them. He cleared his throat with a majestic harrumph that Washington, Jefferson, and Lincoln could never have matched, and began his declamation. When he reached the line "Behind every great man stands a woman," a scantily clad belly dancer slithered out behind him and did a series of bumps and grinds. A handful of onlookers in the studio roared with appreciation, and Swope, as pleased as Professor Lamberti ever pretended to be, spoke grandly on. When he was finally let in on the jape, he took it in good spirits and graciously gave the dancing girl his autograph.

On a real-life level, Swope never aspired to be President, but he would have welcomed some titular award for his long faithfulness to the Democratic cause. Just after the 1936 national convention he wrote to Frankfurter, "Probably you and I are the only ones left who have no hope of reward, or fear of punishment, from the Great White Father." * It was periodically rumored in the 1930s that Swope was slated for an ambassadorship. (President Roosevelt did offer once to send him to Albania, but he was kidding.) A Berlin newspaper reported, shortly before Hitler came to power, that Swope would be the American envoy to Germany. Damon Runyon thought he ought to be dispatched to England, since he would look so good in knee breeches, and the London *Evening Standard* called him a "hot candidate for Moscow." Swope had his own views. Asked one time how it was that, despite all the talk, he'd never become an Ambassador, he said, "Anywhere I was sent, we'd be at war in two weeks if I took Maggie along."

Of all the posts he might have occupied, the one he'd have liked best was a seat in the United States Senate. "I have always regarded the Senate as being the one place in politics which promised to be interesting," he once said. And when Richard L. Neuberger was elected to the Upper House from Oregon in 1954, Swope wrote him, perhaps a mite wistfully, "I am particularly happy that you enter politics from journalism. We need some good men from that source."

Swope might have made a splendid Senator. He had the build, the intelligence, the knowledge, the self-assurance, the deep and probing interest in public affairs, and the sonority. And he would have enjoyed the privileges. "That old toga would have fitted him very well," Robert Moses said. On several occasions Swope was mentioned as a prospect for the Senate; while Harry Hopkins was Roosevelt's right-hand man, Hopkins and Baruch had a serious discussion as to whether Swope might not be the best man to fill a vacant seat from New York. But Swope would probably have found an election campaign tedious and the petty demands of his constituents a bore. And while the hours of the Senate, which normally convenes at noon, would have suited him admirably,

---

* Frankfurter's reward, a place on the Supreme Court, came three years later. Swope was still looking for his in 1946. Having difficulty then getting a newspaperman's widow a post-office-clerk's job, he complained to Farley, "It's a remarkable thing that I, as a Democrat and a *contributing* member of the party, both in brains and dollars, have never had a single preferment from the party. That makes me rather sore. That record dates from Al Smith, including Wilson, you, Roosevelt and everybody else. I think I am entitled to a break."

he might have found it unacceptable to be thrown into a situation where ninety-five other men could argue with constitutional justification that they were his peers.

As it turned out, the highest elective office he ever attained was that of a trustee of the village of Sands Point. He held this post from 1931 through 1937, and at intervals also served, like most village trustees, as mayor and police commissioner. In this last capacity he could sometimes obtain a motorcycle escort when he had to get somewhere on Long Island in a hurry, a state of affairs he found agreeable. After he'd been a trustee for six years, though, it was suggested that he step down, because, as one neighborhood political leader felt impelled to inform him, "It has been somewhat awkward in not having you more regular in your attendance at the meetings." The final blow came when he was asked to yield up his police commissioner's badge.

In the first few weeks of the New Deal, while the Roosevelt Administration was dispensing the spoils that go to victors, Swope had felt that both he and another influential Democrat, Joseph P. Kennedy, who later did become an Ambassador, were being slighted. Like a schoolboy, Swope always had to have a best friend, and during the first five years or so of the Roosevelt era Kennedy probably held that honor. In Kennedy, Swope found many of the qualities he admired. As an Irish Catholic, Kennedy, like Al Smith, was a sort of underdog. Moreover he was a speculator, was wealthy, and was ambitious. Swope and Kennedy had a standing engagement to chat by telephone every morning at eleven o'clock, and they would often talk for a solid hour. Kennedy came to assume that pinnacle of intimacy that Swope reserved for a chosen few: the two men had a joint stock-market account. (They were also gambling cronies at Colonel Bradley's Palm Beach Casino.) In a long footnote to a letter Swope sent Kennedy on March 30, 1933, he said, in part:

Ray Moley has just been in to see me. He spent a couple of hours here. While here Frank Walker and Forbes Morgan came in, by appointment with M. They wanted to go over the list of applicants for jobs. Walker and Morgan urged upon Ray, Steinhardt for Sweden, Bullitt for Budapest or Prague; Dave Hennen Morris for Belgium; some other piece of cheese from the west for Uruguay and five or six other jobs for other people. At the end they all began talking of you, and what a damn shame it was that nothing had been done. My comment was merely that I did not think there was anything they could do for you, but, from an outside position, my view was that the lot of them had been running after you while they needed you, but I had not discerned much running after the need had passed. All agreed, and thought it was a damned outrage. They are going to send for you and have the Great White Father hold your hand. I am told that everybody agrees that not alone should you have what you want, but that you have the right to speak for any job you want for anybody else. I believe there is still a question of trying to put you in as under-secretary of War, though I noticed Woodring mentioned for that post today. I am told that Howe is quite friendly, except he wants to keep you away from finance. That's his method, I suppose, of separating the Administration from Wall Street. They put it on that basis, rather than his having anything personal against you.

As they talked I felt myself getting sore that there should be so much discussion of men who had absolutely no claim upon good nature—certainly, far less than I have. I noticed that Coolidge said in his letter to Everett Saunders that only Smith could win Massachusetts and Rhode Island. Smith did it. You know, Flynn knows, and Farley knows that I alone brought Smith in. *You* know how earnestly and effectively I worked for F.D.R., even *before* the nomination; I am referring to the two weeks preceding Chicago, when we began our talk.

I find myself clutching at the Crown of Martyrdom. I have no desire to wear it, but I find my reactions of soreness are much the same as yours, though, of course, mine rest on a far lesser basis of justification. . . .

Well, anyway, you have them in a stew. They really are concerned, even though nothing happens. Probably the thing to do is to wait and then plump hard for a specific request in your own behalf, or on behalf of somebody else. Let's wait and see how events shape themselves.

Events shaped themselves in June 1934, when Roosevelt appointed Kennedy to the newly formed Securities and Exchange Commission. Swope, Baruch, Moley, and Kennedy were in Roosevelt's office one day, discussing various prospects to serve on the Commission, and Baruch, pointing to Kennedy, said to the President, "What's the matter with that redhead over there?" Roosevelt picked Kennedy on the spot. A few days later the President still hadn't decided whom to make *chairman* of the S.E.C. Baruch and Swope, learning that the President was leaning toward another man, let it be known that since he had appointed Kennedy first, he ought to put him in charge. Roosevelt acquiesced. Swope, overjoyed, wired Roosevelt his congratulations ("IT TOOK GUTS TO DO IT AND AS USUAL YOU HAD THE GUTS") and tendered Kennedy a lunch in New York, so the chairman could become better acquainted with the financial writers for the city's papers. Swope was so enamored of Kennedy that, beseeching some club-house privileges for him at a Florida race track, he said, "I am more interested in him than I would be in myself."

But once again the bonds of friendship began to fray. Certainly after the Second World War started and Kennedy, by then wear-ing the knee pants of an Ambassador to the Court of St. James's, advocated a neutralist position, Swope, an ardent internationalist, would have had a falling-out with him; but the two men managed to achieve this even in advance of those impassioned times. One of Kennedy's many sources of income was importing liquor from Great Britain. He asked Swope to join him in the business when he was setting it up, but there was a dispute over terms. Kennedy felt that Swope should put up some capital—$150,000 is the figure most commonly cited. Swope, on the other hand, felt that he had already given Kennedy a solid $150,000 worth of advice and that he should therefore get his share of the business for nothing.

They drifted apart, and soon Swope would be writing Lord Beaverbrook, "I have an idea that this is the first American Am-bassador to England who is engaged in the liquor business, and, probably our first who is engaged in importing it to the country from which he is accredited. However, with so many beer barons, ale earls, and whiskey lords, perhaps he will feel at home." And to another American Ambassador, Hugh Wilson, stationed in Berlin, Swope would say, "That was a good speech you made . . . sound and clear. It is somewhat better, I think, for an Ambassador's effort to be directed to such subjects as these than to be publicly identified with debutantes and silk knee breeches."

Before the disenchantment between the two friends set in, how-ever, Swope was able to do Kennedy one favor that might have had historic consequences. Swope's son had entered Princeton in the fall of 1932. In the fall of 1935 Kennedy's second son, John Fitzgerald, who was convalescing in London from a summer at-tack of jaundice, wanted to enter Princeton. The academic year had already begun, but to Swope this was no insurmountable obstacle. On October 16, 1935, he cabled the senior Kennedy, who was also in London, conventionally trousered, "HERE'S GOOD NEWS STOP GOT ACTION DEAN GAUSS PRINCETON FOR JACK STOP

380

VIOLATION RULE ADMIT BOY SO LATE BUT IN RESPONSE TO PICTURE I PAINTED YOUNG GALAHAD HE THINKS CAN WANGLE IT THROUGH STOP WANTS BOY HERE IN TWO WEEKS STOP . . . HURRAH FOR NEW TIGER. . . ."

Poor Swope! His life was full of frustrations. After young Kennedy had matriculated at Princeton, he had a recurrence of his illness and had to withdraw at Christmas time. When, the following year, he was fit enough to resume his studies, he switched colleges and eventually became known world-wide, despite Swope's valiant efforts to enshrine him as a son of Old Nassau, as a Harvard man.

The only formal mission ever entrusted to Swope by President Roosevelt turned out unhappily. In June 1933 representatives of sixty-six nations convened in London for an International Monetary and Economic Conference. It was a gathering that, in the most optimistic view, would solve universal fiscal problems by stabilizing foreign exchange—much as the sponsors of the League of Nations hoped their body could stabilize foreign relations. The American delegation was headed by Secretary of State Cordell Hull, who was a croquet player but not in Swope's class. When Hull's associates were being selected, Raymond Moley, then Assistant Secretary of State, proposed that Swope go along as the group's public-relations man.* The suggestion was coolly received at the White House, however, and Charles Michelson got the public-relations job.

---

* The previous January, during the interregnum between Roosevelt's election and his inauguration, Swope had had an abortive idea for another kind of jaunt for Moley and himself. Considerable attention was then being focused on the question of American recognition of the Soviet government, and Swope wrote Kennedy: "Ray Moley, at my house on Sunday, stated there was a real chance in the Russian situation. We have often discussed that, and this new and unexpected affirmation brought it back to my mind. His idea, roughly, was to have you, him and me appointed a commission to investigate Russia and to make recommendations upon our return. I really think there is something in it—especially now, when things are at their lowest ebb. Here is an improvement on the idea: Have Franklin make the offer to you, which you will then decline to accept officially. You can say, however, that you will go unofficially. Moley and I will go, make the necessary exploration, make a report with recommendations for action and you in the meanwhile, in your private capacity, can take advantage of such conditions as promise to be fruitful."

381

The conference got off to a limping start. Some of the Europeans, with the French in the forefront, were all for rigid stabilization, but the United States, which had just gone off the gold standard, wanted to move slowly until domestic prices, cut by the depression, had risen. There was a good deal of jockeying back and forth among the conferees, and a good deal of confusion back in Washington as to just what, if anything, was being accomplished abroad. In mid-June President Roosevelt, never reluctant to pit one of his top aides against another, let Moley go to England as a trouble-shooter. Moley asked if he could take Swope along. Louis Howe, who had never got on particularly well with Swope and had once disdainfully called him "a little brother to the rich," demurred. "But I *like* him," Roosevelt said. He telephoned Swope on June 15 and invited him to make the trip. The next day he sent a confirming telegram:

WOULD BE DELIGHTED IF YOU COULD ACCOMPANY RAYMOND MOLEY FOR SHORT VISIT TO LONDON STOP I AM SENDING HIM SOON AND FEEL YOUR PRESENCE WOULD BE EXCEEDINGLY HELPFUL TO HIM IN MANY WAYS STOP I SHOULD BE PERSONALLY GRATEFUL TO HAVE YOU DO THIS HAVING CONFIDENCE AS I DO IN YOUR JUDGMENT AND YOUR WIDE KNOWLEDGE OF INTERNATIONAL AFFAIRS STOP YOU WOULD BE ABSENT FROM THIS COUNTRY ONLY ABOUT A MONTH.

Moley and Swope set sail on June 20. Each took an assistant. Moley's was the son of the Democratic National Committeeman from Nebraska; Swope's was his own son, who was seventeen and had just finished his freshman year at college. Swope described himself on the eve of their departure as an "assistant to an errand boy" and said his function would be to "carry baggage for a messenger," but his diffidence got him nowhere. "You can't believe all you read in the newspapers," F.P.A. said in the *Herald Tribune*. "Mr. Herbert Bayard Swope, former executive editor of the former New York *World*, sailed on the *Manhattan* yesterday with Mr. Raymond Moley. But the papers said 'Mr. Moley will be accompanied by Mr. Herbert Bayard Swope.' Most of us know that Mr. Swope will be accompanied by Mr. Moley, as Mr. Moley himself probably discovered before the ship reached Ambrose Light."

In London, proceedings all but came to a halt, as the conferees waited to see what instructions or suggestions Roosevelt's liaison man carried. Meanwhile, at home, Baruch moved into Moley's State Department office as a liaison man for the liaison man. At sea, Swope was kept posted by wireless messages from Baruch, one of which said, "SUGGEST UTMOST CAUTION WISDOM ON LANDING AS AMERICAN EUROPEAN PRESS MOMENTARILY UNFRIENDLY. . . . GREAT MODESTY AND APPARENT SELF-EFFACEMENT YOUR AND RAY'S BEST WEAPONS." Moley and Swope prepared statements to be released when their ship docked at Cobh, its first port of call, and at Plymouth; and Swope, concerned at Baruch's message, radioed to Michelson in London, asking how the British press had reacted to their embarkation. Michelson replied, deflatingly, "YOUR DEPARTURE UNCOMMENTED." Actually, though, the London *Times* had already run a dispatch from its Washington correspondent, who said:

The approaching arrival in London of Mr. Raymond Moley, whose official title is Assistant Secretary of State, but who has a relation of special intimacy with President Roosevelt, has given rise to assumptions which are by no means borne out by any knowledge in the possession of the American delegation here. It does not appear that Mr. Moley will bring with him any new instructions whatever; or that he will be armed with any authority, direct or transmissible, which might favorably modify any phase of the negotiations; or, in fine, that his duties will be more than those of fact-finding, tempered by the pleasures of travel in the excellent company of Mr. Herbert Bayard Swope.

Mr. Swope knows, and has long been known by, Europe. He was for many years a newspaper correspondent, in which field of activity his fertility of resource and imperturbability of spirit in the face of great events won him notice. He became executive editor of the (now defunct) New York *World*, and he has more than once been saluted as the greatest natural force in the Western Hemisphere—after Niagara. It is inconceivable that one of so dazzling a temper could be associated with a project of even temporary stabilization.

Other comments quickly followed. The *Daily News Chronicle* described Swope and Moley as "Roosevelt's two mystery men" and said that the American delegates in London were "as perplexed about his [Swope's] status as they were about Mr. Moley himself." It was hinted that "Hurricane Swope," as the *Evening Standard* called him, was not a New Deal emissary at all, but rather a spy for J. P. Morgan. Moley had scarcely reached London when he was at odds with Hull. Moley didn't consider himself to be there on State Department business. He felt that he should report directly to the Secretary of the Treasury, William H. Woodin, and to the President. In Hull's view, however, an Assistant Secretary of State was subordinate to a Secretary of State. The newspapers gaily reported their tug of war, and in the antic atmosphere *Punch* ran a topical poem:

> Said Professor Moley to Mr. Swope,
> "Stabilization is not the dope,"
> "You've said it, kid; I'm with you wholly,"
> Said Mr. Swope to Professor Moley.
> Said Professor Moley to Mr. Swope,
> "Reduction of tariffs. Gee, what a hope!"
> "They rise up fast but they come down slowly,"
> Said Mr. Swope to Professor Moley.
> Said Professor Moley to Mr. Swope,
> "With this world-crisis I've come to cope."
> "On you the world is depending solely,"
> Said Mr. Swope to Professor Moley.
> Said Professor Moley to Mr. Swope,
> "The world will continue to groan and grope—"
> "Till they follow your lead, by all that's holy,"
> Said Mr. Swope to Professor Moley.*

More or less on his own, and without consulting Hull, Moley worked out a tentative agreement for long-range stabilization and sent it to Roosevelt for his approval. Then the President, to Moley's consternation, disapproved of the agreement and, to make matters worse, in issuing a statement expressing his disapproval, used the text of a document Swope had prepared before he and Moley left—a document, though, that was supposed to be used in circumstances precisely opposite to those in which Roosevelt was now employing it.

There was hopeless misunderstanding everywhere. The conference was in danger of breaking up then and there. To save

---

* Swope sent a copy of the verse to F.P.A., who said he didn't like the rhyme of "wholly" and "Moley," but preferred:

> Said Herbert Swope to Raymond Moley,
> "I hate omargarine that's ole."
> "I'd just as soon eat shaving soap,"
> Said Raymond Moley to Herbert Swope.

Roosevelt from being blamed for scuttling the enterprise, Moley and Swope asked Walter Lippmann and John Maynard Keynes to join them in preparing a statement that would at least keep the conferees talking to each other a little longer. The four men toiled most of one night and at three-thirty in the morning began to write out their thoughts. "Lippmann, Keynes, and I each tried to help with the typing process," Moley recalled, "but did so poorly that Herbert, in disgust, shooed us away and did the job himself." Despite Swope's stenographic ministrations, the stabilization conference broke up inconclusively not long afterward, with instability rampant. "You are one writ with me," Moley said to Swope after they returned home, "in sour misfortune's book." Swope had had enough of travel—for the government or on his own. For the remaining twenty-five years of his life, he never again set foot outside the United States.

19

JOURNALISM is a lifelong profession," Swope once said, and throughout his life he kept hoping sporadically that some suitable newspaper opportunity would present itself so he could prove his point. In the spring of 1933, for instance, having by then concluded that Baruch was unlikely to stake him to the Washington *Post*, he turned to Kennedy as a possible substitute patron. To have run a liberal daily in the nation's capital at the outset of the New Deal would have been an absorbing experience, but this particular Swope plan ended abruptly when Eugene Meyer, theretofore a banker, bought the *Post*. (Two and a half years afterward, Meyer wrote him, ". . . I am beginning to appreciate how much I have to learn about the newspaper business. . . . I may never catch up with the old-time speedsters, but I still hope that some day you will talk to me about newspapers as well as banking and politics.") Swope's wish for journalistic resurrection even led him into exploratory negotiations with Ezra Pound, who while in Italy in 1933 conceived the notion of starting up an American paper dedicated to what he perceived as the truth. But Swope forsook this collaboration after Pound sent him one rambling seven-page letter that consisted largely of anti-Semitic jokes.

The trouble, however, was that Swope was all but unemployable. He had such a towering reputation as a newspaperman that there were few jobs open commensurate with his stature. He was in the unhappy situation that sometimes confronts star actors unable to find a vehicle that will bear their heavy load of glitter. His interest in newspapers remained intense. He would read the editorial page of the New York *Times* every day like a conscientious schoolteacher poring over a student's daily quiz, and he would very nearly give it a grade. But despite his ambitions, Swope was never again to get much closer to practicing the profession he worshiped than a race-track handicapper gets to breeding thoroughbreds. Swope, instead, became a sort of super-tipster. By telephone and by mail he fed items to city editors and to syndicated columnists like Walter Winchell, Drew Pearson, George Sokolsky, and Leonard Lyons. "It's been said of me that I can get any newspaperman in America on the phone," Swope once reminded himself in a proud *aide memoire*. (It is hard to figure out why Swope should have felt that any newspaperman was difficult to reach; maybe he thought there were others who, like himself, were sometimes inaccessible.) He would get them at all hours, not infrequently routing them from their beds. While Bill Corum was writing a syndicated sports column, he contended that he had one secretary whose sole job was to handle incoming calls from Swope.

Swope expected no tangible rewards for the help he conferred on newspapers. But to live the way he loved to live required a great deal of money, and like a wild creature that to survive must be constantly aprowl for food, so was Swope always searching restlessly for funds. "I am getting awfully tired of unremunerative jobs," he wrote Baruch in August of 1934. "I think I have got something to deliver in the way of energy and ingenuity, together with decency and a good reputation, yet there seems difficulty in getting a price mark put upon it. But to hell with squawks." For a couple of years, in the mid-1930s, Swope was remuneratively occupied as chairman of the board of Keith-Albee-Orpheum, a corporate offshoot of Radio-Keith-Orpheum. He got thirty-five thousand dollars a year and a percentage of the profits, but he found the motion-picture world unappetizing. "I don't like this thing any too well," he wrote to Florence White in January 1936. "It is more of a racket than a vocation." Three months later, after a disagreement with his associates over carving up the profits and after a realignment of the ownership of the company, Swope severed connections with K-A-O, R-K-O, and a host of appendant film companies in which he had become involved.

There were other business affiliations. Swope served for a few years on a stockholders' committee of the Brooklyn-Manhattan Transit Company, and he was active in the prolonged negotiations that led to New York's subways' switching from private to municipal ownership. He played a key part in the reorganization of the Columbia Broadcasting System, getting together a syndicate to buy a block of its stock that was held by the Paramount-Publix movie company. Swope always hoped that a fat fee would be forthcoming for this catalytic effort. But often what he visualized as quick silver turned out to be quicksilver. All he got out of the CBS deal was a chance to buy some stock cheap and a spot on the company's board of directors.

As a director of CBS, Swope was theoretically concerned merely with matters of over-all policy, but he could not resist plunging into the minutiae of the network's operations. Its two chief executives, William S. Paley and Frank Stanton, on arriving at their offices in the morning, would often find on their desks communiqués from Swope—complaining, perhaps, about a twisted fact or mispronounced word he had heard on a late-night news broadcast. Or, after listening attentively to a question-and-answer program conducted by Professor Quiz, Swope would write to that academician reproving him for his definition of a taxidermist as a man who stuffed birds. "You see," Swope wrote Paley, enclosing a copy of his rebuke to the professor, "I take our broadcasts seriously."

But these activities were of a part-time, stop-gap nature, and Swope wearied of moving in and out of business situations, or simply buzzing at the fringes of them. In 1936 he resolved that as long as everybody seemed to be soliciting his advice and using his connections, he might as well profit from it. Accordingly, he became a paid public-relations consultant—a line of endeavor that he had first looked favorably on when he and Willis Pratt set up their abortive partnership back in 1909. His first, and most durable, client was Lewis S. Rosenstiel, the panjandrum of Schenley Industries, who took Swope on in 1936, retained him for twenty years, and periodically provided him with a California vin rosé that arrived flatteringly labeled "Bottled for Herbert Bayard Swope." While Averell Harriman was Ambassador to Russia, according to Swope's own records, the publicist broached to him diplomatically the possibility of getting Schenley potables admitted and consumed behind the Iron Curtain. (Harriman did not subsequently recall this bold stab at coexistence.)

Swope's own conception of his role as a consultant was that "My job is to keep people from doing what they want to do, unless it is what they ought to do." Sometimes he referred to himself as a diagnostician, and indeed a man who dispenses politic advice is not unlike at least one kind of physician— the legendary Chinese doctor who construes his function to be that of keeping his patients healthy and unneedful of medical treatment. Sometimes Swope called himself a "policy consultant" and sometimes a "publicist." H. L. Mencken defined the latter, bluntly, as "press agent." Swope much preferred Webster's "a writer on, or one versed in, the laws of nature and nations, the science of public right, the principles of government, etc.; now, esp., a writer on current political topics."

Swope would complain whenever he caught somebody following the Mencken line, though there is no evidence that he ever dressed down the Baltimore lexicographer for his impudence. He did protest, however, when the New York *Times* led off a story about a union of Hollywood press agents with the headline "SCREEN PUBLICISTS WIN PAY INCREASES." Swope dashed off a letter to the editor that went: ". . . Publicists? Far from it. A publicist is one interested in public affairs of a political nature. The group about which your story is written is composed of press agents. That is a good old-fashioned name for important work in the entertainment field but it is totally unrelated to the work of a publicist. . . . Let the *Times* consider itself rebuked."

The then managing editor of the paper, Edwin L. James, replied mildly that the *Times* felt quite justified in what it had done, inasmuch as the name of the press agents' group under discussion was the Screen Publicists' Guild. Swope was not appeased. "Publicists are publicists and press agents are press agents," he retorted, "and the twain cannot meet in one word." His own career, though, would demonstrate that the twain could be nearly inseparable and might in fact be not twain at all but instead a double image of a single entity.

Whatever he may be called, an operative such as Swope became can perform a useful service. The executives of large corporations, for instance, find it welcome, and reassuring, and—in view of their ample budgets—not onerously expensive to have an outsider available to try new ideas on, or get ideas from. It is for much the same reason that many corporations seek to maintain a balance on their boards between insiders on the payroll and outsiders with no personal stake in day-to-day affairs. A corporation president or board chairman surrounded by fawning and ambitious yes-men may find it not only congenial but highly desirable to form an affiliation with an astute and potentially argumentative detached consultant—an Edward L. Bernays, say, or an Anna Rosenberg, or a Benjamin Sonnenberg—who can and now and then will utter an objective "No" or, more probably, a "Do you think you really ought to?"

Most big-time public-relations consultants have elaborate offices and bustling underlings and scholarly research assistants to help them. Swope ran a one-man show. Rather, he *was* a one-man show. He had no staff to back him up, and much of his research came out of his own fact-crammed head. But his tastes and his acquaintances were so catholic, and his imagination so fecund, that he could dispense with the ordinary appurtenances of his trade. Conventional functionaries and files would have cramped his free-wheeling style. Like the Pope, he needed no divisions to fight his battles. He brimmed over with ideas, some good, some bad, some inventive, some inane. He was informed, articulate, and aggressive, and he radiated self-confidence.

Best of all were his connections. If a client had an interest in some legislative proceeding, Swope, on a telephone in New York, could lobby in Washington as effectively as could most paid hands operating there out of plushy offices and plushier hotel suites. Sonnenberg confessed once that he doubted he was personally acquainted with more than twelve members of the United States Senate. Swope was fettered by no such handicap. There were hardly a dozen members of any Senate of his adult life he *didn't* know. Once, when a newly elected member of the Upper House arrived in Washington, a veteran solon who had not long before found Swope a useful ally in getting his son commissioned in the Army urged the tyro, during a cloakroom briefing, to waste no time in making Swope's valuable acquaintance.

Before the unremitting demands of money compelled Swope to lower his standards, he had a lofty view of his function as a consultant. He once told Baruch, "There must be a definite and continuous policy serving some public good before I am willing to accept a client." (He interpreted the world "client" loosely. In soliciting business from new clients he once mentioned as former clients Franklin D. Roosevelt, Al Smith, and Woodrow Wilson.) When asked one time to try to put a little gloss on the public image of a man about to be convicted of income-tax evasion, Swope replied, "My work does not include cases such as this."

Yet a few years later, at the urging of a lawyer he respected, he

accepted ten thousand dollars to try to rub some of the taint off
Serge Rubinstein, a man with an almost unique talent for not
serving public good fleetingly, let alone continuously. Swope
didn't do him much private good, either. Few of Swope's friends
knew about his arrangement with Rubinstein, or, for that matter,
knew much about his relationships with any of his paying clients.
Howard Dietz was for many years not only a lyricist but also a
vice-president of Metro-Goldwyn-Mayer. He was for just as
many years a friend of Swope's, but he did not know until after
Swope's death that Swope had been for several years retained by
Twentieth Century-Fox.

Swope, who liked to have all his friends and associates share his
interests, got Rosenstiel into horse-racing. "Seriously, you will
find great satisfaction in owning a horse, provided he is a *good*
horse," Swope advised the Schenley man. "You will see his victories become yours; how his gameness becomes representative of
your own; how his speed is indicative of your own ability. In
short, there comes a transference of identity, which will be helpful
to your ego—not that you need this artificial support, for, in all
frankness, your own record is capable of supplying a natural
stimulus." Rosenstiel acquired a string of horses, and Swope undertook to invest them with suitable names. One of these, "Three
Feathers," was rejected by the Jockey Club, which decreed that
Rosenstiel would have to switch to something less commercial.
Swope worked most closely and contentedly with Bernard
Baruch, whom Margaret Swope once told, "You two are a beautiful and effective combination and greatly needed in this world of
ineffectuality and mediocrity." But privately she was unhappy
about how much time Swope spent on his affairs. She once said,
acerbly, when Baruch was not around, that he and Swope were
working for the same goal—"the glory of God and of Bernie."
Another time she called Baruch the Galatea to Swope's Pygmalion.
The appraisal was probably unfair to Baruch, a man who, after all,
had striking natural endowments; but Swope himself sometimes
seemed to share it. In 1951 he dictated a note to himself that went,
"Krock said to me, in the '20s, that B.M.B. should be deeply grateful to me for having devised a pattern for him to live by and be
known for; that I had kept him from being presented and recognized not merely as a rich man—perhaps a daring rich man whose
only claim to public approbation was money. Instead I had staged

391

him as a pro bono publico—as a servant of the people—as one with a passion for service. I think this is true; it is deeply discerning of what I tried to do and what B.M.B. has become—almost too much so, at times."

Swope's relationship to Baruch, whose function in public life Swope also described on occasion as "evangelism," may have been best summed up by Ferdinand Eberstadt, who knew them both well and felt, as did others who enjoyed their companionship, that it did not hurt the one big man to have another big man make him even bigger. Before Eberstadt became an investment banker he had taught Greek, and as he observed Swope and Baruch in action he was reminded of a passage in Plutarch. Alexander the Great, the historian said, had once paused reflectively at the tomb of Achilles and had remarked, "Oh, fortunate Achilles, who had Homer to sing your praises!"

Baruch was only briefly a contractual benefactor of Swope's. In 1936 they signed an agreement committing Baruch, as a client, to pay Swope fifteen thousand dollars a year for "the right to consult with you on various problems of public relationship"—a right the granting of which inspired Swope to write Baruch:

> To my oldest, my dearest, my most valued client, patron, student, leader, follower and FRIEND:
> This is to acknowledge receipt not of the check that puts you on my books, but of the thought that lay behind it. The flow of spirit between us cannot be measured in price, but I realize you wish to give an outward and visible symbol to the relationship by putting it in terms of a formal connection. It is the spirit which reaches me, and for which I reach.
> My love always from across the years.

Baruch was disinclined to extend that setup beyond two years. However, he later reduced various loans he made to Swope by sums he considered payments for advisory services.

Baruch was always conscious of Swope's financial difficulties and was eager to help him out without being too hard hit himself; he once told Swope that at times he worried more about Swope's affairs than about his own. Swope's pride would never let him disclose that anything like an employer-employee relationship had ever existed between the two of them. He wrote one friend in 1956 that "It occurs to me that you may want to know that I never had a salary arrangement with Baruch. I found a reward in seeing his dedication to public concern." Privately, however, his attitude was different. A 1939 memorandum of Swope's about Baruch went:

I must do something and I want to do it with him. And he, too, has need of sort of companionship I can supply with love and admiration.

I can help him express himself and in so doing express myself. There is much that he has to do, all of which can be done better together.

I'll take office with him or be on hand every day for discussions. Go south with him. (The question of compensation is not the most important point but it is an essential one, for there must always be an external valuation of one's efforts, whether it takes the form of public approval (as is the case with him) or of pay therefor.) Such a relationship will bring us both peace of mind and that means bodily health. In it will be that which cannot be bought—loyalty, affection, understanding and complete faith. . . . The relationship would give me an outlet for my energy and imagination. And, for him, it would coordinate his efforts and help to give them direction. And it would bring two people together who are—at least, one of them is—happiest in each other's company. . . . I'm willing to sink myself into him for the rest of his life.

The question of money, or the lack of it, sometimes momentarily beclouded, but could not eclipse, the intense radiance of an exceptional friendship between the two men. Neither would take a step, for many years, without first consulting the other. "I never did a damn thing without having Swope around," Baruch said. People who wanted to get hold of the sometimes hard-to-get Baruch knew that a word dropped in Swope's ear had a good chance of being transmitted further.

Baruch was twelve years older than Swope. It was nearly the same age differential that separated Swope from his elder brother, and toward Baruch he had much the same attitude as he had toward Gerard—part filial, part fraternal, part deferential, part resentful. Swope could never quite figure out whether he wanted to be closer to Baruch than he was. Frequently he brooded about his ambivalence and expressed his puzzlement both to Baruch and to himself. "Sometimes I wonder if my identification with you is not too complete," he wrote Baruch one time. So much, in fact, did the one become identified with the other that, although apart from being tall they had little physical resemblance, Swope's photograph would now and then be used to illustrate a newspaper story about Baruch.

Swope usually called Baruch "Boss" to his face, but in correspondence he would address him as "Old Sweetheart" or "Baby." In the body of the numerous letters they exchanged there were, however, astonishingly few personal touches; both men were serious-minded and were much less apt to discuss, say, family matters than the rate of growth of the gross national product or the political situation in southeast Asia. But their letters were larded through with professions of affection. Sending Baruch a book as a bon-voyage present before a transatlantic trip, Swope would write: "Dear, dear Bernie: . . . Perhaps it will help you think of me—I like to be kept in your mind, and in your heart. Friendships are too rare not to be nourished and helped in every way. You have my love and trust and confidence. Come back to us soon. . . ." Or, in one of his periods of self-evaluation, Swope would write Baruch:

DEAREST B.M.:

Yesterday's meeting and today's make me certain of this: I'd like to be with you all the time as a sort of alter ego or vicar of Christ.

We supplement each other. I know your mind and your heart, and you know mine. You give me a sense of uplift and faith; I think I stimulate you into a greater and more effective use of your mind (I do not know a better one!) and a surer employment of your extraordinarily devoted sense of public service. I am, to you, a catalyst—I make you self-expressive and, in that way, help the public gain a truer interpretation of your spirit and your work, in keeping with their innate nobility—and I mean just that! . . . I am over-energized but under-hitched—to use the sense of the comment you made yesterday. I want to do something that promises satisfaction. I want to do it, regularly and responsibly, with you. I feel as much pride in the reclamé you gain as I do in my own. You need, from the standpoints of both mental and *physical* health (and the latter is most important) the companionship that an association of this kind will yield. I would be guilty of false modesty if I did not feel that I can supply that element, based on the mutual love, confidence, admiration and faith which have so long existed between us. [This was written a day or two after his sink-myself memorandum.]

Swope once told Margaret L. Coit, a Baruch biographer who summarized her subject as "the greatest living American legend," that the secret of the friendship between the two men was "the

394

abandonment of all civility between us." Swope was probably the lone man Baruch knew who would stand up to him, and even slap him down. "I frequently find myself the only one of those around him who offers dissent," Swope wrote Arthur Krock. Men like Baruch are often isolated from the give and take of ordinary companionships. Baruch found, in Swope, someone who, refreshingly, was not intimidated either by his being an elder or a statesman. Musing on Swope once, Baruch said, "You know, it's a great thing just to have somebody to talk to." And with Swope around, even that was not a certainty. If Swope was in the middle of a lengthy discourse and Baruch tried to get in a word, Swope would say, "Oh, shut up, I'm talking," and Baruch would shut up. Swope would swear at Baruch and he would tease Baruch, and the recipient of this unabashed irreverence was, it should not be forgotten, a man whom Presidents of the United States traditionally held in, if not veneration, at least awe. One time, visiting Baruch's apartment in Manhattan and finding his host clad in a ragged dressing gown, Swope bellowed, "You son of a bitch, can't you afford a better one?" Nobody else would have dared make such a remark; Baruch took it, from Swope, in good spirit.

Swope, however, was no court jester whose function it was to amuse the king. Baruch needed henchmen. Swope once described Baruch as "an independent unbought voice on public issues." It was a useful role, but in playing it Baruch, however independent his views might be, relied heavily on assistants to assess them and to put them into digestible form for public consumption. Sometimes he would come to Swope with the rough draft of an idea and ask, "Did I say anything?" Over the years Baruch had other associates, among them Hugh Johnson and Samuel Lubell. Swope occupied a niche apart from all the rest, but he was nonetheless prone to be jealous of the others. He could not bear to have anyone even momentarily closer to Baruch than he was, and when Baruch asked him to comment on a speech one of his other hands had composed for him, Swope replied, "This is a good speech—fluent and easy. But it is less of an original writing than it is rewriting. You have said most of it before—there is nothing new in the thinking—nothing startling in your suggestions. But, as I say, it is a satisfactory job, even though you are not saying anything new."

Baruch was ever mindful that much of his public luster derived from the image of him that was carried in the press, and he was fond of newspapermen. If they had syndicated columns, so much the better. Mark Sullivan was one of his cronies. So was Frank R. Kent, who sometimes accompanied him on jaunts to Europe. So was Krock, whom he used for an occasional speech-writing stint. But such men as these could hardly spare him many of their working hours. To have a professional journalist like Swope available at *any* hour was comforting. Swope knew how to handle the newspapers from which Baruch so long coveted, and so often received, such special handling. Baruch stood, like the United States Marines, almost above criticism, and the splendid vision of him that the press portrayed was in large measure the result of Swope's persevering efforts to mold his image.

Swope occasionally thought there was *too* much of Baruch in the papers, and he once wrote to Krock, "He has a passion for service and who is to say no to that, even though the service is attended by fanfare of trumpets. I sometimes wonder if his reputation is wholly deserved or if he, like most of us, is occasionally synthetic. . . ."

Stung by a book reviewer who was brash enough to regard him as fallible, Baruch asked Swope one time how he should retort to the fellow. Swope said he should do nothing at all, adding, "Remember: now and then a sour note intensifies the course of understanding approval." On another occasion he told Baruch, "I think you ought to be out of the paper for a while. It will give you a Scarcity Value that is always important." Three years after conveying that counsel, Swope thought it might be helpful to a venture he was in to obtain newspaper rights to some old Baruch speeches. When he asked Baruch for permission to have them reprinted, Baruch, in turning him down, used Swope's own advice as a boomerang to slap him gently with, saying that to accede to Swope's request would be inconsistent with Swope's constant admonitions about Scarcity Value.

For the most part, however, Swope encouraged Baruch to make full use of the obliging journalistic trumpets that played his fanfare. Whenever Baruch made a new speech or issued a statement, Swope saw to it that copies were sent not merely to the news departments of the principal papers thoughout the country but to their editorial departments as well; and whenever, as frequently occurred, an editorial writer saw fit to commend the latest Baruch utterance, Swope would have the recipient of this praise swiftly pen his thanks for the approbation, a gesture that was likely to sow the seeds of still further adulation. (At one point, Baruch's correspondence with newspapermen was so voluminous that he used Charles S. Hand, the *World* reporter, to attend to some of it for him.)

To Swope, there was nothing accidental or uncontrived about getting a good press, or putting on a good performance. "I rehearse each line he utters," Swope observed in a 1945 memorandum about Baruch, and Baruch noted autobiographically that it was Swope who had taught him how to open his mouth when he spoke and that in 1939, when Baruch was making a radio talk after the death of Pope Pius XI, Swope had stood directly in front of him, grimacing, so Baruch would remember to move his lips. When Swope first got to know Baruch the older man was a halting, stammering, soft-speaking orator. Swope changed all that, by prevailing upon his friend to, in Swope's phrase, "ham it up."

Some of Baruch's finest performances, with Swope expertly directing, were at Congressional committee hearings. After Baruch appeared before one such legislative body, its chairman, Senator Lyndon B. Johnson, sent Swope a transcript of the proceedings. Swope thanked Johnson but said that to send *him* Baruch's testimony was like sending "coals to Newcastle." In the spring of 1935 Baruch was summoned before a Senate investigating committee headed by the violently isolationist Gerald P. Nye of North Dakota. Nye and his committee counsel, Alger Hiss, were trying to expose war profiteers, and they hoped to show that Baruch, while chairman of the War Industries Board in 1918, had prospered personally.

It was a false hypothesis. Swope went to Washington with Baruch, and for two days and nights they prepared his case, which included a full disclosure of his income-tax returns for the time under scrutiny. Two of the Southern Senators whom Baruch had befriended and whose campaigns he had supported, Carter Glass and James F. Byrnes, sprang to his defense. Before Baruch could even answer some of Hiss's questions, Senator Glass snorted, "Never heard such dadboomed nonsense in all my born days." *

---

* Thirteen years later, when Hiss was dominating the newspaper headlines, Swope hoped to find in the transcript of the Nye Committee hearings some evidence of Communistic leanings. Instead of reading through the transcript himself, he asked Krock to. Krock did, but reported that after carefully going over Hiss's cross-examination of Baruch, he couldn't find anything ideologically significant.

Nye finally began to wish he'd never called Baruch in the first place, and at one point said lamely, "We are just asking Mr. Baruch to come down and give us the benefit of his great experience." When Senator Byrnes had concluded his affirmation of faith in Baruch's purity, Swope whispered loudly to the committee stenographer, "Have you got that down?" The stenographer said yes. Then Swope turned to Baruch and said, "Now we got the sons of bitches! From here on we just coast in!" They did.

Baruch was so pleased with the way things turned out that he offered Swope twenty-five thousand dollars for his help. Swope declined, but a couple of years afterward he agreed to accept thirty-seven thousand five hundred dollars—in the form of a reduction of a debt to Baruch—as a fee for his services.

For assistance in guiding the conduct of Baruch's own affairs, Swope had no compunctions about seeking or accepting rewards. When, however, Baruch set forth in full panoply to succor his country at some critical moment or other, Swope was almost always at his side, with little expectation either of recompense or of recognition. The sight of the tall, stern-visaged Swope bending over the Solomonic, seated Baruch, whispering hortatorily into the hearing aid that clung jewellike to his ear, became so familiar that it inspired a few small jokes. Sir Alexander Cadogan, an early British representative on the United Nations Security Council, was reported to have remarked, after watching Swope thus urging Baruch into combative action, "I see you're using London prize fight rules—'If you can't get your man into the ring, bite his ear.'"

Of the many government missions entrusted to Baruch, one of the most difficult and most dramatic took place in 1946. At the start of that year the UN established an Atomic Energy Commission, to study and recommend to the Security Council a course of action it could embrace about nuclear weapons, which the United States then exclusively possessed. Most member nations had their regular Security Council representatives serve on the Commission; but President Truman and Secretary of State Byrnes thought the matter of such overriding importance that it deserved a special spokesman. Truman, accordingly, invited Baruch, then seventy-seven, to sit in for the United States. After some hesitation, Baruch accepted.

As usual, Baruch chose to work as the head of a small, trusted, efficient, and congenial team. In this instance he recruited as his principal lieutenants the classically educated Ferdinand Eberstadt, who had not long before completed a stint in Washington as an allocator of priorities for war production; John Hancock, the tobacco-chewing Midwesterner who had first experienced the clash of arms in the Philippine Rebellion at the turn of the century; Fred Searls, Jr., a mining engineer well versed in uranium and other relevant raw materials; and Swope, who four years earlier, at the start of the war, had labored mightily to help Baruch get out a report for President Roosevelt on the nation's rubber resources and whom Baruch now looked to as the team man who would couch his views in prose likely to enhance their chances of winning universal acclaim. These four aides revealed their own assessment of their relationship to Baruch in 1949, when he celebrated his eightieth birthday. As a gift, they commissioned the Hungarian artist Alois Derso to paint them dressed as musketeers in the retinue of a splendidly d'Artagnanian Baruch. (Derso had to do the job twice; apparently under the impression that no d'Artagnan was entitled to more than three musketeers, he unwittingly left out Searls the first time.) On the second echelon of Baruch's team were a host of others—among them such scientists as Dr. Richard C. Tolman, a physicist from the California Institute of Technology; and such military men as Generals Leslie R. Groves and Thomas S. Farrell, late of the Oak Ridge Manhattan Project.*

Baruch set up an office in the Empire State Building, and throughout the winter of 1946 his team worked there, with periodic trips to Washington to confer with the President, or Secretary Byrnes, or Undersecretary of State Dean Acheson, whose name, along with that of David Lilienthal, adorned the first postwar American report on controlling the troublesome new explosive. The Acheson–Lilienthal document, while strongly advocating international control of atomic energy, had shied away from demanding that United Nations inspectors be allowed unlimited access to nations that might ultimately be producing nuclear weapons themselves. Inspection, Baruch's men began to conclude as they pursued their studies, working weekends at

---

* Another general who worked closely with Baruch was Matthew B. Ridgway, then the American military representative at the UN, to whom Swope would subsequently write, "My thanks to the Atom Bomb for having brought me a new friend."

their leader's home, was a critical factor. They were convinced that without it—and without, for another matter, the agreement to abandon the use of the veto in the Security Council if and when violators of an atomic accord should come up for punishment—any plan would have little real meaning.

From conversations with Andrei Gromyko, the Soviet representative on the UN Atomic Energy Commission, Baruch realized that Russia was unlikely to subscribe to any such restrictions on its freedom of conduct, but in the American team's view inspection and the abandonment of the veto in those special circumstances were unnegotiable keystones of any sensible pact. A number of Americans thought that the Baruch position was too inflexible and that its rigidity doomed it to failure from the start, but Baruch would not budge, and to his resoluteness Swope lent a firm supporting hand. There was a near crisis early in June, when Baruch got the impression that the United States had it in mind to go no further, before the UN, than to restate the relatively mild proposals embodied in the Acheson–Lilienthal report. On June 6, a day on which Swope drafted a letter of resignation for Baruch to submit to Truman, the Secretary of State got Baruch on the phone. They talked for an hour, with Swope listening in on an extension and furiously penciling notes. The outcome was that Byrnes said Baruch could proceed as he saw fit.

Baruch was scheduled to submit his plan formally on June 14. A week before this he was on a Central Park bench with Eberstadt and Swope, trying to figure out how to begin his exposition. Baruch muttered that it was a life-and-death issue they were grappling with. Swope, after mulling over *that* for a while, called him excitedly and said, "I've got it!" The introductory remarks he forthwith composed for Baruch to deliver in the auditorium of Hunter College, where the UN was then temporarily housed, started off with the ringing words:

We are here to make a choice between the quick and the dead.
That is our business.
Behind the black portent of the new atomic age lies a hope which, seized upon with faith, can work our salvation. If we fail, then we have damned every man to be the slave of Fear. Let us not deceive ourselves: We must elect World Peace or World Destruction.
Science has torn from nature a secret so vast in its potentialities that our minds cower from the terror it creates. Yet terror is not enough to inhibit the use of the atomic bomb. The terror created

400

by weapons has never stopped man from employing them. For each new weapon a defense has been produced, in time. But now we face a condition in which adequate defense does not exist.

Science, which gave us this dread power, shows that it *can* be made a giant help to humanity, but science does *not* show us how to prevent its baleful use. So we have been appointed to obviate that peril by finding a meeting of the minds and the hearts of our peoples. Only in the will of mankind lies the answer.

It is to express this will and make it effective that we have been assembled. We must provide the mechanism to assure that atomic energy is used for peaceful purposes and preclude its use in war. To that end, we must provide immediate, swift, and sure punishment of those who violate the agreements that are reached by the nations. . . .

Baruch's oration, the Demosthenic touches for which were provided almost entirely by Swope, was widely hailed. Editorials everywhere applauded it, although some commentators, including Walter Lippmann, found its tone a mite intransigent. The Manchester *Guardian*, selecting a nuclearly cataclysmic verb for its accolade, said that in Swope's quick-and-dead sentence "rhetoric and truth were perfectly fused." Eberstadt thought the speech a classic. "The damn thing belongs with St. Paul," he said. But the Russians, whatever their feelings may have been about the statement's style, had little relish for its content. Gromyko and his aides got along well enough personally with Baruch and his— Baruch took a flock of UN men, including the Russian and Trygve Lie, to the Joe Louis–Billy Conn heavyweight fight at the Yankee Stadium, and they all appeared to have a rollicking good time—but they had no stomach for Baruch's proposals.

In the six-month period that followed the presentation of the Baruch Plan—as Swope took pains to see that the American scheme became everywhere known—there were a number of tense moments, by no means all of them foreign in origin. Henry A. Wallace, then Secretary of Commerce, was one of those who had misgivings about the rigidity of the Baruch Plan. He said as much in a private letter to the President, and he said so publicly in a speech that Truman at first declared he'd approved before it was given and then declared he actually hadn't seen ahead of time. Baruch was furious, and when Baruch burned, Swope smoked. They tried to force Wallace into a public confession that he had misinterpreted their proposals, but they never quite got him pinned down. (It was not long afterward that Wallace ran against Truman for the Presidency.) Not that, in the long run, it all mattered very much. The Russians would probably never have gone along with any Western scheme that impinged upon their own development of a nuclear arsenal. When the Baruch Plan came up for ratification by the UN Atomic Energy Commission, at the end of December 1946, it won affirmative votes from ten of the twelve nations involved, but the Soviet Union and Poland, the other Communist country on the Commission, abstained. That was as far as Baruch's proposals ever got. The following month he and his team resigned.

Swope knew Truman least well of all the Presidents of his time. But they had met early in the war, and by 1945 Truman had joined Swope's vast roster of correspondents, though he had not made the somewhat more exclusive club of recipients of the *World Almanac*. While Truman was President, Swope's visits to the White House were rare. When he went there once at the start of 1949, representing an organization called the National Citizens' Council on Civil Rights, he felt so out of things that he wrote in advance to Charles Ross, asking the press secretary to remind Truman that he and Swope knew each other. Swope's relations with Truman were not sweetened, though, after the United Nations episode, by a rift between the White House and Baruch—a rift that Swope made no effort to smooth over. When in the fall of 1947, for instance, the President asked Baruch to represent him at the dedication of a war memorial in Philadelphia, Baruch asked Swope what he should do. Swope at once drafted a declination and told Baruch, "The President had absolutely no right to make so snippy and cheesy a request of you. It is as if he were fobbing you off by giving you entrance to his water closet. Resent it. . . ."

Swope continued briskly to fan the flames of Baruch's resentment. After the 1948 election Truman felt, or was persuaded by others to feel, that Baruch had been niggardly in contributing to his cause, and the re-elected President took a public slap at the elder statesman. This was too much for Baruch, and for Swope, too, who began to figure out ways to try to redress the balance between his senior citizen and the not-so-far removed junior Senator from Missouri. "It occurs to me that perhaps it might be wise to show that there is life in the old dog yet by the use of what I've called a veto power," Baruch was told in April 1949 by Swope, who not so long before had been counseling him to deplore the indiscriminate use of big-time vetoes. "Let us find a subject in which there is a real margin of disagreement—in which your views are opposed to H.S.T., then publicly disagree. Let us, first, assure ourselves that we've got certain Senatorial and journalistic support. Do you see what I mean? I am getting tired of the manner in which a childish egotism pervades certain sections of Washington. It may be time to demonstrate that your long devotion to the true Public Interest has brought with it a public confidence and a faith, not to be ignored. This course might be helpful, too, in showing the public that you still have the right of individual assessment and independence of judgment."

It was not easy to find an issue to take a stand on, however, and three months later Swope would merely be comforting his old-dog friend by pointing out that the President, in having nothing to do with Baruch, was hurting himself more than he was hurting him. "After all, he needs you a darned sight more than you need him," Swope said. But there was one thing about Truman Swope could not help admiring: he was a scrapper. He had a temper, and he sometimes lost it. He could get angry, like Swope himself. Swope's inclination toward ire was so well known that once when he wrote a letter to Captain Joseph Patterson of the *Daily News*, which Patterson decided to publish pseudonymously (the letter was sharply critical of the FBI, and the *News* naturally didn't want to put on anyone it liked the onus of attacking that institution), the publisher chose as an apt signature the acrostic "M.A.D." *

Swope sometimes thought it was a shame that Baruch was not as eager as he was to tilt lances. "B.M.B.'s greatest fault is that he won't fight," Swope once confided to himself. "He gives that impression, but he never hits back. In fact, he tries to conciliate." When, through the conciliatory tactics of General George C. Marshall, Baruch and Truman met face to face in 1951 and more or less made up, Swope had the satisfaction of the last word—

---

* Swope had read that the FBI was investigating sin in Miami, and he wrote to Patterson, "This extension of power is dangerous. If it gets by it will mark the establishment of a centralized authority on manners and morals. It's the inalienable right of every American to go to the Devil—or seek a higher deity—in his own way, without the aid or consent of Mr. Hoover or anybody else."

which he jotted down for his archives: "The President wrote him a letter of peace, this largely due to my insistence that he (B.M.B.) permit no overtures to be made. . . ." *

In a preliminary version of the June 14, 1946, Baruch speech on atomic bombs, Swope had referred to the standoff between the United States and the Soviet Union as a "cold war." Hancock and Eberstadt persuaded Baruch that—what with the State Department being so concerned about implied hostility toward Russia—the phrase might be construed as provocative, and the entire team agreed to delete it. But Baruch and Swope both liked it. "Use 'cold war' note in another speech," Swope reminded himself the day Baruch made the address from which it had been excised.

The opportunity presented itself on April 16, 1947, when South Carolina honored its famous native son by unveiling a portrait of Baruch in its legislative halls at Columbia. Speaking at the ceremonies, Baruch said, "Let us not be deceived—we are today in the midst of a cold war. Our enemies are to be found abroad and at home. Let us never forget this: Our unrest is the heart of their success. The peace of the world is the hope and the goal of our political system; it is the despair and defeat of those who stand against us."

Baruch's remarks were widely disseminated, although Swope did not succeed, as he had hoped he would, in getting CBS to broadcast them over its radio network ("C.B.S. did not display a good spirit," he told himself), and in a number of quarters the "cold war" line was applauded as especially felicitous. The phrase gathered momentum, and Swope was appalled. For from every side Baruch was being acclaimed for *his* frigorific invention. Baruch was perfectly willing to cede all his rights in the matter, and finally, at Swope's behest, he wrote Swope a letter formally crediting him with "cold war." Baruch balked, however, when Swope next asked for a similar set of credentials setting forth his ownership of another pet phrase of theirs: "Every man has a right to his own opinion, but no man has a right to be wrong in his facts."

---

* Always quick to render praise when he thought praise was due, Swope sent Charles Ross a telegram a few hours after the United States entered the Korean War: "PLEASE TELL THE PRESIDENT FOR ME HIS BOLDNESS AND DECISION IN THE KOREAN CRISIS MUST AND WILL WIN THE SUPPORT OF THE ENTIRE COUNTRY."

To be the father of "cold war," which Swope sometimes called "my baby," meant a lot to him, and he conducted an unremitting campaign to make certain there would never be any question of the child's paternity, firing off letters, often with copies of Baruch's quit-claim attached, to the editors of anthologies of quotations. (Swope died, mercifully, before the publication of a two-volume, eleven-hundred-and-fifty-eight-page book that, though entitled *The Cold War and Its Origins*, nowhere mentioned its terminological origins.) The worst trouble Swope had was with his old friend Walter Lippmann, who not only used *Cold War* himself for the title of a series of 1947 columns, and a book containing them, but insisted that he didn't think it mattered much who'd coined it anyhow. It was Lippmann's recollection that as far back as the mid-1930s the French, concerned about what Adolph Hitler was up to across the German border, had been talking of "*la guerre blanche*" or "*la guerre froide*." These phrases had been in his mind, Lippmann told Swope, when he was trying to hit on a suitable title after the war. "I hesitated for a long time whether to call the series the 'White War' or the 'Cold War,'" Lippmann wrote Swope. "I decided against the 'White War' finally because of the confusion which might arise because the Russians were called 'Reds' and their Russian opponents were known as White Russians."

Swope, who in a memorandum to himself had dated his conception of the phrase as "at the very beginning of 1946," replied to Lippmann:

> The first time the idea of the cold war came to me was probably in '39 or '40 when America was talking about a "shooting" war. I had never heard that sort of qualification. To me "shooting" war was like saying a death murder—rather tautologous, verbose and redundant.
>
> I thought the proper opposite of the so-called hot war was cold war, and I used that adjective in the early '40's in some letters I wrote, before our war.
>
> I may have been subconsciously affected by the term cold pogrom which was used to describe the attitude of the Nazis toward the Jews in the middle '30's. I never heard the French expressions to which you refer.
>
> The description became timely again when the Russians were putting pressure on us for the second front, but I used it first in a little talk I made in '45, just before the war ended. Then in '46 at

the time B.M.B. made his speech to the United Nations on the American attitude toward the atomic bomb. . . .

To which Lippmann answered tactfully:

It seems to me not at all improbable that the idea of the "cold war" first came to you in '39 or '40. The phrase had undoubtedly been current in Europe for some years—more or less since the beginning of the Hitler regime—and it is probable that you, as I did and many others, picked it out of the same air.

Lippmann—who was unquestionably the first man to use one metaphorically engaging phrase: "The cold war will smoulder on for generations"—was credited with "cold war" by the *Dictionary of New Words in English*, published in 1956. *American Words*, published in 1959, gave "cold war" to Swope. Meanwhile, the cold war went on.

It was frequently difficult to tell whether Baruch was doing or saying something on his own, or was reciting pure Swope. "I have given my life to wearing the gloves of Esau," Swope wrote in 1944 to Dudley Nichols. But, at that moment feeling no qualms about the sale of his birthright, he added, "I am quite content that way as long as a few knew that certain thoughts and actions have emanated from me. Curious, for at bottom, I am probably an ex-hibitionist. Yet I have taught myself to work from behind and others [his typist's variant of "another's"] façade."

When Swope did get public acknowledgment for something Baruch did it was usually because Baruch, who once called Swope "the man least appreciated by his fellows," preferred it thus. That same year a biography of Baruch, *The Park Bench Statesman*, was published. Neither Swope nor Baruch liked it very much, but still it was a hard-cover book about their favorite subject. Accordingly, Swope, as spokesman for "a group of friends" of Baruch's, bought ten thousand copies, for distribution to school and college libraries. The entire bill for this generous dissemination of literature was footed by Baruch. Similarly, after the magazine *The Churchman* celebrated its one hundred and fortieth anniversary in 1944 with a dinner in Baruch's honor at the Waldorf (Swope recruited the principal speakers and served as toastmaster), Swope arranged for its editor to send out fifteen thousand reprints of a booklet, "The Churchman Award Dinner," the text of which consisted mainly of eulogies about Baruch. The booklets, too, went to school and college libraries, and the bill went to Baruch.

Resigned though he was to letting Baruch bask in most of the glory that rewarded their joint efforts, Swope was determined to get his proper reward in one niche of history that meant much to him—Baruch's obituary in the New York *Times*. When a man is as famous, and has lived as long, as Baruch, his obituary is carefully prepared and periodically revised. In the summer of 1948 a *Times* man assigned to bringing Baruch's obit up to date got in touch, naturally enough, with Swope and let Swope see proofs of the text already set up in type.

Swope was shocked. "The funny part of the Baruch obituary," he confided to himself, "is that, after thirty-five years, there isn't a single reference to me." Swope told the *Times* man that the obit was all right, up to a point, but that "it would achieve more interest if it were to include certain excerpts from the various significant speeches he has made. There comes to my mind now the speech at the United Nations, on 14 June, 1946. . . . Out of these you can weave his political and social philosophy. In them you will find such phrases as: 'Cold war'; and 'Every man has the right to his own opinion, but no man has a right. . . .' " Swope also called Arthur Krock's attention to the obituary's deficiencies. Krock arranged for a paragraph to be inserted about Swope, in which Baruch and Swope were referred to as a close-knit, high-level team comparable to President Wilson and Colonel House.*

Human beings who become as closely knit as Swope and Baruch were for so long are bound to have misunderstandings. The two men were no exception. In Margaret Coit's *Mr. Baruch* she describes as "what must be one of the most remarkable letters of the kind ever written" a communication Swope sent to Baruch on April 22, 1931, which went in part:

> I am worried over our relations. I find that little wrongs . . . are of less importance than the preservation of a friendship in which affection is engaged and the qualities of respect and admiration are present.
>
> For fifteen years we have worked much . . . played a little; quarreled occasionally and fought frequently, but always side by side. . . . For our strengths we had admiration. . . . For our shortcomings we had sympathy. . . .

* Between Swope's death and Baruch's, the obituary was once again revised, and Swope's role in the Baruch drama was cut to less than one sentence.

"Forsake not an old friend, for the new is not comparable to him." . . . Because I feel all this deeply, I am writing frankly. It is the only way I know.

What had brought on this letter—a not at all remarkable one for Swope, incidentally, but merely a fairish example of his loving-petulant style—was his suspicion that Baruch had "backed and filled" and "tried to duck away from" an agreement to help him buy a newspaper. Swope's expression of concern about their friendship was mailed to New York, and the gist of it was relayed to Baruch, in South Carolina, by a secretary. Baruch at once sent a wire that said, in part, ". . . NOTHING COULD REPLACE THE COMFORT AND DELIGHT OF MY DEEPLY AFFECTIONATE FRIENDSHIP FOR YOU AND I WAS HEART AND MIND SICK STOP PLEASE NEVER QUESTION THE QUALITY OF MY FRIENDSHIP STOP I WOULD NOT YOURS AND ANYTHING I COULD DO TO HELP YOU OR YOURS OR MAKE THEM HAPPY WILL ALWAYS GIVE ME PLEASURE. . . ."

Swope wired back: "TOUCHED BY WARMTH AND BEAUTY YOUR WIRE. IT IS SO FINE A THING TO BE BOUND BY AFFECTION THAT ANGUISH ALMOST ALWAYS FOLLOWS ITS DEFECTIONS. I KNOW HOW SINCERE IS YOUR MEANING AND YOU KNOW WITHOUT EXPRESSION HOW DEEP MY SENTIMENTS ARE. BOTH OF US ARE SUBJECT TO A TENSE-NESS WHICH OCCASIONALLY FLARES UP MEANINGLESSLY. . . ." But less than a week later Swope would note diarially, about Baruch, "Did not notify me that Charlie Michelson told him Washington *Post* was for sale. On Saturday, May 2nd, did not notify me that Sarnoff called him up and told him about the *Post*. I had to call Baruch on my own. This might have been so important a matter to me that he should have told me about it, even if he had been pledged to secrecy, which was not the case."

Swope's files bulged with such comments about Baruch: "He said he would have difficulty putting me on his pay roll as advisor, first saying it was not deductible, and then that he didn't want to reveal the fact, yet he had Hugh Johnson on for several years." . . . "He wouldn't come down to my house, but he was able to go to [Henry] Luce's." . . . "He never displayed my photo-graph in his house." * . . . "He has several times been lacking in

---

* In Baruch's New York apartment he had a study lined with original caricatures of himself. The only photographs amid this gallery were two of Swope. One was inscribed, "To America's first citizen from America's latest."

personal courtesy. . . . He asked me to go to Saratoga with him and then said he had no room for me. This is almost studied." . . . "He calls me at will but does not recompense." . . . And, on April 21, 1947, when Swope was sixty-five: "Had I but served myself with half the zeal I served B., I would not, in my age, be naked to my enemies."

In spite of it all, Swope clung to Baruch, because, as Swope once told Krock, "He has great qualities which outweigh his small ones," and perhaps also because one cannot easily shake a lifelong habit. "We must always remember that each of us possesses a dual personality," Swope wrote Baruch in April 1953—"(1) that which we actually are; and (2) which the public believes us to be. Due consideration should be given to preserving, building up and protecting both images."

Swope often talked about some day writing Baruch's biography, though the chances were that even had he embarked on the project, he would never have finished it. Nor would it—nor *could* it, in the singular relationship the two big men enjoyed—have accurately reflected Swope's judgment of Baruch. Baruch was always on the lookout for a suitable biographer and for a while had Marquis James on his string. James produced a manuscript that was never published. In 1950 Margaret Coit won the Pulitzer Prize for her biography of John C. Calhoun. Calhoun was a South Carolinian, and Miss Coit was a South Carolinian, and Baruch's claim to be *the* South Carolinian was contestable, probably, only by James Byrnes.

Swope showed Baruch the Coit book and said, *"There's* your girl!" The author duly came to New York and spent several years on Baruch's payroll, working in his office. (Oddly, Swope, probably the best living source on Baruch, proved all but inaccessible to her; after many efforts, she succeeded in getting just one not terribly revealing interview with him.) When Miss Coit had finished the first draft of her manuscript, Baruch didn't like it—he later changed his mind—and he refused her permission to quote directly from his papers. Instead, he embarked swiftly and competitively on a two-volume autobiography, which he had written for him, for the most part, by Samuel Lubell and another assistant, Harold Epstein. Swope wasn't called in until the first volume was completed, but it evidently disturbed Baruch that Swope's participation in the project was so limited; he paid him twenty-five hundred dollars to read the manuscript and presented him with an additional twenty-five hundred that came in from newspaper serialization rights.

In Swope's last years Baruch had less and less occasion to call on him for help. The older man had Lubell and Epstein to write speeches for him, and Swope, as a rule, was only asked to look these over once they'd been prepared. (He achieved one minor triumph by scornfully pointing out to Epstein, when he brought around a speech Baruch was about to make, that a quotation Baruch planned to ascribe to Woodrow Wilson had been swiped by Wilson from Shakespeare.) Baruch said to the end that Swope was the best friend he ever had, and this was doubtless true. It was no less true that Baruch was probably the best friend Swope ever had. But whether either man, each so egocentric, could ever carry on a friendship in the ordinary sense of the word was debatable. They were unquestionably dependent on each other, and whatever each accomplished would have been of slighter stature but for the aid the other rendered. They were meant for each other.

On the day Swope died he received a request from an advertising agency, which hoped he could prevail upon Baruch to do a one-minute television and radio spot about the contributions of American oil men to the welfare of the nation. Swope never saw this last plea to serve as liege man to his chosen lord. When Swope died in a hospital, early that same afternoon, unexpectedly, Baruch was informed by phone a few minutes later, and he said to Epstein, "Well, Herbert checked out." Epstein misunderstood; he thought Baruch meant that Swope had recovered and left the hospital. "That's good," Epstein said. "No, no!" cried Baruch. "He's slipped away! He's *gone!*" A few minutes later he sat down and wrote to Margaret Swope, "I feel quite alone, for he was the closest to me of all in the world." And subsequently Baruch sometimes seemed quite lost without his Swope to guide him, to goad him, to worry him and worry over him, and to love and hate him all at once in that curious, scrambled, tangled emotional fashion that was his. Once, after Swope was gone, Baruch was meditating about a speech someone had written for him to give. "God damn it!" he exclaimed. "If Swope were alive he'd needle these guys and get this thing in the papers for me!"

410

20

It was symptomatic of the spirited individualism in the Swope household that while Margaret Swope thought horses were the "stupidest, bloodiest animals in the world," to her husband, though he was no particular advocate of their intelligence, horses were irresistible. For a book called *American Race Horses of 1936*, which Alfred G. Vanderbilt published, Swope wrote a foreword that began:

> Racing—what a wealth of memories it conjures up; what hopes; what pride; what satisfaction. No other sport lends itself so wholly to the vindication of the ego—and that means much in these days of neuroses and psychoses. Dropping the Freudian terminology, I mean that there is a great mental fillip in selecting a horse to win a race and have your judgment confirmed by a victory. You don't have to bet on him to obtain this glow of self-esteem. You need only pass an opinion. But a winning wager helps that vindication. You run the race; you win it; you ride the horse; you train it. There is a complete identification, and you get a mental catharsis which should go far toward relieving the nervous strain Americans are supposed to suffer from.

And in a terse second paragraph he added, "Get a horse is the cure. Or go to see a horse race. That's a cure for many ills."

Swope often found himself in disagreement with other guardians of the national health who considered betting to be about as tonic as the plague. When he was a young reporter, in 1910, the New York race tracks were unaccommodatingly shut down for a couple of years, thanks to the efforts of do-gooders who believed that they offered sordid opportunities for working men to squan-

411

der their wages and who omitted to reflect that man's ingenuity has always somehow devised alternatives to savings banks. What was more, Swope contended, people who disapproved of betting on horse races were overquick to blame this agreeable pastime for all the follies of society. "The time has come to call a halt on every absconder, embezzler or other type of thief who falsely blames his downfall on the races," he declared in 1936. "The papers have printed a story to the effect that a lawyer's shortage of his client of more than $500,000 was explained on the grounds that he had lost money at the races. I have had investigations made and find that this man is not known on the New York courses. He owns no horses, nor is he known to any of the bookmakers. Most of the time money claimed to have been lost in this manner has gone in other ways. I am tired of having every misstep laid on a fine sport."

Until the 1930s racing in New York was largely controlled, under a tight rein, by the Jockey Club, a self-perpetuating association with a membership then limited to fifty and with vacancies occurring, as a rule, only upon death. The club members were about the only men around who really cared about raising the standards of horse racing. They worked hard at it, in a leisurely, gentlemanly way, but they had the reputation of being snobbish, and they tended to frown upon gambling. The Jockey Club, Swope once declared, "lived in a fanciful world in which it rose above such a mundane practice."

The Jockey Club was principally concerned with improving the breed of thoroughbred horses. New York State, on the other hand, was interested in improving its revenues, and to secure a portion of the money that everybody knew would be bet on horses every year, whether or not anybody approved of the practice, seemed an enticing prospect. In 1934, accordingly, while Herbert Lehman was Governor, the New York legislature passed a bill authorizing betting at race tracks and at the same time instructed the State Secretary, Edward J. Flynn, to appoint a three-man Racing Commission to watch out for the state's interests. There had been such a commission before, but it had had few responsibilities and little power. The Jockey Club had paid it no more heed than a horse might pay a house fly.

The new commission had more sting. The Jockey Club, the state decreed, could continue to control stud books and breeding records, and—for a while at least—to license trainers, jockeys, and owners, but its jurisdiction was restricted. It could no longer arbitrarily revoke licenses, for instance, on its own, but had instead to have a commissioner present and concurring. Even before the law was enacted Swope was mentioned as an ideal choice for chairman of the commission. Damon Runyon expressed the hope that Swope, "one of the most intelligent gentlemen in this country, or any other country," could be induced to accept the appointment, adding that "his name would give the public more confidence in racing than it has had in a long time."

Immediately after the racing bill was passed and was signed by the Governor, Swope was appointed to the commission, along with the architect John Sloan, who had designed race tracks, and John Hay Whitney, then, at twenty-nine, the youngest member of the Jockey Club. It was traditional for the club to be represented on the commission, and Whitney was regarded in non-Jockey Club circles as perhaps the least stuffy member of that group. In Jockey Club circles it was thought that, as a friend of Swope's and a racing-stable owner with an impeccable heritage, Whitney was in a good position to serve as a safe and sure bridge between the sedate old order of things and the conceivably pyrotechnic new order.

The commissioners were sworn in on May 1, 1934, and Swope at once issued a statement calculated to reassure all hands:

> . . . I think that, in a word, we can reduce our conception of duty to one phrase: "The public." Particularly are we glad to do a job for the sport under non-political conditions. Under the law, the Racing Commission has become vitalized, has become a factor of major importance. So far as I can speak for the other members of the Commission, our purpose will be to function so as not to be in dissonance with the Jockey Club. . . .

Within a year, however, the legislature was to please Swope and displease the Jockey Club by further limiting that organization's authority. This time the commission was empowered exclusively to set dates and specify places for race meetings, as well as to approve all officials anybody else appointed to conduct races. Among other new privileges, the commission got to fix admission charges to tracks.

Swope, thereby winning wide acclaim for gallantry, at once reduced the charge for women from $2.00 to $1.75 and raised it for men from $2.00 to $2.50. He also got women licensed as

413

trainers, and the second one to become eligible gladdened him by buying his old horse Lativich, now aged ten and graying, who had had a hard time of it since shedding Swope's colors, having at one point changed hands, humiliatingly, to square an unpaid feed bill. Perhaps inspired by Swope's elevation to commissioner, Lativich finished in the money seventeen times in twenty-five races he ran in 1936.

In 1934 horse racing was still more of a sport than a business. Its contribution to the state's treasury that year was a mere three hundred thousand dollars. But the future looked bright. The bill that legalized betting at the tracks had also authorized parimutuel machines, the installation of which would presumably increase the volume of betting and increase the state's percentage of the handle. The only hitch was that the legislature declared that parimutuels would have to be sanctioned by an amendment to the state constitution, ratified by the electorate in a referendum. Swope was considered comical when he predicted, in 1937, that the introduction of parimutuels might bring the state as much as twelve million dollars a year. He would probably have been considered daft had he dared predict that New York would within a generation get from horse racing one hundred million dollars a year.

The racing commissioners were unpaid, but they had enough of a budget to hire a small staff. Swope put several former *World* employees on the commission payroll at one time or another, among them Alex Schlosser, George F. T. Ryall, and John F. Shevlin, who had joined the newspaper in 1928 as a copy boy, had become a personal assistant to the executive editor, and remained a faithful adjutant throughout Swope's life. Another ex-*World* copy boy who partook of Swope's patronage was Anthony Zito, who under the name of Toney Betts became a *Daily Mirror* horse-race specialist. He had gone to the *World*, as a teen-ager, upon being expelled from school for devoting too much time to betting. After reaching adulthood Betts joined Swope and Baruch in Swope's box at a race track one day and later told his *Mirror* readers, reverently, "You have the feeling you are in the presence of great Americans like Thomas Jefferson and Benjamin Franklin." He did not disclose which he thought was like which.

Still another onetime reporter who worked for the commission was Eugene Campbell, who'd been on the *Sun*. Swope gave him a job when he was down and out. It was a measure of the devotion that Swope's servitors had for him that Campbell once expressed the hope that his benefactor would some day call on *him* for a favor—"preferably in the middle of the night and with a howling blizzard outside."

The chief salaried administrator of the commission was its steward. For that post Swope and his associates picked Marshall Cassidy, who had an impressive racing background. His father Mars had been a trotting-horse breeder and a starter, and his brother George and he had both gone into starting, too. It was not easy for Marshall Cassidy to work with Swope. Accustomed to race-track hours, the steward normally arose at four-thirty in the morning, and he never lay abed after five. Swope, who as far as Cassidy's routine was concerned might just as well have been on the other side of the International Date Line, would often phone him at six or seven in the evening and suggest that they hold a business session later on that night—at, say, ten or eleven.

Cassidy considered himself a professional racing administrator, utterly detached from politics. When Swope, who at the start of his tenure as a commissioner had provoked the New York Democrats by putting nonpolitical ex-newspapermen on his staff instead of party hacks, remarked pleasantly to Cassidy one day that it might be nice if his subordinates, like the employees of other New York commissions, contributed a day's pay a year to the coffers of the state Democratic organization, Cassidy got so angry the two men almost came to blows. Cassidy, moreover, thought it unwise for racing administrators, salaried or unsalaried, to bet on horse races. He himself had no difficulty observing that policy, for he had stopped betting eighteen years earlier, when, at Pimlico, down to his last twenty dollars, he was given a tip on the final race of the day by a compassionate assistant starter and won eight hundred dollars. Then he quit for good. He thought that while Swope was Racing Commissioner he should quit, too, at least temporarily.

Swope was of another mind. He pointed out to Cassidy and to others who voiced concern that there had never been anything furtive about his betting, that his new job did not provide him with any way of affecting the outcome of a race or the odds on a horse, and that as a commissioner he was privy to no more inside information than he'd had as a layman. (Swope knew everybody of consequence in racing, and he got a lot of tips. He was always looking for more. Before a race he would go to the paddock and talk to owners and jockeys and trainers and would return to his box with such a vast accumulation of advice that, in the view of one professional gambler who often saw him at the races, the information canceled itself out. "You can only have a certain amount of important facts," the man said. "Otherwise it is too difficult to bet properly.")

Furthermore, Swope asserted, dredging from the vast storehouse of his memory the kind of inside information he loved to hoard and bring to light when the occasion demanded, was it not true that George Washington had been wont to put as much as five hundred dollars on a single horse? Swope would allude to Washington so movingly that he made it sound almost unpatriotic *not* to bet on the races. The story went around that Swope asked a dozen men whose opinions he respected whether they thought it was proper for him, as a commissioner, to continue to gamble on horse races. They all replied, with varying degrees of emphasis, that they thought it would be prudent for him to abstain. Then he asked a thirteenth man, who said he could see nothing wrong in it at all. Thus reassuringly confirmed in his own judgment of the matter, Swope went merrily on his plunging way.

Swope's penchant for gambling, which he considered a natural appetite of man no more deserving of censure than eating or sex, became a public issue in the spring of 1937. The New York legislature had passed a bill permitting betting at dog-racing tracks, and while Governor Lehman was making up his mind whether to sign it or not (he vetoed it), there was a good deal of agitation. The horse-racing interests, not to mention the motion-picture-theater interests, were against the bill; Swope said that if the dog-racing act went into effect, it would "not only eventually destroy that sport, but horse-racing as well." A proponent of the bill was Martin W. Littleton, the District Attorney of Nassau County, on Long Island, where a dog track was operating. In seeking to denigrate his opposition, Littleton accused Swope of being a gambler and, what was even naughtier, of being a shameless sponsor of an illegal lottery.

The charge was true, but Swope couldn't have cared less. In this instance he felt strongly that the end justified the means, because the lottery in question was one called the Hospital Relief Futurity Sweepstakes, which was held annually, and somewhat clandestinely, for the benefit of the New York Infirmary for

Women and Children. Thousands of chances had been sold each year since 1932, and the lucky winners drew horses entered in the Futurity Stakes at Belmont Park. The perennial president of the hospital, Mrs. Frank A. Vanderlip, was not a race-track sort, but on her board of directors were such sports-minded women as Mrs. Charles S. Payson, Mrs. Dodge Sloane, Mrs. Harold E. Talbott, and Mrs. Cornelius Vanderbilt Whitney.

Mrs. Talbott was the driving force behind the lottery. As Peggy Thayer, the strikingly attractive daughter of the Pennsylvania judge who'd gone down on the *Titanic,* she had met the Swopes in 1919, while she was visiting the Joshua Cosdens at Saratoga, and she became a Swope protegé. She followed Swope around like a pet puppy and often accompanied him to the races; when he was a delegate to the 1932 Democratic convention he arranged for her to attend, too, obtaining for her some floor credentials that identified her as an observer from the Virgin Islands.

The Hospital Sweepstakes were small stuff compared to their Irish prototype—first prize was only forty or fifty thousand dollars—but in the seventeen years that Mrs. Talbott conducted her charitable lottery she raised more than a million dollars for the New York Infirmary. Since the whole operation had to be *sub rosa,* and since she didn't want to get the hospital in unnecessary trouble if anything went wrong, she would resign from its board each year before starting to sell her chances and would then accept re-election by her grateful fellow directors when she turned up a few months later with a pile of money.

Swope was her chief counselor. To begin with, he introduced her to high-ranking editors of all the New York papers. Each year after that, at lottery time, Mrs. Talbott would stop in at the newspaper offices and beg prettily to have not a word printed about her activities. This was so refreshing a change from the approach of most society women on philanthropic missions that the papers gladly obliged, and Mrs. Talbott exuded such charm that after a while she had a good many newspapermen not only conspiring with her but selling chances for her.

Word of her kindhearted transgressions would occasionally leak out nonetheless, and in 1940 she was called before a Senate investigating committee in Washington. (Harry Hopkins had been selling tickets for her, at Swope's urging, and when one secretary in a government agency drew a winning number, some

417

less fortunate ticket-holding bureaucrats who'd bought their chances from Republicans had aired their jealous complaints.) Young and handsome, her eyes brimming with repentant tears, Mrs. Talbott cast such a spell over the Senators confronting her that after some gruff-uncle throat-clearing all they did was to ask her to promise not to sell lottery tickets any more. She promised not to, at least not until the following year, and then, observing the solons' relief when she dried her eyes and managed a wan smile, she added that if she *did* find herself committing the crime again she hoped they'd all sell some chances for her.

It is a federal offense to use the mails in the conduct of a lottery, and Swope was a big help to Mrs. Talbott in recruiting couriers who, in their travels here and there across the country, would carry chances for her and carry back the proceeds of their sales. (During the Second World War, when gas rationing was in effect, Mrs. Talbott would travel herself, by subway, down to Wall Street, where many of her most faithful customers had their offices, with a suitcase full of tickets, and would ride the subway back uptown a few hours later with seven or eight thousand dollars in cash in her bag.) Mrs. Talbott's success was her undoing. The underworld learned of what was going on and began to muscle in on her. Mobsters would buy up large batches of her chances, would sell them, and would simply keep the money, aware that they were in no danger of being sued by the proprietors of a venture that was itself illicit.

When Senator Estes Kefauver's investigating committee began poking into organized crime in 1949, Mrs. Talbott acceded to Swope's advice that perhaps the time had come for her to stop. Her husband had become finance chairman of the Republican National Committee, and any attention focused on her form of fund-raising might have been embarrassing for his. Not long after she regretfully abandoned her sweepstakes, Mrs. Talbott was dancing with Senator Kefauver one night at a party in Washington. He hadn't caught her name, but he was pleased when she complimented him on the high-principled work his committee was doing. "The only trouble is you've put me out of business," she added, pouting. "I have? What's your business?" asked the Senator. "I ran an illegal sweepstakes," Mrs. Talbott said. Kefauver gulped, missed a step or two, and, trying to switch the conversation to a topic less potentially incriminating, said, "Is your husband here, Ma'am?" "No, he's out of town," she said.

"What does *he* do?" asked Kefauver. "He's raising money to try to defeat you," she replied, with saucy candor that Swope would have applauded.

Swope hugely enjoyed being a Racing Commissioner. At the tracks he would stroll around the paddock or clubhouse or grandstand waving benignly to this trainer, warmly hailing that stablehand, responding with a courtly wave to cries of "How are you, Commissioner?" There were so many outstretched hands to clasp it sometimes took him thirty minutes or so to cover a distance that an unknown punter could have made in five. (On occasion, when Swope was late getting under way to a track and wanted to be there for the first race, he would telephone ahead and ask to have its start delayed until his arrival.)

While Swope and his fellow commissioners waited for the referendum that, if successful, would bring parimutuels to New York, they busied themselves instituting a series of reforms to make the sport more upright than it had previously been and more pleasurable for its watching and wagering followers. Electrical gates were introduced to make starts more equitable and electric-eye cameras to take the guesswork out of judging finishes. Human judges were still around, but now they were required to pass eye tests, to which they had not before had to submit. Jockeys had to take physical examinations before they could ride. Horses were given urine tests and saliva tests, and a commission laboratory was set up as a further deterrent to tampering with animals. The run-of-the-mill grandstand spectators, who understandably suffered now and then from dried lips and parched throats, were provided with drinking fountains. They even got loud-speakers and announcers, so they could find out how the races they had come to see were progressing. The list of innovations went on and on, the crudities that had once been associated with the sport became more and more refined, and the credit belonged in great measure to Swope, who, his fellow commissioner Whitney would later observe, "established many fine principles and fought the good fight for racing in a way nobody else could have."

On Election Day of 1939, two months after Germany invaded Poland, the voters of New York finally got their chance to speak out on parimutuels. By a majority of more than two to one they emphatically endorsed the installation of the machines at race tracks, over the loud opposition of, among others, Mayor La-Guardia of New York City, who thought gamblers were punks and that gambling was punk, too. On April 15, 1940, the first two-dollar ticket ever sold at a New York race track exchanged hands at Jamaica, Long Island. When the total money bet that entire spring day had been added up, it came to $821,946. Swope telephoned Governor Lehman after the last race to announce, triumphantly, "The results of the first day insured a gigantic success for the new system."

It was ironically indicative of the dissimilarity between Swope and his brother that at the very moment the commissioner was being applauded at the Jamaica track for his accomplishment, in another part of that suburb LaGuardia was acclaiming Gerard Swope, then chairman of the New York City Housing Authority, at a cornerstone laying for a $2,325,000 housing project. The Mayor made no comparisons by name, but he did say, "There are two public events in Jamaica today. This is one. The other is at the race track, where the State for the first time is taking an ante from gamblers. This is promise; the other is regret. This is giving something to the people; the other is taking something from the people that they can't afford to lose. I don't believe that the people should be encouraged to spend money needed for food, clothing, and housing. I don't think that gambling is going to be successful in a progressive, enlightened state like New York." LaGuardia couldn't have been more wrong, but then, as he himself often put it, when he made a mistake it was a beaut.

Swope had been appointed to the commission, in 1934, for a six-year term. When the legislature put the final stamp of approval on parimutuels in the winter of 1940 it also decreed that Racing Commissioners should thenceforth be appointed by the Governor and confirmed by the Senate. The legislature was in recess that May, when Swope's term ran out, and the interim appointment that Lehman gave him then would, everybody knew, last only until the beginning of 1941, when he would have to be reappointed for another regular term. Now, the antigambling forces in the state saw a chance to make Swope squirm. The alarm was sounded by the Senate's majority leader, Joe R. Hanley, an upstate Republican who had been both a jockey and a clergyman in earlier days, but on whom sermons had had a more lingering impact than stretch runs. The newspapers liked to call him "Holy Joe." Hanley announced that Swope's retention of his commissionership was by no means certain. "I would absolutely refuse to confirm the appointment of anyone who is a persistent bettor at the races," he declared.

Swope prepared a memorandum that summer, ostensibly on behalf of all three commissioners, that stated his viewpoint. "The whole theory upon which the turf rests is honesty and good faith," he declared. But the following January the Senate Finance Committee, unmoved by his words, sent eighteen out of nineteen gubernatorial appointments along to its parent body, recommending confirmation. The exception was Swope. The sports pages of the New York City papers, which at relatively tranquil moments were not always effusively cordial to Swope, now rose shrilly to his defense. Swope himself interrupted a visit to Florida to go to Albany and present himself before the balky committee. He carried the day. Although he did not retreat from his stand that he had as much right to bet as anyone else, he was unanimously confirmed, and, just before the Senate took the telltale vote, Hanley paid him one of those glowing tributes that politicians often utter when they know they're outvoted.

Victorious, Swope moved the commission's headquarters from a state office building far downtown in New York, an inconveniently long journey from his midtown haunts, to a handier location at Fifth Avenue and Fifty-eighth Street, which doubled as his own office. He filled the premises with so many pictures of race horses that one British visitor who came to see him on nonracing business thought, while sitting in an anteroom and listening to the betting talk that filtered through a closed door, that he'd got the address wrong and had wandered inadvertently into a bookie joint.

Swope was on the best of terms with most of the country's bookmakers, although he sometimes had disputes with them about the precise terms of bets he had made with them, or that Miss Millar had on his behalf. (The 1940 parimutuel law had outlawed bookies from the race tracks, but Swope kept hoping that a few of them could be reinstated there—there was ample precedent; the British sanctioned both systems of betting—and he continued to bet with them as well as through the machines. A big bettor can often obtain superior odds from a bookie; when a large amount of money is dropped into a parimutuel pool, this automatically depresses the odds on the horse concerned.) One aspect of horse racing that disturbed many people who crusaded against the sport

421

was that bookmakers and other unsavory characters were believed to figure in the ownership of certain tracks. In the 1930s, for instance, Frank Erickson had a 20 per cent interest in Tropical Park, in Florida. There were other shareholders of dubious repute there, and because of them Tropical had acquired the nickname of the "Racket Track." In 1941 the Florida State Racing Commission refused to grant an operating license to Erickson and his associates, so they put their stock up for sale. Swope had always hankered after his own race track, and he soon joined a syndicate —it included A. Charles Schwartz and three American Totalisator Company men, Harry Straus and the brothers Charles and Gurnee Munn—that bought Tropical. He became Chairman of the Board. But like a child with a bright new toy, he wearied of the enterprise, and in 1950 he sold out—shortly before a boom in Florida racing that, had he hung on, would have nicely shored up the sagging finances of his last years.

While war clouds were building up over Europe there was concurrent *sturm und drang* at the summit of the Racing Commission. John Sloan was, like Swope, a Democrat, but political affinity proved to be just about all they had in common. Their main point of difference was Sloan's contention that Swope was trying to turn the commission into a one-man show; the chairman would issue statements, the architect complained, without even consulting his fellow members. But the two men tilted no less fiercely over petty matters. The commission had a car and chauffeur assigned to it by the state; Sloan and Swope never could agree on who should get to use the car and in what circumstances. (Whitney had plenty of transportation of his own and kept out of the squabble.) They would exchange curt, stiff notes, addressing each other at such times, although they were theoretically on a first-name basis, as "Sir" or "Commissioner."

Not long before Pearl Harbor, Cassidy left the commission to become the chief full-time executive of the Jockey Club—a defection of sorts, to Swope's way of thinking, into the enemy camp. When the United States went to war there was much talk about the extent to which racing, as well as other sports, should be allowed to continue. Swope's immediate reaction was that racing should go on unbridled. In a statement he issued December 8, 1941, while the nation was still reeling from the Japanese attack, he restated his cathartic view of the sport. He said that sports in general might be more important during the war than ever before, since they constituted a safety valve for the country's tensions, and that horse racing was the best safety valve of all, because it offered betting as a relaxing concomitant. "In time of stress heavy-pressure betting and similar forms of diversion gain an appeal," he said. It was rumored that Swope would be designated a national czar of horse racing to preside over all American tracks during the time of crisis, but the closest he got to that was to become chairman of the executive committee of the Turf Committee of America, which was established in the spring of 1942 by the National Association of State Racing Commissioners and which before the war ended raised seventeen million dollars for Army and Navy Relief by holding special meets at various tracks.

Sloan resigned from the commission early in the war, and then Whitney went off to join the Air Force. They were replaced by David Dows, the sheriff of Nassau County, and Ashley Trimble Cole, a corporation lawyer. Swope was rarely in accord with either of them. "Dows appointed to Commission to get me," he reflected in a memorandum sometime afterward. "He did. Jockey Club knew this; probably arranged it. Why didn't J.H.W. [Whitney] tip me off to help smash conspiracy? Cole was in on play. . . ." But for a time Swope stayed on, and it was a tribute to his forcefulness that he, a Democrat, was retained in this appointive post by the Republican Governor of New York, Thomas E. Dewey.

The new triumvirate disagreed on, among many other things, the desirability of off-track betting. Swope was an early and a perennial advocate of this scheme. As long as people who couldn't get to a track wished to bet, he argued, they *would* bet, and the state might as well establish kiosks at which they could indulge themselves and from which the state could derive more income. (Twenty years after his initial advocacy of the scheme, the voters of New York caught up with him and endorsed it thumpingly in a statewide referendum.) "The greatest factor against legalized off-track betting is political opposition," Swope once said. "Certain politicians think that they can get right with God by opposing what they think is sin. But betting is not sin. Mass betting is merely an extension of degree, not a new invention. However, hypocrisy is a dearly loved American virtue." Cole, like many others who did not consider themselves hypocritical but who just happened to dislike off-track betting, was testifying one time in opposition to it, and he could not resist throwing in what sounded like a dig at Swope. He was not against gambling, Cole said; he used to do a lot of it at the tracks himself—*before* he became a commissioner.

It was increasingly frustrating to Swope to have to deal with two fellow commissioners who not only had dissimilar opinions but, in a showdown, could overrule him. Here was he, of whom the *Thoroughbred Record* had said in 1943, "Herbert Bayard Swope has become almost as familiar an institution in racing as the Kentucky Derby"; and here, holding the whip hand over him, were two tyros who had never even been accorded the institutional stature of a claiming race. There were other irritants. Swope had been unsalaried all along, but the state of New York began to question some of his expenses—principally the massive charges he ran up on the commission's telephones. By the end of 1944 Swope had had enough, and he announced his retirement from the commission, two years before his term expired. It turned out to be a well-timed decision, for just three days after his announcement the Federal government shut down all horse racing for the remainder of the war.

Swope accomplished his primary objective as a Racing Commissioner. He loosened the grip of the men who had formerly overseen the sport, and he gave the public that supported it more of a voice in controlling it. But though many two-dollar bettors rightly viewed him as their champion, and though Bill Corum extolled him as "the human Man O'War," he was never quite forgiven for his heresy by the aristocrats he had unhorsed.

A court ruling in 1951, which further restricted the Jockey Club's authority, added more fuel to the fire Swope had lit under the club. The nominal protagonist in this litigious episode was Jule Fink, an uncommonly successful bettor and horseowner who had irked the Jockey Club and its secretary Cassidy. Fink, born in Poland in 1913, grew up in London and then accompanied his family to Cincinnati, where his father ran a barbershop. The son began to study racing charts and became expert at handicapping horses. He formed a betting syndicate with four Cincinnati friends. Damon Runyon called them the Speed Boys, because they usually backed horses that broke fast from the starting gate.

The Speed Boys came to New York for the first time in 1944.

By then, Fink had done well enough to acquire a string of horses, and the Jockey Club gave him an owner's license. He fell into the pleasant habit of sitting at the races with Swope, or Swope and Baruch, or, when they were not present, using Swope's box to entertain a couple of visiting Speed Boys. In Swope's absence, too, Fink would make bets for him—though, Fink said later, on a modest scale; he doubted he had ever won more than five thousand dollars for Swope in any single year. "He is a good man with a horse," Swope told Jock Whitney in 1947. "I have watched him. He knows as much about the value of speed and its development as anybody I have ever seen."

Success begets envy, and envy begets gossip. Fink was the subject of a good deal of speculative conversation, by no means all of it flattering. To many members of the horse-racing set, the very existence of a man who consistently seemed to make large sums of money betting on races—who, indeed, seemed to earn a comfortable living at it—was insufferable. A number of discreditable stories about him were widely circulated. One had to do with three of his horses, none of which had ever shown much before, winning at a single track in a single afternoon, and all, because of their previous lackluster records, coming in at handsome prices. Another tale was that Fink consorted with bookmakers—a hardly startling accusation in the horse-racing business.

When Fink asked to have his owner's license renewed in New York in 1949, the Jockey Club turned him down. This rebuke was interpreted by some as an indirect slap at Swope, for all the race-track habitués knew how close Fink and he had become. Fink fought the decision all the way up to the State Court of Appeals, which ruled against the club, on the ground that the legislature had no right to delegate its licensing powers to a private group. The Racing Commission was thenceforth to do the licensing, and the Jockey Club found its authority more circumscribed than ever. Swope didn't smooth things over any, as far as his own involvement was concerned, by publicly hailing the Court of Appeals' verdict as the "greatest blow ever delivered to the Jockey Club's dominance of racing in New York State."

The Racing Commission, under Ashley Cole's chairmanship, never did get around to restoring Fink to good standing, and this was thought to be in part, at least, further vengeance upon Swope, who had been a character witness for Fink in court. (Baruch had written a letter on his behalf.) Up until a year before his death

Swope kept trying to get Fink restored to good standing, but he never succeeded. And after Swope died, the old guard of racing continued to punish him for having nettled it while he was alive. The box Swope had had at Belmont Park for thirty years, his widow was informed, would have to be taken away and given to someone on a waiting list. The Swope family pointed out, unavailingly, that upon the death of another boxholder his *mistress* had been allowed to keep his seats, and that a widow with forty-six years of marriage to her credit would seem to merit at least equal treatment.

After Swope's death, when a new racing structure was unveiled at Aqueduct, one of its features was a clubhouse mural depicting seventy-eight men and women who had been prominent in the history of New York racing from 1890 on. Swope, the most consequential commissioner the state ever had, and quite apart from that a man who had been a flashy ornament of racing for half a century, was left out of the picture. (So was Colonel Bradley, who had a celebrated racing stable but also ran a celebrated gambling casino.) It was a cruel, necropsic jab. True, the flags at Belmont Park had been lowered to half-mast when Swope died, but his friends kept hoping his favorite sport might find it possible to pay him some less ephemeral tribute. Baruch was so provoked when none was forthcoming that he self-sacrificially suggested that the only horse race ever named in honor of a living man, a handicap at Saratoga, be rechristened, and that the name of Herbert Bayard Swope be substituted for that of Bernard Baruch. But nobody took him up on it.

21

Back in 1923, when Baruch had a racing stable, Swope thought it would be nice to get his friend into the Turf and Field Club, which had its own restricted enclosures at the big New York tracks and which had a restricted membership policy, too. After Swope ascertained that the club would admit Baruch, Baruch said he was sorry but he wasn't interested. His position was that if most Jews were not considered welcome, he did not wish to be an exception; he felt—using a cliché he was fond of—that all men should be equal on the turf as well as under it. The next thing anyone knew, Swope turned up as a member of the Turf and Field. When he was asked why, in the light of Baruch's attitude, he had taken this seemingly expedient step, he replied, "I can fight this thing better from the inside."

Up to the advent of Nazism there had seemed to be no particular reason for Swope to pay serious attention to his origin. True, *others* might pay attention.* He was in the customary awkward spot of Jews in America who like to be thought of as nothing at all; they can rarely achieve this state of social weightlessness because, more often than not, they are expected by non-Jews to give evidence of Jewishness and by Jews, similarly, to give evidence of non-non-Jewishness. The Jew who goes to work on Yom Kippur and looks blank when a fellow Jew tells him a

---

* When someone unfamiliar with Swope's background asked Woollcott one day if there was any truth to the yarn that Swope had a drop or two of Jewish blood in him, Woollcott replied, venomously, "Yes, and I hear Paul Robeson has a touch of the tarbrush, too."

joke with a Yiddish punch line does not always feel sorry for himself, but he is sometimes ruefully aware of the difficulties of getting elected to anything.

Quite a few urbane, educated, and wealthy German Jews with backgrounds like Swope's sought to avoid the whole bothersome question of what they were (or what other people deemed them to be) by simply passing over into the non-Jewish world as soon as they were a generation or so detached from the family rabbi. This sometimes meant keeping a relative from the old country under wraps, but it was on the whole not hard to accomplish, and it could lead to a wider and freer social life.

Swope saw no need to take any such evasive action. He didn't care whether he was known as a Jew or a non-Jew. There was nothing in his experience to make him *feel* Jewish. His parents had been relaxed about the entire matter, and while his brother Gerard—who might not have got as far as he did at General Electric if he had been publicly identified as a Jew—occasionally dropped in at a Chicago synagogue at the turn of the century, it was mostly because he was fond of the music. Both brothers married Gentiles, and both raised their children in an utterly nonsectarian environment. Herbert Swope's daughter didn't even realize she was Jewish until she was sixteen.*

Nobody knows, of course, precisely what a Jew is. Not even the Supreme Court of Israel could come up with a satisfactory definition as late as 1962. While Swope was aware that in practice a Jew is anyone anybody else thinks is Jewish, he liked to describe himself, when he gave the problem any thought at all, as occupying a "twilight zone" between Jews and non-Jews. He may have visualized himself as being uniquely equipped to serve as a liaison man between the groups—a double agent, as it were, without squalid overtones of espionage.

In consonance with this image of himself, he zealously deplored —at least until the early 1930s—all manifestations of parochialism. Declining once to address a dinner of Jewish war veterans, he said, "I am not in favor of parochializing patriotic endeavors. I think men serve for the colors not because they are Jew, Catholic, or Protestant, but because they are Americans. I do not believe in

---

* Raoul Fleischmann once remarked to George S. Kaufman, a philosophical man, "I didn't know I was Jewish till I was eighteen." "I didn't know I was a boy till I was twenty," Kaufman replied.

schismatizing such service. Religion in charity, religion in spiritual matters is good. Religion in secular matters is not good. I do not believe in organizations of Jewish war veterans, Catholic actors, or Protestant teachers. I may be wrong. I am open to argument. I have heard none that is particularly convincing; until I do, the principle I have set forth will be my guide." (Principle or no, his guidance for President Eisenhower in 1953 was to appoint a Catholic to the Supreme Court, simply because there didn't happen to be one on it. "I do not believe the Catholics or the Jews, or the Protestants, vote as a unit," Swope wrote the President, "but nevertheless there is a large element in each of these groups that is affected by the compliment implied in the elevation of one of their own.")

Swope constantly kept being reminded, however, that, though he might deplore it, he dwelt in an essentially parochial world. This was ironically demonstrated to him not long before he died. One of the phrases he was proudest of having coined, and which he used over and over, was "I cannot give you the formula for success, but I can give you the formula for failure: Try to please everybody." The homily, which he was fond of expressing to friends embarking on new missions—a Joseph Kennedy, for instance, about to take over the S.E.C., or a Winthrop Aldrich on his way to England as American Ambassador—did, to Swope's satisfaction, find its way into several secular publications, such as the *Reader's Digest* and the *Flo-Sweet Diary*, the latter distributed by a syrup company to its customers; but the chief reference book to pick up and immortalize the admonitory formula was a volume with the unabashedly parochial title *A Treasury of Jewish Quotations*.

For someone in the twilight zone there were certain obvious advantages to be gained by neglecting to move firmly toward the moon or toward the sun. New York City had two athletic clubs. The larger and more fashionable, the New York Athletic Club, had hardly any Jewish members; the City Athletic Club was almost exclusively Jewish. Swope joined the N.Y.A.C. In Palm Beach he was admitted to the equally choosy Bath & Tennis Club, and he remained in it until 1935, when its governors asked the members for "hearty cooperation" in observing a resolution requesting them "to refrain from introducing any guest who is not of the Christian faith." This was too much for Swope, who wrote the club:

I am on terms of friendship with men and women, some of whom are Jewish, some Unitarian, some Buddhists, some Shintoists, and some Agnostics. As I am not in the habit of questioning their religious or political beliefs or permitting them to question mine, I am unwilling to take on that rude burden by direction of the Board of Governors of the Bath & Tennis Club. I deny the right of them, or of any other group, to place a restriction upon free association. As this view is in opposition to the attitude assumed by the Club (which I think I have visited twice in the last four or five years), I hereby resign my membership therein to take effect immediately.

In New York that same year Swope joined the River Club, which took in a few Jews but had, all in all, a fairly strict quota on that kind of immigration. Swope was not disturbed by this until, almost a generation later, his old friend Robert Moses asked to be put up for membership. Moses' motives were simple enough: he liked to swim, and he had grown dissatisfied with the Yale Club pool because it was too small. Once, after a dive, his momentum carried him all the way to the other end of the pool, which his head struck with such stunning force he almost drowned. The River Club pool was more capacious and less hazardous. But when Moses' application was submitted, he was blackballed. Swope told him he thought this rejection was "little short of outrageous" and said he would never have joined the club himself if it hadn't had other Jewish members, because "I make it a rule never to be an exception." He forthwith resigned, notifying the governors, "If the Club, for any reason, thinks it can get along without Bob Moses, then I am sure I can get along without the Club."

Swope also liked to describe himself, using a term that was probably first given currency by Supreme Court Justice Louis Brandeis, as a "foul-weather Jew"—one, that was, who, though noncommittal about his background in halcyon days, felt impelled to identify himself with other Jews when the going was rough. When Adolf Hitler came to power Swope donned his foul-weather gear, like a knight putting on armor. His need to be personally involved in world-shaking events was amply and sorrowfully filled by the new order in Germany; like so many other American Jews, Swope had relatives there, and the three sons of his sister Golda all were driven into exile and drifted around the world seeking refuge—in Shanghai, in Australia, in Brazil—while Swope and his brother sought to find them a permanent resting place. Herbert Swope got one nephew an entry permit into England by appealing directly to Winston Churchill.

Initially, Swope was no more perceptive than most Americans about the ultimate horror of Hitler. "It is difficult to take him seriously," he wrote his other sister, Dolly, in Berlin, at the end of 1930, when she was a receptionist at the American Embassy. "It would be so great a reflection upon German common sense." But Swope changed his appraisal faster than many Americans, and in the spring of 1933, a month after Franklin Roosevelt's first inauguration, he would write Baruch:

The Hitler regime is incredible. With Prussianized logic, they protest that there are no atrocities, and thereby convince themselves that none is taking place. All the time they are prohibiting men and women from entering the arts and professions; they are driving out those already in; they are destroying Jewish trade, and they are preventing the departure of Jews from Germany. . . . They say they do not kill men or cut off the hands of children. Probably they don't, but there is such a thing as spiritual oppression; as social disabilities; as civic disqualifications, much more devastating than mere physical violence. By the same process of terrorism they gain the cooperation of the Jews to urge that no steps be taken in other countries to register disapproval of the German program. The very appeals such Jews make give condemnation to the conduct of the Hitlerites. I think it would be a good thing for some Jew in Germany to martyrize himself to decline to bear lying testimony; to tell the truth, regardless of the cost to him. . . . I regard the condition of the Jews in Germany today as being worse than at any time since the Crusades.

No act of the government; no compelled apology; no reestablishment of Jewish rights can possibly repair the damage done. Seeds have been planted that will bear new and bitter fruit for years to come.

I do not believe it is possible for the rest of the world to stand idly by. I saw the fight that Wilson made for the recognition of the rights of minorities, when he was crusading for self-determination, and that same step must be taken to prevent the extermination of a race, or, if not its complete extermination, then the soul destroying experience of the tortures to which it is being submitted; tortures calculated to sap the very wellsprings of self-respect and self-reliance; tortures that certainly will break the Jewish spirit and bring back new and worse slave psychology of inferiority.

Swope got increasingly angry at Germany. By 1935 he was taking to task individuals—Herbert Pulitzer and his brother Jo-

431

seph, Jr., among them—for deigning to travel abroad on a German ship. For the same reason he was cross at Joseph E. Davies, who booked passage on the *Europa* after being appointed Ambassador to Russia late in 1936. Davies and his wife, the former Marjorie Post Hutton, the enormously wealthy General Foods heiress, achieved some unwanted notoriety before they left when it was revealed that they were taking with them a quantity of frozen and refrigerated edibles. At Davies' request, Swope spent part of Christmas Day that year preparing a statement designed to mitigate the adverse publicity he'd received, but after Swope had thus let Christian spirit impinge on Christ's day the Ambassador and the White House decided it would be more politic to say nothing at all and to let sleeping dogs lie. That made Swope even madder—not so much because he minded giving up part of a holiday as because he usually believed in prodding sleeping dogs into yipping wakefulness. "When you let them lie, with wrong thoughts in their heads," he told Baruch a few days after Davies had decided to keep quiet, "they always bark on the same key when they awaken."

One man who influenced Swope's attitudes and actions in the worrisome 1930s was a stockbroker named Arthur J. Goldsmith. Like Joseph P. Kennedy, he had been a member of the class of 1912 at Harvard, and he later shared an office with Kennedy. Goldsmith visited Germany as an undergraduate. He went back there in 1935 and was appalled at the transformation. On returning home, he founded a committee that hoped, vainly, to put Hitler in his place by having the scene of the 1936 Olympic Games, scheduled to be held in Berlin, shifted elsewhere. Goldsmith enlisted Swope's support, which was at once forthcoming. "Why don't you holler against America participating in the Olympics?" Swope wrote to Westbrook Pegler. "That is supposed to be free men in free contest. How can that condition be present when Jews, Catholics, and non-Nazi Protestants are barred?"

In the next few years Goldsmith, who was to become an unflagging do-gooder and to devote himself to such earnest undertakings as a world-wide habeas-corpus movement, started up a private intelligence service, gathering material mostly about Americans suspected of having pro-Nazi leanings, and sharing his findings, when they seemed especially eye-opening, with the FBI. Pegler, in his turn, began to concentrate on Goldsmith. The columnist had many *bêtes noires*, but it is possible that more Peglerian spleen was vented against Goldsmith than any other individual outside of President Roosevelt's immediate family. Many of Goldsmith's acquaintances—or, in Pegler's view, accomplices—shared in the attention and abuse, and Swope was conspicuous among them.

Swope and Pegler had, in more carefree days, been good friends. In 1935 Swope thought the columnist, whom he sometimes addressed as "Peggie-Weggie," was "an essential figure in American journalism," and even five years after that they were still saying nice things about each other—Swope calling Pegler "brilliant" and "just one Hell of a newspaper man" and Pegler stating that Swope, "say what you will about his personal showmanship and the garrulousness which makes it impossible for anyone to break through his service, was a great reporter and a great news editor. . . ." But in the years that followed, the bloom of mutual admiration withered. As Pegler was belaboring Goldsmith, whom he dubbed, because of his proclivity to join organizations, "Abou Ben Goldsmith," so also was he castigating "Horsetrack Herbert Swope," who the columnist said "has made a career of hanging around big people on the theory that a man who does that can rub off some big onto himself."

Things got to the sorry point where, when Swope was asked to a testimonial dinner for Pegler in 1954, to pay tribute to his "brilliant and fearless achievements in the field of Journalism," Swope did not even bother to reply to the first invitation. When a follow-up letter arrived he let fly with "I make a practice of dining with my friends, not with my enemies, especially when an enmity is without reason and in the face of a long-standing series of services that I have performed when I was called upon by your guest of honor. I suggest that you occasionally read his column; then you would not be so pressing in your desire to have me attend the function that is intended to honor him."

Swope got more and more immersed in Jewish affairs. In 1917 a Viennese named Jacob Landau had founded a news service called the Jewish Telegraphic Agency, which had its headquarters first in London and then in New York, with branch offices in Paris, Berlin, Warsaw, and Jerusalem. Part of the agency's income came from newspapers that used its dispatches, part from contributions. Landau's chief American patron was the banker Felix Warburg. In 1931 Warburg wanted an objective analysis made of the outfit he was underwriting and asked Adolph Ochs to recommend somebody to do it for him. Ochs proposed Swope for the assignment, and Swope took it on, despite his being predisposed against parochial organizations. In reporting favorably on the work of the J.T.A., as he ultimately did, he was principally won over by Landau himself. A quiet, lisping man, unprepossessing in stature, Laudau seemed to know almost everybody of consequence in Europe (where he had once been called the uncrowned king of the Jews), and he had the reputation of spending more money than he had—which may have prompted Warburg's concern about his operations in the first place.

Swope kept in touch with Landau throughout the Thirties and learned with growing distress about the difficulties his agency was encountering. The Berlin bureau of the J.T.A., for instance, was closed down by the Gestapo in 1937, a repressive act that triggered Swope into telling Baruch, "If it were not for the J.T.A. I doubt that we or the world would have known a thing about the frightful Polish situation. This agency throws light into the dark places. The purblind fools who failed to support it don't realize that only through being properly intelligenced can they act intelligently." To one plea of Landau's for help, Swope responded, "Christ would have saved the world even more completely than he did had you been his evangel. I will do my damnedest." To which Landau replied, describing himself as Swope's John the Baptist, "I have been talking Swope during the last two years to everybody in Europe, describing liberals, hopeless leaders, and worried Czech, French and British statesmen. And I am so happy that you intend to do your 'damnedest.' John the Baptist has no doubt that the future will prove that he was right in the choice of his Christus."

Swope was charmed with that kind of dialogue, and he felt that he could do even more if the agency were less specialized and didn't concentrate almost exclusively on information about Jews and their plight. Out of conversations that he and others had with Landau, some of them evangelical and some mundane, there evolved the idea of a broader agency, to be known as the Overseas News Agency, which could supplement the big existing wire services by furnishing newspaper clients with stories and features about the persecution of all minorities everywhere.

It was not until the spring of 1940, however, that the O.N.A. became a reality. Then, Swope convened a meeting at his home, where a board of directors was set up consisting of, among others, William Allen White, Hendrik Wilhelm Van Loon, Rabbi Abba Hillel Silver, George Backer, Harold Guinzburg, the Rev. Robert I. Gannon, Jacob A. Blaustein, and Swope. Blaustein, a wealthy petroleum man noted for his philanthropies, was named president. Landau and his wife Ida, who regularly worked with her husband, were to administer the venture. Swope became chairman of the board. When he soon afterward had some O.N.A. business cards made up, he identified himself on them as "Correspondent and Chairman of the Board."

As a correspondent he felt entitled to, and obtained, a working press card from the New York City Police Department. It had been a long time since Swope had had a set of the credentials he liked best. He didn't ever actually function as a reporter, but he would have the O.N.A. correspondents' daily dispatches sent to his office and would vigorously mark them up with red pencil. It was not quite the same thing as running a newspaper, but for a long-starved editor it provided tolerable ersatz nourishment.

The Overseas News Agency flourished during the war. Through the Office of War Information it furnished material in twenty-eight languages for distribution to foreign-language papers in the United States. On its own it serviced twenty-seven American papers with a total circulation of five million, and it had additional outlets in Canada and Latin America. It hired military experts and cultural critics, and it disseminated serializations of books. Once it almost syndicated Baruch. Swope somehow got the impression that it would be all right with his friend if the O.N.A., under the heading "The Park Bench," put out excerpts from Baruch's speeches and statements. He sent Baruch proofs of a few samples. "Look at these," Swope wrote. "You will marvel at their lucidity, profundity, and authority." Baruch swiftly telegraphed his refusal. Furthermore, he wondered who had written the stuff, with some of which, he said, he disagreed. A few of O.N.A.'s full-time contributors were accused, every so often, of being excessively radical. This did not bother Swope. "We have built up a reputation in O.N.A. for always getting into hot water," he said in one report to his board. "We wouldn't have it otherwise. It's proof, if proof were needed, that O.N.A.'s correspondents do not bow to pressures, do not accept muzzling, and go for the story wherever the facts lie."

A single correspondent, Constantine Poulos, was almost always in hot water. He kept getting thrown out of countries, usually by military authorities. The British expelled him from Palestine and the Americans from Greece and from Austria. Every time this happened, Swope took it as a personal affront and girded for battle. He proved an effective fighter. After Poulos' Austrian skirmish, Swope wrote challengingly to Army headquarters in Washington:

> If Poulos is rotten, let's have the evidence and we'll throw him out, but I am damned if I am going to let anybody assassinate by shots in the dark and in the back, a man who works for me. And worse: blacken his character by insinuations and implications without definite charges. Such action becomes a military lynching. . . . Let's have it out in the open. Let's put him on trial. It is possible he may be guilty, but I'm damned if I will permit a judgment to be made in advance of a hearing.

Following that barrage from afar, Swope stormed into Washington himself and talked the Army into backing down.

But while Swope could manage fairly well to patch up O.N.A.'s recurrent troubles with the outside world, he found distasteful the internal bickering that soon became one of the organization's principal—though unsyndicated—features. Several of its directors had grown disenchanted with the Landaus, and after a series of postwar investigations and counterinvestigations and charges and countercharges that seemed to go on as long and be contested as violently as the war itself, the organization broke up, in 1949, in a spate of dissension.

Swope's connections with Landau's agencies brought him into frequent contact with men who were running Jewish philanthropies, and it was perhaps in the natural evolutionary order of things that they, who in the pre-Hitler days had scarcely ever turned to him for either money or guidance, now eagerly sought both. At the start of 1946, when the United Jewish Appeal was setting forth on a campaign to raise one hundred million dollars, it thought so highly of Swope's potential that it agreed to pay him fifty thousand dollars a year for two successive years to help out. Swope was supposed to raise money from a few select individuals, Baruch inevitably included, who it was thought might respond more outgoingly to him than to an ordinary solicitor. In Baruch's case, Swope's first assignment was to have his friend turn up physically at a Washington function, in February of 1946, when the hundred-million-dollar drive would be officially launched. Swope thought he had Baruch lined up to attend, but had a nasty turn when Baruch, working hard on his atomic-energy proposals for the UN, decided that he wouldn't go to the Washington affair. "An atom bomb has struck the U.J.A.," Swope wrote him. "They are fearful that the whole campaign has failed, for you had become the chiefest factor in their strategy."

Baruch replied that he doubted the bottom could fall out of a worthy, hundred-million-dollar project because of a single person's nonappearance at a single gathering, and that if anybody felt that way it merely tended to confirm his belief that he was to be used as a bellwether, which he didn't much relish. But after Swope pleaded with him to reconsider, Baruch came around, and Swope probably earned his fee when the U.J.A. got one hundred thousand dollars from Baruch, another hundred thousand from Rosenstiel, and a scattering of fifty-thousand-dollar contributions from other men he tapped. In any event, the U.J.A. was pleased enough for Swope to be seriously considered, in 1948, as the head of the organization. He declined the honor, saying, "I am quite convinced . . . that I would lose whatever usefulness I may possess were I to become a special pleader. It is far better for me to occupy a seemingly disinterested onlooker's seat than to become a public advocate for a particular need. . . ."

A swarm of Jewish organizations began to retain Swope for various public-relations chores, and he toiled with equanimity both for Zionists, non-Zionists, and anti-Zionists—quite a feat in the maelstrom of Jewish social and political action groups. When in the fall of 1947 the Jews of America were as concerned about politics as philanthropy, with the partition of Palestine then preoccupying the United Nations, Swope was in the thick of the agitation that resulted in the emergence of the state of Israel. Before that came about he had achieved a gratifying close relationship with Dr. Chaim Weizmann.

The more closely identified Swope became with Jewish affairs, the more curious he became about Judaism. Toward the end of his life the Jewish Theological Seminary of America was preparing a revised edition of a book about Jewish history, culture, and religion. Dr. Louis Finkelstein sent a form letter to various men, asking if they had any suggestions. Swope responded at once with a list of what he described as key questions that were often asked about Jews—that, it seemed not unlikely, he had been asking himself—and that he hoped the book would answer:

Are the Jews clannish? Do they avoid contractual relationships with others in their community?

Are they more Jewish than they are American? (Does the Jewish interest outweigh the call of the country?)

Have the divisions of Jewry, such as Orthodox, Conservative, Reformed, et al, and the erection of Israel hurt the group?

Has the influence of Jews upon history been recognized?

What other religious or racial body has given the world three such gifts as: 1, Monotheism; 2, The Decalogue; 3, Sabbatarianism? Are these three elements not basic to the present day civilizations and should they not be more widely emphasized?

Unequivocally Jewish Swope had become, but long after he made no bones about it, there were those who still regarded him as something of an enigma. When in the early 1950s he remarked once that the United States couldn't pull out of Europe "because, for one thing, the Vatican is our first line of defense," the *Herald Tribune*, reporting what he'd said, felt constrained to add, "Mr. Swope is not a Roman Catholic."

While Swope was traveling out of the twilight zone, his brother Gerard was also on the move. In the spring of 1947 the British government announced that, in recognition of Gerard Swope's many services, he had been named an Honorary Commander of the Most Excellent Order of the British Empire. But because it would take a while to have the appropriate regalia and insignia made up, his investiture was to be delayed for a year—the year, as it developed, of England's grudging withdrawal from Palestine. Gerard Swope was incensed at the British behavior. He was to receive his O.B.E. in the middle of June 1948. A month before then Israel attained independence, and three weeks after *that*— only a few days before the scheduled ceremonies in his honor—he announced that he would turn down the award.

If Gerard's metamorphosis at that time into a staunch Israeli sympathizer surprised a good many people, they were flabbergasted, when he died nine years later, by the terms of his will. He left nearly his entire estate, some eight million dollars, to the Israel Institute of Technology, known for short as Technion, at Haifa. An American fund-raiser for Technion had met Gerard through Herbert and had fanned his interest in the Institute. The big bequest was not easy to make, for Gerard, thinking his wife would outlive him, had before her death given her most of his money, in order to reduce the estate taxes that would ultimately have to be paid. When she died, her will authorized him to leave her estate to any relatives or eleemosynary institutions he chose. She did not, however, specify any legatees. Her estate, accordingly, would ordinarily have been liable to a four-and-a-half-million-dollar federal estate tax on the eight million he wanted to give to Technion.

That obstacle was neatly circumvented when Congress, before Gerard died, passed a bill permitting certain individuals—individuals whose circumstances were precisely tailored to his—to choose a charity to receive a decedent spouse's money without having to pay any tax on it. Herbert Swope had soured a bit by then on Israel. It was as hard for a country as for an individual to retain his unflagging attention or affection, and in one note to himself about the new nation he said, reprovingly, "She is becoming as arrogant as Ireland." And he was quite upset at the terms of his brother's testament. "It was not a good will," he wrote a nephew after Gerard's death, "because if he had wished to be philanthropic he should have benefited the country in which he made his money." But it was what Gerard wanted to do, and as a result most of his capital funds were transferred to a nation for whose founding fathers it would have amazed the brothers' friends, not too many years before, to realize either man cared a farthing.

22

SWOPE thrived on contention. He needed no flaming issue to goad him into action; argument *gratia* argument sufficed. When a discussion he was in got pleasingly percussive, he was like a soloist who, while absorbed in his own artistry, does not try to overwhelm his accompanying orchestra. To an acquaintance who was curious about his obvious relish for disputes, he said, "I find my interest in fights of this kind to be bilateral: I am interested in my own position and also in seeing that, when I debate with friends, they do not permit their positions to deteriorate too quickly."

But when debates of global dimension were in progress, Swope could be as unilateral as anyone else. He threw himself vigorously and unfalteringly into the battle that was waged between American interventionists and isolationists in the edgy period before the Japanese attack on Pearl Harbor. From Woodrow Wilson's Administration on, Swope had been a champion of world-wide interdependence, and his sympathies and energies naturally went to the interventionists. As France fell and the English pulled back from Dunkirk, Swope sought to bolster the morale of Winston Churchill and Brendan Bracken, who became Churchill's Minister of Information, with cheery notes of encouragement. They, in turn, sated Swope's appetite for exclusive news with private communiqués on the progress of the Battle of Britain.

While Averell Harriman was running the American lend-lease program to England, he wondered if Swope had any public-relations ideas he'd care to transmit to Bracken. Swope had indeed, and he spelled them out succinctly:

1. The underlying philosophy of British news releases and commentaries should be the unswerving, undying spirit of determination. You know:
   "Come the world against her—
   England yet shall stand."
   (That, by the way, is a Hell of a good quotation I heard Philip Snowden use in the House of Lords several years ago. It is from Swinburne.)
2. I do not think policy or expediency should be permitted to affect news releases. The sanctity of a fact should be preserved. There should be no effort made to turn its edge. Interpretation may be added, but that should be on the responsibility of the Ministry.
3. If Britain has a victory, claim it; if Britain sustains a defeat, admit it.
4. I would not attempt to measure the value of a release by its effect on the public mind; one cannot be sure what that effect is; and, second, one can alienate the reader by attempting to put a ring in his nose. For example:
   In reporting losses in the Atlantic, I suggest that they be stated without qualification. With that can be given the comparative figures on the unrestricted U-boat warfare of late '17 and '18. The comparison, by the way, is not bad.
5. Every possible effort should be made to show that Britain is attempting to wage a war of movement, and is not indulging in a "sitzkrieg"; that she realizes she is on her own and is not waiting for America to pull her chestnuts out of the fire; that she feels herself capable of beating off Hitler and all others who might come against her, and that she is willing to take them all on, if she has to, to preserve her Freedom. (These are answers to the aspersions of the America First Committee.)
6. Do not let the impression gain prevalence that Britain believes she is fighting America's battle. This is her own battle, which may be (as, indeed, it is) the first line of defense for us. But the tendency on the part of some English, and a few Americans, to make it appear that, were it not for England's desire to save us she would not be in the fight, is embarrassing.
7. Give us pictures of the air force; of the women, and especially, of your leaders. With them should come personality stories— America loves that sort of thing. Give us action pictures of the R.A.F. Give us action pictures of the American planes—if any are being flown.
8. While pursuing this positive program, don't forget the negative. Attacks on Hitler are always good. Bring out, whenever possible, his perfidy; how many times he has broken his pledged

word; his treachery, by which he has tried (and succeeded) in debauching nations.

9. Hess was not used to full extent. It is all very well to talk about the great wall of silence in which he has been buried. Why not tell stories, by indirection, of his having flown with peace overtures; his closeness to Hitler—one away—makes anything he does of great significance. He will not be able to deny the stories, and, besides, the stories would be true in their substance.

10. And if the Army has done away with the Old School Ties, and the Col. Blimps, it seems to me, the Navy might well break down its specious reputation of being the "silent service." Don't let America think she is doing all the work in the Atlantic.

11. Print all possible pictures of the various English ships. Ships, next to women, have an irresistible appeal to readers.

12. Give us more stuff about the various commanders—we know about Cunningham, but who are the other fellows who are adding new glory to the Nelson tradition?

13. Play up the Irish Catholics in the service. Too bad O'Connor (of the army) was grabbed in Libya just as he was becoming a romantic figure. Play up all the Irish, but give emphasis to the Southerners.

14. Make plain for American consumption that Russia is not a coequal ally; that she is an associate, or, perhaps, an instrument. In America we are not for Stalin; we are against Hitler, and any stick is good enough to beat that dog with! . . .

P.S. One last thought, even though it is supererogatory:
Be brutally frank with the correspondents. Trust them and if they are unworthy of trust, throw them out. Give them background stuff. Help them to get their stories. You will find most of them, although thoroughly honest, are wholly with Britain and America because, either they feel that way, or because of their environment.

On the home front, Swope enlisted early in William Allen White's Committee to Defend America by Aiding the Allies, and he presided at numerous meetings held by that group and *its* allies. When they needed money, as they generally did, he got some for them from Baruch, who was concerned as always about the laggard mobilization of industry for war production and was anxious to demolish the roadblocks that the isolationists were trying to set up in the path of preparedness. Baruch and Swope, inseparable as ever, turned up together one night on Long Island to direct traffic during a mock air raid and practice blackout conducted by a civil-defense group. Baruch played this unaccustomed role without costume; Swope proudly sported a military-police arm band.

Swope was just short of sixty when the Japanese attacked Hawaii. He was too old for active military duty. His hair had grayed despite the salves and lotions he had lavished on it in the hope of preserving its combative luster, and his health in general was none too good. (During one wartime bout of illness, he wrote to John Hay Whitney, "I don't want to brag, but Maggie told me I had a fever of 105. That fact was widely circulated and false hopes were raised in the bosoms of my enemies—'Good old Swope,' they were saying, 'he wasn't a bad guy.' Their tune changed as I got well.") Still, Swope wanted to participate in the greatest of crusades. Four days after Pearl Harbor he telegraphed an offer of his services to, among others, Archibald MacLeish, who was then director of the Office of Facts and Figures, the precursor of the Office of War Information; and to Secretary of the Navy Frank Knox, Undersecretary of War Robert Patterson, Supreme Court Justice Frankfurter, and President Roosevelt. "I am wholly at your disposal," Swope told the Commander-in-Chief.

Swope's son had already become a naval officer. For a while he was on a patrol ship, and then he spent two years on a minesweeper. This upset his mother, who even after her son and her two brothers grew up was uneasy at night until they were safely home. Margaret Swope felt worse when she and her husband got to chatting with a high-ranking Navy man at a party. He inquired after their son and, on learning of his minesweeper assignment, replied, "Fine! Fine! That's the finest service in the Navy!" He paused to consider whether he had made the doting parents sufficiently proud of their boy, decided he hadn't, and churned on. "Yes, that's the best assignment a man could have. It is, by far, the most dangerous service in the entire fleet." Then he cruised off across the room. "Reassuring little bastard, isn't he?" said Margaret.

Just where the senior Swope could best fit into the rapidly accelerating war machine was hard for him or anyone else to figure out. There were those who thought he should be appointed the American counterpart of Brendan Bracken—a Minister of Information with broad powers of censorship. That job never materialized. It was one of Swope's boys from the *World*, Stanley J. Grogan, who hit upon an acceptable alternate. As a young reporter in Bridgeport, Connecticut, many years earlier, Grogan had come to Swope's attention. Swope summoned him to the Pulitzer Building for an interview and asked the out-of-towner just one question: Did he think he could find his way unaided from Manhattan to the Bronx? Grogan said he thought he could, and Swope hired him.

Grogan had subsequently gone into the Army, where he specialized in press relations. After General Marshall became Chief of Staff, Grogan, a lieutenant colonel, was put in charge of the War Department's Press Branch in Washington. He was under the General Staff and was specifically beholden to its G-2, or Intelligence, Section, which did not construe as part of its rightful function the quick-flowing dissemination of military information. The Secretary of the General Staff, an officer suspicious of journalists, was fond of saying, "I learned how dangerous the press can be while studying the Civil War at West Point." So widespread was the military distrust of the civilian press that before Grogan could issue any kind of release he was obliged to carry it to the Chief of Staff's office and have Marshall approve it personally.

With the nation at war it was obvious that General Marshall would have other things on his mind and that some better system would have to be devised. Grogan managed first to get his department out from under the yoke of G-2, and he began talking to Swope and others about how the Army should handle its relations with the press. Swope hammered away at a point he had been making all his life: that the government owed it to the people to disclose all information that did not violate security. It was at Swope's instigation that the War Department on February 2, 1942, issued a memorandum for the press—it was not for publication, merely for background, but it was at least a step in the direction Swope was pointing to—that went, "While recent reports from our troops in the Philippines and other points in the Far East have been uniformly favorable, there is nothing in the situation to warrant a great amount of optimism concerning the outcome of military operations of the next few weeks. War Department communiqués relative to operations of American ground and air forces have been factual. However, some of the headlines tend to magnify the importance of local successes and perhaps mislead the public into a belief that an early defeat of the enemy may be possible."

Grogan sent Swope a copy—"the first result of one of your good ideas," he observed. Swope responded with a variation on his public-mind theme:

Your outfit should never be content with merely putting stuff out; it is even more important for you to be able to evaluate the effect upon the public mind of your releases. [He had by this time apparently changed his own mind about the fourth of the fifteen suggestions he'd sent to Harriman for Bracken.] You must be able to anticipate the reactions before they occur. In fact, this is a matter that goes to the very root of both Expression and Suppression—in both of which arts your Bureau is engaged.

An opportunity to let Swope himself do some of the evaluating —to have a public mind readily on tap within the War Department itself—soon arose. Grogan brought about a second reorganization of the Army's Bureau of Public Relations in the winter of 1942. Now the bureau would be taken entirely out of the chain of command that led up to the Chief of Staff and would be directly beneath the Secretary of War, Henry L. Stimson. A Regular Army general, Alexander D. Surles, was installed as the head of the bureau, and a civilian deputy was authorized to supplement his uniformed staff.

Several men were considered for this job, Swope among them. Surles and Grogan finally picked him, despite a good-natured warning from Baruch, who told them while their search was on that Swope would make an estimable choice but that they shouldn't expect him to do any work before noon. Having missed his chance of wearing a uniform in the First World War, Swope hoped to be commissioned in spite of his age—and in the 1950s he would refer to having been offered the silver maple leaf of a lieutenant colonel or the star of a brigadier general—but the War Department didn't want any more senior officers in public relations. It wanted a civilian who would not have to worry about rank and its privileges. Swope finally consented to become a part-time civilian consultant to the Secretary of War, on a ten-dollar per-diem basis, and Stimson announced his appointment at a press conference on July 3, 1942. When a reporter asked the Secretary what Swope's duties would be, Stimson, who apparently had not expected to have to spell them out, replied, "Mr. Swope always has a duty of helpfulness, which he performs admirably well in consultation and conference." In whatever line of endeavor Swope found himself, it was never easy for his associates to pigeonhole him.

Most of the consultants in mufti whom the War Department gathered into its fold were formally designated "Consultant to the Secretary of War." Even though they might never lay eyes on Stimson, it sounded good. Swope was different. He was to be a consultant to the Secretary in fact as well as in name. He agreed to go to Washington whenever summoned by the Secretary or, more probably, by General Surles, with whom he was expected to be in closest contact. He had an office at the Pentagon, but in that building of five concentric rings it was considered a status symbol to be on the "E," or outer, ring, and Swope was disappointed to find that an inner, windowless office had been assigned to him. Swope complained to Grogan about his windowless state; Grogan tried to explain that with a war on even an edifice as vast as the Pentagon could not make fenestral concessions to part-time men.

To Swope, who finally argued himself into the "E" ring, it mattered where in the building he was, but to others wandering through that mammoth entomber of individuality it was a comfort just to know merely that he was on the premises. Charles G. Ross was in Washington as a contributing editor of the *Post-Dispatch* during the war. He once recalled whimsically, "Around 1944, when lost one day in the Pentagon, I came across his [Swope's] name on a door; I was so heartened by this evidence of the permanence of fundamental values in a confused world that I was able to make my way out of the building unaided."

There were further logistical complications. Swope kept wanting to be admitted to a high-level dining room in the Pentagon known as General Officers' Mess No. 1, to which fewer than a dozen civilians working for the War Department had regular entrée. Swope never made this elite list, though he sometimes had lunch there at the invitation of a member in good standing. And it was galling to him that, unlike the other high-ranking individuals with whom he contentedly rubbed elbows whenever he was in the General Officers' Mess, he had no transportation assigned to him. For a while, however, he used to brag, he had a "Triple-A Priority," for use on airplanes and trains—a priority also held, it made him feel good to be able to reflect, only by President Roosevelt and J. Edgar Hoover. "How I got it I don't know," Swope said in a note to himself, "although, of course, I never used it." *

Swope had access to Stimson but did not see as much of him as he would perhaps have liked to; the Secretary simply hadn't time to give Swope the kind of attention he needed. The expert consultant's relationship with Surles, too, was less than ideal. The general was a professional soldier with no special flair for public relations; Swope was as unfathomable to him as a submarine. Somebody would sell Surles on a public-relations idea that seemed to have promise—such as sending two teams of major-league baseball players on a round-the-world tour of Army installations after the 1943 World Series—and then Swope would come along and torpedo it. (Swope thought it would adversely affect the morale of men who'd been drafted if healthy physical specimens turned up among them wearing civilian baseball uniforms.) In a letter to an Army acquaintance in the summer of 1944 Swope said, ". . . I have not seen Surles for some time, but I spare him visits. I seem to make him very nervous. I am afraid he is quite insecure and my presence doesn't add to his stability. . . ." To himself, Swope wrote, of Surles, "He is scared to death lest I try to take his job."

It was not readily apparent to anyone else at the Pentagon that Swope constituted a serious threat to General Surles' job security, but to avoid trouble all around, the consultant stayed out of Surles' way and attached himself to Undersecretary Patterson. A former federal judge with a distinguished First World War combat record, Patterson was at the opposite end of the personality spectrum from Swope. The Undersecretary was austere and reserved. He was totally unimpressed by fripperies; he astonished Swope, when they were dining together one night, by being perfectly content with a pick-up meal of scrambled eggs and tuna fish. The simple, unostentatious type of public servant, devoid of sham or guile, had of course always appealed to Swope. He now enshrined Patterson on the pedestal he had formerly reserved for

---

* Just what it was is uncertain. Jonathan Daniels, a member of the White House staff who handled some priorities during the war, said in 1962 that he dimly recalled Swope's having made such a claim and that it might have been correct. "There was a lot of funny business about such priorities," Daniels said, "but I never knew that anybody personally possessed any sort of document providing travel priority. I am sure President Roosevelt was not equipped with any such document." J. Edgar Hoover could shed no light on the matter.

Al Smith. He described Patterson to Whitney as "forthright, understanding, and decisive, intolerant of those of whom he disapproves, but deeply appreciative and faith-giving to those he trusts." Swope hoped that after the war Patterson would become President of the United States.

Patterson found in Swope, as had others before him and would others afterward, someone whose willingness—even eagerness—to argue on any subject provoked thought and clarified judgment. (After one dispute, Swope reminded Patterson of something George Bernard Shaw had said—that there was no point in arguing with G. K. Chesterton, because they were both dogmatic: Chesterton dogmatic and wrong, Shaw dogmatic and right. "Needless to say," Swope told Patterson, "in this case I am Shaw!") Swope was ready as ever, too, with advice on this or that aspect of the war: whether WACs should wear visored caps or plain ones; or whether it might not be feasible for the Quartermaster General to supplement standard Army rations with raisins made from Algerian and Moroccan grapes.

On a more serious level, Swope would try on Patterson's behalf to foresee eventualities. Thus, in February 1944, he would write the Undersecretary:

DEAR JUDGE:
  We ought to be ready for this one, which will be tough:
  Why aren't the allies bombing Rome? Is a political or religious factor interfering? It has been said that Rome is a great supply point for the Nazis. Bombing is the usual treatment; then why not in this case? Are we afraid of protests. . . ?
  These questions do not reflect my own attitude, but they are being asked by intelligent civilians. They are growing in volume. Belief is crystallizing that we are not fighting an all out war at the very front.
  We should have a statement on this subject from the President, the Secretary, you, or from the Chief of Staff.
  Make no mistake, this matter is ripening fast. The way to do is to beat the other fellow to the punch.

One of Patterson's jobs was to try to maintain harmony between the military and the plants that manufactured the matériel the Army needed. The Undersecretary made a good many placatory trips to Army posts and industrial areas. Often he would take Swope with him, both for his lively companionship and his mediative aptitude. One time they jointly inspected the liner *Queen Elizabeth*, which was outfitted as a troop transport and jammed with soldiers about to sail for Europe.* They noticed that the Negro soldiers on board had been sequestered fore and aft, where the accommodations were the least comfortable and the life-saving equipment the sparsest. On Patterson's return to Washington he initiated a move to have the Army put an end to segregation—in Swope's 1954 words, he "loosened a tide that is no longer stoppable." Owing in large measure to Patterson's stubborn prodding, the Army ultimately led the military services and, for that matter, most of the civilian components of the country in integrating its personnel.

On his own, Swope made one small comparable wartime gesture. Some military units, moving from place to place, found themselves with no area to encamp in; they set up their tents at race tracks. In the days before military integration Swope used his influence in racing circles to have a regiment admitted to the Aqueduct track in Queens. It was an all-colored unit, but Swope put it there, adamantly, even though it was not universally welcomed by the permanent residents of that preponderantly white borough. He had a more pleasant time of it when in the fall of 1943 the Army asked him to entertain a visiting Peruvian general. There was racing at Jamaica then, and Swope arranged to have the afternoon called Peruvian Day and to have a couple of races given Peruvian names—one of these honoring a military academy in Lima, over which the South American was then presiding. Swope took the general to the track himself, and the visitor was enormously flattered. A few days later an American major general, thanking Swope for the trouble he'd gone to, wrote him, no less flatteringly, "It is such spontaneous manifestations that help to create that understanding and good will with the Latin American

---

* Visiting the berthed ship was as close as Swope got to an overseas theater. After Patterson's departure on one foreign journey, Swope wrote a friend, "The Judge has went away, bawling me out for not going with him; but I feel no man has the right to go abroad unless he has a specific job to do." Some of Swope's friends thought this attitude was needlessly diffident. After Edna Ferber, at the request of the Air Force, had gone to Germany as a war correspondent early in the spring of 1945 and seen some concentration camps, she wrote him, "I wish you would go to Europe for a few weeks. Men like you should see this frightful sight and use your fine intelligence and your power and your eloquence to check its spread. And the hell with racing."

Republics which are so vital to this country and which can, in many instances, be accomplished only by the personal touch."

For three years Swope spent a couple of days a week in Washington. The war demanded sacrifices, and in spite of Baruch's apprehensions about his hours Swope would sometimes leave New York as early as 9:15 A.M. His brother Gerard tried to phone him one midmorning and was told Swope had already left for the capital. When Gerard had recovered from the shock, he wrote Herbert, "I was surprised when I heard that you had left on the 10:30 train!" It did not matter especially, however, when Swope reached the Pentagon, for his hours were no more fixed than his responsibilities.

As the war went on, though, he did assume one continuing assignment. He became the Bureau of Public Relations man in charge of Walter Winchell. This was no trivial task. The gossip columnist, whose indifference about checking items he printed was notorious, took to running gripes from soldiers, and since he was widely syndicated, every complaint he aired had rippling repercussions. The bureau knew it couldn't stop Winchell from publishing whatever he chose to, but it did hope to soften the blows he might land by at least trying to confine him to gripes that could be more or less substantiated.

Swope was entrusted with this mission. Nobody else in the bureau knew Winchell, and Swope happened, not surprisingly, to be an old friend. He had once offered Winchell a job on the *World*, as a theatrical reporter; he had given the columnist many tips; and in classic Swope fashion, when his wife lost a pet dog, he had prevailed upon Winchell to ask for its return in a hundred-odd papers. Swope had a talk with Winchell, who agreed that he would let the War Department check the substance of some of his gripe letters. The Army, for its part, agreed to investigate whatever complaints he passed along and to submit reports to him, which he could use or not use as he saw fit. A good many of the gripes Winchell got did have merit to them. Once he relayed to Swope an allegation about miserable conditions in an Army hospital in the South. Swope took up the matter with the Surgeon General, who, after looking into it, had the officer in command of the hospital relieved of his job.

But Winchell could not be entirely calmed. When he was convinced that the Army was trying to tell its soldiers what they could read and what they couldn't, he ran one challenging item that went, "Open letter to Herbert Bayard Swope of Sec'y of War Stimson's office: We would like to ask a few simple questions on military law. . . . Under what section can a General deprive a Private of his personal property, if that property happens to be [the book] *Under Cover?* . . . Is there an official list of approved books and newspapers . . . and who makes up the list?" Swope didn't let on to Winchell that he himself was harboring similar thoughts. It disturbed him that the newspapers the Army was sending to soldiers who didn't have ready access to the daily press were the New York *Times* and the Chicago *Tribune*. It was sound policy to give citizen-soldiers a chance to read varying points of view, Swope conceded, but he thought it was ridiculous for an Army to try to appease right-wing critics of the Administration by giving such special recognition to the *Tribune*, a journal stridently hostile toward its Commander-in-Chief.

In 1931, appearing before a Joint Congressional and Cabinet Commission that was studying, in the leisure of peacetime, the stresses of war, Swope had testified on the degree to which a government had the right, or the need, to control and influence public opinion. He was in favor of limited censorship during wartime. "Important as is liberty, life is more important," he said, Patrick Henry's dissenting views notwithstanding. Swope believed, however, as he had told Colonel Grogan before he became a War Department consultant, that too many military men were overfond of censorship and that it should be one of his chief tasks at the Pentagon to argue for broader dissemination of news than was favored by many of the knights of that citadel. It was Swope's idea, for instance, to have the Army's public relations officers retitled "public information officers." Secretary Stimson declined to make this change, but after the war was over the military finally adopted Swope's recommendation.

So determined was Swope to keep the public informed that his attitude sometimes made his Pentagon associates nervous. He had access to confidential information, and to keep a secret had never been easy for him, because of his impulsive eagerness to share whatever he had with persons of lesser privilege. In the summer of 1943, just after the invasion of Sicily, the columnist George Dixon was reminded of a talk he'd had months before with Swope, who had remarked that the Axis powers would begin to crumble when the Allies invaded that island. Dixon wrote that he'd been astounded to hear back then that an invasion of Sicily was even contemplated but that events had proved that Swope knew what he was talking about. The Army reacted differently. Colonel Grogan sent Swope a copy of Dixon's column and appended the crisp notation, "Bad business." Swope hastily wrote an extenuating memorandum to himself:

The Dixon story printed in the *Times Herald* on Tuesday, July 27th, 1943, refers to a conversation I had with a group of people at a social gathering in connection with a statement that was then being made in England and America about the welfare of Italy by the English. I had no knowledge that the American troops were going into Africa; I was referring, merely, to the strategic value of an attack on Italy for the purpose of maintaining dominance in the Mediterranean. Just as Germany had taken Crete, I thought it possible for the British to take Sicily, probably using Gibraltar as a base of operations. . . .

Before the invasion of Sicily, Grogan had gone to North Africa with Assistant Secretary of War John J. McCloy. The First Armored Division had had a bad time at Kasserine Pass, and the Chief of Staff wanted to know from a personal emissary what had happened and what corrective steps could be taken to avoid another such setback. When McCloy returned, Grogan helped him prepare a report for General Marshall. Swope asked Grogan to attend a dinner party for a few individuals—Adlai Stevenson, Arthur Krock, and Thomas K. Finletter—who Swope knew would, like himself, enjoy a firsthand, up-to-the-minute briefing on the North African situation. Grogan had hardly accepted the invitation when he was summoned to the Chief of Staff's office. "I understand you are going to dinner with Swope," Marshall said. "I wish you wouldn't discuss the report." Grogan also felt he shouldn't discuss with Swope his reason for not discussing the report. He went to the dinner and, when Swope tried to draw him out on his trip, gave such discouragingly terse and noncommittal replies that the host, in desperation, finally abandoned that subject entirely and steered his guests into a series of memory games involving the names of the capitals of the states.*

---

* After the war, Grogan retired from the Army and took over public relations for the Central Intelligence Agency, where he was under no pressure, understandably, to try to expand the output of information. Now and then Grogan would call on Swope to perform a small chore for the CIA in

452

Inasmuch as Swope was receiving a pittance for his war work, he had to give some consideration to what he described once to Baruch as "selling my brain." His faithful old customer Schenley Industries was still standing by, and he also managed to get retainers from, among other clients, the Aluminum Company of America, the Standard Oil Company of New Jersey, and Twentieth Century-Fox. Now and then he was able to turn one consultancy to the advantage of another. When Colonel Grogan, for example, was trying to set up a branch of the Bureau of Public Relations that could act as a repository for background material on war industries, Swope wrote him, "I had a few words with Farish, Chairman of the Standard Oil Company of New Jersey. His people have oil and gas information always on tap. He said he would be very glad to see their material would be available to any demand you may make upon it." And when the Army refused to permit the showing of a Twentieth Century-Fox biography of Woodrow Wilson at its post theaters—on the ground that Republican Congressmen might consider its exhibition an attempt to indoctrinate troops with partisan Democratic propaganda—Swope raised such cain that the Army rescinded the ban.

After V-E Day the Army began to cut down on its civilian helpers, and Swope's consultancy was terminated in July 1945. Two months before that he reflected to himself, "I need time for private enterprises. The other day I spent two hours on Freedom House matters, two on War Department work, one on T.C.A. [Turf Committee of America] matters, three on O.N.A., one on Long Island State Park Commission. I must attend to my own knitting, and engage in profit-making. My only capital is myself." Instead, however, he would not long afterward be ignoring his knitting again to assist Baruch on his atomic-energy plan.

In 1947, Swope—in a ceremony presided over by General Eisenhower, then the Army's Chief of Staff—was awarded the Medal of Merit, given to 404 civilians who "distinguished themselves by exceptionally meritorious conduct in the performance of outstand-

New York—an explanation to a newspaper managing editor, perhaps, of why it might be awkward for the intelligence outfit if a certain story were handled in a certain way. Swope might have done much more of this sort of thing for the agency, but he wasn't usable. The CIA ran afoul of his impatience with bureaucratic procedure. When he was asked to submit to a routine security investigation, he refused; he would not be subjected to that sort of harassment.

ing public services." * Among those who convened in Eisenhower's office for the occasion were James Byrnes, Averell Harriman, then Secretary of Commerce, Secretary of the Interior Julius A. Krug and a number of multistarred generals. Eisenhower had called the ceremony for noon. Swope, taking no chances of being tardy, took a plane from New York—he was accompanied by Baruch—that was scheduled to reach Washington a full hour ahead of time. But fate was cruel. The weather turned bad, the flight was held up, and on the one occasion when Swope really wanted to be prompt he was, through no fault of his own, late as usual.

In the postwar years, the United States government was pre-occupied with the disposition of enemy-owned assets in this country that had been seized and turned over to an Alien Property Custodian. In the Custodian's safekeeping were a number of juicy mercantile plums, and when these came up for sale there was customarily much jockeying among potential purchasers and, since the Federal government had the final say, not a little political jostling. In such circumstances a man like Swope could be a valuable ally. It was Swope's reputation as a liaison man that caused an industrialist named Israel Rogosin to call on him toward the end of 1947 and enlist his services.

---

* Eisenhower and Swope were then in the middle of what proved, for Swope, to be a difficult situation. A brigadier general had written an article that Eisenhower liked about United States policies in Greece and Turkey. Being in the armed forces, however, the author didn't want to sign his name to it. Eisenhower asked Swope if *he* would, and Swope consented. Just before sending the piece to the *Saturday Evening Post*, Swope wrote John Wheeler of the North American Newspaper Alliance: "I have got a pretty good story in my system which was inspired by General Ike, and approved by Secretary [of State] Marshall and Secretary [of Defense] Patterson. Baruch is familiar with it. Because I felt it a semi-public duty, I had to put it together and sign it myself. If, when and as it is freed, I shall give you the first shot at it for newspaper use." The *Post* rejected the article. Swope told the actual author this was probably because it didn't have enough sex appeal, and he sent it to *Collier's. Collier's* rejected it. Swope turned it over to the literary agent George T. Bye, who'd been a reporter on the *World* in 1922. Bye tried unsuccessfully to peddle it to the *Reader's Digest, Coronet, Life, Harper's*, the *Atlantic Monthly, Look*, The New York *Times* Sunday Magazine and, coming full circle, John Wheeler's N.A.N.A. Swope finally wrote Bye, "I hope the magazines to which you sent 'A Formula for Firm Peace' were made to understand it was not my original script—that I was merely the covering agent. I should not like these magazines to think that a piece I had actually originated and written myself was of such a nature as to be so readily rejectable."

Rogosin, a Polish immigrant who had prospered and taken over a textile complex called Beaunit Mills, was known for his extreme generosity to Jewish philanthropies. He had met Swope through their common interest in the Jewish Telegraphic Agency. Now Rogosin wanted to put in a bid for two affiliated textile companies in the Custodian's hands, North American Rayon and American Bemberg—or, at any rate, for the majority stock interest in these that the government controlled. In Holland there was a minority group of stockholders in the two concerns. Rogosin knew a lot about yarn and wool and cotton and rayon, but he knew very little about politics. He was prepared to match, or better, any offer anybody else might make, but he wanted to be sure he had a fair chance in the bidding, so he engaged Swope to advise him. "I took him on as a kind of insurance," Rogosin said.

Swope performed smoothly and effectively. He did not happen to know the Alien Property Custodian, David L. Bazelon, but he quickly wangled an introduction through Drew Pearson, and presently, when Bazelon was in New York, he would find himself at the Stork Club, shoulder to shoulder with Leonard Lyons and other important citizens who fluttered mothlike toward Swope's incandescence. When Swope heard that the Custodian was planning a trip to the West Coast, he made sure that Bazelon had warm letters of introduction to such hospitable luminaries there as Darryl Zanuck and Samuel Goldwyn. Swope was in the fortunate position, furthermore, of being able to get word to the Dutch minority stockholders that the Rogosin proposition deserved serious consideration; the American Ambassador to The Hague at that time was Baruch's brother Herman. And there were certain Senators whose states harbored plants belonging to the two companies. It went without saying that Swope knew the Senators, without whose concurrence any transaction involving their home territory might have run into difficulties.

There was nothing underhanded about all this; it was in the conventional American public-relations pattern. Rogosin eventually got the properties he wanted—it cost him more than sixteen million dollars, but he was generally considered to have swung a good deal—and in gratitude he kept Swope on his payroll, as a policy adviser, for another seven years, although by the time the negotiations with the government were over Rogosin had concluded that politicians were just about like any other people and that he could handle them himself instead of having to operate through a third party. Rogosin finally slipped out of the Swope orbit after asking Swope to help him organize a group that he was trying to get together to sponsor a memorial to Jewish victims of the Nazis. Swope said he'd be happy to—for an extra fee. Rogosin had rather hoped he would do it for free, and their business relationship came to an end. Meanwhile, Swope had absorbed considerable information about textiles and had also acquired some shirts Rogosin thought would be suitable for croquet.

As Swope lost one account he was usually able to obtain another. He had had his eye on the National Broadcasting Company and its parent organization, the Radio Corporation of America, since the mid-1930s, and he had long been on amiable terms with David Sarnoff, who presided over both outfits. But Swope's affiliation with CBS had precluded his establishing any remunerative relationship with its big rival. After the war Swope had a falling-out, as he did sooner or later so often, with William S. Paley and switched his allegiance to RCA and NBC, in this instance finding the shift doubly rewarding, for he was engaged by his old friend Sarnoff as a consultant by both companies, getting twenty-five thousand dollars a year from RCA and ten thousand a year from its subsidiary. The work was doubly hard, though, for while in his CBS days there had merely been radio programs for Swope to monitor, now there was television, too. Thus, though still concerned with sounds (he would urge Sarnoff to have his announcers bone up on the correct pronunciation of "Czechoslovakia"), he also felt impelled to worry about sights ("I find that the reflection *from the teeth*, especially the front teeth, is frequently so markedly shiny as to make everyone look rabbit-mouthed," he wrote in 1949 to Niles Trammell, the president of NBC).

Swope continued to demonstrate his adeptness for neatly entwining the proliferating tendrils of his existence. When he arranged for Lyndon Johnson—who as a Senator once summed up Swope as "a great man who earned himself a prominent place in history and the affections of this country"—to be the principal speaker at a 1955 banquet honoring Sarnoff, he wrote Johnson:

> I don't think you will be wanting to devote your whole speech to David Sarnoff. That is an antiquated method that has proven ineffective. A man in the eyes of the public can take advantage of the opportunity to say something apropos of his subject, and then go off into a public discussion of public subjects.

456

In this case, you will want to talk about Sarnoff being characteristic of the type of citizenship that is ever ready for any call—that
is the certain factor of strength in our republic. We run the government through statesmen or, if you please, politicians, but we have
ready at hand the counsel, advice and actual efforts of those who are
in private life, but who feel the obligation of public duty heavy
upon them and respond to every call.

Sarnoff is an example of that group, and so is Baruch, who will
be at the dinner. I will try to have you sit next to B., if you wish.

The fact that Sarnoff is the American story, having come from
poverty-stricken parents and risen through his unaided efforts, is
another inspiration of our hope and pride in America. He has become the head of a company that is almost as fully engaged in
defense work as the Services themselves. And, you can add, he has
just finished a job on a matter infected with public interest. It has
to do with the cold war. . . .

I would like to have you talk on a subject that would be page
one stuff. I'll do all the spade work here, so as to have the press
ready for the Magnum Opus. . . .

Johnson's speech was almost exactly what Swope had asked for.
It was entitled "Winning the Cold War," and it went in part:

In a very real sense, we are here tonight to pay tribute to America.
The strength of a country lies in its people. A country that can list
General David Sarnoff among its leaders need not fear the future.
It is difficult for me to think of America without General Sarnoff.
He is one man who has given as much to his country as he has
received. . . . No man feels a greater sense of obligation. And no
man is more willing to serve; more eager to sacrifice; more anxious
to set aside his personal affairs when duty calls in war or in peace.
. . . His company is almost as fully engaged in defense work as
the Defense Department itself. . . . This is the record of the man
who has arisen to the top through his own unaided efforts. . . .
I feel humble tonight that I have the privilege of paying tribute to
such a man. I feel even more humble because I find myself in the
company of some of our greatest Americans. Here tonight is Herbert Bayard Swope, a towering figure in journalism and one of the
most forceful thinkers of our times; Bernard Baruch, America's
financial genius and advisor to Presidents. . . .

Swope's hope that he could steer Johnson onto the front pages
of the newspapers was not fulfilled, but the occasion worked out
quite satisfactorily. The Senator made page two of the *Times* and

page three of the *Herald Tribune;* the phrase "cold war" appeared in the headlines of both papers; and in the text of their stories the *Tribune* used "cold war" six times and the *Times* a heady seven.

Sometimes, however, the tendrils were hard to enlace. While Swope was working for Twentieth Century-Fox, for example, the company produced *Gentleman's Agreement.* It was based on the book by Laura Z. Hobson; it starred Dorothy McGuire, who was married to Gerard Swope's son John, the photographer; and its theme was anti-Semitism, a subject to which Herbert Swope had been devoting much thought since his involvement with Jewish organizations. The promotion of the movie was from many an angle, accordingly, a natural for Swope.

Shortly before its première a crisis came up. The picture was being released late in December, and to win a nomination for an Academy Award, which its producers very much hoped it would, it had to make its mark before the end of the year. But Hedda Hopper, whose approval of any movie in her syndicated column counted heavily in the minds of people who make nominations for Oscars, was hesitant about giving it a plug. The reason was, Zanuck wrote Swope, that she'd heard that Baruch, an old friend of hers, had some reservations about Mrs. Hobson's book. The solution to this dilemma, Twentieth Century-Fox had concluded, was to get Baruch to see the movie and, if possible, to give it his blessing. That would bring Miss Hopper in line. It went without saying that Swope was the one man who it was thought could carry out this delicate assignment.

Swope arranged a special showing of the film in New York and escorted Baruch to it, assuring Zanuck that, if Baruch liked it, Miss Hopper would quickly learn of his reaction. But something happened that no one had counted on. Baruch had very little reaction to the movie one way or another because he couldn't hear the sound. "I repaired that breach by sending him the script," Swope wrote Zanuck three weeks before the deadline for Academy Award nominations. Five more days went by, and Zanuck begged Swope to get some word about Baruch to Miss Hopper before all was lost. Swope did his best. He wrote the columnist:

Dear Hedda:

Having heard that you had a high opinion of the picture, I took B.M. to see (and hear) *Gentleman's Agreement*. He was deeply impressed—so much so that he sent for the script which Moss Hart supplied personally. I share your opinion. I think it is one of the most fruitful pictures I have ever seen.

Gentleman's Agreement got the nomination its producers wanted. Lacking a testimonial from Baruch, Twentieth Century-Fox proceeded to repair *that* breach by advertising the movie with a tribute that went, "*Gentleman's Agreement* is an important contribution to the literature of today. It deals with a burning question with swift sure touches, never leaving drama even when it teaches its deepest lesson. It is among the great pictures I have seen.—HERBERT BAYARD SWOPE."

Nearly all of Swope's postwar clients found themselves involved, one way or another, in a principal nonprofit pursuit of his to which he was faithful to the end of his days. This was Freedom House, which was formed at the end of 1941 as an offshoot of the Committee to Defend America by Aiding the Allies and a likeminded body, Fight for Freedom. Freedom House was not an activist group. It was conceived of by its founders—Herbert Agar, Thomas Finletter, Mrs. Kermit Roosevelt, Wendell Willkie, and Swope—as an institution antithetical to Hitler's celebrated shrine of oppression, The Brown House in Munich. The new House was open to all and considered its function to be that of a clearinghouse and meetingplace for the many American organizations concerned with freedom.

Freedom House took over a building—ultimately known as the Willkie Memorial Building—on West 40th Street in New York City, across from the Public Library; among the tenants were the National Association for the Advancement of Colored People and the Anti-Defamation League of B'nai B'rith. The structure had once been a private club. After the repeal of Prohibition it was acquired by Schenley Industries. Swope, a director of Freedom House for seventeen years, was mainly responsible for Schenley's letting his group have the building for far less than the asking price. When Freedom House couldn't even raise enough to meet the absolute minimum, Swope cajoled the head of Schenley's, Lewis S. Rosenstiel—a man who knew well from the Volstead Act era how insufferable restrictions on freedom could be—into forgoing a final twenty-five thousand dollars that was due his company.

Many of Swope's fellow directors on the Freedom House

board were men with a strong intellectual bent—the outspokenly liberal Catholic priest George B. Ford, for instance, the crusading editor Norman Cousins, the indefatigable committeeman Leo Cherne. The chief full-time administrator was George Field, a man full of fervent, visionary ideas that he wanted carried out in the name of freedom. He would not infrequently run hard into Swope's pragmatic opposition to fanciful new notions. "Swope would argue and argue against me," Field recalled, "but as often as not he'd finally say, 'Well, if this young man thinks this can be done, why should we try to stop him?' And then he would help me."

Swope was invaluable to Freedom House because of his incomparable ability to attract the interest and the money of important men who had many rival demands on their time and their funds. He persuaded Robert Patterson to become the president of Freedom House and Henry Luce to be the chairman of one of its fund drives. The organization's main attention-getting, and money-raising, device was to hold an annual dinner—Swope was invariably toastmaster—at which it bestowed upon some worthy recipient an award for having contributed the most to the cause of freedom in the previous year. The choice for this high acclaim naturally depended on who was available.* Swope regularly provided Freedom House with a personage of real distinction—an Eisenhower or a Churchill or a Baruch—and since whatever a man of that stripe said at a public gathering was apt to constitute news, Freedom House could always be certain of a gratifying flurry of annual publicity. Reflecting contentedly on the roster of Freedom Award winners—the list also included Dean Acheson, General Lucius D. Clay, Dr. James B. Conant, David Lilienthal, Walter Lippmann, General George C. Marshall, Senator Arthur H. Vandenberg, and Sumner Welles, most of whom had been corralled by Swope—George Field observed, "Swope did twenty times as much work for us as for anybody who ever paid him a fee." Swope worked so hard for the Freedom House dinners that in preparing for almost every one of them he lost his voice—for

---

* In a manipulated society, availability often governs acclamation. One industrialist, a client of Swope's, got an honorary degree from a well-known university because the university hoped that Baruch would speak at its commencement exercises. It asked Swope to bring this about. On learning that Baruch wasn't interested, Swope talked the university into accepting his client as a top-drawer substitute.

him, a real sacrifice. His family had no need to consult a calendar to determine, each year, when the banquet was imminent; there was, instead, the telltale recurrent evidence that the paterfamilias had once again grown hoarse and, in his anxiety to make his remarks and those of others a resounding success, all but inaudible.

23

B Y THE time Swope reached seventy, at the start of 1952, there was nothing unusual about a male American's moving serenely beyond the Biblical life span of three score years and ten. In Swope's case there was ample evidence close at hand that a septuagenarian had every expectation of a vigorous and fruitful future. The two men with whom he had been most intimate for the longest time were flourishing examples; Gerard Swope was approaching eighty and still had a firm seat on a horse, and Baruch, at eighty-two, could still bring down a quail or a woodcock on the wing. Yet the mere fact of becoming seventy had a profound effect on Herbert Swope; the messages of congratulation he received on his birthday in January had the same sour impact on him as the posting of a backstage closing notice has on the cast of a long-running show.

Swope's gloom was accentuated by the deaths, within the first four months of that anniversary year, of three persons who meant much to him. First Robert Patterson, whom Swope had not long before happily seen installed as the president of Freedom House, was killed in an airplane crash. Then Jacob Landau, in whose struggle to survive the infighting that wrecked the Overseas News Agency Swope had been a loyal henchman, died of a heart attack. ("You stuck by him even when you knew it meant you, too, would have to wade through mud," Landau's widow wrote Swope. "Jacob never got over the wonder of it. Jacob said to me over and over again, 'All Swope ever had from me is trouble. I wish I could do something really big for him.'") The death in April of Helen Millar, who for more than thirty years had been

462

an uncompromising ally in Swope's own clashes with a sometimes hostile outside world, was the final blow.

When Swope was in an exuberant mood his gaiety was overwhelming. The dimensions of his despair were no less exaggerated. As when he talked he demanded and generally got the undivided attention of all within earshot, so when he lapsed into glum silence was it nearly impossible for anyone to penetrate the thick pall of his withdrawal. Preoccupied with thoughts of death, he scrawled notes to himself like "Things to do—Get a lawyer to familiarize myself with my Will and other things." (A man who liked to do everything on a grand scale, Swope appointed seven executors in one of several dozen wills he drew up. A lawyer persuaded him to curtail the field, on grounds of unwieldiness.) He had been suffering for sometime from insomnia, and now it got worse, despite his recourse to sedatives, chiropractors, psychiatrists, and books like *Outwitting Our Nerves*, which assured him that the main cause of not sleeping was worrying about not sleeping and that all he had to do was to stop fretting. "The best way to learn to sleep is not to care whether you do or not," Swope read; but it was difficult advice to accept for a man whose stock in trade was caring about whatever he was doing with hot passion. Dourly writing to Baruch in the spring of 1952 about his sleeplessness and concurrent inability to outwit his nerves, Swope said, "I'm a God damned weakling and I don't control myself. I get out of bed much too often; I have anxieties and apprehensions—just a complete fathead. Thank God these spells don't come on me too often!"

Baruch tried solicitously to jolly his friend into a think-younger-and-live-longer frame of mind. When two months later a press agent for a World Beauty Congress asked Swope if he couldn't arrange for Baruch to be photographed on a park bench with fifteen aspirants for the title of Miss Universe, Swope was laggard in passing along the invitation; on finally doing so, he said, "There was a time when they couldn't have held you away from the job. Now we have to be statesmen!" Baruch scribbled a response on Swope's letter: "Why so late in communicating with me. . . . Who wants to be a statesman in these circumstances? You are thinking of someone older than I." But it did not seem to cheer Swope especially to know that older men than he were still capable of feeling coltish. He had periodically been calling on the retired Florence White, twenty years his senior. In 1955, however, Swope, then seventy-three, wrote to another *World* elder, Sherman Morse, that he had stopped visiting White. "I fell out of the habit of seeing him when I got to be afraid of age," Swope told Morse, who was then eighty-five himself.

When not in the grip of one of his spells, Swope tried valiantly to be his old ebullient self. On the eve of his seventy-third birthday, as if to demonstrate that, like Baruch, one could be no older than one thought one was, he sent in his annual dues to an organization called the Affiliated Young Democrats. (A man of wide interests, he also belonged to the Society for the Preservation of Long Island Antiquities.) His concern for politics remained keen; and it was gratifying to him that while in the 1952 Presidential campaign he had not been overtly antagonistic to his good friend Adlai Stevenson, the White House came to be occupied by the even better friend he had supported with advice and with betting money and on whose behalf he had briefly contemplated setting up and running a rump group called Wilson Democrats for Eisenhower. (After the 1952 returns were in, Swope suggested to President Eisenhower that he put Stevenson in charge of the American delegation to the United Nations.) Before Eisenhower's nomination, when the general was in Europe commanding SHAPE, Swope and he frequently communicated about his Presidential prospects.* Concurrently, Swope was urging Henry Cabot Lodge, one of Eisenhower's chief strategists, to have the general bone up on some of the nonmilitary aspects of American public life by conferring with a few representative businessmen. Two of them whom Swope thought it would be especially useful for Eisenhower to get acquainted with were Lewis Rosenstiel and David Sarnoff.

On January 7, 1953, just before Eisenhower's first inauguration, Swope wrote him, "I shall not bother you unless I see a matter of immediate importance, then I will try to jog your elbow."

---

* Swope, of course, had by then been on amiable terms with Eisenhower for several years. Swope had a peculiar way of pronouncing some words. In the winter of 1947, when Eisenhower was Chief of Staff, the general was on a golfing holiday at Miami. Swope, anxious to talk to him one day, telephoned the Pentagon, inquiring of the person who answered whether Eisenhower was "still in Me-ah-me." The response was vague and unenlightening, despite Swope's loud and repeated insistence that he be given the information he'd requested. A few days later Swope was surprised when an FBI agent dropped in at his office; the man wanted to know why it was that Swope had been so determined to ascertain whether Eisenhower was "still in the Army."

Less than a month afterward, though, he could not resist telling the President:

> Just a word that will help to bring a note of cheer in these labor-laden days:
>
> Your responses from the White House are quicker than those from any occupant with whom I have been on friendly terms since Woodrow Wilson.
>
> That shows what a fine system you have instituted. But I doubt that you could have put in any other kind—it's the nature of the beast.

Eisenhower wrote back the same day he received that note that his secretaries had said he had to answer Swope's letter at once. Somewhat muted Swope might have become, but the prospect of incurring his wrath still could make the White House edgy. And in the same mail, what was even more rewarding, Swope had a note from one of the President's assistants, Colonel Robert L. Schulz, who on Eisenhower's instructions was glad to be able to advise Swope of a way of writing personal letters to the President—through a post-office box in Schulz's name—that would reach his desk more swiftly than correspondence that had to fight its way upstream through normal White House channels.

To have such special access to the Presidential eye was, naturally, a delight to Swope, but as he grew older he did not always use it tellingly. He was as eager as ever to transmit ideas to the White House, but he was getting increasingly careless about something he would not tolerate in others—checking his facts. On May 12, 1955, for instance, when he was over seventy-three and in not the best of health, a way occurred to him of bolstering United States prestige in one then troubled corner of the earth, and he at once wrote to Eisenhower, urging him to invite the Prime Minister of Ceylon, Sir John Kotalawala, to Washington sometime soon. Eisenhower was obliged to reply that Sir John had been in America five months before and had had lunch at the White House. The President added that Swope must have missed it in the papers. That must have hurt doubly.

Swope had good reason for giving his beloved newspapers less careful scrutiny than had been his custom. The mere sight of an obituary page disturbed him. There are men still in their forties who regard a day as spoiled if at the start of it they discern that the average age of the top headliners on the *Times* obituary page

465

is less than their age; a morbid man in his seventies has little chance of coming out ahead in that kind of game unless a nonagenarian or two has been considerate enough to die the day before. Still, Swope, though suffering from anxiety, nervousness, and the awful awareness of his age, continued to read his newspapers, clipping shears at hand, more assiduously than most men ever do, and it was a rare day that went by without his telephoning at least one journalist to give a compliment, a reprimand, or a suggestion. The overburdened editor of one New York daily complained to the equally busy editor of another that he'd spent an hour listening to Swope before he could make an excuse to hang up. "I had him for an hour just before you did," said the second editor. "Did he have anything important to say to *you?*" asked the first. "No," said the second, "but what we probably both ought to remember is that some day we'll be in his position ourselves."

One newspaperman who figured importantly in Swope's ebbing years was Turner Catledge, the managing editor of the *Times*. They had met at the 1936 Democratic National Convention, in Philadelphia, when Catledge was a reporter on the Washington staff of the paper. Swope, absenting himself from his delegate's chair for dinner, went to Bookbinder's restaurant. He spotted Arthur Krock presiding over a table of *Times* men and joined them. Swope forthwith tipped Krock off to a newsy morsel he'd picked up during the day and was sure the *Times* would enjoy having exclusively for the following morning. Krock said he already knew all about it.

"How the hell did you know?" asked Swope.

"This reporter here got the story," said Krock, introducing Catledge.

Swope took a long, thoughtful look at Catledge and said, "I'll be God damned. You're the first reporter I ever met who's as good as I am."

Catledge moved to the New York office in 1945 and began to see a lot of Swope. "He had a great enjoyment of life, and a great sense of history in its recent phases—and also, of course, quite an appreciation of his own connection with it," Catledge said. "And he was a big help to me in my editorial job. I felt as if I had a free-lance city editor working for me. He was the sort of goad I needed." Catledge was spending a weekend with Swope at Sands Point when President Eisenhower had his heart attack in Denver, on September 23, 1955. The Swope telephones were soon pre-empted by the *Times*, as one staff man after another called the managing editor for directions on covering the incident. Swope relished every minute of the excitement. For a while it was as though he himself were back at an editorial desk, barking out instructions under pressure. "I had a feeling Herbert was having a vicarious ball," Catledge reflected afterward. "He kept telling me, between phone calls, 'Don't make this play too modest. This is a *big* story!' And I was glad he had a chance to be even that much in on it."

"Growing old is not too happy an experience," Swope wrote in 1953 to Sherman Morse, to whom he also observed at about that time that "life's chief problem" was "blunting the edge of age." An equally pressing problem, for Swope, was to try to blunt the knife-sharp thrusts of continuing financial need. The gushing inflow of money that his scale of living demanded had abated, and he hoped he could somehow stem the outflow, too. (He always carried around a little sterling-silver image, an infant of Prague, that his latter-life secretary, Kathleen E. Gilmore, gave him. The legend was that anyone equipped with such a charm would never be impecunious, but Swope's experience hardly gave credence to the superstition.) One obvious step was to sell the Sands Point house. It was too large, the taxes on it were too high, and too many servants were required to run it properly. And it would fetch, he believed, two hundred and fifty thousand dollars. But it also proved—until Swope's widow finally disposed of it in 1964—to be unsalable.

Swope sought hard, though, to unload it. He was as aware as anyone that in the 1950s few places such as his were attractive to individual owners and that his best chance was to find an institutional purchaser. (The only individuals he considered likely prospects were Mike Todd and King Farouk.) At one time or another Swope attempted to sell the property, through Sarnoff, to the National Broadcasting Company for conversion into television studios; to the United States Navy as a training base; to International Business Machines as a country club for its executives; to the Soviet and Nationalist Chinese delegations to the United Nations; to the Department of State as an official residence for the American delegate to the UN; and to Robert Moses for use as a park and yacht basin. A month before Swope's death he was still trying, and in last-ditch fashion he sent a note to Baruch's secre-

467

tary: "I want to sell my house. Why doesn't B.M.B. buy it?"

Some money kept coming in from Swope's old clients, but the search for new clients went on. Like a young family man who simply must have some kind of job to make ends meet, Swope offered his services to the Ford Foundation, to the Coca-Cola Company, and to the government of Iran. His rosiest prospect for a while seemed to be Liberia. A group of Americans, including his son-in-law, Robert L. Brandt, thought it might be lucrative to import diamonds from that country, and in 1954 they entered into an agreement with Swope, who in return for helping to overcome any obstacles they might run into was to get seven and a half per cent of their net profits.

When the President of Liberia, William V. S. Tubman, visited the United States that summer, Swope arranged a fancy dinner for him at the "21" Club, with a distinguished wine list and an equally eminent guest list, including the Mayor of New York, Ralph Bunche, Jim Farley, and such staunch Swope friends as Sarnoff and Baruch. Swope was eventually thanked for his hospitality by being designated a Knight Commander of Liberia, but the decoration was nearly his entire harvest from the undertaking; his share of the profits on diamond sales was a disappointing three hundred and sixty-five dollars and eighty-five cents, less than the cost of the feast.

His main source of income, toward the end, came from trotting races. At the start of 1954 he was engaged as a policy consultant by both the Roosevelt and Yonkers Raceways. It was difficult for a man who for so long had pledged his allegiance to flat racing to work up real enthusiasm for a plebeian cousin of that aristocratic sport, but there was one solace. Swope had never received a salary as State Racing Commissioner, and the trotting people, who hoped he would bring to their growing sport a measure of respectability they had not much enjoyed, were willing to pay him, in fees and expenses, fifty thousand dollars a year. Margaret Swope was not fazed when a new breed of horse fancier began to turn up in her drawing room. While she professed to think that some trotting men, at least, were "a bunch of absolute thugs," she also professed to find these same ones enchanting. "I've always had a sort of feeling for schlemiels," she said. Her husband, doing his best to cleanse the sport of its raffish repute, acted in his usual forthright fashion; among those he invited to accompany him to the Roosevelt opening in the spring of 1954 was J. Edgar Hoover.

468

All the same, the trotting races never touched Swope's heart. He was pleased to have found a new patron, but he still much preferred races in which a horse's guide sat atop his mount, instead of being dragged behind it in a claptrap caudal chariot. Swope used to love to recite the ancestry of thoroughbred race horses and to devise names for them in keeping with their illustrious origins. For trotters and pacers he had no such feeling. It was almost indicative of his lack of interest in the pastime that, while willing enough to lend his name, for a price, to its furtherance, he began to spend many evenings in affable flat-racing reminiscence at a cottage owned by the trainer Max Hirsch at Belmont Park, in the stable area.

Hirsch was two years older than Swope. They had known each other from 'way back; Hirsch had trained horses for Arnold Rothstein, for Morton and Charles Schwartz, and for Baruch, who in his later years, when going to the races at Belmont, would often stop in first at Hirsch's cottage for a refreshing nap.* Late in the day, after the races, Swope would drop in at Hirsch's, and he would sit there for hours swapping racing yarns, so relatively at ease that, despite his ordinary fastidiousness, he would let Hirsch's dogs climb all over him and shed hair in his lap. Sometimes,

---

* Hirsch liked to tell one story about the fun-loving 1920s. Baruch decided while having breakfast at Saratoga with the trainer that it would be nice to try to make a killing off the bookmakers. He asked Hirsch to buy a horse for him and get it, without too much fanfare, into winning condition. Hirsch found a onetime robust runner that had turned seedy, and began to freshen it up. When he decided the horse was ready to run, he called Baruch and said he had entered it in a race. He warned Baruch, though, not to pass the word on to Swope and the Schwartz brothers; they would probably start betting and depress the odds. Instead, Hirsch would bet surreptitiously for Baruch and for his three friends. The day of the race, the horse opened up at ten to one. Hirsch had commissioners scurrying around on his behalf from one bookmaker to another, and they were so busy that by post time the price on the horse had been driven down to eight to five. Then, as the race was starting, Hirsch joined Baruch, the Schwartzes, and Swope. Baruch asked how much had been bet. "Thirty thousand dollars," Hirsch said. The foursome stood to win around two hundred thousand, which might not have ruined the bookies but would have given them a memorable jolt. In the back stretch, Baruch's horse opened up a lead of seven or eight lengths. Swope and the Schwartzes, by then aware how much money was on the horse, began pummeling one another and screaming with joy and hugging Baruch—began celebrating their triumph so wildly, indeed, that nobody except Hirsch had his eyes on the track when another horse sprinted up on the outside and beat out Baruch's horse by a nose.

Swope, whose own meal schedule was of course quite different from that of an early-bird race-track man, would sit and chat contentedly while the Hirsch family had its dinner. Hirsch's cook called Swope Sitting Bull.

At Swope's own homes the atmosphere was more subdued than it had been. He didn't entertain quite as much as formerly, and he didn't go out quite as much, either. To his friends, in years gone by, it had been irritating, but not critical, for the Swopes to show up outrageously late at dinner parties. But now most of the people Swope knew had reduced staffs, and their cooks liked meals to be served on time. There were not a few hostesses who were more concerned about staying in the good graces of servants than of Swopes. Ironically, as these precautions were being taken against Swope's spoiling front-stairs–back-stairs harmony, he himself was now and then exhibiting belated signs of promptness. He began turning up on time at Freedom House board meetings. ("H.B., what the hell has *happened?*" his dumfounded fellow directors would exclaim.) Told one evening that if he arrived for a poker game as much as five minutes late he wouldn't be dealt in, Swope, who in prior years would have remained imperiously impervious to any such threat, was on hand five minutes early. He even got to an occasional theatrical first night before the curtain was up.

He no longer went to all the important premières, however. The new genre of playwrights, with their emphasis on neurosis and aberrant sexuality, were not to his taste. He had so many depressing thoughts in real life that he could do without more of the same when he sought make-believe distraction. After the first act of one Tennessee Williams opus Swope excused himself to his wife, walked up the aisle and disappeared until the final curtain. Margaret had not much use for stark plays, either. Most of the modern dramas that others hailed as classics she dismissed, in and out of their authors' hearing, as crashing bores. When an exasperated playwright asked her once what she *did* like, she said, in her customary ironical fashion, "I like plays about the problems of the rich, and I like them solved in attractive settings." In this instance, however, she remained in her seat, though she suspected something dreadful had probably happened to her husband and was tempted to enjoin the police to drop everything else and search for him. When Swope reappeared it turned out that he'd simply been unable to stand the sad and sordid play and had gone

470

to a movie. He thought that walking might help cure his insomnia, and he would sometimes insist, after a show or late dinner party, on going home on foot. Margaret, aware that her lion had grown old, was terrified that he would fall prey to muggers. She would climb into their car after he'd set out and have the chauffeur follow him, at a discreet distance, until he'd reached his destination.

In some notes for a 1950 speech about Baruch, Swope mused, "He has vanity—who hasn't? Vanity is another term for conscientiousness; always do the best you can." This was a variation on a theme upon which Swope had dwelt before, publicly. Ten years earlier he had said, "Conceit is usually a mark of self-faith." The columnist Albert Edward Wiggam, in his syndicated feature "Exploring Your Mind," had picked this up and asked his readers, "Do you agree?" Without waiting for their response, he indicated he did not. "This may be true of a man betting on race horses," said Wiggam, who knew Swope was then a Racing Commissioner. "And I understand it is one of Mr. Swope's duties to try to regulate the races, but it is surely not true of human nature in general. Conceit is simply another name for egotism and egotism is another name for swell-head, and swell-head is another name for show-off, and they are all merely other names for fear. The very essence of conceit is fear. Real self-faith is vastly different. It is a genuine and usually intelligent belief in one's capacity to succeed in whatever he undertakes."

Conceit Swope certainly had. He had self-faith, too. And as far as achieving what he set out to do was concerned, he certainly appeared to be a successful man. He had resolved at an early age that he would make Herbert Bayard Swope someone to reckon with and listen to and talk about, and there was no doubt he had brought this splendidly to pass. There were few in his time who would deny his uniqueness. His disdain for conventionalities had won him many enemies and lost him just as many friends, but even those who could not bring themselves to like him had to concede that his vitality and curiosity and prickliness made the world in which he grandly moved more interesting than it would otherwise have been. "I must confess I am living a sort of aimless existence," Swope said at the start of 1958. That at seventy-six he should still be searching for a goal was perhaps indicative that whatever anyone else might think about him *he* considered his high promise by no means completely fulfilled. He could, and often morosely did, look back on what seemed a bitter dose of disappointments. There were so many stock tips he should have had but didn't get, so many finder's fees he thought he'd earned but had not received, so many deeds undone, and so many others done but unacknowledged.

The trouble was that the character he portrayed was of such heroic stature that his friends expected a good deal more of him than he was actually capable of giving. It was the same with some of Swope's business clients, who, being men who had to decide things, could not altogether comprehend an associate who was largely a man who gave advice. Swope himself liked to say toward the end of his life, when pressed for an accounting of precisely what services he had rendered this or that client, that to enumerate them would be not only difficult but meaningless, inasmuch as he operated in an area of intangibles. It was a tough spot for a man to be in, especially when so many of those from whom he derived his income were concerned with tangibles—case sales of whiskey, for instance, or the nightly attendance at a trotting track. Perhaps it was Swope's misfortune to end his life in an era when egocentricity was in low repute, and when what a man did counted for more than what one was. In an age of status symbols he insisted on being his own status symbol. But it did not seem to matter so much to others, any longer, that here was a man who could proudly advertise to the world that he could never be successfully imitated. He had only himself to comfort with the reflection that there was no reasonable facsimile of a Herbert Bayard Swope, and little chance that, even in an age of technological marvels, one could ever be credibly synthesized.

A year before he died Swope left RCA and NBC when he failed to make much of an argument for his being kept on. He could have hung around on a severely curtailed basis, but his pride wouldn't let him, and anyhow he had decided he couldn't get along with John L. Burns, whom RCA installed as its president early in 1957. That June, just as Swope was severing his connections with the organization, Burns made a commencement address in which he said that the country's greatest shortage was of "men who know people and who can work effectively with and through them." Swope thought there was bitter irony in that remark coming at that time from that source, and, calling the words to Sarnoff's attention, added, "I hope this statement of Mr. Burns's is true, for I think I know as many people as the next one, and

I have no difficulty in working through them or having them work through me."

"We are both of us passing into the Danger Zone," Swope wrote Arthur Krock early in 1958, employing his emphatic capitals. He still now and then behaved in character—he was prompt to congratulate President Eisenhower when the United States sent its first satellite into orbit that February—but his enthusiasm for life was waning. In his last months his son, trying to shake him out of his apathy, pointed out to him that Baruch and Churchill and others of his friends, far older than he was, were still bustling about. "People want you to be important, informative, exciting, brilliant," the younger Swope adjured his father, "part-sage, part-Caesar." Swope could not bring himself to meet this demand. He did, however, write an indignant letter to the *New Republic*, which in its April 28, 1958, issue referred to him chillingly as "the late Herbert Bayard Swope."

To the end, he protected his name like a trademark, and he gloried in its every legitimate use. Only ten days before he died the *Herald Tribune* daily crossword puzzle had as its "4 down" definition "Herbert ——— Swope." Swope snipped out the puzzle and, before having it pasted up in a scrapbook, ignored all the squares except the "4 down" one, which he neatly and accurately filled in with red crayon. Even then, he must have needed and welcomed further reassurance that people were aware that he existed.

Swope had been hospitalized late in April 1958 for a hernia operation. The ailment gave him a new area of information to get concerned about. He would write notes about his own symptoms and pass them along, as he had relayed so many other bits and scraps of knowledge to others, to his own attending doctors. He was out of the hospital for only a month before he had to be readmitted, this time suffering from diverticulitis. (What worried him almost more than the impending surgery was that while sitting in a restaurant, on his way to the hospital, he lost a gold pencil, his favorite note-maker. Without it he felt defenseless.) The surgery he had to face this time was not especially serious, but he seemed to have no strong will to survive it. "I'm not coming out of here," he told one visitor, George Backer, before the operation. Baruch stopped by to see him, with Billy Rose in tow, and Rose said later, in his peculiar Broadway jargon, "I got the feeling that the fellow in the black suit was with him, too."

The friend Swope seemed most eager to be with was a relatively new one—Father George Ford. Swope was not a religious man. He had a habit of filching Gideon Bibles from hotel rooms, but he was motivated not so much by belief as by acquisitiveness. He took ashtrays, too. Detached though Swope was from any formal religious adherence, though, he had always been fond of priests. He had got to know quite a few of them through Al Smith, and one of Swope's favorite Smith stories had to do with an upstate political campaign, during which Smith arose at six one bleak and snow-gripped winter morning and urged his entourage to accompany him to early Mass. The invitation went unheeded. Smith set off alone into the shivery outdoors, saying, "God, if I'm wrong, what a penalty I'm paying!"

The comfort Swope derived from Father Ford's presence in his hospital room apparently had nothing to do with any contemplated deathbed conversion. "He'd ask me to come to the hospital every night," Father Ford said, "even as late—for me, that was—as midnight. He seemed to look forward to my coming. It had nothing to do with religion. He had no religious faith that I knew of, and I always just assumed that he was a good agnostic. But, toward the end, he would always say, 'George, please say a prayer for me,' and I did, and I participated in his funeral afterward, for which I guess I could have been excommunicated."

Swope caught pneumonia after the second operation and died four days later, on June 20. The funeral service in which Father Ford took part was held at the Sands Point house. The service was different from what Swope had had in mind when he had dwelt on the subject thirty-one years earlier. "I should like to have John Haynes Holmes say a few words," Swope had told himself then, "as he is one of the few clergymen I know who is free from hypocrisy and false religion. If not him, then someone of his type. While making acknowledgment to God, I want the service to be as freed from religiosity as possible. I should like to have the music consist of something stirring rather than funereal —perhaps something like the Battle Hymn of the Republic, or the Marseillaise; perhaps also Old Black Joe." There was no music, when the time finally came, but the service was simple, and Father Ford was probably as close as a Catholic clergyman could come to Holmes.

The priest read a couple of psalms and said a prayer. (He was not excommunicated.) Martin Gabel recited two poems, one of them Swope's old favorite "Invictus," which Swope himself had intoned to the banker Charles Morse, riding to the penitentiary in Georgia, forty-nine years before. Baruch said a few words, and Robert Moses delivered the principal eulogy: "His was the sharp, probing, challenging, incisive mind, the astonishing memory, the biting speech vitriolic only as a fine teacher is vitriolic, the supreme impatience with mushiness, sloppiness, fustian and clichés. He was a tireless battler for the right word, a purist in the practice of our matchless English language. . . ."

Then, seeking to borrow an apt phrase from Thoreau, Moses said, "No chronicler of small beer, he did not roam the wide world to count the cats in Madagascar." Had Swope been there, and in top form, Moses would probably have got no further. With a roar of scornful indignation, Swope would have pounced on him in mid-paean and announced, using a liberal dosage of the didactic acid so well known to Moses and the eighty or so other mourners present, that the speaker was a flathead of the most egregious sort and that, as anybody in his right senses knew—or, at any rate, as *he* knew—the cats that Thoreau's nonchronicler of small beer did not roam the world to count were not in Madagascar but in Zanzibar.

There were two other memorial services—one at Freedom House and one at the Columbia School of Journalism, where a room already consecrated to the *World* was redecorated and rededicated in Swope's name. On neither occasion did any of the men who spoke happen to quote one phrase from Swope's past that might have served as a fitting epitaph. It was an excerpt from the official chart of the running of the Belmont Stakes in 1925. The race horse that Bud Fisher named after Swope was entered, and while those who had bet on the horse to win were disappointed when he came in only third, the chart said, "Swope ran a good race all the way and finished well."

475

BIBLIOGRAPHICAL NOTE

HERBERT SWOPE was not a sentimental man, but he saved everything about himself. A magazine article about him that he professed not to like he had done up, as a preservative, in natural linen. It is hard to figure out what, if anything, he proposed to do with them, but until his death he kept more than one hundred copies of the issue of *Editor & Publisher* that announced his retirement, thirty years before, from the *World*. He saved old, worthless tote tickets—the dismal spoor of all the horses he'd backed that ran out of the money. (He told his secretary once that when she had nothing better to do she might get an adding machine and calculate how much of an investment this heap of scrap paper represented, but she never found the time.) He saved old cardiograms, old dog licenses, and rubber bands of any vintage. (His son recalled that, when he was small, his father's hands always used to smell of newsprint and rubber bands.) He couldn't throw anything away. At the *World* he dictated a long telegram to a reporter on an out-of-town assignment. Just as Swope was finishing, a message came in from the man that made his editor's instructions obsolete. Swope could not bring himself to destroy his telegram, so he tacked onto it a "Disregard the foregoing" and sent it along.

Every now and then Swope would make a vague effort to reform and would remind himself, in writing, to start weeding things out. Then he would add the reminder to his files. He saved ticket stubs from prize fights ("Loughran knocked out Sharkey," he would scribble on a stub) and from baseball games (he would inscribe the score and the names of the winning and losing pitchers). He saved a card showing that a pressed duck he'd eaten at La Tour d'Argent in Paris in 1918 was Number 44971, and with it a pass issued that year by the Adjutant General of the American armies in France—which had stamped on it "This pass must be returned to the office of the assistant Provost Marshal, Paris." He saved form letters he had no

476

intention of answering inviting him to charity functions he had no intention of attending. Curiously, the one thing he did not save, to the distress of a researcher who becomes fretful if exposed overlong to libraries, was a complete file of his *World*.

Swope's own accumulation of material about himself—a couple of dozen fat scrapbooks and a hundred or so bulging filing cabinets—was the documentary lode from which much of the information in this book was dredged. Other sources were the correspondence files of Bernard Baruch and a set of the minutes of *World* Council meetings, from 1920 through 1926, in the possession of Arthur Krock. Gerard Swope, Jr., provided material relating to his father. The New York Public Library, the Library of Congress, and the Yale University Library all furnished assistance. Columbia University was good enough to make available, in its Oral History series, the transcribed reminiscences of Rev. George B. Ford, Mrs. Florence Jaffray Harriman, John H. Hettrick, DeWitt Clinton Poole, Benjamin H. Reese, William Jay Schieffelin, and James P. Warburg. The New York *World* was much consulted, naturally, as was the New York *Times*, an invaluable aid to any researcher. Many other newspapers and magazines have provided bits and pieces.

The main books and articles drawn on were:

ADAMS, FRANKLIN P., *The Diary of Our Own Samuel Pepys*. Simon and Schuster, New York, 1935.

——, *Nods and Becks*. Whittlesey House, New York, 1944.

ADAMS, SAMUEL HOPKINS, *Alexander Woollcott: His Life and His World*. Reynal & Hitchcock, New York, 1945.

American Racehorses of 1936. The Sagamore Press, Maryland, 1937. (Foreword by Herbert Bayard Swope.)

AMORY, CLEVELAND, *The Last Resorts*. Harper & Bros., New York, 1952.

Ask Me Another!, ed. by Lucien Esty and Justin Spafford. Simon and Schuster, New York, 1927.

BARAGWANATH, JOHN, *A Good Time Was Had*. Appleton-Century-Crofts, New York, 1962.

BARRETT, JAMES W., *The World, the Flesh, and Messrs. Pulitzer*. The Vanguard Press, New York, 1931.

——, *Joseph Pulitzer and His World*. The Vanguard Press, New York, 1941.

——, ed. *The End of the World*. Harper & Bros., New York, 1931.

BARRYMORE, ETHEL, *Memories*. Harper & Bros., New York, 1955.

BARRYMORE, JOHN, *Confessions of an Actor*. The Bobbs-Merrill Co., Indianapolis, 1926.

BARUCH, BERNARD M., *Baruch: My Own Story*. Henry Holt & Co., New York, 1957.

——, *Baruch: The Public Years*. Holt, Rinehart & Winston, New York, 1960.

BEAZELL, WILLIAM P., "Death Comes to a Crusader," article in *Outlook and Independent*, March 11, 1931.

BETTS, TONEY, *Across the Board*. Citadel Press, New York, 1956.

BOLITHO, WILLIAM, *Italy under Mussolini*. The Macmillan Co., New York, 1926.

BOWERS, CLAUDE, *My Life: The Memoirs of Claude Bowers*. Simon and Schuster, New York, 1962.

BROUN, HEYWOOD, *The Boy Grew Older*. G. P. Putnam's Sons, New York, 1922.

——, *It Seems to Me*. Harcourt, Brace & Co., New York, 1935.

BURNS, JAMES MACGREGOR, *Roosevelt: The Lion and the Fox*. Harcourt, Brace & Co., New York, 1956.

——, *John Kennedy: A Political Profile*. Harcourt, Brace & Co., New York, 1960.

BUSCH, NOEL F., *Briton Hadden: A Biography of the Co-Founder of TIME*. Farrar, Straus & Co., New York, 1949.

BYRNES, JAMES F., *All in One Lifetime*. Harper & Bros., New York, 1958.

CERF, BENNETT, *Try and Stop Me*. Simon and Schuster, New York, 1944.

CLARKE, DONALD HENDERSON, *Man of the World: Recollections of an Irreverent Reporter*. The Vanguard Press, New York, 1950.

COIT, MARGARET L., *Mr. Baruch*. Houghton Mifflin Co., Boston, 1957.

CONNELL, BRIAN, *Knight Errant: A Biography of Douglas Fairbanks, Jr.* Hodder and Stoughton, London, 1955.

COURTNEY, MARGUERITE, *Laurette*. Rinehart & Co. New York, 1955.

COX, JAMES M., *Journey Through My Years*. Simon and Schuster, New York, 1946.

CREEL, GEORGE, *Rebel at Large*. G. P. Putnam's Sons, New York, 1947.

CROWTHER-SMITH, H. F., *The Art of Croquet*. H. F. & G. Witherby, London, 1932.

DANIELS, JOSEPHUS. *The Wilson Era: Years of Peace—1910–1917*. University of North Carolina Press. Chapel Hill, N.C., 1944.

ELDER, DONALD, *Ring Lardner*. Doubleday & Co., Garden City, N.Y., 1956.

FARLEY, JAMES A., *Behind the Ballots; the Personal History of a Politician*. Harcourt, Bace & Co., New York, 1930.

——, *Jim Farley's Story: The Roosevelt Years*. McGraw-Hill Book Co., New York, 1948.

FERBER, EDNA, *A Peculiar Treasure*. Doubleday & Co., New York, 1960.

FLYNN, EDWARD J., *You're the Boss*. The Viking Press, New York, 1947.

FOWLER, GENE, *Beau James: The Life and Times of Jimmy Walker.* The Viking Press, New York, 1949.

———, *Skyline.* The Viking Press, New York, 1961.

GELB, ARTHUR and BARBARA, *O'Neill.* Harper & Bros., New York, 1962.

GERARD, JAMES W., *My Four Years in Germany.* George H. Doran Co., New York, 1917.

———, *My First Eighty-three Years in America.* Doubleday & Co., Garden City, N.Y., 1951.

GORDON, RUTH, *Over Twenty-one.* Random House, New York, 1944.

GREEN, PAUL D., *Fabulous Freddie and the Saints and Sinners.* Wilfred Funk, New York, 1951.

HARRIMAN, MARGARET CASE, *The Vicious Circle.* Rinehart & Co., New York, 1951.

HECHT, BEN, *A Child of the Century.* Simon and Schuster, New York, 1954.

———, *Charlie.* Harper & Bros., New York, 1957.

HOBSON, LAURA Z., "Freedom Pavilion," article in the *Nation*, April 29, 1939.

HOLTON, LEONARD T., and LONGSTRETH, EDWARD, *What'll We Do Now?* Simon and Schuster, New York, 1928.

HOOVER, HERBERT, *Memoirs.* The Macmillan Co., New York, 1952.

HOWARD, LESLIE RUTH, *A Quite Remarkable Father.* Harcourt, Brace & Co., New York, 1959.

ICKES, HAROLD, *The Secret Diary of Harold L. Ickes.* Simon and Schuster, New York, 1953.

JACKSON, JOSEPHINE A., and SALISBURY, HELEN M., *Outwitting Our Nerves.* The Century Co., New York, 1932.

KAHN, E. J., JR., "Master of All, Jack of None," article in *The New Yorker*, July 24, 1948.

KATCHER, LEO, *The Big Bankroll: The Life and Times of Arnold Rothstein.* Harper & Bros., New York, 1959.

KAUFMAN, BEATRICE, and HENNESSEY, JOSEPH, eds., *The Letters of Alexander Woollcott.* The Viking Press, New York, 1944.

KELLOCK, HAROLD, *Houdini: His Life Story from the Recollections and Documents of Beatrice Houdini.* Harcourt, Brace & Co., New York, 1928.

KERNEY, JAMES, *The Political Education of Woodrow Wilson.* The Century Co., New York, 1926.

KIRK, DONALD, Unpublished history thesis on Herbert Bayard Swope for Princeton University, 1959.

KRAMER, DALE, *Heywood Broun: A Biographical Portrait.* A. A. Wyn, New York, 1949. (Foreword by Herbert Bayard Swope.)

LEVANT, OSCAR, *A Smattering of Ignorance.* Doubleday, Doran & Co., New York, 1940.

LEWIS, THERESE, " 'The World' Well Lost," article in *Town and Country*.

LILIENTHAL, ALFRED M., *What Price Israel*. Henry Regnery Co., Chicago, 1953.

LINDLEY, ERNEST K., *The Roosevelt Revolution: First Phase*. The Viking Press, New York, 1933.

LOTH, DAVID, *Swope of G.E.* Simon and Schuster, New York, 1958.

MANEY, RICHARD, *Fanfare*. Harper & Bros., New York, 1957.

MARX, HARPO, and BARBER, ROWLAND, *Harpo Speaks!* Bernard Geis Associates, New York, 1961.

MERRILL, ARCH, *The Lakes Country*. Reprinted from the *Democrat & Chronicle*, Rochester, N.Y., 1944.

MICHELSON, CHARLES, *The Ghost Talks*. G. P. Putnam's Sons, New York, 1944.

MOLEY, RAYMOND, *After Seven Years*. Harper & Bros., New York, 1939.

NICOLSON, HAROLD, *Peacemaking: 1919*. Houghton Mifflin Co., Boston and New York, 1933.

PRINGLE, HENRY F., "The Newspaperman as an Artist: Frank I. Cobb," article in *Scribner's Magazine*, New York, 1935.

PRIOR, R. C. A., *Notes on Croquet*. William & Norgate, London, 1872.

PROSKAUER, JOSEPH M., *A Segment of My Times*. Farrar, Straus & Co., New York, 1950.

RODGERS, CLEVELAND, *Robert Moses: Builder of Democracy*. Henry Holt & Co., New York, 1952.

ROOT, JONATHAN, *One Night in July*, Coward-McCann, New York, 1961.

ROSENBLOOM, MORRIS V., *Peace Through Strength: Bernard Baruch and a Blueprint for Security*. Farrar, Straus & Young, New York, 1953.

ROSS, CHARLES G., "Department of Amplification," article in *The New Yorker*, August 19, 1948.

SCHLESINGER, ARTHUR M., JR., *The Age of Roosevelt, II: The Coming of the New Deal*. Houghton Mifflin Co., Boston, 1958.

SCHWAB, ARNOLD T., *James Gibbons Huneker*. Stanford University Press, Stanford, Calif., 1963.

SCUDDDER, HORACE ELISHA, *The Game of Croquet: Its Appointments and Laws*. Hurd and Houghton, New York, 1866.

SEITZ, DON C., *Joseph Pulitzer: His Life & Letters*. Simon & Schuster, New York, 1924.

SHERIDAN, CLARE, *In Many Places*. Jonathan Cape, London, 1923.

SHERWOOD, ROBERT E., *Roosevelt and Hopkins*. Harper & Bros., New York, 1948.

SMITH, MORTIMER, *William Jay Gaynor*. Henry Regnery & Co., Chicago, 1951.

SPEWACK, BELLA and SAMUEL, *Clear All Wires*. Samuel French, New York and Los Angeles, 1932.

STEFFENS, LINCOLN, *The Autobiography of Lincoln Steffens*. Harcourt, Brace & Co., New York, 1931.

SULLIVAN, MARK, *Our Times; The United States*. Charles Scribner's Sons, New York, 1926–1935.

SWANBERG, W. A., *Citizen Hearst*. Charles Scribner's Sons, New York, 1961.

SWOPE, HERBERT BAYARD, *Inside the German Empire*. The Century Co., New York, 1917.

———, *Journalism: An Instrument of Civilization*. Publication of Phi Beta Kappa address delivered at Hobart College, Geneva, N.Y., June 16, 1924.

———, "An Instrument of Civilization," article in *An Introduction to Journalism*, ed. by Lawrence Murphy. Thomas Nelson & Sons, New York, 1930.

———, "The Aims of the New York *World*," article in *Newsmen Speak*, ed. by Edmond D. Coblentz. University of California Press, Berkeley and Los Angeles, Calif., 1954.

TALMEY, ALLENE, "First-Nighter," article in *Stage* magazine, January 1935.

TEBBEL, JOHN, *The Life and Good Times of William Randolph Hearst*. E. P. Dutton & Co., New York, 1952.

THOMPSON, CHARLES T., *The Peace Conference Day by Day*. Brentano's, New York, 1920.

TRAIN, ARTHUR, *Yankee Lawyer: The Autobiography of Ephraim Tutt*. Charles Scribner's Sons, New York, 1943.

A Treasury of Great Reporting, ed. by Louis L. Snyder and Richard B. Morris. (Preface by Herbert Bayard Swope.) Simon and Schuster, New York, 1949.

A Treasury of Jewish Quotations, ed. by Joseph L. Baron. Crown Publishers, New York, 1956.

WALKER, STANLEY, "Symphony in Brass," article in the *Saturday Evening Post*, June 4, 1938.

WARNER, EMILY SMITH, *The Happy Warrior: A Biography of My Father*. Doubleday & Co., New York, 1956.

WEINGAST, DAVID ELLIOT, *Walter Lippmann: A Study in Personal Journalism*. Rutgers University Press, New Brunswick, N.J., 1949.

WEITZENKORN, LOUIS, *Five Star Final*. (Preface by Herbert Bayard Swope.) Samuel French, New York, 1931.

WHEELER, JOHN N., *I've Got News for You*. E. P. Dutton and Co., New York, 1961.

WHITE, W. L., *Bernard Baruch, Portrait of a Citizen*. Harcourt, Brace & Co., New York, 1950.

481

WINKLER, JOHN K., *W. R. Hearst—An American Phenomenon.* Simon and Schuster, New York, 1928.

WOOLLCOTT, ALEXANDER, *Enchanted Aisles.* G. P. Putnam's Sons, New York, 1924.

———, *The Story of Irving Berlin.* G. P. Putnam's Sons, New York, 1925.

———, *Going to Pieces.* G. P. Putnam's Sons, New York, 1928.

E. J. K.

INDEX

487

Hotel Belmont (New York), 181–82
Hotel Carlton (Washington), 81
Hotel de Crillon (Paris), 228
Hotel Grand Horta (Fayal), 161
Hotel Metropole (New York), 147, 149
Hotel St. Francis (New York), 122
Houdini, Harry, 245–47
Hough, George A., Jr., 207–8
House, Col. Edward M., 189, 196, 214, 218, 222, 407
  Cosgrave on, 230
  described, 206
  as Swope's source, 226
Houston, David, 191, 203
Houston *Chronicle*, 350
Howard, Leslie, 295
Howard, Roy W., 308, 371
  sale of *World* and, 342, 346–47, 351
Howe, Louis, 379, 382
Hudson Dusters, 107
Hughes, Charles Evans, 65, 180–82
Hughes, Charles Evans, Jr., 180
Hughes, Mrs. Charles Evans, 65
Hughes, Howard, 20
Hull, Cordell, 285, 381, 384
Hull House, 96
Humes, Gregory T., 168–69
Hummel, Abe, 133
Huneker, James G., 263
Hunter College, 400
Hurley, Patrick J., 191
Hutton, Marjorie Post, 432
Hyde, Charles H., 136–38
Hylan, John F., 205–6, 231, 282

Ickes, Harold, 72
"Impossible Interview," 12
"Information Please," 298–99
Intergroup Relations, Commission on, 34–35

International Business Machines Corporation, 320, 467
International Harvester, 204
International Monetary and Economic Conference (1933), 381–85
International News Service, 227
"Ireland, Baron," 262
Irish Sweepstakes, 318
Ismay, J. Bruce, 143
Israel Institute of Technology, 438–39
Ittleson, Blanche Frank, 44, 93, 95
Ittleson, Henry, 93, 95, 121, 330

Jack's restaurant, 110
Jackson, Robert H., 60
James, Edwin L., 389
James, Marquis, 409
James, Schell and Elkus, 120
Japan *Times*, 184–85
Jefferson, Joseph, 18
Jefferson, Thomas, 54, 251
Jeffries, Jim, 170
Jewish Telegraphic Agency, 433–34, 455
Jewish Theological Seminary of America, 437
Jockey Club, 16, 118, 357, 391, 412–13, 422–25
Joffre, Marshal Joseph Jacques Césaire, 219–20
John Jacques & Son, Ltd., 327
Johnson, Albin, 350
Johnson, Davy, 117
Johnson, Hugh S., 371, 395, 408
  column by, 71
  on W.I.B., 204
Johnson, Jack, 170–71
Johnson, Lyndon B., 154, 397, 456–58
Jones, Jesse, 71
Joseph Pulitzer Employees' Association, 350
Joya, Moku (Mock), 184–85
Judge (periodical), 269

493

ABOUT THE AUTHOR

E. J. KAHN, JR., *a staff writer for* The New Yorker *since 1937, is one of America's most brilliant reporters and writers. His work for* The New Yorker *and other major magazines has ranged from profiles of important people to coverage of the Olympics, from humor to combat reporting. In addition he has written eleven books, dealing with such diverse subjects as the Coca-Cola Company, Frank Sinatra, and the story of the Japanese holdouts in the Pacific Island after World War II ended. He worked for four years on this definitive biography of Herbert Bayard Swope.*

Mr. Kahn was born in New York City and has traveled extensively in Europe, Australia, Japan, Korea, the U.S.S.R. and the Pacific Trust Territories. He was graduated from Harvard cum laude, with a B.A. degree, and in 1962 his alma mater awarded him an honorary Phi Beta Kappa degree.

Mr. Kahn is married and has three teen-age sons. He lives in Westchester County, New York, and spends his summers at Cape Cod. There, in addition to writing books and magazine pieces, Mr. Kahn plays fierce—and usually victorious—tennis and contributes a weekly guest column to Park Here, *a mimeographed newspaper published by his sons.*